Mysore Inscriptions

Mysore Inscriptions,

TRANSLATED FOR GOVERNMENT

BY

LEWIS RICE

GYAN

Published by

GYAN

Gyan Publishing House
5, Ansari Road
Daryaganj, New Delhi-110002
Phone: 011-47034999, 9811692060
E-mail: books@gyanbooks.com

Distribution Network
gyanbooks.com
India, USA, Canada, UK, Australia

ISBN: 978-81-212-5526-4 (HB)
First Published, 1879

2nd Impression 2024

Printed at: Gyan Press, Delhi.

MYSORE INSCRIPTIONS
Translator: LEWIS RICE

BEGUR STONE—NO. 113.

Mysore Inscriptions,

TRANSLATED FOR GOVERNMENT,

BY

LEWIS RICE,

Director of Public Instruction, Mysore & Coorg.

BANGALORE:

PRINTED AT THE MYSORE GOVERNMENT PRESS.

1879.

CONTENTS.

PREFACE.

A few words of explanation are needed as to the origin and purport of the present volume. When Mr. L. B. Bowring, C. S. I., (previously Private Secretary to the Governor General, Lord Canning), was Chief Commissioner of Mysore, the garrison of Bangalore included the 22nd Regiment, Madras Native Infantry, one of whose officers, Major H. Dixon, had taken a series of photographs of the celebrated temples of Orissa, and dedicated them by permission to Lady Canning. He was now commissioned, about 1865, to take photographs on behalf of the Mysore Government of the principal inscriptions in this Province. How the selection was made I am not aware, but all he took belong to the north of the country. There were 150 altogether—129 from inscriptions on stone and 21 from those on copper-plates—nearly a half of the whole number being from Balagámi and Taldagundi, close to it, both in the Shimoga District.*

Sets of the photographs were sent to the India Office and Asiatic Societies, but without a translation they could be regarded only as curiosities. Some native officials here, with the aid of pandits, attempted the translation of a few for Mr. Bowring, but, as might be expected, with very imperfect results.

About seven years ago the collection was put into my hands, to translate for Government when I had leisure. Though familiar with the language of the country, the subject of inscriptions was not one I had paid any attention to. I also found no one who could read the ancient characters, and had besides little time to give to the matter.† However, gradually setting to work, after many repeated attempts, I had at length the satisfaction of deciphering the whole of the obsolete characters ; and continued practice not only gave me facility in reading inscriptions but familiarized me with their general style and

---

* Of the execution of these it is not my province to speak : but owing to imperfect clearing of the inscriptions before the photographs were taken, and the microscopic scale of the greater number, the difficulties involved in deciphering them were greatly multiplied.

† The Pandit placed at my disposal, Somayáji S'iva Ráma S'ástri, (since, I regret to say, deceased), was a clever man and an excellent Sanskrit and Kannada scholar, but he did not know the old characters and took but feeble interest in transcribing inscriptions.

method of arrangement, so that on meeting with any, during tours of inspection in the country, I was enabled to pick out the essential historical facts they contained.

This success greatly enhanced the interest of the subject, though other engagements (such as compiling the Gazetteers of Mysore and Coorg) obliged me often to put aside the work for months together. But the notes I continued to take of inscriptions in various parts of the country convinced me that a very limited and imperfect collection had been made. I therefore drew up a tabular form, a copy of which was despatched to each Amildar, with orders from Government to return it filled up with particulars of every inscription existing in his taluk. The result was, as I had hoped, to bring to light some ancient inscriptions of great value—witness Nos. 151 and 153, which opened as it were a new chapter in the early history of Mysore.*

The returns received from the various taluks shewed the existence of at least 3,722 inscriptions throughout Mysore, † besides those in Coorg. But with regard to the particulars of their contents, where the entries were not entirely erroneous, the columns for page on page were simply in most parts filled up with the equivalents for "unknown," "illegible," or "not understood." General attention, however, having been drawn to the subject, I found it easier to get access to inscriptions in any part of the country visited, and from time to time came across more valuable ones than had been produced for entry in any of the lists. Some of these I thought it well to publish at once, and they have appeared in the *Indian Antiquary* with fac-similes of the originals. A select number I have appended to the present work as Part III.

No pretence can of course be made to have in any way exhausted a subject the materials of which are so numerous, so generally distributed, and which require individually so much time and study to reproduce in English. But in addition to all those photographed by Major Dixon—which I have felt in duty

* It appears that Chikka Deva Rája, who reigned from 1672 to 1704, caused a register to be made of all the inscriptions in Mysore, no doubt as a check upon the endowments; but the document seems to have been one of those which Tippu found in the palace and contemptuously ordered to be taken for boiling the *kulti* or gram for the horses.

†

District.	No. of inscriptions registered.	District.	No. of inscriptions registered.
Bangalore	332	Hassan	464
Kolar	840	Shimoga	791
Túmkúr	148	Kadur	323
Mysore	403	Chitaldroog ...	421

bound to translate, as undertaken, for Government, but for the selection of which I am in no way responsible—I have given from among those known to me such as in my opinion will best serve to present a somewhat complete view of the ancient history of Mysore : and in the Introduction have combined the information thus obtained with such as I have gathered from other sources, in an attempt to treat the subject in as exhaustive a manner as the space at disposal would allow. A summary of results deduced with reference to the language and other matters has also there been similarly included.

And should this work have the effect of, in any measure, promoting, in the case of others, as it has with me, an interest in the people, the country, its institutions, its important language and valuable literature, whether on the part of European scholars or more especially on the part of the sons of the country itself, my labour will not have been expended in vain in elucidating these records and monuments of bygone times—a labour which those alone are in a position to appreciate who have done similar work.

Bangalore, July 1878.

ADDENDA ET CORRIGENDA.

Page,

xi, omit 3rd Hoysala grant.

xii, add to end of Hoysala grants
3, 1310, *Ballála Deva*, *Chitaldroog*, 6.

„ under Yádava, add *Mahadeva Ráya* to No. 15.

xiii, lines 3 and 4 from bottom, for pages 326, 329, read 302, 304.

xxv, line 2 from bottom, read *sallekhana*.

xxxiii, „ 23, for Naga, read *Nagar*.

„ „ 2 from bottom, for *henda* read *henḍa*.

xliv, „ 4, after Mákunda, read or Mankunda.

xlv, note ‡, for Thumbler, read "humbler."

liv, end of para. 2, add—A more credible account is that they were introduced in the 3rd century by Mukunti Pallava.

lvii, line 19 of note, after out insert a semicolon.

lxiv, „ 15, after Malla, add—whose governor of Banavase, &c., in 1019 was Kundamarasa (p. 150).

lxvi, „ 10, for no doubt, read perhaps; and for Gangavaḍi, read Kumbhakoṇa.

lxvii, „ 16 „ 1394, read 1094.

„ „ 30 „ Achchupa Nayaka, read Barmmarasa.

lxviii, add to foot note, A somewhat different account is given at p. 84 of the descent of the Páṇḍya named Tribhuvana Malla Káma Devarasa, with the title Nigalanka Malla, ruling Haive in 1112 from Sisugali.

lxxiii, line 20, after 1157, add—But in 1155 Mahadevarasa held that position (p. 10).

lxxvii, „ 2, read Hoysalas.

lxxviii, „ 30, after time, add (p. 106).

3, date of No. 3, alter to 1310.

3, „ „ 4 „ about 1150.

, end of para 4, after Hiḍumbes'vara insert a comma; for Videyáditya read *Udeyáditya*.

9, line 8, for 1045 put a dash.

7, para. 2, for Víra read *Vijaya*.

9, end of para 4, for just in punishing, read *a generous prince, the punisher of Ayyana*; and add foot note *Vengi-Manḍales'varan udára-mahes'varan Ayyana-danḍa*.

60, omit foot note †

72, line 5 from bottom, for *Káli* read *Koḍi*.

97, date of No. 44, alter to 1149.

99, line 10, for *nád* read *náḍ*.

121, date of No. 56, alter to about 1150.

155, line 12, for *Hárana* read *Holala*.

183, para 2 of description, for nine read *seven*, and omit the three words after hoods.

187, date of No. 100, for 1196 read 1169.

„ line 3 „ „ Chálikya read *Bálikya*.

209, line 12, for I will describe, read *will be described*.

210, „ 4 of note, for *védipe*, read *vendoḍe*.

„ last 3 lines of description, after thereby, read *the daughter of Ayyapa taken prisoner* (*see Introduction*, *xliv*).

213, date of No. 117, alter to 1136.

236, „ „ 132, „ 695.

240, „ „ 134, „ 693.

256—260, alter numbers as 141 to 145.

282, last line, for the line of gurus to, read *and the Des'ika gaṇa, by*.

283, line 9, for he, read *was*.

285, last line of notes, for *narpatim* read *narapatim*.

286, line 24, for 14 read 4.

326, date of No. 173, alter to 1184.

328, para 4, for Sátavve read *S'ántavve*.

„ last line, omit 18.

Chronological and Classified List of the Inscriptions.

No.	*Date.*	*Ruling Sovereign.*	*Locality of Inscription.*	*Page.*
		Pandava (!)		
130	...	Janamejaya	Anantapur	232
133	...	Do	Sorab	238
139	...	Do	Tirthahalli	251
		Mahavali.		
	A. D.			
163	c. 300	Baṇarasa	Gulganpode	304
164	„ 500	Báṇarasa	do	305
		Ganga.		
156	? 350	Vishnu Gopa	Harihar	293
154	454	Kongaṇi...	Mallohalli	289
151	466	Do	Mercara	282
157	481	Do	Bangalore	294
155	513	Avinita...	Mallohalli	291
152	762	Pṛithuví Kongaṇi	Hosur	284
153	777	Do	Nagamangala	287
113	c. 850	Ereyapparasa (usurper) ...	Begur	209
		Pallava.		
115	c. 750	Nolamba	Nandi	212
		Chalukya.		
158	444	Víra Noṇamba	Bangalore	296
159	c. 640	Ambera...	Hosur	298
98	c. 690	Vinayáditya	Balagami	186
134	693	Do Satyás'raya ...	Sorab	240
132	695	Do do ...	Harihar	236
160	758	Kírtti Varmma	Vokkaleri	299
99	997	Ahava Malla	Taldagundi	186
72	1019	Jaya Simha	Balagami	148
80	c. 1020	Do Jagadeka Malla ...	do	166

No.	*Date.*	*Ruling Sovereign.*	*Locality of Inscription.*	*Page.*
	A. D.			
107	...	... ...	Taldagundi	203
75	1202	Víra Ballála Deva	Balagami	162
59	1202	Do	Balagami	128
65	1205	Do	do	137
50	1206	... ...	do	113
51	...	... ...	do	„
64	1207	Do	do	137
20	1223	Víra Narasimha Deva ...	Harihar	30
171	1250	Víra Somes'vara	Bangalore	321
166	1253	Do	Nirgunda	307
147	1262	Narasimha Deva	Belur	270
27	1269	Do	Harihar	48
172	1270	Do	Somnathpur	323
120	1275	Do	Halebid	219
148	1278	Do	Belur	275
6	1287	Do	Chitaldroog	11

Yadava.

No.	*Date.*	*Ruling Sovereign.*	*Locality of Inscription.*	*Page.*
101	? 1189	Billaha Rája	Taldagundi	188
37	1215	Simhana Deva	Balagami	72
54	1269	... ...	do	115
15	c. 1270	... ...	Davangere	24
12	1271	Mahádeva Ráya	do	20
26	1277	Rámachandra Ráya... ...	Harihar	44
57	1282	Do	Balagami	127
111	1283	Do	Sorab	207
82	1284	Do	Balagami	169
52	„	Do	do	113
81	1286	Do	do	168

Vijayanagar.

No.	*Date.*	*Ruling Sovereign.*	*Locality of Inscription.*	*Page.*
131	1354	Bukka Ráya	Harihar	234
1	1355	Do	Chitaldroog	2
2	1356	Do	do	4
29	1379	Harihara Maháráya... ...	Harihar	55
125	c. 1380	Do	Belur	222
128	„	Do	do	226
146	1382	Do	do	267
149	1395	Do	Hassan	277
150	1406	Deva Ráya Maháráya ...	do	279
18	1410	Do	Harihar	26
5	1412	Do	Chitaldroog	9

D

INTRODUCTION.

Hindu literature is remarkably deficient in works of history. But the value of inscriptions has of late years been more and more recognized as one of the chief sources from which trustworthy materials may be drawn for supplying that deficiency. The inscriptions translated in this volume are concerned entirely with the Karṇáṭa or Karṇáṭaka country, as represented by the existing state of Mysore (Mahishúr). The modern history of this State is well known to all who are conversant with Indian affairs as forming one of the most important chapters in the records of the progress of British dominion in the East. But the ancient history of the country is, even to its own people, almost, if not altogether, a blank.

The present inscriptions cover a period embracing the whole of the Christian era. Some profess to go back much farther, but their claims to such antiquity will be considered in their proper places. Before, however, presenting in detail the history of nineteen centuries as derived from these monuments of the past, it may be well to describe briefly their nature and character.

As a general rule any inscription is called a *s'ásana*, a word derived from the Sanskrit *s'ás*, to command or proclaim, and signifying a royal grant, charter, or edict. A s'ásana engraved on stone (*s'ilá*) is thence called a *s'ilá s'ásana*, while one engraved on copper (*támra*) plates is similarly called a *támra s'ásana*. A s'ila s'ásana is sometimes a counterpart of a támra s'ásana: the latter being portable and intended for private custody, the former to be set up in a public place for general information. Some portion of the present collection, as will be explained farther on, does not consist of s'ásanas properly so called.

A s'ilá s'ásana is generally engraved on one side of a large slab of stone (*lipi kallu* or *s'ásana kallu*) erected at the entrance or within the enclosure of a temple, or on the outer wall of the edifice. Sometimes the inscription is on a pillar in front of the temple. Where the site is favourable, inscriptions are also cut on the face of the natural rock. Inscriptions on the ground or on the floor usually record the votive offerings of private persons in return for recovery from sickness or other favour received.

A támra s'ásana consists of several plates of copper strung together on a stout metal ring, the place where it is joined being secured by an impression in metal of the royal seal or crest. Such grants are often kept buried in the earth for security.

But some of the inscriptions in this collection are not, as before stated, charters or s'ásanas in the proper sense of the term. They may more accurately be described as epitaphs. The monumental stones on which these occur are of two kinds, sculptured with figures in relief but most usually without any inscription. The first are called *víra kal*, hero stones, being monuments erected in memory of warriors slain in battle. They are also in a few places called *bóru kal*, war stones, and *kollu kal*, slaughter stones. These trophies are met with in every part of the country, sometimes in the middle of open fields, sometimes in the hearts of lonely forests, sometimes singly or in groups by the wayside or in the centre of a village; and probably mark the scene of the hero's last fight.

The other class of monument, called *másti kal* (that is *mahá sati kal*) consist of the memorials of *sati*, and denote the spots on which women were burnt along with their deceased husbands in obedience to the rules for *sahágamana*,* or the ceremony of "going along with" their departed lords by immolation on the same funeral pyre. They are met with at the entrances of villages, more especially, I think, if not entirely, in the west of Mysore. They very rarely bear any inscription, but the figures sculptured on them are so singular as at once to arrest the attention.

An account of the general style and arrangement of the inscriptions on these several kinds of monuments may not be unacceptable to those who perchance have often gazed upon such memorials of the past and wished for some guide or clue to an interpretation of the time-worn characters and shapes upon them.

To begin with the *S'ilá S'ásana*, or grants inscribed on stone slabs, which are the most numerous. They present the aspect of an unbroken expanse of writing, surmounted by a few sculptured images. The inscription is without any interval or gap from top to bottom, the engraving being rude and rough or skilful and regular, according to the period, and the ability of the sculptor. The most ancient (as Nos. 163 and 164) are in large and deliberately deep-cut letters, on massive and ponderous slabs, seeming as if the work of giant hands. The letters become smaller and more artistically shaped as the period of the Hoysala grants is approached. The inscriptions of this time, or the 12th and 13th centuries, are perfect works of art, being incised on beautifully

* Also called *anugamana* and *anumaraṇa*.

polished slabs of black hornblende, in regular and ornamental characters, varied in design to suit their position; and the whole so well arranged and fitted together, that no space is left where a single additional letter could be inserted. From this time the character of the engraving deteriorates, until the later grants, after the fall of Vijayanagar, came to be engraved, without selection, on any kind of stone however unsuitable, in very rude characters.

The great majority of s'ilá s'ásana have several sculptured images at top. These do not occur in the most ancient, and their introduction I am inclined to think marks the rise of sectarianism. The figure in the centre represents the donor's chief object of worship. If he be a S'aiva, the linga or symbol of S'iva will appear, often with a priest officiating; if a Jain, the figure of a Tírthankara; and so on for the various sects. On either hand of this deity are other figures. On one side the animal which is the peculiar *váhana* or vehicle of the god, as the bull Nandi for S'iva, the kite Garuḍa for Vishnu, and so on: on the other a cow suckling a calf, the former representing the land presented, the latter the recipient who is to enjoy its produce. Above are the symbols of the sun and moon, both as being the two great witnesses of all treaties and human transactions, and as emblematic of the perpetuity of the gift. Some stones also shew the figure of the royal crest, as a boar for the Chálukyas, a sword for the Kalachuryas, &c. In many S'aiva stones will be noticed a human figure, seated in meditation on one side of the linga. This is the donor himself, modestly represented by anticipation as already enjoying the reward of his meritorious donation. According to the S'aiva faith there are four stages of future bliss—*salokya*, dwelling with God; *samípya*, nearness to God; *sarúpya*, likeness to God; and *sayujya*, absorption into God. The last two are unattainable by those who live in this sinful age or Kali yuga: the other two are the reward of works of merit and devotional acts. To one of these states of holy blessedness the donor's piety has raised him. In No. 38 he may be seen in the presence, wrapt in profoundest abstraction, undisturbed by the gambols of his attendant boar, which is anxiously offering its services. In No. 21 the royal donor appears in a higher state of glory, as himself officiating in the heavenly temple, arrayed in a costume somewhat resembling that of the Coorgs, but with a singular head dress which also occurs in No. 17.

Following immediately upon these images, which are in relief within the rounded or arched top of the stone, is the inscription, which commences with an invocation or proem, generally in Sanskrit verse, engraved on the raised margin or frame forming the base of the arch above mentioned.

The couplet most frequently met with at the beginning of S'aiva inscriptions is as follows :—

Namas tunga-s'iras chumbi-chandra-chámara-chárave
Trailokya-nagar-árambha-múla-stambháya S'ambhave.

Adored be S'ambhu (S'iva), beauteous with the chámara-like crescent moon kissing his lofty head; the original foundation-pillar of the city of the three worlds.

The same verse occurs when the inscription is in honor of Harihara, the combined form of Hari (Vishnu) and Hara (S'iva); while the relation of this dual deity to Lakshmi and Párvati, the consorts respectively of Vishnu and S'iva, affords an opportunity of enlarging on a theme upon which a Hindu poet rarely suffers the veil of modesty to remain unlifted.

Vaishnava inscriptions often commence with the following :—

Jayaty ávishkṛitam Vishnor varáham kshobit-árṇavam
Dakshiṇonnata-damshṭrágra-vis'ránta-bhuvanam vapuh.

Supreme is the Boar form of the resplendent Vishnu, which scattered the waters of the ocean and raised up the peaceful earth on the tip of his long right tusk.

Jaina inscriptions generally begin with the following :—

S'rímat parama-gambhíra-syád-vád-ámogha-lánchhanam
Jíyát Trailokya-náthasya s'ásanam Jina-s'ásanam.

May the doctrine of Trailokya-nátha, the supreme profound *syád váda*, prevail, the Jain doctrine which is a token of unfailing success.

Other verses are of course used in many cases, according to the taste of the composer, but these specimens are the most common. It is not however to be understood that only one such verse is used : one or several occur according to the inclination of the composer.

The second portion of the inscription contains the name of the reigning sovereign, with all his titles, generally in prose ; preceded in many cases by his genealogy, traced back to the progenitor of the line, or even to the creation of all things ; this portion being in verse, with connecting phrases in prose. The language here is for the most part Sanskrit, often largely intermixed with Haḷe Kannaḍa, the verses being some in the one and some in the other language according to the subject, and so as to display the skill and taste of the composer. More rarely the whole is in Haḷe Kannaḍa. For historical purposes this, in connection with the date, is the most important part of the s'ásana.

The lines of kings whose descent is elucidated by the present collection will be given farther on. It may here be noted that every person directly connected with the s'ásana—as the reigning monarch, the donor, &c.,—is introduced with the expression *Svasti* (Sans.—May it be well!) a term of good omen, probably designed to avert any evil consequences such as orientals apprehend from mention or utterance of a person's name, much more of that of royalty. The character of the sovereign's reign is represented as one of Arcadian simplicity, for he is always stated to be ruling *sukha-sankathá-vinodadim*, in the enjoyment of security and good conversation (literally, good stories). I have generally translated the phrase more freely, in the enjoyment of peace and wisdom.

Next after the style and dynasty of the monarch, comes frequently an account of the family and pretensions of the great feudatory or officer ruling over the province in which the land lay which was the subject of the endowment, followed by similar statements regarding the donor,—the whole in a strain of hyperbole and excessive adulation, which, by a common infirmity of human nature, becomes more extravagant as the social scale is descended. Each subordinate is presented with reference to his immediate superior as *tad-páda-padmopajívi*, dwelling (like a bee) at his lotus-feet. Sometimes a greater distance is implied than even this measure of personal contact would admit of between one step of dignity and the next in the social scale. As in No. 147, where, to illustrate the unapproachable superiority of the queen, it is stated that to move within the space illuminated by her toe-nails was sufficient to confer honour on other king's wives.

A difficulty in determining the rank of these nobility and gentry arises from their freedom in assuming the name of king (*rája* or *arasu*), a title which seems in former times to have been used by all hereditary landholders of noble birth or *quasi* independent position. Speaking of a similar practice in the charters of the Saxon kings in England, Sir H. Nicolas says,* "It was a common practice for a man to style himself Rex though not supreme king, that is, king in the modern sense. Probably all of the blood royal who had appanages of land may have laid claim to the title, at least before Egbert's victories threw the preponderance into the lands of Wessex."

We next usually, though not invariably, come to the date of the s'ásana, which is given with great apparent minuteness, mentioning the year of the cycle, the month, the lunar date, the day of the week, with any astrological or astronomical phenomenon or conjunction of auspicious import when making the gift, as an eclipse, an equinox, &c., &c. But though all these particulars are thus minutely stated, it is evident they do not, in the absence of a reference to some known determinate era, suffice to fix the date, as the cycle of Hindu years contains a recurring period of only 60: the name of any single one can therefore

---

* *Chron. Hist.* 363.

only confirm the evidence otherwise obtained and cannot of itself give a clue to the age of the inscription.

The most clearly dated of the s'ásanas in this collection mention the year of the well known S'áliváhana S'aka, or era of Sáliváhana, and are thus easily assigned to their proper time.* Many, on the other hand, date from the Chálukya Vikrama era, and others from the eras of obscurer sovereigns. The difficulty of fixing the year according to our reckoning is thus greatly increased. A different kind of difficulty arises from the deliberate falsification of the historical data, for the purpose of enhancing the antiquity of the grant. Some instances of this, in which we are required to go back to the time of the deluge, will be adduced farther on.

But some s'ásanas contain the precise date concealed in a phrase, capable sometimes of various interpretations, and determined to be arithmetical from the context alone ; or in letters of the alphabet, combined into a word which may or may not be significant of anything. Add to this that the figures thus to be unearthed (if I may so speak) must, when brought to light, be read backwards, and the precautions are pretty complete against any casual reader coming at the date. The initiated in astrology however are in possession of keys for unlocking these mysteries.

The system by which certain words have a numerical value is a very elaborate one. The principle however is easily intelligible. Supposing, for instance, a date were expressed in English by the words *eyes*, *gospels*, *poles* and *moon*. Taking them backwards, according to the rule, as we have *one* moon, *two* poles, *four* gospels, and *two* eyes, the date would, according to this system, be 1242. But even when this result is arrived at, the era must also be known to determine the date. Though the above is the simple principle on which the system is based, in practice it is much more complicated, as any synonym of the representative word for a number may be used instead of the word itself. The variety thus introduced is almost inexhaustible, and controlled alone by the fancy of the composer.

The following is a list of words arranged under the numbers they express : the list is compiled from three manuscript works—*Muhúrta-dípike*, *Kavikalpa-lata* and *Sankhya-ratṇa-kos'a*, of which the copy of the last is unfortunately incomplete. All the words are stated to have been taken from actual use.

1. *S'as'i, soma, s'as'ánka, indu, chandra, kalánidhi, ṛájá, vidhu, sudháms'u, yama, eka, jana* | *átma, indra, hasti, as'va, gaja, S'ukladṛik* | *Parabrahma, viráḍrúpa, múlaprakṛiti, bhúmi, airávata, s'ukranetra, vighnes'aradana, dhruva, uchais'rava, átmá, prapancha, chandramas, svishṭakṛit, uktá.*

---

* An inscription at Taḍa Málingi is dated by both the Kali and S'aka eras in the following elaborate manner.—*Kali varushada pramáṇula* 432000 *ke sanda varusha* 3179 *S'aka varusha* 1435 *ubhayam* 4614 *neya varusha sandu naḍuva varusha S'rímukha samvatsara.*

2. *Akshi, chakshu, kara, netra, lochana, báhu, karṇa, paksha, dṛishṭi, dvaya, yugma, ambaka, nayana, íkshaṇa | pakshi, nadíkúla, asidhára, Rámanandana | asidhára, vibhúti, páda dvandva, kara, bhru, kucha, grahana, násatya, nadíkúla, úru, báhu, vishuvat, karṇa, jánu, gulpa, jangha, agnis'írsha, oshṭha, paksha, hora, kapála, Rámanandana, ayana, netra, atyuktá.*

3. *Vahni, Ráma, s'ikhi, agni, pávaka, dahana, anala, s'ankarákshi, puri, loka, tríṇi, kála, traya, guṇa | traya, kála, agni, bhuvana, Gangámárga, ís'adrik, grívárekhá, kávya, s'ula s'ikhá, sandhyá, pura, pushkara, Ráma, Vishnupada | Trivikramapadanyása, drekkáṇa, Haralochana, sandhyá, kárya, íshna, ṛiṇa, dosha, linga, agni, maṇḍala, Ráma, nádí, s'akti, múrti, loka, bháshya. guṇa, bhṛingipáda, tyájyapáda, gáyatrípáda, pushkara, grívarekha, vahnipála, vachana, savana, tanu, triyakpuṇḍra, s'úlas'ikhá, Vishṇupatni, pura, das'asyandanapatni, sandhyá.*

4. *Abdhi, ságara, chatvári, Vanarás'i, yuga, ambudhi, chatur, várdhi, gati, jaladhi, níradhi | chatvári, deva, brahmásya, abdhi, Haribáhu, svardantidanta, senánga, upáya, yuga, ás'rama | yuganátha, agnis'ringa, khaṭvápáda, gostana, vidhivaktra, Das'arathaputra, Airávatadanta, yuga, veda, vyúha, kendra, upáya, mṛigánghri, senánga, varṇa, gati, purushártha, ás'rama, abdhi, haribáhu, pratishṭhá.*

5. *Indriya, panchama, jnána, ishu, bána, márgaṇa, vrata, bhúta, s'ara, parva, práṇa, vishaya | pancha, Páṇḍava, rudrásya, indriya, agni, mahápápa, mahábhúta, mahákávya, mahámakha, puráṇalakshana, anga, indriyártha | bhúta, indriya, s'ara, práṇa, s'ikhá, kshára, pallava, s'ivásya, gavya, tanmátra, kanyá, Gauḍa, artha, Páṇḍava, kos'a, pátaka, loha, Dráviḍa, klesha, kola, lavana, pitá, mátá, kachcha, tvak, devapádapa, puránalakshana, pakshi, maháyajna, as'vadhárá, supratishṭá.*

6. *S'ástra, shaṭ, ruchi, kála, ṛitu, rasadravya, kos'a, shaḍdars'ana, shaḍágama | shaṭ, vajra, tris'ironetra, tarka, anga, dars'ana, chakravarti, mahásenavadana, ritu, rasa | rasa, s'ástra, anga, ves'yá, úrmi, kumárásya, átatáyi, karma, ṛitu, jíva, bhringánghri, tarka, ari, káraka, chakravarti, dehachakra, anádi, bala, mata, upas'ástra, prayoga, bháshá, ámnáya, angadevata, pralaya, gáyatri.*

7. *S'aila, adri, dvipa, váyu, muni, sapta, achala, giri, turaga, as'va, naga, gotra, mahídra, rishi | sapta, pátálabhuvana, mani, dvípa, arkaváji, vára, abdhi, svara, rájyánga, vríhi, vahnis'ikha | mátṛiká, táṇḍava, vára, dvípa, rájyánga, parvata, ṛishi, svara, nadí, vyádha. vibhakti, vyasana, kratu, paṭṭaṇa, chirajívi, agnijihvá, kalpa, as'va, dhátu, pákayajna, pátála, havi, agnipáṇi, Páṇḍusena, ushnik.*

8. *Ashṭama, gaja, karṇi, diggaja, danti, hasti, sámaja, matamátanga, dikpála, vasu, váraṇa | ashṭau, yoga, anga, vasu, ís'amúrti, diggaja, sidhi, brahma, s'ruti, vyákarana, dikpála, ahi, kulácha̋la | siddhi, bhairava, dikpála, siddhánta, vasu, kunjara, ísámúrti, mada, gandha, lakshmí, sarpa, mangala, rahasyayogini, píṭhapála, vidyes'vara, s'arabhánghri, sphoṭa, pára, praṇáma, gayá, yogánga, viváha, garbhavarjyángana, áya, yáma, guptatarayogini, kashṭa, anushṭup.*

9. *Navama, navaratṇa, brahma, kamalásaná, nidhi, graha, khaṇḍa, randhrabháva, labdhaka | nava, anga, dvára, bhúkhaṇḍa, kritarávanamastaka, vyághristana, sudhá, kuṇḍa, rasa, graha | durgá, ratṇa, nidhi, nanda, megha, ballálanáyaka, gopya, varsha, khaṇḍa, mána, dhánya, anka, ḍhanáyaka, chakres'vari, náthasiddha, nṛisimha, upadhánya, randhra, graha, víra, chola, dhenu, pás'ána, bhakti, vyághristana, vyákaraṇa, ávaraṇa, bṛihati.*

0. *A'kás'a, gagana, s'únya, antariksha, marutpatha.*

10. *Das'a, hastánguli, S'ambhubáhu, Rávanamauli, Krishnávatára, dik, avasthá, indraváji, | kula, vishnukalá, mudrá, avatára, rudrakalá, agnikalá, rávanásya, brahmakalá, nighantu, dik, avastá, dharmapatni, snána, dhúpa, nagnaka, rúpaká, lakára, dohala, nátya, putra, phalgunanáma, pankti.*

11. *Ekadas'a, mahádeva, kurubhúpatisena | rudra, karana, parimána, trishtup.*

12. *Dvádas'a, arka, mása, rás'i, sankránti, gurubáhu, arikoshtaka, senáninetra | garbhasandhyanga, sankránti, mása, s'anmukhabáhu, vigárambha, súryakalá, ritupatni, nátyapada, rás'i, divakara, bhávasandhi, jagati.*

13. *Trayodas'a, támbúlaguna | vis'vedeva, pratimukhasandhyanga, sámagácharya, vidhyanga, támbúlaguna, atijagati.*

14. *Chaturdas'a, vidyá, yama, Manu, bhuvana | purandara, nirvahanasandhyanga, Manu, mrigábhirujya, vidyá, sampradáyayogini, s'akvari.*

15. *Panchadas'a, tithi | nityádevi, strikalá, tithi, atis'akvari.*

16. *Shodas'a, indukalá, ambiká.*

18. *Ashtádas'a, dvipa.*

20. *Vims'ati, Rávanabhuja, anguli.*

100. *S'ata, dhártaráshtra, s'atabhishak, purusháyus, Rávanánguli, abjadala, s'akrayajna, abdhiyojana.*

1000. *Sahasra, jáhnavivaktra, s'eshas'irsha, ambujachala, ravibána, arjunakara, vedas'ákha, indradrishti.*

The system by which certain letters of the alphabet have a numerical value is called *katapayádi sankhya*. The rule for it is thus briefly stated—*kádi-nava tádi-nava pádi-pancha yádyashtau*—from *ka* nine, from *ta* nine, from *pa* five, from *ya* eight; that is to say, the nine letters commencing with *ka* count in order as one to nine, and so for the others. The following is the scheme:—

1	2	3	4	5	6	7	8	9
k	*kh*	*g*	*gh*	*n*	*ch*	*chh*	*j*	*jh*
t	*th*	*d*	*dh*	*n*	*t*	*th*	*d*	*dh*
p	*ph*	*b*	*bh*	*m*				
y	*r*	*l*	*v*	*s'*	*sh*	*s*	*h*	

No provision, it will be seen, is made for the cipher: this is expressed by the words *ákás'a* or one of its synonyms, or by *s'únya*. Should the significant letters be involved in words or a phrase, only the last pronounced of combined consonants is counted, while vowels have no value.

The next portion of the s'ásana is generally in Haḷe Kannaḍa or Old Kanarese, and describes the gift itself, with the boundaries, if the endowment be of land. The transfer is made with the ceremony of pouring water, a practice still observed in closing an agreement or sale. The person who resigns the proprietary rights pours a little water on to the hand of the purchaser in token of his entire renunciation of all claims. Often a presentation of a coin is also made at the same time.

The land thus bestowed is given in permanence, and rent free, with release from all burdens and the assignment of all present and prospective profit it may yield. These are generally termed *ashṭa-bhoga-teja-swámya*, the eight rights of perfect possession, which are described p. 3.

Grants to a temple are usually made to a guru or priest of the temple, with the ceremony of washing his feet. The good qualities and professed doctrines of this holy man are often eulogised at great length, giving rise to a suspicion that he must have had a hand in the composition.

The concluding portion of a s'ásana is occupied with quotations of texts in Sanskrit or Haḷe Kannaḍa, denouncing the crime of revoking or alienating in any way gifts of land to a god or to the Brahmans, and inciting to works of merit. One or more of the following most commonly occur, the first nearly always.

Svadattám paradattám vá yo hareta vasundharám
S'ashṭhir-varsha-sahasráṇi vishṭáyám jáyate krimih.

Whoso usurps a gift made by himself or by another shall assuredly be born a worm in ordure for sixty thousand years.

Dána-pálanayor madhye dánáchchhreyonupálanam
Dánát svargam avápnoti pálanád achyutam padam.

Of making a gift oneself or maintaining another's, the maintaining is the best: for he who makes a gift obtains svarga, but he who maintains one obtains final beatitude.

Na visham visham ity áhur devasvam visham uchyate
Visham ekákinam hanti devasvam putra pautrakam.

Poison is no poison, a gift to the gods that is the real poison: for poison kills one man, but a gift to the gods (if usurped) destroys sons and descendants.

Sámányoyam dharma-setur nripáṇám kále kále páliniyo bhavadbhih
Sarván etán bhávinah párthivendrán bhúyo bhúyo yáchate Rámachandrah.

Merit is a common bridge for kings, this should you support from time to time, thus continually cries Rámachandra to the kings who should come after him.

Bahubhir vasudhá-bhukta-rájabhis Sagarádibhih
Yasya yasya yadá bhúmih tasya tasya tadá phalam.

The earth has been enjoyed by Sagara and many kings, according to their (gifts of) land so was their reward.

Dharmmaman ávan obban pratipálisidam Gayeyoḷ Gangeyoḷ Kurukshetradoḷ Váraṇásiyoḷ Prayágayoḷ sásira kapileyam koḍum koḷagamam pancha-ratnagaḷim kaṭṭisi veḍaparágarappa Bráhmaṇargge koṭṭa puṇyamam aiyugam.

Whoso maintains a gift derives the merit of presenting a thousand tawny cows in the holy bathing places of Gaya, Ganga, Kurukshetra, Váraṇási and Prayága, and of presenting koḷagas decked with the five precious stones, to Brahmans versed in the vedas.

The s'ásana sometimes winds up with the names of witnesses and the royal signature. Also the names of the composer and the engraver.

Támra S'ásanas or grants on copper do not materially differ in style from those on stone, but are more rarely decorated with the images at top. It is manifestly easier to tamper with such s'asanas, or even to fabricate forged or *kúṭa s'ásanas,* than to alter an inscription on stone set up in a public place, or in such a position to palm off one not genuine. As previously stated, the ring on which the plates of a támra s'ásana are strung is secured by an impression of the royal seal, which is an additional mark of attestation beyond what occurs on s'ila s'ásana. But this of course can be forged equally with the grant.

We now come to a description of the *Vírakal,* the prominent features of which are, three tableaux sculptured in relief. Where there is an inscription, it is short; and introduced between, on the frame as it were of the bas-reliefs. Being rudely cut, and filled with rustic or obsolete forms of letters and words, it is difficult to decipher or translate. The lowest of the sculptures represents the fight in which the hero fell. As a composition it is spirited, and the grouping not unartistic: but the attitudes are conventional rather than natural, and the hero always of heroic proportions. The elaborated details of armour and weapons are often very interesting: witness the devices on the shields in No. 81.

According to the generally received notions, the warrior falling in battle is at once conveyed to paradise by the apsaras or celestial nymphs, who are allotted to be the portion of the brave, there to enjoy the voluptuous pleasures of Indra's heaven. The middle bas-relief exhibits the translation of the hero from the field of battle to the upper world, and is a most fantastic compound. Sometimes the hero is being bodily borne aloft, supported by the apsaras or celestial nymphs, the whole procession ascending in a triumphal dance, with poses and attitudes that defy description, but no doubt intended to convey the notion of spirits treading the air. In many cases, however, the hero is seated in a *vimána* or car during the ascent, though the dignity of this mode of locomotion is somewhat impaired by the frantic manner in which the celestial attendants who convoy him are represented as holding on to rings in the side provided for that purpose. In many cases the gandharvas or celestial musicians accompany the procession, performing on their various instruments. The hero is sometimes not alone in his glory but accompanied by his wife, or 'life's lamp' as she is gracefully termed (No. 81), though this pleasing picture of connubial devotion is marred by our recollection that she must have performed the act of *sati* thus to accompany her husband.

The upper portion of a vírakal is not unlike that of a s'ila s'ásana, and nearly all I have met with are of the S'aiva sect, as indicated by the linga. The figure of the hero here appears seated in meditation in the presence of the deity, as also that of his wife if she is introduced in the car below. The identity of the hero's features in the three tableaux is well preserved and often unmistakeable.

A word or two on the epitaph.* It generally commences with the name of the reigning sovereign and the date. Then follows a brief account of the expedition which proved fatal to the hero, and winds up with *palabaram kondu sura-loka-práptanáda*—" He killed many and gained the world of gods." A short Sanskrit verse often follows, inspiring to valour and glorifying the death of the brave : thus—

Jitena labhyate lakshmí mriten-ápi surángand
Kshaṇe dvandvam kámayatám ká chintá maraṇe raṇe.

Who wins in fight gains spoil, who falls enjoys the celestial nymphs, what need he then care for death in war who for a moment seeks the close encounter.

---

* A different class of epitaphs are the Jain memorials of religious suicide (*salle khana*), as Nos. 161, 162, 120. A full description of such has been given by me in *Ind. Ant.* II, 265, 322.

These monuments introduce us to scenes very different from the listening in security to a recital of good stories which we are required in the s'ásanas to imagine was the pleasing pastime of the sovereigns of the day. Cattle-raids, marauding expeditions, the treacherous ambuscade reveal the violent and disorderly character of the times.

The *Mástikal* also consist of a stone slab, on which is represented in relief the figure of a post or pillar, with a human arm of the natural size, or larger, projecting from the middle of it: the hand is held up straight, with the fingers distended, and in the hollow between the thumb and forefinger is often placed a lime. Below this striking symbol is in many cases a representation in miniature of a man and woman: sometimes seated side by side with the linga above them, sometimes with the man seated and the woman dancing round him, and other arrangements. These stones never have any inscription so far as I have noticed.

What is symbolised by the pillar I regret that I am unable to explain, but the extract given below may throw some light on it. I have seen one stone in which it had the head of a woman. The human arm I have heard called *Madana kai*, the hand or arm of Mada, that is, of Cupid, love or passion. Some mástikal have two arms projecting from the pillar, one on each side.* Limes are the common offering of respect on approaching a superior, and are always distributed to the guests at the conclusion of a durbar or any native assembly. What they signify, or what determines the number presented, I am not informed, but they appear to be considered in some way efficacious in averting anger or the evil eye.

The following extract about *sati* as performed in Mysore was copied from *Household Words*, four or five years ago, but I cannot trace the title and date of the article† "The Canarese, in the early part of the last century, used to dig a shallow pit, ten feet by six feet, which they filled up with logs of wood, placing erect at one end a ponderous piece of timber, weighing five hundred pounds or thereabout, to which a cord was attached. When all was ready, oil and clarified butter were poured upon the wood, and the corpse, decently shrouded, laid in the middle of the pile. A torch was then applied by the nearest male relative of the deceased, and, as the flames leaped up, the devoted widow took

---

* Those with one arm are called *wonṭi kai másti*; those with two, *yeraḍu kai másti*.

Though a S'aiva emblem, I do not think the *Vyásana-tólu* (Ind. Ant. II, 49, 133) is the same as the *Madana kai*.

† For a full account of the ceremonies prescribed for the performance of Sati, consult Colebrooke's *Duties of a faithful Hindu widow* (*As. Res.* IV.)

leave of her friends and acquaintances, and with cheerful countenance walked once or twice round the blazing heap, scattering flowers and repeating a form of prayer or invocation. Suddenly she would spring on to the burning logs, amidst a tremendous din of discordant music, and the frantic shouts of the bystanders. At the same instant a Brahman pulled the cord, and the erect beam fell heavily upon the living and the dead, cutting off all means and hope of escape."

"At times, of course, the hapless victim would shrink back at the last moment, appalled by the fierceness of the flames; but it was then all too late for second thoughts. The surrounding Brahmans would thrust her back with long poles, while her agonising shrieks were drowned in the uproar of drums, trumpets, and cymbals, heightened by the multitudinous yells of the spectators. Such instances of natural timidity were, however, of comparatively rare occurrence, for when there was reason to suspect a premature collapse of resolution, narcotics were previously administered, and the stupefied victim fell upon the pile."

The másti kal sometimes takes the form of a statue of the woman. This was especially the case with the Náyak race or Bedar chiefs. The woman is partly in wedding attire. Her cloth, from the waist downwards, is tied in the mode called *ganḍa kás'i*, resembling the tight-fitting ladies' dresses of the present period of European fashion. The upper part of the figure is bare, but decked with garlands. On her head she wears the *bháshinga* or bridal coronet. The left hand holds a small shield, or a spouted vessel like a tea pot (*ginḍi*): the right arm is raised, with the fingers extended as in the *Madana kai*, and a lime is placed in the hollow between the thumb and the forefinger, or the forefinger is folded down, which appears to be a sign known as *abhaya hasta*, the fearless hand.

The only másti kal in the present collection is No. 50, which introduces the husband also, and contrary to the usual custom bears an inscription giving the date.

History.

But, as before stated, it is the historical information to be derived from these ancient inscriptions which gives them their main value, and the present collection, it will be found, presents us with a pretty complete outline of the history of Mysore during nearly the whole of the Christian era.

There is at least one Jain inscription (161) which, of whatever date in itself, refers to an earlier period even than that, namely to the 3rd century B. C., a time that may be described as the very dawn of authentic history in India. It does not, however, supply any political information, and will be considered in connection with religious sects.

Of the legends and traditions relating to the pre-historic period still farther back, a summary has been presented by me elsewhere.* They chiefly refer to Paras'u Ráma, Ráma distinguished as Rámachandra, and the Páṇḍavas. The present collection includes three grants (Nos. 130, 133, 139) professing to be made 3000 years B. C. by the emperor Janamejaya of the Páṇḍava family, one of them being dated according to the era of Yudhishṭhira his grandfather. These will be shewn further on to belong to a much more modern period.

But it is desirable, before dealing with the historical facts presented to us in the inscriptions now translated, to indicate certain coincidences and points of contact between the legendary stories and what may be considered accounts of a more authentic character in connection with the pre-historic times.

At some remote period the regions south of the Vindhya mountains were invaded by the Haihayas, who put to flight Báhu, the king of Mahishmati (now Mandla) on the upper Narmadá, and established themselves in his capital. Subsequently his son Sagara recovered the sovereignty and became the paramount ruler in India. We however find the Haihayas again powerful at Mahishmati in the person of their king Kártavíryárjuna. He, attempting to wrest from Jamadagni the possession of Surabhi (Sorab, in the north-west of the Mysore), was slain at, it is said, Koláhaḷapura or Koláḷapura (Kolar, in the east of the Mysore), by Paras'u Ráma, the valiant son of the latter. But Jamadagni was in his turn cut off by the sons of Kártavíryárjuna, in revenge for which, a general slaughter of the Kshattriyas by Paras'u Ráma ensued, and twenty one times he swept them off the face of the earth.

Eventually the Haihayas established their capital at Ratanpur (in the Central Provinces), and continued in power until deposed by the Mahrattas in 1741 A. D. Inscriptions have been found proving the dominion of the Haihayas over the upper Narmadá valley up to the 2nd century A. D., and there are grounds for inferring that they were at that time Buddhists.†

" Tradition asserts that at the end of the Satya yuga a monarch named Sudhyumna presided over the destinies of the East. Of his descendants, one son,

* *Gazetteer of Mysore and Coorg*, Vol. I, II, III, *passim*.

† *C. P. Gaz.*, Int. *l.*

Níla Dhvaja, got the throne of Mahishmati (Mandla or Maheswar); a second, Hamsa Dhvaja,* became monarch of Chandrapur, supposed to be Chándá; and the third received the kingdom of Ratanpur, then called Manipur, by which name it is known in some of the Puránas. The two former kingdoms of Mandla and Chandrapur, after the lapse of some generations, were overthrown by the Gonds, and the Manipur or Ratanpur kingdom alone survived till the advent of the Mahrattas."†

The ancient Jain Rámáyana, composed in the Haḷe Kannaḍa language in about the 12th century, enables us to carry on the history from the time of Sagara with a considerable show of probability. According to that work there existed in the south three great empires or kingdoms. These were the Rákshasa kingdom, with its capital at Lanka; the Vánara dhvaja kingdom, or kingdom of the monkey flag, with its capital at Kishkindha; and the Vidyádhara kingdom, with its capital at Ratha-núpura-chakravála-pura. The first embraced Ceylon, in which Lanka was situated, and the maritime districts of the south; the second, whose capital was on the Tungabhadra at the site of the modern Vijayanagara and Anegundi, occupied the country above the Ghats watered by that river, corresponding with the greater part of the present

---

* Sudhanva, a son of Hamsa Dhvaja, is stated in the traditions of the Mysore to have been the founder of Champaka-nagara, a city represented by the present village of Sampige in the Kadaba taluk.

† The following is the list of Haihaya rajas supposed to have ruled at Ratanpur:—

	A. D.				
		Moha Deva		Kaval Sinha	1407—1426
Múrta Dhvaja		Sur Deva	749	Sankar Sahi Deva	1426—1451
Támra Dhvaja		Prithvi Deva	860	Mohan Sahi Deva	1451—1462
Chitra Dhvaja		Brahma Deva		Dádú Sahi Deva	1462—1487
Vis'va Dhvaja		Rudra Deva		Purushottam Sahí Deva	1487—1509
Chandra Dhvaja		Jájal Deva	950 to 990	Báhu Sahi Deva	1509—1536
Mahipál Dhvaja		Ratna Deva		Kalyan Sahi Deva	1536—1573
Bikram Sen		Bír Sinha Deva		Lachhman Sahi Deva	1573—1581
Bhim Sen		Ratna Sinha Deva		Sankar Sahi Deva	1581—1596
Kumár Sen		Bhúpál Sinha Deva	1088—1126	Mukund Sahi Deva	1596—1607
Karna Pál	115—194	Karma Sen Deva	1126—1156	Tribuvan Sahi Deva	1607—1622
Kuar Pál		Bhau Sen Deva	1156—1195	Jagmohan Sahi Deva	1622—1635
Mer Pál		Narsinha Deva	1195—1225	Adli Sahi Deva	1635—1649
Mohan Pál	310—370	Bhú Sinha Deva	1225—1250	Ranjit Sahi Deva	1649—1675
Jájal Deva		Pratáp Sinha Deva	1250—1293	Takht Sinha Deva	1675—1689
Deva Pál		Jay Sinha Deva	1293—1311	Rája Sinha	1689—1712
Bhú Pál		Dharma Sinha Deva	1311—1333	Sardár Sinha Deva	1712—1732
Bhúm Deva		Jagannáth Sinha Deva	1333—1371	Raghunath Sinha	1732—1745
Kám Deva		Bir Sinha Deva	1371—1407		

C. P. Gaz., 89, 159.

Mysore, Ceded Districts and Dharwar; the third kingdom was north from these, and its capital may possibly be the Ratanpur in the Central Provinces.*

The victories of Sagara, before mentioned, drove a prince named Toyada Váhana (=Megha Váhana or Jímúta Váhana) to take refuge in Lanka, where he was adopted by the Rákshasa king, who was childless, and succeeded to the government. A connection of this family at a later period founded Kishkindha. The Lanka and Kishkindha sovereigns, down to the time of Rávana the Rákshasa emperor, were in constant alliance. On one occasion, Kishkindha being attacked by the Vidyádharas owing to the quarrel which arose out of the success of the Kishkindha prince at a svayamvara, the Rákshasas supported the latter. But the allies were defeated, and the Vidyádhara emperor, overrunning both their kingdoms, placed a creature of his own on the throne of each. The Lanka princes after a time recovered their capital, but marching to aid in the reconquest of Kishkindha, were again defeated and deprived of their kingdom. Eventually Rávana drove out the Vidyádharas† and both kingdoms were once more ruled by their own princes.

An estrangement now sprang up between Rávana the king of Lanka and Váli the king of Kishkindha, because the latter was unwilling to give his sister in marriage to the former on account of his notorious character. Being, however, powerless to refuse, Váli abdicated in favour of his brother Sugríva. The latter by some stratagem was ousted from his throne just about the time that Rávana accomplished the abduction of Síta, the beautiful wife of Ráma. These royal exiles from the court of Ayodhya or Oudh had arrived near the Pampa or Tungabhadra when this calamity occurred. Sugríva obtained the aid of Ráma in regaining his throne, and forthwith placed all the resources of the kingdom at the disposal of his benefactor for the recovery of Síta.‡ Reports having been received that the ravisher was Rávana, and that he had carried off his victim to Lanka, Sugriva sent for Hanuman, the chief of Hanuvara dvípa (Honávar or Honore on the Canara coast) and despatched him, as being of Rák-

* The Silaháras of Karaháṭa (Karhad) near Kolapur claim to be Vidyádharas and connected with the royal race of Ceylon. A Chalukya inscription of A. D. 1008 says, "the Silára family of the Simhala kings are descended from Jímúta-váhana, son of Jímúta-ketu, the lord of the Vidyádharas, who was preserved by the celestial Garuḍa" (See *J. Bo. Br. R. A. S*, No. V, p. 221.)

† In one purána Rávana is said to have been seized and tied up by Kártavíryárjuna, thus making them contemporary.

‡ The so-called monkey army which assisted Ráma is thus evidently a poetical travesty for the army bearing the monkey flag. But it may be noticed that the names of certain tribes, as the Kóta of the Nilagiri, the Koḍagas of Coorg, &c., easily suggest monkeys (*kóti, kóḍaga*). Compare the story at p. 96 of the *Gazetteer of Coorg*.

shasa descent, to Lanka to ascertain the truth of the tidings. He brought back tokens from Síta, and the forces meanwhile assembled for her deliverance immediately set out. The story of the triumph of Ráma, the fall of Rávana, and the recovery of Síta are familiar to all.*

To pass to the accounts of the Páṇḍavas. The Mahá Bhárata, in describing the expeditions sent out by Yudhishṭhira to the four quarters to enforce the acknowledgment of his supremacy preparatory to the performance of the Rájasúya sacrifice, represents Sahadeva as commanding the one to the south.† In the course of his march he comes to a region called Guha which he subdues.‡ This is by tradition the name of the country round Harihara on the Tungabhadra. He then goes to Kishkindha and reduces to submission the Vánara rájas, of whom there appear to have been two. Thence he crosses the Kávérí to the city of Mahishmati (Mahishúr, Mysore) and attacks Níla Rája its king. A series of terrible battles ensues: Agni comes to the help of Níla Rája, and Sahadeva's army is in the point of destruction, when he propitiates Agni and peace is made. The reason of Agni's interference is explained at some length. The king Níla Rája, it is said, had a most lovely daughter, of whom the god Agni (Fire) became enamoured. He contrived to pay her many secret visits in the disguise of a Brahman, until one day he was discovered and brought up before the king. When about to be condemned to punishment, he blazed forth and revealed himself as the god Agni. The council hastened to appease him, and he granted the boon that the women of Mahishmati should thenceforth be free from the bonds of marriage, in order that no adultery might exist in the land; and that he would befriend the king in time of danger.

Now, in the celebrated Samudra Gupta inscription on the Allahabad pillar following upon one of As'oka's edicts, Níla Rája is mentioned among the southern kings. The passage was read by Prinsep § as follows:—*Kánchiyaka Vishnu, s'ápávamuktaka Níla Rája, Vaingeyaka Hasti Varma, Pálakka Ugrasena, &c.*

---

* As alleged tokens of the time of Ráma, the so-called coins known as *Rámaṭenki* are interesting. They are of gold, about the size of a crown piece and concave. Within the concavity are delicately executed figures of Ráma, S'ita and Lakshmana, seated on thrones. On the convex reverse is a figure of Hanumán, and arranged in a square around him, an inscription in what look like Páli or debased Greek characters. It is pretended that these are coins struck under the government of Ráma. They are rare, and found only among the Kómaṭis, the highest banking and trading class, who profess to be the sole Vais'yas. By these they are preserved with the utmost care as priceless heirlooms, and periodically worshipped as household gods. It is very difficult to get even a sight of one, and they are only sold under the direst necessity, as during the late terrible famine, which brought out a few.

† Sabhá Parva, 31st adhyáya. ‡ See note below, p. xxxii. § *J. A. S. Beng.* VI, 972.

But, as revised by Bhau Dáji,* it appears it should be—*Kánchíyaka Vishnu bhúpa, Avamuktaka Níla Rája, &c.* We have thus, according to him, Vishnu Bhúpa of Kánchi, Níla Rája of Avamukta, Hasti Varma of Viñga (? Vengi), Ugrasena of Pálaka, &c. But it seems doubtful if Avamukta is the name of a country.† On the other hand, whether the original be the one or the other of the above versions, the "freed from a curse" of the former or the "liberated" of the latter might be taken as an epithet of Níla Rája, and it is conceivable that it might have reference to the circumstances related in the Mahá Bhárata as above. But however this may be, the evidence for the existence of a Níla Rája is explicit, and taking into account the other localities mentioned, where can he be assigned to with greater probability than to Mysore? The period of Samudra Gupta, according to the latest authorities, would appear to be about the 1st century A. D. ‡

In No. 71 the Páṇḍavas are expressly stated to have visited Balligráme after the performance of the Rájasúya. Other points of connection with the Páṇḍavas may perhaps be found in the following circumstances. The *vánara-dhvaja* or *kapi-dhvaja*, the monkey flag, gave its name to the rulers of Kishkindha; and Kapi-dhvaja is a name of Arjuna, the most popular of the Páṇḍavas. Again, there is reason to believe that Hánagal, just over the north west frontier of Mysore, was the Viráṭa nagara in which the Páṇḍavas passed their last year of exile *incognito*.§ Now, the Kadambas, the earliest historical line of rulers in that region, had the *kapi-dhvaja* or monkey flag as one of their insignia (see pp. 53, 320) and when they were reduced to the position of feudatories under the Chalukyas, it was to the district of Hánagal that their jurisdiction was circumscribed.

With the commencement of the Christian era we enter upon more certain and authentic history. There is evidence that by the 2nd century the Kadam-

---

* *J. Bo. Br. R. A. S.* IX, cxcviii.

† Seeing that *s'ápávamuktaka* on closer examination resolved itself into *bhúpávamuktaka*, possibly still further investigation might result in the discovery that it should be read *bhúpála Mahisha* (or Mahishaka).

‡ See the learned investigations of Mr. E. Thomas in *Report on Archæological Survey of Western India* for 1876, Chap. III. Also article by Sir E. C. Bayley, in *Ind. Ant.* VI, 57.

The Guptas have been supposed to be the same as the Nágas. The *Vishnu Purána*, using the prophetic style, says, "the nine Nágas will reign in Padmávatí, Kántipuri and Mathurá; the Mágadhas and the Guptas will rule over Prayága on the Ganges; . . . the Guhas will possess Kalinga, *Máhishaka*, and the mountains of Máhendra." Bk. IV, Chap. xxiv.

§ *Ind. Ant.* V, 177.

bas were supreme in the north west of Mysore, and the Gangas in the south and centre: while the east was ruled by the Mahávali line, and the north east by the Pallavas. To take these up in the order mentioned.

Kadambas.—The dominions of the Kadambas embraced all the west of Mysore, together with Haiga (N. Canara) and Tulava (S. Canara). The founder of the line is variously styled Jayanta, Trilochana Kadamba and Trinetra Kadamba; and their original capital was Banavasi (Jayantipura or Vaijayantipura) situated on the river Varada on the western frontier of the Sorab taluk. It is mentioned by Ptolemy. It is also mentioned (in the Mahawanso) together with Mahisha-maṇḍala (Mysore) as a place to which a Buddhist missionary was sent after the third convocation, held in the 18th year of As'oka or B. C. 245. The thero Mahadeva was sent to Mahisha, and the thero Rakshita to Wanawasi.

As for the origin of the family,—it is said that after his conquest of the Asura Tripura, some drops of sweat fell from S'iva's forehead at the root of a *kadamba* tree: and thence was born the progenitor of the line, called in consequence the Kadambas (see p. 59). The tree itself is said to have been produced by a drop of nectár which fell upon the earth from the churning stick, namely the Mandara mountain, at the churning of the ocean.

The kadamba tree appears to be one of the palms from which toddy is extracted.* Toddy drawing is the special occupation of several primitive tribes spread over the south west of India, and bearing different names in various parts:—The Hale-paiki or Hale-paika of Naga, the I'ḍiga of other districts in the west of Mysore, the Kumára-paika of N. Canara, the Bilvar of S. Canara, Vastara and Coorg, the Tíyar of Malabar and Coorg, &c. In Manjarabad the Hale-paiki hold a higher social position, and are called *Dévara makkaḷu*, sons of God. The Todas of the Nilagiri clearly betray a common origin, for among them the Paiki form the highest clan, from which alone the *páláls* or priests are chosen, and these also style themselves *Der mokh* (that is *Dévara makkaḷu*) sons of God.† The Hale-paiki are said to be brave, and good sports-

* Toddy from the *ichalu* (*elate sylvestris*) resembles milk in appearance. It is obtained by making a triangular incision in the stem of the tree, just below the head, and tying an earthen pot under the incision so as to catch the juice as it exudes. Trees are successively tapped in this manner at about a foot apart as long as they continue to grow. When the toddy ferments, it has a strong and unpleasant odour. From it is distilled arrack. Toddy is also extracted from the *táḷé* or palmyra palm (*borassus flabelli-formis*). The juice of the bagni or baini palm (*caryota urens*), when fresh drawn, resembles lemonade. The general name for toddy in Kannaḍa is *henda, séndi*.

† Col. Marshall, *A Phrenologist among the Todas*.

men. They were employed by former rulers as foot soldiers and body guards, being noted for their fidelity. Besides extracting toddy from the bagini palm, they now engage in the cultivation of rice, and of woods containing pepper vines. The Bilvar are bowmen, as their name indicates. The Todas are acknowledged as the lords of the soil by the remaining tribes on the Nilagiri, and do no manner of work. They hold sacred the buffalo, (*mahisha*) from which animal Mysore, properly Mahish-úru, derives its name, and maintain large herds of it for the sake of the milk.

A strong belief has been expressed that the Todas are connected with the Æthiopians,* a term applied by the ancient Greeks to certain dark races occupying the modern countries of Beluchistan in Asia and Nubia and Abyssinia in Africa. Now in the account which Herodotus gives† of a mission sent by the Persian monarch Cambyses, when he was in Egypt, to the Ethiopians, some curious coincidences present themselves, which may be thought to lend support to the theory; and it is well known that in the language of Beluchistan traces are found of a connection with the south Indian languages.‡ To quote the passage from Herodotus referred to: "When the Ichthyophagi had arrived from Elephantine, Cambyses despatched them to the Ethiopians, prescribing what they were to say; and carrying gifts, consisting of a purple cloak, a golden neck-chain armlets, a stone jar filled with myrrh, and a *flask of date wine*. These Ethiopians, to whom Cambyses was sending, are described as the most gigantic and the handsomest of men: their customs, it is added, are totally different from those of other nations, and especially so far as regards the royal power; these people investing with the sovereignty that citizen whom they regard as of most gigantic stature, and of strength commensurate to his size.

---

* Id. p. 4. † Thalia, 20 ff.

‡ Bráhui, the language of the mountaineers in the khanship of Kelat in Beluchistan, contains not only some Dravidian words, but a considerable infusion of distinctively Dravidian forms and idioms. ....The Bráhuis state that their forefathers came from Haleb (Aleppo). Dr. Caldwell, *Gram. Drav. Lang.* intro. 43.

The Ethiopians from the East (for there were two kinds of Ethiopians in the army) were drawn up with the Indians; they resembled the other Ethiopians in appearance, but differed in their language and their hair; for the Ethiopians of the East are straight-haired, whereas those of Libya have hair the most curly of all men: for the most part, these people were accoutred after the fashion of the Indians, but they wore on their heads the skins of horse's foreheads stripped off together with the ears and mane; the mane answered the purpose of a crest, while the ears of the horses were fastened in an erect position; in lieu of bucklers they made themselves a sort of armour from the skins of cranes. *Laurent's Herodotus*, vii, 70. The following is the translator's note—It is probable they occupied, E of Persia, a part of Gedrosia, and even the country of the Oritæ conquered by Alexander. Mecran, a province of Persia, on the bounds of Hindustan, appears to me to answer to the country of these Eastern Ethiopians.

"The Ichthyophagi having reached to this nation, presented the gifts to the king, saying as follows: 'Cambyses, king of the Persians, desirous to become your friend, has sent us with his behests to us to have an interview with you and present you with these gifts, in the enjoyment of which he himself delights.' The Ethiopian, already informed that spies were coming to him, made this reply to them: 'It is false that the king of the Persians' said the prince to them 'sent you with gifts, esteeming it such an honour to have me for his friend: neither do you speak the truth, for you have come hither as spies upon my kingdom. If your king were an honest man, he would neither covet another's territory besides his own, nor would he reduce to thraldom men from whom he has never received any offence. Now, therefore, do you give to him *this bow*; and say to him these words:—The Ethiopian king advises the Persian king, when the Persians can thus easily string a bow of this size, then to head his overwhelming multitudes against the Macrobian Ethiopians: until that time, let him thank the gods they have never turned the minds of the sons of the Ethiopians to possess themselves of any country than their own." He spoke thus, *unstrung the bow and gave it to the new comers*: then he took up the purple cloak, asked what it was, and how it was made. The Ichthyophagi describing to him all the exact particulars respecting purple and the mode of dyeing; the king said, 'The men are full of deceit; and full of deceits also are their garments.' Then he asked about the neck-chain and the armlets: the Ichthyophagi representing the beauty of such ornaments, the king burst into laughter; he knew, he said, they were chains, and observed that the Ethiopians had stronger ones than those. Next he inquired about the myrrh; and when informed how that ointment was manufactured he made the same remarks as he had done respecting the cloak. *But when he came to the wine, and was informed how it was obtained, he was beyond measure delighted with the beverage*; and then asked, what was the chief food of the king, and what was the greatest extension of life among the Persians. The spies replied, that the king ate bread, and described the nature of wheat; and stated that the longest duration of life prescribed to man is eighty years. Whereupon the Ethiopian prince observed, he was not at all surprised that living upon dung and muck, they should be so short lived; nor indeed would they even be able to attain to that age if they did not refresh their vigour by the use of the beverage, *pointing to the wine, and confessing that in that particular, the Ethiopians were inferior to the Persians.* The Ichthyophagi, in their turn, questioned the king on the length of life, and the diet of his people: he told them, that most of his subjects reached their hundredth year, and some even exceeded that; their food was boiled meat: *and their drink milk.*"

This digression will be pardoned if it may be supposed to throw any light on the remote origin of the interesting races engaged in toddy drawing, from one of which, the Halepaika* for instance, we are probably to understand that the Kadamba family in reality sprang. These races, though now free, formed for ages, until quite recent times, the servile class; and should there be any reason, as is alleged, to connect them with the Chaldæans, the Turanian inhabitants of ancient Babylonia†, the vista is carried back to the very cradle of the human race and the sources of the Mosaic history of the creation.‡

To return to the founder of the Kadamba line of kings. Perhaps he was selected for the crown as the fittest of his race, after the custom of the Ethiopians as related above; but according to tradition, the people of the country being at the time without a ruler, had recourse to the state elephant, which being turned loose carrying a wreath, presented it to the youth whose birth was so miraculous, and he was consequently proclaimed king. The royal line thus founded continued independent till the 6th century, and during this period they claim to have performed many as'vamedhas or horse sacrifices, indications of supreme authority. They were then subdued by the Chalukyas and reduced to the condition of feudatories, their jurisdiction being confined to the province of Pánungal or Hánagal in Dharwar. From the 10th century they appear to have been entrusted with the government of a larger portion of their ancestral dominions, and in the 12th century their capital was at Goa (Gopaka-paṭna). The founders of the Vijayanagar empire in 1336 seem to have been connected with the Kadamba family, and from that time no trace is met with of the latter.

The following are lists of the Kadamba kings as derived from various inscriptions. There is not sufficient information to admit of their being exactly synchronized, and there may have been branches of the family, but some of the names in each of the lists evidently correspond.

---

* The name Halepaika is said to be derived from *haḷe* and *páyika*, meaning the Old Foot: others say from *haḷe* and *páyaka*, the old drinkers. Their occupation may have suggested the latter; and if the peculiarity which Colonel Marshall has remarked in the Todas, that they always keep step in walking—said to be very unusual even among trained sepoys when off duty—be common to the Haḷepaiki, it may have suggested the other. And with regard to this latter peculiarity, may it not account for the Ekapáda or Ekapádaka, the one-footed men of the Sanskrit writers? (pp. 123, 222).

† *Phren. am. Todas*, p. 4.

‡ *Hist. of Babylonia from the Ancient Monuments*, by the late George Smith, edited by Rev. A. H. Sayce.

a *	A. D.	*b*	A. D.	*c*	A. D.
Jayanta, Trilochana, Trinetra ...	109				
Madhukes'vara.					
Mallinátha.					
Chandra Varmma.					
Chanda Varmma,					
Chandra Varmma.				Mayúra Varmma.	
Purandara.					
Mayúra Varmma.				Mukanna.	
Kshetra Varmma, Chandragada, Trinetra.		Krishna Varmma ...	438	Krishna Varmma...	420
Krishna Varmma.		Deva Varmma.			
Nága Varmma.		Kákustha Varmma...	538		
Vishnu Varmma.		S'ánti or S'ántivara Varmma			
Mriga Varmma.		Mriges'a Varmma, Mriges'avara Varmma ...	570		
Satya Varmma.					
Vijaya Varmma.		Ravi Varmma ...	...		
Jaya Varmma.		Bhánu Varmma ...	600		
Nága Varmma.		Hari Varmma ...			
S'ánta Varmma.					
Kírtti Varmma.					
A'ditya Varmma.					
Bhattaya Varmma.					
Jaya Varmma.					
Mayúra Varmma ...	1034—1044				
Tailapa	1054				
S'ánti Varmma.		Guhalla Deva ...	...	Kirtti Varmma ...	1068
Tailapa	1077—1108	Shashta Deva ...	...	Barmmarasa ...	1108
Namra Bhúpa Permadi.		Jayakes'i ...	...	Boppa Deva.	
S'ánti Varmma.		Vijayáditya ...	...	Purandara ...	1121
Taila	1157	Jayakes'i, Jayas'iva	c 1125	Taila...	1129
Karna.		Permadi, S'iva Chitta	...	Soma, Soyi ...	1157
Sovi, Somes'vara.		Vijayáditya, Vikramárka Vishnu Chitta ...	...	Ketarasa, Nagati arasa	1171
Víra Malla ...	1241—1251			Toppa Devarasa, Nigalanka Malla ...	1179
		Jayakes'i... ...	1187	...	1277
S'ankara Deva ...	1336				

Of the early kings, Mayúra Varmma was the most celebrated: but the Chandra Varmmas who preceded him are of high interest, if, as seems probable, they respectively represent, one, Chandrahása, the hero of the popular and romantic story of that name†, and the other, the progenitor of the Kodaga or Coorg race.‡

Chandrahása's capital is said to have been at Kubattur in the Shimoga District. He was the son of a king of Kerala (Malabar), but on the death of his father and mother, was carried to Kuntala (N. Shimoga, Dharwar and neighbouring districts) by his nurse, where she also died, and he was reduced to

* *a* From Sir Walter Elliot, (*Mad. J. L. and S.*, XVIII, 227): *b* from Mr. Fleet, (*Ind. Ant.* V, VI and VII; *J. Bo. Br. R. A. S.* IX): *c* from inscriptions in the present volume, except Purandara, who is mentioned by Buchanan.

† See *Gazetteer of Mysore and Coorg*, Vol. I, 187—8. ‡ *id.* Vol. III, 91—3.

subsist by begging. The minister, Dushṭa-buddhi, (a statue of whom is shewn at Kubattur), having learnt from astrologers that the boy had signs of greatness upon him indicating that he would one day become ruler of the country, took measures to have him secretly murdered. But the executioners merely conveyed him into the forest and let him go, where he was found by an officer named Kulinda, who was childless, and adopted by him. (Kulinda is said to have been the lord of Chandragutti in the Shimoga District).

The boy grew up as a valuable assistant to his protector; but the minister one day, on visiting the latter, discovered that the young man was no other than the boy he had thought was murdered long ago. Another plan was contrived to get rid of him, but, by a series of romantic circumstances, it came about that he married the king's daughter and succeeded to the throne, on which the minister destroyed himself.

As regards Chanḍa Varmma, there is a story that he rescued from the flames of a forest fire a serpent named Manjista, which, entering into his mouth, took up its abode in his stomach. He was forced to wander about in search of a cure, which was eventually effected by an old woman at Kalyáṇa-pura. The truth probably is that his kingdom was usurped by some Nága chief. According to the *Kávérí Puráṇa*, Chandra Varmma was a son of Siddhártha, king of Matsya (Viráṭa's capital, Hánagal in Dharwar). He left his country, and went on a pilgrimage to all the holy *tírthas* or bathing places, until Párvati appeared and offered him a boon, in consequence of which he received a kingdom at the source of the Kávérí, and a S'údra wife, from whom he, as a Kshatriya, should beget a valiant race called Ugras. For the eleven sons he had by her, the hundred daughters of the king of Vidarbha (Berar) by S'údra mothers were obtained as wives. Each of these bore more than a hundred sons, who, to provide accommodation for their growing numbers, levelled the hill slopes and settled over a district five yojanas in extent at the sources of the Kávéri river in Coorg.

Mayúra Varmma seems to have restored the authority of the Kadambas, and is sometimes represented as the founder of the line. He became king of Banavasi, and there obtained 'the sword of sharpness, the shoes of swiftness, and the garment of invisibility.' He is said to have rescued Sasiprabhé, the wife of Rája Vallabha, prince of Kalyánapura, from a *yaksha* named Kandarpa Bhúshana, living in Hemanta-guhe, who had carried her off. He received in consequence a large accession of territory, together with the Kalyána princess S'as'anka-mudre in marriage. He is also stated to have introduced Brahman colonists from Ahichchatra (in Rohilkand), and distributed the country below the Ghats into 64 portions, which he bestowed upon them. In the reign of his son Kshetra Varmma, Chandragada or Trinetra, these Brahmans attempted to leave the province, but they were brought back; and in order to prevent a repetition of the attempt were compelled to leave unshorn a lock of hair on the forehead as a distinguishing mark. From these are descended the Haiga or Havika Brahmans of the north-west of Mysore. They would appear (p. 196) on this occasion to have been settled by Mukanna, that is Trinetra, above the Ghats, at Sthánagundúru (Tálagundi). During his reign, a kinsman named Chandrasena ruled the south of Tulava, and the Brahmans were spread into those parts. Lokáditya or Lokádípya, the son of Chandrasena, married Kanakávati, the sister of Trinetra, and had by her a daughter, whom Hubásiga, the king of the mountain Chaṇḍálas, sought as a wife for his son. In pretended compliance, he was invited to Tripura and there treacherously murdered. The authority of the Kadambas was extended in consequence above those Ghats, and the Brahmans followed this accession of territory. Lokádípya is said to have reigned 50 years.

Of Krishna Varmma we have several notices, to the effect that his sister was given in marriage to the Ganga king Mádhava II, whose reign ended in 425. Krishna Varmma's son was Deva Varmma, who makes a grant, but without date, from Triparvata. He claims to be in the enjoyment of a heritage not to be attained by the Nágas.* From the grants of the others who follow him in column *b*, it appears that Kákustha Varmma was ruling at Palásika (Halasige in Dharwar); Mriges'a Varmma at Vaijayanti (Banavasi). The latter king is described as a fire of destruction to the Pallavas, and the uprooter of the lofty (*tunga*) Gangas. Ravi Varmma is stated to have uprooted Chaṇḍa Daṇḍa the lord of Kánchi†, who should therefore be a Pallava. Bhánu Varmma was his brother, and in his reign may have occurred the Chalukya invasion which terminated the independence of the Kadambas, for Jaya Simha, who effected the conquest, reigned at the end of the 6th century. Accordingly, we find Hari Varmma's grant issued from Uchchás'ringi (Uchchangi-durga near Harihara, the seat of government for the Noḷambavāḍi Thirty-two Thousand province); but the family are not prominent again till the 11th century, when their alliance seems to have been sought by the Chálukya Vikrama in his plans against his brother, and on his success they were advanced in honour.

The group among whom Jayakes'i occurs had their capital at Gopakapaṭṇa (Goa). It will be seen (p. 98) that the first Vijayáditya married the

* *Ind. Ant.* VII, 34. † *id.* VI, 30.

sister of the king of Hombucha. His son Jayakes'i married Mailala Mahádeví, 'the ruby of the Chálukyas.' The daughter of the last Jayakes'i married Karṇa, Rája of Chedi or Bandalkhand.*

Of the names in column *c*, Kírtti Varmma was governor of the Banavase Twelve Thousand province under the Chalukya king Trailokya Malla (p. 320). Barmmarasa was an official of Noḷambavádi under Tribhuvana Malla (p. 18). Taila appears as the head of the family in the time of Somes'vara (p. 89). Soma, grandson of Barmmarasa before mentioned, was an official of the Nágara-khaṇḍa Seventy in the time of the Kalachurya king Bijjala (p. 59). Ketarasa's son Nágati-arasa is described (p. 53) as lord of a Thousand náḍ and in authority at Uchchangi durga. Many particulars of the family are given in this place. Toppa Devarasa appears as the chief of the family in 1179 at Balligámve (p. 161). Finally, a Kadamba king, whose name is not mentioned, is said (p. 47) to have been established in his authority by Tikkama, the general of the Yádava king Rámachandra Deva in 1277.

It seems probable from a consideration of the above particulars, that the branch of the Kadambas at Uchchangi-durga, &c., was different from that at Goa. The former seem to have had the management, and perhaps an hereditary claim to some portion, of the public taxes, referred to as the *manneya, pannáya*, &c. Though holding a subordinate position, they are always mentioned with great respect, as became the representatives of an ancient royal family of so high distinction.

Their grants of the 5th and 6th centuries, when they were independent, describe them in certain terms which it is singular are those a little later adopted by the Chálukyas, namely—their connection with the group of mothers (the seven mothers), and their being of the Mánavya gotra, and sons of Háriti.

Gangas.—The true history of this important line of kings—apparently purely Mysorean in their origin—may be said to have been entirely brought to light and authenticated by the inscriptions No. 151—157 included in this volume. They were previously supposed to be identical with the Chera kings mentioned in the earliest traditions of the south, but not one of their various grants so far known contains any reference to the Cheras.† An old Tamil chron-

* See the romantic story about this from the *Dvyás'raya, Ind. Ant.* IV, 233.

† It will be noticed (p. 263) that the Hoysala king Vishnu Varddhana after he had acquired the whole of the Ganga kingdom gives Chera as one of the southern limits of his dominions; that (p. 70) Ganga is distinguished from Chera; also that (p. 143) a Ganga professes to subdue a Chera king.

Chera probably corresponded with Travancore, Cochin, &c.

icle,*—which was, until the present grants were discovered, the principal, if not only, source of information regarding them—simply styles them kings of the Kongu country without any dynastic name.

That document further states that they were preceded in the government of Kongu by seven kings of the Raṭṭa line. Of these no memorial has hitherto been found, but the following are their names, &c.—

	A. D.		A. D.
Víra Ráya Chakravarti.		Govinda Ráya.	
Govinda Ráya.		Chaturbhuja Kanara Deva Chakravarti.	
Krishna Ráya.		S'ri Vikrama Deva Chakravarti	178—188
Kali Vallabha Ráya.			

In the section on the Raṭṭa kings, it will be seen that some of these names correspond with those of later rulers of that line. Little is known of the first six kings, save that a learned Jain named Nága Nandi was *guru* to the last three. S'rí Vikrama or Tiru Vikrama abandoned the Jain faith for that of S'iva, and after his conversion is said to have made many conquests in the Choḷa, Páṇḍya, Keraḷa and Malayála countries. He is mentioned as if the first who ruled over Karṇáṭaka or Mysore.

No reason is stated for the change of dynasty which followed, but it seems highly probable that the Gangas of Mysore threw off his yoke and superseded him in the government, which thenceforward remained in their family for many centuries. The Ganga kingdom may be described, generally, as having extended over all the region drained by the river Kávéri and its tributaries, with the exception of the delta of Tanjore: that is to say, over the south of Mysore and Coorg, with Salem, Coimbatore, the Nilagiri and parts of Malabar. Their territory in Mysore was called the Gangaváḍi Ninety-six Thousand, as containing perhaps 96 náds; while their territory in Coimbatore and Salem was called the Kongu country.† Down to the middle of the 3rd century their capital was at Skandapura, which Lassen has placed at Gajalhaṭṭi, on the old ghat road from the south of Mysore to Trichinopoly: the seat of government was then removed to Talavana-pura or Talakáḍu on the Kávéri.

The Ganga crest was an elephant, and with the use of this animal, which abounds throughout the mountain ranges on the southern frontier of Mysore, they seem to have been very familiar. They were evidently a hardy and manly race; for one king reckons a wound received in war as his principal ornament, of another it is said his arms were grown stout and hard with athletic exercises and were adorned with hard knobs produced by the discharge of

* *Kongu-des'a rájakal,* Mad. J. L. and S. XIV.

† The subjects of Gangaváḍi are represented by the present Gangadikára ryots (Gangavádikara, p. 296); while those of Kongu are the present Kongas, and a form of that name may also perhaps survive in Koḍagu, which has been corrupted by Europeans into Coorg.

his bow as if with brilliant gems. Their skill in horsemanship is more than once mentioned. But they were distinguished alike in letters as in arms, for two of them are described as authors of books, and others as deep students of political and other science.

The following is the list of the Ganga kings from inscriptions,* with their dates, to a great extent verified by grants.

	A. D.
Kongaṇi Varmma Dharmma	188 to 239
Mádhava	239
Hari Varmma	...247 to 288..
Vishnu Gopa	350
? Rája Malla	
Mádhava	to 425
Kongaṇi	425 to 478
Avinita, Duvvinita, Kongaṇi Vriddha, Kongaṇi	478 to 513
Mushkara	
S'ri Vikrama	to 539
Bhú Vikrama	539

	A. D.
Vilanda Rája [Kongaṇi]	620
S'rí Vallabha [Govinda Ráya, Nandi Varmma]	
Sivamára, Nava Káma, Kongaṇi	668
? Bhíma Kopa	
? Rája Kesari, A'luva Ganga	690
Prithuví Kongaṇi	727 to 777
Rája Malla Deva	
Ganda Deva	
Rácha Malla, Satya Vákya Kongaṇi	837 to 869
Permmanaḍi do do	869
Malla Deva	...878 to 894

It will be seen that Kongaṇi was a sort of family name, and held by several of the kings. It also appears in the forms Konguḷi, Konguṇi and Kongiṇi.

The first king is invariably described as having distinguished himself by the renowned, but rather unintelligible, feat of dividing with a single stroke of his sword a great *s'ilá stambha* or stone pillar. It seems not improbable that the term should properly be *s'ila stambha*, the name given to the pillars on which the edicts of As'oka were inscribed. None has hitherto been found in the south, but no reason appears why one should not have been erected in this part of India, which Kongani I. overthrew. The conversion by the uninitiated of so artificial a term as *s'ila stambha* into the more common collocation *s'ilá stambha* seems a most natural error. This king is also said (p. 289) to have been a wild-fire in consuming *Baṇa*, to whom further reference will be made later on.

The next king, Mádhava I, seems to have been a learned man, and is stated to have written a treatise on the law of adoption. Hari Varmma it was who removed the capital to Talavana-pura or Talakáḍu, and there all the subsequent kings were crowned. Vishnu Gopa's claim to notice is generally a vague statement of his religious devotion; but in one inscription (p. 289) he is with more apparent truth to nature described as a skilful ruler, who retained his mental energy unimpaired to the end of life; from which it would appear he must have lived to a great age.

* The names in brackets are from the Chronicle and not found in the inscriptions.

According to one inscription (p. 293) he seems to have had a son Rája Malla, who was governor of Talavana-pura during his father's lifetime. But his successor, according to all the fuller inscriptions, was a son called Mádhava, whether the same is not clear.* Mádhava married the sister of the Kadamba king Krishna Varmma, and their son was Kongani II, who, from the fact of his receiving his coronation anointing while an infant in his mother's lap (pp. 292-295), seems to have been born only shortly before his father's death. An important revival of Brahman influence is implied under Madhava II. from the statements (pp. 290, 291, 295) that he renewed many thousands of long ceased donations for the festivals of the gods and Brahman endowments. Kongani II. seems to have pursued the same policy.

Avinita, the son of the last, appears to have been a remarkable character: his names are singular, and he is credited with a mastery of magical incantations. He was the author of a commentary on the Kirátárjuníya. He is said (pp. 285, 292) to have waged sanguinary wars for the possession of Andari, A'lattúr, Paurulare, Pennagara and other places. Of these, Pennagara or Pelnagara is the place still so called situated near the left bank of the Kávéri in the north west of the Salem district: the others have not been identified. He is also described (p. 292) as ruling the whole of (?) Pákhád (possibly Pálghát, south west of Coimbatore, near which too is an A'lattúr) and Punnád, as if he had added these provinces to the Ganga kingdom. Punnád was a Ten Thousand country (p. 283), which apparently means that it contained 10 nads, for it is identical with the Padi-nádu of more modern times (p. 334) occupying the south-east of the Mysore District. Its chief at the time was Skanda Varmma, and his daughter, we are told (pp. 222, 295), fell in love with Avinita and became his wife, although her father had betrothed her to some one else. By his conquests Avinita is said to have exacted tribute from the kings of Kerala, Pándya, Chola, Dravida, A'ndhra and Kalinga.

Of the succeeding kings, under Vilanda Raja (? Kongani IV), his brother. S'rí Vallabha, who was commander-in-chief, gained a great victory at a place called Bhimes'a gráma over the Pallava king Narasimha or Narasimha Pota Varmma—who was trodden to death in the fight by his elephants (p. 285) He is said to have carried his victories over the whole of the Peninsula, up even to the river Narmadá, taking tribute from Chola, Pándya, Dravida,

* The Chronicle previously referred to gives a different account of what occurred. According to it, Vishnu Gopa, being childless, adopted a son named Mádhava, who was installed in the government in subordination to the king. But the latter afterwards had a son born to him, Krishna Varmma, who was anointed as his successor and Mádhava provided with some territory below the ghats. Krishna Varmma dying childless, Dindikara Ráya, a connection of Mádhava's, obtained the kingdom: but the ministers set him aside in favour of Kongani the son of Krishna Varmma's sister.

A'ndhra, Kalinga, Viráṭa, Maháráshṭaka and other countries. On his return from this expedition, he strongly fortified Talakáḍu. Meanwhile he took up his residence at Muganda-patna or Mukunda-patna, which was situated at the present village of Mákunda, near Molur, close to Channapatna. His successor also resided here, but it is at about this time that the Kadamba king Mṛiges'a Varmma speaks of uprooting the lofty (*tunga*) Gangas, and the Chálukya king Vinayáditya of being served by A'luva Ganga (p. 237). The succession is not very clear until Prithuví Kongani, who had a long and prosperous reign. His queen was named S'ríjá (p. 288). It must have been his successor Rája Malla, whom, according to Raṭṭa inscriptions, the Raṭṭa king Dhruva or Nirupama defeated and imprisoned; the Gangas, it is stated, having never been conquered before. This Raṭṭa king's son Govinda, on coming to the throne about 785, released from his long and painful captivity the Ganga king whom his father had confined, but eventually was forced again to seize and imprison him.*

It is to this period, both from its style and from some of its historical allusions, that I would assign the reign of Ereyappa of the elaborately sculptured stone brought from Begur, 10 miles south of Bangalore (p. 209). He is described as descending with the brilliance of lightning among the stars in the clear firmament (a phrase indicating a peaceful and untroubled succession, specially used with relation to this line) of the world-renowned Ganga kings,—a pretty plain statement that he was an usurper. He is represented as the independent ruler of the Gangavádi Ninety-six Thousand; 'the protector of the mighty Valala and Mekhala kings, and the chosen lord and possessor of the auspicious Taila's dominion.' The former of the above phrases may be doubtful, but the latter is clear; and I consider refers to the Chálukya king Taila or Tailapa, in whose time that powerful dynasty, as will appear in the section relating to them, met with some reverse, and did not recover the possession of their dominions until 973, when a more illustrious Tailapa won back the lost throne of his fathers.

The important Rudra Deva inscription at Anumakonda or Warangal † must also refer to this period, as it speaks of Proli Raja capturing and subse-

* *Ind. Ant.* VI, 69, 70.

† *J. A. S. B.* vii, 901: revised and corrected by Bhau Dáji *J. Bo. Br. R. A. S.* x, 46. There must be some great mistake about the date: the former giving it as S'aka 1054, the latter as 1064, and both as the year Chitrabhánu; but Chitrabhánu does not agree with either by 20 and 30 years! The reference to the Chálukya king Tailapa and his successor Bhíma, as also to the Raṭṭa king Govinda, unmistakeably fixes the period as the middle of the 9th century; moreover the Ayyapa of the Begur stone, who attacked Ereyappa and was defeated, was doubtless the Chálukya of that name, Bhíma's son.

quently releasing the Chálukya king Tailapa Deva. The latter, however, afterwards, when Rudra Deva had come to the throne, died, and was succeeded by Bhíma (the next on the list of the Chálukyas) "the vilest of kings" &c., who "ventured to defy the terrible Rudra Deva." He was eventually forced to submit, together with "all the rájas like him living between Kánchimaṇḍala and the Vindhya mountains"—the latter is the region of the Mekhalá or Narmadá river. But to connect Ereyappa more directly with this inscription, it will be seen that Proli is said to have given a kingdom taken from Tailapa (and Govinda Rája the Raṭṭa, who, it will be seen in another place, had at this time acquired supreme control of the Chálukya territory,) to "king Erha" in the first version, "king Udaya" in the second, of which I take the former to be correct.

To pursue the history of the Gangas.—Gaṇḍa Deva seems to have re-established their authority and is stated to have conquered Kánchi and levied a tribute upon Draviḍa. He also fought with the Chola king, and impressing him with fear, afterwards made friendship with Chola and Páṇḍya. Of the two Satya Vákya Konganis there are inscriptions in Coorg, from which the dates are determined.* The first, Rácha Malla, is spoken of as ruling at S'ripura, which was situated (p. 286) near Gúdalúr, the existing place of that name on the north west of the Nilagiri, on the borders of that district and Wainád. He assumes the titles "lord of Kovaláḷapura or Koláḷapura (Kolar) and of Nandagiri (Nandidurga)" †. Malla Deva, the last on the list, is related to have defeated an attack by the Páṇḍya king.

Soon after this (about 894) it seems that a Chola king took Talakáḍu, and the Gangas were driven from their kingdom; but we continue to meet with notices of members of the family in subordinate positions. The first I can adduce is in a stone inscription, without date, of the Pallava king Bíra Noḷamba, at Goribidnur. He claims to be 'the protector of Ayyapa Deva's daughter' ‡ and is, I take it, the Bíra Mahendra of the Begur stone (p. 209), while Ayyapa, as already stated, may be identified with the Chálukya prince of that name. If this be correct, he lost his life in that battle, and his daughter, taken prisoner §, became the prize of the ruling sovereign. In this inscription, whose

---

* *Ind. Ant.* vi, 99.

† He appears to have admitted the claim of a son of Ereyanga gámunda to an estate in Kalnáḍ on his doing homage and paying tribute. Now Kal-naḍ is the name of the district bestowed by the usurper Ereyappa on similar terms (p 209). Might the son possibly be his? But if so, it is difficult to account for the grant being set up in Coorg.

‡ *S'ríman mahá ... Ayyapa Devana magaḷ aṇaga*; the last word would also mean Thumbler :' but I have adopted the more gallant interpretation.

§ Can this be the female, bound, apparently blind-folded, to the king's standard in No. 113?

date would thus be about 900, we find a Ganga, lord of Kolá|apura, and *nanniya Ganga*, a Ganga of truth—a title evidently derived from the *Satya Vákya* of the later kings of his line—fighting under the Pallava king and losing his life in the battle.

Then we have (p. 148) *Satya* [*Vákya*], lord of Kuvalá|apura, chief of Nandagiri, having the ensign of a lusty elephant, *nanniya Ganga*, &c., making a gift at Balagami, apparently in 1058, in succession to the Chálukya king Jaya Simha. Though making no direct acknowledgement of dependence, he was probably subordinate to the Chálukyas; but the names have been deliberately mutilated. Next (p. 307) we have *Gangarasa*—retaining the titles, now shorn of their meaning, Konguli Varmma Dharmma Mahárájádhirája—and lord of Kolálapura, with the crest of a lusty elephant, and also calling himself *nanniya Ganga*, holding the position of governor of the Arabala Seventy and Melála *manneya* under the Hoysala king (? Ereyanga) in 1065.

A little later, or in 1070, we find (pp. 134, 144, 164) *Udayáditya* as minister for peace and war to the Chálukya king Bhuvanaika Malla. He seems (p. 165) to have gained some important victories, and by 1075 we find him (p. 142), after having subdued the neighbouring Chera*, Chola, Pándya and Pallava kings, appointed as governor of the Banavase Twelve thousand, the Sántalige Thousand, the Mandali Thousand and the eighteen agraháras. His titles are Ganga Permmanáḍi Bhuvanaika Víra, and he is lord of Kolá|apura and Nandagiri, has the crest of a lusty elephant, and is a Ganga of truth (*nanniya Ganga*). He seems (p. 173) to be still in power in 1102. We next find (p. 216) a *Ganga Rája* as a minister and general in 1136 under the Hoysala king Vishnu Varddhana, who (pp. 262, 332) had about 20 years before possessed himself by conquest of the whole of the former Ganga kingdom: the significant Ganga titles are now dropped by the representative of the family. This Ganga Rája's wife was Nágalá Devi, and they had a son *Bappa*.

Further, in 1158 there appears (p. 158) *Ekkalarasa*, 'a moon in raising the fortunes of the Ganga family', appointed to superintend an agrahára established in the reign of the Kalachurya king Bijjala by the governor of Banavase; while his son *Tailapa Devarasa* and his son-in-law Eraharasa remit the claim to certain dues in the same place (p. 160). These two appear (pp. 77, 119) in the same connection down to 1181.

The expression applied to Ekkalarasa, that he was a moon in raising the fortunes of the Ganga family, seems to imply some revival of their power, and

* This is worthy of note in connection with the hitherto supposed identity of the Cheras and Gangas.

accordingly we find an inscription bearing the dates 1173 and 1181 mentioned (*As. Res.* IX, 436) as having been found at Kurugóḍ, a few miles north of Bellary, from which it would appear that the Gangas had been established by the Chálukyas in a principality situated at about the site of the modern Vijayanagar on both sides of the Tungabhadra, as there are temples and grants by the Gangas at Lakshmesvar. Possibly the union of the Ganga princess with Víra Páṇḍya (p. 70) had something to do with this. The first of the princes that ruled at Kurugóḍ is stated to be Ráksha Malla. His wife was Somala Devi, by whom he had a son Nerungala Rája. The latter married Pakshala Devi, who bore him two sons, Ráksha Malla and Soma Bhúpála, of whom the elder, Immaḍi (or the second) Ráksha Malla, succeeded his father and was ruling at the time of the grant. It is interesting to note that the Chálukya king under whom this grant was made must have been the last of his line, and he is stated to have made Kurugóḍ his capital. See also p. 155 for Ráchche Malla's territory.

Having traced the Gangas thus far after their downfall in Mysore, and seen how on the occurence of that catastrophe members of the family found refuge with the neighbouring powers to the north, and were admitted to positions of influence and honour under them, we have now to direct our attention to a more distant quarter, where the Ganga sovereignty was revived and Ganga kings ruled with great glory for several centuries. This was in Orissa, where the Ganga vams'a dynasty—also called Gajapatis or elephant lords, and acknowledged to have come from Karṇáṭaka*—was established at the end of the 11th century and continued to rule that country down to 1534, soon after which it was subdued by the Muhammadans. The first of the line was Ananta Varmma,† also called (according to Wilson) "Koláhala, sovereign of Ganga Rárhi," which is no doubt a mistake for lord of Koláhaḷa-pura, and sovereign of Ganga-váḍi.

The following is the succession of the Ganga-vams'a kings of Orissa, as given in the chronicles preserved in the temple of Jagannátha at Puri.‡

Chor Ganga (Churanga, Saranga Deva, Rudra Deva)...	1132—1152
Gangesvara ...	1152—1166
Ekajátaka Deva ...	1166—1171
Madana Mahadeva ...	1171—1175
Ananga Bhíma Deva ...	1175—1202
Rájarájesvara Deva... ...	1202—1237
Lánguliya Narasimha Deva ...	1237—1282

Of these kings, Ananga Bhíma Deva was one of the greatest of the rulers

* Lassen. *Ind. Alt.* IV, 14.

† *McK. Coll.* I. cxxxviii.

‡ *id.* and Dr. Hunter's *Orissa* II, App. 187.

of Orissa. He made a survey of his whole kingdom, measuring it with reeds. He also built the present temple of Jagannáth. Rája Narasimha Deva built the great Sun temple at Kanárak on the sea, the black pagoda, 'the most exquisite memorial of sun worship in India or perhaps in any country.'*

The line continued in power down to 1534, soon after which the country fell a prey to the Muhammadans; but the only kings that claim notice here are Purushottama Deva, ruling in 1479—1504, and Pratápa Rudra, 1504—1532. The former sought in marriage the daughter of the king of Kánchi, famed for her beauty. But on the ground of his performing the office of sweeper to Jagannáth his suit was rejected. He therefore attacked Kánchi and was at first repulsed. At length he captured it, and took the princess prisoner, whom he vowed in revenge should be married to a sweeper. The minister charged with the execution of this order kept the girl in concealment until the festival of Jagannáth, at which the king was accustomed to sweep the ground before the god; and while he was engaged in that act, placed her beside him and they were married. The reign of Pratápa Rudra is remarkable for the reformation of the Vaishnava religion by the preaching of Chaitanya, whose views the king finally adopted; and Buddhism, to which he had previously inclined, was banished the country. Pratápa Rudra is said to have extended his conquests southwards as far as Cape Comorin, and his name occurs in many local traditions in the east of Mysore.

Not yet however have we done with the Gangas. About this time, or the first part of the 16th century, a Ganga Raja returned to the scene of their former dominions and established a principality at S'ivasamudram, the island at the falls of the Kávéri, about 12 miles north-east of Talakáḍu.

Ganga Rája, after a prosperous reign, was succeeded by his son Nandi Rája, who, to atone for some ceremonial offence, leaped into the cataract at Gagana Chukki on horseback with his wife. His son, Ganga Raja the second, enlarged the city greatly, and lived with much splendour. He had two daughters, whom he gave in marriage to the two chief Pálégars in the neighbourhood. The one was married to the Rája of Kilimale, a place now in ruins, about 12 miles from Satyagála: the other daughter was married to the Rája of Nagarakere, 3 miles east from Maddur. These marriages were very unhappy; for the pride of the ladies gave their husbands constant disgust. They were continually upbraided for not living in equal splendour with their father-in-law; and at length, having consulted together, they determined to humble their

* *id*; 288; Fergusson however now inclines to the opinion that it is really three centuries older. *Hist. Ind. Arch.* 426—7.

wives, by shewing that their power was superior to that of Ganga Rája. Having assembled all their forces, they besieged S'ivasamudra ; but for a time had very little success.

The siege had continued twelve years without their having been able to penetrate into the island, when the two Rájas found means to corrupt the Dalaváyi or minister of Ganga Rája. This traitor removed the guards from the only ford, and thus permitted the enemy to surprise the place, while he endeavoured to engage his master's attention at the game of chess. The shouts of the soldiery at length reaching their ears, the prince started up from the game. The Dalaváyi, who wished him to fall alive into the hands of his sons-in-law, endeavoured to persuade him that the noise arose merely from children at play ; but the Raja, having drawn his sword, first killed all his women and children, and then, rushing into the midst of his enemies, fought until he procured an honourable death. The sons-in-law on seeing this were struck with horror, and immediately threw themselves into the cataract at Gagana Chukki ; and their example was followed by their wives, whose arrogance had been the cause of such disasters.

Jagadeva Ráyal of Channapatna and S'ri Ranga Rája of Talakáḍ, the two most powerful of the neighbouring Pálégárs, then came, and removed all the people and wealth of the place.

Mahávalis.—The rule of this ancient house is established by the inscriptions Nos. 163 and 164, but their name, though connected with one of the most interesting places in the south of India, has been very rarely met with, and the dynasty has hitherto found no niche in history.

The first inscription (p. 304) belongs to the reign of a king named Mahávali Bāṇarasa of the Mahávali-kula, ? door-keepers (*pratihára*) to Parames'vara adored by all three worlds as the lord over gods and giants (*sura* and *asura*). The second inscription (p. 305) is of the reign of Mahávali Báṇarasa, who seems on account of his victories to have been called Vikramáditya, and to whom other kings gave the celebrated name of Báṇa Vijyádhara.*

Mahávali is evidently the same as Mahábali, after whom Mahábalipur or the Seven Pagodas, on the eastern coast a few miles south of Madras, was named. According to Hindu mythology, Mahá-Bali or Bali was a powerful Asura emperor, who become so elated with his prosperity that he omitted the essential ceremonies and offerings to the gods. To punish his arrogance, Vishnu

* This term is more commonly met with as Vidyádhara (see above, p. xxix). The interchange of *ja* and *da* is according to rule, and is well exemplified in the name of Vijayanagara, which was originally Vidyánagara.

assumed the form of a Brahman dwarf—the *vámana avatára*, the fifth incarnation—and appearing before him, asked a boon, which was promised. Vishnu requested only as much ground as he could pace in three steps, declining anything more, and this much was confirmed to him with the pouring of water. As the water fell into his hand, the dwarf's form expanded till it filled the world; and Vishnu, now manifesting himself, deprived Bali at two steps of heaven and earth, but on account of some virtues the latter possessed, left Pátála or the infernal regions still in his dominion.

With regard to the Mahávali-kula, they are mentioned in an inscription obtained by Sir Walter Elliot, * from which it appears that the Chálukya king Vikramáditya I (? 650—681) conquered the chief of the Mahámalla† kula, besides by the capture of Kánchi subjecting the Pallava king Jayates'vara Pota Raja. 'From these facts it may be inferred' adds Sir Walter 'that the rulers of Mámallaipura were in a state of independence in the 6th and beginning of the 7th centuries.' The present inscriptions not only support this view, but, for reasons to be further stated, make it likely that from the 2nd century the Mahávali line ruled the whole tract of country through which the river Pálár flows, from its source near Srinivaspur, where these stones were found, past Kánchi (Conjeveram), to Mahábalipur near its mouth.

To revert again to the legends of Mahábalipur ‡ "The son of Bali, its reputed founder §, was Báṇásura (Banácheren in *As. Res.*), who is represented as a giant with a thousand hands. Aniruddha, the son (or grandson) of Krishna, came to his court in disguise, and seduced his daughter; which produced a war, in the course of which Aniruddha was taken prisoner and brought to Mahábalipur: upon which Krishna came in person from his capital Dváraka and laid siege to the place. Siva guarded the gates and fought for Báṇásura, who worshipped him with his thousand hands; but Krishna found means to overthrow S'iva, and having taken the city, cut off Báṇásura's hands, except two, with which he obliged him to do homage. He continued in subjection to Krishna till his death, after which a long period ensued in which no mention is anywhere made of this place." It was subsequently destroyed by an inundation of the sea.

Whether the Báṇarasa of the inscriptions under notice had anything to do with Báṇásura of the foregoing story or not, the coincidence of names is singu-

* *Seven Pagodas*, 127; see also *Ind. Ant.* VI, 76.

† Another form of the name, which variously appears in that of the city as Mámallaipura, and Mahábalipura.

‡ See *Sev. Pag.* 13; *As. Res.* I, 156.

§ Balipura is also given (p. 119) as a form of the name of Balligámve (the mother of cities, *paṭṭanangala tavarmane*, see p. 89), the capital of the Banavase province in the north west of the Mysore, and its origin attributed to Bali, while the name Banavase itself, which was Sanskritized into Vanavási, might possibly have had some connection with Baṇa.

lar. But we are not without a direct reference to Báṇa which enables us to place him with certainty not later than the 7th century. This is in the Nágamangala inscription (p. 287), where Duṇḍu, the king of Nirgunda, is described as the confounder of the Báṇa-kula, a designation which may be considered as applied to the kings of the Mahávali line who came after Báṇa. But even with regard to Baṇa, assuming that he is not the same as Báṇa, there is probably a reference (p. 289) which makes him contemporary with the Ganga king Kongani I, and therefore to be assigned to the end of the 2nd century.

That the Mahávalis did not continue in power beyond the 7th century not only follows from the known fact that the Pallavas were in possession of Kánchi early in the 7th century—their former capital of Vengi having then passed into the hands of the Eastern Chálukyas,—and the improbability of their tolerating the existence of an independent kingdom in such close proximity to their capital, but from a Pallava inscription of 768 occurring on a stone at the very site where the two Mahávali inscriptions are, with others from that time onwards in various parts of the Kolar District, and from the existence at Mahábalipur itself of Pallava inscriptions of about this period.

Pallavas.—The Pallavas are an ancient line of kings of high interest who played an important part in the history of the south of India throughout the region in which the Telugu language now prevails. Their architectural remains at Amarávati and Mahábalipur are among the finest in the country, and shew that they were at first Buddhists.*

Their origin is uncertain. They are mentioned in the Puránas along with the Haihayas, S'akas, Yavanas, &c., as Pahlavas, which would imply a Persian source.† "As the name of a people, the word Pahlav" says Weber "became early foreign to the Persians, learned reminiscences excepted: in the Pahlav texts themselves for instance it does not occur. The period when it passed over to the Indians, therefore, would have to be fixed for about the 2nd—4th century A. D., and we should have to understand by it, not directly the Persians, who are called Párasikas rather, but specially the Arsacidan Parthians."‡

* See Fergusson's *Tree and Serpent Worship.*

† Wilson's *Vishnu Purána* (Hall's edn) II, 187: III, 292 &c.

‡ *Hist. Ind. Lit.* (Trubuer's Or. Ser.) 188. There are Pahlavi Christian insciptions at St. Thomas's Mount near Madras and other places in the south, supposed to be of the 7th or 8th century. See *Ind. Ant.* III, 113.

The Parthians revolted from the Seleucidæ about B. C. 250, under a chief named Arsakes (Askh, Arsaces) who founded an independent monarchy. The Parthians subsequently overran the provinces east of the Euphrates, and about B. C. 130 overthrew the kingdom of Bactria, so that their empire extended from the Euphrates to the Indus and from the Indian Ocean to the Paropamisus or even to the Oxus. The memorable wars between the Parthians and the Romans eventually weakened the former and gave the Persians the opportunity of throwing off the Parthian yoke. Led by Artaxerxes (Ardashir) they put an end to the Parthian kingdom of the Arsacidæ, after it had lasted 476 years, and established the Persian dynasty of the Sassanidæ A. D. 226.

General Cunningham considers them Skythians * and it will be seen that their descent is described as being from S'áliváhana the S'aka king. "The Scythians, who had previously been in some measure allied to the Parthians, were a portion of the great nomad hordes of Central Asia who often swept down on the fertile, cultivated and comparatively refined south, like a whirlwind of locusts. To check their first advance the Parthian princes had paid them a sort of black mail, but Bactria, less fortunate, was rapidly overwhelmed to the north and west. . . . It was on the accession of the Parthian king Mithridates the Great, B. C. 124, that the tide of Scythian victory (over Parthia) was arrested, and they were driven back and compelled to pour their superabundant numbers into Seistan and the eastern provinces of Persia.† Thus was formed the famous Indo-Scythic kingdom of whose chieftains we have so many monetary records. Occupying, as they did, the plains south of the Hindu Kush between Bactria and the Punjab, and occasionally extending their power even to the mouth of the Indus, this Scythian kingdom effectually separated India from Greece, and arrested the growing influence of Greek manners and civilization; indeed, but for these intervening hordes, there seems no reason why the Greek language should not have been as well understood on the Jumna and the Ganges as on the Nile." ‡

Though several grants made by the Pallava kings have come to light, and there are frequent references to the line in contemporary records, yet, owing to the former being undated, and the references being generally to the Pallavas without any specification of names, no chronological list has hitherto been published of the rulers of this line; and, indeed, they have received but scant notice. Having obtained, as I consider, materials for drawing up such a list, subject to the corrections which further discoveries may shew to be needed, it is given below. On certain points there seems to be no doubt, namely, that the Pallavas to the 6th century ruled a country whose name was Vengi, situated between the mouths of the Krishna and the Godávari. Early in the 7th century (? 605) they were dispossessed of this region by the eastern branch of the Chálukyas, and then established their seat of government at Kánchi (Conjeveram), where it remained in all probability till the 12th century: their inscriptions of about the 7th century are found at Mahábalipur.

* *Arch. Rep.* III, 4. The Parthii were a people of Scythian origin. Dr. Smith, *Class. Dict.*

† The present name of this portion of Persia, Seistan (or on the coins Sejestán), is a memorial of this Scythic invasion, the district they occupied having been naturally called Sacastene—the land of the Sacæ.

‡ Vaux's *Hist. of Persia from the Ancient Monuments*, 125.

As regards their connection with Mysore, a grant on copper plates of the 4th century* shews them in possession of Videnúr, that is, the present Goribidnur, which was formerly called Bidanúr. Pallava inscriptions on temples and stone slabs occur throughout the Kolar District, of which I have found several, at Betmangala, A'vani, Nangali†, Srinivaspur, Nandi, Goribidnur and Molkalmuru‡. Their titles in these grants generally correspond with those at p. 312. The name of the Noḷambaváḍi or Noṇambaváḍi Thirty-two Thousand province, extending over most of the Chitaldroog and Bellary districts, specially connects itself to all appearance with the Pallavas, but the earliest mention of it, so far as I can find, is in 1066 (p. 19). There is a gold coin in the Bangalore Museum bearing the image of Harihara on the obverse and the name Noṇambaváḍi in Haḷe Kannaḍa characters in the middle line of the reverse. The following is the proposed list of the Pallava kings:—

	A. D.
Mukunti	200
Trilochana, Trinetra... ...	
Chanda Varmma	300
Vijaya Nandi Varmma ...	to
Vijaya Buddha Varmma ...	400
Skanda Varmma	
Víra Varmma	400
Skanda Varmma	to
Simha Varmma	
Vishnu Gopa Varmma ...	500
Simha Varmma	
Rajendra Varmma	
Devendra Varmma	c. 570
Chanda Danda, ? Ati Raṇa Chanda	„ 600
Káma Rája, Raja Jaya, ...	„ 610
Narasimha Pota Varmma, Narasimha	„ 620
Jayates'vara Pota Varmma or Jayates'vara Pota Rája	„ 660

	A. D.
Trairájya Pallava	685
Nandi Pota Varmma ...	735
... ...	745
... ...	760
Noḷamba Rája, A'hava-duggan, Ahitara javanam	768
Hemas'itala	788
Vattiga, (? Battiga, or Chattiga) ...	804
Ereva Noḷamba	
Bira Noḷamba, Bira Trinetra ...	
... ...	898
... ...	944
... ...	988
Sthira Gambhíra Noḷamba, Víra Tala Prahári, Doḍḍanka ...	1050
(A'hu Malla)	1070
Narasimha Varmma	1120
... ...	c. 1140

The data on which the above list is based it is now necessary to state.

Sáliváhana, whose era used throughout the south of India dates from A. D. 78, is acknowledged to have ruled at Pratishthána, now known as Paithan, on the Godávari. From him are said to have descended Mádhava Varmma, Kulaketana, Nílakaṇṭha and Mukunti Pallava. The last appears as the founder of the Pallava line, with his capital at Dharanikoṭa, and is

* *S. Ind. Pal.* Pl. xx.

† This is not certainly Pallava, as the most important part of the inscription has gone, the upper half of a fine slab having been recently broken off and carried away; for the repairs of a well, I was told, but did not find the missing piece.

‡ Two inscriptions here, on a rock, but the names and chief particulars have been deliberately mutilated, so they cannot be put down as undoubtedly Pallava, but there is reason to suppose they are: one is dated in S'aka 910.

said to have been a son of Mahadeva (Siva) by a girl of the mountain tribe called Chensuars (Chensabaras). * He is placed in about the year 200, and is, according to local tradition, the king under whom was erected the splendid tope or *stúpa* at Amarávati, which is called on the spot the Dúpa Mogasála (or assembly hall) of Mukunti Mahárája.†

Trilochana Pallava was ruling in the 4th century when Jaya Simha, surnamed Vijayáditya, of the Chalukya kula, invaded his territories, but failed to obtain a permanent footing. Jaya Simha seems to have lost his life in the attempt, for his queen, then pregnant, is described as flying after his death and taking refuge with a Brahman named Vishnu Somayáji, in whose house she gave birth to a son named Rája Simha. On attaining to man's estate, the latter renewed the contest with the Pallavas, in which he was finally successful, cementing his power by a marriage with a princess of that race. ‡ A Trinetra Pallava is said to have introduced Brahmans into his territory, and an inscription to this purport dated 2000 of the Kali (1100 years B. C!) we are told is to be found at Upatur in the Guntur district.§

For the next three on the list, we have a grant by Vijaya Nandi Varmma ruling at Vengi-pura, son of Chanḍa Varmma, in the 7th year of his reign, of certain dues at Videnur (Goribidnur), in the province of Kuduhára (? the same as Kuvaláḷa or Koláḷa, the present Kolar). ¶ Vijaya Buddha Varmma, is also mentioned, in a grant§§ by the same, as his Yuva-rája. For the next six there is a grant‖ by Vishnu Gopa Varmma, made from Palakkada (which might suggest Pulicat) while Yuva rája, in the 11th year of Simha Varmma; and one ** made by Simha Varmma, the son of Vishnu Gopa Varmma, in the 8th year of his reign, from Dasanapura, of a village in Vengo ráshṭra. Rájendra Varmma, and his son Devendra Varmma also appear in a grant†† and the latter is perhaps the Pallava to whom the Kadamba king Mriges'a Varmma, about 570, describes himself as a wild-fire. Chanḍa Danḍa is mentioned‡‡ as king of Kánchi and uprooted by the Kadamba king Ravi Varmma,

---

* Wilson, *McK. Coll.* I, cxxiv, cxx.

† Fergusson, *Tr. Ser. Wor*, 171. The building is supposed to have been under erection from about A. D. 200 to 380, and the statements of the Buddhist pilgrim Hiouen Thsang lead to the supposition that it was abandoned about 550.

‡ Sir Walter Elliot, *Mad.* J. IV, 78.

§ Wilson, *McK. Coll.* I, cxx.

¶ *S. Ind. Pal.* Pl. xx; *Ind. Ant.* V, 176.

§§ *Ind. Ant.* VI, 175.

‖ *id.* V, 50.

** *id.* V, 154.

†† *id.* III, 152.

‡‡ *id.* VI, 30.

which would be about 600 ; and as the name Ati Raṇa Chaṇḍa Pallava appears on a temple at Mahábalipur * I have supposed him to be the same, but this might be a name of the next, Káma Rája or Raṇa Jaya, who is also mentioned in an inscription at Mahábalipur† as the Pallaves'vara. Either he or his predecessor should, from the evident period of the inscriptions, be the Pallava whom the Chalukya king Satyás'raya (608—634) forced to hide behind the ramparts of Kánchi ‡ which seems to be an allusion to the ejection of the Pallavas from the Vengi country by the Chalukyas.

Narasimha § or Narasimha Pota Varmma ‖ (p. 301) must be the Pallava king who, about 620, fell at Bhimes'a gráma in a battle with the Ganga king (but at that time commander-in-chief) S'rí Vallabha, and was trodden to death by the elephants (p. 285). He it is who is described (p. 301) as having made (or created) a remarkable collection of statues in stone consisting of Rája Simhes'vara and other *deva kula*, which, as there is no god of that name, I suppose to refer to deified members of the royal family, and perhaps to the Chalukya named Rája Simha who married a Pallava princess as before stated. Jayates'vara Pota Raja or Pota Varmma appears¶ as the name of the Pallava monarch defeated by the Chalukya king Vikramáditya I (650—681), who, with reference to this victory and one over the Mahávali king, claims to be the real S'rí Vallabha and the real Rája Malla**, both Ganga titles referring to the victory gained at Bhimes'a by the king bearing the former name. The idea seems to be, that as the Pallava was killed in that battle—and came by his death, perhaps accidentally, by falling under the elephants, it may be of his own side, which charged over him—he could not be considered as conquered. But Vikramáditya actually defeated the king, "who had never before bowed to any other man", and made him kiss his feet with his crown. Hence he was more the favourite (*Vallabha*) of fortune (*S'rí*). The claim to be Rája Malla need not necessarily imply that the Mahámalla line continued in power till this

---

* *Sev. Pag.* 59, 120. † *id.* 58. 128, 224.

‡ *Ind. Ant.* V, 73. § *id.* VI. 78.

‖ Pota Varmma is doubtless a corruption of Buddha Varmma. But there is a local god named Pota. C. P. Brown says (*Tel. Dict.*) "he is a rustic god, like Pan, worshipped (chiefly by herdsmen) throughout the Telugu, Kannaḍa, and Maratha countries; after him many men are named. His wives, after whom some women are named, are called Gangamma and Polakamma or Poleramma. These answer to Punch and Judy."

In Mysore, Potappa is represented as a man with a sword in one hand and a buffalo's head in the other. His figure is invariably placed in temples of Dharma Ráya, the chief object of worship among the Tigalar, a class of cultivators from the Tamil country.

¶ *Ind. Ant.* VI, 78. ** *Sev. Pag.* 127.

period; which, though just possible, is hardly probable: it is sufficient if he conquered the Pallavas who had but recently conquered the Mahámallas, to constitute him Rája Malla, and the verbal resemblance to the Ganga title gives occasion for a side thrust at them too beyond what is contained in claiming to be the true S'rí Vallabha.

Trairájya Pallava, which does not seem to be a name, is the king defeated (p 237, 241) by the Chalukya king Vinayáditya (681—695). Nandi Pota Varmma is explicitly stated (p 300) to be the name of the Pallava king who was slain in battle in the Udáka province by the Chalukya king Vikramáditya II (733—747), when all the royal insignia fell into the hands of the conqueror, who made a triumphal entry into Kánchi, but refraining from plundering the city, commemorated his entry by causing the statues before mentioned to be gilded; while his queen Loka Mahádevi caused a temple to be erected * at Paṭṭadkal to celebrate the victory. In about 745 the Chalukya prince Kírtti Varmma, then Yuva rája, attacked a Pallava king (p. 301) whose name is not given, and forcing him to take refuge in a hill fort, plundered him of all his treasures and scattered his troops: while in 777 a grand-daughter of the Pallava king, and therefore perhaps this one, is the wife of the king of Nirgunda in the Chitaldroog District (p. 288)

About 760 the Raṭṭa king Dhruva or Nirupama claims † to have conquered a Pallava king. As a Pallava inscription of 768, at Gúlgánpode near Srinivaspur where the Mahávali stones were found, gives the king's name as Noḷamba, he may be the one. It is some confirmation of this that the name Nirupama occurs in a mutilated Pallava inscription on the Rámalingesvara temple at Avani, in which the Pallava king's name is Noḷambádhirája, with the *upavákya* or cognomen *áhava duggan ahitara ȷavanam.* It would appear that his wife was a Kadamba princess, and named Devámbiká. There is also an inscription of Noḷambádhirája at Nandi (p. 212). The next Raṭṭa king, Govinda or Prabhúta Varsha, also defeats a Pallava king about 790 or 800.‡ Now, according to Wilson, the king of Kánchi in 783 was Hemasitala, whom he describes as the last Buddhist monarch of that place. Akalanka, a Jain from S'ravaṇa Belgoa, disputed in his presence with the Buddhists, who were defeated, and banished to Kandly in Ceylon. The same Raṭṭa king, Govinda,

---

* *Ind. Ant.* VI, 85. She was a Haihaya princess, 61. † *id.* 69. ‡ *id.* 71.

appears * in 804 as receiving from (?) Vattiga, then ruler of Kánchi, certain tribute collected for him by the Chálukya king Kírtti Varmma III, who, as I gather, may have married the Raṭṭa king's daughter, and to whom this tribute had been assigned, perhaps as her dowry, with authority to her husband to collect it. This was no uncommon condition attached to a gift in turbulent times, of which many instances might be adduced; and was nothing more nor less than setting one rival on to levy war against and plunder another, a course sure to result in damage to one of the two, and perhaps to both.

Of the next on the list, there is an inscription of Ereva Noḷambádhirája, of about this period, on the Vijaya Rangaswámi temple at Betmangala, and as the Ganga king Gaṇḍa Deva is stated † to have conquered Kánchi, which would be about 830, I associate this event with Ereva. Bíra Nolamba is the donor of the Goribidnur grant, in honour of the Ganga king who fell in his service. He is the one described as taking charge of the unfortunate Chálukya princess Ayyapa's daughter, ‡ and his name occurs three times in the inscription. For the reasons previously stated he may be placed with some confidence at about 850. Bíra Trinetra, mentioned in an inscription on a *mána stambha* at A'vani, is perhaps the same.

---

* *S. Ind. Pal.* Pl. xxiv and p. 88. As this interesting inscription has not been accurately deciphered, and has been erroneously called Chera, I proceed to transcribe and explain it.

Svasti S'aka-nṛipa-kálátíta samvatsarangaḷ élnúr-irppatt-iraneyá Subhánu-emba varshadá Vaisákha-mása-krishṇa-panchame Bṛihaspati-váramági Svasti prabhúta-varsha s'rí-pṛithuví-vallabha mahárájadhirája parames'vara Goyindara-bhaṭárará Gámunḍabbe-mahádeviy-kági rájy á pro[va]rddhamána-káladoḷ Kanchiyan-áḷva Vattigana me . . . kappan gaḷal bandalli Tungabhadreyá taṭiyoḷ tan á . . . dugaḷ iḷdu Rámes'vara emba tírtthadá modale deppikki porada pandigaḷan iriyal bandalli tírttha meppu kaṇḍu S'ivanári emba goravarge . . dumbeya manu . . .Kirtti-Varmmo rája-parames'vara datta . . . . dank aḷisidar odar appode itta pránta svadatta paradattam bá yo hareti vasandarán shashṭi varsha sahasráṇi vishṭá[yám] jáyate krimi api varsha sahasráṇi . . mre . . nyato bhayam púrvva sthiti kuḍembu toṛe mere mahá-sandhi-vigrahádhikáradhipate S'ridharasya likhitahsya

In the S'aka king's years the 726th, the year Subhánu, the month Vais'ákha, the 5th day of the dark fortnight, Thursday.—May it be well. On coming having levied the tribute imposed during his reign upon *Vattiga*, the ruler of Kanchi, by *Prabhúta-Varsha*, the favorite of earth and fortune, great king of kings, supreme lord, *Goyinda bhaṭára*, on account of [his daughter] *Gámunḍabbe Mahádevi*; halting his . . on the bank of the Tungabhadra, netting (or? knocking down) the crocodiles of the *tírtha* called Rames'vara, and sticking the pigs which ran out being pleased with the tírtha, *Kírtti Varmma*, supreme lord of kings, with a mind fixed like a bee . . . . presented it to the *gorava* (Kuruba priest) named S'ivanári, &c.

Rámes'vara tírtha is an island in the Tungabhadra at a bend a few miles north of the junction of the Tunga and Bhadra. This Kírtti Varmma I conclude must be the Chálukya prince. Govinda or Prabhúta-varsha is a Raṭṭa king. The ruler of Kánchi should be a Pallava: there is a Baddiga among the Raṭṭas.

† *Mad. J. L. S.* No. 32, p. 12.

‡ See above, p. xlv.

Three dates then follow without any names. The two first are clearly expressed in words, in Haḷe Kannaḍa, according to the *S'aka nripa kála*, and are cut on two long narrow stones at Betmangala, which are now enclosed in a small temple and worshipped as gods under the name of Gangamma. They are completely smeared with saffron and dotted over with vermilion spots; the usual offerings of flowers, &c., are placed on the heads of the stones and at foot. Both are very brief, and record some grants apparently by Kadamba princesses. From the locality, and comparison with the one above mentioned, I consider them Pallava. The date 988 is that of one of the two mutilated rock-inscriptions at Molkalmuru. A more careful examination than I had leisure at the time to make, now some years ago, may clearly identify them with the Pallavas.

There seems reason to believe that about this period, the Cholas, having upset the Ganga kingdom, overran the Pallava possessions in the north-east of Mysore and then supplanted the Eastern Chalukyas at Vengi. But the Western Chalukyas must have recovered the present Chitaldroog District, which was formed into the province of the Nolambavádi Thirty-two Thousand, and placed under the prince Vijayáditya, who was also viceroy of Vengi (as will appear further on under the Chalukyas). About 1050 we have (p. 327) a Sthira Gambhíra Noḷamba, who distinguished himself in the army of the Chálukya king A'hava Malla and received the titles *Víra-tala-prahári* and *Doḍḍanka*. His son was A'hu Malla. About 1070 we have a Pallava made to pay tribute to the Chálukya king Bhuvanaika Malla by his general Udayáditya of the Ganga family (p. 143). In 1079 we have (p. 396) the Chálukya prince Jaya Simha, the brother of Vikrama, calling himself a prince of the Pallava line, and it seems to follow that his mother must have been a Pallava princess. In 1081 we find mention of a Pallava subordinate to the Chálukya king Vikramárka. About 1120 we have (p. 331) the Hoysala king Vishnu Varddhana defeating a Pallava, whose name appears to be Narasimha Varmma, and taking Kánchi. And lastly, the Chálukya king Jagadeka Malla (1138—1150) boasts (p. 58) to have driven the Pallavas from their kingdom, which he added to his own dominions, thus terminating the continual rivalry and contests of seven centuries. It would appear (pp. 8, 52) that this victory was achieved by his general Vijaya Pándya Deva of Uchangi, who was in consequence granted the title 'lord of Kánchipura'; and he calls himself 'defeater of the designs of Rájiga Chola', who will be noticed in connection with the Chálukyas. I have not met with any further reference to the line.*

* It appears that a Pallava is said to have been conquered in 1223 by the Yádava king Singhana Deva of Devagiri. *Ind. Ant.*

Chalukyas.—The memorials of this powerful line are perhaps more abundant, exact and varied than those of any line of sovereigns in the south. Their first appearance south of the Narmadá was in the 4th century, previous to which they are said (p. 149) to have had 59 predecessors on the throne of Ayodhya (Oudh). On entering the Dekhan they encountered the Kalachuryas the Raṭṭas, the Kadambas, and the Pallavas. The three first were reduced to the condition of feudatories ; the Pallavas however drove off the invader, who was slain, but his successor defeated them and then formed with them an alliance cemented by a marriage with a Pallava princess. The Chalukya capital was established at Kalyána, still known by that name, situated in Bidar in the Nizam's dominions, about a hundred miles west of Haidarabad ; their country was called Kuntala des'a and Karṇaṭa des'a.

At the commencement of the 7th century the Chalukyas separated into two branches, of which the Eastern Chalukyas made Vengi, taken from the Pallavas, their capital : the Western Chalukyas, with whom chiefly Mysore is concerned, continued to rule from Kalyáṇa. From the name of the founder of this branch they were called the Satyás'raya-kula. In the 8th century the Raṭṭas appear to have regained an ascendancy, and the Chalukya power was for some time obscured : but at the end of the 10th century their authority was restored, and they reigned with increased glory to the end of the 12th, when they were subverted by the Kalachuryas.

The Chálukyas were of the Soma vamsa or lunar line, and the Mánavyasa gotra. They claim to be the sons of Harita, nourished by the *Sapta mátrike,* or seven mothers. The boar was the principal emblem on their signet, obtained from Bhagaván Náráyana (Vishnu) ; but their insignia included a peacock fan, an *ankus'a* or elephant goad, a golden sceptre, and other symbols. The titles on their inscriptions, which are very numerous in Mysore, especially in the Nagar Division, are nearly invariably as follows—*Samasta-bhuvanás'raya, S'rí-prithvi-vallabha, Mahárájádhirájá, Parames'vara, Parama-bhaṭṭáraka, Satyás'ra-kula-tilaka, Chálukyábharaṇa.*

Although the above details are very circumstantial, the account of the origin of the Chalukyas is evidently puránic *, and the real source from which they sprang is far from clear. Moreover, while on the one hand the name Chalukya bears a suggestive resemblance to the Greek name Seleukeia, on the other

* They are stated (p. 68) to have miraculously sprung from the moisture or water in the hollowed palm (*chuluka, chulaka*) of Harita's hand ; see also p. 153. According to another account (*Ind. Ant.* VI, 74), from a libation to the gods poured from his *chulka, chuluka* or *chaluka* by Háriti, who wore five tufts of hair on his head, that is, he was a Brahmachári or bachelor student.

hand it will be seen (p. xl) that the title to be descendants of Harita or Háriti, nourished by the seven mothers, and of the Mánavya gotra, may have been adopted from the Kadambas, on their being subdued; while as to the 59 previous kings, who are said to have occupied the throne of Ayodhya, not a single trace has been discovered. May not the Chalukyan kings have been of Seleukeian or Seleucidan origin; and the prolonged struggles between them and the Pallavas,* supposing these to be of Parthian connection, have been but a continuation of the contests between Seleucidæ and Arsacidæ, transferred from the banks of the Tigris and Euphrates to those of the Krishna and the Palar?

The succession of the earlier Chalukya kings, down to the commencement of the 7th century, when the family separated into two branches, has not been very decidedly made out. The following seems to be the probable order:—

		A. D.			A. D.
Jaya Simha, Vijayaditya.			Pulikes'i, Raṇa Vikrama,	...	489
Rája Simha, Raṇa Raga.			Kírtti Varmma		
Buddha Varmma, Vira Noṇamba	...	444	Mangales'a, Mangales'vara	...	566—578
Vijaya Varmma, Vijaya Rája	...	472			

Jaya Simha is said to have defeated and destroyed Krishna the Raṭṭa Raja. He himself, however, was slain in an encounter with Trilochana Pallava. His queen, then pregnant, fled and took refuge with a Brahman called Vishnu Somayáji, in whose house she gave birth to Rája Simha or Raṇa Rága. On growing up to man's estate he renewed the contest with the Pallavas, in which he was finally successful, and married a princess of that race.† The memory of this Rája Simha it was, I have conjectured, that was preserved in the statue bearing that name erected by the Pallava king (p. 301). His son was Buddha Varmma, a name evidently Pallava in its associations: with it, therefore, I connect Víra Noṇamba, a name also clearly connected with the Pallavas (p. 306), and assign them to the date of the grant No. 158, which date may not be inaccurate, though, as it is, the grant is of a much later period; this will be shewn further on. Vijaya Varmma was Buddha Varmma's son.‡

Pulakes'i or Paulakes'i was the most powerful of the early kings and performed the horse sacrifice. He appears as the lord of Vátápi-nagara or Bádámi.§ His second name was Raṇa Vikrama (p. 298). His date is taken from a grant in the British Museum. His son was Kírtti Varmma, who was the conqueror of the Kadambas (p. 299). Mangalís'a, his younger brother, subdued

* An expression used of the Pallavas in a Chalukya grant (p. 300), describing them as "by nature hostile" (*prakrity-amitra*), seems to imply something mutually hostile in their origin.

† *Mad. J. L. & S.* IV, 75.

‡ *Ind. Ant.* VII, 249.

§ *id.* V. 69. The date of this inscription is singular, being given as 3730 from the war of the Bhárata, 3550 of the Kali yuga, and 506 of the S'aka era.

the Kalachuryas. He attempted to establish his own son in the succession, but Satyás'raya, the elder son of Kírtti Varmma, obtained the throne, about 585. About 20 years later, or 605, his younger brother Vishnu Varddhana, surnamed Kubja, crooked or hunch-backed, captured the city of Vengi from the Pallavas. From this time the family separated into two branches: the Western Chálukyas continuing to rule from Kalyáṇa to the end of the 12th century, while the Eastern Chálukyas remained in power in the Rájamahendri country till the beginning of the 11th century.

The following is the succession of kings in the western line, as confirmed by numerous grants:—

	A. D.
Satyás'raya, Pulikesi	? 585 to 634
Ambera, Amara	
Aditya Varmma	
Vikramáditya ...	? 658—681
Vinayáditya, Yuddha Malla	681—695
Vijayáditya ...	956—733
Vikramáditya ...	733—747
Kírtti Varmma ...	747—758...
Kírtti Varmma ...	...799—844...
Tailapa	
Bhíma Rája	
Ayyapa, Ayya	
Vijayáditya, Vijitáditya	
Tailapa, Taila, Núrmmaḍi Taila ...	973—997
Satyás'raya, Sattimanta, Irivi Bhujanga, A'hava Malla	997—1008
Vikramáditya, Vibhu Vikrama, or Núrmmaḍi	1008—1018
Jaya Simha or Jagadeka Malla ...	1018—1040
Somes'vara, Trailokya Malla, or A'hava Malla	1040—1069
Somes'vara, Soma, Sovi, or Bhuvanaika Malla	1069—1076
Vikramáditya, Kali Vikrama, Vikramánka, Permaḍi, or Tribhuvana Malla ...	1076—1127
Somes'vara, Soma, Bhúloka Malla, Tribhuvana Malla	1127—1138
Permma, or Jagadeka Malla	1138—1150
Tailapa, Núrmadi Taila, Núrmaḍi Tailapa, or Trailokya Malla	1150—1182
Somes'vara or Tribhuvana Malla ...	1182—1189

Satyás'raya or Pulikes'i II, was a great conqueror and subdued all the neighbouring nations. He is said (p. 299) to have gained victories on simply riding forth alone, mounted on his splendid charger Chitrakanṭha. His greatest victory was over Harsha Varddhana, king of Kanoj, and the most powerful monarch in Northern India (pp. 236, 299). By this conquest Satyás'raya obtained the title of Parames'vara or supreme lord, ever after borne by the Chálukyas. Of his son Ambera there is a memorial in the grant No. 159 (p. 298). Vikramáditya I. was successful in war against Páṇḍya, Chola, Kerala and Kalabhra* (p. 299) but his greatest achievement was his capture of Kánchi (pp. 237, 241) and forcing the Pallava king 'who had never bowed to any other man' (pp. 237, 241, 299) to kiss his feet with his crown. Vinayáditya, his son, captured and destroyed the army of Trairájya Pallava, the king of Kánchi (pp. 237, 299), was served by the Pallava, Kalabhra, Kerala, Haibaya, Vila, Malava, Chola, and Páṇḍya kings, as well as by A'luva Ganga (p. 237); and levying tribute from the rulers of Kavera, Párasíka, Simhala and other islands,† churned all

* Perhaps the Kalabhuriyas or Kalachuriyas.

† Simhala is Ceylon. Kavera may be some island in the Kávéri, as Srirangam, Sivasamudram or Seringapatam; Párasíká, a name of Persia, introduced between the two, is difficult to explain, unless indeed the Pallavas, retaining some tradition of a Persian origin, may have given the name to an island in the south.

the kings of the north and gained possession of the Páḷi dhvaja* (p. 299). His son Vijayáditya completed the conquests of the two preceding reigns, both in the south and the north, and in addition to the Páḷi flag, gained the Gangá and Yamuná flags (p. 300). His son Vikramáditya II. gained an important victory in the Udáka province over the Pallava king Nandi Pota Varmma, whom he slew in battle, and capturing all the royal insignia, made a triumphal entry into the capital city Kánchi, which he refrained from plundering, and ordered the remarkable statues he found in the royal palace to be gilded (p. 300, 301). He then, after withering up Páṇḍya, Chola, Kerala, Kalabhra and other kings, took up his residence at Jayamambha, situated on the shore of the southern ocean, called the Rolling Ocean (*ghúrṇamánárṇa*). Kírtti Varmma II, his son, while yet Yuva Rája under his father, obtained permission to make an expedition against the Pallava king, whom he drove to take refuge in a hill fort, and dispersing his army, plundered his treasures (p. 301).

But the Chálukyas were now to suffer a reverse, and their glory under Kírtti Varmma III was obscured by the ascendancy of the Raṭṭas:† the proof

---

* What this flag was is not clear. Páli is the name of the language of Magadha, the sacred language of the Buddhists.

† The Raṭṭa, Ráṭhor or Ráshṭra kúṭa family of kings "rose to power in the Dekhan about the middle of the 8th century, and for the space of two centuries obscured and almost took the place of its older rival the Chálukya race of Kalyáṇa. During the time of its prosperity, it extended its rule not only over the Dekhan proper but over the Konkana, a portion of Gujarat, and Central India up to the Vindhyas. Its power sank again towards the close of the 10th century, when the Chálukyas, under Tailapa of Kalyána and his successors, regained their ancient position. But even after that period we find Ráshṭra kúṭa states at Devagiri, at Belgam, &c., in the Dekhan, in Central India, and even as far north as Kanoj, some of which played a considerable part during the last period of Hindu rule, and branches of which flourish even in the present day." (*Ind. Ant.* VI, 59).

The following is the list of Raṭṭa kings:—

	A. D.		A. D.
Govinda	660	Amoghavarsha	810
Karka	685	Akálavarsha	835
Indra	710	Jagadrudra	
Dantidurga, Danti Varmma, Prithvi Vallabha, Khadgavaloka ...	725—755	Indra Nripa	
Krishna, Vallabha	755	Amogha Varsha	
Govinda, do	765	Govinda Rája	
Dhruva, Dhora, Nirupama, Kali Vallabha, Dhárávarsha ...	770	Baddiga	
Govinda, Jagattunga, Jagadrudra, Prithvi Vallabha, S'ri Vallabha, Prabhútavarsha	785—810	Krishna Rája	
		Khotika, Khodviga	
		Kakkala, Karkara	973

Dantidurga subdued a prince named Vallabha, and obtained the title Rájádhirája Parames'vara. His successor Krishna humbled the Chalukyas. Dhruva subdued the Pallavas and made a prisoner of the Ganga king, whose family had never been conquered before. Govinda III was the most eminent of the dynasty. He released Ganga, whom his father had imprisoned, from his long and painful captivity, but had again to reduce and imprison him; he also went to the Tungabhadra and again subdued the Pallavas: he also ordered the lord of Vengi (the Eastern Chálukya king) to build him a fort, which was done apparently at Mányakheta (now Málkhed, in the Nizam's dominions), which, under the next king, became the capital. *Ind. Ant.* VI. 59—72; *J. Bo. Br. R. A. S.*

of this in 804 has already been given (p. lvii). Of the next three kings, it is considered, as previously stated, that Taila and Ayyapa correspond with those of that name in No. 113 (p. 209). But fuller particulars, as already described (p. lix), are contained in the Rudra Deva inscription.* There the Kákatiya king Proli Deva is said to have in an instant bound down Tailapa, the head ornament of the Chálukyas, but on being pleased with his faithfulness as speedily released him; he dealt in the same way with Govinda, and gave the kingdom (*i.e.* Taila's kingdom, as it is called in the Begur inscription, which had come under the power of Govinda the Raṭṭa) to king Erha. Then (v. 18) "from sheer fright of the valorous king S'ri Rudra Deva (Proli's son), king Tailapa was afflicted with diarrhœa and became emaciated. And although this resulted in death, Bhíma ventured to succeed to the fleeting royal dignity." And (v. 20) this "Bhíma, the vilest of kings, a brute among men, the husband of his step-mother, who killed an eminent brother at dinner, intent upon attempts at swallowing the skies, ascended the point of the great peak of the mountain of pride, and incensed by envy, ventured to defy the terrible S'ri Rudra Deva." The latter went against him, burnt the suburbs of Chodádaya (or Bodádaya) and forced Bhíma, with all the Rájas like him living between Kánchi manḍala and the Vindhyas, to submit. Ayyapa, according to the Begur inscription (p. 209) seems to have attempted to attack Bíra Mahendra, whom I conjecture, for reasons already given, to be the Pallava king; but was defeated, probably at Begúr, or Bevúr as it is written on the stone, by Irugange Nágatta, an officer under Ereyappa, and slain; his daughter (as represented in the sculpture) being taken prisoner. She, according to the Goribidnur inscription mentioned p. xlv apparently became the prize of the Pallava monarch.

The Chálukyas, thus thoroughly beaten and disgraced, had no resource but to flee from their kingdom. The representative of the line, Jaya Simha, perhaps a second name of Vijayáditya's, fled to Anhalvara in Gujarat, the court of Bhoja Raja, the last of the Chawuras or Sauras. There his son Moolraj married the daughter of Bhoja Rája, and in 931 succeeded the latter on the throne, the Salic law being set aside in his favour. He ruled at Anhalvara for the space of 58 years, and his descendants occupied the throne of that country with great glory till 1145.

Meanwhile Tailapa defeated the Raṭṭas (p. 149) in the person of the Raṭṭa king Kakkala†, and retrieved the Chálukya fortunes. He ascended the throne

* *J. Bo. Br. R. A. S.* X. 46.

† *Ind. Ant.* VI, 65.

at Kalyána in 973, and transmitted to his posterity a kingdom which increased in splendour and prosperity under each succeeding reign for nearly two hundred years. The Cholas, who, taking advantage of the late collapse of the Chálukya power, had pressed northwards, brought the Ganga kingdom to an end, and overrun much of Mysore, were now the chief opponents of the Chálukyas; and Tailapa is described (p. 149) as full of desire to fight with the Chola Rája, and as being a destroying fire to the Cholas. In fact the tide of Chola conquest seems to have been thus turned aside to the eastwards, and accordingly we find the Eastern Chálukya king Vimaláditya forced into a matrimonial alliance with the Cholas, with the result that his kingdom passed in 1023 to Rájendra Chola or Rájarája Chola, said to be his son.*

To Tailapa and his wife Jakabbe was born Satyás'raya, who succeeded him and married Ambiká Devi. Their sons were Vikrama and Das'a Varmma (p. 87). The former, dying without issue, was succeeded by his nephew Jaya Simha, the son of Das'a Varmma and Bhagavati Devi. Jaya Simha or Jagadeka Malla is said (p. 149) to be a lion to Rájendra Chola, and appears to have gained some advantages over them which led to a formidable invasion by the Cholas in the reign of his son Somes'vara. They burnt Pulikara nagara, the modern Lakmes'var, and destroyed its famous Jain temples erected by Permaḍi Ganga. But Somes'vara, having the titles Trailokya Malla and A'hava Malla, inflicted a signal defeat upon the enemy, and the Chola king would appear to have been killed. Somes'vara, on returning from the pursuit and defeat of the Cholas, halted at Puliyappaṭṭana or Puliyar-paṭna (the modern Huliyar in Chitaldroog District) and made a grant of Sivanur (now Sávanur) to Nága Deva his chief general and minister, in 1059. Somesvara's son, named Vishnu Varddhana or Vijayáditya, who calls himself (p. 19) the Vengi manḍales'vara and the punisher of Ayyana (? his uncle: there is a similar reference to Ayyana at p. 327,) was in 1066 ruling the Noḷambavádi Thirty-two Thousand (which seems

---

* For convenience of reference it is desirable here to give the succession of the Eastren Chálukyas.

	Reigned		Reigned
Kubja Vishnu Varddhana ...	18 years.	Gunánka Vijayáditya	... 44 years.
Jaya Simha Vallabha ...	33 „	Chálukya Bhima ...	... 30 „
Indra Rája		Kollabhiganda Vijayáditya	... 6 months.
Rájanandana, Vishnu Varddhana	9 „	Amma Rája ...	... 7 years.
Mangi Rája	25 „	Tálapa, Tádapa (usurper)	... 1 month.
Jaya Simha Vallabha ...	13 „	Vikramáditya ...	... 11 months.
Kokkili, Kaikkili ...	6 months.	Yuddha Malla (usurper)	... 7 years.
Vishnu Varddhana ...	37 years.	Rája Bhima ...	... 12 „
S'akti Varmma, Vijayáditya.	18 „	Amma Rája ...	... 3 (945)
Vishnu Varddhana ...	30 „	Dánárnava ...	... 25 „
Vijayáditya, Narendra Mrigarája	48 „	S'akti Varmma ...	... 12 „
Kali Vishnu Varddhana	1½ „	Vimaláditya ...	... 7 (to 1023 A. D.)

to be the earliest mention of the province by this name). Meanwhile Rájendra Chola, before mentioned, who ruled 41 years or till 1064, we are told* "was succeeded by his son Vikrama Deva surnamed Kulottunga Chola. On the death (which, from what follows, must have been in 1077) of his uncle Vijayáditya, who had been viceroy of Vengi-des'a, the king deputed his son Rájarája to assume the office; but after holding it for one year, 1078, he resigned it in favor of his younger brother Víra Deva Chola, who assumed the title of Kulottunga Chola. His grants are found in great numbers from 1079 up to 1135." It seems to me clear that A'hava Malla must have formed an alliance with the Pallavas against the Cholas, and married a Pallava princess: that he recovered the north east of Mysore, which had belonged to the Pallavas but was at this time overrun by the Cholas, and formed the new province of Noḷambavádi—whose name connects it with the Pallavas,—as a barrier against Chola encroachments on the Western Chálukya dominions.

To continue our history. Bhuvanaika Malla was apparently a weak prince and did not long retain possession of the crown. But he had a powerful minister and general in Udayáditya of the Ganga family (p. 144). His title of *Mane Verggaḍe Daṇḍanáyaka*, corresponding to Lord High Chamberlain, is deserving of notice as indicating the growth of luxury at the Chalukya court, which will be remarked on again. Udayáditya, it is said (p. 164), defeated before 1071 a secret conspiracy against the throne and against the guru, and seizing the property and jewel-laden women of the conspirators, handed them over to his emperor. By 1075 we find him (p. 142), after many victories, raised to the dignity of viceroy of the Banavase province and other districts, and in the enjoyment of regal honours.

Vikrama in 1076 expelled his brother, seized the throne, and became the most powerful of the Chálukya monarchs, uniting (p. 87) the qualities of the sixteen preceding kings, that is, up to his namesake Vikramáditya I. He set aside † the ancient era of S'áliváhana, and from his accession established the Chálukya Vikrama era, which continued in use as long as the Chálukyas were in power. Many interesting particulars regarding him are contained in Bilhana's *Vikramánka Deva Charita*.‡

Previous to his accession to the throne he had gained so many important victories, chiefly against the Cholas and other powers south of the Tungabhadra, that his brother, moved by jealousy, sent forces into the Banavasi country

* Sir Walter Elliot, *Mad. J. L. and S.* VII.

† Literally *rubbed it out*, as figures are swept out of the sand by school boys.

‡ Edited, with an introduction, by Dr. G. Buhler, Bombay.

(the Shimoga District) to seize him ; but Vikrama destroyed them. He seems however to have taken the precaution of strengthening himself by alliances. For he married his daughter to Jayakesi, king of the Kadambas, whose capital was then at Goa ; and formed a friendship with his former enemy the Chola Rája, which was cemented by his marriage with the Chola princess. The Chola king died soon after, and his kingdom was thrown into a state of anarchy. On hearing this, Vikrama, who was still tarrying on the Tungabhadra, at once started for the south, in order to place his wife's brother on the throne. He entered Kánchi and put down the rebels there; then destroyed the enemy throughout Gangakuṇḍa, (no doubt the same as Gangaváḍi); and re-established the Chola power.

But not long after his return, he learned that his brother-in-law had lost his life in a fresh rebellion, and that Rájiga, the lord of Vengi, had taken possesion of the throne of Kánchi. Vikrama at once prepared to march himself against the usurper ; but the latter opened negotiations with Somes'vara at Kalyáṇa, who, thinking a favourable opportunity had offered itself for the destruction of his hated brother, eagerly entered into alliance. He followed so closely on Vikrama's march to the south, that when the latter come up with Rájiga's army, Somes'vara's forces were encamped not far off in his rear. A terrible battle ensued, in which victory declared for Vikrama : Rájiga fled, and Somes'vara was taken prisoner. This was in 1076.

Vikrama placed his younger brother Jaya Simha in the government of Banavase and repaired to Kalyáṇa. He there heard that a *svayamvara* was proclaimed for Chandralekha or Chandala Devi, daughter of the Silabara prince of Karaháṭa, and possessed of marvellous beauty. He also ascertained that the lady on hearing of his valiant exploits had fallen in love with him, and therefore hasted to the festival, where he was chosen as the bridegroom from among the assembled princes of Ayodhya, Chedi, Kanyakubja, Kalinjara, Malava, Gurjara, &c., who, though filled with anger at the result, were restrained from violence through fear of the great Chálukya.

Next year his brother Jaya Simha rebelled, and collecting a large army advanced to the Krishna. Vikrama being forced in self defence to take the field against him, a battle was fought, in which Jaya Simha was defeated and taken prisoner. The remainder of Vikrama's reign seems to have been peaceful, with the exception of an expedition in 1081 against Kánchi and the Pallavas, and one north of the Narmada in 1083. But towards the close he was invaded by the Hoysala Ballála king, who was driven back by his general Achyugi Deva.

In the present volume an account of Vikrama's conquests will be found at pp. 129, 175, 14 and 88. In 1077 he appears as residing at Tagiri (pp. 130, 163), perhaps the modern Daulatabad. In this year, on his son's birthday,* he makes a grant (p. 131) to the Chálukya Ganga Permmaḍi Jinálaya at Balligámve. His governor of Banavase and associated districts at this time was Barmma Deva (pp 130, 163, 18). In 1079 his younger brother Jaya Simha, who before long rebelled against him, was viceroy of Banavase (p. 306), with the titles S'rímat Trayalokya Malla Vira Noḷamba Pallava Permmanaḍi Jaya Simha Deva. Moreover, though styling himself head jewel of the Chálukyas, he also claims to be prince of the world-renowned Pallava race. Perhaps his father A'hava Malla's queen was a Pallava princess. If so, Vikrama himself must have borne the same relationship to them. Before the next year must have occurred Jaya Simha's rebellion and defeat, for we then find (p. 166) Vikrama's chief minister Anantapála appointing Govindarasa to rule the Banavase province, while (p. 135) Gundamarasa, a Mane Verggaḍe Dandanáyaka, had the management of the taxes and duties. In 1394 the Hoysala king appears (p. 326) as subordinate to Vikrama. In 1096 a general named Kálidása is named (p. 170) as gaining great distinction against the Lála, Magadha, Nepála, Panchála and Pánḍya kings.

The luxury of the court continued to increase with the growth of its power and wealth, and in 1028 we find (p. 108) Bivanayya, a great minister and (?) senior Lála-Kannaḍa ambassador, bearing among his titles, besides Palace Chamberlain, officer over the female apartments, and president of the concubines! Perhaps he was an eunuch. He causes Padmanábhayya to to be appointed governor of Banavase. In 1102 Govinda appears (pp. 78, 127) still as a dependent of Anantapála's, in charge of the taxes of Milvalli. In 1103 he is again (p. 140) governor of Banavase. Anantapála has by this time received a title as Bánasa Verggaḍe Danḍanáyaka, lord high chief of the kitchen! In 1107 he is (p. 200) Bánasa Mane Verggaḍe and Govinda still at Banavase. In 1108 we have (p. 18) Achchupa Náyaka appointed by him governor of Nolambávaḍi. In 1112, Govinda, still ruling Banavase under the orders of Anantapála (p. 85), makes a gift at the request of Káma Deva, with the title Tribhuvana Malla, of the Pánḍya line, said to be the ruler of Konkana and Haive. In 1114 Anantapála is still in power (p. 177), with Govinda under him, who has now the title of Mane Verggade Danḍanayaka and claims to have

---

* The 22nd December 1077: this must have been Soma who succeeded him, and the offspring of his bride won at the *svayamvara* already mentioned. There is a lively description of his childhood at p. 88.

'washed away the stain of the ignorance of the other generals who commanded in the palace of the king Vikramárka.' In 1115 he appears (p.185) as making war in the south, and neither his name nor Anantapála's occurs after this. But in 1121 we find (p. 15) a Pándya Deva, perhaps Víra Pándya, with the title Tribhuvana Malla, ruling Nolambaváḍi. He also bears the title lord of Kánchipura, which would indicate some victory gained over that city; and a succession of these Pándyas continued to rule Nolambaváḍi for a considerable time from Uchchangi durga. the district around which is even called the Pándya mandala.* Víra Pándya is said (p. 70) to have plucked off the crown of Paundra on the field of battle, while Vijaya Pándya is described (pp. 8, 52) as defeater of the designs of Rájiga Chola.

Soma, called Bhúloka Malla or Tribhuvana Malla, Vikrama's son, succeeded in 1127 to a kingdom powerful and prosperous on every hand (p. 88). To him all kings applied the name Sarvajna mahípála (p. 68). In 1138 we find (p. 329) Vinayáditya of the Hoysala line in subordination to him, ruling the centre and west of the present Mysore; while in 1142 Víra Pándya Deva appears (p. 6) as the governor of Nolambaváḍi. Jagadeka Malla, it is said (p. 58), ruled over the Pallava kingdom, from which he had driven the king; thus bringing to an end the long succession of alternate hostilities and alliances between the Pallavas and Chalukyas from the very time when the latter first appeared in the Dekhan in the 4th century. In 1149 we have an account (p. 97) of the S'ántara kings of Hombucha or Humcha (Paṭṭi Pombuchchapura), in the Nagar country, who were feudatory to him. At that time Jagadeva, with the title Tribhuvana Malla, appears as ruling in the place called Setu

---

* The origin of these Pándyas, who are found ruling the same district to the beginning of the 13th century, when they were subdued by Víra Ballála (p. 266), is related at p. 69. They claim to be Yádavas, and the following is the succession as gathered from that and other notices of them in this volume.

A'ditya Deva ...	Pándya Rája (*m.* Sávala Devi,) whose sons were ...	
Pándya Rája ...	Pándya Deva	
Chedi Rája ...	Víra Pándya Deva, Tribhuvana Malla,	
Dampala ...	(*m.* Ganga Devi, Vijaya Devi,) and	1121 to 1147
Víra Pándya ...	Káma Deva, Nigalanka Malla	
Dampala ...	Tailapa (son of Pándya Deva)	
Kavela ...	Trinetra (son of Víra Pándya Deva)	
	Vijaya Pándya Deva (son of Káma Deva)	1151 to 1171
	Pándya Deva	1200

(I think in Canara)*. He is mentioned among the kings overcome by Vishnu Varddhana of the Hoysala line (p. 263).

Under Núrmaḍi Taila, having the title of Trailokya Malla, the Chálukya dynasty, which had reached its zenith under the last Vikramáditya, began rapidly to decline. A powerful noble named Bijjala, of the Kalachurya race, had been appointed general of the Chálukya armies, and the influence which he thereby obtained he turned against his sovereign, and expelled him from the throne. This event occurred in 1157. The Chálukya king retired south and maintained himself in the Banavase country. The religious feuds which raged at Kalyána in connection with the establishment of the Lingáyat creed kept the hands of the Kalachuryas fully occupied. The Chálukya influence therefore was not extinguished, and Somes'vara, the last of his race, succeeded to the fallen fortunes of his house in 1182. What ultimately became of him does not appear, but the Hoysala Ballála̤s of Dorasamudra from the south and the Yádavas of Devagiri from the north, soon closed in upon the disputed dominions; and the great and powerful Chálukya name disappears from history as that of a dominant power, though certain descendants of the line appear to have ruled in some parts of the Konkan till the middle of the 13th century.

---

* The following is the account, as given in this place, of the S'ántara kings, who were Jains:—

S'ántara, S'antares'vara, several kings of this name.
Kámana.
Singi Deva.
Taila.
Káma (*m.* Bijjala Devi. Her sister Battala Daivi was *m.* to Vijayáditya Deva of the Kadamba family, whose son was Jayakesi).
Jagadeva, Jagaddeva, Tribhuvana Malla 1149
Singi Deva, his brother.
Bammarasa, his son.

But the kingdom of Hombucha was established soon after the subjection of the Kadambas by the Chálukyas in the 5th century. Jinadatta Ráya, its founder, was of the solar line, and his descendants claim to be of the Ugra race, lords of the northern Madhura (*Gazetteer of Coorg*, 26). The latter would make them of common origin with the Páṇḍyas of Madhura in the south. Jinadatta subdued the country as far as Kalasa (Kadur District) and the capital of the kingdom was subsequently removed to Sisila or Sisugali on the Manjarabad frontier, and later on to Kárkala in S. Canara; lieutenants being appointed to Bárkur, Bangádi, Múḍu Bidare and Mulki (see *Gazetteer of Mysore*, II, 374). The rulers of Sisugali are expressly called Páṇḍyas (p. 83). The Kárkala rulers had the general name of Bairasu Woḍeyar and continued in power to the 16th century.

The first of the Humcha kings who took the name of S'ántana or S'ántara would appear to have been Varmma or Barmma, born in 925 and ruling in 977. He was suceeded by his brother Vikrama S'ántana, and then follows Víra or Bíra S'ántana.

And here it becomes necessary to notice more particularly the professedly Chálukya grant of Víra Noṇamba, No. 158, and to show its connection with the alleged Pándava grants of Janamejaya Nos. 130, 133, and 139, with the view of establishing their real dates. The best known of these is the Gauj agrahára inscription, No. 130, which has been the subject of much controversy. It was first brought to notice by Colonel Mackenzie about 1801 and examined by Colebrooke (*As. Res.* IX, 446), who denounced it as unauthentic, and declared that the astronomical data in it would not bear the test of a critical examination. These data, as interpreted by Colebrooke, were given by Colonel Ellis to Sir G. B. Airy, the Astronomer Royal, who therefrom calculated that the eclipse mentioned in the grant occurred on Sunday the 7th of April 1521 (*J. Bo. Br. R. A. S.* X, 81). On this high authority it was concluded that the grant was a forgery of the time of the Vijayanagar kings in the 16th century.

Of these grants by Janamejaya, the one at the Bhímankaṭṭe maṭh, No. 139, is dated in the year 89 of the Yudhishṭhira era, which would be 3012 B. C! The three others, belonging respectively to the Gauj agrahára, No. 130, the Kuppagadde agrahára, No. 133, and the Begur agrahára (not in this collection), all correspond in their contents and date, which is not referred to any era, and profess to have been granted at the sarpa yága to the officiating Brahmans. But they also correspond in the descriptive portion with No. 158, which is dated in 366 of the S'aka era, only that this grant is attributed to Víra Noṇamba of the Chálukya line, instead of to Janamejaya of the Páṇḍava line. They are all in the Nandi Nágari character, but employ a second form of *r* to express the now obsolete Haḷe Kannaḍa letter. A minute comparison of them has been made by me elsewhere (*Ind. Ant.* VIII 80) and I will here only state the grounds on which Sir G. B. Airy's date must be rejected, and the grants assigned with some probability to the end of the 12th century.

The dates of the three Janamejaya grants are thus given :—

Tungabhadra - Haridrá-sangame s'ri-Harihara-Deva-sannidhau kaṭakam-utkalita Chaitra mása
(*Begur*) krishṇa-pakshe Bhauma-dine tritiyáyám Indrabha-nakshatre sankránti vyatí-páta tan nimitta.
(*Kuppagadde*) krishṇa-pakshe Soma-dine Bharaní-mahá-nakshatre sankránti vyatí-páta-nimitte.
(*Gauj*) krishṇa-(pakshe So.........) karaṇá uttaráyana sa................vyatí-páta-nimitte súryya-parbani-ardhdha grása-grahita-samae.

and the exact part of the sacrifice at which the grants were made, thus :—

Begur. Sarppa-yága árambha-samae.
Kuppa. Sarppa-yága-purṇṇáhuti-samae.
Gauj. Sarppa-yága-purṇṇáhuti-tad-anga-samae.

Now, the *So* of the Gauj inscription, which, with the preceding *rakshe*, being at the edge of the plate, has got broken off since Colebrooke's time, (see his transcript in *As. Res.* IX) was the beginning of the words *Soma-dine* or Monday, as clearly appears from the Kuppagaḍe inscription. This, of course, Colebrooke could not guess. He attributed the grant to "the time of a partial eclipse of the sun which fell on a Sunday in the month of Chaitra, when the sun was entering the northern hemisphere, the moon being in the nakshatra As'vini"; adding in a note, "such is the deduction from the text, which states a half eclipse of the sun in Chaitra on the sun's entrance into the uttaráyana or northern path at the moment of vyatipáta (which imports new moon on a Sunday in any one of the undermentioned nakshatra *viz*: As'vini, S'ravaṇa, Dhanishṭha, Ardrá, Aslesha, and Mrigasiras, the first of which is the only one compatible with the month)". Sir G. B. Airy very naturally calculated from the data as interpreted by Colebrooke. But that he was wrong is evident from the fact that the eclipse is said to have happened on Monday and not on Sunday.

The actual calculations, as made for me by the native astronomer Siddhánti Subrahmaṇya S'ástri, result in giving the year 36 of the Kali yuga, or 3066 B. C., which is of course fabulous. But by accepting the phrase *kaṭakam ulkalita* as embodying the date, and taking the letters in the direct order, *ka ṭa ka m* give us 1115, or in the usual manner reckoning that year as complete, A. D. 1194; and from Struyk's *Catalogue of Eclipses* it appears that a partial eclipse of the sun occurred on the 22nd of April 1194. So much for the agrahára grants. With regard to No. 158, which, in addition to *kaṭakam*, gives us S'aka 366 as its date, the only way that occurs to me of reconciling the two is, to take the sum of these figures, 15, as expressing 1115 without the hundreds, a system of which there are examples, and which is common enough among Europeans, as when we speak of 78 meaning 1878, &c. At the same time, S'aka 366 may notwithstanding be a real date, preserved in the annals of the Chálukya house, as that when the first alliance with the Pallavas was formed, and now made to do duty in this corresponding case.

In favour of A. D. 1194 being pretty near the actual date the following evidence may be adduced. In the Gauj grant the village is called the Gautama agrahára; now, Gautama was one of the line of munis who were ácháris of the Kedáres'vara temple at Balligráme, and it is evident that he was officiating from A. D. 1130—1150 (see pp. 87, 97, 99, 102, &c.). Again, No. 56 whose date is also about A. D. 1150, mentions (p. 126) the "mahájanangalu of Kuppagaḍe": which village was therefore an agrahára at that time. Moreover the sarpa yága, according to the traditions of the place, was performed at Hiremagalur, near Chikmagalur, and an inscription there shews that it was an agrahára in the time of Trailokya Malla (1150—1182). Furthermore, the Kilva Ráya of No. 158 corresponds with the Kilvogoḍeyarasa of No. 13, dated in 1169. And further, the origin of the unusual title *Tala-Prahári* is related in the inscription No. 173, dated about 1184, and it is applied to a Noḷamba. Moreover, from the names and description of Jaya Simha, the younger brother of Vikrama, as given in No. 165 it is evident that Víra Noḷamba implied a prince who was the offspring of a Chálukya-Pallava union.

For these and otherrea sons, which will occur on comparison of the grants, I incline to the opinion that they may be of the latter part of the 12th century. Also, from the royal titles in the three agrahára grants being distinctively Chálukyan, and the entire descriptive portion corresponding so closely with No. 158, which is expressly stated to be of Chálukya origin, that the grants emanated from a Chálukya prince by a Pallava mother. There were not wanting reasons for falsifying the date at this period. For the representative of the Chálukyas, driven from power by the Kalachurya king Bijjala, was maintaining a doubtful authority in the Banavase country, soon to end in the extinction of the dynasty. The Pallavas had equally lost their kingdom and lately become dependents of the Chálukyas. Moreover, in the religious world the triumphs of the Lingayet faith were rapidly overthrowing in the north of Mysore the authority of the Brahmans. The merchant Máro S'eṭṭi in No. 158 had no objection to attribute his grant to a prince of Buddhistic associations, such as the Pallavas were, but the agrahára Brahmans thought it safer to go back to a vague antiquity and an orthodox prince.

Kalachuryas—The Kalachuryas or Kalabhuryas were one of the royal houses subjected by the Chalukyas on their first arrival in the south. They were apparently connected with the Haihayas in descent. From the inscription at p. 64 we learn that the founder of the line was named Krishna, and that he was born of a Brahmani girl by Siva. 'He slew in Kálanjara an evil spirit of a king who was a cannibal and followed the occupation of a barber; and taking possession of his kingdom reduced the nine lakh country of Dahala manḍala (Chedi or Bandelkhand) to obedience, and ruled in peace.' After several generations, Kannama Deva arose in this line of kings. His sons were Bijjala and Sanda Rája. The latter had four sons, Nammugi, S'ankha Varmma, Kannara and Jogama; of whom the first and last seem to have ruled in succession. Jogama's son was Permáḍi, who was the father of Bijjala.

The latter, as has been related, took advantage of his position as general of the Chálukya armies, and perhaps induced by carelessness or weakness in the sovereign, to usurp the throne. But for several years he did not assume the royal titles, and it would appear (from p. 61, 189 and similar passages in his grants) as if he had formed on expectation of being recognized as a legitimate successor of the Chálukyas. It was not till the fifth year of his usurpation, or 1161 (p. 94), that he marched to the south, whither the Chálukya prince had retired, and there proclaimed himself supreme.

The following is the list of the Kalachurya kings :—

	A. D.		A. D.
Bijjala, Bijjana, Nis'sanka Malla or Tribhuvana Malla ...	1156—1165	Sankama, Nis'sanka Malla or A'hava Malla ...	... 1176—1181
Ráya Murári Sovi, Somesvara, Vira Vijala or Bhuvanaika Malla,...	1165—1176	A'hava Malla, Aprati Malla	... 1181

Among the titles in their inscriptions, of which there are many in the north of Mysore, are the following :—lord of the city of Kálanjara (the well known fortress in Bandalkhand), having the flag of a golden bull, Malla of the S'anivára Siddagiri durga.

It appears (pp. 93, 192, 159, 66) that Bijjala had a minister named Kasavaya or Kasapaya. While the former was still a general of the Chálukya army (p. 58), Kasavaya was the governor of Banavase, in 1157. Under his orders, Kesi Rája (p. 154), Kes'imayya or Kes'ava Rája (p. 190) was the Hergga de Danadnáyaka and governor of Banavase from 1157 to 1160 (p. 182). The conquests by which the latter had raised himself to favour are given at p. 155, and embrace all the region about the Tungabhadra in the Bellary and Shimoga Districts and westwards to the coast.* In 1160 we find (p. 66) Kasavaya's nephew Barmmarasa ruling the Banavase country, after having gained a victory over the Hoysala forces on the banks of the Tungabhadra. In 1161 he is still in that position (p. 93). In 1165 we have (p. 61) Vijaya Pándya, the son of Káma and nephew of Víra Pándya, ruling the Nonambavádi country. Subordinate to them was an officer of the Sindha family, whose origin is related at some length, though unfortunately the inscription is legible only to a certain point. The founder of the line was born from the union of S'iva and Sindhu, and nursed on the milk of a tigress created for the purpose!

* His name is the same as that of the author, living at about this time, of the *S'abdamani-darpana*, the ancient grammar of the Kannada language in Kannada, and we find him (p. 192) making special provision for good teachers of Kannada, but his genealogy as given pp. 154 and 117 does not accord with that of the grammarian as given in his work. Balligráme is specially described (p. 94) as containing grammarians of many schools.

Málati Devi was appointed his family goddess, and Karabáṭa given him as a kingdom. The Sindhas had a blue flag (*níla dhvaja*) and a tiger signet (*vyághra mṛiga lánchhana*) and ruled many lands within the Four Thousand of Sindha and Karabáṭa.

Vijaya Páṇḍya rules Noṇambavádi down to 1169 (pp. 17, 71, 23) but it will be noticed that he makes no acknowledgment of any higher authority, as if the Páṇḍyas were now independent. There is little doubt that the commotions connected with the establishment of the Lingayet faith by the minister Basava, as will be noticed under religious sects, ending in the murder of the king Bijjala, must at this time have weakened the authority of the government.

But we find (p. 110) mention of what seems like an act of abdication on the part of Bijjala in favour of his son Ráya Murári Sovi Deva, who sends for Byálike Kesimayya (perhaps the former governor of Banavase, before mentioned) and directs him to take the government of all the countries forming the treasury of the south. These, it appears (p. 111), were the Taddavadi Thousand, the Hanugal Five Hundred, and the Banavase Twelve Thousand, which he ruled for a long period in peace, a statement which is confirmed by finding him (p. 161) still in power there in 1179.

In 1171 we find (p. 52) Vijaya Páṇḍya, still apparently independent, calling himself "defeater of the designs of Rájiga Chola" an epithet already adopted 20 years before under the Chálukya king Jagadeka Malla (p. 8). His chief minister is Vijaya Permáḍi, and he also has under him the representatives of the Kadamba family. In 1173 Permáḍi's son Durgarasa appears as *adhikári* of Banavase (p. 54).

Under Sankama Deva luxury had attained to that pitch of excess which presaged the speedy overthrow of the sovereignty of the Kalachuryas. A graphic description of this appears (p. 76) in the gifts presented to him by foreign powers, among whom Láḷa (the Konkan) sends young girls. In 1180 we accordingly find (p. 138) Kesimayya, the experienced governor of Banavase, dubbed "chief of the female apartments".

In 1181 it appears (p. 116) that A'hava Malla, the younger brother of Sankama, had come to the throne. He also sends for Kesimayya (p. 117) and appoints him to govern the south 'so that the country may have quiet' and he, accepting the charge, appears, with the names Krishna Kes'ava Deva, as ruling (p. 119) Banavase, Hayve, S'antalige, Yeḍedore and other associated countries. Among A'hava Malla's generals was Chanḍugi Deva, who claims (p. 117) to have burnt the territory of Vijayáditya (of the Kadamba line, ruling in the

Konkan, see p. 119) and taken the Chola and Hoysala kingdoms. But from p. 119 it would appear that tho Hoysala king Víra Ballá!a reduced these chiefs to subjection.

Hoysalas.—This dynasty, like that of the Gangas, was essentially Mysorean, and ruled this country with great glory from the 10th to the 14th century. The earlier kings were Jains. They claim to be Yádavas and therefore of the lunar line.

The founder of the family was Sala, and the exploit which raised him to a throne is related in many inscriptions (pp. 214, 31, 322, 260, 271, 324, 275). Going one day to worship Vásantika his family goddess, whose temple was in the forest near S'as'akapura, his devotions were interrupted by a tiger, which bounded out of the jungle glaring with rage. The *yati* * of the temple, snatching up a *saláki*—a slender iron rod—gave it to the chief, saying in the Karṇáṭaka language *Hoyi Sala !* Strike, Sala ! on which the latter discharged the weapon with such force at the tiger as to kill him on the spot. From this circumstance he adopted the name Hoysala, formed from the words of the yati's exclamation ; and the dynasty so called descended from him had a tiger (*s'árdúla*) as the device on their flag.

The following is the list of the Hoysala kings, with their dates as obtained from the sources indicated, but their inscriptions are not so dated as easily to establish the exact year of each king's succession. There is every reason to believe that Sala was a chief of some district immediately to the south of the Chandra Drona or Bába Budan mountains in the Kadur District. According to the *Channa Basava Puráṇa*, Hoysala was crowned in A. D. 878† but this seems too early.

Inscriptions.		Channa Basavana Kálajnána.	Kongu Desa Rájakal.
	Sala, Hoysala	984—1043	...
...1039—1047...	Vinayáditya	1043—1073	—1068...
1065	Yereyanga, Pereyanga, Víra Ganga ...	1073—1114	...
...1117—1138...	Biṭṭi Deva, Vishnu Varddhana, Tribhuvana Malla...	1114—1145	...1099—1147...
...1142—1191	Vijaya Narasimha, Víra Narasimha ...	1145—1188	1147—1174
1191—1207...	Víra Ballála	1188—1233	1174—
1223	Víra Narasimha	1233—1249	—1237
1252	Soma, Víra Somes'vara	1249—1268	1237—1283
...1262—1287...	Víra Narasimha	1268—1308	1283—1313
1310	Balláḷa Deva	...	...

* He seems to have been one of the Humcha gurus, and named Vardhamána munindra.—*Gas. Mysore,* Vol. I, p. 373.

† Kittel, *Naga Varmma's Chhandas.* Intro. I.

Till the beginning of the 12th century the Hoysalas were apparently feudatories of the Chálukyas, but Vishnu Varddhana then made them independent. Vinayáditya, the son of Sala, is said (p. 329) to have ruled over a territory bounded by Konkaṇa, Bhaḍada-vayal-náḍ, Talakáḍu and Sávi-male, and also (p. 261) described as threatening the Konkanas and (p. 329) the Malapas. His wife was Keleyabbe or Keleyalá Devi, who appears (p. 329) as taking a great interest in Mariyáne Danḍanáyaka, promoting his marriage, and on that occasion obtaining for him in 1039 the lordship of Sindigere near Chikmagalur. She bore to the king a son Ereyanga or Pereyanga, who succeeded him, and perhaps from assuming the protection (p. 307) of the Ganga prince, who had lost his kingdom, took the name of Víra Ganga. The conquests of Ereyanga are somewhat vaguely described (p. 261). He married Achala Devi and had three sons,—Ballá]a, Biṭṭi Deva and Udayáditya. Of these, Ballá]a does not seem to have come to the throne. The principal thing related of him in the inscriptions here collected is (p. 330) that in 1103 he was living at Bélápura (Belur), and on the same day, in the same marriage hall, married the three accomplished daughters of Mariyáne Danḍanáyaka of the second generation, renewing the gift to him of the lordship of Sindigere bestowed on the family before.

Biṭṭi Deva, under his subsequent name of Vishnu Varddhana, was one of the most celebrated kings of this line and of his time. He was converted, probably in 1117, from the Jain faith to that of Vishnu by the Vaishnava apostle Rámánujáchári, who had taken refuge in the Hoysala kingdom from the persecutions of the Chola king Karikala, an uncompromising S'aiva. Vishnu Varddhana would appear (pp. 326, 328) to have been feudatory to the Chálukya king Vikrama or Tribhuvana Malla, and commander of a considerable part of his forces (p. 330). His ambition was fired (p. 262) by the stories of the valour and glory of the Sauvíra kings.* As soon as he had made himself independent master of the Hoysala kingdom, 'taking up the circle of the points of the compass,' he burnt Talakáḍu†, the capital city of the Gangas, and took possession of the Ganga kingdom, being the first of his line to rule it (p. 262). From this conquest he took the titles Bhujabala Ganga. It would appear (p. 332) that he was assisted by Mariyáne Danḍanáyaka.

During the 200 years which intervened from the capture of Talakáḍu by the Cholas and their overthrow of the Ganga kingdom to this time when the Hoysalas acquired possession of them, a period of anarchy no doubt prevail-

---

* Probably kings of Rajputana.

† Talakáḍu has been described (Wilson, *McK. Coll.* I. cix) as the early capital of the Hoysalas. This is an error: Dorasamudra was their capital during the whole time of their power.

ed in the south of Mysore. But there are accounts of the springing up of a kingdom there during that interval, which, but for the triumphs of the Hoysalass absorbing the whole country, might have secured a greater place in history. The stronghold of this young power was Beṭṭada-koṭe on the well known Gopalswámi hill. It belonged to a family of nine brothers, called the Nava Danáyak. Bhíma Danáyak, one of four of the brothers the chief of whom was named Perumál Danáyak, and who had quarrelled with the other five, gained possession of Nagarapura (Nanjangud) and Ratnapuri (Heḍatale) and set up a separate government. After a time they returned to attack Beṭṭada-koṭe, which, after a siege of three years, was taken by stratagem. Mancha Danáyak, who conducted the defence, seeing the citadel taken, leaped from the hill on horseback and was killed.* The four victorious Danáyaks, placing a junior member of the family in the government of Beṭṭada-koṭe, set forth on expeditions of conquest, in the course of which it is said they penetrated as far as Goa on the north; to Davasi Beṭṭa (the southern limit of Coorg) on the south; to the Bisale ghat (in the north west of Coorg) on the west; and to the pass of Satyamangala (to the north east of the Nilagiri) on the east. This includes the whole of the hill region to the west and south of Mysore, and these Danáyaks may possibly be the Male Rájas (or hill kings) and Malapar whom the Hoysalas claim to have subdued.

To return to Vishnu Varddhana. His conquests in the south (pp. 263, 215, 32, 331) extended over Kongu, Kovatúru (Coimbatore), and Toreyúru; and in the east, to Kolálapura (Kolar), Nangali, Vallúru (Vellore), and Kánchipura (Conjeveram). Westwards he acquired the whole of the Male and Tulu countries (p. 215, 263). The range of his expeditions northwards (p. 308) was as far as Vengiri, Uchangi, Viráṭa, Polalu, Bankapura and Banavase. He subdued Jayakesi (p. 216) the Kadamba king, Jagat Deva (p. 263) ruling Tuluva, Narasimha (p. 263) or Narasimha Varmma (p. 331), the Pallava king; overcame Chola, Kerala, and Páṇḍya; subdued As'vapati, Gajapati and other kings, &c. In short, 'he disturbed all the world with the noise of his armies' (p. 216), 'trod it to dust with the squadrons of his Kámbhoja horse' (p. 263), and 'overwhelmed his enemies as if the great deep had been broken up, the coursers of the sun being borne away in the deluge and all the points of the compass filled with the sounds of their neighing' (p. 215).

The boundaries of his kingdom in 1117 are thus stated (p. 263)—the lower ghat of Nangali on the east; Kongu, Cheram, Anamale on the south; the Barkanúr ghat road of Konkana on the west; and Sávi-male in the north.

* The site of this leap is still pointed out.

And in 1136 the provinces of his kingdom are given (p. 216) as Talakáḍu, Kongu, Nangali, Gangaváḍi, Noḷambaváḍi, Máraváḍi, Huligere, Halasige, Banavase, Hánungalu, and Náḷugonḍa; that is, the whole of the present Mysore, with Coimbatore, Salem, parts of Bellary, Dharwar, Canara and Malabar. His chief ministers were (p. 332) two Jain brothers, Mariyáne Danḍanayaka and Bharataṇa Danḍanáyaka. His wife, and the mother of Narasimha who succeeded him, is called (p. 32) Lakuma Devi and (p. 264) S'ántala Devi. From the continuation of No. 117 it would appear that the birth of his son took place in 1136 at the time when he had gained some victory at Bankapura, and that both events were attributed to the favour of Párs'vanátha, whose temple he had recently caused to be built at Hanasoge (Hassan District). He accordingly named his son Vijaya Narasimha, and the god Vijaya Párs'va.

Vijaya Narasimha would seem to have succeeded to an established and peaceful kingdom. He must have been a minor at the time, and this may account for his mother S'ántavve being mentioned (p. 328) among his counsellors. He is said (p. 327) to have been like a god, enjoying the pleasures of the gods; and his glory to exceed that of the elephant kings, doubtless the Gangas. His standards are described (p. 308) as being planted as far north as Devagiri.

His queen was Achalá Devi and they had a son Víra Balláḷa, who rivalled even Vishnu Varddhana in the glory of his reign and the extent of his conquests, so that the Hoysala kings are also called after him the Balláḷa kings. Víra Ballála's conquests are described at p. 104. They were principally to the north, where a fierce contest arose between the Hoysalas and the Yádavas of Devagiri for the possession of the late Chálukya-Kalachurya dominions. The Páṇḍya ruling at Uchchangi was reduced to submission (p. 266) and his power restored to him. After a defeat of the general of the Kalachuryas, in consequence of which he appropriates their titles of Giridurga Malla and Malla of the S'anivára Siddigiri durga, and carrying his dominions up to and beyond the Krishna, Víra Balláḷa made Lokigonda (Lakkundi in Dharwar) his residence for some time, and here took place the great and sanguinary battle (described p. 32) between him and Soma the general of the Devagiri king Jayatuga Deva. In 1192 his minister Eraga was governor (p. 104) of Banavase and Sántalige. In 1205 it appears (p. 137) that Pananappa Arasu was ruling Banavase.

Víra Narasimha, the son of Víra Balláḷa by Padmalá Devi, succeeded his father. His army was chiefly employed in the south (p. 34). He is described (p. 33) as churning with the Mandara mountain of his powerful right arm the ocean of the Kádava army into which the Páṇḍya alligator had plunged, and thus acquiring numerous elephants of great strength. He overthrew, it is said, the Kádava king, Makara, the Pándya king and others and gave the crown to Chola. Also (p. 272) that he dragged out the Chola king, who had been overwhelmed under the clouds of dust raised by the march of hosts of enemies, and set him up again in power. Whatever the incident referred to may have been, the Hoysalas claim in their later inscriptions to be "thrusters out of the Pándya Ráya, and setters up of the Chola Ráya." Narasimha's wife was Lokámbiká, whose native place was apparently at Turuvekere (Túmkúr District). His general and minister was (p. 34) Polálva, who had also held that position under Víra Ballála. He erected the temple of Harihara on the Tungabhadra, and was called Tolagada Kamba (unshaken pillar).

Soma or Víra Somes'vara apparently (p. 272) had a generally peaceful reign. His queen is stated (p. 272) to be Bijjali Devi, 'to move within the space illuminated by whose toe-nails made the wives of other kings honourable'! But he appears (p. 322) to have married Somala Devi, and with her taken up his residence at Vikramapura, 'which he had established for his own pleasure in the Chola country, conquered by the power of his own arm'.

Narasimha, the son of Soma by Bijjali, succeeded him on the throne. He had a general Perumála (p. 273, 11), called the king of the Ráuttas, who gained some victory over a chief named Ratnapála and thence had the title Javanike Nárayana. Soma, the son of the king's elder sister, was his minister (p. 324). He founded the agrahára of Somanáthapura on the Kávéri, and erected the celebrated temple there (p. 325, 50). Narasimha's son, it would appear (p. 7), was Ballála Deva, who, as commander of the army, together with his cousin Soyana, ably supported his father and eventually succeeded him on the throne. His ministers were Mendige Deva and Aliya Mácheya.

The grant containing these particulars falls in the very year that the Ballála dominions were invaded by a Muhammadan army under Káfur, the general of Ala-ud-Din, the second king of the house of Khilji or second Pathan dynasty. A great battle was fought, in which the Ballála king was defeated and taken prisoner. Dorasamudra was sacked, and the enemy returned to Delhi literally laden with gold. Another expedition, sent by Muhammad III of the house of Toghlak in 1326, completely demolished the city. After the first defeat the seat of government seems to have been removed to Belur, the king now retired to Tondanur (Tonnur), 9 miles north of Seringapatam, at the foot of the Yádava hills. He is said to have borne the name of Vishnu Varddhana.

Thus ended the rule of this powerful line, consisting of nine chief princes, and thence called the Nava Ballála; which, from a very small beginning, had, by the valour of its several members, subdued the whole of Karnáṭaka up to the Krishna, with Tuluva on the west, Drávida on the east, and part of Telingána on the north-east.

Yádavas.—This line of kings arose in the northern part of the old Chálukya kingdom, the founder being contemporary with Víra Ballála of the Hoysala line. They overcame the Kalachuryas and became masters of all the Western Dekhan, having their capital at Devagiri, the ancient Tagara, and now known as Daulatabad. Their standard bore the device of a golden garuḍa.

The following is the list of the kings :—

	A. D.		A. D.
Ballam, Bhillama ...	... 1188—1193	Mahadeva ...	... 1260—1271
Jayatuga, Jaitugi, Jaitpala	... 1193—1210	Rámachandra, S'rí Ráma	... 1271—1310
Simhana, Singhana ...	... 1210—1248	S'ankara	... 1310—1312
Kandara, Kanhara, Krishna	... 1248—1260		

If the inscription No. 101 belongs to the first king of this line, it would appear that he had taken possession of the Banavase country. But the Hoysala king Víra Ballála soon drove the Yádavas beyond the Krishna. Their genealogy is given at p. 44. It was not till the time of Simhana Deva that they re-appear in Mysore. Among the conquests of the latter (pp. 20, 72) he claims to disperse the dark clouds the forces of the Karnáṭaka kings. His minister was Hemmaya Náyaka, who 'so discharged his duties that the king was not disturbed in his enjoyments'! (p. 72). An amusing description of the proclamation of Mahadeva's accession to power is given (p. 45), where his heralds summon all the neighbouring kings forthwith to submit to him. He is said to have acquired the Telunga kingdom and established the kings in their three cities. Rámachandra was the first to regain a footing in Mysore. His general Sáluva Tikkama claims (p. 47) to have taken Dorasamudra, the Hoysala capital, and levied tribute from the Hoysalas. The Yádavas accordingly from this time assume the title of lords of Dvárávati paṭṇa, and the general proclaims himself 'establisher of the Kadamba king, disgracer of the Hoysala king.' He built a temple at Harihara. Rámachandra also styles himself (p. 127) 'disgracer of the Hoysana Ráya, establisher of the Telunga Ráya.' The Yádavas would seem at this time to have made Bettur* in the Chitaldroog District the seat of their government in Mysore.

The Muhammadans now first appeared in the Dekhan, and Ala-ud-Din took Devagiri in 1295. By 1318 the Yádava power was completely overthrown, and in 1338 Muhammad Toghlak removed the capital of his empire from Delhi to Devagiri, giving it the name of Daulatabad.

---

* Whether the old name Bemmattanúr belonged to this place or to Chitaldroog I do not feel sure.

Vijayanagar.—The last great Hindu sovereignty of the south was founded in 1336, and brings us back, after a lapse of more than two thousand five hundred years, to the site of Kishkindha, whose annals engaged our attention near the beginning of this historical survey. Though the details vary, all accounts attribute the origin of the Vijayanagar empire to two persons named Hakka and Bukka, assisted by the celebrated scholar Mádhava, surnamed Vidyáraṇya or forest of learning,* who was the guru of S'ringeri (Kadur District), and is also known to literature as S'ayana, the most celebrated commentator on the vedas.

Hakka and Bukka, of whom the former assumed the name of Harihara, were the sons of Sangama, described as a prince of the Yádava line and the lunar race. Mádhava was minister to Sangama. Nothing is known of the situation of Sangama's kingdom, but one inscription describes him as S'ailankanátha, and his father's name appears to have been Kampa. The earliest of the inscriptions of the Vijayanagar kings are found in the north and west of Mysore.

The site selected for the new capital was a remarkable one, on the banks of the Pampa or Tungabhadra, where the ancient Kishkindha had stood. In the words of an inscription (p. 55) 'its rampart was Hemakúṭa, its moat the auspicious Tungabhadra, its guardian the world-protector Virupáksha, its ruler the great king of kings Harihara.' The Vijayanagar sovereigns adopted the *varáha* or boar as the emblem on the royal signet, and their family god was Virupáksha, the name under which S'iva was worshipped in a celebrated temple erected at the capital. Their grants are signed *S'rí Virupáksha.*

The succession and dates of the Vijayanagar kings as traditionally handed down are much confused. The following list is approximately correct, based on many inscriptions I have examined.

	A. D.
Harihara, Hakka, Hariyappa	1336—1350
Bukka, Víra Bukkanna	1350—1379
Harihara	1379—1401
Deva Ráya, Vijaya Ráya, Vijaya Bukka	1401—1451
Mallikárjuna, Víra Mallanna, Prauḍha Deva	1451—1465
Virupáksha	1465—1479
Narasa, Narasimha	1479—1487
Víra Narasimha, Immaḍi Narasinga	1487—1508
Krishna Ráya	1508—1530
Achyuta Ráya	1530—1542
Sadás'iva Ráya (Ráma Rája, regent, usurps the throne till 1565).	1542—1573
Srí Ranga Ráya (Tirumala Rája, brother of Ráma Rája, 1566—).	1574—1587
Víra Venkatapati, &c.	1587—

* The capital was apparently called Vidyánagara (city of learning) at first, in honour of the sage Vidyáraṇya, who was chiefly instrumental in its foundation; but by a natural transition it passed ere long into Vijayanagara (city of victory), the Bijanagar of Muhammadan historians, and the Bisnagar of

Sangama—'the lady of whose brilliant fame was like an ornament of musk adorning the brow of a sky as dark as the shade of the *honge** tree'—by his wife Kámámbika had five sons, Harihara, Kampa or S'ankara, Bukka, Márapa and Muddapa.† Harihara was the first ruler of Vijayanagar, and was succeeded by Bukka. Márapa ruled over the Kadamba territories, as *yuva ráṭ* or viceroy, at Chandragutti (Shimoga District). What became of the others does not appear. Bukka Raya married Gaurámbika, and had a son Harihara, who succeeded him on the throne. Harihara's son was Deva Ráya, whose queen was Mallayavve, and by her he had Víra Mallanna, perhaps the Mallikárjuna who succeeded him, and who seems also to have borne the title of Prauḍha Deva. But Víra Pratápa Prauḍha Deva are epithets commonly applied to the Vijayanagar kings in inscriptions.

Their dominions up to this time seem to have been most extensive under Harihara and his son Deva Ráya. The former had a general named Gunḍa, whose conquests are referred to pp. 227, 228, and with most extravagant detail at p. 222. Of the king himself it is with more truth said (p. 268) that he conquered Chola, Kerala and Pánḍya, besides by his victories causing the days to appear ever cloudy to the Yavanis (the wives of the Muhammadans) through their blinding tears. Harihara's minister was Mudda (pp. 56, 268) who had been his father's adviser. This king repaired the great temple at Belur,—which the Hoysala king Vishnu Varddhana had erected, but which the Muhammadans had damaged by fire,—and renewed its endowments (p. 222). Deva Ráya's coronation is referred to (p. 279). An account is given (p. 28) of a dam erected during his reign in 1410 across the Haridra, the stream which flows from the Sulekere into the Tungabhadra at Harihara. This work appears to have been executed with the funds of the Harihara temple. But (p. 40) there is also an account later on of the breaching of the dam in 1424, on which Náganna, the king's minister, seems to have brought official pressure to bear on Cháma nripála, the commander of the forces, and induced him to

---

the French. It is also commonly known as A'negundi, properly the name of a village on the other side of the river, said to have been the capital of the Yavanas, regarding whom so little is known. A'negundi, a Kannaḍa name, meaning elephant pit, was translated into Sanskrit as Hastinapura and Hastinavati, which is the designation in the Mahá Bhárata of the capital of the Pánḍus near Delhi. (Vidyanagara may, however, become Vijyánagara according to rule see Vijyádhara, p. xlix.)

* The *Pongamia glabra* or Indian beech.

† Another inscription says he had five sons by S'árada, the youngest of whom was named Hariyappa. S'áradamma is the name under which Sarasvati is worshipped as the tutelary goddess of S'ringeri.

undertake its repair. During this reign the eastern districts of Mysore seem to have been administered from Mulbagal (pp. 213, 259, 208) by two brothers Akhanna and Mádanna, called the Heggade Devas. It was this Deva Ráya between whom and Firoz Shah, the Sultan of the Bahmani kingdom, which had been established at Kulbarga not long after Vijayanagar, arose the alternation of sanguinary wars and alliances of which Ferishta's *History* gives long and interesting accounts (see *Gaz. Mysore*, I, 225 ff).

With Narasa or Narasingha the line was changed. The origin of Narasa is traced (p. 243) to the Tuluva kings, among whom S'ekhara, of the family of Krishna Rava, was his father, and Bukkamma his mother. An important account is given of his conquests, p. 243, and he appears to have established his residence at Seringapatam. He had two sons Víra Narasimha and Krishna Rája, by different mothers. These ruled in succession to each other, and an account is given (pp. 244, 245) of their dominion and power.

Krishna Ráya was one of the most powerful and distinguished monarchs of the Vijayanagar line. About 1520, the Muhammadans sustained a severe defeat from his armies, in consequence of which a good understanding prevailed between the courts of Vijayanagar and Bijapur for a considerable period. He not only restored the kingdom to its former limits but extended them in every direction. He kept possession of all the country up to the Krishna; eastwards he captured Warangal and ascended to Cuttack, where he married the daughter of the raja as the bond of peace; while westwards his conquests extended up to Salsette. He was also a great patron of Sanskrit and Telugu literature. Eight distinguished poets, called the *ashṭa-dig-gaja*, were maintained at his court.*

The Hindu traditions represent Krishna Ráya as conducting his affairs both in peace and war in person. But they acknowledge that he owed much to the Brahman minister of his father, who had saved his life, and who continued to be his minister until his death, three years preceding that of the raja. His name was Timma Rája, the Hemraj of the Muhammadan historians. At no period probably in the history of the south did any of its political divisions equal in extent and power that of Vijayanagar in the reign of Krishna Ráya.

Achyuta Raya, who next came to the throne, was probably the cousin or nephew of Krishna Ráya. He was succeeded by Sadás'iva Ráya, his son (p. 228), who was only nominally the ruler, under the guardianship of Ráma Rája (supposed to be the son of Timma Rája before mentioned) and Tirumala

---

* The principal one was named Appaya Dikshita.

Rája (pp. 228, 225). These are described (p. 253) as brothers and their genealogy is given. Tirumala Rája, the maternal uncle of Sadásiva, managed for a short time to gain the supreme power, but being overcome by Ráma Rája, destroyed himself. Ráma Rája's arrogance provoked the hostility of the Muhammadan powers to the north—Bijapur, Golkonda, Ahmednagar and Bidar—who, uniting their armies, advanced against him, and in the great and decisive battle of Talikota, fought on the 25th of January 1565, slew Ráma Rája, routed his army and virtually brought the Vijayanagar empire to an end.

From this point it is unnecessary to pursue in detail the later history of Mysore: it has been given by me with sufficient fulness elsewhere (*Gazetteer of Mysore*), and the task undertaken in the present sketch, of delineating more especially the ancient history of the country as contained in its inscriptions, has been accomplished. Moreover, from this time inscriptions on stone or copper are less frequent, their place being supplied by *sannads*, written on paper, which confine themselves more to the immediate object of the document and are not, as with the ancient grants, made the medium of enlarging on the genealogy of the royal family and the achievements of their ancestors, nor a vehicle for exhibiting the powers and taste of the author in poetical composition.

At the same time, a few inscriptions of modern date framed on the ancient models have been included by me in this collection. The most interesting of these are the Yelandur grant (No. 175), and the grants by the Mysore Rájas (Nos. 167, 168, 169).

Geography.

The ancient geography of Mysore, as contained in the inscriptions to the time of the Vijayanagar empire, is best exhibited in the form of the accompanying map, which will shew at a glance, better than any description, the former divisions of the country, and identify the sites of ancient cities, towns and places of interest.

Of the various states into which Mysore was broken up after the fall of Vijayanagar, a sketch map has been given by me elsewhere (*Gazetteer of Mysore*, Vol. I, p. 234), to which I have only to add that a small state, omitted there, should be marked off from the north east corner of Chikka Ráya's territory and the east of the Chikka Ballapur territory, with its chief town at Yerukálve in the former.

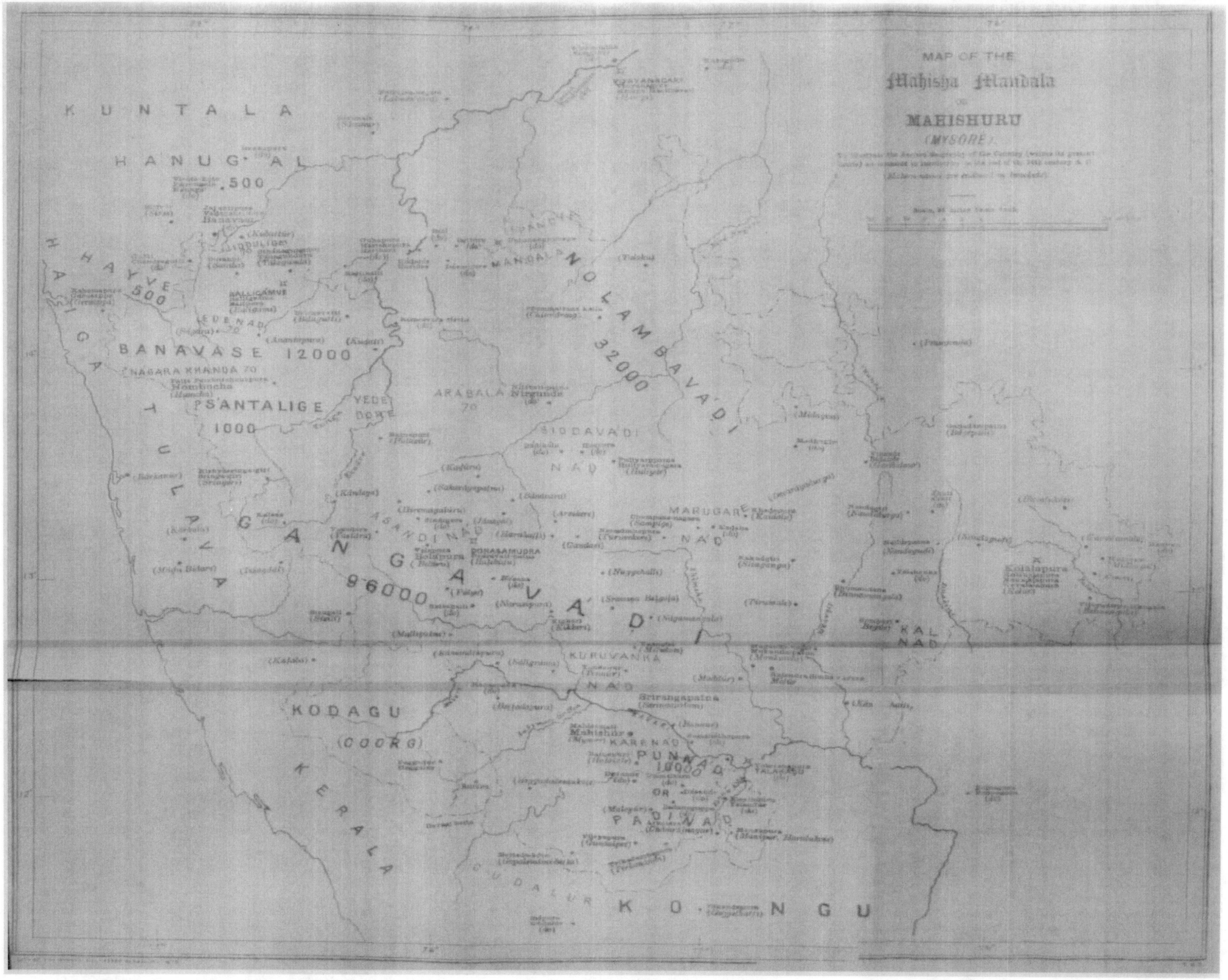
MAP OF THE
Mahisha Mandala
OR
MAHISHURU
(MYSORE)
KUNTALA
HANUG·AL 500
HAYVE 500
BANAVASE 12000
NAGARA KHANDA 70
PSANTALIGE 1000
EDENAD 70
YEDE DORE
ARABALA 70
NOLAMBAVADI 32000
SIDDAVADI NAD
MARUGARE NAD
ASANDI NAD
GANGAVADI 96000
TULAVA
HAIGA
KURUVANKA NAD
KAL NAD
KODAGU (COORG)
KERALA
PUNNAD 10000 OR PADINAD
KARENAD
TALAKAD
KONGU
Srirangapatna
Mahishur
Kolalpura
Dorasamudra
Nirgunda

The rise and extension of the modern State of Mysore at different periods of its history have also been shewn in a separate map in the same work (p. 268). To that I have nothing to add, save to remark that, although the existing State was constituted by the treaty of Seringapatam in 1799, the actual present limits date from the subsequent treaty of 1803, when an exchange was made with the British Government of certain border districts, as described at p. 297 of the first volume.

Language.

These inscriptions are a permanent record of the forms and style of the Kannaḍa or Karnáṭaka language, called Canarese by Europeans, at successive stages of its growth. To enter into this question fully would need a separate treatise of considerable dimensions. If it should be my good fortune to complete the publication proposed to myself of the two standard ancient grammars of the language, namely the *Karnáṭaka Bháshá Bhúshana* of Nága Varmma, and the *Karnáṭaka S'abdánus'ásana* of Bhaṭṭákalanka Deva, with its two commentaries the *Bháshá Manjari* and the *Manjari Makaranda*, no slight contribution will have been made towards the elucidation of the subject.

Here I can only refer to certain inscriptions as characteristic of their respective dates, of which I have transcribed the Kannaḍa of the original in whole or in part in foot notes. The earliest are unquestionably those on pp. 304 and 305 (Nos. 162—164). Reference may also be made to pp. 293 and 283. These passages are none of them later than the 5th century. There is a specimen for the 7th century in No. 98.*

For the 9th century, see pp. 209—210 :
for the 10th century, p. 187 :
for the 11th century, pp. 149—150, 145—146, 143, 131, 107 :
for the 12th century, pp. 81, 83, 85, 18, 199, 214—5, 261—5, 87, 90, 122—4, 101, 94, 61, 104, 110, 116—7, 119—20, 153—5, 182, 187, 196, 327—8 :
for the 13th century, pp. 30, 33, 308, 323, 45, 219 :
for the 14th century, pp. 235, 223, 267 :
for the 15th century, p. 259 :
for the 16th century, p. 220 :
for the 17th century, p. 221 :
for the 18th century, pp. 320 and 257.

* The other inscriptions in this volume of the 6th, 7th and 8th centuries happen to be in Sanskrit.

Religion.

Jains.—The oldest of the inscriptions in this volume, No. 161, refers to a great migration of Jains from Ujjayini to the south under the leadership of Bhadra Báhu, in order to escape a twelve years famine which he had foretold. On arriving at the present S'ravaṇa Beḷgoḷa, feeling a premonition of his approaching death, he resolved to remain there to perform the final ceremonies of a sannyási, dismissing the multitude who followed him on their journey southwards under another leader. One single disciple he retained with him to minister to his last moments. From the account of these transactions derived from the *Rájávali Kathe* as published by me elsewhere*, we ascertain that this Bhadra Báhu was one of the *s'ruta kevali* or hearers of the first masters, as those were called who were disciples in the second generation from Mahávíra or Varddhamána, the great Jain apostle, whose death in 527 B. C. is the era from which Jain chronology dates.

Bhadra Báhu is said† to have lived 170 years after Varddhamána, or 357 B. C., and the single faithful disciple who elected and was suffered to remain with him to the last was, it is alleged, no other than the emperor Chandra Gupta, whose period, from his identification with the Sandrokoptos or Sandrocottus of the Greeks, has long formed one of the most certain landmarks in Indian chronology. According to Jain accounts he abdicated the throne, which most Jain kings are represented as doing, and took *díkshe* in order to devote his last years to religious exercises, joining himself to Bhadra Báhu. The latter expired in a cave at S'ravaṇa Beḷgoḷa, where his footprints are still worshipped, and the sanctity with which the spot was thus invested led to the formation there of the existing Jain settlement, the seat of the chief guru of the sect in the south. The bare granite hill on which the inscription is cut is also scored over in all directions with memorials of Jain saints, who selected this since holy spot in which to end their days by keeping the vow of *sallekhana*, an account of which, and of the epitaphs of which No. 162 is a specimen, has been published by me elsewhere.‡

The religious leader to whose direction Bhadra Báhu committed the company of pilgrims who followed him from Ujjayini was, according to the history already referred to, named Vis'ákha muni, one of the *das'apúrvis*, as the disciples who come next after the s'ruta kevalis were called. He, on the termination of the famine in the north, led back those of the emigrants who wished to return, and visiting on his way the hill where Bhadra Báhu had remained

* *Ind. Ant.* III, 153. † *J. Bo. Br. R. A. S.* IX, 150. ‡ *Ind. Ant.* II, 265, 322

behind to die, found Chandra Gupta muni there, awaiting the time when he too should quit the body, and from him received an account of the last hours of Bhadra Báhu. As this interesting inscription mentions several gurus in succession to Vis'ákha, the inference is that it was inscribed some time after the period to which it actually refers, and I have assigned it to the 1st century B. C.

It would appear that at the time of Bhadra Báhu's death there were no Jain settlements in the Mysore, though there are said to have been some in the countries further south whither the emigrants went. But it may be also inferred that Jains had settled at S'ravaṇa Beḷgoḷa by the date of this and cognate inscriptions. The history previously referred to describes the settlement as being formed in the time of Chandra Gupta's grandson.

At what time the colossal image of Gomaṭes'vara was erected there, is not known, but it appears from Jain chronicles that it is attributed to Rávaṇa, and that its existence was revealed in a dream to Chávuṇḍa Ráya, who caused it to be consecrated afresh and endowed it with lands for the permanent maintenance of its worship. The account of Chávuṇḍa Ráya's action is confirmed by the inscriptions at the foot of the image. He is said to have been the minister of Rája Malla the Páṇḍya king of the southern Madhura, which may be the existing place of that name, or possibly Humcha in the Nagar Division. Who Gomaṭes'vara, Gommaṭes'vara or Gummaṭes'vara was, is not clear.* He is also described as Bhuja Bali and Báhu Bali. It is singular that Gomates is discovered in the cuneiform Persian inscriptions of Behistán to be the name of the Magian known in history as the Pseudo-Bardes, who personated Bardes the

* The account given in the *Bhujá Bali Charita* is that Bharata (after whom India is called Bharata-varsha) and Bhujabali were sons of Náṭi. At a city in the north, called Pádana-puri, the *rájarshi* bharates'vara, son of A'di Brahma, set up a *bimba* or image of Bhujabali, in the form of a man, 525 bow-lengths in height, so natural that he seemed as if smiling and speaking. This Bhujabali received the new (*abhinava*) name of Gummaṭa. A merchant who visited the court of Rája Malla gave such a description of this image that Chávuṇḍa his minister resolved to go and see it. He set out, with his mother Kálikámba and their guru Simha Nandi, taking a vow that he would not taste milk until he had seen this wonder. In the course of their journey they meet with unexpected difficulties, and while resting one night at a Jinálaya near a small hill, each of them has the same dream, in which a muni appears and informs them that an image of Bhujabali, set up by Rávaṇa, is on that very hill, 10 palmyra (*tále*) trees in height or 20 bow-lengths. They accordingly find the image, and in the year 600 of the Kali yuga, the year Vibhava, Chaitra s'uddha 5, Sunday, under the Mrigas'ira nakshatra, saubhágya yoga and kumbha laghna, Chávuṇḍa consecrated this Gommaṭes'vara, who thus appeared to him in Beḷaguḷa in the Kushmáṇḍáraṇya, endowing it with lands to the value of a lakh and a half of pagodas. The king Rája Malla on hearing of his munificence gave him the title of Ráya.

Only three of these images are known to exist—the one at S'ravaṇa Beḷgoḷa, 60 feet high; the other two in South Canara, at Karkala and Yennur, 40 and 35 feet high respectively.

brother whom Cambyses the Persian monarch had murdered, and usurped for a time the Persian throne.* The Jain chronicles too, apparently, connect their Tírthankara Párs'vanátha with Persia. Chávuṇḍa's consecration of the statue of Gomaṭes'vara is assigned to the year 600 of the Jain Kali yuga or 50 B. C.†

Of the early spread of the Jain faith in this country, apart from the fact of the Raṭṭa kings of the beginning of the 2nd century A. D. having a Jain guru, we have the evidence of No. 151, which shews by the middle of the 5th century six generations of gurus down to the one in favour of whom the grant there recorded was made by the Ganga king Avinita. From No. 153 we find Jains in high consideration in the 8th century, and numerous other memorials down to No. 120 of the 13th century. They still continue to form an important section of the population of Mysore. Their religious establishments are, and have long been, in a state of decay, but in trade and commerce the Jains hold a prominent place.

Buddhists.—The oldest reference we have to Buddhism in connection with Mysore is the passage in the *Mahawanso* previously referred to, which states that Buddhist missionaries were sent to Wanawasi (Banavase) and Mahisha maṇḍala (Mysore) after the third Buddhist convocation, or 245 B. C., in order to propagate the faith. That the early Pallava kings were Buddhists, there is abundant evidence both in monuments and names, and possibly the Mahávalis too.‡ The Ganga king Kongani I of the 2nd century is said to have overthrown a *s'ilá stambha*, which I have already given reasons for supposing was a *s'ila stambha* or pillar inscribed with Buddhist edicts under As'oka.

The Chinese pilgrim Hiouen Thsang of the 7th century, who visited only Buddhist scenes, is well known to have halted at a place somewhere in the Mysore, which he calls Konkaṇapura, the site of which has been the subject of much controversy without resulting in any certainty as to its site (see *Gazetteer of Mysore*, Vol. I p. 206). As late as the 12th century we find (p. 90) a Bauddhálaya among the five maṭhas of Balligráme, and from p. 109 it would appear that a Buddhist nun was the head of it in 1098.

Hindus.—Brahmans are stated to have been introduced into the countries east of Mysore in the 3rd century of the Christian era by Mukunti Pallava: and into the countries to the west a little later, below the Ghats by the Kadamba king Mayúra Varmma and above the Ghats by his son.§ But the revival of

* Vaux's *Hist. of Persia from the Ancient Monuments*, 28.

† That the Madura kingdom existed in the time of Augustus Cæsar we know from Strabo, and the author of the *Periplus* describes the Malabar coast as subject to the Pandion king. Wilson, *M. K. Coll.* I, lvi.

‡ Buddhists are said to have come from Benares in the 3rd century A. D. and settled about Kánchi. *id.* lxv.

§ *id.* lviii, lix; see also above, pp. xxxviii-ix, liv.

the modern Hindu sects dates from the time of Sankarácharya, the first Sringeri guru, in the 8th century. The main result of his labours was to displace the Jain and Bauddha faiths by the supremacy of S'iva worship. In the 12th century took place the revival of Vishnu worship under Ramánujáchári, the first guru of Melukoṭe. These forms of faith had probably been all along in existence, though not so actively influential as they became after the periods referred to.

That there was much religious toleration is evident from many circumstances. Thus the five maṭhas of Balligráme were, even in the 12th century, respectively dedicated (p. 90) to Vishnu, S'iva, Brahma, Jina and Buddha. At the same period the virtues of the queen of Sámanta Bhaṭṭa are described (p. 328) as including all that were embraced by "the Mahes'varágama, the Jina-S'rídharmma, the Sad-Vaishnavágama and the Bauddhágama," thus putting them all on an equality.* Even in the 14th century, the god Kes'ava of Belur is declared (p. 226) to be identical with "whomsoever the Vedántins in their hearts adore under the name of Brahma and S'iva, or the Bauddhas under the name of Buddha, the Naiyyáyikas, skilled in the sacred scriptures, adore under the name of A'tma (soul), whomso the Jainaka understand by Tanu (body), whomso the Mímámsaka call Karma (action)."

This toleration embodied itself in a palpable manner in the form of the god Harihara, which united in one deity both Vishnu and S'iva. He is called (p. 41) "god of all the chief gods, reconciler of the disputes between the S'aivas and the Vaishnavas." And again this incarnation is thus explained (p. 30), "Some saying there was no god on earth but Hari (Vishnu), and some saying there was no god on earth but Hara (S'iva), to remove their doubts the *Harihara múrti* was revealed in Kúḍalúr † in a single form. The S'íva that was, obtained the form of Vishnu; Vishnu obtained the mighty and celebrated form of S'iva; in order that the saying of the Vedas ‡ might be established.

This liberality in religious thought co-existed with the acts of charity which are its best outcome. An eminent example is found in the description at p. 94 of the Kóḍiya maṭha attached to the Kedares'vara temple at Balligrame, which temple it appears from No. 98 was in existence as far back as the 7th century. At this maṭha "food was freely distributed to the suffer-

* I cannot forbear noticing the chivalrous regard with which women are generally mentioned in these inscriptions. And what single term have we for all that is becoming and attractive in feminine accomplishments so simply expressive as the *woppuva vidhya* of p. 21?

† At the junction of the Haridra with the Tungabhadra.

‡ That they are the same, or that there is only one God.

ing, the destitute, the lame, the blind, the deaf, . . . the naked, the wounded, &c., and to poor from all countries," while, more remarkable still, "suitable medicine was dispensed to various kinds of diseased persons."* Moreover, among the ceremonies prescribed at p. 194 is that of "pronouncing a blessing on the reigning sovereign", a practice which is new to me in connection with Hindu worship.

At a later period we have what appear to be distinct traces of Christian knowledge in the following ascription to the god Kes'ava of Belur :— "the giver of sight to the blind, who raises up the poor to royal dignity, who causes the lame to be the swiftest of the swift, makes the dumb as eloquent as Brihaspati, the barren to be crowded with offspring."

No account of religion in the Karṇáṭaka would be complete without a notice of the great sectarian movement that resulted in the establishment in the 12th century of the Lingáyet faith, which so largely prevails throughout the Kannaḍa speaking countries. It was founded by Basava, the minister of Bijjala the Kalachurya king, who being enamoured of Padmávati the beautiful sister of Basava, gave himself up to the charms of his bride, leaving all power in the hands of her brother, who was thus in a position to carry out his views of religious reform. He rejected the authority of the vedas and the Brahmans, together with the observances of caste, pilgrimage and penance. The symbol of the S'ivabhakta or S'ivachár, as his followers are called, is the *jangama linga*, or portable linga, worn upon the person. (For further accounts see Gazetteer of Mysore.)

These principles were largely adopted by the mercantile and trading class, known as the Banajigaru, or in these inscriptions (pp. 120, 123, 73,) as the Víra Bananju dharma. Nothing can be more humorous than some of the descriptions here given of the sect, their praises being so expressed as to convey a double meaning, attributing to them in one sense royal birth, heroic deeds, &c., as if they were kings, and in another sense alluding to their travels and business tranctions. Perhaps the best specimen is at pp. 123 and 124, but it is impossible in English to convey the raciness of the allusions, while some are so far-fetched that they are positively untranslateable.

---

* The following, as gathered from the inscriptions in this volume, was the succession of gurus of the Kedares'vara temple in the middle ages, and the dates when they are mentioned as in office.

Kedára S'akti.		Vádi Vidyábharaṇa	1129
S'ríkaṇṭha.		Gautama	1129—1149
Somes'vara...	1071—1112	Váma S'akti	1155—1215

The Lingáyet faith was the state religion of the Keladi, Ikkeri, or Bednur rulers; and at p. 250 one of these dignifies himself and his creed by assuming the title "establisher from beginning to end of the *forbidden* veda"!

An endless variety of topics might be noticed in this Introduction, such as the system of government (*náḍ áḍiya rúḍhi*, p. 99), the elaborate machinery of taxes and transit, duties, the land tenures, the land measures, &c., but this would extend it beyond the limits proposed. What has been written will, it is hoped, suffice to shew how great a wealth of information lies around on every hand to reward the researches of diligent students.

From Major Dixon's Photographs.

I.

S'ILA' S'A'SANAS,

OR

INSCRIPTIONS ON STONE SLABS.

1. S'ila S'asana at Chitaldroog, date A. D. 1355.

Size ft. 3 × ft. 3.—Haḷe Kannaḍa Characters.

Cow sucking calf. Sword. Nandi Sun. LINGA Priest. Moon.

The s'ásana given by *Mallinátha Voḍeyar*, son of *Aḷiya Sái Náyka*, is as follows :—

Fortune. Reverence to the gurus. Obeisance to *S'ri Siddhanátha.* Adored be *S'ambhu*, beauteous with the chămara-like crescent moon kissing his lofty head; the original foundation-pillar of the city of the three worlds.

Beyond the reach of slander, a thunderbolt to the mountain chains the hostile kings, is *Bukka Ráya*, at the brandishing of whose glittering sword the earth trembles, kings steal away in terror and hide themselves ; by their evil designs they bring ruin on themselves and are beaten however strong. What king in truth can stand before him? A lion to the rutting elephants the hostile kings, a crowning ornament of the wisest monarchs, firm as mount Meru, delighting in battle with opposing kings, the treasury to which all kings and rulers come, who, O *Bukka Ráya*, among the kings of the earth is king above you?

May it be well.—While the Mahá Manḍales'vara, the king who is a destroyer of rulers, the conqueror of opposing kings, the punisher of kings who break their word, the lord of the eastern and western oceans,* *Víra S'ri Bukka Ráya Voḍeyar*, was in *Hosa paṭṭaṇa*, a city possessed of all titles, the capital of *Nijagali Kaṭaka Ráya*, in the *Hoysaṇa* country, ruling the kingdom in peace and wisdom :—†

The noble *Mallinátha*, son of *Naḍegonṭa Sáyyana*, was the exalted commander of the *Turaka* army, the *Sevana* army,‡ the *Telunga* army, the powerful *Pánḍya* army, and the *Hoysaṇa* army. This valiant king was respected as a great hero among all the forces of his enemies. To describe the prowess of *Naḍegonṭe Malla* :—To his own army he towered above the earth like a fort of

---

* These titles in the orginal are :—*S'rimanu Mahá Manḍales'varam, manḍalika-khanḍiya ráya, ari-ráya-vibháḍa, bháshege tappuva ráyara ganḍa, púrva paschima samudrádhipati.*

† *Sukha sankathá vinódadim*, literally, in the enjoyment of agreeable conversation, or in the enjoyment of happiness and good stories, supposed to be the same as *dharma kathá*, moral tales, or anecdotes of the justice and administration of former kings (see expression in No. 28), especially of such acts as resulted in the acquisition of merit. It is a set phrase, used in the majority of the inscriptions, and has been rendered in this and all other places "in peace and wisdom" as conveying the idea probably intended to be expressed.

‡ Perhaps *turaga*, the horse or cavalry, and *sevana*, the slaves or mercenaries.

adamant, but to the forces of the enemy as if surrounded with ditches, ramparts, bastions, batteries, and embankments constructed for their ruin.*

May it be well.—While the Mahá Mandales'vara, the king who is a destroyer of rulers, the worshipper at the divine lotus feet of the god Amara Gunḍa, *Mallinátha Voḍeyar*, son of Aḷiya Sái Náyka, was in *Bemmattana-kallu*, ruling the kingdom in peace and wisdom :—

May it be well.—In the S'aka year 1277, the year Manmatha, the month Jyeshṭha, the 7th day of the moon's increase, Monday; having built an upper storey of stone for the god *Siddhanátha* of that *Bemmattana-kallu*, and having dedicated a pinnacle thereon to the god, and constructed a stone swing; in order that this work of merit may endure as long as sun and moon, and bear fruit, having repaired the village of *Chikkapura* in that *Bemmattanakallu náḍu*, which formerly belonged to the god, we have presented it to that god Siddhanátha, for the decorations and processions, for the illuminations and presentation of food ; † and within the four boundaries of the village, the *akshina*, *ágámi*, *nidhi*, *nikshepa*, *jala*, *páshána*, *siddha*, *sádhya*, together with the *siddháya*, *hodike*, *hadike*, *kánike*, *kaḍḍáya*, *biṭṭi*, *koṭṭana*, *aḷivu*, *annyáya*, *sunka*, *haṭṭidere*, *tappu*, *tovudi*, *púrbbáya*, *apúrbbáya*, and all the *ashṭa-bhoga-tejas-swámya* rights, ‡ free of every burden. Thus has *Mallinátha Voḍeyar* presented, with pouring of water, to the holy priest, the worshipper at the divine lotus feet of the god Siddhanátha, *Sovanna*, the son of *Hiriya Siddanna*.

Mallinátha Voḍeyar's own signature of approval :—

S'ri Amara Gunḍa (in Devanágari characters).

Whoso usurps a gift made by himself or by another shall assuredly be born a worm in ordure for sixty thousand years. Of making a gift or maintaining one made by another, the maintaining another's is the best. He who makes a gift obtains svarga, but he who perpetuates one obtains final beatitude. Whoso maintains this gift will exalt his progenitors of both lines ; whoso opposing it, brings it to ruin, will cast his ancestors for twenty one generations into hell.

* The verse is full of a play of words, between *gônṭe* a part of his name, and *gónṭe*, a fort.

† *Anga ranga bhóga dipti amṛita paḍi.*

‡ *The ashṭa-bhóga-tejas-swámya*, or eight rights of full possession, recur in many inscriptions. They are, *akshina*, present profit ; *ágámi*, future profit ; *nidhi*, hidden treasure ; *nikshepa*, underground stores ; *jala*, springs ; *páshána*, stones or minerals ; *siddha*, actualities ; *sádhya*, possibilities.

Besides these, are here specified a variety of imposts as follows ;—*siddáya*, land rent ; *hodike*, a tax paid by merchants on piece goods ; *hadike*, a tax paid by tank diggers ; *kánike*, offerings or gifts ; *kaḍḍáya*, distraint ; *biṭṭi*, impressed labour ; *koṭṭana*, beating the husk from paddy ; *aḷivu*, waste or ruin ; *annyáya*, injustice ; *sunka*, customs duties ; *haṭṭidere*, tax on cattle pens ; *tappu*, fines ; *tovudi*, burrowing ; *púrbbáya*, old rights ; *apúrbbáya*, new rights.

Signature of *Karnika Devanna.* Signature of *Devappa.*

The builder of the upper storey for the god, of the tower and the stone swing, and the engraver of this s'ásana was the stone-mason Jadaya Ramajja.

This is genuine, any letter deficient or in excess notwithstanding. Prosperity! Fortune, fortune!

---

2. S'ila S'asana at Chitaldroog, date A. D. 1356.

Size ft. 2 9' × ft. 3.—Haḷe Kannaḍa Characters.

Sun Moon

Nandi. LINGA Priest. Cow suckling calf. Sword.

Fortune. Reverence to the gurus. Obeisance to *S'ri Siddhanátha.* Adored be *S'ambhu*, beauteous with the chámara-like crescent moon kissing his lofty head; the original foundation-pillar of the city of the three worlds. Do thou the supreme, the five-faced, embodiment of all above and below, supreme lord, wearer of the serpent ornament, benefactor of all worlds, a wild-fire to the forest of sin, supporter of all worlds, great in might, friend of Paras'u Rama, the purifier, have mercy on me.

Beyond the reach of slander, a thunderbolt to the mountain chains the hostile kings, is *Bukka Ráya*, at the brandishing of whose glittering sword the earth trembles, kings steal away in terror and hide themselves; by their evil designs they bring ruin on themselves and are beaten however strong. What king in truth can stand before him? A lion to the rutting elephants the hostile kings, a crowning ornament of the wisest monarchs, firm as mount Meru, delighting in battle with opposing kings, the treasury to which all kings and rulers come, who, O *Bukka Ráya*, among the kings of the earth is king above you?

May it be well.—While the Mahá Manḍales'vara, the king who is a destroyer of rulers, the conqueror of opposing kings, the punisher of kings who break their word, the lord of the eastern and western oceans, * *Víra S'ri Bukka Ráya Voḍeyar*, was in *Hosa-paṭṭana*, a city possessed of all titles, the capital of *Nijagali Kaṭaka Ráya*, in the *Hoysaṇa* country, ruling the kingdom in peace and wisdom*:—

---

* See note, p. 2.

As Indra dwells in Amarávati on the summit of mount Meru, as Krishna in Dváraka, as S'iva in Kailása, so, worthy of all praise, the king *Sávaya Mallinátha*, the sole champion, famed throughout the world, having the title of *Naḍagóṭe Malla*, resides in his hill-fort. The noble *Mallinátha*, son of *Naḍegonṭa Sáyana*, was the exalted commander of the *Turaka* army, the *Sevana* army,* the *Telunga* army, the powerful *Pándya* army, and the *Hoysaṇa* army. This valiant king was respected as a great hero among all the forces of his enemies. To describe the prowess of *Naḍegonṭe Malla* : to his own army he towered above the earth like a fort of adamant, but to the forces of the enemy as if surrounded with ditches, ramparts, bastions, batteries, and embankments constructed for their ruin.†

May it be well.—While the Mahá Manḍales'vara, the king who is a destroyer of rulers, the worshipper at the divine lotus feet of the god Amara Gunḍa, *Mallinátha Voḍeyar*, son of Aliya Sáyi Náyaka, was in *Bemmattana-kallu*, ruling the kingdom in peace and wisdom* :—

May it be well.—In the S'aka year 1278, the year Durmukhi, the month A'sháḍha, the third day of the moon's increase, Thursday; having built an upper storey of stone for the god *Siddhanátha* of that *Bemmattana-kallu*, and having dedicated a pinnacle thereon to the god, and constructed a stone swing; in order that this work of merit may endure as long as sun and moon, and bear fruit, having repaired the village of *Musuvadiya-pura* in that *Bemmattana-kallu náḍu*, which formerly belonged to the god, we have presented it to that god *Siddhanátha*, for the decorations and processions, for the illuminations, and presentation of food; and within the four boundaries, namely, the Linga mudre stone of Ketana khandi formerly existing in the east, the Linga mudre stone of Musuvadiya khandi, the Linga mudre stone at the boundary of the fields south of Gondamanhalli, the Linga mudre stone at the boundary of the fields west of Gondamanhalli.—within these four boundaries, the *akshína, ágámi, nidhi, nikshepa, jala, páshána, siddha, sádhya*, together with the *siddáya, hodike, hadike, káṇike, kaḍḍáya, biṭṭi, koṭṭana, aḷivu, annyáya, sunka, haṭṭidere, tappu, tovudi, púrbbáya, apúrbbáya*, and all the *ashṭa-bhoga-tejas-swámya* rights, † free of every burden. Thus has *Mallinátha Voḍeyar* presented, with pouring of water, to the holy priest, the worshipper at the divine lotus feet of the god Siddhanátha, *Sovanna*, the son of *Hiriya Siddanna*, to endure as long as sun and moon.

Mallinátha Voḍeyar's own signature of approval :—

S'ri Amara Gunḍa (in Devanágari characters).

* See note, p. 2. † See note, p. 3.

Whoso usurps a gift made by himself or by another shall assuredly be born a worm in ordure for sixty thousand years. Of making a gift or maintaining one made by another, the maintaining another's is the best. He who makes a gift obtains svarga, but he who perpetuates one obtains final beatitude. Whoso maintains this gift will exalt his progenitors of both lines; whoso opposing it, brings it to ruin, will cast his ancestors for twenty one generations into hell.

The thief who, wandering here by day or by night, shall steal so much as a stick; the great lord of the country, or the emperor who rules in the city, or the sovereign who rules the world, if he shall with an evil mind think to plunder the rent-free villages, or fields, or property within this region; cast his mother and father and all his relations for 27 crores of years into the hell full of worms, and swallow them up at last, O sin, do you see? * Whoso fearing to touch this sacred land and property, like a frightened serpent drops from a branch, so slips away and respects it; with him speedily and at once unite, and bring him along with joy, O merit, do you see? Sin or merit will a man contract according to these two prayers. This is true, this is true, do you see, all people? Whoso doubts it will sink into hell.

Signature of *Karnika Devanna.* Signature of *Sovarsa Virappa.*

In this village the gauḍa will give five days sowing and maintain the property of the god.

The builder of the upper storey for the god, of the tower and the stone swing, and the engraver of this s'ásana, was the stone-mason Jadaya Ramajja.

This is genuine, any letter deficient or in excess notwithstanding. Prosperity! Fortune, fortune!

3. S'ila S'asana at Chitaldroog, date A. D. 1190.

Size ft. 4 4' × ft. 1 5'.—Haḷe Kannaḍa Characters.

Cow suckling calf. LINGA Priest. Nandi

S'ri Somanátha. Adored be *S'ambhu*, beauteous with the chámara-like crescent moon kissing his lofty head; the original foundation-pillar of the city of the three worlds.

When the tiger rushed out of the forest, the muni saying *hoyi sili*, that moment *S'ala* piercing it (*hoyi sili*), dragged it along, and in a wonderful manner raised up the tiger on the point of his iron rod, which thence stood for his banner, and he became famous throughout the world as *Hoyisaṇa.*

---

* *Kanḍiyá yele pápavé!*

To the auspicious *Hoysaṇa* emperor *Vinayáditya* was borne, by his virtuous queen, *Yereyanga Deva.* From him (came) the king *Vishṇu,* the king *Narasimha* and the king *Ballála.* Then, famous for victories, *Narasimha Raya.* From him *Vira Somes'vara.* To *Somes'vara Chakri* and *Bijjala Ráni,* whose form was that of the Lakshmi of victory, was born, a cause for the prosperity of the world, of great might, *Sri Narasimha,* who as an abode of victory, in prowess equal to Indra, versed in all the poems, a hero incarnate, was famed throughout the world.

To Narasimha, the splitter of the skulls of his enemies, and to his queen the Paṭṭa Mahádevi, was born through their virtue, the brave king *Ballála Deva Hoysaṇa Ráya.* Who in the earth is a king? who brave? who the support of the king Nárasimha? who the immovable, a bheruṇḍa to other kings' sons? He is the king; he is the brave; he is the support of the king Nárasimha; he the immovable, the bheruṇḍa to other kings' sons. Brave, in generosity as Meru, commander of great forces, by the valour of his cousin (*mayiduna*) *Soyana*

. . . . . .

May it be well.—While the auspicious king *Hoysaṇa Bhuja Bala Ballála Deva,* protector of all lands, favorite of earth and fortune, great king of kings, supreme ruler, first of monarchs, the sun in the sky of the *Yádava* race, a chúdámaṇi to the wise, king over the *Male* rájas, a champion among the *Malepas,* ganḍa bheruṇḍa, unassisted hero, immovable champion, sole champion of the earth, *Malla* of the *S'anivára Siddhigiri* hill fort, * in bravery like Rama, a lion to the elephants the hostile kings, the establisher of *Chóḷa Ráya,* the . . of *Páṇḍya Ráya,* the uprooter of the *Magara* kingdom,*—together with his great minister *Mendige Deva Dannáyaka* and his great minister *Aliya Mácheya Dannáyaka,* was in his residence at *Dorasamudra,* ruling the kingdom in peace and wisdom:—†

In the S'aka year (*figures obliterated*), the year Sádhárana, the month Vaishákha, the 3rd day of the moon's increase, Friday; a gift was made by the great ministers . . . . . . *Dannáyaka* and *Aliya Singeya Dannáyaka,* to the god *Somanátha,* set up in the . . . . . . maṭha in *Bemmattana kallu,* as follows:—

(*Rest illegible*).

---

* *Samasta-bhuvanásrayam, s'ri-prithvi-vallabham, mahárájádhirájam, paramesvaram, parama-bhaṭṭárakam, Yádava-kulámbara-dyumaṇi, sarvajna-chúḍámaṇi, Male rájara rájam, Maleparoḷu-ganḍa, ganḍa bheruṇḍan, asaháya súra, kadana-prachanḍa, yekánga víra, Sanivára Siddhigiri-durga Malla.*

† See note, p. 2.

4. S'ila S'asana at Chitaldroog, date A. D. 1063.

Size ft. 3 7' × ft. 2 1.' Haḷe Kannaḍa Characters.

(Indistinct and partly broken.)

Priest. LINGA. Moon. Sword. Sun. Calf. Cow.

Adored be *S'ambhu*, beauteous with the chámara-like crescent moon kissing his lofty head; th original foundation-pillar of the city of the three worlds. Reverence to the gurus.

May it be well.—While the victorious kingdom of the auspicious *Jagadeka Malla*, protector of all lands, favorite of earth and fortune, great king of kings, supreme ruler, first of monarchs, glory of the *Salyás'raya kula*, ornament of the *Chálukyas* * was increasing in prosperity to endure as long as sun, moon, stars and sky;—

The dweller at his lotus feet; May it be well, the auspicious Mahá Manḍales'vara, *Vijaya Páṇḍya Deva*, entitled to the five great drums, great lord of the earth, lord of *Kánchipura*, sun in the sky of the *Yádava* race, a head-jewel to brave warriors, a sun to the lotus of his own family, defeater of the designs of *Rájiga Choḷa*, ... a bee at the lotus feet of the auspicious Jagadeka Malla Deva, having these and all other titles, was in his residence at *Uchangi*, ruling the *Noḷambavádi* 32,000 in peace and wisdom, punishing the evil and protecting the good:—

The dweller at his lotus feet, a bee at the lotus feet of Kámarasa Deva, possessed of these and many other titles, chief of great tributaries, favorite of the Lakshmi of victory . . . . . . a sun to the waterlilies the faces of the wives of hostile kings, an ornament to the lady fame, in purity like Bhishma, subduer of his enemies' forces, chief of mighty kings, worshipper at the lotus feet of the god Hiḍumbes'vara I'rugaya Náyaka, was *Videyáditya Náyaka*.

To describe his bravery:— When any hostile force essayed to attack him and he with great fury surrounded it, or when if it seemed more numerous than his own he raised a terrific war cry like the roar of a lion, and sprang upon them with the charge of a great tiger, as about to swallow them up like Ráhu,—whose faces did not turn? When the neighbouring tributary kings,

---

* *S'rí-prithvi-vallabham, Mahárajádhirájam, Paramea'varam, Parama-bhaṭṭárakam, Salyás'raya-kula-tilakam, Chá[lu]kyábharaṇam.*

losing confidence in their commanders came themselves crowding together to fight against him, then as Suyodhana and the other kings who came to fight against Bhima turned their backs and fled, so they turned the back and ran.

While he was in his residence at *Bemmattanúru*, ruling the Thirty-two, the Haḍuvagere Five Hundred, and the (?) Sagalunga Seventy, in peace and wisdom, punishing the evil and protecting the good; his excellent sons *Kámaya Náyaka*, *Chólaya Náyaka* and *Yeme Náyaka* being with him, discoursing on the merit that arises from a gift of land:—they, in the S'aka year 1045, the year Shobhakrit, the month Phalguna, the 10th day of the moon's increase, Sunday, at the time of the equinox; for a lofty tower to the god *Siddhi Hiḍumbes'vara*, at the *Nága tirtha* of the hill south of *Hiḍumba vana*; for the illuminations, the daily offerings, and a procession in Chaitra; * presented to the *Máheshvaras*, pure in gotra, friends of the good alone, famed throughout the world,—with pouring of water,—the land bounded east by the Budhivanta rock, ... by the Gavaya pond, west by Bemma, north by the Kambhagara tank; 200 *kummas* of paddy land under this.

Whoso usurps a gift made by himself or by another shall assuredly be born a worm in ordure for sixty thousand years.

5. S'ila S'asana at Chitaldroog, date A. D. 1412.

Size ft. 4 × ft. 2 4.—Haḷe Kannaḍa Characters.

Sun. Nandi. Sword. Linga with Priest. Cow suckling calf. Moon.

Fortune! May subjects prosper, may kings rule in justice, may cows and Brahmans be daily nourished, may all worlds be in peace. May we have long life, strength, health and concord; through thy favor may our enemies be diminished; may we obtain fame and our ancestors be satisfied with our offerings; mayst thou receive auspicious praises from all, O lord merit, may all have faith in thee. May we prosper and obtain all manner of good fortune.

May it be well.—In the S'aka year 1334, the year Khara, the month Kártika, the 15th day of the moon's increase, full-moon day, Tuesday; the auspicious Maha Mandales'vara, filled with justice, generosity, benevolence and wisdom, his mind purified by the praise of the lotus feet of Tryambaka, *Vira Mallanna Voḍeyar*, son of Vira Pratápa Deva Ráya, great king of kings,

* *Nandá dívige nivédyakam Chaitra pavitrakam.*

supreme ruler, conqueror of hostile kings, lord of the four oceans, eastern, western, northern and southern; * daily bestowing streams of gold and camphor; a lord over the courtezans the hostile kings (!); a terror to the kings at the eight points of the compass; gave the following s'ásana:—

In the aforesaid year, on the aforesaid day, at the auspicious time of full-moon in the month Kartika, having made a great feast, and dedicated a tower to the incarnation of the supreme lord Sada S'iva which was manifested at the time when Vrikodara the son of Pandu slew Hidimbikásura, (namely) the god *Hidimbanátha* of the auspicious great city of *Bemmattana-kallu*, situated in Jambu dvipa, which lies south of Maha Meru, the centre of the world 50 crore yojanas in extent:—the auspicious Maha Mandales'vara, *Vira Mallanna Vodeyar*, in order that his mother might obtain merit; at the auspicious time of full-moon, on the 15th day of the moon's increase, in the month Kartika, naming Kunchiganahalli, one of the eastern villages belonging to Bemmattana-kallu, after his mother *Mallayavve*, presented it to provide for the decorations, processions and illuminations of the god *Hidimbanátha*.

And for the erection of a stone tower to the southern gateway of that god's temple, in order that his mother Mallayavve might obtain merit in the other world, he presented within the four boundaries of that *Mallápura*, late Kunchiganahalli, the *nidhi*, *nikshepa*, *jala*, *páshána*, *akshina*, *ágámi*, *siddha*, *sádhya*, with all the *ashta-bhoga-tejas-swamya* rights, † with freedom from every burden, as long as sun and moon endure; and for the service, processions and illuminations of the god *Hidimbanátha*, the remission of all taxes.

This s'ásana of the gift for the service of god of the late Kunchiganahalli, named Mallapura after our mother, bestowed with presentation of a coin and pouring of water, in sole possession, for the sake of future merit, have we, the Mahá Mandales'vara, *Vira Mallanna Vodeyar*, given of our own free will and consent. When offering the daily service and prayers to the god *Hidimbanátha* at the three seasons, may the devotees of the place enjoy this; and Parvati grant her blessing that *Mallayavva* may obtain the heaven of merit May the people eat with joy the food presented to the god.

Approved—S'ri Tryambaka.

Whoso usurps a gift made by himself or by another shall assuredly be born a worm in ordure for sixty thousand years. Therefore let all acquire the merit of preserving this gift. Whoso with an evil mind destroys a gift presented to the gods or to Brahmans loses all the merit of his own gifts.

Great prosperity! Fortune, fortune!

---

* See note p. 2.

† See note p. 3.

6. S'ila S'asana at Chitaldroog, date A. D. 1287.

Size ft. 5 5′ × ft. 2 9′.—Haḷe Kannaḍa Characters.

Sun. Moon. Nandi

Linga with Priest.

Chakra. Vamana avatara. Cow suckling calf. Sankha.

Adored be *S'ri Ganádhipati*. Adored be the lord *Rámakrishna*. Adored be *S'ambhu*, beauteous with the chámara-like crescent moon kissing his lofty head; the original foundation-pillar of the city of the three worlds.

The *Hoysaḷa* emperors, king *Vinayáditya* of glorious fame, *Yereyanga Deva* the valiant, the king *Narasimha Chakri*, the powerful king *Ballála*, *Narasimha Rága* exalted with victory; from these (was descended) *Vira Somes'vara*. To Somes'vara Chakri and Bijjala Ráni, whose form was that of the Lakshmi of victory, was born the king *Narasimha*, a collection of all good fortune to the world.

To that brave king Narasimha, like a limb in carrying out all his wishes the manager of all his affairs, of a benevolence which benefitted all who looked on him, of exalted honor, *Perumála* was the minister (*mantri*), whose acts were full of glory.

An ornament to those who were born in the excellent Atreya gotra was *Vishnu Disha*. To him and to *Trivitta manchale*, praised by all the world, was born the exalted son *Perumála Deva Mantri*, the Ráutta Ráya, of good character, worshipper at the two lotus feet of his guru *Ramakrishna*. With his sword he offered up the head of the powerful *Ratnapála* to the Lakshmi of victory though there was a screen between them, and capturing that tent (*javanike*) he obtained the name of *Javanike Náráyana*, such was the might of this Ráutta king.

May it well.—While the heroic emperor, that *Hoysaḷa S'ri Narasimha Deva*, possessed of all titles, was in the royal city of *Dorasamudra*, ruling the kingdom of the earth in peace and wisdom :—*

The dweller at his lotus feet, the auspicious Mahá Pradhána, *Perumála Danḍanáyaka*, punisher of the slayers of swamis, king of the Ráuttas, Javanike Náráyana, worshipper of the lotus feet of Ramakrishna; the s'aka year 1208 having passed, and the year Byaya being then current, in the month Chaitra, the 10th day of the moon's increase, Wednesday; within the *Bemmattanáru*

* See note p. 2.

vritti, at the hands of *Benaka Gauḍa*, son of Kama Gauda, on the application of the giver of gifts the Adhikári Viṭhappa, son of Vissanna, and on the application of the people of that Bemmattanúru, of the Náḍ prabhus to whom the vrittis belonged, and of all the persons having an interest in the lands and dues; that *Perumále Deva Dandanáyaka*, paying the proper value of that time into the hands of that *Benaka Gauḍa* by the hand of *Vokkalaya*, took as a regular purchase, with presentation of a coin and pouring of water, *Kurubara Káleya's* tank situated in the *Nagaréri S'ime*, and the paddy land attached to that tank, together with the *ágámi* * within the sluice of the tank; also the tract of dry-cultivation land within these four boundaries, within the stones erected by that nad, namely, from the tamarind tree, on the north Bamiya Benaka, on the south the Benne pond, on the west Holaveri, on the east the Bella hollow.

And on this tract of dry-cultivation land, that *Perumála Deva Dandanáyaka*, erecting stones within the four boundaries as far as the Hule well of that Bemmattanuru durga; divided it into 24 vrittis according to the two dozen sacred names, and attaching it to the Brahmapuri belonging to *Perumálapura* which he had built, gave it with pouring of water to the Brahmans.

And in this kshetra he presented, with pouring of water, 10 *kolagas* of paddy land for offering of food to *Hidimbes'vara*; 1 *sulige* of paddy land for offering of food to *Choles'vara*; 1 *salige* of paddy land and 100 *kamba* of dry land to *Benaka Gauḍa* as *koḍige* for building the tank; 10 *kolaga* of paddy land to *Báchaya*, the nad shanbhog; and 10 *kolaga* of paddy land to the Heggade *Chámaya*. All the rest belongs to those Brahmans.

And the s'ásana of this gift which the citizens of *Bemmattanúru*, (namely) *Chaṭṭe Seṭṭi, Bomma Setti, Bhrántiya Malla Setti, Voḍeya Piḷḷe Setti, Sankeya Náyaka, Bomma Setti*; the master of the nád, that *Benaka Gauḍa*; *Baraḍa Gauḍa* of the Sigali stone quarry; *Hála Bomma Gauḍa* of Sádarahalli; *Balla Gauḍa*, the son of Káma Gauḍa of Benne-dóni; that *Bamma Gauḍa; Keta Gauḍa*, the son of Bomma Gauḍa of Siddhapura; *Báchanna*, the son of the Volageri Vittiya Nád Prábhu, Ampaleya Hiriyanna; *Malla Gauḍa*, son of Boppa Gauḍa of Manale; *Nága Gauḍa*, son of Naga Gauda of Maleyanuru; the Nád Setti *Gutta Chaladanka Rama Setti*; the Nád Rája-guru *Mála Guru*; that *Chola Guru*; Volageri Vitti *Dhammana Guru*; that *Bomma Guru*; the Nád Senabhova *Báchanna;* that *Chámaiya* Heggade; *Káma Bhova*, the son of Kabbela Kála Bhova—caused to be written, and gave to *Perumála Deva* with pouring of water, as of a Brahmapuri themselves had made, was as follows:—Within this kshetra whatever *aḷivu* or *annyáya* is included in the *siddáya, kaṭaka, sese*, and

* See note p. 3.

kirukula * we ourselves discharging it, have presented this gift free of all burdens, and free of rent, as long as sun and moon endure, and have given it with pouring water as a gift presented by the nad.

And within this kshetra, that *Perumála Deva Dandanáyaka*, rebuilding that *Kurubara Káleya* tank which he had bought from the hands of that *Benaka Gauda*, and naming it *Perumála samudra*, presented it for the maintenance of the *Aindra parva* rites of the god *Panchakes'vara* to be performed in *Perumálapura* ; and of the land under that Perumála samudra 1 *salige* of paddy land, and of the dry cultivation land he had purchased, 100 kamba of dry land, these he presented with pouring of water for the rites of that *Panchakes'vara*. The *mahajuns* of that *Perumálapura*, exacting no *hodike* or *hárane*† from that kshetra, or from the cultivators of that kshetra, shall preserve the kshetra free from all burdens, as long as sun and moon endure, for the *Aindra parva* rites.

In confirmation of which, the signatures of that *Perumála Deva Dandanáyaka*, of Alada *Masari Virappa*, of the seller (of the land) *Benaka Gauḍa*, of the *âgâmika*, and the nad people are attached.

The writing of the Nad Sénabhóva *Báchanna*.

Great prosperity ! Fortune, Fortune !

Merit is a common bridge for kings. This from age to age deserves your support, O kings of the earth. Thus does Rámachandra from age to age beseech the kings who come after him. Whoso usurps a gift made by himself or by another shall assuredly be born a worm in ordure for sixty thousand years.

(Signatures) *S'rí Yallalenátha* ; *S'ri Bis'ves'vara* ; that Benaka Gauḍa's approval,—*S'rí Bhimanátha* ; the approval of the citizens,—*S'rí Vitarága*, (? 3 letters in Tamil) *S'rí Báches'vara* ; the approval of the chiefs of the Náḍ Gauḍas, *S'rí K . . . Náráyana*, *S'ri Brahmésvara*, *S'ri Somanátha*, *S'ri Somanátha*, *S'ri Kallinátha*, *S'ri Somanátha*, *S'ri Mallinátha*, *S'ri Kallinátha*, *S'ri Harihara*, *S'ri Cholanátha*, *S'ri Cholanátha*, *S'ri Dharmes'vara*, *S'ri Mallinátha*, *S'ri Gopinátha*, *S'ri Kallinátha*, *S'ri Billes'vara* ; approval of the nad,—*S'ri Hidimbanátha* ; approval of the city,—*S'ri Hidimbanátha*.

---

* *Aḷivu*, waste or ruin ; *annyáya*, injustice ; *siddáya*, land rent ; *kaṭaka*, city or army ; *sese*, coloured rice presented on ceremonial occasions ; *kirukula*, petty taxes.

† *Hodike*, tax on piece goods ; *hárane*, special gift.

7. S'ila S'asana at Davangere, date A. D. 1121.

Size ft. 5 × *ft.* 2 6'.—*Haḷe Kannaḍa Characters.*

Cow suckling calf. Sun. Linga with Priest in a temple. Moon. Nandi.

(*very indistinct.*)

Adored be S'iva in the form of *Om*. Adored be *S'ambhu*, beauteous with the chámara-like crescent moon kissing his lofty head; the original foundation-pillar of the city of the three worlds. Obeisance to the wearer of the crescent moon, the embodiment of pure wisdom, the three vedas being his eyes, the bestower of all happiness. Manifest to the senses, benefactor of the world, cause of the preservation, destruction and creation of the universe, the soul of all things, conqueror of anger and love, lord of the three worlds, to thee, O S'iva, obeisance.

Vallabha of fortune, vallabha of the victorious spoils of his enemies, vallabha over the proudest aspiring kings and all the earth with its wealth, vallabha of the Lakshmi of a pure unsullied fame, is the auspicious *Vallabha* emperor *Vikrama Bhúpa*. What kings can compare with the lord of *Kuntala*, shining as the protector of the kings who sought his protection? All other kings he defeated without opposition. This being true, how can they compare with him in greatness or like him become famous? Will they rush into the flames of his valour and equal him? Dismiss the idea (*tege*). Will they capture his victorious army shouting with a lion-roar? What enterprise will those who become his enemies undertake against him? The famous and fearless kings of *Vanga*, *Anga*, *Kalinga*, *Páṇḍya*, the mightiest among the *Ballá'as*, with those of *Sauráshṭra*, *Varáṭa*, *Láṭa*, *Karaháṭa*, *Chedi*, *Káshmira*, *Gurjara*, *Sindhu*, *Trigarta*, *Málava*, *Turushka*, and other countries, he subdued by the power of the sword in his hand, the *Chálukya* emperor.

May it be well.—While the victorious kingdom of the auspicious *Tribhuvana Malla Deva*, protector of all lands, favorite of earth and fortune, great king of kings, supreme ruler, first of monarchs, glory of the *Satyás'raya kula*, ornament of the *Chálukyas*,* was increasing in prosperity to endure as long as sun and moon:—

The dweller at his lotus feet, whose wealth and authority in the world were in the form of Lakshmi and Vishnu, glorious in his splendid fame, of

---

* *Samasta-bhuvanás'rayam, s'ri-prithvi-vallabham, mahárájádhirájam, parames'varam, parama-bhaṭṭárakam, Satyás'raya-kula-tilakam, Chálukyábharaṇam.*

great might, the famous *Malla Deva*, possessed of great and royal wealth, bearing up the burden of the world surrounded by the four oceans, surpassing Vikrama in bravery, was *Pándya Bhúpa.*

Breaking down the pride of the *Chola* kings, tiring out the *A'ndhra* kings, terrifying the *Kalinga* king, scaring and pursuing after the kings of *Anga, Vanga, Magadha*, and slaying by his bodily might many other kings, he became famous. That he left the *Gurjara* king, was it because he was defeated, that Páṇḍya Bhupála? 'Tis false. This great king gave up his enmity (!). Punishing the mightiest among the groups of brave kings and wearing them out, ... an ornament of the *Pándya manḍalikas*, a joy among the mandalikas, king over all the mandalikas, of great fame, was *Vira Pánḍya.*

May it be well.—The Maha Mandales'vara, *Tribhuvana Malla Pánḍya Deva*, lord of *Kánchipura*, sun to the sky of the *Yadu* race, a head jewel among heroes of the battle field, a sun to the lotus of his own family, a chief among victors over their enemies, a terror to meaner kings, a bee at the lotus feet of *Tribhuvana Malla* ;—ruling the *Noṇambavádi* Thirty-two Thousand, punishing the evil and protecting the good, being in his residence of . . . . ruling the kingdom in peace and wisdom :—*

Over all the people belonging to . . . *ttur* praised for its Lakshmi of wealth as *Bhogibhúshana-pura*, attached to *Kari*-náḍ, situated in *Sávira náḍ*, belonging to *Noḷambavádi*; were the three chiefs *Bomma Náyaka, Sankara gámunda*, and *Hommarasa*, chiefs of the beautiful villages . . . great with all high qualities, eager in performing works of merit, counted as jewels of governors for their skill in governing, versed in all wisdom :—And, may it be well.—*S'aiva Deva Seṭṭi*, possessed of all titles, a collection of all good qualities, chief of the *Mummuri danḍa* of the *Kannaḍa* 4,000, praised by all the people in the world as a Meru to merit, the bearer up of merit, the birth place of merit, a sea to the greatness of the glory of merit, a jewel to pure merit, a seed to merit, a mine of merit, the illustrious lord promoter of merit, and of *Parasiva* works of merit :—

In the 46th year of the Chálukya Vikrama era, the year Plava, the month Ashvija, the 5th day of the moon's increase, Sunday ;—the auspicious Mahá Mandales'vara, *Tribhuvana Malla Pánḍya Deva*, gave into the hands of the aforesaid chiefs and Saiva Deva Setti . . . . . for repairing the temple of *Bhimesvara*, for the daily service, for the illumina-

* See note p. 2.

tions, and for feeding the priests of the place,—* gave, with pouring of water,
. . . . 15 *máru*
. . . . north of the *Dávangere s'íme.*

And this much that *Saiva Deva Setti*, with those chiefs, gave over, pouring water, and washing the feet of *Brahma S'iva Deva*, priest of Tribhuvana Malla Pán!esvara, and *Rudra S'akti Deva*, guru of Mallikarjuna.

---

8. S'ila S'asana at Davangere, date A. D. 1142.

Size ft. 5 8′ × ft. 3 1′.—Haḷe Kannaḍa Characters.

Linga. Nandi.

(Greater part illegible.)

While the victorious kingdom of the auspicious *Bhuloka Malla*, protector of all lands, favourite of earth and fortune, great king of kings, supreme ruler, first of monarchs, glory of the *Satyás'raya kula*, ornament of the *Chálukyas*, was increasing in prosperity to endure as long as sun and moon :— †

The dweller at his lotus feet, *Vira Pándya Deva*, ruling the *Noṇambaváḍi* Thirty-two Thousand, punishing the evil and protecting the good, being in his residence in the fort on the *Uchchhangi* hill, governing the kingdom in peace and wisdom :— ‡

. . . .
for the offerings, illuminations, daily service, distribution of alms, and repairs of the temple of the god *Jagadis'vara*, gave, with pouring of water .
. . . . of *Arasinakere*
. . . . to *Lokábharana Pandita*,
distinguished for *yama*, *niyama*, *svádhyáya*, *dhyána*, *dharma*, *yoga*, *anushṭhána*, *japa* and *samádhi* § . . . .

In the year Dundubhi, the month Pushya, the 11th day of the moon's increase, Monday, at the vyati páta, the auspicious time of the sun's entering Makara (Capricornus) on his northern course . . . . . .
Vira Pándya Deva, to the god *Jagadis'vara* . . . . . .
. . . .

---

* *Khanḍa sphuṭita jírnoddhárakam, nitya naimittikakam, dêvara nandá d'vi pópahárakkam, sthánáchâryara grâsakkam.*

† For these titles see note p. 14. ‡ See note p. 2.

§ *Yama*, penance; *niyama*, fasting; *svádhyáya*, reading the vedas; *dhyána*, meditation; *dharma*, religious merit; *yoga*, spiritual devotion; *anusṭhána*, performance of devotional exercises; *japa*, prayer; *samádhi*, religious abstraction.

9. S'ila S'asana at Davangere, date A. D. 1165

Size ft. 6 10′ × ft. 2 8′.—Haḷe Kannaḍa Characters.

Nandi — Sun. — Linga in a temple. — Moon. — Cow suckling calf.

(*Very indistinct.*)

Obeisance to the wearer of the crescent moon, the embodiment of pure wisdom, the three vedas being his eyes, the bestower of all happiness.

While the auspicious Mahá Mandales'vara, *Vira Páṇḍya Arasu*, purified by meditation on the lotus feet of S'ankhara Náráyana, was ruling the *Noḷambavâḍi* Thirty-two Thousand, punishing the evil and protecting the good, being in his residence at *Huchangi*, governing the kingdom in peace and wisdom :—

The dweller at his lotus feet, *Gopála Deva Danḍanáyaka*, for the offerings, the illuminations, the daily service, and repairs of the temple, of the god *Somes'vara*, gave . . . . under the Sovigere tank . . . in the S'aka year 1087, the year Parthiva, the month Bhadrapada . .

(*Rest illegible*).

10. S'ila S'asana at Davangere, date A. D. 1108.

Size ft. 4 9′ × ft. 1 7′.—Haḷe Kannaḍa Characters.

The Donor. — Sun. — Linga. — Moon. — Cow suckling calf.

(*Indistinct*).

Fortune! Adored be *S'ambhu*, beauteous with the chámara-like crescent moon kissing his lofty head; the original foundation pillar of the city of the three worlds.

May it be well.—While the victorious kingdom of the auspicious *Tribhuvana Malla Deva*, protector of all lands, favourite of earth and fortune, great king of kings, supreme ruler, first of monarchs, glory of the *Satyás'raya kula*, ornament of the *Chálukyas**, was increasing in prosperity to endure as long as sun, moon, stars and sky :—

* See note p. 14.

The dweller at his lotus feet, the auspicious *Barmarasa*, entitled to the five great drums, chief of great tributaries, ... great minister, Báṇasa Verggaḍe Danḍanáyaka, having by the support of *Anantapála* been appointed to the government of the whole country, possessed of all ministerial and lordly qualities, an eloquent speaker, purifier of the . . gotra, son of a well-born mother . . . . lord over *Achchupa Náyaka*, having these and other names and titles;—was ruling in peace the *pannáya* of the *Noḷambaváḍi* Thirty-two Thousand, punishing the evil and protecting the good:—

May it be well.—Adorned with good qualities, of great valour, the object of universal praise, giver of rewards to his friends, his head placed with great joy at the lotus feet of S'iva, his breast against the full bosoms of the youthful fair, of a life of virtue, thus was *Barmarasa* in the world. In Kogali nád, among the dependents (?) of the noble *Kadamba* chiefs, from the half share of customs duties which he received, having with affection made a grant of one tenth for a temple and Jinálaya, dancing girls (?), a tank, a well, and a chattram*, famous was *Barmarasa*, a setting for the gems of good qualities.

For the service and decoration of the god *Sarve'svara*, bright as the sun with his flaming eyes, lord of the daughter of the mountain king, (*i. e*, Parvati), for the great illuminations, for the daily processions, and the monthly processions, *Barmarasa* made the following gift with great joy. In the 33rd year of the Chalukya Vikrama era, the year Sarvadhari, the month Pushya, the 5th day of the moon's increase, Thursday, at the time of the sun's entering on his northern course, at the moment of vyati páta; *Barmarasa*, washing the feet of *Nílakanṭha Panḍita*, made the grant, with pouring of water, as a gift to the god, of 5 *pana* a month from the half customs duties (*sunka*) which he received, for the illumination and service of the god *Sarves'vara*.

Whoso maintains this gift will derive the merit of presenting a thousand tawny cows, and kolagas decked with the nine jewels, to a thousand Brahmans versed in the vedas, in the holy bathing places of Varanas'i and Kurukshetra. Whoso resumes this gift will incur the sin of killing a thousand cows and a thousand Brahmans versed in the vedas, in the holy bathing places of Varanas'i and Kurukshetra. Whoso usurps a gift made by himself or by another shall assuredly be born a worm in ordure for sixty thousand years.

May it be well.

---

* *Kogaḷi náḍoḷ aggada Kadamba dísáyara dásarangadoḷ degulakam Jinálayakam váravegam keṛe bávi satrakam rágade tanna pannayada sunka daḷam das'avannavitta.*

11. S'ila S'asana at Davangere, date A. D. 1066.

Size ft. 3 10′ × ft. 1 11′.—Hale Kannada Characters.

The Donor.	Nandi.	Sun. LINGA. Moon.	Cow suckling Calf.

The gift made by *Suliya Bomma Nayaka*, garden watchman (*toṭada talára*) to Mulasthana Deva.

Adored be *S'ambhu*, beateous with the chámara-like crescent moon kissing his lofty head; the original foundation-pillar of the city of the three worlds.

May it be well.—While the victorious kingdom of the auspicious *Trailokya Malla Deva*, protector of all lands, favourite of earth and fortune, great king of kings, supreme ruler, first of monarchs glory of the *Satyás'raya kula*, ornament of the *Chálukyas*,* was increasing in prosperity to endure as long as sun, moon, stars and sky:—

His son—may it be well—*S'ri Vishnu Varddhana Mahárája Vijayáditya Deva*, a protector of all, patron of the learned, an embodiment of the name *Ahava Malla*, the fort defended by whose army was impregnable to the bravest of the enemy's troops, promoter of those who extol him, destroyer of the pride of his enemies, in valour a Janardana, of virtuous life, a jewel to the *Chalukyas*, a stage for the Lakshmi of victory to dance on, the modern Manmatha, to the race of his enemies the rod of Yama, a sun among the brave, like S'iva to Manmatha the hostile kings, a surpassing wrestler, to the poor a chintamani-like benefactor, a head jewel to the diadem of kings, protector of the *Vengi Mandales'vara*, just in punishing; was ruling the *Noḷambavádi* Thirty-two Thousand in peace and wisdom. †

By his permission, the Pergaḍe *Devappa*, minister for peace and war, and other *karnams*; *Nágari arasa*, lord of a thousand villages; *Pokarasa*, chief of twelve villages; *Machana Pandita*, *Mala Gámunda*, and *Udayáditya Náyaka*, chieftains of the place; uniting:—In the S'aka year 988, the year Parábhava, the month Bhádrapada, at the time of new moon, Tuesday, during an eclipse of the sun; for the service and decoration of the god *Múlasthana Mahádeva*, and for repairs of his temple, gave, with pouring of water, to *Sonangi Deva*, rent free, in *Bala Betturu* the first of the Twelve, the following land:—the *modaleri* fields of the Nagara tank, 1 *matta* of paddy land; west of that, at the watercourse of the Kenchekere weir, 1 *matta* of paddy land;

---

* See note p. 14. † See note p. 2.

near the first garden at the great sluice of Mudagere 400; east of the god's temple, 1 *matta* of dry land; near Billa in Múdagere 1 *matta* of dry land. For the god's lamps they presented 3 oil mills; and for the enjoyment of the god placed 12 dancing girls within his precincts.

Whoso heartily maintains this gift will derive the merit of presenting a thousand tawny cows with gold to a thousand Brahmans at Kurukshetra and Banarasi. Whoso resumes this gift will be guilty of the sin of slaying tawny cows in Banarasi, Brahmans in Kurukshetra, and rishis in S'ri Parvata. Whoso usurps a gift made by himself or by another shall assuredly be born a worm in ordure for sixty thousand years. Poison is no poison, the property of the gods that is the real poison. For poison kills a single man, but the property of the gods (if usurped) kills sons and descendants.

---

12. S'ila S'asana at Davangere, date A. D. 1271.

Size ft. 4 11′ × ft. 2 6′.—Haḷe Kannaḍa Characters.

Table or Book rest.	Sun. Crooked sword.	A Tirthankara enthroned, with chamaras on each side.	Moon. Cow suckling a calf.

(*Much of this s'ásana is illegible and obscure.*)

The doctrine of *Trailokya Nátha*, distinguished by the fruits of the supremely profound *syád váda*, the Jina doctrine, may it prevail.

. . . destroyer of powerful enemies, . . . *kates'vara*, in bravery unequalled as the lord of Lanka (Ravana).

A sun to the sky of the *Yádava* race, of rare bravery, a casket for the gems of good qualities . . . . . . was *Rámachandra Bhúpála*, whose descent was as follows:— . . . . *Málava*, the *Konkana* king, . . *Vanga*, the *Kalinga* king, *Nepála*, *Varáṭa*, *Láṭa*, *Gurjara*, the *Turushka* king, *Varáḷa*, *Maráṭa*, *Gaula*, . . these kings could not exist, such was his bravery. A head jewel in a mine of splendid bravery, *Kanda nripa* . . . had no equal on earth. His brother was *Mahadeva Ráya*, whose bravery was as follows:—a terror to the greatest heroes of the battle field . . splendid as , ... Moreover that *Kanda Raya's* son was *S'ri Ráma Deva*, whose bravery was as follows:— . . . .

The servant of his lotus feet was *Kúji Rája*, whose royal guru was *Márdangi Deva*, the glory of whose descent was as follows :—chief among the *Víra Sena senácháryas*, firm as mount Meru . . . . The Chakreshvara *Madusena Yogi* . . . . . the glory of the *agraganya* of his line was as follows :— . . . . *Munipada Sena Yati* . . . . . . chief of the *bhaṭṭárakas* . . . . A sun to his adherents, of blameless character, in learning a wonder, a patron of distinguished wise men, ... an axe to cut down the spreading creeper of sin, a friend to the humble, an abode of morality, was *Padma Sena Yatinátha*, son of *Chitra Bhúpati*.

And devoted to the two lotus feet of the king, a Meru in firmness, his chest like a broad rock, the mere dust thrown up by the troops of his horse covering up all other kings, glorious with many titles, was *Kúji Rája*, whose greatness was as follows :—The son of *Nimba Deva* praised by all the world, and of *Mallámbika* whose fame resembled the full moon in autumn, younger brother of *Chaṭṭa*, the husband of *Lakshmi*, reverencing the lotus feet of *Padma Sena*, of established merit, of distinguished fame, an abode of learning and truth, such was the glory of *Kúja*.

Through affection like the life to one another, celebrated in the world as were Rama and Lakshmana, in strength like Bharata, who can compare with these, thus did poets and their relatives praise *Chaṭṭa Nripati* and *Kúja Rája*.*

And the excellence of that exquisite *Lakshmi* was as follows :—Like the embodiment of the spells of Manmatha, of a colour like that of the most beautiful champaka, of a blameless character, glorious in good qualities, skilled in all useful learning (*woppuva vidhya*), praised by the whole circle of the earth, having the gait of a lusty elephant, thus was *Lakshmi Devi* the wife of *Kúji Rája* famed throughout the world.

And the glory of Kúji Rája's son was as follows :—the son of a hero, of surpassing excellence, all offering gifts to him on account of his bravery, like the chief embodiment of valour, deriding the courage of the sun, devoted to the lotus feet of the guru Padma Sena, of great fame was *Yaro Deva*.

---

* See No. 15.

And in the middle of the *Pándya des'a* was *Betlúru*, whose beauty was as follows :—Having matchless temples, delightful rows of shops, with a street of dancing girls, and surrounded with ramparts, beyond which were extensive pleasure gardens. And the greatness of its *Manneya S'etti* and *Guttara Gauda* was as follows :— an assemblage of the three branches of wisdom, lords of the *Pándya des'a*, descendants of the *Manneyaru*, of great bravery, abodes of all good qualities. Forsaking the companionship of the evil, ... making good use of their abilities, of distinguished fame in the world, were the sons of the *Mandala S'etti*. And one son of *Mácha* was *Hariva Gauda*, of extensive fame, profound as the sea, of a form like that of Manmatha. And the other son of *Mácha* was *Yoga Gauda* of great glory. . And great by fortune was *Ráma Gauda*, firm as mount Meru, descended in the family of *Sámanta Gauda*, to which sky he was the sun. .

Kúji Rája, having obtained possession of *Betlúru* and other towns, while dwelling there at ease, by the instruction of *Padma Sena* erected a Lakshmi Jinálaya, in order that his wife *Lakshmi* might obtain the blessings of *svarga* and *moksha*. Of incomparable beauty was the temple erected by *Kúja*, the light of the celebrated Sena gana, and the Pogari gachcha.

Moreover that *Kúja Rája*, in the year Prajotpati, at the time when *S'ri Víra Mahádeva Ráya* was establishing the *Báluma* agrahára, obtaining from him the village of *Hunasehalli* and 12 *honnu* as a free grant in permanence, came and presented them on a fortunate day to *Párs'vanátha Deva* of that Jain temple, writing a s'ásana and washing the feet of *Padma Sena Bhattáraka*.

And with the consent of the Gaudas, the Manmatha-like *Kúja* also gave the following :—a shop, an areca garden, an oil-mill . . . 2 *matta*, with pouring of water.

The mine of good qualities presented *Hunasehalli*, with pouring of water, to the *Párs'vanátha* temple, in perpetual gift.

13. S'ila S'asana at Davangere, date A. D. 1169.

Size ft. 4 4' × ft. 2 7'.—Haḷe Kannaḍa Characters.

Sun. Moon.

Nandi. Linga with Priest in a temple. Cow suckling calf.

Adored be *S'ambhu*, beauteous with the chámara-like crescent moon kissing his lofty head; the original foundation-pillar of the city of the three worlds. . . . .

May it be well.—While the auspicious Mahá Manḍales'vara, entitled to the five great drums, lord of the city of *Kánchipura*, sun to the ocean of the *Yádava* race, a head jewel to the bravest warriors* . . . . *Vijaya Pánḍya Deva*, was in his residence at *Huchangi*, ruling in peace and wisdom, the *Nonambavâḍi* Thirty-two Thousand :—

At that time; may it be well.—In the S'aka year 1091, the year Virodhi, the second (or intercalary) month S'ravana, the 15th day of the moon's increase, full moon, Monday; the lands which had been formerly given rent free for the service and decoration of the god *Avimuktes'vara*, which was set up in the old ruins (*haleya biḍu*) of the royal city *Hiriya Betúru*, in the kingdom of the warrior *Kilvog-oḍeyarasa Deva*,† (namely) under the first sluice of the king's tank, 1 *matta* 450 *kamba* of paddy land; also . . . 200 *kamba* for a garden: on the east 1 *matta* 100 *kamba* of dry land for a flower garden; and near it 100 *kamba* of dry land :—

These lands, having made inquiry that they formerly belonged to the gift which had been alienated, he gave again, with pouring of water, rent free, for the service and decoration, the daily worship, the illuminations and repairs, of the god *Avimuktes'vara*.

Whoso usurps a gift made by himself or by another shall assuredly be born a worm in ordure for sixty thousand years. Merit is a common bridge for kings. This from age to age deserves your support, O kings of the earth. Thus does Rámachandra from age to age beseech the kings who come after him.

Sakapura Tille Náyaka . . . . the S'iva Kalyána Nambi, received the vritti.

---

* *Samadhigata pancha mahás'abda, mahá manḍaḷésvaram, Kánchipura varádhisvaram, Yadu vams'ámbudhi dyumaṇi, samara bhaṭa chúḍámaṇi.*

† See *Kilva Ráya*, in Chalukya grant of A. D. 444.

14. Virakal at Davangere, date? A. D. 1169.

Size ft. 6 11′ × ft. 2 7′.—Haḷe Kannaḍa Characters.

A weapon (?) Sun. Moon. A weapon (?)
The hero. Linga with Priest. Nandi.

May it be well.—The great minister *Mácharasa**, possessed of all titles, ... the year Sarvadhári, the month Jyeshṭha, the 10th day of the moon's increase, Tuesday . . . .

The hero seated in a car, with attendants bearing chamaras.
A fight between horsemen armed with swords and spears.
A similar scene. Two men in the back ground escaping in terror over a wall. A horseman in the left hand corner holding up some article with a threatening gesture.

15. Virakal at Davangere, date about A. D. 1270.

Size ft. 6 5′ × ft. 2 4′.—Haḷe Kannaḍa Characters.

Sun. Lotus. Lotus. Moon.
The hero. Linga with Priest. Nandi.

The promoters of the glory of the kingdom of Mahádeva Ráya, their grandfather (*pitámaha*), a king over hostile kings, and of his gentle queen, were *Chaṭṭa Rája* and *Kúcharasa*. To the elder sister of these two, *Mailu Bái*, his mother, was born *Sena*, to describe whose departure (or death) the lord of the thousand tongues (Adisesha) alone is able.

The hero seated in a towering car, attended by celestial nymphs bearing chamaras, and by celestial musicians.

The rain of flowers descended, the heavenly drums beat, and the heavenly nymphs loving her son *Sena* bore him to heaven.

A battle scene. Two horsemen engaged in combat, each attended by a number of followers, horse and foot.

16. Virakal at Davangere, date A. D. 1169.

Size ft. 5 7′ × ft. 1 10′.—Haḷe Kannaḍa Characters.

Moon. Sword. Sun.
The hero. Linga with Priest Nandi.

In the s'aka year . . . . the year Sarvadhari, the month Chaitra, the 10th day of the moon's increase, Tuesday, the father-in-law of *Mallara Bhima*,

The hero ascending to heaven in a car with celestial attendants bearing chamaras.

*See No. 28.

Vira, at the west tank of the *Kundu ko!a*, fearlessly cut down the horses of *Kodavára* and destroyed the force. *Vira*

A fight between horseme armed with swords, one of them distingui hed by an umbrella.

while . . . from his camp, fell and went to heaven. Great good fortune (attend him).

Another fight between horsemen, one side armed with spears, the o he with swords. A shield bearer in the left corner.

---

17. S'ila S'asana at Harihara, date A. D. 1555.

Size ft. 4 11′ × ft. 2 2′.—Ha!e Kanna!a Characters.

The Donor worshipping. Sun. Linga. Moon. Nandi.

Adored be *S'ri Harihara*. Adored be *S'ambhu*, beauteous with the chámara-like crescent moon kissing his lofty head; the original foundation-pillar of the city of the three worlds. The mighty tree of bounty in the form of *Harihara* do I adore, which is entwined by the vines the shining arms of Lakshmi and Parvati.

May it be well.—In the year 1477 of the victorious increasing S'álivábana era, the year Ananda, the month Vaishákha, the 14th day of the moon's increase, Monday :—While the auspicious great king of kings, the supreme ruler,* *S'ri Vira Pratápa Sadás'iva Deva Mahárάya* was in *Vidyánagara*, in the enjoyment of peace and wisdom† ruling the empire of the world, seated on his diamond throne :—

May it be well.—To the god *S'ri Prasanna Harihara*, lord of all worlds, original god over all gods, the supreme, punisher of his enemies and subduer of their shouts, the giver of boons to Márkandeya rishi, the one (joint) incarnation of Hari-Hara, the planter of his lotus feet upon the breast of *Guhásura* who opposed the vedas in *Guhápura*, worshipped by the three worlds of heaven, earth and hell, granter of the desires of his votaries, the remover of all fear in the sacred forest of *Guháranya*, dwelling on the eastern bank of the *Tungabhadra*, lord of the city of *Kú!alúru;—Krishnappa Náyaka*, son of *Bayappa Náyaka*, worshipper of the lotus feet of that *Sadás'iva Ráya*, terrible as the white-bodied bearer of the moon (S'iva), boon lord of *Maninágapura*,‡

**S'riman Mahárajádhirája, Rája parames'vara.*

† See note p. 2.

‡ *S'itakara ganda dhavalánka Bhima, Maninágapura varádhisvara.*

on the auspicious occasion of the birth day of Narasimha,* in order that his father *Bayappa Náyaka* and his mother *Kondamamma* might obtain merit; presented the village *Beluvádi* to provide for the mid-day meal in the chatram of the god Harihara; and the money obtained from the *harigóḷu*† fees at the river of Harihara (he assigned) for furnishing the evening meal and lamps; and presenting a silver tray for offering the evening food, felt as if every desire were satisfied.

Whoso maintains this gift will derive the merit of performing countless horse sacrifices. Whatever sinner unable to let it live, destroys it, will incur the sin of killing cows and Brahmans in the Ganges, of parricide, and of causing a mother to eat the flesh of her son.

Thus is the stone writing (!)

To maintain a gift made by another is twice as meritorious as to make a gift oneself. To resume a gift made by another is to lose all the merit of one's own. Of making a gift or maintaining one made by another, the maintaining another's is the best. He who makes a gift obtains svarga, but he who perpetuates one obtains final beatitude.

Great good fortune be to *Dásappa*, the son of *Kámarasa*, who caused the village of Beluvádi to be written down for the chatram of the god Harihara.

---

18. S'ila S'asana at Harihara, date A. D. 1410.

Size ft. 9 9' × ft. 3 10'.—Haḷe Kannaḍa Characters.

Adored be *S'ri Harihara*. Adored be *S'ambhu*, beauteous with the chámara-like crescent moon kissing his lofty head; the original foundation-pillar of the city of the three worlds. The mighty tree of bounty in the form of *Harihara* do I adore, which is entwined by the vines the shining arms of Lakshmi and Parvati. A pearl in the frontlet of the pleasures of Parvati and Lakshmi, a chintámani granting all the desires of his votaries, a head jewel to the *upanishads*, the . . . . of the three worlds, that *Harihara* ever protect us. The god who in sport assumed the form of a boar, and shone forth tossing up the earth on the tip of his tusk which resembles a jasmin bud, ... , may he protect us. By virtue of whom the earth is called the firm, the jewel wombed, the mine of hidden wealth, the fertile with crops, the sustainer of all. . . May

* *S'ri Narasimha jayanti punya káladalu.*

† A coracle, or round basket-boat covered with hides, commonly used in Mysore at the ferries.

he who adorns the crest of S'ambhu with glory, the brother of Lakshmi, *Chandra* protect us.

Considering that in this Kali yuga the earth was filled with *kali* (sin), Vishnu formed the intention of being born in the lunar line as *Sangama.* The lady of whose brilliant fame was like an ornament of musk adorning the brow of a sky as dark as the (leaves of the) *honge* tree. In that line, as Rama in the line of Das'aratha, so was born *Bukka Ráya,* distinguished with all auspicious marks, destined to be the deliverer of the world. While he with his great strength was supporting the burden of the world, Vishnu and S'iva enjoyed complete rest in their beds (they had nothing to do!) His son was *Rája Harihara,* in the milk sea of whose fame the mundane egg (Brahmánḍa) floated as a bubble. The fire of his valour, as flame fed with ghee, so it increased, watered by the rain of the tears of hostile kings' wives. Again and again without end had he bestowed the sixteen kinds of gifts, and others besides.

As from S'iva was born Senáni, so from this king sprung *Daiva Rája,* the punisher of the evil. When he went forth to war the dust thrown up by the hosts of his cavalry caused the sun to set, and his enemies were drowned in the streams of blood drawn forth by the clouds of his arrows, thus was *Daiva Rája* famed in the world. During his reign no lesson was taught but the veda, agitation was only in the waves of the river, trembling only among the leaves of the vine, . . . none of these things occurred among men. By the brightness of whose fame all the world shone with white, and the fear of Agastya forsook this milk sea. . The conqueror of the hosts of his enemies, a Bhoja to learning, a kalpa vriksha in bestowing, a Kubera in wealth, a Manmatha to women, to all manner of wisdom a refuge, a devoted worshipper of S'iva, thus shines *Daiva Rája.*

May it be well :—An ornament to all the world, bearing in his mighty arms a bow skilled in destroying the groups of powerful enemies, rejoicing S'iva with his unintermitting devotion, lord of the eastern and western, the southern and northern oceans, whose inexhaustible arrows are the envy of all other kings, destroyer of the serpents the kings who break their word, to Hindu rájas a divine protector, granter of life, land and wealth to the kings who seek his protection, displaying his power in uprooting and destroying the trees the evil, remover of the fears of all by his might, devoted to the worship of the lotus feet of the self-born S'iva ; by the worship of the feet of the royal guru *Kriya S'akti,*—auspicious royal *áchárya* of the *rája-guru manḍala,* chief *áchári*, invincible king of the *Ráhuṭas*, the united dwelling place of the Lakshmi of penance and the Lakshmi of government,—having obtained all manner of wealth and the kingdom, the auspicious king of kings, the supreme ruler, **S'ri Vira Pratápa Daiva Rája Mahárája*, in the S'aka year *netra, agni, vahni, indu*, the year 1332, the year Vikruti, the month Bhádrapada, the 12th day of the moon's increase, Monday, made an agreement (*vyavahára*) between the god *Harihara* and the Brahmans residing in *Harihara kshetra*, as follows:—

On the Brahmans at their own expense building a dam to the river *Haridra*, and leading a channel through the land of the god Harihara into *Harihara-pura*; of all the lands irrigated by the thus led channel, two shares (thirds) shall be for the god Harihara, and one share (third) for the Brahmans who at their own expense constructed the channel, to be by them enjoyed, free of all burdens, as long as sun and moon endure. Thus was it given in a copper s'ásana.

In order that it may be known with certainty what Brahmans have a right to this land, their *gotra* and *sútra* are here set down.

(*Here follow the above particulars relating to* 108 *Brahmans.*)

And for the daily service of the god Harihara one *vritti*, and for the food of the Brahmans (in his temple) two *vritti*, altogether 111 *vritti*.

Taking together all the land which is irrigated under the channel made to *Barani*, *Kandu*, *Beluvádi*, *Hanagavádi*, *Harihara*, *Guttúru*, as far as *Ganganarasaiya* tank:—the god Harihara shall enjoy two shares thereof, and the Brahmans who built the dam and led off the channel at their own expense shall enjoy one share.

And the expense of annual repairs of the channel, and expenses arising in course of time from any orders of kings, or the judgment of God, shall be borne at the rate of two-thirds by the god, and one-third by the Brahmans.

The water of the channel moreover shall be distributed at the same rate of two-thirds to the (land of the) god, and one-third to (that of) the Brahmans.

And the expense of cleaning out the channel and building sluices shall be borne at the same rate of two-thirds by the god and one-third by the Brahmans.

Thus is it written in a copper s'ásana, of which this stone s'ásana is a copy.

At the time of building the dam to the river *Haridra*, the god Harihara and the Brahmans, the past present and future possessors of the vrittis, gave to

---

*See note p. 25.

Bharata arádhya, the son of *Krishna Malláchárya*, of the Gautama gotra and the Rik shákha, with pouring of water; 10 *maṇuvina koḷaga* of paddy land under the channel; namely, 5 from the god and 5 from the Brahmans; altogether 10.

And to the preparer of this s'ásana, the god Harihara and the Brahman vritti-holders uniting, gave from the god 4 *koḷaga*, and from the Brahmans 4 *kolaga*, altogether 8 *kolaga* of paddy land; namely, to *Cháyanáchári*, the son of *Vishnukarma*, called *Kalli Rája*, a *kaikripa taksha* (? poor working carpenter) of the Yajus shákha, and skilled in stone work, they gave 8 *maṇuvina koḷaga*.

And at the time of building the Haridra dam, the god and the Brahmans gave to *S'ankhara Bhaṭṭa*, performer of the *anga pradakshana*, with pouring of water, from the god 2 *kolaga* and from the Brahmans 2 *kolaga*, altogether 4 *maṇuvina koḷaga* of paddy land.

Whoso usurps a gift made by himself or by another shall assuredly be born a worm in ordure for sixty thousand years.

May the god Harihara, whose feet trampled to death the rakshasa Mura, and hasten to the assistance of all pure kings who praise them, protect us as long as sun, moon and stars endure.

(*A few lines at the end illegible.*)

---

19. S'ila S'asana at Harihara, date A. D. 1539.

Size ft. 3 7' × ft. 1 4'.—Haḷe Kannaḍa Characters.

Sun — Moon

Nandi. — LINGA — Cow suckling calf.

Adored be *Ganádhipati*. Adored be *S'ambhu*, beauteous with the chámara-like crescent moon kissing his lofty head; the original foundation-pillar of the city of the three worlds. The glorious form of *Harihara* do I adore, bearing the lucky mark on the breast, having a throat like a shining conch, beautiful to the sight, enveloped in saffron garments.

The praise of the gift made by the auspicious great king of kings, the supreme ruler, **Vira Pratápa S'ri Vira Achyuta Deva Mahárája*, is thus described in two verses:—†

In the S'aka year reckoned as *chandra, rasa, amarendra* (1461) the year . . . the month Bhádrapada, the 12th

* See note p. 25. † *Padya dvayam likhyate.*

day of the moon's increase, Tuesday, the nakshatra being S'ravana; the king *Achyuta* saying 'My name is my wealth, what is this property to me?' presented a mine of happiness delighting the Brahmans.

Nourished by all manner of merit, conspicuous by the crowds surrounding him, claimed by the assemblies of good men as their own, famed among all kings as the most liberal, who can obtain equality with him?

---

20. S'ila S'asana at Harihara, date A. D. 1223.

Size ft. 11 2' × ft. 3 7'.—Haḷe Kannaḍa Characters.

Sun. Nandi. Gandharva. Linga with Priest. Gandharva. Garuda. Moon. Cow suckling calf.

Adored be *S'ri Harihara.* Adored be *S'ambhu,* beauteous with the chámara-like crescent moon kissing his lofty head; the original foundation-pillar of the city of the three worlds.

* The abode of the spirit of Lakshmi (or of the poison), bearer of the serpent and the chakra, wearing the moon as an ornament, the granter of desires (or the consumer of Manmatha), eager in the assistance of Arjuna, a form pleasing to the *gopa* (or preserving the world), pure as the moon, the mighty, the original male (*ádi purusha*), the supreme lord, the crowning ornament of the original gods (*ádi devata*), this *Harihara* is ever the protection of the world.

Some saying there was no god on earth but Hari (Vishnu), and some saying there was no god on earth but Hara (Siva), to remove their doubts the *Harihara múrti* was revealed in *Kúḍalúru* in a single form, which form of glory may it protect us. The S'iva that was obtained the form of Vishnu, Vishnu obtained the mighty and celebrated form of S'iva, in order that the saying of the veda might be established; and settled in Kúḍalúr in one single form, praised by all lands, the god *Harihara* is engaged in the protection of the world. † May he the blameless, the unchanging, of ineffable peace and joy, without be-

* Most of the epithets can be interpreted in two ways, as referring either to Hari (Vishnu) or to Hara (S'iva).

† *Hariyindam biṭṭu daivam dharaṇitaḷadoḷ illendu pélvar kkelambar Haranindam biṭṭu daivam dharaṇitaḷadoḷ illendu pélvar kkelambar nnarar á sandéhamam pingisal atis'ayadim Kúḍalúralli s'obhákaram appant ondé rúpam taḷeda Hariharam kúṭu rakshirke nammam. Sanda S'ivange Vishṇuvina rúpam ad ádudu Vishṇuvinge pempóndi negaḷte vetta S'iva rúpam ad ádadu véda váky ad indend adan eydi, nis'chayisuvantire Kúḍalúrnoḷ éka múrtiyim ninda jagan anutam Hariharam parirakshisutirkke dhátriyam.*

ginning or end, the perfect, the form of wisdom, without growth, the being without form who took upon himself a form in the celebrated *Guháranya*, receiver of the praises of the chief gods, *S'ri Harihara*, protect us.

The Lakshmi of fortune dancing on the stage of his breast, the Lakshmi of victory disporting in the pleasure garden of his powerful arms, Sarasvati reposing on the lotus of his face, his orders being borne upon the diadems of hostile kings, his pure fame spreading light all around, the king *Narasimha*, the mightiest of kings, ruled the earth as far as the ocean shore.

The genealogy of this first of the monarchs of the world was as follows:— The veda (*sruti*) being his throne, Lakshmi with lightning glances fanning him with chámaras, the changing lustre of gems in the crowns of the adoring gods rising up as the wave offering (*árati*) of a lotus before him, Nárada rishi hymning his praises in the assembly, shone Padmanábha (Vishnu) as a kalpa vriksha, granting the desires of the world. From the midst of the lotus of his navel sprung Brahma, having the four vedas as his four faces, the cause of the creation of gods and men.

From the lotus of the heart of Brahma, as pure fragrance worthy of it, came forth the pure Atri. To him was born Chandra, his beams filled with the streams of nectar.

To Chandra, delighting all worlds with his growing rays of glory, was born the gentle Budha. From Budha that was, sprung Purúrava. From Purúrava Ayu. From Ayu Nahusha. From him Yayati. From this Chandra kula sprung the *Yadu kula*, in which was born the incomparable *Sala*.

He being a friend (or disciple) of the muni, was with devotion offering praises to the goddess *Vásantika* of *Sas'akapura*, in order that he might obtain the dominion of all kingdoms, when a tiger rushed forth, with its waving tail lashing the earth so that it trembled, its eyes flaming forth streams of fiery rage, its tongue stretched out as if the river of fire so formed, roaring like a thunderbolt, terrific in form. The muni saying *Hoyi Sale*, he slew it and dragged it along, and thus became *Hoyisala*.

To the sky of the kings of that Hoyisala race was *Vinayáditya* the sun. Glorious was *Yereyanga*, who on those that with obeisance resorted to him for protection descended in showers of gold like the rain, but on others he fell as a destroying thunderbolt. The sons of this Yereyanga were the powerful *Ballála*, *Biṭṭi Deva* (and) *Udayáditya*.

Among them *Vishnu nripa* was celebrated as the most handsome in form, a great king of the earth. . . . . When he set out for the conquest of other kings the dust raised by his hosts covered the ocean and turned its waters to clay, but by their march treading it down firm, they passed over, subdued mighty kings, and brought them into subjection, thus was *Biṭṭiga* the chief among the three. When this Biṭṭiga, the jaṭṭiga (boxer) of the battle field, set out for victory, *Kánchi* was breached, *Kongu* was overthrown, *Viráṭa-kóṭe* cried out, *Koyatúru* opposing was destroyed, the seven *Konkanas* unable to stand against the (chariot) wheels of his command threw down their arms and cast themselves into the sea.

To that *Vishnu Varddhana* and to *Lakuma Devi*, resembling the royal queen of Manmatha, was born the king *Narasimha*, a lion in battle. More powerful than Bhima, stronger than Parasu Rama, purer than Ganga, firmer than the chains of mountains, profounder than the ocean, more glorious than the incomparable sun, braver than the lion, a swift [illegible] in the field of battle, was *Narasimha*.

As if sprung from the sharp edge of Narasimha's terrific sword, was born *Ballála*, conspicuous for his bravery. . . . With the army of *Somana* he fought in the battle field, till the earth could no longer drink in the streams of blood which covered it, the paths were choked up with headless bodies, and . . . Though accompanied by 200,000 troops besides 12,000 horse and numerous mounted chieftains all regarding him affection, he (Ballála) on his single elephant routing that immense army of *Somana nripa*, pursued him, and stopping him between *Sovatúru* and *Krishna veni*, slew him, this *Vira Ballála Ráya*. And escaping the hostile chiefs who with fury singling him out came to fall upon him, when he had halted and re-formed the pursuing army, he marched to *Viráṭa kóṭe*, and speedily laid siege to the hill forts within *Belliṭige, Raṭṭapalli, Sovatúru* and *Kurugoḍa*; how shall I praise him, this *Giri Durga Malla?*

From the love of the mighty *Ballála Ráya* and his queen *Padmala Devi* was born the king *Narasimha*, to women a form of love, to fame a royal lover, to poetry an ocean, to the most powerful kings a budding Yama, to all others a kalpa vriksha. Thinking he had conquered but one, two or three, others opposed him, but lost their lives as soon as they appeared against him. How shall I describe him? As there was no part of the Kuru land which Bhima had not traversed with his *gada* weapon, so was there no battle field which the state elephant of this paramount king *Narasimha* had not trodden: why should I count the victories? When he went forth mounted in a splendid howdah on his caparisoned elephant, and the bravest of the brave, the lotus of their jewel-

led heads swaying before its gold-covered shoulder, addressed him as *Bhala!* (well done), *Jagadeka Vira!* (sole champion of the world), *Maruddeva!* (god of the gods), *Púrbápúrba Deva!* (the ancient and modern god), *Náráyana! Narasinga!*—the waving of the banners at the top appeared as if nodding in token of approval. This ornament of the Yadu race, the king *Narasimha*, churning with the Mandara mountain of his powerful right arm the ocean of the *Káḍava* army into which the *Pánḍya* alligator had plunged, acquired numerous elephants of great strength, though the gods and rákshasas churning the ocean with the Mandara mountain obtained but a single elephant. Having first on the one hand slain *Vikramapála* . . . .
on the other hand he overthrew that *Káḍava Ráya*, *Makara*, the *Pánḍya* king, and *Konḍa*, and being charmed with a certain elephant he placed it before *Choḷa* and gave him the crown, and in that Bridge (*setu*) he set up a pillar of victory, this *Narasimha*.*

May it be well:—While the protector of all lands, favourite of earth and fortune, great king of kings, supreme ruler, lord of the city of *Dvárávati*, sun in the sky of the *Yádava* race, a crowning ornament of the wisest, king of the *Male* rájas, *ganḍa* among the *Malepas*, *ganḍa bherunḍa*, unassisted hero, sole champion, Malla of the Shanivára Siddigiri hill fort,† in war like Rama, a lion to the elephants the tributary kings, a thunderbolt to the great *Pánḍya* rock, a Janárdana to the Kaiṭabha the *Káḍava* king, the rooter up of the *Makara* rája's kingdom, the setter up of the *Chola* raja's kingdom, thus celebrated, *Hoysaḷa S'ri Vira Narasimha Deva*, surrounded by *mahá manḍalika*, by great commanders, by tributary kings, and fair women, was in his own capital of *Dorasamudra*, ruling the kingdom of the earth in peace and wisdom:—

To that valiant emperor as the reflection of his glory . .
the power of his council, to his kingdom as a wall of adamant, of sincere mind, lord of the office of the prime minister, having the title of Tolagada Kamba (immovable pillar), . . the theme of song, the refuge of the good, the manager of state affairs, the supporter of fame, an ornament to poets, a moon filled with the nectar of good works, rejoicing in liberality, an abode of Lakshmi, the Vaishnava emperor, in the form of the world-adored Brahma, virtuous by nature, was *Poldḷva Deva*.

To describe his greatness:—

---

* *Modaloḷ Vikramapála pá . . saran ittalu kondan attalu poraḷ bidan á Káḍava Ráyanam Makaranam Pánḍes'anam Konḍam unu mada gandábhaman oldu paṭṭaman adam Choḷange munḍiṭṭu kaṭṭidan á Sétuvinoḷ Nrisimham aduvim neṭṭam jaya stambhamam.*

† See note p. 7.

Gay with the tinkling of the golden ornaments of beautiful dancing girls and of the bells of young and lusty elephants, and with the lively strains of singers, giving joy to all people on earth, a continual source of happiness, thus shone *Náraṇapura*, in the *Andhra* country. In that royal city, a favourite of Lakshmi, of pure fame, a Manmatha in form, famed for liberality, was the glorious *Atti Rája*.

To the beautiful *Naviládeyakka*—a kalpa vine to all her dependents, a Lakshmi to the *Olvas*,—and to *Atyarasa*, was born a son *Poláḷva*, a Vishnu to all titled commanders. In battle a weapon, in giving a hand, prudent in council, a favourite minister, in liberality a Karna . . . a jewelled ornament to the assembly, thus praised, he was the life to *Balláḷa Rája* and to king *Narasimha*, this *Poláḷva Daṇḍádhipa*. In war when he subdued the south (*tenkaṇa*) sending his troops of four kinds, this minister being in friendly consultation with the other councillors as to who was the bravest in the fight, all exclaimed 'Who in government and in war is equal to this minister *Polálva*? All testified that among kings and ministers there were none besides these, saying, 'Among kings that *Narasimha*, among all the ministers we have seen this *Polálva*, you two in bravery and government have surpassed all in the world, ... Who in these days has protected all the dominions of the *Hoysaḷa* kingdom like you?' . . . . in government, in dignity and energy like Brahma, accomplished in virtue, reverenced by all the world as the abode of uprightness and energy in the army of *Narasimha*. In beauty without a peer, single in speech, liberal without intermission, in discerning merit knowing no party, in the king's business without thought of profit, in wealth without pride, after praising him to whom will praise apply? After taking milk what more can one take?* Wealth and learning without opposition are both found in him, and ever young ever increasing have like the flood of the Ganges spread through all the world, thus was the greatness which *Poláḷva Daṇḍádhipa* had acquired in the world.

. . . . . .

May it be well:—In the year 1145 of the victorious increasing era, the year Svabhánu, the month Mágha, the 11th day of the moon's increase, Thursday; *Poláḷva Daṇḍanátha*, the *mahá pradhána* of *S'ri Víra Narasimha Deva*, the setter up of the Chola king, caused to be erected a temple adorned with 115 golden pinnacles for the god *Harihara*.

---

* *Hál uṇḍu mél umbudo?* a Kannaḍa proverb.

To describe the glory of that temple :—

Celebrated through all the world as of unequalled magnificence, of lofty eminence, such as none in any former age had constructed, the temple thus built he caused to be constructed so that it should endure, an ornament to the earth. Placing on the eight cardinal points images surrounded by hills, surmounted by numerous pinnacles, with towering golden domes shining like the disks of the sun and moon, after this manner did *Polálva Dandádhipa*, a Dharma Ráya among the liberal, erect it. Is it a hill or the peak of a mountain? Is it a sun or a kalasa? The groups of figures, are they the ladies of the points of the compass or shining creepers? That all might thus say, *Polálva Dandanátha* caused this marvel of a temple to be erected for Harihara. A place of brightness expanding like the sun, of lofty fame like donations to the good, like a pond of waterlilies, like the elephants at the points of the compass adorned with bells, thus did he cause the residence of Harihara to be adorned, this *Polálva Dandinátha*, the chief commander of the Yadu king. With a tower adorned with figures having smiling mouths, with numerous lotuses, with high raised knees (?), with plates of precious stones, like the stem of a vine adorned with leaves of pictures and bells, thus a marvel to all, painted with many colors, did the temple of Harihara shine.

Praised by all as the sole chief among Vaishnava emperors, this *Polálva Dandes'a* alone has obtained the fruits of merit, for he obtained the treasure for the creation of the Harihara temple, shining with 100 golden pinnacles. Formerly there was a king *Hermmádi** who thought to build a temple for Harihara and besought the god, who in a dream said to him, 'You forbear, a devout one will arise who shall accomplish this.' And this *Polálva* being directed in a dream saying 'You do this' he accordingly erected the temple and gained great fame. The temple of Harihara, which neither the king Sagara, nor the king Bhagiratha, nor Kártiviryárjuna, Bharata, Purúrava, Prithu, Dilípa, none of these chief kings of old had erected, this *Polálva Dandanátha* caused to be built, surmounted with golden pinnacles. In the Harihara kshetra, greater in the earth than Setu, Varanás'i and Kurukshetra, and surpassing them in beauty, in this region, attracting all like a magical charm, did *Polálva* erect the temple of Harihara with golden pinnacles towering to heaven.

And 104 holy Brahmans, the embodiment of the meaning of the vedas, to the law like its lips, to the *mantra* its excellence, to the *tantra* its origin, thus possessed of all ability, caused a metal roof (*vajra kavacha*) to be made for the sake of merit, but Polálva of greater merit erected the temple.

* More commonly met with as *Permádi*.

In this Harihara kshetra, famous as *Dvárávati*, known as *Guháranya*, celebrated with the name of Java Lakshmi Náráyana, with dvárapálaka at the four points of the compass, was *Bánavalli* . . . . . . at *Holehálu*, in the noble *Bánavalli*, this liberal king presented them to the 104 -Brahmans in order, with pouring of water, *Polálva Dandanátha* the chief minister of the Indra-like great king *Narasimha*.

What shall I say ? Making the temple of Lakshmi Náráyana a joy to all, he presented certain vritti in *Bánavalli* for that temple, to endure as long as sun and moon, this *Polálva*, the chief commander of the Yadu king.

None truly besides you was worthy to make these two gifts in the past and none will be in the future. This from a love of merit did you do. Who before erected such a beautiful temple for Harihara.

Whoso with joy preserves this gift will obtain life and wealth. Whoso destroys it will incur the sin of slaying many rishis, Brahmans, cows, and Brahmans versed in the vedas, in Kurukshetra and Varanás'i. Whoso usurps a gift made by himself or by another shall assuredly be born a worm in ordure for sixty thousand years.

---

21. S'ila S'asana at Harihara, date A. D. 1538.

Size ft. 7 7′ × ft. 2 11′.—Hale Kannada Characters.

The Donor? worshipping. Sun. Linga. Moon. Nandi.

Praise to *Harihara*.—Adored be *S'ambhu*, beauteous with the chámara-like crescent moon kissing his lofty head ; the original foundation-pillar of the city of the three worlds. May the god *Harihara*, happy in the side-glances of Parvati and Lakshmi, grant prosperity to the three worlds. May the god Harihara, destroyer of the Daitya race, humbler of the pride of Manmatha, terrifier of the city of Lanka, who brought low the desires of Duryodhana, the only being in the world, consumer of the three cities of the rákshasas, like Yama in the destruction of the world, the cavity of whose mind is filled with the three worlds,—protect the universe.*

Prosperity ever to *Achyuta Deva Ráya*, who resembles in brightness the rising sun or the pleasure-giving crescent moon. His fame, which fills the three worlds, shines as would the mundane egg if split in two (?). Who sooner forms

* Two verses of an erotic character omitted, bearing on the double relation of Harihara to Parvati and Lakshmi alike.

a merciful intention than the king *Achyuta*? Hari to Vyasa and others his friends who have served him long grants moksha, but king Achyuta to such as are not his friends too.

While this *Achyuta Bhúpála*, king of kings, the resplendent, the supreme monarch, champion over the three kings,* a terror to hostile princes, a Vishnu among Hindu rajas,† conspicuous with these and other titles—was ruling the whole world :—

Under his orders in all things was *Achyuta Malappanna Nripati*, a sea of mercy, like a bee at the lotus feet of S'iva, his mind ever bent on the worship of S'iva.

He on one occasion with great trembling, in order that his master might obtain the fame of merit, made a proposal to him, and receiving from him the reply 'I will assuredly present to the god Harihara, husband of Parvati, the village of *Kundaváḍa* which will speedily bear fruit' :—

Thereupon, in the year *vyoma, tarka, chatur, chandra,* (1460) of the era of S'áliváhana, the year Vilambi, the month Kartika, the day of full moon, Wednesday, at the auspicious time of the moon's eclipse ;—*Achyuta Malappanna Mahipati*, skilled in moral science, learned, prudent, the home of bravery and other heroic qualities, just by nature, true of speech, without vacillation, a nest filled with affection for cows, Brahmans and gods, of righteous life, of the highest wisdom, versed in all moral stories, sagacious, great by nature, understanding well morality and prudence, walking in the ways of merit, having obtained authority over all the Brahman agraharas and temples in Harihara.—That the fame and merit of his master *Achyutendra* might be increased, presented to the good god *Harihara*, who—a resting place for the lotuses of the hearts of multitudes of yogis, an assemblage of unnumbered good qualities, resplendent as a crore of suns, of an immortal form which has no parallel, the enemy of Mura (a rákshasa), the preserver, creator and destroyer of the three worlds,—dwells on the banks of the *Tungabhadra*, overflowing with goodness, eternally the same ;—the village of *Kundaváḍa*, fertile to bear all manner of fruits, in the beautiful *Uchchangi-venṭhe* of the pure *Páṇḍya nad*,—(its boundaries) west of the village of Sebanuru, north of Sálakaṭṭe, east of the village of Báti, south of the village of Yeraguṇṭa—with the rights of

---

* ? As'vapati, Gajapati and Narapati.

† *Rájádhirájas tejasvi yo Rája-parames'varah, múṛu-ráyara-gaṇḍánkah, para-ráya-bhayankarah, Hindu-ráya-suratráṇa.*

nidhi, nikshepa, jala, páshána, siddha and *sádhya,** freed from all burden, in the manner approved by all. And renaming it *Achyuta Rajendra Mallapura,* assigned it in permanence, as long as sun, moon and stars endure, for the mid-day offering to the god, and for the food of the Brahmans in the *chattra.*

Mallanárádhya, sun of Timmanárádhya, follower of the Yajur veda, of the Vádhúla gotra, a learned man, born in the Koṭisha family, prepared this inscription by order of his master.

---

22. S'ila S'asana at Harihara, date A. D. 1530.

Size ft. 5 8′ × ft. 2 8′.—Haḷe Kannaḍa Characters.

Moon.

Nandi. LINGA. The donor worshipping. An attendant bearing his umbrella.

Praise to *Harihara.*—Adored be *S'ambhu,* beauteous with the chámara-like crescent moon kissing his lofty head; the original foundation-pillar of the city of the three worlds. Praise to that excellent kalpa-vriksha, the form of *Harihara,* which is entwined by the vine the arms of the shining Lakshmi.

In the year 1452 of the era of S'áliváhana, the year Vikruti, the month S'rávana, the 8th day of the moon's decrease, Monday, on the auspicious birth-day of Krishna, at the moment of the Krishna avatár,†—while the great king of kings, supreme monarch, ‡ *S'ri Vira Pratápa Achyuta Ráya Mahárdya,* was ruling the earth in peace and wisdom :—

Of the village of *Achyutaráyapura,* otherwise called *Baḷḷápura,* in the *Harihara* country, belonging to the *Pándya* náḍ of the *Uchchangi-venṭha,* and which the king had assigned to me for the office of *Amara-náyak*—*Narayana Deva,* the son of Timmarasa of the treasury of gold, of the Vasishtha gotra and As'valayana sutra,—presented two shares (two-thirds) for the *chattra* of the god *Harihara,* and one share (one-third) to *Vis'ves'vara Arádhya,* son of Harihara Rámachandra Arádhya, of the Gautama gotra and As'valáyana sútra—in the presence of the god Harihara, with the ceremony of receiving a coin and pouring water.

---

* See note p. 3.

† *Jayanti puṇya káladalli S'ri Krishnávatára samayadalli.*

‡ See note p. 25.

This third part may you enjoy from generation to generation, as long as sun and moon endure.

Than making a gift, preserving one is better. By making a gift svarga is gained, but by preserving a gift final beatitude is obtained. To all kings land presented to Brahmans is a younger sister, whom neither may any other possess nor take away by force. Than making a gift oneself, to preserve the gift made by another is doubly meritorious. To alienate another's gift is to lose all the merit of one's own gift. Whoso violently takes away a gift made by himself or by another will be born a worm in ordure for sixty thousand years. Those who by force take away land given to Brahmans will boil in the hell called Kumbhipáka as many years as the Brahmans from whom they seized it, with their families and descendants, are in suffering therefrom. Whoso carries off the money of an agrahára, saying it is for the tribute to the king, or the gift to obtain a wife, or a contribution to save the village, incurs the guilt of incest with his mother. Support the bridge of merit, continually cries Rámachandra to the kings who come after him.

---

23. S'ila S'asana at Harihara, date A. D. 1424.

Size ft. 4 4′ × ft. 2 3.′—Haḷe Kannaḍa Characters.

Sun. Moon.

Nandi. Linga with priest. Cow suckling calf.

Praise to *Harihara.*—Adored be *S'ambhu*, beauteous with the chámara-like crescent moon kissing his lofty head; the original foundation-pillar of the city of the three worlds. I praise *Harihara*, the moon to the ocean of eternal mercy, the father of Manmatha and Karimukha (Ganesha), the diadem of the upanishads, adorned with the crescent moon, wearer of the serpent and the kaustubha, the remover of fear.

May it be well.—By order of *Nágaṇṇa Dhaṇṇáyaka*, the Mahá Pradhána of *S'ri Vira Pratápa Deva Ráya Mahárája*, son of *S'ri Vira Pratápa Harihara Mahárája*, an ornament to all worlds, supreme ruler, sole master of the southern and northern countries, a serpent to kings who break their word, a divine protector of Hindu rajas, a cage of adamant to those who seek his protection :—

At the request of the king *S'ri Deva Ráya*, did *Bukka Raja* eagerly undertake the following work of merit, ... the river *Haridra** . . . . . .

---

* See No. 18, p. 28.

The messengers of *Náganna Dhannáyaka* the Mahá pradhána of *S'ri Víra Pratápa Deva Ráya Maháráya*, having brought intelligence that the *Haridra* dam had breached,* on inquiring who would undertake the meritorious work of restoring it, looking upon *Cháma nṛipála*, the commander-in-chief of all the forces of the auspicious great king of kings, the paramount sovereign *Sri Víra Pratápa Deva Ráya Maháráya*, a devoted worshipper of the lotus feet of the Somes'vara linga, worthy with all good personal qualities, son of *Boppa Deva*, a kalpa vriksha to his dependents, a Manmatha to women, a victor in the battle field, skilled in the four branches of policy, protector of works of merit, fond of songs—(he said) 'the dam which by order of *Deva Ráya Maháráya* I built to the river Haridra having breached, to restore by the assistance of merit the provision for the service and decorations of the god Harihara and the property acquired by the Brahmans resident in that kshetra, except you there is no one else. That the fruit of the merit of building this dam will according to the veda and the dharma s'ástra be beyond calculation you are well aware. You therefore must repair this work of merit.'

Hearing this order, and with submission undertaking the work, in the S'aka year 1346, the year Krodhi, the month Kartika, the 12th day of the moon's increase, Monday, at an auspicious time, *Cháma Nṛipála*, with his own hands pouring water on behalf of the god Harihara and the Brahmans, and committing the work with pouring of water into the hands of *Bukkarasa*, sent him saying 'Do you in my behalf build this dam and excavate the channel' and had it repaired. Whose great glory is as follows :—

Of a form shining with firm friendship, gainer of the praises of all the world, filled with the highest good qualities, a moon to the ocean of a good race, devoted to good works, disposed to virtue and merit, glorious as the sun, thus shines *Cháma nṛipála* in the earth. Of a form granting all desires, of a fame which aimed at the points of the compass, unshaken as mount Meru, a Yama to his enemies, to his own family shining as an island of jewels, beautiful as Manmatha, an abode of all good qualities, son of the king Boppa Deva, who can bestow praise worthy of your greatness, *Cháma nṛipála?* To the world as a Bhoja, to his enemies a Bhima, in protecting the world of great glory, in firmness as mount Meru, hymned by all the poets, conspicuous among the meritorious, to the poor as a kalpa vriksha, thus famous was *Cháma rája*. Distinguished as the faithful protector of those who sought refuge with

---

* See No. 18.

him, a mighty hero, to the forest of his enemies a wild fire, a new Bhoja was *Cháma rája*. Thus did all the world praise *Cháma rája*, the son of Boppa-nripála, the driver off of hostile kings, a lion to the elephant foreign kings, a kalpa vriksha to the learned, of undying glory. . .

(*Several more verses in the same strain, containing nothing of importance*).

---

24. S'ila S'asana at Harihara, date A. D. 1560.

Size ft. 6 1′ × ft. 2 1′.—Haḷe Kannaḍa Characters.

Sun. Moon.
Nandi. Harihara. Garuda.

Praise to *Harihara Ráya*.—May it prosper.—Adored be *S'ambhu*, beauteous with the chámara-like crescent moon kissing his lofty head ; the original foundation-pillar of the city of the three worlds. I praise *Harihara*, the moon to the ocean of eternal mercy, the father of Manmatha and Karimukha (Ganesha), the diadem of the upanishads, adorned with the crescent moon, wearer of the serpent and the kaustubha, the remover of fear. Grant me joy, O merciful god Harihara, who on the rákshasa (Bali) the great tormentor of gods, men and the serpent world, didst place thy foot and force him down to hell. May the god Harihara protect us, who shining in happiness with Lakshmi and Parvati is to them a diadem of pearls, the chintámani glittering with generosity to the sorrowful and destitute, the diadem of the upanishads, the amulet of protection to the assembly of the gods.

In the year 1482 of the S'áliváhana era, the year Durmati, the month Magha, the 15th day of the moon's increase, Monday, at the auspicious time of the moon's eclipse,—while the great king of kings, supreme ruler, * *S'ri Víra Pratápa Sadá S'iva Máháráya*, was in *Vidyánagara* ruling the kingdom of the world in peace and wisdom :—

May it be well.—To the gracious god *Harihara*, lord of all the earth, god of all the chief gods, reconciler of the disputes between the S'aivas and the Vaishnavas, who to give a promise to Markandeya assumed the single Harihara avatár, who destroyed the arrogance of Guha, whose pair of feet were placed on the breast of Guha, worshipped by the worlds of Svarga, Martya, and Pátála, gratifier of the desires of the faithful, remover of the fears of the dwellers in the auspicious forest of *Guháranya*, lord of *Kúḍalúru*, situated on the eastern bank of the excellent *Tungabhadra* ;—

---

* See note p. 25.

Márga Saháya Náyaka, son of Velúr Kálappa Náyaka, the chief agent of *Krishnappa Náyaka*, son of Haḍapa Bayappa Náyaka, who was an officer of that *Sadá S'iva Mahárúya*, a Govinda to the Haḍapa sea, * terrible as the white bodied bearer of the moon (S'iva), lord of *Maninágapura*, †—in order that Krishnappa Nayaka might obtain merit—presented to the god S'ri Prasanna Harihara and his wives Mahá Lakshmi Devi and Parvati Devi, for a car procession on the full moon day of Chaitra, in order that Krishnappa Nayaka might obtain merit, the village named *Ganganarasi*, free of all imposts; this he repaired, and presenting, felt as if all his desires were accomplished.

Whoso protects this s'ásana will acquire the merit of performing the horse sacrifice and of giving shelter to many Brahmans. The extreme sinner who does not protect it will incur the guilt of slaying innumerable Brahmans versed in the vedas at Kás'i, Prayága, Gaya and Kurukshetra, of patricide and matricide, and of causing a mother to devour the flesh of her son.

To maintain a gift made by another is twice as meritorious as to make a gift oneself. To resume a gift made by another is to lose all the merit of one's own. Whoso usurps a gift made by himself or by another shall assuredly be born a worm in ordure for sixty thousand years. Of making a gift or maintaining one made by another, the maintaining another's is the best. He who makes a gift obtains svarga, but he who perpetuates one obtains final beatitude.

One in form says the *s'ruti* are Hari and Hara, and thus is he revealed. Whoso causes their division Yama will thrust into hell. That god Harihara, the sole ruler of the world, may he protect us.

Great good fortune be to *Súrappaiya*, son of Chadupurála Kondama Raja, who making application to *Márga Saháya Náyaka* repaired the village of *Ganganarasi*, and gave it up for the car procession of Harihara and Lakshmi. Fortune, fortune!

* *Haḍapara sindhu Govinda.*

† See No. 17.

25. S'ila S'asana at Harihara, date A. D. 1531.

Size ft. 4 × ft. 1 11'.—Haḷe Kannaḍa Characters.

Nandi. Sun. Linga Moon. Cow suckling calf.

Adored be *Ganádhipati.* May all obstacles be removed. Adored be *S'ambhu,* beauteous with the chámara-like crescent moon kissing his lofty head; the original foundation-pillar of the city of the three worlds.

May it be well.—In the year 1453 of the victorious increasing S'áliváhana era, the year Khara, the month Ashvija, the 10th day of the moon's increase, Wednesday:—while the auspicious great king of kings, the supreme ruler,* *S'ri Víra Pratápa S'ri Achyuta Ráya Mahúráya,* was in *Vidyánagara,* ruling the kingdom of the world in peace and wisdom:—

The villages named *Beluváḍi* and *Gaṅganarasi,* situated in the *Pánḍya nád,* belonging to *Uchangi venṭe,* within the *Harihara* country these two which the swámi had granted for the office of *Amara Náyak,* have we, *Avasarada Dikshita,* son of Annáji Deva, of the Gárgya gotra, the Apastambha sutra, and the Yájus shákha, so as to provide for the offerings of milk and rice to the god Harihara . . . presented to the god Harihara, in order that *Avasarada Devarasa,* of the Apastambha sutra and Bádaráyana gotra, might attain to the world of eternal merit.

In that *Beluvádi* village, have we, *Avasarada Dikshita,* son of Annáji Deva, of the Gargya gotra, the Apastambha sutra and the Yajus shákha, presented this to . . . . of the Atreya gotra, Apastambha sutra and Yajus shákha, with pouring of water and presentation of a gold coin in the presence of . . . . in order that . . . . . might obtain eternal merit.

Thus is the s'ásana given that you may enjoy it from generation to generation.

Of making a gift or maintaining one made by another, the maintaining another's is the best. He who makes a gift obtains svarga, but he who perpetuates one obtains final beatitude. Whoso usurps a gift made by himself or by another shall assuredly be born a worm in ordure for sixty thousand years. To maintain a gift made by another is twice as meritorious as to make a gift oneself. To resume a gift made by another is to lose all the merit one's own.

Avasarada Dikshita, son of Annaji Deva, ... the dwelling of the god Harihara . . . .

* See note p. 25.

26. S'ila S'asana at Harihara, date A. D. 1277.

Size ft. 10 2' × ft. 3 4'.—Haḷe Kannaḍa Characters.

Cow suckling calf. Moon. Harihara. Sun. Garuda.

Adored be *S'ri Harihara*. Adored be *S'ri Ráya Mahádeva Lakshmi Náráyana*. Adored be *S'ambhu*, beauteous with the chámara-like crescent moon kissing his lofty head ; the original foundation-pillar of the city of the three worlds. May the four arms of *Vishnu* protect you, black as a cloud, hard with the blows of the Sharnga bow-string, the pillars of the mantapa of the three worlds.

May the boar form of Vishnu protect you, on the tip of whose tusk the earth is firmly fixed like a female bee clinging to the shining white bud of a lotus. May the boar form of Vishnu with great affection preserve this gift, on the tip of whose tusk the earth rests like a female bee in the centre of the pure lotus. May *Harihara* protect this holy gift, who in the beginning took the form of the boar * . . . .

May *Ganapati* grant our desires, the elephant-faced, the son of S'iva, with broad eyes like the lotus, son of Parvati, free from old age and death, the light from the jewelled heads of the serpents which bind his waist causing the lotus of his feet to open even by night, lord of the three worlds. May *Saraswati* dwell on my tongue, who holding in her hand, as a jewel of the rosary, the mundane egg created by Brahma, is ever praying both night and day for the good of her votaries.

From Soma (Chandra,) who rose so glorious as their great original from the ocean which gave birth to Lakshmi, arose the mighty Kshatriyas. To their dominion succeeded Yadu, from whom all the kings of that line have been famed as *Yádavas*. From the appearance of Rama and Krishna to remove the burdens of the world, from that time has the line been greatly renowned.

In which, as the sole lords of the lady Earth, were ruling *Billama* and others. After whom came *Jaytugi Deva*. His son, powerful, of increasing greatness, of great bravery, by excellence established as superior to all, lord of the earth, was *Singhana*.

When he with joy marched forth to war, and seeing the dust raised by his hosts, all kings fearing brought their wealth and offered it to him, so that the feet had no standing room for the money spread on the ground, he caused

* An indecent allusion omitted.

the waters of the ocean to recede and to leave a plain for them. The sun *Singhana* by his power evaporating the waters in the lotus ponds of the hearts of hostile kings, caused the waterlilies the eyes of their queens to close, while it expanded the lotus the face of the Brahmans with joy.

His grandson, born in love, lord of the earth, was *Kandara Deva*, through fear of whom all kings forsook their kingdoms. By his great fame, by the strength of his capital city, by the might of the power of a Kshatriya, by his skill and valour in seizing upon the royal wealth of hostile kings, he was as renowned as the friend of the Páṇḍavas (Krishna), the brave *Kandara Deva*. As if in order to bring great glory to the Yadu line Hari were born as a king in the form of *Kandara Deva*, such was the fame he acquired.

And as if Hara, in order to subdue his proud enemies, were born from love (for him), so did Kandara's younger brother, the great *Mahadeva* shine. *Mahadeva* being now the sole lord of the world, you, *Kerala*, give up the pride of your kingdom, do not ruin yourself by excess of courage ; you, *Konkana*, come at once and quickly present your gifts and tribute ; *Chola*, what can you do with your forces ?—thus do the heralds (or door-keepers) make proclamation. *Gauḷa* being afraid of war went and stood by the snake hole, *Utkala* forgetting shame ran away, *Choḷa* losing his composure ran and took to the sea, the *Máḷavas* trembled, the *Láḷas* gave tribute and had audience, all the other kings were subdued and ruined, how shall I extol that king's great power. Had his power not been thus, would he have acquired those *Telunga* kingdoms and established the kings in their three cities ?* What other king in the world had gained such great fame by subduing the herds of lusty elephants ? Thus is it certain that S'iva was incarnate as *Mahadeva Ráya*.

The son of that *Kandara*, who possessing himself of the wealth of his enemies became the lord of Lakshmi, the favourite of the earth, was *Rámachandra Mahindra*. Of a secure and mighty kingdom, served by hostile kings, remover of the troubles of the world, of a great fame filling all the points of the compass, a sun to the lotus the face of the Brahmans, the son of Kandara, a

---

* *Biḍu nîm Kéraḷa ninna rájya madamam ham miranim viradim keḍabéḍ igaḷe bandu kánṇikeyamam kappangaḷam bégadim | kuḍu nîm Konkaṇa Chôḷa ninna balupinn én appudend ágaḷu poḍavisem Mahadevan arbban avutam duvárádhipar saárwar || Gauḷar khilagak anii putt aḍaridar unán biṭṭu póg Utkaḷar Chchoḷa pritiya biṭṭar ôḍi jalavam pokk anjidar Mmáḷavar|| Láḷar kkáṇike goṭṭu kanḍar uḷida kshmápáḷar ellágaḷum veḷ áḷág iharendaḍ ém pogaḷven á bhûpa pratápôgramam || vṛi || Dhórrakoḷge balup intadalladaḍy á Tilunga rájyangaḷam pura mûṛakk iṣayági máḍi kalad á téjógram antádudo |*

collection of all good qualities, thus shines *Ráma Ráya.* A moon to the water-lilies the faces of the fair, an embodied Manmatha, of surpassing brilliance, a jewel to the wealth of the Yádavas, lord over the whole circle of the earth, universal emperor (*sárva bhouma*), worthy of his illustrious name, thus did he shine, this *Ráma.* Delighting Devendra with his sacrifices, protector of the Brahmans, lord over the world, capturer of the finest elephants among the elephants of his enemies, a lion to the elephants and their lofty vine-covered mantapas his enemies, a white elephant of the points of the compass, shining with fame, may this *Rámachandra* prevail.

May it be well.—During the rise of the victorious kingdom of *S'ri Ráya Náráyaṇa, Prauḍha Pratápa Chakravarti, S'ri Víra Rámachandra Ráya,* favourite of earth and fortune, great king of kings, supreme ruler, first of monarchs, lord of the city of *Dvárávati,* a sun in expanding the lotus bud of the *Yádava* race,* a S'iva to the Manmatha the *Málava* king, an elephant-goad to the elephant the *Gurjara* king, the establisher in his kingdom of the *Telunga* king, mighty of arm in seizing upon the wealth of the *Hoysaṇa* kingdom, skilled in beating time upon the group of hostile kings (!) :—

The commander of all his household troops was the auspicious *Sáluva Tikkama Deva,* whose descent and glory were as follows :—Born like the commander of the forces of the gods, of unequalled good qualities, ... commander of the army of Ramachandra Deva king of the world, thus great was *Tikkama mantri.* A hero, liberal, sporting from his great bravery with his shining sword which subdued the valour of all others, master of all the forms of greatness, a bee at the lotus feet of Vishnu and S'iva, of powerful strength, of great fame in the world, was *Sáluva Tikkama Deva.* He shone like a faithful son to the heart's affection of the auspicious *Mahadeva,* like the moonlight of the *chandra* (moon) the mighty king *Rámachandra.* When this *Sáluva Tikkama* with joy went forth to war, the dust raised by his hosts covering the mountains and causing all the sky to appear like the earth, enlarged the (surrounding) ocean ; his valour cutting off the heads of hostile kings, brings the spoils of their wealth and lays them at his feet.

May it be well.—The auspicious Mahá Maṇḍales'vara, mighty of arm in smiting the heads of the groups of the strongest and bravest of hostile kings, devoted to war, a Revanta in putting his horses through their five paces, the creeper of his fame having spread into the utmost corners of all the points of the compass; in encountering the hardest butts from the muscular heads of the

---

* *S'rí-prithiví-vallabha, mahárájádhirája, parames'vara, parama-bhaṭṭáraka, Dvárávati-pura-varádhís'vara, Yádava-kuḷa-kamaḷa-kaḷiká-vikasa-bháskara.*

wrestler Chamira (*viz.*), the hostile kings, and shutting up their shouts, an able antagonist like the *purána* Náráyaṇa: by the favour of Tryambaka and Harihara having obtained the kingdom in protecting which he was a powerful right arm, in liberality of gifts a growing Karna, establisher of the *Kádamba* king, disgracer of the *Hoysaḷa* king,* rejoicing in the abiding prosperity obtained by favor of the Brahma of a virtuous life, commander of all the forces, *Nissanka Pratápa S'ri Sáleya Tikkama Deva Rana*, having in an expedition to the south captured the city of *Dorasamudra*, accomplished his object, and taking a tribute of all manner of wealth, especially of horses and elephants; while coming thence :—†

The liberal *Tikkama* saw the city of *Harihara*, the residence of Vishnu the conqueror of Guha, and the place where his faithful votaries obtain mukti. Kuru, Kás'i, Varanás'i, Himagiri, Gaya, Godávari, S'rinaga, are famed in the world each for some single excellence, but this Guháraṇya des'a surpasses them, for it owns the power of the Boar (*váráhi*), has 104 Brahmans the gods of the earth, and is the dwelling place of Vishnu. Is it a city or is it the residence of Devendra? Is it the silver hill on which the lord of Gauri dwells, standing in the ocean from which Lakshmi rose, this wonder of the world? Never have we seen so rare a place. Thus saying, the minister of *Mahadeva Ráya* made there with joy some gifts of land in the name of his sovereign.

His various free gifts in this Harihara agrahara were as follow :—

On account of his victorious expedition to the south, and his visit to the Harihara incarnation, he presented a tank, free of all dues and *siddháya*.

And *Sáluva Tikkama Deva* besought that he might have the honour of building a temple in the city of Harihara in the name of his sovereign *Mahadeva Ráya*, thus ;—That as this god had with affection granted what his worshipper prayed for, he had with the consent of the mortal creatures there made a free gift, and requested that he too (the king) as a divine incarnation might ever abide in that city. Thus did he this minister *Tikkama*. Accordingly, to the god who had accepted his prayer, he resolved to set up a Lakshmi Náráyana incarnation of his master *Mahadeva*, and having bought the land, rejoicing the hearts of those 104 (Brahmans), he informed the king of the date on which he proposed to commence the erection of the temple, (namely) on Friday, the 13th day of the moon's increase, in the month Chaitra, the year Is'vara, the s'aka year 1199. And in the following year, Bahudhanya, the

* *Kádamba Ráya sthápanáchíriyanum, Hoyisaḷa Ráḷ disápaṭṭanum.*

† *Dakshiṇa digvijaya Dorasamudrákramana krita káryya kari turaga mukhya samasta vastu sahitam kappam goṇḍu bandalli.*

month Magha, the 6th day of the moon's increase, Wednesday, the powerful Mahá Mandalika *Tikkama Deva* set up the image of *Mahadeva Ráya* in the form of *Náráyaṇa* the universally adored lord of Lakshmi.

And in the year following, the year Pramádi, the month Phalguna, the 5th day of the moon's increase, Tuesday, the nakshatra being Asvini, he set up golden pinnacles to that temple, and presented the following lands to provide for the service of the god reigning in Harihara.

That *Tikkama Deva* having purchased with joy 4 *matta* of paddy land belonging to the Betta Gauda tank, at the price fixed by the *sabhe*, presented it to the god.

And in the excellent Satradundige, paying due respect to the 104 Brahmans, ...

(*Rest illegible*).

27. S'ila S'asana at Harihara, date A. D. 1269.

Size ft. 10 1' × ft. 3 1'.—Haḷe Kannaḍa Characters.

(*The photograph does not include the symbols*).

Adored be *S'ri Harihara*. Adored be *S'ambhu*, beauteous with the chámara-like crescent moon kissing his lofty head ; the original foundation-pillar of the city of the three worlds. May he protect us from danger . .

(*Much illegible.*)

From the lotus of his navel sprung Brahma, from him Atri, from him Chandra . . . .

In that line was born, a wild-fire to the forest of the ornaments of the moon-faced wives of hostile kings, a moon to the ocean of the *Yádava* race, an ornament of ministers to the lord of *Kalyána*, destroying with the pillar of his right arm the hostile Kshatriyas, growing in power. The poison of the serpent of calamity he admits not into his throat, association with serpents he does not form, he bears not throughout the three worlds the name of cruel, yet is he truly characterized as (or named) *Rudra*.

From him was born *Mailaya*, celebrated for his great fame, preventing the wives of hostile kings from painting their eyes (*i. e.* widowing them.) Thus having reduced all hostile kings to be his servants, was the *Heggaḍa Maila*, a moon to the ocean of the treasures of the lord of Kalyána, a kalpa vriksha born on the earth, whose words were as sweet as nectar. His wife, brilliant with the colour of gold, was *Revallati,* conquering by her good qualities and wealth, by her bright smiles and splendour putting the moon to shame.

By her to the Heggada Nayaka was born *Soma*, the central gem in the garland of the pearls of good qualities, of a fame like the light of the moon, great by the perfume of his goodness, a moon (*soma*) in causing the lotus faces of the wives of hostile kings to shut up, a moon (in raising the tides) to the ocean of the *Hoysaḷa* line.

To the lord of the earth *Soma*, the brave *Narasimha* was son, who setting up the wealthy *Chola, Páṇḍya* and other kings, had acquired great renown as a commander of the army. Truly was *Soma* a herd of elephants filled with the water of wealth, else whence flowed the river of his bounty.

By this king, devoted to merit, were many agrahâras erected on the banks of the joyful *Kávéri*, which are praised by many great poets. And in those agraháras (even) the parrots had a knowledge of *niti*, and were nourished upon the *mimámsa*. In one place they assembled together arguing in the severest critical terms of the *turka*, in another they beautifully recited *subda*, *yajna* and *kavitva*. Thus was it in the mine of learning *Somanátha-nagari*, a brilliant ornament to the world.

And by him were many gods and goddesses set up on the banks of the Kávéri, namely Purahara, S'ri Narasimhes'vara, S'ri Lakshmi Nrihari, Murahara, S'ri Yoga Narayana. And on the north east he set up the five-faced S'iva, Bijjales'a and others; in the centre Gopála, Janárdana, S'ri Kes'ava, the Matsya and other the ten avataras, Murahara, Narayana. And on the walls Kes'ava and others the twelve murtis, Sankars'ana and other murtis, Vishvaksena and numerous other minor deities, Padmasena, Indra and other gods. Gira and all these gods were set up in *Somapuri.*

His elder brother was the great commander *Melaiya*, of great good fortune. His elder sister's son was *Malli Deva*, a spear to the bodies of hostile kings, a wild fire to the forest of his enemies, the gratifier of the desires of his dependents, who continually extol his good qualities.

Of great strength was the commander *Soma*, resembling Karna, giving his assistance to all the kings of the east he set them up on their thrones and increased their power, the wealth of his enemies he destroyed, *Gaṇḍa Peṇḍára** . . Chandis'a (S'iva) had granted him the boon of prosperity as long as sun and moon endure.

Thus in his line was born the reverend *Gangádhara*, praised by all and of great wealth, a sun in chasing away the darkness of the Chárváka and

* A jewelled anklet, denoting championship.

Bauddha doctrines, in *tarka* an independent authority, an Agastya avatára in his skill in swallowing up the ocean of the Jainas; this great pandit illuminated the assembly like a gem.

To that god *Harihara* was this *Soma* the servant, who had become incarnate in face of the world that he might establish the *advaita* (the non-duality or unity) described in the vedas of Vaikun*t*a (Vishnu) and Nilakan*t*ha (S'iva); who had stopped the growth of the world (in wickedness); by whom the Kaivalya Lakshmi (or Lakshmi of moksha) had settled on the lotus hands of all people; who had devoured the flesh of the rákshasas. To Gauri life, to S'ri a lord, adorned by Bhadra, indivisible (*advayam*) and thus a bigamous husband, the crowning glory of the *tatva*, O Harihara, do thou remove my sins; thy lotus feet are my refuge, which will not spare in trampling upon every cause of sorrow; who enjoying unending happiness art of boundless generosity.

The S'aka year 1190 having passed, and the year Vibhava being current, *Somanátha* caused a temple with golden pinnacles to be erected at the door of the temple of the god *Harihara*. May the joy-producing meritorious work of the chief commander, Gan*d*a Pendára *Soma*, prevail as long as sun and moon endure.

*An ornament to the beautiful country bordering on the *Kávéri*, having lofty towering walls surrounded by a deep moat, containing a *soma* street and an *árka* street, the numerous houses of which were filled with people, was the city bearing the name of *Somanátha*, a joy to the eyes of all. There congregated, the excellent Brahmans increased, performing the ceremonies prescribed by the vedas, understanding the meaning of the *ágama*, *tatva*, *mantra*, *tantra*, and *tarka*; engaged in their individual daily rites, works of merit, and sacrifices; pure, single minded, devoted to acts of virtue, good men. Astonishing was the greatness that *Somanáthapura* had acquired from the many great men who had their origin there. Surrounding it were numerous pleasure gardens, in which the trees bent down with foliage, and the fields were filled with grain, . . . On all sides were tanks filled with lotuses and waterlilies, and with the motion of the waves in the moat the hanging boughs of the trees were waved. Thus was this *Somanáthapura*, like the name of the jewel of the earth.

In the middle of this celebrated *Somanáthapura* having erected a great temple and adorned it with a god-like incarnation of Vishnu which continued

* The foregoing part of the s'ásana is in Sanskrit, the remainder is in Kannada and repeats a good deal of what was stated before.

ever as bright as if just set up, highly distinguished became *Soma chamupati.* And in the Vishnu temple which by his order had been erected in the middle of *Somanáthapura,* S'ri Kes'ava distinguished by the name Prasanna Chenna, surrounded with brightness, to the south of him Gopála the beloved of the world, Janárdana the embodiment of the desires of all; these three múrti were the chief and the most richly endowed with all manner of gifts.

And as if in this scene of many victorious processions Vishnu had strung together all the varieties of his forms, many other gods did he there set up, namely, the Matsya and others the ten avataras, Kes'ava and other deities, Sankars'ana of auspicious form, the Varáha form, Náráyana and other gods the givers of wealth and prosperity, Krishna and twelve other gods the merit of whose worship is incalculable. The excellent Ganapati, Bhairava, Bháskara, Vishvaksena, Durgi and other gods. Altogether 74 gods adorn the temple which he built in the middle of the city.

And on the north-east side he set up the five-faced S'iva, which in order are Bijjales'vara, next to it Pergaḍes'vara, the four-fold Abales'vara, and the splendid Jayavales'vara, and in the middle Somanátha S'ivalinga. Having securely established these, *Soma Danḍádhipa* gained great renown. And the excellent form of Narasimhes'vara, the auspicious Yoga Náráyana, the ever abiding Lakshmi Narasimha, being established in it, the city of Somanátha, shining in the middle of the Kávéri as the residence of so many gods, was thus rendered worthy of reverence from all the world by the mighty *Soma Danḍádhinátha.*

(And so on, the conclusion being illegible.)

28. S'ila S'asana at Harihara, date A. D. 1171.

Size ft. 6 5′ × ft. 2 3′.—Haḷe Kannaḍa Characters.

Nandi. Sun. LINGA. Moon. Cow suckling calf.

Adored be *S'ri Harihara.* May the kalpa vriksha embodied as *S'ambhu Náráyana* ever grant our desires, whose smiles resemble the brightness of its white shining flowers, whose powerful arms are its branches, whose hands are its ruddy young shoots, encircled by the creepers of serpents, enriched with the four manner of fruits.

. . . .

May it be well.—While the victorious kingdom of the auspicious *Vijaya Pándya Deva*,—entitled to the five great drums, Mahá Mandales'vara, lord of *Kánchipura*, sun to the sky of the *Yádava* race, a head jewel of brave warriors, his mind purified by meditation on the lotus feet of the god S'ankara Náráyana, an ornament of the *Yádavas*, sun to the lotus of the *Pándya kula*, champion over the smiters of their enemies, . . . defeater of the designs of *Rájiga Chola* * of surpassing greatness, splendid with these and other titles, reverenced by crowds, an abode of glory,—was increasing in grandeur and prosperity, to endure as long as sun, moon, stars and sky :—

All the chiefs who heeded not his commands were driven out; those brave ones who came to fall upon him, being seized, disgraced, tormented, their bodies worn out, forsaking their places they fled in all directions; how great was the bravery of the king *Vijaya Pándya*.

The dweller at his lotus feet; May it be well.—the Mahá Pradhána was the auspicious *Vijaya Permadi Dandanátha*, a lion to the herd of elephants the most powerful tributaries, terrible in the field of battle, his forehead adorned with a wafer made of the dust from the lotus feet of *Vijaya Pándya*, a mill-stone to the slayers of swámis, skilful as Chánakya in driving off with powerful incantations the rákshasas the hostile kings, a central jewel to the diadem of the group of ministers, a powerful new Anjaneya in leaping over the ocean the forces of hostile kings, his fame was stamped as an ornament of sandal powder on the swelling breasts of the ladies of the points of the compass, having received from his king the honor of the name of *Kumára*, a promoter of wealth, protecting all the people with even greater care than if his own children, splendid with these and many other titles, in firmly establishing the great kingdom of the king over kings, *Vijaya Pándya Deva*, his able right arm. Braves who do not ask him for orders there are not in the land, proud ones who despising him will not serve under him there are not, obstinate ones who twisting his orders carry out something different and live, there are not; thus did he manage the kingdom of king *Vijaya Pándya*, what an abode of consummate ability was *Permadi Dandádhipa*. Whoso refused to do obeisance, them he forced first to do obeisance to himself and then made them do obeisance to king *Vijaya Pándya*. And so celebrated was his government in all the world, that all did him obeisance, this *Vijaya Perma Dandádhis'a*.

Moreover a dweller at the lotus feet of *Vijaya Pandya Deva*, that abode of the Lakshmi of self-secured victory was; May it be well.—*Ketarasa*, en-

* *Rájiga Chóla manóbhangam.* See No. 4, p. 8.

titled to the five great drums, Mahá Maṇḍales'vara, lord of the city of *Banavási*, having a monkey flag and a lion signet, lover of the sound of Permaḍi's drums, the setter up in 84 cities of the frontal-eyed (S'iva) and the four-armed (Vishnu), universally known as having performed 18 as'vamedhas in strict conformity with the vedas, having by his power set up in the cave and on the peak of Himavat the chief of mountains a stone pillar describing the surpassing glory of his line, splendid with the mighty elephants he had bound, born in the line of *Mayúra Varmma*, the *Kádamba chakri*, lord of *Uchchangi-giri*, obtainer of a boon from S'ankara Náráyaṇa. *

To him and to *Kanakabbe arasi*, the moonlight to the chakora and the waterlilies of his heart and eyes, . . . was born *Nágati nripála*, whose fame made havoc of the lotus gardens the hostile kings. To describe the greatness of his qualities. The terrible shadow of the bodies of hostile kings smitten by the shining sword in the hands of *Nágati*, the chief of kings, resembled the moon at sunrise (being bloody). Moreover, the serpent of the surpassing strength of king *Nágati* snatches away as flesh the poverty of the learned, and the best of the lands of hostile kings.

His younger brother, of surpassing bravery, of great good qualities, a dazzling light to the swarms of grasshoppers the hostile kings, was *Hari arasa*.

To that king *Nágati* was born; as Karna in former times to Súrya, distinguished by gifts of liberality, an abode of virtue, a friend of the learned, *Ketarasa*.

And to that king *Nágati* was born another son, skilled in all learning, an ornament to all kings, a Karna to supplicants, the celebrated *Mácharasa*.

One day, while that abode of praise and glory, *Nágati arasa*, chief of a Thousand nad, with his uncles *Hamparasa* and *Sattiyarasa*, and that Nágati arasa's younger brother *Hari arasa*, and his sons *Ketarasa* and *Mácharasa*, were in the enjoyment of peace and security, listening to the history of the early kings, and the account of their meritorious works †; perceiving that they were as devoted to merit as eager to carry off the lady victory from the forces of opposing kings; remitted the tribute which they received from

* *Svasti samadhigata-pancha-mahá-s'abda mahá-maṇḍales'varam* | *Banavási-pura vará dhís'varam* | *vánara dhvaja mṛigéndra lánchchhanam* || *Permaḍḍi túrya nirghoshanam* | *chatur ás'iti nagaradhishṭita laláṭa lochana chatur bhbhujam* | *jagadvidhitáshṭadas'ás'vamedha dikshádikshitam* | *Himavad girindra rundra s'ikhara s'akti samsthápita nijanvaya prakaṭitorjjita pratápa s'ilá stambha* | *baddha mada gaja mahá mahimabhirámam* | *Kádamba chakri Mayúra Varmma vams'odbhavan Uchchangi-giri nátham S'ri S'ankara Náráyaṇa Deva labdha vara prasádan enisida Ketarasam.*

† *Suka sankathá vinódadin irdd ondu divasav ádi rája charita dharmma kathá s'ravanodatta s'ravaṇarági.* See note p. 2

Kúḍaluru, the ancient agrahára of the god Svayambhu S'ankara Náráyaṇa, together with the dues they received from the cultivation of the beautiful channel; and in the S'aka year 1093, the year Vikriti, the month Pushya, the 1st day of the moon's increase, Friday, at the time of uttaráyana sankramana, presented them, with pouring of water, at the divine lotus feet of *Svayambhu S'ankara Náráyaṇa*, to endure as long as sun and moon.

Whoso maintains this gift will obtain the merit of presenting at Varanás'i, Kurukshetra, and holy bathing places; at Gaya, Prayága, in the dwelling of S'ankara Náráyana and other most sacred places; at the auspicious times of new moon, the sun's eclipse, *uttaráyana sankramana* and *vyati páta*; to a *s'ankha* (a trillion) and a *mahá-s'ankha* (a quadrillion) of Brahmans, versed in the four vedas and their vedángas, masters of all learning, of incalculable merit; to each one separately, a crore of golden coloured cows, and golden *koḷagas* decked with jewels, together with milking cups of bell metal, according to the s'ástras. Whoso destroys it will incur the guilt of slaying with his own hand that number of Brahmans and cows in those holy places at those times. Of making a gift or maintaining one made by another, the maintaining another's is the best. He who makes a gift obtains svarga, but he who perpetuates one obtains final beatitude. Merit is a common bridge for kings. This from age to age deserves your support, O kings of the earth. Thus does Rámachandra from age to age beseech the kings who come after him. Whoso usurps a gift made by himself or by another shall assuredly be born a worm in ordure for sixty thousand years.

(Here follows another s'ásana, dated 2 years later.)

May it be well--In the S'aka year 1095, the year Nandana, the month Bhádrapada, the 3rd day of the moon's increase, Wednesday: the auspicious Mahá Pradhána, *Durgarasa Danḍanáyaka*, adhikári of the *Banavasi* 12,000, whose father, a worshipper of Indra and Vishnu, a mine of good qualities, was *Permaḍi Danḍádhinátha*, his mother the celebrated and fortunate *Mahádevi*, his younger brother, served by all the learned, *Soma Deva*;—this *Durga Danḍádhinátha*, obtaining greatness in the world, a moon to the ocean of the Vishvamitra gotra and thus no common man: presented in the ancient agrahára of *Kúḍalúru*, 100 gadyána to the 104 Brahmans, in order that they might devote one hága a month for the lamp of the god, as long as sun and moon endure; thus did he give, with pouring of water, that the Brahmans might provide for the god *S'ankara Náráyaṇa*.

29. S'ila S'asana at Harihara, date A. D. 1379.

Size ft. 7 4′ × ft. 1 10′.—Haḷe Kannaḍa Characters.

Cow Nandi. Sun. LINGA. Moon. The Donor* Priest.

Adored be *S'ri Harihara.* Adored be *S'ambhu,* beauteous with the chámara-like crescent moon kissing his lofty head; the original foundation-pillar of the city of the three worlds. Obeisance to *Ganes'a,* on the drops of moisture exuding from whose temples the bees delight to cluster. Supreme is the original Boar, by whom uplifted the earth with its growing crops appears as if still horripilated with joy. May the glory in the form of *Harihara,* the creator of the world, ever grant prosperity, who boasts in the rivalry of the joint wives Párvati and Lakshmi, who presents the appearance of the rain-cloud associated with the cloud of autumn, the supreme cause of the creation and destruction of the world.

Ever active in the world is the mighty *Yádava* race, an ornament to the earth, an abode of great minds, beautiful, the birth-place of good qualities. As the bright spring causing the flowers to bloom adorns all the other seasons, so did the king named *Sangama* adorn that race with his high qualities. The streams of moisture issuing from the temples of the herds of his lusty elephants caused all other streams to appear like the river of Yama.

The kings *Harihara* and *Bukka* protected the earth as if Bala Ráma and Krishna had again united for its preservation. *Harihara,* the elder brother of Bukka, having subdued by his might all hostile kings, ruled over the earth, all kings in which desiring his service continually wore his commands like garlands around their necks. Afterwards his younger brother *Bukka Ráya,* celebrated in the world, governed the city named *Vijaya* in the same manner as Krishna ruled the beautiful city of Dváraka.

. . . .

From that *Bukka Ráya* was born the glorious *Harihara,* as the splendid moon arose from the milk sea. In that same city did *Harihara* dwell, as in former times Ráma dwelt in the midst of the city of Ayodhya. Its rampart was *Hemakúṭa,* its moat the auspicious *Tungabhadra,* its guardian the world-protector *Virupáksha,* its ruler the great king of kings *Harihara.* The golden zone of the land *Kánchi,* the incomparable *S'ákhapura,* words fail to give a description of these.

---

* Or Garuḍa.

Harihara, the successor of *Bukka Ráya*, at the time of obtaining the government also obtained a minister, *Mudda Daṇḍádhipa*, who by his policy alone daily overthrew the might of hostile kings, resembling Sumantra the minister of the heroic Rama. (*Much illegible.*) Whose sword was a creeper through fear of whose falling upon them the wisest of kings were continually in a tremble, the rivulets springing from the water poured forth by him in making his gifts united into a great river and converted an unirrigated into an irrigated land.

This *Mudda Daṇḍesha*, a kalpa vriksha to his supplicants, forming an agrahára by the name of *Mudda Daṇḍanáyaka-pura*, at *Kottúru*, near *Uchchangi durga*, and making a large tank :—In the S'aka year reckoned as *s'as'i, kha, s'ikhi, chandra*, (1301), the year Siddhárti, the month Kártika, the 12th day of the moon's increase, Monday, at the auspicious time of Hari-pada ; making 36 vrittis for Brahmans, presented to the god Harihara 12, and to the Brahmans 24. Thus were all given.

That all may clearly understand, the boundaries of the land are here written in the Karṇáṭaka language. North-west, the white stone of Tugilappa at the boundary of Muduhadade Bisalahalli ; thence east, the black stone of the Beddana-doddi of Kindadaratti ; thence east, the Doneya-kola ; thence east, the white stone at the three rocks below the Basaru-kaṭṭe ; thence south . .

(*A great part of the inscription knocked off here, in which apparently the boundaries were continued, and the names of the Brahmans entitled to the land, with their gotra and sútra, given.*)

Merit is a common bridge for kings. This from age to age deserves your support, O kings of the earth. Thus does Rámachandra from age to age beseech the kings who come after him. Whoso usurps a gift made by himself or by another shall assuredly be born a worm in ordure for sixty thousand years. Land presented to Brahmans is to kings as an only sister, neither may she be enjoyed nor ravished away, (otherwise, nor subjected to taxation.) Of making a gift or maintaining one made by another, the maintaining another's is the best. He who makes a gift obtains svarga, but he who perpetuates one obtains final beatitude.

May this gift of *Mudda Daṇḍesha* continue without disturbance as long as sun and moon endure. Great prosperity! Fortune, fortune!

S'ri Harihara Ráya's approval ;

S'ri Virupáksha.

From the whole of this agrahára created by Harihara Deva one vritti was given to *Bhaktadara Bhaṭṭa*, a celebrated Vásishṭa, which, added to the 36 given before, made 37.

The agrahára holders' approval:

S'ri Harihara.

Aruna the carpenter engraved this great s'ilá s'ásana for the god Harihara and the worthy Brahmans of *Danḍanátha-pura* named after the minister *Mudda*. Fortune, fortune!

---

30. S'ila S'asana at Harihara, date about A. D. 1157.

Size ft. 7 × ft. 2 6'.—Haḷe Kannaḍa Characters.

Nandi. LINGA Cow suckling calf.

A glory there is in the form of *Harihara*, in colour like a blue waterlily, eternal, causing the roots of the kandali tree the joy of its worshippers to spread. May *Harihara*, beloved by Lakshmi and Párvati, of a splendour uniting both light and shade, lord of the earth, a beloved jewel to svarga, having Garuḍa and Vrishabha as his vehicles, of a brilliant form, grant to *Soma Bhúpati* lasting prosperity and long life.

. . . . . .

. . were the *Chalukya* emperors. In succession to whom,* destroying a certain son of a rákshasa (*dana suta*) who with enmity had carried off . . . *Taila*, born as a lord of justice, in valour Vikrama himself, subdued the dominions ruled by the *Ráshṭra kúṭa* kings, and restored the *Chalukya* race.

Afterwards his son *Satyás'raya* ruled the world. And after him *Vikramánka* his younger brother's son ruled the world. After whom, his younger brother, with a fame as splendid as the light of the moon, the able *Appaya* ruled the earth surrounded with the seven oceans. *Jaya Simha* then ruled the lady Earth, whose breasts are the swelling mountains, the leafy *honge* trees her tresses, engirdled by the sea as with a zone.

Afterwards when *Ahava Malla*, a crowning ornament of kings, accomplishing what even Brahma had not done, ruled the world, the regents at the points of the compass forgot their cares and were at ease. His son, who caused the hearts of his enemies to burn, superior to all kings, ... *Soma Deva* obtained renown. His younger

---

* *Atikramanadóḷ*.

brother *Vikrama*, tying up the mouth of Nepála, and shewing the might of his arms by conquest of many other kings, ruled over the whole circle of the earth. His son, distinguished in all learning, having made the tour of victory, a Manmatha to women, praised throughout the world, *Bhúloka Malla*, gained renown. His son, *Jagadeka Malla* then governed the earth. Destroying the *Pallava* and *Málava* kings, he ruled over the *Pallava* kingdom, from which he had driven the king; lord was he over the *Láṭa* kingdom, the king of which stood with folded hands placed to his forehead; the *Kalinga* king and land he reduced to the greatest straits, and by his great might subduing many kings he gained great fame. His younger brother was *Núrmaḍi Tailapa*, shining with a sword which was solely engaged in smiting through the groups of his enemies, of a fame as pure as the moon.

At that time *was *Bijjala* king, who shone with a sword which destroyed all the enemies of the earth, able in subduing the mightiest enemies, excellent in victory . . . . The whole of the *Chalukya* army did he protect, devoted to the service of the feet of the *Chalukyas*, adorned with the gems of good qualities, obtaining the name of *Sadáya Náyaka* (the bountiful chief).

At that time, while the abode of good qualities *Kasavaya Náyaka*† was ruling the *Banavasi* Twelve Thousand, punishing the evil and protecting the good:‡—An asylum of peace was that *Vanavási*, the native land of wealth, the stall in which prosperity was tied, the cradle of virtue, the birth-place of the learned, the region free from fear. The people in all parts of that nád on every side shone with the colour of gold, all the points of the compass were filled with perfume, the gardens were filled with trees, the land was full of running streams and ponds, in which appeared lotuses and waterlilies with swans between. And the land was full of pleasure gardens . . . . And it shone with the brightness and beauty of women's faces . .

And in that nád was the *Nágara khanḍa kampana*, in which was no garden that was not surrounded with amorous bees clustering on the lotuses in the ponds, no ponds in which the lotus did not grow, no town around which cool streams did not flow. And ever was it bright with groves of punnága trees, of nága and champaka trees, and of the nága creeper. Thus was the

* *Tat káladoḷ.*

† *See Nos. 33 and 43.*

‡ *Dushṭa nigraha s'ishṭánugraha púrvakam.*

Nágara khaṇḍa a splendid setting for gems of beauty. Containing numerous sandal trees filled with most fragrant oil, it enraptured the minds of all like the young new moon.

Ruler of the *manneya* of this beautiful Nágara Khaṇḍa Seventy,* a moon to the waterlilies the faces of women, famous in the earth was *Soma nripála*, who by his supremely excellent government converted this Kali yuga into the Krita yuga, raising the waters of the ocean of pleasure, surrounded by the splendour of his fame even by day he shone with the moon-like radiance of Ramachandra. The pure race from which sprang a portion of the glory of the master of that maṇḍala, the jewel of the region, was as follows :—

As if Rudra had himself become incarnate under the excellent *kadamba* tree, so was born the king *Mayúra Varmma*, the disperser of his enemies, reverenced by crowds of kings. Shining with an eye in his forehead, he assumed the government by his might, as if all the kings had assembled and placed the crown on his head. Increasing under the thick shade of the numerous kadamba trees, that race became (known as) the *Kadamba kula*.

And when many great kings had been born in that fortunate race after *Mayúra Varmma* with the flaming eye in his forehead :—*Barmma Deva* †arose, the sole ruler of the world, the rays of whose fame sported like swans at the ten points of the compass, whose form gave delight to the eyes of all, whose unflinching bravery troubled all the hostile kings, whose Kshatriya qualities overcame all the Kshatriyas, thus did he shine. As no kings are in the world to compare with the king born in the kadamba grove, so gaining great superiority his fame filled all the points of the compass, this *Barmma*. That king's wife, *Kálala Devi*, like the moon in autumn, like a kalpa creeper of the modern Manmatha, praised by all people in the world, an abode of learning, to her dependents a cow of plenty, was greatly celebrated.

Their son was *Boppa Deva*, famed as in great bravery like Arjuna, in liberality like Karna, in purity like Bhishma . . . . .
Can the sea compare with him as a treasury of good qualities, can a mountain compare with him in grandeur, or Hari in valour, or the moon shining at night in splendour, or Manmatha in beauty of form ? Far was he above these, *Boppa Deva*. His wife was *Siri Devi*, a kalpa creeper to her dependents, a jasmin creeper to the bees the eyes of her husband, a bhúta creeper to the kógile the learned, ...

* *Antu sogayisuva Nágara khaṇḍav eppatara manneyakk adhipatiyam.*

† See No. 10.

To these two, as to Hara and Párvati was born Kumára, to Náráyana and Siri Manmatha, to Indra and Indráni Jayanta, so, lord of a pure fame, was born *Soyi Deva*, praised by all the world. His son was *Soma* . . . . . .

(The rest of the inscription is knocked off. Apparently records a gift to Harihara by the last named Soma.)

---

31. S'ila S'asana at Harihara, date about A. D. 1180.

Size ft. 6 10′ × ft. 3 5′.—Haḷe Kannaḍa Characters.

Nandi.	Harihara with Garuda * in a temple.	Cow suckling calf.

(The inscription is so much defaced, a great part being knocked off, that no more than the following can be connectedly made out.)

While the mighty *Kalachurya* emperor *Nissanka Malla Sankama Deva* was ruling in peace and wisdom in his capital of *Kalyána* :—

The dweller at his lotus feet . . . .

---

32. S'ila S'asana at Harihara, date about A. D. 1165.†

Size ft. 7 9′ × ft. 2.—Haḷe Kannaḍa Characters.

Nandi.	A weapon (?)	Sun.	LINGA.	Moon.	A weapon (?) Cow suckling calf.

May it be well—Obeisance to Vishnu, having the lotus navel, the able, the giver of the boon of happiness to gods and Brahmans, an ocean of power. May the tusk of the original mighty Boar protect you, to which the earth clings as its consort, whose light irradiates Pátála and the earth.

Surrounded by an ocean fearful from its mighty roar, luminous with the rays of glittering gold and clusters of gems, casting up spray which filled the sky and reached to all the points of the compass,—was Jambu-dvípa. In the exact centre of Jambu-dvípa, thus surrounded by an ocean full of jewels, shone the Mandara mountain, whose peaks overturned by the gods were the landmarks of countries, around the summit of which the constellations revolved, the abode of the chief gods. An ornament to the south of the Mandara

---

* Or the donor worshipping.

† From No. 9 it appears that *Vira Páṇḍya* was ruling in 1165; and from No. 35 that *Vijaya Páṇḍya* was ruling in 1167. The present grant seems to belong to the close of Vira Páṇḍya's government.

mountain, was the *Kuntala des'a,* lovely with its beautiful fields, splendid towns, and groves which resembled the tresses (*kuntala*) of the lady Earth.

Of that *Kuntala-des'a* were many *Chalukya* emperors the rulers. In succession to whom (*atikramaṇadol*) :—The world was obtained by *Jagadeka Malla*, who utterly despoiled the wealth of the *Málava* kings, who forced the group of *Pallava* kings to hold the sprout, * the kings of the *Láṭa* country to place their folded palms to their forehead, who increased the troubles of the sign of the *Kalinga* kings, so that all the world praised him as the exhibitor of terrible valour.

At that time, (*tat káladoḷ*) was *Bijjala* king, whose mighty arms were a refuge to the earth, the serpent of whose sharp sword swallowed up the air of the lives of boasting enemies, the bounty lovingly bestowed by whom filled all lands with satisfaction, whose glory filled the ears of the elephants at the points of the compass, thus was he praised by all people.

Devoted to the service of the feet of that king, was *S'ri Víra Páṇḍya Bhúpa*, an ocean to the gems of all good qualities, subduer of trouble from his enemies. His younger brother was *Nigalanka Malla Káma nripala* †, versed in all learning, receiving the submission of many brave hostile kings, devoted to happiness, Harihara and Brahmans. His eldest son was *S'ri Vijaya Páṇḍya*, son of the learned Páṇḍya Ráya, a sun to the group of lotuses the learned, a splitter of the manḍalika with the vajra of Ganḍagiri, brave in war.

While the lords of the *Páṇḍya-manḍala* were ruling the *Noṇambavádi* Thirty-two Thousand with justice, the origin of him of the *Sindha vams'a* who was serving them, was as follows :—

By the union of S'iva and Sindhu was born a son, to whom S'iva himself with affection gave a name *Saiv* . . . . , together with the protection of Indra. Considering that unless nursed with tigress' milk he would not be brave or pure, S'iva with affection created a tigress, and that infant drinking the tigress' milk grew. ‡ Moreover appointing *Málati Devi* to be his assistant in war, § he gave him a second name of *Kshoni Sindha.* On receiving

* A sign of submission. The treatment of each king is described in a play upon the name.

† See No. 41.

‡ *Sindhánvayad avatárav entendoḍe* || *Siva Sindhu sangadind udbhavisidan orbba kumáran átana pesaram Bhavan iṭṭan oldu Sai . . van ivanendar Agári Rája raksha sahitam* || *puliválam kuḍidallade kaliyágam pavitran endu Gauripati tann olavim puliyam nirmmise puliválam kuḍidu beḷedan á s'is'u dhareyoḷu* ||

§ *Sangrámakke sahíyeyágendu besase.*

that, and being directed that *Karahâṭa*, the residence of yogis (*yogi piṭha*), was to be his abode, thither he came, and by the might of his arms speedily slaying the groups of kings there, this king born of the *Sindha* line ruled the country, all the people ever praising him as the mightiest among kings, the bravest, the best, and the most illustrious by birth.

May it be well.—The Mahá Manḍales'vara, entitled to the five great drums, lord of the city of *Karaháṭa*, possessor of all lands through the boon bestowed by *Málati Devi*, to the Lakshmi of victory an earring, conspicuous with a blue flag (*niḷa dhvaja*), a Karna in bestowing gifts, rejoicing in the sound of the *mallali* (a drum), adorned with the gems of good qualities, a sun to *Sindha*, of a victorious arm, of the family of . . *ni Rája* an ornament to the good, having the signet of a tiger (*vyághra mṛiga lánchhana*), donor of gifts of gold, the abode of bravery, to enemies as fearful as Vishnu, an elephant-goad to those bearing the emblems of the . . . the *s'anka* (conch), and the *karagasa* (saw), a wild-fire to the grove his enemies, this *Sindhera Deva*, with his long arms (*niḍu dól*) ruled many lands within the 4,000 of *Sindha* and *Karaháṭa*.

And in his line many more ruled. Among them, an ornament of surpassing valour, possessed of many royal spoils won by the might of his powerful arms from hostile kings, bold as a lion, an Agastya to the ocean of his enemies' forces, thus praised by all people in the world, *Piria Beṭṭarasa* obtained great renown. His wife, a combination of all good qualities, more illustrious than Sita or Párvati, was *Dorabarasi*, famous as if the originator of conjugal affection then first discovered.

By the merit of that husband and wife a son was born to them of surpassing bravery, *Nágarasa*, who ruled the world. To him was born a most fortunate son, *Beṭṭarasa*.

(*Some unintelligible,—praises of Beṭṭarasa.*)

Afterwards in that line, arose *Deva narapála*, glorious with wide-spread fame, chief among the number, of great bravery in defence, ever increasing in policy, reverencing the worthy, promoter of bravery, glorious in fame, splendid as the sun of exalted fortune, of great valour.

(*Some illegible, referring to the same.*)

Like the milk sea from which sprung Lakshmi, or as S'iva unites with Parvati as his other half, so did he with the Lakshmi of prosperity; as mount Meru is a refuge to the gods, so was he a refuge to the learned; as Vishnu for lofty valour, as the sun among the stars, so was he a sun among the virtuous, a sea of modesty (*vinaya*), a mighty one in the world, of exalted merit was *Deva narapála*.

To this prince (*kumára*), who was as a moon to the ocean of the *Sindha* race, *Beṭṭala Devi* was the chief queen (*agra mahishi*), in beauty, grace and conjugal affection, superior to Rati, Parvati and Arundhati, the mistress of his house. All the world praised her as in descent, in strength, in stature, in grace, in good fortune, in resolution, in the charms of beauty, in wealth, in disposition, in affection, a jewel of women, in devotion to her husband a Sita.

His younger brother, of virtuous life, delighting in exercise with chariots, able in putting down the boasts of the proud, was *Malli Deva*, of wide-spread fame. His younger brother (a second one), whose renown filled all the world, an abode of all high qualities, bearing great affection to his elder brother, was *Ayvarasa*, like Krishna to Bala Rama, like Bhimasena to Dharma Ráya, like Lakshmana to the world-renowned Rama, possessed of firm faith, virtue and purity, modesty and courage, esteemed as a man of preat purity, he remained with his elder brother. As if liberality had once more opened its eyes, or Karna was again born into the world, so was he esteemed for his gifts, this *Ayvarasa* revered by all.

The eldest son of that Devarasa was *Ráyarasa*, whose fresh glory in his father's kingdom was as follows:—Of great power in protecting with his arms the world, in war terrible as a lion, to courtesans a Manmatha, the king was to him like his minister (!), his enemies, whither had they fled? a prince ever mindful of the learned in order that his fame might never diminish. To this ornament of the *Sindha* line, the loving *Buchala Devi* was the wife, whom all the world praised as akin to virtue, in all graceful charms resembling Parvati, Sarasvati and Lakshmi.

To this husband and wife, as the moon from the milk sea, as the sun from the eastern mountain, as Brahma from the lotus of Vishnu's navel, as an offspring of the Lakshmi of good fortune, was born a son *Is'vara nṛipála*.

(A few verses in praise of him and his sword. The rest of the s'ásana illegible.)

33. S'ila S'asana at Harihara, date about A. D. 1160.

Size ft. 8 4' × ft. 2 11.'—Hale Kannada Characters.

Moon.

Nandi. LINGA. Cow suckling calf.

Obeisance to the divine form of *Harihara*, of surpassing glory, the eternal, the one, he who causes the kadali tree the joy of his worshippers to flourish. May *Harihara-múrti*, uniting in a single form both S'iva and Vishnu, lord of all worlds, exceeding the comprehension even of Harihara the chief priest (*paramárádhya*,) ever establish the desires of his favourite Daṇḍádhipa *Barmmarasa*.

A Brahmani girl (*ilámara putri*) having paid worship to S'iva, seated on a hide, in order to obtain the fulfilment of her desires, she had a dream, in which S'iva himself embraced her and she conceived a portion of his glory. Having thus conceived, when nine months were accomplished, it happened that she bore a son named *Krishna*, possessed of great beauty, of surpassing courage, bearing all the marks of fortune, famous in all learning.

He slew in *Káḷanjara* an evil spirit of a king who was a cannibal and followed the occupation of a barber,* thus obtaining great fame among all people. Placing him between the teeth of Yama, this king *Krishna*, by the might of his arms, took possession of the government of his kingdom, and reducing the nine lakh (country of) *Dahala maṇḍala* to obedience to his word, ruled in peace, an ornament of the *Kalachuri kula*.

And in his line many kings ruled, in succession to whom (*atikramaṇadoḷ*), *Kannama Deva* obtained a name in the world, by his form, his beauty and his skill, the founder of the science of captivating haughty women, the originator of bravery in the subjection of proud enemies, the creator of a fame which resembled the brightness of the moon when it rises in the east. To this illustrious king, like an additional pair of arms, favourites of the Lakshmi of victory, were born two dear sons, *Sanda Rája* and *Bijjala*. The elder of these, *Bijjala Deva*, a treasury of emulation, established himself in that excellent kingdom, and with the point of his sword causing the groups of hostile kings to bow before him, engaged in the task of conquering the world, that he alone might be worthy of estimation.

To that king's younger brother, shining like the four arms of Vishnu, or

* *Udiyisi nápita-karmmadin ad órvva nara-mámsa-bhakshiyam nṛipanam durmadanam samharisi.*

the four tusks of Airavata, were born four famous sons, *Nammugi, S'ankha Varmma*, *Kannara* and the celebrated *Jogama*.

The eldest of these, *Nammugi* . . . . After-wards his younger brother *Virata Jogama* became conspicuous by his policy; those kings who came near to fight him he seized in a grove, those kings who escaped and fled he cast in Yama's face, thus punishing them according to his pleasure, while those who fell at his feet he treated with the utmost respect, thus obtaining the praises of all the world. His son, who when engaging in war with hostile kings was seized with great fury and cast them headlong into an ocean of trouble, who was the promoter of his dependents, whose life put to shame the purity of the life of Manu, how great was he *Permaḍi* Bhúpálaka.

To that king was born, a treasury of valour, *Bijjala Deva* with whom was born benevolence, with whom was born the love for him of the haughtiest women, with whom was born . . . . for the groups of boasting hostile kings, and a time of festival for kings who were his friends. To all the world his powerful arms were a refuge, the serpent of his sharp sword swallowed the air of the lives of boasting enemies, his donations lovingly bestowed filled all lands with gratification, while his glory filled the ears of the elephants at the points of the compass; thus was he praised this *Bijjaḷa Kshonipála*. Some kings who came trembling with fear biting their fingers and letting the betel drop out of their mouths, to beseech that he would not bear them enmity any longer, these ignorant chiefs he guided as with an elephant goad. Save giving such protection, could he protect the elephants, the horses and chariots of those who came to him? When he placed the crown of the kingdom on his head, all the bravest were filled with alarm, and by his might and his rage he soon poured boiling water on the roots of the manḍalika and at last exterminated them altogether, this ornament to the glory of mighty emperors, *Bijjaḷa Kshonipála.*

How with one tongue can I praise the growing greatness of this *Giridurga Malla*, for he so destroyed the might of many kings who came against him with united forces, as if all the elephants and horses in the world could not avail against him. The heads of those kings who opposed him . . . . . . those who thought themselves unconquerable would he leave with life? those who came to overthrow him would he leave without cutting in pieces? . . . . , so mighty was this *Bijjala Deva*. As Agastya born from a pot drank up the ocean, so did this ornament of kings swallow up all the earth.

May it be well—While the victorious kingdom of *S'rimad Bhuja Baḷa Chakravarti Tribhuvana Malla Bijjaṇa Deva*, entitled to the five great drums, great king of kings, lord of the city of *Káḷanjara*, having the flag of a golden bull, with the damaruga, turya and nirghoshana (kinds of drum,) a sun to the lotus of the *Kalachuri* race, invincible hero, a Meru in honour, a light among great warriors, an elephant-goad to the mighty, master of elephants, a cage of adamant to those who sought his protection, in valour a Rávana, a brother to the wives of others, Malla of the S'anivára Siddagiri-durga, valiant as Ráma, a lion to the elephant the hostile kings, *Nissanka Malla*, distinguished by these and other titles ;* was increasing in wealth and prosperity, to endure as long as sun and moon :—

The dweller at his lotus feet was *Kasavaya Náyaka*,† of sincere wisdom in benefiting his master, of a form of beauty like that of Manmatha, liberal as Kámadhenu, distinguished in gratifying the desires of Brahmans, of surpassing ability in destroying the groups of elephants the boasting hostile kings, famous was the land which owned him. Resting with great affection at the two lotus feet of the great king *Bijjaḷa*, the chief of the monarchs of the world, by valuable gifts, by eloquence, by promoting the performance of meritorious vows, he increased his wide-spread fame until it filled all the points of the compass. In discrimination a Rukmánga, a second Dharma Raya, a new Prahláda, in purity of life a Bali, thus was he prasied by all the people in the world.

His nephew (*maiduna*) was *Barmmarasa Danḍanátha*, praised in all lands for every good quality, of great fame and courage. His father was *Munjala Deva*, born in the line of the emperor Sagara, his mother was *Bayila Devi*, famous for her matchless beauty, his father-in-law was *Dobha chamupati*, a treasury in making gifts of horses. Thus pure by descent was this *Barmma*. Beautiful as Manmatha, glorious as Chandra, of great wealth . . .

Having slain without exception the hostile kings, he cared naught for the opposition of *Hoysaḷa*, and meeting him on the battle field drove his wounded forces into the Tungabhadra, whose waters were as red with their blood as if

* *Svasti samadhigata pancha mahás'abda mahárájadhirájam, Kálanjara-pura varádhisvaram, suvarnna vṛisabha dhvajam, ḍamaruka túryya nirghoshana, Kalachuri kula kamala márttanḍam, kadana prachanḍam, mána kanakáchalam, subhaṭaráditya m, kaligal ankus'am, gaja sámanta, s'araṇágata vajra pinjaram, pratápa Lankes'varam, para nári sahodaram, S'anivára Siddhigiri durgga Mallam, chaladanka Rámam, varíbha kanṭhiravam, Nis's'anka Malla námádi pras'asti sahita.*

† See No. 43.

dyed with kunkuma from the bathing place of women, and such they were. On destroying the force, every one exclaimed that he had surpassed Adisesha and was an ornament to the most illustrious, thus exalted was *Barmma Dandanátha's* greatness.

To his king *Bijjaḷa Ráya*, he with devotion gives advice, saying, 'From this fort alone we may subdue the hill forts, the sea forts (or forts with a moat) we may cast into the sea, the fire forts we may consume with the fire of our valour.' How brave was this *Barmmarasa*.

Food to eat, clothes to wear, and many other benefits does he confer on the people. Weapons of war does he bestow and thus subdue all hostile kings. He with his ministers, all of whom were truthful, sincere, mighty of arm and meritorious, was a treasury of favour to his friends, in promoting Brahmanical rites a place of their daily growth. His high descent, his worth in war, his commanding person, his disposition befitting that form, his fortune equal to his disposition, his prudence equal to his fortune, his skill equal to his prudence, all these qualities uniting adorned him.

Among his *karnams* was *S'ridhara Náyaka*, a gyeat warrior, of excellent life, glorious as the sun among the *karnams*. By youth, by generosity, by power of administration, in gratifying the desires of all applicants, *Vengana Náyaka* was famous among the *karnams*.

. . . .

While *Barmmarasa Danḍanáyaka*, surrounded by all these *karnams*, was ruling the *Banavase* Twelve Thousand punishing the evil and protecting the good, one day when the subject of *dharma* and its greatness were the topic of discussion—

(*A few lines follow which appear to be in praise of the town Harihara. The s'ásana then ends and is evidently incomplete*).

34. S'ila S'asana at Harihara, date A. D. 1147.

Size ft. 9 3' × ft. 3 5'.—Haḷe Kannaḍa Characters.

(*The commencement and much of the body of the inscription illegible.*)

To the south of it shone *Bharata varsha*, in the middle of which was the *Kuntaḷa des'a*, shining like the tresses (*kuntala*) of the lady earth. The rulers of that *Kuntaḷa des'a*, matchless in valour, of immense wealth, who, adorned with every good quality, were as bridegrooms to that land, were the *Chalukya* kings. The origin of whose line was as follows :—

From the profound ocean of the navel of Vishnu, the lord of Lakshmi, sprang a lotus, fragrant with delicious perfume; from the ovary of the lotus of that navel came forth Brahma, from the lotus of whose heart sprung the true founder of this race, the highly renowned *Harila*. His son was *Harila*, from the moisture of the palm of whose hand was miraculously born *Sattima Deva*, holding a drawn sword and teeming with all wisdom.*

From that *Satyás'raya Deva* the *Chálukya* line acquired fame. And in that line many kings ruled with power and glory. By their valour acquiring greatness, by their splendour striking terror into the hearts of their foes, for whose greatness no simile can be found, they were lords of the beauty the *Kuntaḷa des'a*.

An ornament of the *Chálukyas*, his breast embraced by the Lakshmi of prosperity, of terrific valour, drinking the blood of his enemies, *Tailapa* ruled the world. Giver of immeasurable wealth, surrounded with obedient kings . . . . . . a conqueror of the world was *Taila*. The son of this *Tailapa* of exalted bravery, was *Sattimanta* Nripála. His son was the able *Vikrama*, whose younger brother was *Sandayya* (?) . . . : . . . . the mighty king *Jaya Simha*. His son was *Ahava Malla* with the designation of king *Trailokya Malla*. His son was *Somesvara*.

His younger brother was a king revered by all, a fire in consuming the hostile kings, whose sword never stayed from slaughter on the field of battle, in possessing whom the earth was blessed with a good king. Celebrated on the shores of the four oceans, with the tongue of the cobra his sword drawing out the life of his enemies' souls, illustrious from his great valour, in the pastime of destroying his enemies on the field of battle enjoying the sports of S'iva, this king *Vikramánka* protected the circle of the earth.

His son, a treasury of all wealth and learning, bearing the distinguished name of *Sarvajna Mahibhrit* (all-knowing king), a moon surrounded by the light of a pure fame, the king *Soma* increased in greatness. This king *Bhúloka Malla* ruled the world, and to him all kings applied the name of *Sarvajna Mahipála* . . . . :

His son, *Permma* Nripa, having uprooted his enemies, a thunderbolt in splitting the mountains his enemies, a protector of the virtuous, ruled the earth. By the pride of his greatness and bounty the equal of Sagara and Bhagiratha,

---

* . . *tan nija kuḷádi bhúta Haritan ati vikhyátam* ‖ *A'tana tanúbhavam Haritam tachchuḷuka jaḷadoḷ abbari yenal utkhátási verasu puṭṭidan átata* . . *pra* . . . . *Sattima Deva.*

how can he be compared to the emperors Manu and Nrigu, say. Of matchless valour and surpassing courage, this *Jagadeka Malla* protected the earth.

To this illustrious *Chalukya* king . . . . . . of great renown was *Víra Pándya Deva.*

All praise of the descent of that *Víra Pándya Deva* is impossible, by him the lunar line became known to all.

From the lotus which sprung from the lotus of Vishnu's navel was born Brahma, from the lotus of whose heart came forth, a joy to all, the excellent rishi Atri. From the dazzling light of his eye was born *Chandra*, adorned with tresses of glorious rays, an ornament to the forehead of Lakshmi. Though really born in three ways, from water, from Brahma's navel, and from the muni's eye, yet is he strangely called Atrijanana.* In this Chandra-vams'a was born *Yadu*, and from him the royal race of *Yádava* is known, of wide-spread glory.

In that line was born . . by whose birth the line was greatly purified. Then *Aditya Deva*, an ornament to all the Yádava race. From his arm sprung *Pándya*, and to that *Pándya Rája* a son named *Chedi Rája* was born.

The kings descended from that Chedi Raja were famous above all for their mighty deeds. That Chedi Rája's son, esteemed as an ornament of the Yádavas, was *Dampala*, whose son was *Víra Pándya.* To Víra Pándya of the Yadava descent, *Dampala* was son . . . . beloved of fortune *Kavela nripála* was born. To that king was born, great as Indra, a great general . . . . . the beloved king *Pándya.* Assuming the government of all the world he gained great fame. . . . . . . with his powerful arms he ruled all the world as Indra rules svarga. His wife was *Sávala Devi*, in exalted qualities the equal of the king. . . . .

Of this husband and wife the eldest son, praised by all the world, of great distinction in policy, of a fame pure as the stream of the Ganges . . deriding the government of Bhoja Raja, of king Vatsa, and of S'ri Vikramáditya who ruled from Himáchala to Setu, saying 'Who was a witness of their greatness?' thus did *S'ri Pándya bhúpálaka* rule.

Instructed in all wisdom by *Madhu Súdana Deva*, and thus possessed of all learning and beloved by all the wise, what comparison could other kings

* A pun on the word, which may mean either *a-tri-janana*, not born in three ways, or *Atri-janana*, born from Atri.

bear to him? His younger brother, distinguished for all learning, having subdued many brave hostile kings, reverencing gods and Brahmans, was *Víra Pándya Deva*.

His younger brother was . . . . His younger brother was *Káma Deva*, of exalted character and great generosity. . . . . The son of the learned Pándya Deva, a sun to the group of lotuses, the learned, a thunderbolt to the mountain of the neighbouring kings was *Tailapa*.

A crown of great ministers born in an imperial line, excellent in all the world, thus shone . . . Dandanátha. *Ganga Devi*, the daughter of that lord, by her distinguished qualities and pride of beauty becoming the queen of *Víra Pándya Deva*, obtained the name of *Maha Devi*. Seeing this, S'ankhara (S'iva), Indra and Upendra (Vishnu) of their own will bestowed on her the boon to take the place of *Piri Arasi*, and from the lady *Ganga* was born *Trinetra*, worthy of praise from all the learned, in order to destroy *Ugra Shonita asura*. And the eyes of *Vijaya Devi* were as the petals of the open lotus, her commands like those of Vikramáditya, to Víra Pándya she was lik his own arms, to the learned a kalpa vine, thus was she celebrated. On account of the great love of *Vijaya Devi*, may S'ankhara, the lotus of the earth and sky, filling the moon and all worlds, having fire, sun and moon as his three bright eyes, beautiful as the moon, wearing the moon in his crest, now grant her desires.

Among the kings of the earth *S'ri Víra Pándya Deva* being the chief, the most liberal, the greatest destroyer of the forces of hostile kings, he obtained the name of *Jagadeka Malla vallabha*. The mighty kings of *Ganga*, *Kalinga*, *Vanga*, *Maru*, *Ghurjara*, *Kerala*, *Chera*, *Chola*, *Gauda*, *Anga*, *Varáta*, *Láta*, *Khasa*, *Barbbara*, *Kosala*, *Pundra*, *Párasi*, *Kongana*, *Koga*, *Konkana*, *Kuru*, *Drupada*, *Andhra*, *Turushka*, and *Magadha* he causes to weep, so greatly do all people praise this *Pándya bhúpaja*.

(*Very much illegible, apparently in praise of the same.*)

May it be well.—*Víra Pándya Deva*, entitled to the five great drums, Mahá Mandales'vara, ornament of great warriors, sun to the lotus of the *Pándya* race, a wild fire to hostile kings, who plucked off the crown of *Paundra* on the battle field . . . a bee at the lotus feet of the assembly of gods, of mature wisdom, worshipper of the feet of the god S'ankara Náráyana, ... ruling the *Nonambavádi* Thirty-two Thousand and several other countries .

. . . in the 10th year of the emperor *Jagadeka Malla*, the year Prabhava, the month Ashvija, new moon day, Sunday . . . . . worshipping with devotion the feet of S'iva . . . for decorating with sandal and vermilion the god *S'ankara Náráyana* . . . .

(*Rest illegible.*)

35. S'ila S'asana at Harihara, date A. D. 1167.

Size ft. 11 × ft. 2 6'.—Haḷe Kannaḍa Characters.

Nandi. Sun. LINGA. Moon. Cow suckling calf.

(*The inscription is almost entirely illegible. The following has been made out.*)

Vijaya Pándya Deva, the sun to the lotus of the *Pándya kula*; ruling the *Noṇambavádi* Thirty-two Thousand and other countries . . . In the year 1089, the year Shubhakrit, the month Pushya, the 12th day of the moon's increase, Monday, the nakshatra being Rohini . . . for the service of *Harihara*, and the illuminations at the three seasons . . . . . for the Brahmans of *Kúḍalúru* who repeat the veda . . .

(*Bestows an agrahara, from which 300 pagodas are assigned to Harihara and the rest to the Brahmans.*)

36. S'ila S'asana at Harihara, date about A. D. 1166.

Size ft. 4 × ft. 0 9'.—Characters Devanagari at first, then Haḷe Kannaḍa.

Linga.

The sun of the lands between the *Tunga* and the *Haridra*. . . *S'ri Vijaya Pándya* . . being lord of the *Harihara kshetra* :—

It being stated in the *Skánda Purána* that by bathing, making gifts, or fasting in this spot, the four objects of human desire * will be obtained ten millionfold,—this was erected by *S'ri Vembarasu*.

* These are *káma, artha, dharma* and *moksha*; or pleasure, wealth, religious merit, and final beatitude.

37. S'ila S'asana at Balagami, date A. D. 1215.

Size ft. 4 2' × ft. 2 1'.—Haḷe Kannaḍa Characters.

Cow suckling calf. LINGA with Priest. Moon. Nandi.

Adored be *S'ambhu*, beauteous with the chámara-like crescent moon kissing his lofty head; the original foundation-pillar of the city of the three worlds. This S'iva do I praise, who dwells in the mountains united with Párvati, destroyer of the world, wearing the moon as his crest.

May it be well. The glory of *Simhana Deva*, protector of all lands, favourite of earth and fortune, great king of kings, supreme ruler, first of monarchs, lord of *Dvárávati-pura*, a sun in causing to unfold the lotus bud of the *Yádava* race,* a goad to the elephant *Gurjara*, the pairer (?) with the *Málava* woman, the plucker up by the root of the lotus the *Tellunga Ráya's* head, a Rudra to the group of hostile kings, Ráya Náráyaṇa—was as follows :—A piercing light in dispersing the darkness the forces of the *Karṇáṭaka* kings, a lion in destroying the herd of bellowing elephants the kings of *Málava*, an Agastya to the roaring ocean the mighty forces of *Taila*, a head ornament to all kings, victorious over all, is this king *Simhana*.

The dweller at his lotus feet, the mahá pradhána, the sarvádhikári, of great benevolence, was *Hemmaya Náyaka* whose greatness was as follows :—

Making known to *Simhana nripála* all his intentions, he so discharged his duties that the king was not disturbed in his enjoyments

. . a master to all the families, bestower of residence for traders, a chief giving joy to all. And the greatness of the mahá pradhaná's wife was as follows ;— in brightness and amiability the equal of Arundhati and Lakshmi, how shall I compare others with her?

This husband and wife, in the enjoyment of pleasant discourse, having come to *Balligáve*, where was the chief of the gods, the self-born, Dakshina Kedáres'vara, whose glory was as follows :—chief among Brahma, Vishnu and all the gods . . praised by the vedas, in the form of the siddhánta of the upanishads. There all are worshippers of the god Virupáksha, and there is the *Káli maṭha* where *Váma S'akti* resided and *Upamanyu* performed great penance.

Beholding with delight the happiness of the god, and the perfection of *Váma S'akti* the disciple of S'ri Ráya S'rikanṭha Deva ;—in order to provide for the daily illumination of the god *Kedáres'vara*, for sandal, incense, lights,

* S e note, p. 46.

oblations, betel and nut, vessels, distribution of food, a brass throne at S'ivarátri, and a car at the five seasons :—* in the year 1137, the year Yuva, the month Bhádrapada, new moon day, Thursday, . . *Hemmaya Náyaka*, manager of the *sunka* (customs) of *Banavase Nád*, washing the feet of Váma S'akti Deva the áchári of the place, and pouring water, passed, free of all tolls, 25 bullocks laden with pearls, emeralds, silk and grain, free from *hejjunka*, *manneya*, *méydere*, *vokkalu tere* and *mukhya kirukula sunka*.†

Whoso maintains this gift will obtain the fruit of the high merit of presenting in Varanás'i, Kurukshetra and other holy places, a thousand cows decked with gold to Brahmans versed in the four vedas. Whoso destroys this gift will incur the fate of those who commit the five great sins. Whoso destroy the property of gods or Brahmans will be born as serpents dwelling in the hollows of trees.

Be it the customs officer, or the king, or the minister, if he resume this custom he shall be destroyed.

A man with hand extended towards some figure which has been erased by the photographer.

---

38. S'ila S'asana at Balagami, date A. D. 1093.

Size ft. 4 7′ × ft. 1 11′.—Haḷe Kannaḍa Characters.

Sun. Moon.
Boar dancing. ? Somesvara Pandit. LINGA. Sword. Cow suckling calf.

Adored be *S'ambhu*, beauteous with the chámara-like crescent moon kissing his lofty head; the original foundation-pillar of the city of the three worlds. Supreme is the Boar form of Vishnu, on whose long right tusk the shining earth was supported when he agitated the ocean.

May it be well.—While the victorious kingdom of *Tribhuvana Malla Deva*, protector of all lands, favourite of earth and fortune, great king of kings, supreme ruler, first of monarchs, glory of the *Satás'raya* kula, ornament of the *Chálukyas* ‡—was continually increasing in prosperity, to endure as long as sun, moon, stars and sky :—

May it be well.—Famous in all lands, having acquired 500 heroic monuments, possessed of truth, virtue, good character, morality, and modesty, protectors of the Víra Balanji rights, conspicuous with the flag of the holy hill,

---

* *Nitya-divige gandha . . . dúpa dípa naivédya támbúla pátra paḍi S'ivarátri s'itáḷa gadige pancha parva váhaná káraṇam.*

† *Hejjunka*, heavy customs dues; *manneya*, ? seigniorage; *méydere*, grazing tax; *vokkala tere*, family tax; *mukhya kirukula sunka*, chief miscellaneous customs dues.

‡ See note p. 14.

. . . birthplace of fortune, enriched with 32 worthy abodes (?) 18 towns, 64 *yoga piṭha* and 64 *ghaṭika sthána*, chief lords of *Ayyávole-pura*, cages of adamant to those who seek their protection, giving largely and forgetting, ... to strange women as brothers, to their dependents as kalpa vrikshas; having these and all other titles, * the Paṭṭana Swámis of the great royal city Balligráme, *Hanumanta Seṭṭi, Padma Seṭṭi, Mebi Seṭṭi, Sovore Biddimaya, Nandaswami S'ankaraya, Senabrinda S'ankaraya,* . . . . Manigára *Nága Seṭṭi*, together with all the *Nagarthas*, the *mummuri daṇḍa*, *Mundara Bala Deva Seṭṭi, Mohari Koṭe Bidiyanna, Pattakeri Kála Seṭṭi*, having assembled together all the people of the land, the 40 . . . , the 60 chief men (*kottale*), and others the proprietors of the town:—

Famous in all the world for his great power, a peak to the triple chain of mountains, an ornament to his line, was *Kedára S'akti muni*. The chief disciple of that great rishi was *S'rikanṭha Paṇḍita*, like the vajra weapon able to execute every undertaking, shining with universal knowledge. That muni's disciple, perfect in *yama*, *niyama*, *svádhyáya*, *pranáyáma*, *pratyahára*, *dhyána*, *dhárana*, *mauna*, *anushṭhána*, *japa*, and *samádhi*, † distinguished for his attainments in *siddhánta*, *tarka*, *vyákaraṇa*, *kávya*, *náṭaka*, *bharata*, and all the branches of *sáhiṭya*, ‡ the áchári of *Nakharesvara Deva* of the *Távaragere* on the south, was *Somes'vara Paṇḍita*.

In the 19th year of the Chalukya Vikrama era, the year S'rimukha, the month Phalguna, new moon day, Sunday, during the sun's eclipse; washing his feet and pouring water, they gave for the decoration and service of the god, for repairs of the temple, and for feeding the disciples and rishis, § one shop

---

* *Svasti samasta bhuvana vikhyáta pancha sata vira s'ásana labdháneka gaṇa gaṇáḷankṛita satya s'ádáchára cháru cháritra naya vinaya Vira Balanji dharmma pratipálana vis'udda guḍḍa dhvaja virájitánúna khanḍadivyila bhadrodbhava dve trimsad oláyavamam ashṭa das'a paṭṭaṇamam chaushashṭi yoga piṭhamam aṛuvatta nálku ghaṭika sthánamum Ayyavole pura parames'vararum, s'araṇágata vajra panjararum, piridittu maṛevarum, maṛege chalekávarum para nári sahodararum, ásrita jana kalpa vriksharum námádi samasta pras'asti sahitam.* (Cf. No. 56.) These were apparently what are now called Linga Banajigas, the chief sect among the Lingayets.

† See note p. 16. The additional terms here used are *pránáyáma*, closing one nostril and breathing through the other while reciting the names of the god; *pratyáhára*, abstraction; *dhárana*, restraint; *mauna*, silence.

‡ *Siddhánta*, philosophy; *tarka*, logic; *vyákaraṇa*, grammar: *kávya*, poetry; *náṭaka*, drama; *bharata*, dancing or acting; *sáhitya*, classical knowledge.

§ *Deva ranga bhógakkam khanḍa sphuṭitakkam alliya vidyárthi tapódanar áhára dánakkam.*

with its profits (*madabala teruvangadi,*) for each shop one *pana*, from sellers of betel leaf and areca nut (*támbúligaru*) one *pana*, from oil pressers (*téligaru*) one *pana*, from *jagati bhuvugalu* (those who live by the land) one *pana*, from the cultivators 10 viss, from the 60 *kottali* (? houses of palanquin bearers) 10 viss, the (?) sellers of cloth in the town 10 viss, from *mánya* rights one *pana*, from the trade of the *mummuri danda* one . . . and 50 families . . for the perpetual lamp of the god and the light of the matha from the oil mills.

This gift did all the townspeople united make. Let all, young and old, support this gift.

Whoso protects this gift will obtain all his desires by the merit thereof. Whoso destroys it will incur the guilt of slaying women boys and sanyásis in Kurukshetra and Varanás'i, and will with all his line sink into the deepest hell.

39. S'ila S'asana at Balagami, date A. D. 1180 and 1186.

Size ft. 5 4' × ft. 2 6',—Hale Kannada Characters.

Cow suckling calf. Sun. Linga with Priest. Moon. Nandi.

Om. Obeisance to S'iva.—Adore be *S'ambhu*, beauteous with the chámara-like crescent moon kissing his lofty head; the original foundation-pillar of the city of the three worlds. Adored be *S'ambhu*, with a form of eternal wisdom and fortune, through the fulfilment of his designs the foundation of the Brahma-pillar. Obeisance to the royal guru.

May it be well.—The protector of all lands, favourite of earth and fortune, great king of kings, supreme ruler, first of monarchs, lord of the city of *Kálanjara*, having the flag of a golden bull, possessor of the damaruga, turya and nirghoshana, sun to the lotus of the *Kalachurya* line, fierce in war, in honour Meru, a light among great warriors, an elephant goad to the brave, lord of elephants, a cage of adamant to those who seek his protection, in valour Ravana, to others' wives a brother, Malla of the S'anivára Siddhagiri-durga, brave in war, a lion to the elephants the hostile kings, Nissanka Malla ; having these and other truthful titles,* *S'rimat Bhuja Bala Chakravarti Tribhuvana Malla Bijjana Deva*, thus acquired the permanent dominion of the earth :—

The earth which through the ignorant king Prithu for many ages remained as a cow, that earth having now become the crowned queen of *Bijjana Deva*.

* See note p. 66.

continually rejoices. As a gem shining first in the sea, then on the shore, then in a stone on a mountain, at last became the kaustubha on Vishnu's breast, thus through connection with this mighty king did the earth become worthy of praise.

To describe the glory of the dear son of that king of kings *Bijjaḷa.* The birth of this *Soma* resembled that of the moon (*soma*), the darkness of the crowd of hostile kings was dispersed, the waterlily of the earth's joy opened its petals, while the lotus of the faces of hostile kings' wives shrivelled up; shining with wisdom as the moon among the stars, lord of a fame resembling the light of the moon, thus did he rise from the ocean of *Bijjaṇa mahípála.* Such being his birth, he ruled the whole world under his single umbrella, *Ráya Murári Sovi Deva*; whose younger brother's government was as follows.

At length becoming equal to him (his elder brother), by the performance of rites maintaining a continual festival on the earth, in purity a Bhishma, a new Purukutsa, thus did *Sankama Deva* rule the world. They wrote humble letters offering—*Gauḷa* to send him elephants, *Turushka* horses, the great king of *Simhala* pearls, *Chola* milk-white cloths, *Magadha* musk, the *Malaya* king sandal, *Láḷa* young girls; and his councillors read them to the lord *Sankama Deva Bhúpa.**

Those who in various ways having rid the earth of all enemies, the ministers of that great king of kings and chief emperor, reckoned as mahá pradhána, were—the Piriya Daṇḍanáyaka *Lakshmi Deva,* the officer through whom all the numerous orders were delivered *Chandangi Deva,* the chief officer for the land *Rechanayya Daṇḍanáyaka,* the sarvádhikári *Soranayya Daṇḍanáyaka,* the commander of all the forces *Kavanayya Daṇḍanáyaka.*

Coming with all these ministers to the south for his pleasure, and seeing in *Balligráme,* belonging to the *Banavasi* Twelve Thousand, the temple of Dakshina Kedáresvara, with its three towers, the *lata manṭapa,* the golden pinnacles decked with precious stones, the charitable gifts for learning, for food, and for many good works,—he was convinced that this was truly the southern Kedára, and considering 'Here we must certainly perform some work of merit,' he gazed for a long time with great astonishment at the áchári of that place, the royal guru, and observed the greatness and power he had acquired by penance. In grammar a Pánini pandit, in *níti* a Sri Bhúshanácharya, in *náṭya* and other *bharata s'ástra* Bharata muni, in *kávya* the poet Mágha, in *siddhánta* Naku-

* *Utpala* || *Gauḷa gaja Turushka turagam vara Simhala nátha mauktikam Choḷa suḍámbaram Magadha katturiyum Malayes'a chandanam Láḷana bála kanakiyir aindubarar sale binnapangalam keḷisutirppar ólogidoḷam vilhu Sankama Deva bhúpana* |

lisvara, in worship of Siva's feet a Skanda, such in disposition and attainments, *Váma S'akti yuti* is ever supreme.

To this master of many great qualities, the beloved son of Gautama; the king *Sankama* bearing a sincere attachment: May it be well.—In the 5th year of Sankama Deva, the year Vikári, the month Vaishákha, new moon day, Monday, at the *vrisha sankramana*, and *vyati páta*; in order to provide for the decoration and processions of Kedáresvara Deva, for repairs of the temple, and for food to the Brahmans performing penance; *S'rimat Sankama Deva Chakravarti* pesented *Kiru Balligáve* in the *Jiddulige kampana*, washing the feet of the Rája-guru Váma S'akti Deva, the áchári of that place, and pouring water; to last as long as sun, moon and stars endure.

This gift whoso protects will obtain the merit of a hundred sacrifices. Whoso destroys it will incur the sin of interrupting those hundred sacrifices and of killing Brahmans, and will go to Naraka.

(*Here follows another gift*),

May it be well.—Mahá Manḍales'vara *Tailaha Deva* and Mahá Manḍales'vara *Yeraharasa* coming and seeing this gift, and saying 'This is connected with our family, this is the native place of our guru, here we must perform some work of merit,' the wisdom to perform a work of merit entered them.

To describe their glory:—The cruel enemy who came to war against him he sent to svarga, on him who came as a friend he bestowed wealth, on whom he defeated a good fate . . . . the son of Kála nripa, *Tailapa kshonipála*, daily with pride and affection bestowing on all the object of their wishes. Those kings who fled before him in war have never again even to this day seen the light of the love of their queens, for terrified at the brilliance of the new flashing sword of *Yeraharasa* they have never even to this day returned to their countries.

Thus in many ways the abodes of praise and fame, S'riman Mahá Manḍales'vara *Tailaha Deva* and S'riman Mahá Manḍales'vara *Yeraharasa*, in order to provide for the great services and illumination of Kedáres'vara Deva, in the same *tithi* as before written, washing the feet of the Rája-guru Váma S'akti Deva, and pouring water, presented the *manneya*, *kirukula*, *áya* and *dáya** united, of Kiru Balligave in the Jiddulige nád, in the manner approved by all, to endure as long as sun, moon and stars.

Whoso without fail protects this gift will obtain the merit of presenting in Varanás'i, Kurukshetra and other holy places, a thousand tawny cows and kola-

* *Manneya*, seigniorage; *kirukula*, petty dues; *áya*, fees to village servants; *dáya*, presents.

gas decked with gems, to Brahmans versed in the vedas. Whoso destroys this gift will incur the guilt of killing those cows and Brahmans with his own hand, and go to Naraka. In witness whereof it is said, 'Whoso resumes a gift made by himself or by another will assuredly be born a worm in ordure for sixty thousand years.'

(Here follows another gift).

May it be well.—In the s'aka year 1108, the year Parabhava, the month Vaishakha, the 5th day of the moon's decrease, that *Rája-Guru* approving of the *mantapa* of Kedáres'vara Deva which they had newly built, gave to *Bisadoja*, *Bávoja*, *Singoja*, to these three, in the manner approved by all, *háligúṭada kéyi** *kamma* 150, to the south of the *valagere* of Hálneri in Kiru Balligáve, to endure as long as sun and moon endure.

(Apparently a subsequent addition).

Moreover he gave in the manner approved by all, *Samavolalu* in that Jiduge Seventy, to be enjoyed for three generations.

. . . . this S'iva s'asana.

---

40. S'ila S'asana at Balagami, date A. D. 1102.

Size ft. 5 9′ × ft. 2 10′.—Haḷe Kannaḍa Characters.

Boar. Linga with Priest. Cow suckling calf.

Prosperity.—Adored be *S'ambhu*, beauteous with the chámara-like crescent moon kissing his lofty head; the original foundation-pillar of the city of the three worlds. May *S'iva* the lord of Párvati protect us, worthy of worship from gods and giants, the tide of the ocean of whose heart's joy is raised by the moon the beauty of Párvati.

May it be well.—With a broad chest for the Lakshmi of fortune to rest upon, his feet placed on the heads of crowds of enemies, of a fame extolled by all, was *Vikramáditya nripa.*

Devoted to the service of his feet, having pulled off the powerful arms of brave enemies, worthy of reverence from the learned, an ocean to the gems of good qualities, was *Anantapála chamupa.* Among the friends of his lord the chief friend, among the pure the purest, among the able the ablest, was *Anantapála Danḍádhis'a.* A Yama in destroying the mightiest of his enemies,

---

* These words may mean a pole or measure "belonging to the school," as *pallikúṭa* is a common name for a school in some parts of the country.

a swan to the group of lotuses the learned, how greatly did he extend his fame in the world, *Anantapála*. . . .

May it be well.—While the auspicious *Anantapála Dandanáyaka*,—entitled to the five great drums, lord over great feudatories, a mighty general, the arrow of S'iva to Tripura the cities of his enemies, of great liberality in gifts to dancers, to the naked, to beggars, to singers and to eulogising bards, an abode of the Lakshmi of valour, a lion to his enemies, in prudence a Brahma, adorned with the garland of the jewels of good qualities, the patron of the learned, moonlight to the waterlily the *Láṭa kula*, resting like a bee on the lotuses the feet of S'iva,—having obtained two five hundreds (?), the *Banavase* Twelve Thousand, the *vaḍḍa rávula* and *perjjunka*, was protecting them in the enjoyment of peace and wisdom :—*

The dweller at his lotus feet, his breast filled with the embraces of the breasts of the Lakshmi of fortune, shining with a garland of the gems of good qualities, the giver of joy to the assemblies of the learned, was *Govinda*. Who is the only one able to subdue those who refuse to bow to him? Who but *Govinda*?—Who is he that turns back only from troubling the worthy and trampling on them? Who but *Govinda*?—Who thus acquiring fame has obtained from all people the name of Jiya? Who but *Govinda*?—

Besides him no other did all the people thus praise. Save they cast themselves on his mercy, to all who come against him with forces he assumes the terrible aspect of Ranaranga Bhairava, with a great blazing eye, with fearful serpent earrings, in his lotus hand a piercing trident, on his face shining tusks. His terrible wrath blazing forth in an eye of the fiercest flame, the keen sword in his hand like the terrible trident, his groups of brave warriors the attendants, thus appearing before all the enemies' forces, this Ranaranga Bhairava had the aspect of the Bhairava of the final deluge.

The lightning he takes by force, confronting lusty elephants he breaks their tusks, with his broad chest rushing upon great tigers he swings himself by their whiskers, the bravest who come against him with great shields, in his pride he drinks their blood, not letting it fall to the ground. The two lotus feet of the s'akti dwelling in the creeper of his shining sword he constantly worships with offerings of flowery crowns—the curly frontlets of brave warriors, of brilliant vermilion—their fresh flowing blood, and of lotuses—their fallen heads. The mightiest enemies by the high road formed by his dreadful arms he carries up to heaven, O wonder!

---

* *S'rímad Anantapála Daṇḍanáyakan eraḍ ainúrumam Banavase pannirchchhásiramum vaḍḍa rávuḷamum perjjunkamumam paḍedu sukha sankathá vinódadim pratipálisuttam ire.*

It is not clear what the *vaḍḍa rávuḷa* was: the *perjjunka* is the same as the *kejjunka* of previous inscriptions, and means the large *sunka* or customs dues.

A Yama to titled kings, cutter of the throats of the brave, great punisher of the proud, Mrityu to shouting enemies, valour his ornament, such is *Govinda*, the Ranaranga Bhairava. The Ranaranga Bhairava, chief among those adorned with the gems of good qualities, reverencer of his elder brother, mightiest of great warriors, thus did this *Govinda*, a Vishnu to the rákshasas his enemies, shine forth in the world. In valour, in might, in stature, in ability, without an equal; a great warrior, victor in many wars was *Govinda*, the Ranaranga Bhairava.

To the treasury of wisdom *Kes'i Rája* and *Nílabbe* (his wife) was born, beloved on account of his great fame, a gem of good qualities, *Dási Rája*. This sun to the sky of the *Parásara gotra* being his father, and the mine of all pleasing good qualities, *Somámbike*, his mother, how honourable was *Govinda* in the world. To describe the greatness of his bounty. Question . .

. . . .

Answer—*Kali kálu Karna* (the Karna of the Kali age).

While the auspicious Dandanáyaka *Govindarasa*—adorned with such a cluster of good qualities, patron of the learned, the waterlily of the circle of the earth illuminated by the moonlight of his self-acquired fame, the Ranaranga Bhairava, a kalpa vriksha to good poets, Vatsa Rája to the horses the evil, abode of the Lakshmi of valour, displaying to all the points of the compass the wealth acquired through the favour of *Anantapála*—having obtained the *vaḍḍa rávula*, the two *bilkoḍe* and the *perjjunka** of Milvaḷḷi, was protecting them in the enjoyment of peace and wisdom :—

Chief among those of greatest ability in the world, . .

. . . security for three boons (?),† an ornament to his line, was the celebrated *Kedára S'akti yatipati*. The disciple of that Kedára munindra, praised by all the world, was *S'rikanṭha*, a collection of pure qualities, fame his flag, a cuckoo to the mango grove the learned. His heart on the lotus feet of Hara, in his face the beauty of Bharati, in his life purity, among all the points of the compass he established the fame of the elephant of the west (Indra), the collection of virtues, ornament of great munis, light of the wise, ocean of logic, *S'rikanṭha Deva*.

To describe his disciple the king (*dore*) :—The month of Chaitra to the tree of sound eloquence, a moon to the ocean of the Lokáyata, able among the

---

* *S'rímad Dandanáyaka Govindarasar Milvaḷḷiya vaḍḍa rávuḷamum eraḍum bilkoḍeyum perjjunkamumam paḍedu*. The expression *eraḍum bilkoḍeyum* seems to mean transit dues both ways, *i. e.* on imports and exports ; for the other terms see preceding note.

† *Múvarakoṇeya*.

Sánkhya, a pearl in the necklet on the shell-like throat of the lady Mimámsa, a sun to the lotus the Sugata, chief among the Naiyáyika, thus was he famed, the tárkika *Somes'vara Suri*. Some excel in logic, some in well chosen words, some are skilled in the drama, some know to compose verses and poems, some are clever in grammar, but all these being united in him who can fully comprehend him, such is the fame obtained by this sea of learning.

May it be well.—*S'ri Somanátha Pandita Deva*, perfect in *yama*, *niyama*, *svádhyáya*, *dhyána*, *dhárana*, *mauna*, *anushthána*, *japa*, *samádhi*, and *s'íla*,* favourite of the learned, sun to the lotus grove of *nyáya*, the autumn moon in raising the ocean the *vaiseshika*, a jewelled ornament to the *sánkhya* philosophers, a bee at the lotus feet of gurus, spring to the mango grove the science of grammar, ... the flood of Ganges in pouring forth streams of unequalled eloquence, having a multitude of disciples exalted by the influence of his mantras, a sea to the great river the *sáhitya*, rejoicing in the faith of Parames'vara, chief abode of the purest qualities of penance, having these and other names, the moonlight of whose fame illuminated the circle of the world :—This illustrious muninátha making application to the younger brother of Krishna Rája, whose fame was his wealth,—to the mine of glory *Govinda*, the subjector of numerous enemies :—

May it be well.—While the victorious kingdom of *Tribhuvana Malla*, protector of all lands, favourite of earth and fortune, great king of kings, supreme ruler, first of monarchs, glory of the *Satyás'raya kula*, ornament of the *Chálukyas*,† was continually increasing in prosperity, to endure as long as sun, moon, stars and sky, and he was in his residence at *Kalyána*, ruling the kingdom in peace and wisdom :—‡

In the 27th year of Chalukya Vikrama, the year Chitrabhánu, the month Pushya, the 13th day of the moon's increase, Wednesday, uttaráyana sankránti; washing the feet of Somesvara Pandita Deva, áchári of the temple of Dakshina Kedáresvara Deva at the Távaragere of *Balligáve*, the ornament of the *Banavase* Twelve Thousand, which shone like the tresses of the head of the lady the *Kuntala* country—and pouring water, the auspicious Dandanáyaka *Govindarasa*, to provide for the decorations and illuminations of Kedáres'vara Deva, freed the *perjjunka*, *vaḍḍa rávuḷa* and both *bilkoḍe* on 2 lakhs of areca nut sold in the street of that quarter.§

---

* See note p. 16 and 74. *S'íla* is virtue. † See note p. 14. ‡ See note p. 2.

§ *á vágaradoḷ viḍidelli máṛuvaḍam eraḍu lakkav aḍakege perjjunkamum vaḍḍa rávuḷamum eraḍum bilkoḍeyum sarvva namasyam endu biṭṭar.*

Whoso respects and preserves this gift thus made will obtain the fulfilment of all his desires. Whoso destroys it will incur the great sin of wantonly killing in Ganga, Gaya, Kedára and Kurukshetra, Brahmans, tawny cows, women, boys and recluses, together with his own family. Poison is no poison, the property of the gods that is the real poison. For poison kills a single man, but the property of the gods (if usurped) kills sons and descendants.

The *ás'u kavi* (? improvisatore) *Niṭaláksha* composed this splendid s'ásana with choice of sweetest words, so as to display his ability to all the world. Considering that none was worthy to compare with the lord Malli Deva, he undertook to write it and wrote it. He could, whenever required, by his ability compose modern poetry, but how was he able to compose this ancient poetry, with its innumerable poetical beauties? Auspicious, of finished learning, a Brahma in eloquence, an emperor in establishing principles, *Mallikárjuna Bhaṭṭa* rejoices the hearts of all poets.

---

41. S'ila S'asana at Balagami, date A. D. 1112.

Size ft. 6 5′ × ft. 3.—Haḷe Kannaḍa Characters.

		Sun.		Moon.	
A rod ?	? Somesvara Pandit.*	A vessel.	LINGA with nagabharana.		Cow suckling calf.

The whole surmounted with a scroll.

Supreme is the command of . . . of *Trailokya Chandra*, which bestows upon the faithful benefits of things seen and unseen. Supreme is the command of him who dances bearing the rod of the vedas, who controls *dharma* and all the gods, and bestows happiness on the three worlds. Supreme is the god whose crest is adorned with the moon, whose praise as expressed in the collection of the vedas shines forth from the heart of the lotus-navelled (Vishnu) as if inscribed on a tablet of stone, able in controlling the three worlds, of inestimable glory.

. . . . the eloquent muni named *Somesvara*, who is acquainted with the fate and fortune of all living things—Prosperity!

May it be well.—The full moon of autumn in the sky of the *Chalukya* line, the theme of poets, of a self-acquired fame brilliant as the rays of the moon, his lotus feet placed on the heads of hostile kings, gratifier of the desires of Brahmans, chief of universal emperors (*sárvva bhaumi*), of mighty strength,

---

* Seems to be the same figure as in No. 38.

is *Vikramáditya Deva.* The occupation he provides for his enemies is to give up their titles, to forsake the pleasures of the lands they ruled and to dwell in caves on the mountains, thence on returning again to battle to leave their wives behind and to form alliance with the celestial nymphs.

While having obtained such glory and fame, *S'rimat Tribhuvana Malla Deva*, protector of all lands, favourite of earth and fortune, great king of kings, supreme ruler, first of monarchs, glory of the *Satyás'raya kula*, ornament of the *Chálukyas*,*— his own victorious kingdom continually increasing in prosperity to endure as long as sun, moon, stars and sky; being in his residence at *Kalyána*, in the constant increase of supreme happiness (*parama kalyána*), and protecting the whole circle of the world under his single umbrella—was in the enjoyment of peace and wisdom.†

In former ages great fame had *Chandra* obtained in the world, being named a rája in the veda; but bearing that same title, they being really such and he so but in name, he also having spots and they being spotless, how greatly have they exalted the name, having become the theme of all poets' praise, the worthy among the illustrious *Páṇḍyas*.

And after many sons of kings (*arasu makkalu*) had been born. In the Krita yuga, to the accomplisher of his desires Jamadagni, the husband of Renuki, was born the powerful bearer of the Paras'u (axe), the slayer of the son of Kritavirya, who murdered the guru. And twenty-one times slaying all the kings in the world, he bestowed the circle of the earth upon the Brahmans, and remained among them; but thinking that he should not dwell in the property of the Brahmans, departing, he turned back the sea with the tip of his bow, the universally praised son of Renuki. And that prince saying 'Cannot the western ocean spare me a *kana* of ground?' took the seven *Konkanas* for his residence. Thus was it called the creation of Paras'u Ráma.

And to the lady Konkana, *Haive* was as a *kankana* (bracelet), in which like the beautiful chief gem shone *Sisugali.* The children there born even to enemies through this name acquired courage, for as being considered the seat of learning was this chief city among royal cities called *Sisugali.* ‡

There many *Páṇḍya* kings ruled and governed. Among them was born *Chandra*, whose fame was as moonlight rejoicing the hearts of all people in the world, who rose shining from the sea of this race as Chandra rose from the sea of the veda. Among women the best, worthy of praise from all, was *Kammala Devi*; like the moonlight to her husband Chandra, by her union with him she increased his glory.

* See note p. 14. † See note p. 2. ‡ *i. e. Sisu kali*, instructor of children.

To that husband and wife, as if from Lakshmi and Vishnu, was born a worthy son *Káma*, rejoicing the hearts of the coyest fair ones. And *Bágala Devi*, clever, of high qualities and beauty, praised by all, a gem among king's daughters, became his beloved wife, to this Káma a Rati. And to that Bágala Devi and that great king Káma was born a son of great strength, *Chandra*, of pure fame, surpassing Indra in the splendour of his wealth.

While Kali is surveying the place with the view of establishing his practices there, while the enemy is preparing to display his strength, while the proud boasters are preparing to shout, at the mere sight of his face they are driven away; thus did all people praise this *Chandra narendra*. Reverenced by all women, her fame her wealth, of firm conjugal devotion, was *Sovala Devi*; and as Rohini to the famous Chandra, so was this Rohini the beloved wife of this Chandra. To that Sovala Devi and that king was born a son, devoted to S'iva, of pure fame and great wealth, famous among the brave, *Káma Deva*.

All the people on earth called him Manmatha, the Lakshmi of his valour was to him as Rati, great wars the spring season to him, with him truly abode the power with showers of poisoned arrows to send brave enemies to the society of the celestial nymphs, . . . this was in truth *Káma Deva*.

While like the nose (!) to the face of the lady the *Páṇḍya* line,* seated on the Páṇḍya throne, *Tribhuvana Malla Káma Devarasa*, entitled to the five great drums, the mahá maṇḍales'vara, lord of the city of *Gokarna*,, head jewel of the Páṇḍya race, a garland to brave men, a Bhishma to strange women, a glory to the learned, ruler of the *Konkana* ráshṭra, to liars an impaling trident, a favourite of fame, *Nigalanka Malla* †, his crest adorned with the lotus feet of *S'rimat Tribhuvana Malla*, a root to the kandal tree of valour, having these and other names,—was ruling the kingdom in the enjoyment of peace and wisdom :—

One day in a discourse on S'iva dharmma, the *S'iva dharmmánus'ásana* being quoted, to the effect that,—dharmma is the root of the vine of fame; dharmma is beloved in both worlds; save the man devoted to dharmma there is none worthy of reverence in the world :—and from the divine discourse thereon of *Somes'vara Paṇḍiṭa Deva*, a worshipper of spirit, of great learning; having conceived a desire to perform the works prescribed for S'iva dharmma :—

---

* *Antenisi Páṇḍyánvayávaḷiyemba mániniya mugakke múg irppante Páṇḍya piṭhikeyoḷ irdda.*

† See No. 32.

Tribhuvana Malla having bestowed the government of the Vanavási country on *Anantapála*, protector of the vine the Lakshmi of his fame, a patron of all the learned ; when he, accepting the same, was governing it ; and by his command, the dweller at this lotus feet, *Govinda*,—the Raṇaranga Bhairava, brave as a lion, splendid in valour, of glorious qualities, affectionate to his elder brother, famous in praise, to *Krishna Rája* the little younger brother, without pride carrying out orders as being a great distinction and hence called *Maleya* (humble),—was protecting *Banavase* and the *Malapara júju* (?) also,* with pure shining fame :—

Washing the feet of Mebi Seṭṭi, the son of Bhuvanaika Seṭṭi, the son of Mebi Seṭṭi, called the Paṭṭaṇa sámi, the chief officer (janapam) in the beautiful royal city *Ballipura*, which was an ornament to the four quarters of *Banavase;* making an agreement regarding the gift of the freehold land attached to the lotus garden, and buying 110 *kamma* of excellent land, with pouring of water, and with the knowledge of as many as belonged to that great royal city *Balligáve* (to wit) of the five *maṭha sthána nagara* and of the three *pura* :—

Thereupon, in the presence of the five *maṭhas* of that great royal city *Balligáve*, (namely) of S'ánta S'iva Paṇḍita, áchári of the Piriya Maṭha ; S'akti Paṇḍita, áchári of the Pancha Linga ; Kriya S'akti Paṇḍita, áchári of Tripurántaka ; Múliga Ponneya Jíya ; Nagarada Panneya Barmma Seṭṭi, and others—with the knowledge of all these the five *maṭha sthána nagara* and the three *pura*, he presented that land—situated in the tract belonging to the Távaregere beloved by all the people of the earth, having on the east the garden formerly presented to Kedáres'vara, on the south Ponneya Jiya's garden, on the west a stone he set up, on the west (? north) the garden of Purige Deva,—the land within these boundaries, Daṇḍádhísha *Govinda*, the king of that nád, worthy of praise from all people, gave, with a heart filled with devotion to S'iva.

And at that time, in that manner, the lord of the land settling with Mebi Seṭṭi for freeing it from all imposts, gave a permanent order that the five *maṭha nagara* should continue it free of all dues.—

Moreover, among the Kálamukha, descended in the line of the security for three boons (?),† obtaining fame among those great *S'aktis*, the rainy season to the cháṭaka birds his disciples, was the pure *S'rikanṭha*, praised by all the learned, son of Kedára S'akti, bearing S'rikanṭha (S'iva) ever on his breast,

---

* *Maleyade besakeyva besam maleyad enal pálisuttam ire Banavaseyam Malapara júju sudá. Malapara júju* would mean the games or gambling of the Malaparu. The Hoysaḷa kings had a title *Maleparoḷu gaṇḍa*, champion among the Malepara. See note p. 7 &c. † See note p. 80.

of a s'rikaṇṭha (a holy throat) filled with the choice words of the veda. Deeply versed in the science of mind he was invincible in argument, like pure gold perfumed, placing the feet of S'iva as an ornament on his head, possessed of the secure merit of great penance, self-chosen husband of the lady wealth, adorned with all good qualities, such was *S'rikaṇṭha yogisvara*.

The son of S'rikaṇṭha was *Somes'vara*, reverenced by all the world of yatis, S'rikaṇṭha (S'iva) himself in the form of a muni, a Vishnu to the rákshasa of sin. *Somes'vara Paṇḍita Deva*, thus praised by all people,—perfect in *yama*, *niyama*, *svádhyáya*, *dhyána*, *dhárana*, *mauna*, *anushṭhána*, *japa*, *samádhi*, and *s'íla*; * promoter of the learned, a Brahma to the dhárana, a sun to the lotus of a good race and to poetry, of pleasant speech, master of eloquence, having acquired the greatness of penance,—although angry (*ágraha!*) when requested to accept this gift, (Govinda) having won his favour;

In order to provide for repairs of the temple of the lord of the three worlds, Dakshina Kedáres'vara, situated on the bank of the Távaragere which is on the south of the royal city *Balligáve*, the head of the *Banavása* Twelve Thousand; and for flowers, incense and lights for the god, for the daily worship and various other services, and for the food of the rishis:—in the manner approved by all; in the year reckoned as *giri* and *bhavalochana*, the 37th of Vikrama, the year Nandana, the month Pushya, the 4th day of the moon's increase, Tuesday, the uttaráyana:—this ornament of kings, amid the plaudits of the universe, washing the feet of that great sun of learning praised by all the world, and pouring water, this king of illustrious fame presented it (that land) to endure as long as earth, sun and water continue.

Whoso destroys this gift will incur the guilt of slaying Brahmans, tawny cows and sanyásis in the Ganga and Yamuna and at their confluence with the sea. Whoso protects it will derive the merit of bestowing in those holy places a crore of tawny cows upon Brahmans. Whoso by violence takes away land presented by himself or by another shall assuredly be born a worm in ordure for sixty thousand years. Consider this.

Mallikárjunácharya, a most able poet, disciple of that great sun of learning, wrote this s'ásana of a S'iva dharmma, although newly erected, so as to be praised by all poets.

(? Signature). *Gobbúra* dhárana sárvva bhauma sukavíndra *Mallikárjuna Bhaṭṭa Shanmukham*.

May it endure, this S'iva s'ásana.

* See note p. 16, 74 and 81.

42. S'ila S'asana at Balagami, date A. D. 1129.

Size ft. 9 6′ × ft. 2 10′.—Haḷe Kannaḍa Characters.

Cow suckling a calf, in a mandapa.	Sun. Linga with Priest, in a temple.	Moon. Nandi in a mandapa.

(One line illegible)

Obeisance to S'iva and Párvati, surrounded by their worshippers.

May that *Gautama* grant protection, who by favour of the pure rishi *Vidyábharanárya* having obtained the management of the *Kedára maṭha*, through constantly beholding the amrita of the favour of Kedáres'vara has become like the ancient Gautama.

From the lotus of Vishnu's navel sprung Brahma, the lord of Sarasvati. From Brahma's terrible arms came forth, like emanations of Vishnu, the earliest of the *Chálukya* kings, masters of a dominion surrounded by the sea and protected by their invincible arms.—Among them, bringing to mind the Vishnu who with matchless powers slew on the field of battle the rákshasa that carried away the earth, and thus restored the world—so by his power did *Taila nripa.*

The eldest son of Tailapa Deva was *Sattiga.* His son, lord of fortune, was *Vikrama*; whose younger brother, an axe to the creeper the lands of hostile kings, was *Das'a Varmma.* His son, lord of the lady Earth, *Jaya Simha*, obtaining the land, governed it. His son was the brave *Ahara Malla.* His eldest son, lord of the earth, unequalled wrestler, was *Bhuvanaika Malla.*

Afterwards, of superior fame among those *Chálukya* kings, uniting the qualities of the sixteen (preceding) kings,* praised by all the world, was *Permmáḍi Deva* his younger brother. Not as Hari, who to prevent the continual overthrow of the order of things established by him, assumed the tortoise avatára and unsteadily bore up the earth; this Hari, fearing such an unstable base, more immoveably established his government, and thus ruled all the world without anxiety, *Vikramáditya.* In the ocean of the sword of the *Chalukya* emperor *Vikramáditya* ever dwells the Lakshmi of victory, in order by its ablution to purify the world of the evil which under many kings of the Kali age had accumulated and increased.

The palace of the king was flooded with the streams of the sweat of rutting elephants and of the foam of horses, offerings of the troubled kings to

* *Allim baḷiya tach Chálukya nṛipáḷaroḷ achchari jasimi nṛipange shoḍas'a rájôdyachcharitam enisi.*

secure their safety. The *Málava, Chola, Gauda, Magadha, Anga, Turushka, Kalinga* and *Vanga* kings, trembling and panic stricken, despaired of their kingdoms . . the anger of the *Kuntala* lord.

To *Permmádi Ráya* thus famous, was born,—as from the Rohana mountain all manner of beauty, from the milk sea the moon, from the eastern mountain the sun,—*Soma Mahija*, of wide spread glory, an ornament to the line of kings. Then was fame born to Bhárati, then to the earth was born royalty, then was born sorrow to hostile kings, such was the birth of this exalter of the *Kuntala des'a*. Even in his boyhood he was an unyielding opponent, a head jewel of princes, the gem taken from the forehead of the elephant all good kings, a palace to all the worthy, in eloquence a parrot, able in bending the bow. As soon as he learned to walk all hostile kings began to walk away into the forest, as soon as he began to talk their talk was restricted to hermits.

The sea of *Vikrama chakri's* joy was full, the lotuses the hands of hostile kings withered away, the waterlilies the eyes of the singers opened wide their mouths with laughter, when *Soma vallabha* rose like the sun upon the eastern mountain. The Chalukya king *Soma* with his powerful arms supported all the earth, relieving Adisesha of the continual load of which he was weary, and the tortoise from the perpetual attitude which prevented its turning to behold any object on one side or the other. His broad chest was a spacious palace for the abode of the Lakshmi of fortune, his sword was a jewelled residence for the Lakshmi of valour, the lotus of his face was a dancing stage for the Lakshmi of learning, thus great was this *Bhúloka Malla*.

A moon surrounded by the stars the gems on the crowns of prostrate kings, the moonlight of his pure fame rejoicing the chakora birds the good, such were the praises he received, this *Somes'vara* the Chalukya king. Though the brightness of his rays gratifies all the gods, though a jewel on the head of S'iva rejoicing the waterlily the circle of the earth, can the moon (*soma*) in the sky compare with this *Soma*, who shines not only by night, and who has no spots? The brightness of his terrific sword, at the mere mention of its name, eclipses the glimmering light of the glory of hostile kings.

The *Kuntala des'a* being like the tresses (*kuntala*) of his loved one, *Kánchi* like her glittering zone (*kánchi*), the streams poured forth with his gifts the birth place of the naiads of his palace; he set himself to conquer on every side, till his valour reached to the farthest limit of the points of the compass. Thus did he rule the whole world, *Soma vallabha*. His only anxiety was that he had not yet punished Yama for disrespect in killing even those he had protected, that he had not secured Maha Meru to bestow in gift, that Mainaka and other great mountains continued to shelter the earth (while he was its shelter), such was the sea of anxiety in which was he plunged.

When this king *Somes'vara*, with the intention of making an expedition of victory over the whole world, came to the south, and encamping his forces in the tírtha of *Hulluni*, was in the enjoyment of peace and wisdom,* discussing the question of merit ;—seizing the opportunity,—

Taila, a head jewel to the *Kadamba* race, a central gem in the diadem of rulers, a chintámani to the learned, in firmness a great mountain ; *Taila*, the joy of *Viráṭa-nagari*, lord of *Vanavása-pura*, a pearl necklace to the Lakshmi of victory, beloved by all the kings of his line ; rising and standing, folding the petals of his lotus hands, (said) 'Deva! A petition !

"Among all the countries the famous *Kuntala-des'a* is the best ; in it the *Banaváse-nád* is the best ; and in it, if well considered, *Balligáve*, the mine of virtuous men, the mother of cities,† is essentially the best, whose fame has filled all the world surrounded by the ocean. Like Amarávati it is the abode of the gods (or the wise) ; like the famous and splendid Bhogávati, the abode of bhogis (snakes, or happy people) ; like Alakapura, the abode of Kubera (or wealth) : thus celebrated throughout the sea-encircled earth, what city can compare with this *Balligáve* ?

"To describe the qualities of its citizens (*nagara janangaḷu*) :—Hospitable to strangers, sincere of speech (*eka vákyaru*), the birth place (*tavarmane*) of prudence, the dwelling place of dharma, a theatre for the performance of excellent poets, to prosperity simply an inexhaustible mine, where in the world but among the citizens of the great *Balligáve* will be found worshippers of such pure merit devoted either to Harihara, or to Pankajásana (Brahma), to Jina or to other gods. As by bestowal of perishable articles they can obtain neither this world nor the next, they from time to time stock their shops with the imperishable, the citizens of that famous town. Who among the citizens of the famous Balligáve but as Surapati (Indra) among the gods so is the resort of the learned ; as Indra's elephant shines with moisture, so glitters with wealth ; as the moon is surrounded with light, so beams with wisdom ; as Adiraja supports all the world so is a supporter of the whole earth. And in that city, the *prabhus* of the people are like the tusks to the elephant, like the dreadful canine teeth to the lion, like the great wings to the s'arabha.

* See note p. 2.

† *Paṭṭaṇangaḷa tavarmmane.—Tavar-mane* is a woman's birth place, the home from which she was taken as a bride.

"And there in that city are the five *maṭhas* of Hari, Hara, Kamalásana (Brahma), Vítarága (Jina), and Bauddhálaya, which are like five garlands to the land.* And there are three *puras*, which are like three eyes of Samagra Lakshmi, or like three pearl necklets on the throat of that lady.

"In this Balligáve, the native home of all beauty and all merit, at a short distance from the southern quarters, is a garden of white lotuses. And there, as if all the great merit of the citizens had combined into one abode of S'iva, is the beautiful temple to the god called Nagares'vara. This Dakshina Kedára is the means of the absolution of sin, the very presence of S'iva manifested to all, visibly displaying all the glory of the Krita yuga. Moreover the course of the sacred bathing streams is like that of the holy Ganges at Kedára, and the lofty tower of this S'iva temple pierces the heavens and rises up like the peak of Kedára, and the rishis there performing penance are in austerity equal to the ascetics of Kedára, thus is this a new Kedára, the standing crops of its fertile fields resembling the horripilation arising from the worship of S'ivalinga, its temple the abode of Parames'vara.

"May the god Kedára therein, who, thinking with supreme benevolence upon his faithful worshippers—fearful of the falling mist (*manju*) and unable to make the distant pilgrimage (to Kedára)—frees them from all sins (here); reverenced by all the chief gods, a head-jewel of wealth and glory, the brilliance of the lotus of whose feet dazzles all people, may that god, wearing the crescent moon on his head, protect you. And in that holy temple reigns the lord of the Krita yuga, whose lofty tower proclaims to all that he is the remover of the sins of the Kali yuga, that let their sins be ever so numerous all may here obtain release from the fear of them.

"And to describe those *maṭhas*. A refuge are they for all people; as Purusha simha (Narasimha) was distinguished for the *dána* (smiting) of Hiranya-kas'ipu, so are they distinguished for *dána* (gifts) of *hiranya* and *kas'ipu* (money and food); as Kurukshetra is rendered fruitful by Saraswati (the river), so are they by Saraswati (learning); as the Khachara mountain is surrounded by the *vidyádhara* (inferior deities), so are they by *vidyá dhara* (masters of learning); as the Mandara mountain they are the most excellent in all quarters; as Vásudeva was enchanted by the words of Akrúra, so are they by the sound of *akrúra* (gentle words); as the grove of Bhaváni honoured with *brahmachári* (celibates), so are they honoured with the *brahma chári* (observance of the vedas) as a prudent woman whose beauty is adorned with

* *Hari Hara Kamaḷásana Vitarága Bauddháḷayangaḷ ind entuva sundareg eseva pancha saradant ire pancha maṭhangaḷ esevuv á paṭṭaṇadoḷ* ‖

wisdom ; like the banks of the Godávari in being rendered illustrious by the footsteps and vessels of Gautamárya : such is their glory.

"And the descent of the line of its *gurus* is as follows : In the line of the múvarakoneya (?)*, devoted to the gods, was born on the chain of mountains, *Kedára S'akti Paṇḍita Deva*, of wide-spread fame. And after him was his disciple *S'rikanṭha*, resembling the throat of Saraswati surrounded with a necklace of pearls, a touchstone to the golden ornaments of learning, reverenced by all. That muni's disciple, a great milk sea to learning, his face like the moon (*soma*), was the famous *Somesvarárya*. Afterwards, the friend of that great áchári, the worshipful muni's younger brother, the tapasvi *Vidyábharaṇa*, an ornament of all learning, a jewel to the lady fame, became celebrated. The energy of the thunderbolt in smiting through the great mountain the Bauddhas, the strength of the lion in tearing open the forehead of the elephant the mimámsa, the brightness of the sun in piercing through the darkness the *syád váda*, the summit of the nyáya philosophers, was *Vidyábharana muni*.

. . . .

. . . and saying 'I will protect this Váma S'akti maṭha,' there he now dwells."

When on his thus making application, the king, hearing the greatness of the merit of that maṭha, and the power of the penance of the áchari of that maṭha, was filled with joy so that the hair stood erect over the whole of his body ; and, with his eyes wide opened, his voice resembling the note of the kálamba bird, thinking we must perform in this place some work of merit, inquired what towns are there near here—(he replied,) 'If the Deva has a mind to perform a work of merit, I have already made a gift for the increase of the glory of the Deva's kingdom, let it by pouring of water from the Deva's hands be confirmed to endure as long as sun, moon and stars.' Accepting which proposal, for the repairs of the maṭha, for food to those performing penance, and for gifts for the support of learning in that place ;—

May it be well—In the third year of Chálukya Bhúloka [Malla], the year Kilaka, the month Mágha, new moon day, Thursday, the vyati páta ; sending for Vidyábharaṇa Deva, ...
presented the village of Hakkalu Hálanu, in Tadavaṇaleyumana náḍ, belonging to Jiddulige náḍ, as a *sthala vritti*, to be enjoyed for three generations.

(*Rest illegible*).

---

* See Nos. 40 and 41.

43. S'ila S'asana at Balagami, date A. D. 1161.

Size ft. 8 3′ × ft. 4 3.′—Haḷe Kannaḍa Characters.

Sun. Moon.
Nandi. Brahma in temple. The donor? Linga with Priest in temple. Ganesha. Vishnu in temple. Cow suckling calf.

Om. Obeisance to S'iva. Prosperity.—Adored be *S'ambhu*, beauteous with the chámara-like crescent moon kissing his lofty head; the original foundation-pillar of the city of the three worlds.

May the kalpa vriksha in the form of *S'ri Váma S'akti muni* grant your desires, whose root is the *veda* surrounded by the fibres of the *nyáya*, whose sprouts are the various kinds of *smṛiti* tinged with the ruddy hue of *dharmma*, whose blossoms are the rites of the S'iva faith, whose sap is the meditations of the heart.

May S'iva in the form of the párijáta tree, whose branches are his arms, whose sprouts are his hands, whose blossoms are his gentle smiles, . . waving with tresses down to his feet, entwined by Parvati as by a creeper—daily grant to king *Bijjala* all his desires.

May it be well.—Entitled to the five great drums, Mahá Manḍales'vara, his foot stool irradiated with the brilliance of the jewels in the crowns of great feudatories, lord of the city of *Kálanjara*, having the flag of a golden bull, possessor of the ḍamaruga, turya, and nirghoshana, sun to the lotus of the *Kalachurya* line, fierce in war, in honour a Meru, a light of good warriors, an elephant goad to the mighty, master of elephants, a cage of adamant to those who seek his protection, in courage the lord of Lanka, to others' wives a brother, Malla of the S'anivára Siddagiri-durga, in character like Rama, a lion to the elephant his enemies, *Nissanka Malla*, possessed of these and other titles,* is *S'rimat Bhuja Bala Chakravarti Tribhuvana Malla Bijjala Deva*, whose power and glory are as follows :—

The streams of glory issuing from the dazzling sword in his powerful arms quench the fierce flames of the courage of his enemies, so that this great king *Bijjala* rules the world as its sole monarch, there being no king besides. The black serpent of his mighty sword enters the snake holes—the faces of hostile kings, and drinks up thence the milk—the blood which none else were able to draw out, swallows up the air of the lives of his enemies, terrific with its tongue of consuming flame. The battle field in front of *Bijjala Deva* resembles the rainy season, for the jewels from the crowns of fierce opposing kings

* The titles commence—*Svasti samadhigata pancha mahá s'abda mahá manḍales'vara mahá sámanta makuṭa máṇikya manjari punja ranjita páda píṭha*—and continue as in note p. 66.

lie scattered on all sides like hailstones, the flashing of weapons is like lightning, the blood falling in all parts runs along forming rivulets. Wonderful is the war of this Giridurga Malla, entrails are poured out in rolls, warriors sinking covered with wounds lie side by side with their horses, while headless trunks dance around, and the abandoned female rákshasas assemble and enter the field for a feast of blood. A single word uttered by him is like a s'ásana engraved on the Mandara mountain, to a supplicant he grants all his desires . . . . whomso he fights meets with destruction, whoso seeks his protection he delivers from old age and death. What kings can compare with this Rudra of the battle field, *Bijjala Deva.*

A dweller at the lotus feet of *Bijjala Deva Mahipála,* the birth place of honour and fame, is *Kasavaya Náyaka,** to describe whose qualities :—

Any thing reckoned as mere rubbish (*kasa*), at a single glance of his that moment appeared as shining gold (*kasavara*) to all his friends and in all the houses of those born in his family, thus did his name of *Kasavaya Náyaka* become famous throughout the sea-engirdled world. Laying his heart at the lotus feet of S'iva, distributing the wealth he had justly acquired among the worthy, shewing the fierce might of his arm in the battle field against the enemy, no common lord was he, this jewel in the crown of the people. Such was *Kasavaya* in the circle of the world. Resting like a bee on the lotuses the feet of Hara, surrounded with men famous for every branch of learning, a jewel to all the worthy, an ornament to good warriors, was he a common lord? In governing, in bringing a land into order, and increasing its strength, in benefiting his friends, who can compare with this *Kasavaya Náyaka?*

By the approval and command of that great benefactor, was *Barmmarasa* † ruling the *Banavase* náḍ. To describe the greatness of his qualities :— By his government nourishing as with showers of milk the crops the worthy among the Brahmans, obtaining universal praise as a collection of all wisdom, all folded their hands in reverence to *Barmmarasa* as the bestower of happiness on all his dependents. Those who know nothing of *adhikára* (government) are called *adhikári* (rulers), but who can compare with him as an *adhikári* (benefactor) to the learned? Thus was *Barmma* esteemed as a refuge of all the learned.

At the time when the Lakshmi of the government of that *Barmmarasa* was innocent of adultery (*i. e.* having him alone as lord and master), the officers standing before his face were *Sridhara Náyaka, Achana Náyaka, Chaddi-*

* See Nos. 30 and 33.

† See No. 30.

maya Náyaka, *Malleyanna Náyaka*, and *Tikkamaya Náyaka*; which five karnams were as the five senses (*karnangalu*) of Bijjala Deva. The greatness of their qualities was as follows :— Benevolent to others, powerful as the ocean, in ministerial skill unmatched, bold as lions, able in collecting tribute, superior to all opposition, of great fame, possessed of the sound of mighty drums, strengthened with all manner of self-acquired merit, devoted to the faith of the feet of S'iva, how great were these *karnams?*

Moreover a *ravi* (sun) in causing to unfold the lotus of the face of the lady the great fame of that Barmmarasa, was the great minister *Ravi Deva*, the greatness of whose qualities was as follows :—Why by the rays of his ministerial plans do the wide-open lotus faces of other ministers close up and the petals of their hands fold together, while the water-lilies the bright eyes of the lady his great ministerial influence open? This is a great wonder in all the world.

While all these united, in the enjoyment of peace and wisdom, were one day discoursing on merit,—the place *Dakshina Kedára* was mentioned as a field (*kedára*) the crops standing on which resembled the hair of the body standing erect from the joy of the worship of S'iva linga ; . . . . as the place where many S'iva munis performed penance, of which it yielded the fruit ; whose *anga* were the Rig, Yajus, Sáma, and Atharvana, of which four vedas it was the place of recital ; where commentaries were composed on the Kaumára, Pániniya, S'ákaṭáyana, S'abdánus'ásana and other grammars * ; where commentaries were written on the *nyáya*, *vaiseshika*, *mímámsa*, *sánkhya*, *baudhya* and others the six systems of philosophy ; where glosses were composed on the *Akula siddhánta*, on Pátanjala and other *yoga s'ástras*, on the eighteen puránas and the *dharmma s'ástra*, as well as on all kinds of *kávya* and *náṭaka*; a place for all kinds of *náṭika* (dancing) ; the place where food was freely distributed to *dínaru* (? sufferers), to the destitute, the lame, the blind, the deaf, to story tellers, singers, drummers, genealogists, dancers, and eulogists, to the naked, the wounded, *kshapanaka* (Jain sanyásis), *ekadaṇḍi*, *tridaṇḍi*, *hamsa*, *parama hamsa*, and other beggars from various countries ; the place where suitable medicine was dispensed to various kinds of diseased persons † ; a place of security from fear for all living things.

And while thinking we will perform in the *Koḍeya maṭha* there some work of merit, in order to consecrate our vows, our wealth, and our three times seven generations ;—*Bijjala Mahárája* coming to take possession of the

---

* *Kaumára Páṇiniya S'ákaṭáyana S'abdánus'ásanádi byákaraṇa byákhyána sthánamum.*

† *Nánú nátha rógi jana róga bhaishajya sthánamum.*

southern districts, encamped his army in *Balligáve*: and when in the enjoyment of peace and comfort, at that time, all these united coming before him and seating themselves, entered upon a discourse of merit. In which discourse *Kasavaya Náyaka*, rising and standing with his face towards the great king, folding his lotus hands, said, "Deva! a petition," and spoke as follows :—

"This Dakshina Kedára is a place for the destruction of sin, the very presence of S'iva openly manifested in the sight of all people, the visible embodiment of all the glory of the Krita yuga. Besides, this Kamaṭha* resembles the primeval tortoise (*kamaṭha*) in being a support to all the world; is like the man-lion's *dána* (smiting) of Hiranyakashipu in its *dána* (gifts) of *hiranya* and *kashipu* (gold and corn); as Kurukshetra is watered by the Saraswati (river) so is it the abode of Saraswati (learning); like the world of gods surrounded by *vidyádhara* (inferior deities) so is it surrounded with *vidyá dhara* (masters of learning); like the Mandara mountain in being superior to all in the world; like Vásudeva was enchanted at hearing the words of Akrúra so is it delightful with the sound of *akrúra* (gentle) words; like the dwelling of Bhaváni in being dignified with the pure life of *brahmachúris*.

"And descended in the line of the gurus of that maṭha is *Váma S'akti munisvaráchárya*, the disciple of Gautamácharya. To describe his glory :—Before the time that this munisvara appeared in that line of gurus, several munisvara gifted with all good qualities illuminated that matha, but this *Váma S'akti muni*, like the ovary of a bud composed of the brilliance of jewels, or like the moon, or the rays of the sun, filled the whole world with light, while all its inhabitants, with reverence folding their hands and doing obeisance, exclaimed *Jiyá!* His face was a stage for Saraswati to dance upon, his mind was a jewelled dwelling for the destroyer of Madana (Siva), celebrated throughout the world is this *Váma S'akti Paṇḍita Deva.* Though in the creepers of the arched eyebrows of the fair Manmatha had placed his sugar-cane bow, in their glancing eyes his flowery arrows, and thus grown very great; yet from fear of the severity of the penance of this *Váma S'akti muni*, he hid his operations, confining them to the thoughts of the mind.†

"Therefore, were the Deva to perform in that matha some work of merit, it will endure as long as sun and moon."

On his saying thus, instantly taking it to mind, *Bijjala mahipála*, to provide for the decorations of the god Dakshina Kedáresvara, for food for the rishis who resort thither, for the support of learning, for repairs to the temple,

---

* Apparently another name for the place, or for some part of it.

† Alluding to Manmatha's (Cupid's) being bodiless.

and for the gratification of the beloved and the worthy,—in the 6th year (? of his reign), the year Vishu, the month Pushya, new moon day, at the time of the sun's eclipse, washing the feet of Váma S'akti Paṇḍita Deva, the disciple of Gautamácharya,—presented, with pouring of water, *Kirugere* in *Nírumbáḍa*, with enjoyment for three generations.

Whoso protects this gift will derive the merit of presenting in Váranási and Kurukshetra a thousand tawny cows, and kolagas decked with gold and gems, to Brahmans versed in the four vedas. Merit is a common bridge for kings: this from age to age deserves your support, O kings of the earth. Thus does Rámachandra beseech the kings who come after him. Sagara and many kings have enjoyed the world. According to their (gifts of) land so was their reward. Those who alienate the property of gods or Brahmans will be born as black serpents inhabiting the hollows of trees in the forests of the Vindhya mountains. Poison is no poison, the property of the gods that is the real poison. For poison kills a single man, but the property of the gods (if usurped) kills sons and descendants. Whoso usurps a gift made by himself or by another shall assuredly be born a worm in ordure for sixty thousand years.

(Further gifts, apparently inscribed afterwards.)

Ayiranya, in the . . *kampana*, of the Páṇḍya Rájya, *Konya Neralagere* in the *Kálaḍi* nineteen, *Siddiyanurudivi* in *Sattalige kampana*, (who ?) gave, with pouring of water, to be enjoyed for one life. Also *Changaru Mattihalli* in *Basulu kampana*, *Chavalli* in *Nagara khanda*, washing the feet of the royal guru Váma S'akti Deva, to be enjoyed for three lives.

Moreover *Bandanike Soyi Devarasa*, *Chanḍugi Deva*, and *Káma Deva Dannáyaka*, making application in a discourse,—for the service of the god Kedáresvara of the Koḍi maṭha, and the service of the god Somanátha, and the service of the god Brahmesvara of Byalur, gave in the manner approved by all, . . . *Muriganhalli* and *Kundangi* in the *Nágara khanḍa kampana*, *Chikka Kanigya* in *Hánugalla kampana*, with enjoyment for three generations.

May it be well! Fortune!

44. S'ila S'asana at Balagami, date A. D. 1029.

Size ft. 5 2' × ft. 2 10'.—Hale Kannada Characters.

Sun. Linga with Priest. Moon. Cow suckling calf.

Om. Obeisance to S'iva and Párvati, surrounded with worshippers.

S'ri Gautamácharya, the kalpa vriksha of thy dharma gratifies all desires,—its root the veda, the firm nyáya its fibres, the smriti its branches, the desire of dharma its shoots, the observances of the S'iva doctrine its blossoms, the thoughts of the mind its sap.

From the lotus navel of the lord of Párvati sprung Brahma; from his arms came forth several kings who became famous under the name of *S'ántaresvara.* Mines of the quality of *s'ántama* (the highest good fortune), of great *s'ánta* (patience), victors over all their enemies by the great might of their arms, released from the fear and desire of family, they obtained in the world the name of *S'ántara.*

Among them, able in protecting the feudatory kings, a king named *Kamana*, became famous in the world. His brother (*sahajáta*), of great power in the world, famous in the group of the chief kings of the earth, had the name of *Singi Deva.* The son of that famous king, a spear to the head of all hostile kings, a treasury of fortune to his dependent kings, in valour immovable as a great mountain, was *Taila.* The son of that king Taila was *S'ri Káma Bhúpála*, lover of Rati the Lakshmi of the great wealth of the *S'antara maṇḍalesvara*, a Manmatha in attacking the mightiest kings, punisher of all the world in afflicting the inhabitants with the showers of his cruel arrows, thus did he obtain fame. That king's wife was *Bijjaḷa Devi*, esteemed as herself the Sita praised by all the world, in conjugal affection having reached the acme of perfection as the purest in all the world.

To these two was born, great in immortal wealth, as if sprung from the union of *níti* and *viveka*, the *S'ántara* king named *Jagadeva.* To describe his qualities:—The autumn moon to the milk sea of Jina dharma, garlanded with the pearl necklace composed of the large (elephant) pearls the shining good words of the most learned, possessor of the lofty palace formed of the rays of the moonlight of his fame which shot up to all the points of the compass, grateful to the eyes of all people, was *Jagaddeva Bhúpa.* His good disposition was seconded by his arm; and the wealth acquired by the learned dependent on him was an assistant to the glory of the might of his arm; the amount of jewelry set with gems which the wives of hostile kings cast off from their arms and ears, who shall tell it to the king ?—this *Jagadeva Bhúpala.* The company of the women in the palaces of kings not friendly to *S'ri Jagaddeva Bhúpála,* had their hair bunched up unadorned with the weight of chaplets of flowers, their bare waists glittered not with the brilliance of golden zones, the twin globes their swelling breasts were not confined with bands of shining pearls.

To *Battila Daivi,* born at the same time as that Jagadevarasa's mother Bijjala Devi, and to *Vijayáditya Deva,** was born *Jaya Kes'i,* a pure Kshatriya son, considered as the elder brother of that Jagaddeva.—To describe the royal qualities and disposition of that great king :—By the might of his arms forcing to fall at his feet all the hostile kings who refused to do him obeisance, lord of the Lakshmi of the great wealth of the seven *Konkanas,* this *Jaya Kes'i Bhúpaja,* by the exercise of the policy of great kings, obtained the fame that there was no king more mighty than him. There was no beggar who did not receive his charity, there were no ambitious ones who attempted to govern as kings and lived; when he went forth to war there was no country into which his arrows did not fall ; such was *Jaya Kes'i,* his elder brother, whose fame filled all points of the compass. Who then was so great as *Jagadeva ?*

The younger brother of that Jagadeva, who obtained fame as a head-jewel of kings, a kalpa vriksha in the world to the learned, was *Singi Deva.* Seizing immense poisonous serpents by the throat, he forced them to discharge their poison, saying, 'Spit it out, spit it out'—then tearing open their venomous throats, and scratching through their hoods, he snatched out thence the fresh-formed jewels, saying 'I will add them as shining ornaments to my elder brother's armlet.'—Who then in the world can fully describe the valour of that *Singi Deva?*

Thus to fame and wealth a supreme lord, the beloved younger brother of Jaya Kes'i, the beloved elder brother of Singi Deva, entitled to the five great drums, Mahá Maṇḍales'vara, lord of *paṭṭi Pombuchcha-pura,* the obtainer of a boon from Padmávati Devi, fragrant as musk, skilled in the níti s'ástra, perfectly accomplished in sáhitya, a snare to the thighs of kings, an impaling post to the titled, *S'rimat Tribhuvana Malla Jagadevarasa,* while in the place called *Setu,* ruling the kingdom in the enjoyment of peace and wisdom :— †

---

* A Kadamba king, see No. 55 and *J. Bo. Br. R. A. S.* IX, 231.

† *Intu kilti s'rigam S'rigam adhináthan enisid á Jaya Kés'i Devange priyánujanu* | *Singi Devange priyágrajanum enisida samadhigata pancha mahá s'abda mahá maṇḍaḷes'varam* | *paṭṭi Pombuchcha pura varádhis'varam* | *Padmávati Devi labdha vara prasádam* | *kastúriká-modam* | *niti s'ástrajnam* | *sáhitya sarbbajnam* | *arasanka gálam* | *birudara s'úḷam* | *S'rimat Tribhuvana Malla Jagadevarasam Setuvina biḍinoḷ sukha sankathá vinódadim rájyam geyyuttam irdd ondu divasam.*

One day, surrounded by skilful wise men and his attendants, discoursing on merit, said thus—' As water though of one substance is worshipped under many names, so God though essentially one is worshipped under many modes of life (? or systems.)* On saying which in that discourse,—A bee at the lotus feet of Hara, protector of the worthy and of his dependents, a *karnam* whose hands were able in subduing the bravest in war, walking according to the rules of the dharma s'ástra, a kalpa vriksha to supplicants, a Yama in swallowing up those who came with force to fight against him, an effectual cage of adamant to those who threw themselves on his protection, ... having acquired a great name by his experience in governing provinces (*nád ádiya rúḍhi*), the able *Bammarasa*,—His lotus hands being folded in obeisance, said,—' A petition'—and spoke as follows :—

' Dakshina Kedára is a place for the absolution of sin, the manifest presence of S'iva surrounded by the most learned, the visible embodiment of the glory of the Krita yuga. If I should describe the qualities of *Gautamárya*, the áchári of that Kedára stkána :—Several munisvara adorned with the highest qualities having like great and brilliant lights illuminated that matha, at last *Gautama muni*, like the blossom of the perpetual light of a jewel lamp, has attained an established fame which enlightens all the world, while all the inhabitants thereof with folded hands exclaim *Jíyá !* Therefore any work of merit there performed will be a permanent means of the absolution of sin.'

Taking that to mind, and coming to *Balligáve* ;—May it be well. In the 13th year of *S'rimat Chalukya Pratápa Chakravarti Jagadeka Malla Deva*, the year S'ukla, the month Kartika, full moon day, Monday, during the eclipse of the moon,—in the presence of the holy feet of the god Dakshina Kedáresvara,—*Jagadevarasa*, united with his son (*kumára*) *Bammarasa*, washing the feet of Gautama Paṇḍita Deva, the disciple of Vádi Vidyábharaṇa Paṇḍita Deva, and pouring water ; gave, in the manner approved by all, for the illuminations of the god, for repairs of the temple, for food to the rishis, and the support of learning, *Kundúru*, situated within the Kodanáḍ 30 in the Sántalige Thousand with enjoyment for three generations.

Moreover he gave on the north-east of the Madumba stream, below the lower bank of the Kabbilaketa tank, 2 mattas of paddy land, in the manner approved by all.

**Ekam eva payas tatvam náná náma nishevitam, tathaikam Devatá tatvam nánásrama nishevitam.*

This gift whoso maintains will derive the merit of presenting in Váranási, Kurukshetra and other holy bathing places, a thousand tawny cows, with kolagas decked with precious stones, to Brahmans versed in the four vedas. Whoso usurps it will incur the guilt of slaying in those holy bathing places those tawny cows and those Brahmans at the time of the sun's eclipse. Whoso usurps a gift made by himself or by another will assuredly be born a worm in ordure for sixty thousand years.

(*A further gift, apparently inscribed afterwards.*)

And in consequence of that discourse, (who?) gave, pouring water, *Abbase* and *Hosavalli* in *Kodanáḍ kampana*, in the manner approved by all; and *Givindanahalli* in *Muduvalalu kampana*, with enjoyment for three generations.

May it prosper, this S'iva s'asana.

45. S'ila S'asana at Balagami, date A. D. 1155.

Size ft. 6 × ft. 2.—Haḷe Kannaḍa Characters.

Nandi. LINGA. Cow suckling calf.

Om. Obeisance to S'iva. Adored be S'ambhu, beauteous with the chámara-like crescent moon kissing his lofty head; the original foundation-pillar of the city of the three worlds.

May it be well.—While the victorious kingdom of the auspicious *Trailokya Malla Deva*, protector of all lands, favourite of earth and fortune, great king of kings, supreme lord, first of monarchs, glory of the *Satyás'raya kula*, ornament of the *Chálukyas*,* was continually increasing in prosperity, to endure as long as sun, moon, stars and sky:—

At that time,—May it be well. While the auspicious Mahá Mandales'vara, *Bijjana Devarasa*, entitled to the five great drums, Mahá Maṇḍalesvara, lord of *Kálanjara-pura*, having the flag of a golden bull, in beauty a Manmatha, possessor of the ḍamaruga, túrya and nirghoshana, a jewelled ornament to kings, a sun to the lotus the *Kalachurya kula*, fierce in war, in honour a Meru, a sun to good warriors, an elephant goad to the mighty, master of elephants, a cage of adamant to his dependents, in courage the lord of Lanka, to others' wives a brother, Malla of the S'anivára Siddagiri-durga, in character a Rama, a lion to the elephant his enemies, Nissanka Malla, having these and all other titles,†—was ruling all lands, punishing the evil and protecting the good;—

---

* See note p. 14.

† See note p. 66.

His great and able Dandanáyaka, a terror to his enemies, a friend to the people of the lands he had subdued, purifier of his family, the most accomplished among the skilful, *Mahadevarasa* was ruling the Banavase Twelve Thousand.

While united with the four karnams,— *Potarasa*, *Cheddimarasa*, *Padmarasa*, and *Sovarasa*, embodiments of the mind of Bijjana Deva, royal swans among the spreading lotuses the minds of the learned, chintámanis in granting all the desires of their dependents, suns in dispersing the clouds of poverty of the humble and destitute, he was ruling in peace :—

His mahá pradhána was *Mayi Devarasa*, a jewelled ornament of ministers, in the form of Manmatha, a bee at the lotus feet of Hara, the sole patron of the learned, a Náráyana to auspicious kings, worthy and familiar in the pura tantra, the beloved son of the teacher (*upádhyáya*) Nanda Bhatta, rejoicer of the assemblies of the learned, by his merit purifying his family, the beloved son of Gaurala Devi, conspicuous with these and other names. Besides this, how came Chánikya, who with such great effort destroyed eleven Nanda kula, to be called a minister, say,—for without the slightest effort this *Mayi Dandádhipa* subdued all the enemies of his master and greatly increased his joy and prosperity. Whoso clearly coming into his hand, goes and seeks aid from another, he never suffers to remain without defeat on the battle field; whoso comes against him with the bow, he humbles his pride and befriends him : can he be compared with other ministers, this *Mayi Deva*.

This great minister, the Herggade Dandanáyaka of the *vadda rávula* and *hejjunka* of the Banavase Twelve Thousand, *Mayi Devarasa*, being in the royal city of *Balligráme* in the enjoyment of peace,—one day, surrounded by all the learned and his attendants, delivered a discourse on merit :—when, they taking that to mind, spoke as follows :

"Dakshina Kedára is a place for the absolution of sin, the presence of Siva openly manifested to all the citizens, the visible embodiment of the glory of the Krita yuga. And the matha there, like the primeval tortoise is a support to all the world and its inhabitants, like the milk ocean in giving birth to the Lakshmi of prosperity, like the pleasure garden of Bhaváni pervaded with the pure life of brahmacharis, like Kurukshetra watered by Sarasvati (or learning), like Deva loka surrounded with vidhyádhara (or the learned), like Kailása protected by deformed s'aktis and gods (or Váma S'akti Deva).

"And to describe the descent of the line of gurus of that matha : Born in the line of the múvarakoneya (?)*, reckoned as the deva vrata, born on

* See Nos. 40, 41, &c.

the chain of mountains, though ancient ever new, was *Gautama munipa*. The son of that Gautama, an intoxicated bee at the lotus feet of the lord of Párvati, with a face free from passion, of worthy life, was *Váma S'akti Pandita Deva*. The glory of the Kedára sthána was as a kalpa vine in the world, whose branches were covered with shoots by the unmoved penance of Somes'varárya and Gautamárya, until filling all the world it blossomed in *Váma S'akti munindra*. His face a pleasure house for Sarasvati, his mind a jewelled casket for S'iva, thus is he famed in all the world, *Váma S'akti Pandita Deva*.

"Therefore here should be performed some work of merit". On saying which, taking that to mind,—

May it be well.—In the 6th year of S'rimat Chalukya Trailokya Malla, the year Yuva, the month Mágha, new moon day, the uttaráyana sankránti, Monday, at the vyati páta—washing the feet of—May it be well—S'rimat Váma S'akti Pandita Deva, perfect in *yama*, *niyama*, *svádhyáya*, *dhyána*, *dhárana*, *mauna*, *anushthána*, *japa*, and *samádhi*,* devoted to the learned, áchári of the sthána of Dakshina Kedáresvara Deva of the royal city of Ballipura,—and pouring water,—to provide for the food of the rishis, for the illumination of the god, and for the repairs of the temple, freed the areca nut produced in the garden of the god S'ri Kedáres'vara from the *vadda rávula* and the *hejjunka*, from the whole of the *bilkonde sunka* (or transit duties both ways) and the betel leaves of that garden from all customs duties, that they might be conveyed free of all imposts.†

Whoso maintains this gift will obtain the merit of presenting in Váranás'i, Kurukshetra and other holy bathing places, a thousand tawny cows, and kolagas decked with precious stones, to Brahmans versed in the four vedas.

(*Rest illegible*).

---

* See notes p. 16 and 74.

† *S'ri Kedáres'vara Dévara tôntadalu puttuvávupannada gontadakeya vadda rávula hejjunkav eradum bilkondeya sunkav anitumam mattam á tônt'ad elleya pannáyad ellá sunkamumam sarvvá bádhá parihára vági nadavantágiralu bittu kotta* [See No. 40.

46. S'ila S'asana at Balagami, date A. D. 1192.

Size ft. 5 3′ × ft. 2 8′.—Haḷe Kannaḍa Characters.

Cow suckling calf. Sun. Linga with Priest. Moon. Nandi.

Obeisance to *S'iva.* May *Soma*, powerful to create with ease the three worlds, which grew with the nourishment of his pure shining body composed of the substance of the earth and all matter, the object of the love which he creates in Párvati, dwelling on the peak of Meru, the abode of happiness, the residence of surpassing glory and wealth, wearer of the crescent moon, lord of the bhútas, be for your wealth. May *Vishnu*, who supporting Lakshmi on his breast, bearing up in his hand the great mountain of Govardhana, having on his left Brahma, the stable earth at his back, the beauty of lotuses in his eyes, immortal glory in his body, the lord of the *Yádavas*, be the protector of all worlds.

May it be well.—Protector of all lands, favourite of earth and fortune, great king of kings, supreme lord, first of monarchs, glory of the *Yádava kula*, ornament of the *Hoysaḷas*,* was *S'rimat Pratápa Chakravarti Víra Ballá!a Deva*, the origin of whose race was as follows :—

To the great (*mahá*) *Víra Balláḷa*, the brother was *Vishnu Varddhana*. His son was *Nṛisimha*, famous in the world. Through him the earth with joy obtained the glory of a good king, by him the herds of elephants his enemies were smitten ; the destroyer of hosts, who had hung the lamp of his fame on the forehead of the earth, greatly celebrated in the world was *Víra Nṛisimha Bhúpati*.

The destroyer of brave enemies with his claws and the deep roar of his drums, his rolling eyes green (*hasaru*) with rage, conspicuous with the cluster of rays of glory, in all matters bringing happiness to the three worlds, to the circle of the world the Chakri (Vishnu) himself, the chief of the *Yádavas*, the glorious *Narasimha Bhúpála* shone like Indra himself. A kalpa vriksha not sprung from the ocean which the muni (Agastya) had swallowed, a Mandara mountain which had not been disturbed by Vishnu (at the churning of the sea) and hastily returned to its place, a lion which driving off the beaters had established himself as the king of the herd, such was *Narasimha Bhúpála* in surpassing valour. The Káli his sword danced with joy in the battle field when smiting through the hostile kings who would not yield, marking its fore-

---

* *Svasti samasta-bhuvanás'rayam s'rí-pṛithví-vallabham mahárájádhirájam paramés'varam parama-bhaṭṭárakam Yádava-kuḷa-tiḷakam Hoysaḷábharaṇam.*

head with their blood, and by splitting the heads as they rolled off on every side surrounding itself with a garland of brains, it drank its fill of blood from their skulls.

To him was born a son *Ballá!a Bhúpála*, an ornament to all the world, who enriched with great fame, reigned over all the earth. To describe the glory of that king's valour :—*Chola* was driven out of his mind ; *Pándya*, forgetful of his honour, fled by night with his army, and greatly trembling took refuge on the top of a mountain ;* besides these, *Vanga*, *Kalinga* and *Magadha*, kings over mighty hosts, hearing the victorious sound of the *Hoysala* emperor's bow, fled in terror. A Bhima in personal strength, a moon to the ocean of policy, a Ráma in victory on the battle field, a Manmatha in beauty, a jewel to the group of the kings of his line, a light to the world, thus does *Víra Ballála Bhúpa* prevail. *Lála* stood in the open plain (having no city or kingdom), *Magadha* . . . . *Gaula* was defeated, the *Konkana* king was terror stricken, *Nepála* was deprived of his bow, *Málava* was worn out, and *Chola* he terrified and defeated before coming and entering Málava with great speed, that *Víra Ballála Deva*. † And through fear of him hostile kings deserted their kingdoms, saying ' we may chance to live somewhere.' Some got up into trees, some ran away, some took to boats, some chewed the grass (a sign of submission.) In like manner many groups of kings took refuge in hill forts. Thus did the fame of the mighty warrior *Ballála Bhúpálaka* mount and ride forth like the sun chasing away the darkness the groups of hostile kings.

And a moon in raising the tide of his wealth, without a second, was the *Dandarát Eraga*, who shone with great ability as a minister. May he live as long as the earth endures, *Ereyana Chamunáyaka*, whose ability was set up in the temple of the world in order to create merit, whose bounty is devoted to bestowing benefits on all in the world, whose valour is devoted to the destruction of all the enemies in the world. Like a moon does he shine this *Ereëna*, raising the tide of the milk ocean of learning, nourishing the moonlight the cluster of works of merit . . . . , . daily rejoicing the hearts of the learned and Brahmans, acquiring unusual fame.

That Chamunátha, while governing the *Banavase* Twelve Thousand and the *Sántalige* Thousand as the sole ruler (*ekádishtitamági*), one day in a discourse

---

* *Chólas'chálita chitta vrittir abhavat Pándyah pratishtáspruhántyaktvánaktamagán nagágra s'ikharam bhítyá sa sainya svaem.*

† *Lála bailági ninda Magadhan alid anyapadim dánam tanda gádam Gaulam sóládan á Konkana nripati bhayas'ankanágirddan á Nepálam chápa vichyutam Málava madavalidum Málavam bokku baldim Chólangoluntigodam jadidadisi en á Vira Ballála Devam.* ||

on merit, closely observing the glory of the sthala of *Kedára Deva*, and the merit of the penance of its áchári, the royal guru *Váma S'akti Deva* ; of that great one who, perfect in *yama, niyama, svádhyáya, dhyána, dhárana, mauna, anushṭhána, japa, samádhi,* and *s'íla*,* had instructed and confirmed the kings of the Chandra vams'a in the performance of the *ashṭánga yoga*, the glory of the Dakshina Kedáresvara sthala, which was a support to the whole world adorned with the girdle of the sea and filled with all manner of substances ; the lotus of his feet conspicuous with the clustering bees the Hari (dark) sapphires in the beautiful crowns of the faithful doing him obeisance ; a kalpa vriksha in satisfying the desires of poets, of the orthodox (*gamaki*), the eloquent, those of good conversation and others of the learned ; an authority in establishing the meaning of the vedánta, siddhánta, ágama, the six tarka, the whole of grammar, the dharma s'ástra and all other branches of science ; possessor of numerous weapons of argument for splitting through the rocks his opponent disputants ; a chakora feeding on the moonlight of the moons the toe-nails of S'iva (!), which eclipses the pure radiance of the glittering pearls in the diadems of the countless gods ever prostrate before him ; a support to good poets ; devoted to gifts of food, gold, virgins, cows, lands, freedom of fear, medical advice and other things ; a bee at the lotus feet of Hara ; the circle of the ten cardinal points illuminated with the brilliance of his fame, whose whiteness was like that of autumn clouds, or quicksilver, Kailasa, the milk ocean, the autumn moon, the light of the moon, a globe of crystal, a gentle smile, the milk of kine, hoar frost (*nihara*,) a conch, or the body of S'iva ; the beautiful abode of penance and glory ; a rain-cloud streaming down showers of gold which revive the forest the multitude of his supplicants devoured by the flames of the wild-fire of poverty ; far removed from sin ; free from all blame of falsehood : beloved by his dependents ; worshipper of the divine lotus feet of Dakshina Kedáresvara Deva of *Balipura*, the capital among ancient cities ; practiser of many kinds of holy mantras ; the royal guru *Váma S'akti Deva* : the descent of whose line of gurus was as follows :—

A wondrous muni was *Gautama* in the world, for though enjoying all delight with the woman the brightness of his penance, which illuminated the summits of the mountains ; though having a son the wisdom of the wise, and though loving the woman *níti s'ástra*, yet was he called a *yati*. This Gautama, the most excellent in the world, in the same manner as the gods at the beginning by churning the ocean obtained Indra's elephant, Lakshmi the jewel

---

* See notes p. 16 and 74.

of womankind, the kaustubha ornament and the Apsara nymphs,—so obtained *Váma S'akti*, a virtuous son of good qualities, having a knowledge of dharma. May this *Váma S'akti yatindra*, praised by all the world, prevail, whose commands are placed on the heads of kings, whose growing wealth is in the discourses of the eloquent, having the knowledge of the eternal, whose actions are a sufficient security to all the world. This *Váma S'akti yati*, the perfection of wisdom, do all the wise thus celebrate,—as the mountain on which rises the sun of tarka, as an ocean to the gems of good deeds, as skilled in discriminating between the enduring and the perishing, the chief in understanding of the vedas, the principal resting place of the heart's desires of his disciples, the original expounder of the tatva. Skilful is *Váma S'akti vratindra* to rejoice the hearts of the *Chálukya* kings by the notes of wind instruments sounding *sa, dha, ri* and other *rágas*; by the modulations of the seven notes (or octave)* combined in the enchanting songs of singing women; and by the sounds of the *mridanga* and other drums.

. . . .

While that great emperor, from his residence at *Lokkigundi* carrying his victories to the north, was ruling the kingdom of the world in the enjoyment of peace and wisdom :—†

The dweller at his lotus feet, the *mahá pradhána, sarvádhikári*, a giver of great gifts, saviour and protector of the Yádava army, consumer of great kings, despoiler of the possessions of his enemies, worshipper of the divine lotus feet of S'ri Vis'vanátha Deva, punisher of the enemy's forces, a mill stone to his enemies, terrible on the field of battle, a commander of great fierceness, a terror to his enemies, was *Yereyanna*; whose pure descent was as follows :—

A king over the whole world was *Máramayya*; to whom and to his beloved wife *Nágala Devi*, devoted to her husband, adorned with all good qualities, was born a son *Barmma*, clad in the armour of goodness. Him and his younger brother, the originator of great fame, worthily named *Eraga*, these did she bear into the world. This superior in strength, born with great glory in order to purify the region of *Báli* (? *Báliya baḷiyam*), was famed throughout the world as the refuge of the learned, the chamupa *Eraga*.

That chamunátha, for the worship of Dakshina Kedáresvara Deva of *Ballipura*, the capital of the *Banavase* Twelve Thousand, for the illuminations and lamps, the processions in Chaitra and other numerous festivals, for food for

---

* The seven notes are *sa, shaḍja*; *ri, rishabha*; *ga, gándhára*; *ma, madhyama*; *pa, panchama*; *dha, dhaivata*; *ni, nishadha*.

† See note p. 2.

the rishis, and for repairs of the temple; for all these purposes, gave from the vritti of *Kundáni*, situated in *Sántalige nád* which he was ruling, three in the ruined street, the first of the new ones, together with fifteen *gadyána*, free from *guttage*, from *pinda dána*, and from all other imposts;* to endure as long as sun, moon, and stars.

In the s'aka year 1114, the year Paridhavi, the month Pushya, the 6th day of the moon's decrease, Friday, the uttaráyana sankramana, performing the ablution of the holy feet of the royal guru Váma S'akti Deva, did he present it, with pouring of water, from his Mahárája (*tan mahárájanim*).

This gift whoso maintains will obtain the merit of presenting at the union of Ganga and Yamuna tawny cows adorned with precious stones, to chief Brahmans versed in the vedas and vedángas. Whoso resumes it will incur the guilt of slaying those Brahmans and those cows at those holy places. Whoso by violence takes away land presented by himself or by another shall assuredly be born a worm in ordure for sixty thousand years.

The poetry is *Málaiya's*, the pandit of chief poets. The engraving is *kalloji* (stone mason) *Bhattaiya's*.

---

47. S'ila S'asana at Balagami, date A. D. 1098.

Size ft. 5 4' × ft. 2 4'.—Hale Kannada Characters.

Moon. Sun.

Linga with Priest. Cow suckling calf.

Adored be *S'ambhu*, beauteous with the chámara-like crescent moon kissing his lofty head; the original foundation-pillar of the city of the three worlds.

May it be well.—While the victorious kingdom of *S'rimat Tribhuvana Malla Deva*, protector of all lands, favourite of earth and fortune, great king of kings, supreme lord, first of monarchs, glory of the *Satyás'raya kula*, ornament of the *Chalukyas*† was continually increasing in prosperity, to endure as long as sun, moon, stars and sky :—

---

* *Intinitakkam tannáleya Sántalige náda madhya Kundániya vrittiyolagana biyáni sáli miram pothada modal gadyánam hadinaidu sarvva namas'ya kottu guttage pindá dána sarvva parihára, &c.*

† See note p. 14.

The dweller at his lotus feet,—May it be well.—Entitled to the five great drums, chief of great feudatories, commander of great fierceness, officer over all the property of the court (*ásthána vastu náyaka*), a moon to the waterlily the Brahman race, an ocean of virtue, in managing the royal affairs a Yogandhara, skilled in the game (!) of making gifts, worshipper of the feet of Tribhuvana Malla Deva, punisher of his enemy's forces, possessed of these and all other titles, the auspicious Mahá Pradhána, officer over the female apartments (*antahpura*), president of the concubines, the great Lá!a Kannaḍa ambassador, * the Mane Verggaḍe, (? palace chamberlain) † was S'riman Mahá Pradhána Danḍanáyaka *Bivanayya.*

By means of whom (*deseyim*) while,—May it be well.—S'riman Mahá Pradhána Danḍanáyaka *Padmanábhayya*, possessed of all titles, was ruling in peace the *Banavase* Twelve Thousand; the extent (*vistára*) of the capital was as follows:—With groups of lotuses, with lines of bees, with swans, parrots and kokile; with groves of sweet-scented mango trees, of new nága trees, of areca palms, of the trumpet-flower, of the muchukunda, and of jasmin; *Balligáve* shone like the curly tresses (*kuṭila kuntala*) of the lady the *Kuntala des'a.*

As from the womb of Konti were born the five Páṇḍavas, so, obtaining great fame in the world, adorned with all the beauty of Manmatha, were born five from the womb of *Chikkavve.* Among them was *Bamma Devarasa*, next younger to him *Devaya Náyaka*, next to him *Tikkarasa*; and next to him were *Lokarasa* and *Jogarasa*, the minds of which two were ever devoted to merit, to government, to valour, and to doing good to others. These two, considered as rare human oceans of glory and wealth, setting up on the south of the royal city *Balligráme*, to the north of the Távaragere, the gods Lokes'vara Deva and Joges'vara Deva; in order to provide for the decoration and services of those gods, for the procession in Chaitra, for the illuminations, and for the food of the pújári;—While Paṭṭana Sovi *Hanumanta Seṭṭi*, *Bammi Seṭṭi* and *Mebi Seṭṭi* were holding in comfort the office of Paṭṭaṇa Sovi (*paṭṭaṇa sovitana*), *Lokarasa* and *Joga Deva Náyaka*, giving pagodas (*honnu*) to *Bammi Seṭṭi* and buying from his freehold (*umbali*) the land within these four boundaries,—east from the temple, west and south from S'álaya's land, north from Bammi Seṭṭi's tank, and south from Kommajja's garden;—gave

* Compare note p. 76.

† *S'riman mahá pradhánan, antarpurádhyakshaka, sahavásinádhishṭáyakam, héri Láḷa Kannaḍa sandhivigrahi, mane verggaḍe.*

that land in the presence of the Paṭṭana Sávi; of the chiefs of all the citizens, Gammanḍa Sávi *Sankarayya*, Senabhova *Sankarayya*, Sodore *Chiddimayya*; of *Gauḷa Panḍita Deva*, áchári of the Piriya maṭha Bherunḍes'vara; *S'rikanṭha Panḍita Deva*, áchári of the Pancha Linga; *Chaturánana Panḍita*, áchári of the Tripurántaka; *Múliga Honneya Jíya*, áchári of the five maṭhas, especially of the Múlasthána; *S'úleya Parpeya*; the Bauddhálya sávási *Nágiyaka**; and all the unequalled great ones of the Brahmapuri, the Manegar *Nági Seṭṭi*, Togara *Máchi Seṭṭi*, Mindaguddali *Námi Seṭṭi*, and all the *mummuri danḍa*;—Thus in the presence of the whole city; in the 22nd year of the Chálukya Vikrama era, the year Bahudhánya, the month Pushya, new moon day, Sunday, uttaráyana sankránti, vyati páta; that *Bammi Seṭṭi* gave to *Lokarasa*, for the god, 50 *kéyi kamma* out of his freehold.

Whoso without fail maintains this gift, will derive the merit of presenting in Prayága, Váranás'i, Kurukshetra and other holy bathing places, a thousand tawny cows decked with gold and precious stones, to a thousand Brahmans versed in the vedas. Whatso great sinner resumes it, will incur the guilt of slaying in those holy bathing places a thousand tawny cows, a thousand Brahmans versed in the vedas, and a crore of rishis. Whoso by violence takes away land presented by himself or by another shall assuredly be born a worm in ordure for sixty thousand years.

---

48. S'ila S'asana at Balagami, date A. D. 1168.

Size ft. 5 11′ × ft. 2 4′.—Haḷe Kannaḍa Characters.

Cow sucking calf. Linga with Priest. Moon. Nandi.

Om.—Obeisance to *S'iva*. Adored be *S'ambhu*, beauteous with the chámara-like crescent moon kissing his lofty head; the original foundation-pillar of the city of the three worlds.

. . . .

May it be well.—The protector of all lands, favourite of earth and fortune, great king of kings, supreme lord, first of monarchs, lord of the city of *Kálanjara*, having the flag of a golden bull, possessor of the ḍamaruga, túrya and nirghoshana, sun to the lotus of the *Kalachurya* race, able in war, in honor a Meru, a sun to good warriors, an elephant goad to the mighty, master of elephants, cage of adamant to those who seek his protection, in courage the lord of Lanka, a brother to the wives of others, Malla of the S'anivára Sid-

* Apparently a Buddhist nun.

dagiri durga, in character a Ráma, a lion to the elephants his enemies, Nissanka Malla,* . . . . . *Bhuja Bala Chakravarti Tribhuvana Malla Bijjana Deva*, daily enjoying the lady Earth ; to describe whom :—Earth, which through the ignorance (*múḍha*) of Pṛithu was for long turned into a cow, having in the present age become the crowned queen (*paṭṭa mahishi*) of Bijjana Deva, greatly rejoices, shining with the brilliance of the precious stone, which lying first in the ocean, then cast on the shore, then on a rock, at last became the kaustubha on Vishnu's breast. Thus was the earth, exalted by this king, praised by all mankind.

While thus, without a second or a superior, he was ruling the whole world under the protection of his sole umbrella, he made an order conferring his own government (*átmarájyabháram nirúpaṇam máḍida*) upon his son.

To describe the glory of that favourite of the Maharája :—This *Soma*, worthy of the name of *soma* (moon), was born from the ocean Bijjana Mahípála, dispersing the darkness of the clouds the groups of his enemies, causing the waterlily the joy of the world to unfold, and the lotuses the faces of the wives of hostile kings to fade away, lord over the rising of the stars (otherwise, lord preventing the rise of other Kshatriyas), shining with streams of glory, radiant with learning, possessor of the moonlight of his brilliant fame.

While that son of Bhuja Bala Tribhuvana Malla Deva, king of kings, a sun to kings, with glory as dazzling as the rays of the sun, grantor of their heart's desires to all supplicants, terrifier of his enemies, *Ráya Murári Sovi Deva Chakres'vara*, accompanied by his ministers, was governing the kingdom in the enjoyment of peace and wisdom :—†

Calling for *Byálike Kesimaya Danḍanáyaka*,—entitled to the five great drums, great tributary, the issuer of orders to the generals and officers, establisher of the policy consisting of prabhu, mantra and utsáha, the mahá pradhána, sarvádhikari, of great liberality,—favoured him, saying, "Take charge of the countries forming the treasury of the south, and govern them, punishing the evil and protecting the good :" which was accepted as a distinguished favour by that great and powerful Danḍanátha‡ ; to describe the glory of whose valour :—

---

* See note p. 66. † See note p. 2.

‡ *Samadhigata pancha mahá s'abda mahá sámanta sénádi báhattara niyogadhishṭáyakam, prabhu mantrotsáha pramukha níti nishṭáyakam, s'ríman mahá pradhánam sarvádhikári mahopasáye Byálikeya Kesimayya Danḍanáyakaram karadu dakshiṇa dis'ávarada bhanḍáraváda dés'angaḷ ellavam dushṭa nigraha s'ishṭa pratipálana málpudendu káruṇyam máḍal mahá prasádam endu kaikonḍa.*

This is not the world of *vidyadharas* this crowd that fills all the sky, it is not the hosts of *svarga*, it is not the group of *gandharvas*, it is not the shining ranks of *kinnara*, it is the immense host of powerful kings who, falling as soon as Byálike Kesamaya's victories began, have ascended to heaven. His life is that of the Manus worthy of reverence, his policy that of the ancient kings, all the wealth acquired by his mighty arms is for the benefit of others, the promotion of his government he counts as his own promotion, the happiness of his dependents he reckons as his own happiness, thus during his life-time does the glory of *Kes'ava Daṇḍandyaka* increase.

That great one, thus increasing in every kind of glory, ruling the *Taddaváḍi* Thousand, the *Hánugall* Five Hundred, and the *Banavase* Twelve Thousand for a long period (*aneka kála*) in peace; coming to the immemorial (*anádi*) capital *Balligáve* for the purpose of inspecting his own country (*svades'ávalokanárthavági*), and seeing there the elegant tower (*máṭa kúṭa*) of (the temple of) Dakshina Kedáresvara, its palatial buildings, its decorations of precious stones, its golden pinacles, its gifts for learning and food, and other holy rites; thinking, 'This is double of Varánasi, a hundred fold of Kedára, a thousand fold of S'ri Parvata, therefore here must I perform some work of merit and thus obtain all my desires,'—he came into the presence of the Rája-Guru Deva, the áchári of that place, and took note for a long time of the variety and extent of his learning. In *s'abda* a Páṇini paṇḍita, in *níti* Bhúshanáchárya, in *náṭya* and other *bharata s'ástras* Bharata muni, in *kávya* Subandhu, in *siddhánta* Lakulisvara, at the feet of S'iva a Skanda adorning the world, thus is *Váma S'akti yati* truly described.

To him, famous in these and many other ways, on making known his wish to perform there a work of merit, and he replying, 'Be it so (*tadastu*), whatever dharma you bestow we will accept':—In the 16th auspicious Kalachurya year, the year Sarvadhári, the month Vais'ákha, full moon day, Sunday, during the eclipse of the moon, at the sankramana and vyati páta; having made application to *Ráya Murári Sovi Deva*, and obtaining from him a támra s'ásana, *Byálike Kes'imaya* Daṇḍanáyaka, pouring water, gave *Chikka Kannugi*, situated in Yelanchi kampana of Hánugall náḍ, to provide for the worship and decorations of Dakshina Kedára Deva, for repairs of the temple, for food to Brahmans and rishis, and for the support of learning; washing the feet of the áchári of that place, the Rája-Guru Deva, the beloved disciple of Gautama Deva, with enjoyment for three generations; to endure as long as sun, moon, stars and sky.

This gift whoso maintains will derive the merit of presenting in Varanás'i, Kurukshetra, and other chief sacred places, a thousand tawny cows together with gold and many precious stones, and decorated kolagas, to a thousand Brahmans versed in the vedas and s'ástras, performers of the *soma yága*, and born in the line of somayájis. This gift whoso resumes will descend to the Naraka appointed for him who should slay in those sacred places, at that time, those Brahmans and those cows with his own hand. In witness whereof is the *s'ruti*, Whoso by violence takes away land presented by himself or by another shall assuredly be born a worm in ordure for sixty thousand years.

---

49. Virakal at Balagami, date A. D. 1422.

Size ft. 5 2′ × ft. 2 2′.—Haḷe Kannaḍa Characters.

(*Upper figures indistinct.*)

Two men, each kneeling on one knee, engaged in a fight or wrestle. An armed attendant behind each.

May it be well.—While the protector of all lands, favorite of earth and fortune, great king of kings, supreme lord, first of monarchs, *Vija* . . . . . son of *Víra Pratápa Deva Ráya*, was in his residence of *Hastinávati*, governing the kingdom in the enjoyment of peace and wisdom :—

(*Much illegible.*)

. . . . who in the earth is able to praise the valour of . . . *Deva*?

In the s'aka year 1344, the year S'ubhakrit, the month As'vija, the 5th day of the moon's increase, Sunday, the *Ballipura* people . . . . conquering . . . . *Deva* ascended to the world of gods, Indra and all the apsaras, with renewed beauty, dancing and shewing him respect.

---

50. Mastikal at Balagami, date ? 1206.

Size ft. 4 6′ × ft. 2 7′.—Haḷe Kannaḍa Characters.

. . . . . the year Kshaya, the month Chaitra, the . . . . of the moon's increase

Sun. LINGA. Moon.

THE HERO in the attitude of devotion. THE HEROINE arrayed for the sahagamana

51. Virakal at Balagami, date unknown.

Size ft. 3 1′ × ft. 1 4′.—Haḷe Kannaḍa Characters.

Sun. Moon.

The hero. LINGA.

(*The inscription altogether illegible.*)

The hero, supported by celestial nymphs bearing chamaras.

A fight between two men with bows and arrows. A wounded man is lying under one of them, and a herd of cattle standing behind, some turning tail.

52. Virakal at Balagami, date A. D. 1285.

Size ft. 5 6′ × ft. 2 8′.—Haḷe Kannaḍa Characters.

May it be well.—In the 14th year from the commencement of the reign of the *Yádava Náráyaṇa Bhuja Bala Prauḍha Pratápa Chakravarti S'ri Rámachandra Ráya*, the year Tárana,

The hero. Linga with Priest, in temple. Nandi.

the month Vais'akha, the 10th day of the moon's increase, Wednesday, the auspicious *Mari Seṭṭi*. . . . . . destroying men upon men, and piercing them, entered the world of gods dancing.

The hero ascending to heaven in a car, attended by celestial nymphs bearing chamaras, and by celestial musicians.

The hero under a canopy, shielding himself from an attack with swords and spears. Two mounted attendants coming to the rescue.

(*The group is mutilated.*)

53. S'ila S'asana at Balagami, date A. D. 1048.

Size ft. 4 2' × ft. 2 10'.—Haḷe Kannaḍa Characters.

The Donor.	Sun.	A Jain Yati seated.	Cow suckling calf.

May it prevail, the supreme profound *syád váda*, the token of the fulfilment of all desires, the doctrine of *Trailokya Nátha*, the Jina doctrine.

May it be well.—While the victorious kingdom of *S'rimat Trailokya Malla Deva*, protector of all lands, favourite of earth and fortune, great king of kings, supreme lord, first of monarchs, glory of the *Satyás'raya kula*, ornament of the *Chálukyas* * was increasing :—

He whose head was adorned with the sprouts of his feet,—May it be well. Entitled to the five great drums, the mahá manḍales'vara, lord of the city of *Banavase*, having obtained a boon from Mahá Lakshmi, delighting in bounty, *áyadácharya* (?), unassisted hero, male of males, ganda bherunda, having the title of the brave in the assemblies (or at the courts) of three kings †, like S'ankara to the bull the manḍalika, a hand (slapping) on the faces of the valiant, a sun to the titled, the manifest Vikramáditya, Jagadeka Dáni, having these and many other titles, S'riman Mahá Manḍales'vara *Chá(vunḍa)*‡ *Ráyarasa*, while in his residence in the royal city of *Balligáve*, ruling the *Banavase* Twelve Thousand;

In the s'aka year 970, the year Sarvadhári, the month Jyeshṭha, the 13th day of the moon's increase, Sunday, gave to the *basadi* (temple) of the *ashṭopavási* § Bhalára, Kes'ava Nandi, the disciple of Megha Nandi Bhattáraka of the Balagara *gaṇa*, belonging to (the god) Jajáhuti S'ri S'ántanátha, 5 *mattas* of paddy land by the Bherunḍa pole in the Pulleya (deer) plain of the royal city Balligáve, situated in the Jiddulige Seventy. Its boundaries; north, the hollow at the boundary of Tánagundúr; east, the new black stone; south Ashṭopavási gaṭṭa (the bathing ghat of the *ashṭopavásis*); west, an upright stone.

In religious merit, in courage, truth and liberality no equal has there been in the earth to Ganḍa Bherunḍa, nor shall be.

---

* See note p. 14. † *Múru ráyasthána kali biruda.*

‡ Only one letter of this name appears, the rest having apparently been cut off in trimming round the edge of the photograph. There is little doubt that it should be *Chávunḍa* or *Chámunḍa*. See No. 92.

§ *i. e.* accustomed to fast for eight days in the month.

Merit is a common bridge for kings. This from age to age deserves your support, O kings of the earth. Thus does Rámachandra from age to age beseech the kings who come after him. The earth has been enjoyed by Sagara and many other kings, whose empire was extensive in proportion to their gifts of land. To make a gift oneself is an easy task, to maintain that of another is difficult. But of giving or preserving (another's gift), the preserving is the best. Whoso by violence takes away a gift made by himself or by another shall assuredly be born a worm in ordure for sixty thousand years.

In the *Banavase* country, a Jina temple, a Vishnu temple, an Is'vara temple, an abode (*nilaya*) for munis, these by order of the king did the lord *Nága Varmma* cause to be built.

---

54. Virakal at Balagami, date A. D. 1269.

Size ft. 3 × ft. 1 ½.—Haḷe Kannaḍa Characters.

Moon.

A Jain yati
with an attendant on each side.

. . . . . *Yádava* . . . . . . emperor,
Ráya Ná[ráyána] . . . .
the year S'ukla . . . .

The hero in a car
attended by celestial nymphs.

attained to the world of gods. Thus did *Eene Voja's* younger brother *Máru Voja* cause it to be made. Great prosperity! Fortune!

---

55. S'ila S'asana at Balagami, date A. D. 1181.

Size ft. 8 2' × ft. 3.'—Haḷe Kannaḍa Characters.

Cow suckling calf. Linga with Priest Nandi.

Om. Obeisance to *S'iva* and *Párvati*, surrounded by worshippers. Adored be *S'ambhu*, beauteous with the chámara-like crescent moon kissing his lofty head; the original foundation-pillar of the city of the three worlds. Adored be S'ambhu, of a form of eternal wisdom and glory, by the accomplishment of his designs the origin of the Brahma pillar.

Obeisance to *Ganes'a*. May that *Mahes'a*, whose lotus feet are tinted with the brilliance of the rubies in the crowns of the hosts of gods prostrate before him, which (feet) rest on the heaven of the hearts of the lords of the Trimúrti, of exalted qualities, the creator of the threo worlds, sovereign of the sky and of all other matter,—ever grant to *Kes'i Rája* his desires.

In that universe the world of mortals is the most pleasing, * and in it the *Bharata mahitala* (continent) the most glorious (*samrájita*,) and in it the *Kuntala kshiti* (land,) the most beautiful (*bhrájita*). That land with great joy did the glorious emperor lord *Bijjana Deva* rule, in the same manner as Vishnu having brought back the earth carried off by Maya protected it.

That protector of the dwellings of all lands, † favourite of earth and fortune, great king of kings, supreme ruler, first of monarchs, sun to the lotus of the *Kalachurya* kula, able in war, in honour a Meru, light of great warriors, elephant goad to the powerful, master of elephants, cage of adamant to those who sought his protection, in courage the lord of Lanka, to others' wives a brother, Malla of the S'anivara Siddagiri durga, in character a Rama, a lion to the elephants his foes, Nissanka Malla ‡ ; having these and all descriptive titles, which with him were real § ; *S'rimat Bijjana Deva*, ruled the circle of the world as follows :—As a gem which first lay in the ocean, was then cast on the shore, then on to a rock, and at last became the kaustubha on Vishnu's breast, thus was the earth exalted by this king the praise of all.

The son of that mighty emperor, a Manmatha among men, king of kings, sun of kings, able in war, fragrant as musk, lover of bounty, *Ráya Murári Sovi Deva*, having ruled the whole world in peace :—After him, *Sankama Deva*, in truth and purity the equal of the son of Ganges (Bhishma), a new king Purukutsa, ruled the earth as if celebrating a festival.

After that, his younger brother *Ahava Malla*, of great bravery, glorious as the sun, Aprati Malla, was in peace as the lord of the earth. With joy did king *Ahava Malla* govern the whole world, an enraged lion to the lusty elephant the *Gauḷa* king, a net cast upon the shoal of fish the *Chauḷika* (Chola) army, a south wind to the rain-cloud the *Andhra* king, a thunder-clap to the royal swan the *Máḷava* king. That imperial king's powers of government became his chief ministers, whose natural ability was as follows ‖ :—*O Laksh-*

---

* *A jagaddalli martya bhuvanam kaḍu ramyavu.*

† *Samasta bhuvana bhavanás'raya.*

‡ See note p. 66.

§ *Samasta guna námangaḷ ellam yathárttha námangaḷ áda.*

‖ *A' rája chakrés'ana rájya pradhána s'aktigaḷé mahá pradhánar ádar avara svabháva sámartthyam entendaḍe.*

mana Dandes'a! on you has the lady earth set her heart, at the mere sight of your *Kuntala* (otherwise, curly locks) her *Kánchi* (otherwise, zone) slips off with agitation. *Chandugi Deva*, burning the territory of the brave *Vijayáditya*, taking the *Chola* and *Hoysala* kingdoms, troubled the hostile kings who were burning with envy.* The lustre of the beautiful pale (*pándura*) cheeks of the crowned queens of the kings hostile to the lord *Rechana Dandanátha*, chátaka birds taking for the moon, bees for white waterlilies, swans for the stalk of the lotus, wander about causing the world to laugh.

In doing favours to others a S'ibi, in giving charity a Karna, in benevolence to mankind a Dharma, . . . in extensive liberality and unshaken truth the only one, who in the earth was a king but *Sevana Chamupati*. Among the elephants of the points of the compass Airávata, among animals the lion, of gold the Meru mountain, among the gods Indra, of the oceans the shining milk sea, such great fame did *Kavana Dandanáyaka* obtain and increase his glory in the world.

The auspicious *Ahava Malla Mahipála*, surrounded by these great ministers adorned with all exalted qualities, calling for *Kesimayya Dandanáyaka*,—the mahá pradhána, the birthplace of all virtues, purifier of the Bharadvaja gotra, grandson of *Kes'ava Deva* and *Pampámbika*, son of *Holalamarasa* and *Durggámbika*, the loved one to the heart and eyes of *Lakshmi Devi*, unassailable by fear or avarice, in war the three-eyed (S'iva), friend of the learned, a combination of all good qualities which unite in ministers of long service, entitled to the five great drums, great feudatory, the issuer of orders to numerous great commanders, master of all wealth, terrifier of his enemies, possessor of these and other true titles:—and saying "Govern the treasury of the south so that the country may have quiet †, punishing the evil and protecting the good,"—gave him *Banavase nád*, which was accepted as a distinguished favour by that great minister ‡; to describe whose qualities:

His life was that of the Manus worthy of reverence, his policy that of the ancient kings, all the wealth acquired by his mighty arms was used for the benefit of others, the promotion of his government he counted as his own promotion, the happiness of his dependents he reckoned as his own happiness, thus during his life time did the glory of *Kes'ava Dandanáyaka* increase. In the kingdom of this lord *Krishna Kes'ava Deva Chamupati* there were none conceited, none conspicuous in splendour, no opponents, none great in possessions,

---

* *Gandina Vijayádittyana mandalaman suttu Chóla Hoysala rájyan gond ulida ripu nripálaran andalavam Dandanátha Chandugi Deva* ‖ For Vijayáditya see note p. 119.

† *Dakshina dig bhágada bhandárav ada dés'amam bappanane.* ‡ See note p. 110.

none envious, none who went forth to battle and came back weeping, none who unmindful of their proper title gave heed only to the flattery of poets' songs. The double of Chánakkya, twenty fold of S'akaluka, a hundred fold of Bhrigu (Parasu Ráma), a thousand fold of Háli (Bala Ráma), thus much did he exceed them in glory, *Kes'ava Deva*.

And that mahá pradhána *Krishṇa Kes'ava Deva Danḍanáṭha's* excellent ministers were the following :—His life like that of Manu, never uttering vain words, his faith having obtained him a place equal to that of the son of S'iva, possessed of such glory, who could compare with *Singa Náyaka*? In affection and speech free from the sins of the Kali age, except to *Tikka Rája*, to apply to others as frail as grass (*pul mánasaram*) the name of "king" was like calling a stone a jewel. This is true. What I wish for will come at my wish, all else I prevent from coming, thus used to say *Báchayya*. The treasurer *Sovi Deva* was to his dependents a treasury, why praise him? for others called treasurers, what connection have they with the assemblies of the learned, what manner of kings are they? Considering as his own all the intentions in the mind of his lord, to the envious like the messengers of Mrityu (death), to supplicants like a Surabhi (cow of plenty), thus did *Bámayya* appear. His faith at the feet of S'iva, gentle in speech, eager to do deeds of benevolence, possessed of such qualities, *Bibi Rája* shone to all the points of the compass. Only for the purpose of gratifying the desires of supplicants did he take the trouble of acquiring wealth and for no others *S'iva Tirtha S'ri Dási Rája* of great glory.

Moreover, to describe the greatness of the karnams who were like the embodiments of the benevolent wishes of the ministers of that great king of kings. Of qualities praised by skilful poets, born from the face of Brahma, able in doing good to others, excellent in the delights of good speech, beloved by the assembly of the Brahmans, profound as the sea, devoted to the faith of the feet of S'iva, with what esteem should those karnams be regarded!

Besides these were *Hiriya Viṭṭarasa*, like the embodiment of the royal glory of Lakshmi Deva Danḍanátha: *Chanḍugi Deva Danḍanáyaka*, the embodiment of fierce might; the Desiya Danḍanáyaka *Chikka Viṭṭarasa*, the glory of the Váji kula, purifier of the Bharadvaja-gotra, the beloved son of Iṭṭige Duggi Seṭṭi; *Kes'ava Deva*, the chief friend of the world, follower of the life of Rechanayya Danḍanáyaka, an abode of the science of war; *Kávanayya Náyaka*, like a son to the rája Lakshmi of Sovanayya Danḍanáyaka; *Rechannayya Náyaka*, glittering like the formidable bow in the hand of Kavanaya Danḍanáyaka.

While surrounded by all these ministers and royal attendants, the Indra of the wealth of the three worlds, like a cooling moon, was ruling the *Banavase* Twelve Thousand, with *Hayve, Sántalige, Yeḍedore* and other associated countries*, in the enjoyment of peace and wisdom, †—on the occasion of this great assembly, there was started a discourse on merit, describing the (king's) skilful policy and the glory of the city, as follows, by *Swámi Deva*, whose life was that of a muni, of high birth like Kapila, himself the glory of all beauty, considered as equal to Kes'ava, the son of Nachchi, his head marked by the lotus hands of the excellent muni Váma S'aktis'a the S'iva seer, in greatness the noble Rama, the minister of the three puras,—who with great tact entering suddenly,—

'In firmness, of Meru,—in holy life, of Manu,—in providing a theme for the first chief poets, of Sarasvati, —the equal, the peer, the fac-simile‡; to good qualities a quarry; of that firmness the abiding place, of that character the abode, of that sweet theme the home; thus is this lord truly celebrated in the world'—said the minister *Sávi Deva*, with joy.

'For the glory of the city: the rákshasa Bali having dwelt in this kshetra, made gifts, and in the course of manvantaras been considered as Indra himself; *Balipura* is of such immense antiquity that it is beyond my power to praise it. Therefore here perform some work of merit.'

Immediately saying 'Be it so' (*tad astu*), the *S'riman Mahá Manḍales'-vara*, with *Tailaha Deva*; *Eraharasa* § their brother-in-law; *Máli Seṭṭi*, paṭṭaṇa swámi of the royal city Balipura; paṭṭaṇa swámi *Mebi Seṭṭi*; *Múliga Dharmma S'iva Deva*, áchári of the Hiriya maṭha of the five maṭhas; *Rudra S'akti Deva*, áchári of the Pancha Linga maṭha; *Jnána S'akti Deva*, áchári of the Tripurántaka; with other citizens of the five maṭhas and the three puras; *Sávi Deva*, Sandore Herggade; his colleagues (*pratihasta*) *Chaṭṭana* and *Tippana*; the celebrated chiefs of . . . . . . the suns of chiefs who subdued Konkaṇa and took tribute from *Vijayáditya*, those who having given pleasure to *Hoysaḷa Víra Balláḷa*, chief among the *Malapas*, had obtained from him respect and were reverenced by all. ||

---

* *Banavase pannirchchhásiramumman'antah pravishṭavappa Hayve Sántaḷige Yeḍedore pramukha des'amam.*—Hayve is probably the same as Haiga, North Canara; Yeḍedore, the region between the Tunga and Bhadra rivers.

† *Sukha satkathá vinodadim.* See note p. 2. ‡ *Tóḍu pásati samam.* § See p. 77.

|| *Kannaranakarumáḍadoḷamban tettisida jasadatti ganḍarum Konkaṇamam sádhisi Vijayádityanal kappamam konḍa ganḍa máttanḍarum | Malaparoḷ ganḍam Hoysaḷa Víra Balláḷa Devange santóshavam máḍim mananeyam haḍada janaika mányarum enisidar antam.*

This Vijayáditya was the grandson of the Vijayáditya mentioned p. 98, and son of Jayakes'i the Kadamba king who married a Chalukya princess.—*Cf. J. Bo. Br. R. A. S.* ix, 231.

And besides these, the *Bananju dharmma* (a sect)*, firm, of great prudence, granters of their desires to their dependents, of one word, faithful to the feet of Isvara, observers of the policy which raises the prosperity of countries at the right seasons, of good character, of great strength, of exalted merit, beloved by all people, all which is no flattery :—Among the auspicious *Ayyas*, thus in many ways praised, in *Bhallunki* and other *grámas*, *nagaras*, *kheḍas*, *kharvvaḍas*, *maḍambas*, *dronámukhas*, *puras* and *paṭṭanas*; inhabitants of *Láḷa*, *Gauḷa*, *Karṇṇáṭa*, *Bangála*, *Kás'míra* and other quarters and countries: the local heads who united the glory of both classes of the *Des'is*; Manigára *Mahadevi Seṭṭi*, Manigára *Maili Seṭṭi*, Manigára *Padma Seṭṭi*, Manigára *Mánika Seṭṭi*, *Mari Seṭṭi* who had the feet of S'iva as his crest, *Sovi Seṭṭi*, *Holli Seṭṭi*, *Sálige Máchi Seṭṭi*, making joyful all these meritorious ones among the merchants :—

May it be well.—In the 3rd year of S'rimat Kalachurya Bhuja Bala Chakravarti Vira Náráyana Ahava Malla Deva, the year Plava, the month S'ravana, the 13th day of the moon's decrease, . . . day, sankramana, vyati páta: all the property of Bananjigas of Balligáve dying without sons, for the máṭa and sacred rites of Gavares'vara Deva; the property obtained from Nagaras dying without sons, to Nagares'vara Deva; and in all the five maṭhas, the three puras and the seven brahmapuris, in whichever unclaimed property acrues, to the god of that quarter †; these at the holy feet of Gavares'vara Deva, did *Kesimayya Danḍanáyaka*, with his karnams, pradhánas, and taḷári, pouring water, bestow, free from all imposts, to endure as long as sun, moon, stars and sky.

This gift let the *náḍ arasugaḷu*, the *adhikáris*, the *nagaras*, the five *maṭhas*, the three *puras*, and the *mummuri danḍagaḷu* maintain.

This gift whoso resumes will be guilty of the sin of murdering the king or destroying the institutions of the náḍ.‡ Whoso maintains this gift will obtain the merit of presenting in Varanás'i and Kurukshetra a thousand tawny cows, with kolagas decked with gold and precious stones, to a thousand Brahmans in the vyati páta during an eclipse of the sun.

---

* See No. 38, page 73.

† *Baḷḷigaveya Baṇanjigaralliya aputrika mṛitaka dhanav ellam S'rimat Gavareśvara Devara máṭádi deva kâryyakke | Nagaradalliyaputrika dhanav appudu Nagares'vara Devarge | mattam pancha maṭha múrum purav éḷum brahmapurigaḷal ellav allalliya mṛitanav appud allalliya Dévarige.*

‡ *I' dharmmaman âvanágiyuv aḷidavam arasinge rája dróha | náḍinge samaya dróha ||*

Whoso resumes it will incur the guilt of slaying with his own hand in Váraņási and Kurukshetra a thousand cows and a thousand Brahmans. Whoso by violence takes away land presented by himself or by another shall assuredly be born a worm in ordure for sixty thousand years. Poison is no poison, the property of the gods that is the real poison. For poison kills a single man, but the property of the gods (if usurped) kills sons and descendants.

56. S'ila S'asana at Balagami, date A. D. 1054.

Size ft. 3 7′ × ft. 2 7′.—Haļe Kannaḍa Characters.

Cow suckling calf, in a mandapa.	Sun. Linga with Priest in a temple. Moon.	Nandi in a mandapa.

May the three persons (*tri purusha*), the lords (respectively) of S'rí (Lakshmi), Váṇí (Sarasvati) and Girijá (Párvati), seated on Garuḍa (the kite), *hamsa* (the swan) and *uksha* (the ox); dwelling in the ocean, in the lotus and on the mountain (Kailása); having the colour of the bee, of the red lotus, and of the moon: possessed of the qualities of *satva*, *rajas* and *tamas*; having two, eight, and three eyes; *Govinda* (Vishnu), *Abjaja* (Brahma) and *S'ankara* (Siva), ever protect us. Adored be *S'ambhu*, beauteous with the chámara-like crescent moon kissing his lofty head, the original foundation-pillar of the city of the three worlds.

May it be well. While the victorious kingdom of the auspicious *Trailokya Malla Deva*, protector of all lands, favourite of earth and fortune, great king of kings, supreme lord, first of monarchs, glory of the *Satyás'raya kula*, ornament of the *Chálukyas*,* was continually increasing in prosperity, to endure as long as sun, moon, stars and sky:—

As mount Meru is a refuge to the gods so he to the learned, as S'iva the lord of Uma . . . . as Indra continually showering rain so bestowing gifts, as Ahisvara so able to support the burden of the world, as the moon surrounded with rays so with wisdom, as the ocean the birthplace of the beautiful Lakshmi so he of prosperity: thus was the king *Ahava Malla* celebrated.

A lion to the elephant *Choļa*, a mighty wind to the heavy cloud *Kaļinga*, a sun to the darkness *Pánchála*, a wild-fire to the forest *Magadha*, a thunderbolt to the chain of mountains *Máļava*, a Garuda to the serpent *Keraļa*, a Ba-

* See note p. 14.

ḍabánala to the ocean the *Nepáḷa* army, was king *Ahava Malla*. In unsullied fame, in wealth, in character, in courage, in victory, in great wars, in exalted qualities, who can say 'I am equal to *Ahava Malla?*' Can Yayáti, or Bhagiratha, or Purukutsa, or Purúrava, or Dilípa, or Bharata, or Nala, or Nahusha ? Braves who did not do him obeisance, proud ones who did not fear him, kings who did not seek his protection, lords of the forest (*aṭavisvararu*) who did not come to him begging, warriors fond of fighting whom he did not cast into Yama's power, those who invincible by all else did not hide their faces from him, chiefs of hill forts who did not descend from their strongholds and run away, those blinded with pride who did not tremble and quake ; there were not,—such was the bravery of *Ahava Malla Deva*. The seven *Máḷava* who came against him, in a moment he sent to destruction ; the seven *Konkaṇa* and seven *Male*, which united together, he terrified and made to obey him ; *Chauḷika* (the Chola king) in the middle of the fight going into a hole . . . died ; the kings of all the islands gave tribute* ; how great a warrior was this *Ahava Malla*.

May it be well.—S'rimat Vaḍḍa Byavahári, *Hálikabbe Sovi Seṭṭi*, possessed of all titles : in the middle of the ancient city †, the royal city *Balligráme-paṭṇa ;* in the s'aka year 976, the year Jaya, the month Vais'ákha, the dark fortnight, the *akshaya tritiya* new moon day falling on Sunday ; being moved to perform a work of merit, set up a *linga*, and giving it the name of Abhinava Somesvara Deva, in order to provide for the ablutions and offerings, the illuminations, and the food of the áchári presented as a *taḷa vritti*, two *mattas* of paddy land by the katsavi pole under the Are-kere, and within (above) that tank four *mattas* of paddy land with dry land.

The boundaries of that land : east, the land belonging to Chandresvara Deva ; south, the stream running west from the southern sluice of the Bedeya-kere ; west, the bank of the Are-kere ; north, the land belonging to Chaturmukha Deva. The boundaries of the two *mattas* of land under the Are-kere ; east, the garden land of Múlasthána Deva ; south, the land belonging to Pancha linga ; west, the land of Bhagavati Devi ; north, the waste land of the tank.

(Moreover), under the bank of the northern sluice of that tank one flower garden ; and the shops north of the high road running along the south side of that

---

* *Kshaṇadim Máḷavam éḷum meyde viḷaya keydittu sandirdda Konkaṇav éḷum Male yeḷum anji besakeydattovaṭántákaránganadoḷu Chauḷika nammi sattan akhila dvípávanipálakágraṇigaḷu kappaman ittar.*

† *Anádi paṭṭaṇam.*

god, with the street behind the shops south of that high road—he gave, washing the feet of the árádhya, Paṭṭaṇada Múliga, *Jnána S'iva Deva*, and pouring water, in the manner approved by all, with freedom from all imposts.

And that temple in course of time falling into disrepair; in the presence of Paṭṭaṇa Sávi *Mebi Seṭṭi*, *Kirtti Seṭṭi*, of all the *nagaras* and the five *maṭhas*, (namely) *Múliga Madhukesvara Paṇḍita Deva*, áchári of the Hiriya maṭha Bherunḍhesvara; *Sarbbesvara Paṇḍita Deva*, áchári of the Pancha Linga; *Jnána S'akti Deva*, áchári of Tripurántaka:—all the *mummuri daṇḍagalu*, the various *des'i byavaháris* (or merchants of different countries), and Manigára *Mahadeva Seṭṭi*, acknowledging this as a work of merit belonging to them, gave to that god the name of Gavaresvara Deva and repaired the temple.

Titles of the five hundred (who united in the work):—May it be well. Famous were they throughout the world as five hundred *víra s'ásana*; adorned with many acquired good qualities, as truth, purity, good conduct, character, morality, obedience, prudence; protectors of the *Víra Bananji dharmma*; conspicuous with the flag of the holy hill (Kailása); their breasts embraced by a Lakshmi who causes their honour to excel; great in the earth through bravery; born in the *Chandra vamsa*, the root of the khandali tree Vásudeva; having obtained a boon from Bhagavati; possessed of thirty two honourable maṭhas, eighteen paṭṭaṇas, sixty four *yoga píṭhas*, and *ásramas* in the four points of the compass *; the descendants of those called travellers over many countries (?) †; of the sect of Brahma, Vishnu and Mahesvara, of the Krita, Treta, Dvapara and Kali yugas. The earth as their sack, the eight regents of the points of the compass as their load or destination, Vásuki as their girth, the serpent race as their cords, the cow as their secret pocket . . . . the invaluable produce of the soil the articles in their pack ‡. Visiting—in the various countries of *Chera*, *Choḷa*, *Páṇḍya*, *Maleya*, *Magadha*, *Kaus'ala*, *Sauráshṭra*, *Dhanushṭra*, *Kurumbha*, *Kámbhoja*, *Golla*, *Láḷa*, *Barvara*, *Párasa*, *Nepáḷa*, *Ekapáda*, *Lambakarna*, *Strirájya* and *Gholámukha*§—the *grámas*, *nagaras*, *kheḍas*, *kharváḍas*, *maḍambas*, *paṭṭanas*, *dronámukhas*, and *samváhanas*, with the cities of the elephants at the cardinal points; and by land and by water (*páda márgga jala márggadoḷ*) penetrating into many regions (*khaṇḍa maṇḍalan-*

* See No. 38.

† *Náná des'a bhramántukaravargge puṭṭiyum.*

‡ *Prithviye hasumbeyáge ashṭa lokapáḷakare gonṭáge Vásugiye baḷaságe phaṇi kuḷangaḷe dáravági bokkaṇa voḷavasumbeyági chakrame beḷavági kárasiye marasurigeyáge hasumbeyoḷ amúlya vastugaḷe vastugaḷági.*

§ The last four names indicate countries whose inhabitants are respectively one-footed, long-eared, amazons, and buttermilk-faced!

gaḷam): with superior elephants, well bred horses, large saphires, crystals, pearls, rubies, diamonds, lapis lazuli, onyx, topaz, carbuncles, coral, emeralds, *karkkatana*, and various such articles: cardamoms, cloves, red sandal, sandal, camphor, musk, kunkuma and other perfumes: which by selling wholesale, or by hawking about as pedlars, they completely fill the emperor's treasury of gold, his treasury of jewels and his treasury of silk cloths; and the balance they devote with affection to daily bestowing benefits on paṇḍits and munis distinguished for their knowledge of the *chatus-samaya* * and the *shaṭ dars'ana*; and the hundred thousand heavenly blessings these invoke, placing on their hands and bearing on their heads, counting them as Mahádeva and their *ishṭa-deva*; enjoying in great comfort, merit, wealth, pleasure and property (the four objects of human desire). Supporters of the drivers of herds of asses and buffaloes (carriers), of the sixteen of the eight náds (?), of *gavaregaḷu* (?), of *gátrigas*, *seṭṭis*, *seṭṭiguttas*, *ankekáras*, *bíras*, *bíravaṇigas*, *gandhigas*, *gámaṇḍas*, and *gámaṇḍa swámis*. Thus powerful, bearing bows in their hands, having the elephant as a *bheri* (kind of drum), *Bheri* (a sect) as a *maddale* (a drum), white umbrellas as a canopy, the mighty ocean as a moat, Indra as the power of the hand, Varuna as the standard bearer, Kubera as the treasurer, the nine planets as a belt, Ráhu as the sheath, Ketu as the sword, the sun and moon as the backers, the 33 gods as the spectators; they drew forth the sword *kshame* (patience), and with it piercing the enemy named *krodha* (anger), they fought and conquered, these *bhaṭári makkalu* (sons of warriors), possessed of the ḍavaruga, para and nirghoshana: five hundred lords of the auspicious Ayyávoḷe, the best among their people, of unsullied fame, great in brilliant splendour, in truthfulness like Gángeya, in enmity like Duryodhana, in might like Bhima Sena. Like the elephant, they pursue and kill; like the cow, they stand and kill; like the serpent, they kill with poison; like the lion, they spring and kill; wise as Brihaspati, fertile in expedients as Náráyána, perfect in disputes as Nárada rishi . . . . .
The gone Mári (small-pox or any epidemic) they keep up the fear of, the coming Mári they face,† the pursuing tiger they excite, under the moving cart they place their feet, clay they go into and will not leave, of sand they make ropes, the thunderbolt they catch and exhibit, the sun and moon they draw down to the earth. Knowing the contents of the *Guḍḍa s'ástra* (?), which directs the conversation of the three worlds, they converse about things great and small, such as the brow, the eyes and the four arms of Isvara's *bhanṭaru*, the loud

---

* Said to be four sects or schools;—*kempu*, *murige*, *maraḷu* and *múliga*.

† *Hóha máriya chhallaváḍuvarum baha máriyanidirggoḷuvarum.*

laughter of the Brahmans, and the overthrow of Bhagavati. Their merchandise, the spoil of all the points of the compass, lays hold of those who come to their shops and binds them as with a vow; . . . .
they dance carrying the head of the enemy as a bunch of flowers and with the enemy's hand tied as a badge on a pole; . . . .

To the five hundred swámis of the auspicious *Ayyávoḷe**, thus possessed of all titles, making *sáshṭánga*, present offerings of food, O Seṭṭi! To the five hundred swámis of *Ayyávoḷe* present the *támbúla* in a tray, for this is auspicious.

May it be well.—The *dharmmáya* which the ever bountiful auspicious five hundred, Pattana Sávi *Mebi Seṭṭi*, *Kirtti Seṭṭi*, and the chief *nagaras* under them, gave for the decoration and processions of Gavaresvara Deva, and for repairs of the temple:—

The shops of the *nagaras* ten *vísa* each a year; the gold merchants ten *vísa* each a year; the *sihala gavaregaḷu* one *paṇa* a year per sack; the *gavare* of other countries one *hága* a year per sack; for camphor, musk, kunkuma, sandal, pearls and all such articles sold by weight, two *káṇi* per *ponnu*; cloth merchants of the place and foreign cloth merchants two *káṇi* per *ponnu*; for black pepper, cummin seed, mustard, *sada* flower, bishop's weed, aud coriander one *vísa* per *pon*; for sugar, assafœtida, dry ginger, long pepper, cardamoms, green ginger, turmeric, and all fibres and roots sold by weight, one *vísa* per *pon*.

The Danḍanáyaka managing the *hejjunka* and *vaḍḍa rávuḷa* † freed the *sunka* on one load in ten loads; the merchants who load from the place and all merchants from abroad one *mána* per load; the forty families of flower-sellers, one garland for each basket; the thousand *támbúligas*, a thousand leaves for each family in Chaitra for the procession; the fifty families of oilmen one *sondige* for each mill, for the lights of the god.

The worthies (*manneya*) of the Jidduḷige Seventy:—Ekkalarasa the chief, the náḍ prabhu, Chiṭṭi Mára Kála gávunḍa, Sigga Báva gávunḍa, Ságavadde Báda gavuḍa, Avali Jakka gavuḍa, Hampa gavuḍa, Hosa Valliyúr Sávimeya, Sankara Bhaṭṭa, Kúdali Sánta gavuḍa, Tottúr Royda gavuḍa, and all the prabhu gávunḍas gave for the god five *paṇa* a year for each village.

The worthies of the Nágara Khanḍa Seventy: Sovi Deva the chief, Konavatti Prithivi Seṭṭi, Begúr Keta gavuḍa, Mágunḍi Sanka gavuḍa, Malavaḷḷi Keta gavuḍa, Elambaḷḷi Keta gávunḍa, Maḍalúr Kála gávunḍa, and all the prabhu gavunḍas, gave for the god five *paṇa* a year for each village.

---

* See No. 38, p. 74 † See note p. 79.

The worthies of the Edenáḍ Seventy :—Sovarasa Práṇamarasa the chief, the mahájanangaḷu of Agrahára Elase, the mahájanangaḷu of Kuppageḍe, Basamára Bira gávunḍa, Taramára Koḷa gávunḍa, Barige Jakka gávunḍa, Guḍuve Jaka gávunḍa, Veramára Billa gávunḍa, Tavaniddhi Duṭṭa gávunḍa, Soramba Kalla gávunḍa, Kúdali Báka gávunḍa, all these prabhu gávunḍas gave five *paṇa* a year for each village.

The property of those who die without heirs among the *hegala gavare* Bananjigas of the *mummuri danḍagaḷu* in the city and in the náḍ goes to the god.

The goldsmiths of the city gave one *paṇa* a year for each chafing dish ; the washermen of the city gave ten *vísa* each a year ; the basket makers of the city gave five *vísa* a year for each knife : the weavers gave five *vísa* a year for each *kúṭe* (? loom).

What person soever with affection maintains this gift, will obtain the fruit of the merit of bestowing at Kurukshetra, Gaya, Ganges, Varaṇás'i, and other holy bathing places, to a crore of Brahmans, versed in the vedas and s'ástras, lovers of vows, a crore of tawny cows about to become two-faced (*i. e.*, to calve), with humility, in the *punya tithi.* What doubt of this ? Whoso complaining resumes this gift will incur the great guilt of wantonly killing those Brahmans and those tawny cows in those holy bathing places.

To the kings of my own race or the kings of any other race who with minds freed from sin shall faithfully maintain this my gift, to them do I with folded hands placed to my head do obeisance.

Merit is a common bridge for kings ; this from age to age deserves your support, O kings of the earth. Thus does Ramachandra beseech the kings who come after him.

Whoso by violence takes away land presented by himself or by another shall assuredly be born a worm in ordure for sixty thousand years. Poison is no poison, the property of the gods that is the real poison. For poison kills a single man, but the property of the gods (if usurped) kills sons and descendants. The wild-fire though it consumes all the trees in the forest, spares their roots ; but . . destroys both the *kula* and its root.

Múliga Madhukesvara Panḍita Deva, áchári of the Hiriya maṭha, and his son *Dharmma S'iva Deva*, presented in the streets of their Múlasthána Deva ;—in the west street, one house of ten hands (*kai*) to Manigára Mahadevi Seṭṭi ; in the south street, one house of ten hands to Manigára Lakmi Seṭṭi ; in the manner approved by all, to endure as long as sun, moon, stars and sky. The auspicious Mahá Manḍalesvara Ekkalarasa's Danḍanáyaka *Kámarasa* remitted for Gavaresvara Deva the *koḍavísa* on ten bullocks.

57. Virakal at Balagami, date A. D. 1282.

Size ft. 6 6′ × ft. 2 6′.—Haḷe Kannaḍa Characters.

Sun. Moon.

(Inscription here illegible.)

The hero in the presence. Linga with a Priest and a woman in a temple. Nandi, fanned by an attendant.

(Inscription here illegible.)

The hero ascending to heaven in a car, attended by celestial nymphs and a band of celestial musicians.

May it be well.—Entitled to the five great drums, lord of the city of *Dvárávati*, ... sun to the lotus the *Yádava kula*, . . . disgracer (*dis'ápaṭṭa*) of the *Hoysaṇa Ráya*, establisher (*sthápanáchárya*) of the *Telunga Ráya*, (was) the auspicious *Yádava Náráyaṇa Bhuja Bala Prauḍha Pratápa Chakravarti Rámachandra Deva*: In the 14th year from the commencement of whose reign, the year Chitrabhánu . . . the 1st day of the moon's increase, Sunday . . . . . .
Baḷḷigráme, the city of the Víra Bananju of various countries .

The hero under a canopy, and attended by standard bearers and men armed with spears and bows, in the act of stabbing his enemy, whom he has seized by the plume of his head dress. On the side of the latter are a horse and some men armed with swords and shields.

(Inscription here illegible.)

58. S'ila S'asana at Balagami, date A. D. 1102.

Size ft. 5 1′ × ft. 2 4′.—Haḷe Kannaḍa Characters.

Sun. Moon.

Nandi. Linga with Priest in a temple. Cow suckling calf.

(The inscription is almost wholly illegible. Much of the first part consists of praises of Gopati Náyaka, an officer under Govinda Rája Daṇḍanáyaka ruling the Banavase Twelve Thousand.)

. . . in the presence of *Govindarasa*, in the 27th year of Chalukya Vikrama, the year Chitrabhánu, the month Phálguna, new moon day, Sunday, the sankramana and vyati páta : *Gopati Náyaka*, in order to provide for distribution of food, buying in the Balliya plain one *matta* (of land) according to the kachchave pole, and a house, presented them in the manner approved by all, for the purpose of providing food for twenty Brahmans . . .

Whoso maintains this gift will obtain the merit of presenting in Váranás'i, Kurukshetra, and Prayága a thousand tawny cows decorated with precious stones to the Brahmans. Whoso resumes it incurs the guilt of killing those tawny cows and those Brahmans in those holy places. Whoso by violence takes away a gift made by himself or by another shall assuredly be born a worm in ordure for sixty thousand years.

---

59. Virakal at Balagami, date A. D. 1202.

Size ft. 4 8′ × ft. 1 1′.—Haḷe Kannaḍa Characters.

Sun. Linga with Priest. Moon. Nandi.

. . . . . *Yádava Náráyaṇa Bhuja Bala Pratápa Chakravarti Víra Balláḷa Deva* . . . . . ruling the kingdom in peace ; at that time, ... of all worlds, ... adorned with all good qualities, protector of the *Víra Bananju dharma*, supreme lord, a cage of adamant to those who seek his protection . . . five hundred swámis . . . . . son . . . . the year Dundubhi, the month Asháḍha,

The hero being borne to heaven in a car by celestial nymphs waving chamaras.

(Inscription here illegible.)

The hero armed with a bow and standing over a dead body, encountering an enemy similarly armed. Each attended by men armed with swords and shields.

quickly returning, killing, fighting and gaining the victory, entered the world of gods . . . . *Sáleya Bommeya* bore him from the field.

60. S'ila S'asana at Balagami, date A. D. 1077.

Size ft. 9 × ft. 3.—Haḷe Kannaḍa Characters.

Sun. Moon.

Elephant. Jinendra in a temple. Cow suckling calf.

May it be well.—May the command of Jinendra, praised as the universal protection, be pleasure-giving as the moon to the faithful; washed by the streams of the united brilliance from the crowns on the heads of gods and rákshasas, may it ever grant prosperity. May the doctrine of *Trailokya nátha*, the supreme profound *syád váda*, a token of unfailing success, the Jain doctrine prevail.

May it be well.—Protector of all lands, favourite of earth and fortune, great king of kings, supreme ruler, first of monarchs, glory of the *Satyás'raya kula*, ornament of the *Chálukyas*, * was the auspicious *Tribhuvana Malla Deva*.

The *Choḷa* king he caused to shake, (his) great ones (*aniyaru*) he took no count of; to the *Láḷa* king he displayed the power of his arms, and overcoming him destroyed him: the feudatory kings of both emperors (*ubhaya chakresvara sámanta bhúbhrit*), mounting his furious elephant, he tormented and took their kingdoms, and became the lord of the shining Lakshmi of the *Páṇḍya* kingdom, (this) *Vikramáditya Deva*, praised by all. To *Dáráná-tha* (?) a great and dreadful fever; to *Choḷa* a cruel Yama; his feet reverenced by the crowns of the lines of the kings of *Saurásḥṭra*, *Anga*, *Kalinga*, *Vanga*, *Magadha*, *Andhra*, *Avanti*, *Panchála*; the Chalukya regent elephant (*dig gaja*) sported in the forests and mountains on the shores of the eastern and the western oceans. As the form of Narasimha tore open the breast of the rákshasa king, ... bore up Kailasa on his chest, ... presented with joy the gold of the earth to Indra, subduing all the mightiest destroyed twenty-one times the kings of the earth,—even so, O *Vikramáditya*, is your enmity implacable! Saying, "Why share it with others? If I take it upon myself alone shall I be overcome with fatigue?"—from the back of the great tortoise, from the head of the lord of serpents, from the company of the elephants at the cardinal points, from the caves of the mountains (at the points of the compass), boldly lifting off the whole weight of the world, by his might he placed it securely in his arms, *Vikramáditya Deva*.

---

* See note p. 14.

When thus having freed the world from every enemy he was in his residence at *Tagiri*, ruling the kingdom in piece and wisdom :—

The dweller at his lotus feet ; May it be well. Entitled to the five great drums, lord of great feudatories, a commander of great power, a terror to evil doers, a moon to the tall waterlily the company of his relatives, a light to the Brahmans, a benefactor to Sarasvati Devi, adorned with good qualities, a Brahma in skill, a lion in courage, an aid to valour, a Garuḍa in devotion to his master, punisher of the evil, destroyer of the garden of lotuses his enemies, of modest aspect, fame his flag, great in emulation, a bee at the lotus feet of Tribhuvana Malla Deva, having these and other names and titles, was the auspicious Danḍanayáka *Barmma Deva.* *

A security to all the world by the might of his arms, causing great astonishment in the world by his power, the brightness of his terrible glory, his ability, his single word and his exalted fame, an ocean to the gems of all good qualities and happiness, was *Barmma Deva.* He himself an eye to all people, he their fate, a sun through whose brightness the shining of the stars his enemies was eclipsed, the darkness of evil was dispersed, and all the earth shone with exceeding glory, in order to confirm the dominion of the fame of Vikramáditya did he obtain power, *Barmma Deva*, of matchless might. The mountain was removed by Hari, by the Daitya the earth was confined in the womb of Pátála, by the hurricane of wind at the destruction of the world the points of the compass were blown away ;—laughing at these as having no stability, his real firmness despises them, *Barmma Danḍádhipa.*

. . . .

While this abode of praise and fame, the auspicious Mahá Senádhipati, Mahá pradhána, the Danḍanáyaka *Barmma Devarasa*, enjoying (*anubhavisuttam*) the *Banavase* Twelve Thousand, the *Sántalige* Thousand, and the eighteen agraharas, punishing the evil and protecting the good, was in the royal city *Baḷḷigáve* :—

His god Jinanátha swámi, his own guru the great vrati Gunabhadra . . . . his mother Jakkabbe, his father Soma, his younger brother Mebi, his wife Bhogabbe, his father-in-law Kali Deva reverenced by the world, a nest of good qualities, a patron of the learned ; thus blameless in every relation, was *Singa*, distinguished for the collection of tributs and discourse on merit. Of modesty the limit, of merit the home, of virtue the birth place, of reverence the abode, of greatness the summit, to prudence, learning, liberality and patience a mine, thus praised by all the circle of the

* See No. 10, p. 18.

world, was the bee at the lotus feet of Jinapati, of great qualities, *Pratikaṇṭha Singa* . . . . . . on examination he is the perfect equal of the son of S'ankara, of Sarasvati and of Brahma, thus does all the world praise him, how excellent then is *Singa's* greatness of fame among the worthy. Pure was the son of Ganga (Bhishma), purer than the son of Ganga was the beloved son of Váyu (Hanuman), purer than the son of Ganga or the son of Váyu was Suka; but praised as surpassing in purity that son of the river, that king of the apes, and that Suka rishi, is *Pratikaṇṭha Singa.* As birds to a mango tree laden with fruit, as bees to a strong perfume, so to do the crowds of the learned flock to the Diváli festival of his bounty; and he causes them all so to rejoice that they extol it as imperishable and ever new, *Singa Raja.*

With great ardour did he learn the method of bestowing benefits, he learned how to invite the learned to him and to shew them respect, he learned to maintain the great praise of protecting his dependents, he learned to astonish all as the king among the worthiest, all these were the acquired qualities of *Pratikaṇṭha Singa.*

A sun to the sky of Jina dharma, a moon in raising the tide of the milk sea of Jina dharma, a bee at the lotus feet of Jinapati, these being his true qualities, *Pratikaṇṭha Singa* thus praised, originating a discourse on merit, said "You should present to the S'rimat Permmáḍi basadi (Jain temple) one báḍa, obtaining it from S'ri Ballavarasa." *

On his thus making application to his governor, and the auspicious Danḍanáyaka *Barmma Deva* making known the whole matter to his own swámi; *S'rimat Tribhuvana Malla Deva*, in the 2nd year of Chalukya Vikrama, the year Pingala, the month Pushya, the 7th day of the moon's increase, Sunday, it being the uttaráyana sankránti parbba: in the royal city *Balligáve*, on the birthday of his son (*tamma kumára gáladandu*), made the gift to the god of the S'rimat Chálukya Ganga Permmanaḍi Jinálaya, to provide for the services, the worship, the anointing, the decoration, the food of the rishis, for repairs of the temple and the new work of the upper basadi.

Greatly conspicuous by the bright glory of his fame, and the lines of shining lotuses his worshippers, driving away the clouds of darkness evil deeds, brilliant as the three beautiful gems in the sky of the Jainágama worthy of praise from all, a temple of all the qualities of fortune, was (the god) *Gunabhadra Daiva*, the sun to the lotuses chief munis. A treasury of geat penance,

* *Dharmma katha kadhana prasanganam puṭṭisi S'rimat Permmáḍiya basadig ondu báḍanam S'ri Ballavarasaralli paḍedu kuḍim endu tannáḷdange binnapam geyyal.*

lord of the assembly of munis, distinguished for wisdom combined with merit, was the celebrated *Mahasena brati.* And famous was that vratis'a's disciple: in the extensive *s'abda s'ástra* he was like the world-renowned Pújyapáda, in skill in *tarka s'ástra* he was like Akalanka Daiva, in poetical power like Sámanta Bhadra, thus greatly was *Ráma Sena* the chief of the learned praised, as the king of the world.

To him, who had thus reached the furthest shore of the ocean of all science, devoted to the performance of supreme penance: to *Ráma Sena Pandita*, of the S'ri Múla Sangha the Sena gana and Pogari gachchha, with pouring of water and all ceremonies, he gave Manevane one (village), situated in the Jiddulige 70, in the Banavase Twelve Thousand kampana.

This gift whoso maintains, will derive the merit of presenting in Bánarás'i and Kurukshetra, to a thousand Brahmans, a thousand tawny cows and kolagas decked with precious stones. Whoso resumes it will incur the guilty of slaying that number of Brahmans and that number of tawny cows in those holy places.

To the kings of my own race or the kings of any other race, who with minds freed from sin shall faithfully maintain this my gift, to them do I with folded hands placed to my head do obeisance.

Merit is a common bridge for kings. This from age to age deserves your support, O kings of the earth. Thus does Rámachandra beseech the kings who come after him. Whoso by violence takes away a gift made by himself or by another shall assuredly be born a worm in ordure for sixty thousand years. The earth has been enjoyed by Sagara and many other kings, whose empire was extensive in proportion to their (gifts of) land.

Chávundamayya, of the hill of Gunabhadra Deva, wrote it. Great prosperity! Fortune!

---

61. S'ila S'asana at Balagami, date about A. D. 1070

Size ft. 4 3′ × ft. 3 1′.—Haḷe Kannaḍa Characters.

Cow. LINGA with Priest in a Temple, surrounded with an elaborate scroll. Nandi.

May he (S'iva) who like the wild-fire in the forest drinks up the first of rivers (Ganges), its stream widened by the breeze from the waving chámaras in the hands, laden with tinkling ornaments, of the celestial nymphs as they fan him; god of gods; worthy to be praised by the three worlds; the husband of Gauri, grant our desire. May he who is as a thunderbolt to the mountains of trouble, who rejoices in the (movement of the) heads of his serpents, whose prowess is a source of joy, lord of heaven and all worlds, at the kalpa vriksha of whose feet is a place of rest from all care, the sight of whom is a joy to all people, who shines with the light of the moon, *Mahes'a*, grant every desire. May the god who is conspicuous by the light upon his lotus feet from the rows of jewels in the crowns of the celestial inhabitants prostrate before him, adorned with long arms like shining serpents, protect us.

The auspicious *Chalukya* emperor, peerless in might, *Tailapa*; a combination of all splendour, *Satyás'raya*; *Vikramáditya*, the home of bravery; *Jaya Singa*, excellent in wisdom, a treasury of surpassing ambition, kind to all; *Trailokya Malla*, encircling (as a garland) the fortune of the world—these being famous brought the Chálukya kingdom to renown.

That celebrated *Ahava Malla*, conqueror on the field of battle, lord of victory, lord of the sea-engirdled earth, a moon filled with the nectar of his good works, the source of fortune to the Chálukya kingdom, acquired great fame by the power of his own arms.

Trailokya Malla, (was such that) whoever refused him obeisance with folded hands, he went against them, O astonishment! in the greatness of his power, surrounding them, broke them, tossed them up, sacked them, dragged them violently along, beat them, slaughtered them, pierced them, cut them in two, plucked them up by the root, transported them, it is impossible to think of all the ways in which he destroyed his enemies.

Bhuvanaika Malla, his son, with qualities worthy of praise from all the inhabitants of the world, a beloved ornament to the wife his father's kingdom, his crest the dust from the lotus feet of S'iva, of the highest fame, the whiteness of the nectar of his splendid features shone into all lands. The elephants of *Bhuvanaika Malla* chased afar those who made war upon him, streams of blood flowed on all sides, so that wild animals came in groups to drink it; the enemy's elepnants fell here and there exhausted, their heads staggering with giddiness; the enemy's army completely routed, fled panting away.

May it be well.—While the victorious kingdom of *Bhuvanaika Malla Deva*, protector of all lands, favourite of earth and fortune, great king of kings, supreme ruler, first of monarchs, glory of the *Satyás'raya kula*, ornament of the *Chálukyas**—was continually increasing in prosperity, to endure as long as sun, moon and stars.—

Serving with diligence the lotus feet of this great king was the Vishnu-

* See note p. 14.

like *S'ri Ganga*, who could overcome all difficulties, who had subdued hosts of enemies, whose lotus feet received the homage of all rival kings bearing his orders on their heads, the greatest hero in the world.

Like a sea of good fortune, chief of all the Brahmans, a conqueror by his might in every point of the compass, a head jewel to Brahmans and Kshatriyas, a king of kings was *Udayáditya*. Is there any equal to you in the field of battle? you destroyed all the kings of the earth who came against you.

(The s'ásana stops here and is evidently incomplete.)

62. S'ila S'asana at Balagami, date A. D. 1138.

Size ft. 4 5' × ft. 1 7'.—Haḷe Kannaḍa Characters.

Nandi.	Linga with Votary in a temple.	Cow suckling calf.

Om. Adored be *S'ambhu*, beauteous with the chámara-like crescent moon kissing his lofty head; the original foundation-pillar of the city of the three worlds.

I am obedient to the words of Dhrivésvara Guru, the disciple of S'ri Vádi Rudra, and (am) like the possessor of the kalpa vriksha to the ears of the wise.

Om. Praise to S'iva. May it be well. While the victorious kingdom of the illustrious *Bhuloka Malla Deva*, protector of all lands, favourite of earth and fortune, great king of kings, supreme ruler, first of monarchs, glory of the *Satyás'raya* kula, ornament of the *Chálukyas**—was continually increasing in prosperity, to endure as long as sun, moon and stars.—

The sculptors *Byávaṇa* and *Rávaṇa*, adorned with all good qualities, of great reputation among the good, brothers, perfect workmen. Their father was *Goḍa*, their mother named *Ballave*, their friends and relations were *Gauris'a Dásas*, and they revered *Gautamárya*, worthy to be worshipped by munis, the áchári of the Koḍiya maṭha, whose praise is in all the world.

These two, *Byávaṇa* and *Rávaṇa*, in order to clear an aspersion on their own race of the sculptors,† set up an image of the god *Kusuves'vara*, and calling together *Mebi Seṭṭi*, *Kirtti Seṭṭi*, and others, with all the *nagara janangaḷu* and the five maṭhas, as well as their own house people, gave the temple of that *Kusuves'vara* to the illustrious *Gautama Deva*, in the same manner as the god *Kedáres'vara*.

* See note p. 14.

† *Nija s'ilpi kuḷa kaḷankamam kaḷeyadu.*

And that *Gautama Deva*, in the year Siddhárti, the month Pushya, the 13th day of the moon's increase, Sunday, the day of the sun's entering the northern signs—in presence of all the Nagaras and of the five maṭhas—pouring water, gave for the pleasure and daily service of the god, by the hand of *Narasimha*, 60 *kamma* of wet land from the eastern portion of the land in his possession. And *Mebi Seṭṭi* and *Kirtti Seṭṭi*, and the other *Nagara* people, experienced in all works of merit, gave in permanence the land rent of the house in which *Byávana* lived*, for the repairs of the temple of *Kusuves'vara*. And fifty householders of the oil-makers gave to the eternal god one solige of oil for each mill. And all the (?) tailors gave one *paṇa* per house per annum, and one *paṇa* for every wedding among them, for a splendid car procession of the god in the month Chaitra. (*Some defaced*).

Whoso protects this gift as long as sun, moon, stars and sky endure, obtains the merit of presenting a thousand tawny cows to Brahmans at Váranási, Gaya, and Kurukshétra. Kings should from age to age support the bridge of merit, thus prays continually Rámachandra. Whoso alienates any gift made by himself or by another will be born a worm in ordure for sixty thousand years. Of making a gift and continuing it, the continuing it is the best, for he who makes a gift obtains svarga, but he who continues it obtains final beatitude.

Praise to S'iva.

63. S'ila S'asana at Balagami, date about A. D. 1080.

Size ft. 3 × ft. 1 4.′—Haḷe Kannaḍa Characters.

Cow suckling calf. Linga with Priest. Nandi.

Om. Praise. Adored be *S'ambhu*, beauteous with the chámara-like crescent moon kissing his lofty head; the original foundation-pillar of the city of the three worlds.

May it be well.—While the victorious kingdom of the illustrious *Tribhuvana Malla Deva*, protector of all lands, favourite of earth and fortune, great king of kings, supreme ruler, first of monarchs, glory of the *Satyás'raya kula*, ornament of the *Chálukyas*†—was continually increasing in prosperity, to endure as long as sun, moon and stars.—

And the servant of his lotus feet, *Guṇḍamarasa* entitled to the five great drums, chief of great tributaries, a master in the use of missile weapons,

* *Byávaṇan irdda maneya siddáyamam.*

† See note p. 14.

Mane Verggaḍe* Danḍanáyaka, was ruling the Sokampana agrahára, the *vaḍḍa rávula, hejjunka* and two *biḷkoḍe* † within the Banavase náḍ.—

Channamarasa of his family, subduer of fierce kings, entitled to the five great drums, chief of great tributaries, subduer of the rebellious, destroyer of difficulties, like the horse, fish and Ráma incarnations, lord over all kings, the source of ruin to his enemies, the fearful, the ready for war, and with many other names.—

Making obeisance to the god *Sarves'vara* of the village of *Bárahá-koṭi*, filled with piety on beholding the divine Linga, in order to provide for the ablutions and daily worship of that god, (ordered to be given).—From each large rent free betel garden in . . one *paṇa* a month,—from the imposts in all the customs stations, two *paṇa*,—for each heap of fallen areca nuts, two areca nuts,—moreover for the annual festival the Paṭṭana S'ávi of the royal town Baḷḷigráme, and all the other citizens gave five *paṇa*,—for the service on the days of the changes in the moon, one paḍi of raw husked rice from each shop for the puddings,—in the Jiḍḍulige Seventy one *paṇa*, . . all the families of the betel sellers gave five *visa*, ... the goldsmiths . . . five *vi* . . . ‡. Thus let it be.

As much as the foregoing is also to be given if any repairs are required to the temple of Sárves'vara.

The writing of Kávala Sena is genuine (*a few words illegible.*)

---

* See No. 47, p. 108. † See notes pp. 79, 80.

‡ *Pên̩ṭhayoḷ tingaḷinge yeleya peṛu mánya vondakkam paṇa* 1, *samasta sunkada ṭhánántarangadoḷ kanṭháyavana yeraḍu, baḍinav aḍikeya peṛinge yeraḍ aḍike, mattam s'ri rájadháni Baḷḷigráme paṭṭaṇa s'avi modalági samasta nagaram pavitrakke koṭṭa paṇa* 5, *angaḍiyalu parva nivédyakke akki ba* 1, *Jiḍḍulige eppattaṛalu koṭṭa kanṭhavana* 1, *pênṭṭhayamm antará Baladevarum yeleya tambúligaru ellum vokkalol koṭṭa vi* 5, *pênṭṭha* . . . *námunam koṭṭaru sovanigaru koṭṭa vi* 5, *akasále* . . . *vi* 5, *kodatiya* . .

64. Virakal at Balagami, date A. D. 1207.

Size ft. 4 2′ × ft. 2 1′.—Haḷe Kannaḍa Characters.

Sun. Moon.
The hero in the presence. Linga with Priest. Nandi.

May it be well.—In the 17th year of *Vira Ballála Deva*, the year Prabhava, the month Kártika, the 10th day of the moon's decrease, Monday.—*Símeya Maimappa Arasu*, lord of Balligráme, with Sodeva, Deva Sikura, and Sole, though wounded by his enemies, dragged them into his town, killed many and went to heaven. May it be well.

The hero ascending to heaven in a car, attended by celestial nymphs, waving chamaras.

The hero with two attendants fighting in a gateway with several men armed with spears and shields.

65. Virakal at Balagami, date A. D. 1205.

Size ft. 5 2′ × ft. 2 4′.—Haḷe Kannaḍa Characters.

Sun. Moon.
The hero in the presence. Linga with Priest. Nandi.

May it be well.—In the 15th year of the Yádava emperor *Vira Ballála Deva*, the year Krodhana, the month Chaitra, the 11th day of the moon's increase, Monday.—

May it be well.—While the great minister *Panunappa Arasu*, possessed of all titles, a minister of great renown, chief of all the officers, head of all the braves, wed like Yugandha to the goddess of victory, always attentive to his master's affairs, skilled in conciliating the commanders of the army, was ruling in peace and wisdom the nád belonging to Palligráme, the royal city of the Banavase Twelve Thousand, punishing the evil and protecting the good.—

The ancient agrahara *Jambúru* . . . .

The hero ascending to heaven in a car attended by celestial nymphs, some waving chamaras, and accompanied by celestial musicians playing on drums.

The commander with his sons and brothers fought against his enemies (*rest illegible*)

The hero armed with sword and shield, attended by a horseman of rank, a trumpeter and footmen, fighting men armed some with bows some with swords and shields.

66. Virakal at Balagami, date unknown.

Size ft. 3 3′ × ft. 1 6′.—Haḷe Kannaḍa Characters.

The hero in the presence. Linga with Priest. Nandi.

May it be well.—The great minister possessed of all titles,—*Piriya . yaṇa Danáyaka* went against *Singa Deva* and fought.

The hero ascending to heaven in a car, attended by celestial nymphs waving chamaras.

In the inner gate of Tripura, *Tippa* . . *Deva* killed many and went to heaven. The monument of his bravery*.

Men armed with bows fighting with others armed with sword and shield.

67. Virakal at Balagami, date A. D. 1180.

Size ft. 5 1′ ft. 2 5′.—Haḷe Kannaḍa Characters.

Sun. Moon.

The hero in the presence. Linga with Priest. Nandi.

OM. Praise to S'iva. May it be well.—In the reign of the *Kalachurya* emperor, *Ahava Malla Deva*, the year S'árvari, the month Phálguna, new moon day, Monday. While the great minister *Kes'imaya Danḍanáyaka*, chief of the female apartments†, great . . . punishing the evil and protecting the good in the Banavase Twelve Thousand, was carrying on the government in the great royal city of Balligráme in peace and wisdom, one day, .

The hero ascending to heaven in a car attending by celestial nymphs waving chamaras.

the punisher of those who . . the head of great commanders, . his head placed at the feet of Siva, the great lord Talári Keta Malla Náyaka and others, when many were going to the Máyile war‡, marching so that all stooped down and cried out, in front of all killing many and carrying out his master's orders, he went to the world of gods. On the day of his disappearance§ his brother-in-law Kálaya Náyaka, his son Mahádeva Náyaka, and Padmavve Náyakiti erected this *víra s'ásana*. Great good fortune. Prosperity.

A fight between men armed with spears and shields, one of them carrying a banner, and men armed with bows and arrows. A figure in the centre begging for mercy.

---

* *A'tana bira gallu.*

† *S'rimanu mahápradhánam antahpura verggaḍe mahápasákkatam* (?) Cf. No. 47.

‡ *Máyileya bavarakke halaram hógalu.*

§ *Yederantaram halaram kondu svámi káryyavam naḍahi sura loka práptanádan átange paroksha dina.*

68. S'ila S'asana at Balagami, date A. D. 1103.

Size ft. 6 6′ × ft. 2 3′.—Haḷe Kannaḍa Characters.

Sun. Moon.

The Donor. Narasimha destroying Hiranyakashipu. Cow suckling calf.

(Four lines at top illegible.)

May it be well.—*Vikramáditya* was a king whose navel was occupied by the goddess of fortune, his feet were placed on the head of his enemies, he was praised by all people and of spotless fame. With a gentle smile as white as the body of his fame, which resembled in purity curds or the elephant's tusk, he had brought all the world under one umbrella, a crowning ornament to the lunar race. In strength of body, strength of shoulders, strength in wielding the sword, who in the world can excel you? Are there any kings in the earth so conspicuous when the bravest of the enemy are engaged amid the roar of battle?

May it be well.—While the victorious kingdom of the illustrious *Tribhuvana Malla*, a protector of all lands, favourite of earth and fortune, great king of kings, supreme ruler, first of monarchs, glory of the *Satyás'raya kula*, ornament of the *Chálukyas**, was continually increasing in prosperity, to endure as long as sun, moon and stars—and while he was ruling in peace and wisdom in his residence of *Kalyáṇa*.—

Resting at his feet as the bee upon the lotus, was *Anantapála* Danḍádis'a, endowed with titles of honor and virtue, who had exhibited his prowess among the brave enemies, was worshipped by the learned, an ocean to the gem of goodness, the purest of the pure, the ablest of the able.

May it be well.—While entitled to the five great drums, the Mahá manḍales'vara, lord over great feudatories, giver of their wishes to the learned, attentive to the good, purifier of the other family (into which he married), son of a superior mother, a fourth Revanta, like Yama to his enemies, able to overcome impossibilities, a new Narasimha, possessed of all titles—the great minister, Báṇasa Verggaḍe (chief of the kitchen!) Danḍanáyaka *Anantapálarasa* having received the Puḷvala (or Purvala) Three Hundred, the Puligeṛe Three, the Banavase Twelve Thousand, the seven and a half lakh *pannáya*, was governing them in peace and wisdom.†

---

* See note p. 14.

† *S'ríman mahá pradhánam, báṇasa verggaḍe danḍanáyakan Anantapálarasam Puḷvala múnúṛu Puligeṛe múṛu Banavase pannirchchhasiramu saptárddha lakshaya pannáyamam paḍedu sukha sankathá vinodadim pratipálisuttam ire.*

Through his favour, *Góvinda Rája*, brilliant with all good qualities, obtained the government of the Twelve Thousand country of Vanavási.

With a navel greatly enlarged by the goddess of fortune, shining with a garland of good qualities, was *Góvinda*. Like Vishnu to the rákshasas his boasting enemies, like Bhairava his feet were worthy of reverence as those of a king, if seen in anger like S'iva when his central eye flames forth in the forehead, adorned with a snake-like crest, lotus ornaments in his ears, his arms shining with the spear, with a brilliant tusk in his mouth, he was fearful to behold in war. To *Kes'i Rája*, distinguished in all learning, and his wife *Nilarbe*, was born *Dás'i Rája*, beloved by all the earth, filled with all good qualities, a sun in the firmament of the *Parása* family. He was the father, and *Somámbika*, the abode of all virtues and good qualities, the mother of *Góvinda Rája*.

While this *Góvinda Rája*, the gem of all such good qualities, protector of the learned, enlightening the water-lily of the world with the moonlight of his spotless fame, Ranaranga Bhairava, like Vatsa Rája to the river of poison, like the kalpavriksha to the great poets, subduer of all fierce enemies, having received the Banavase Twelve Thousand, the *vaḍḍa rávuḷa*, and the *pannáya* dues of the fifty six (i. e. merchants) within the shadow of his umbrella (i. e. within his jurisdiction)* was protecting them in the enjoyment of peace and wisdom.

His minister for peace or war was *Is'varaya Náyaka*, whose descent was as follows.—

From Brahma was born *Vasishṭha*, a crowning ornament to the body of great munis, continually worshipped by all the people in the world, of perfectly spotless fame, of distinguished greatness, possessed of all the highest qualities, best of the Brahmans. From the family of the great muni *Vasishṭha* sprung the *Siriga* race, celebrated by all people, in which was born *Chaṭṭa*, an ocean of all good qualities, a grinding stone to the heap of sin. To *Chaṭṭarasa* thus reputed, and his famous wife *Nágámbika* were born two sons, *Bábi Rája* and *Basava*, praised of all people. From the devotion of these brothers to the god Virupáksha, of surpassing splendour grew up *Is'vara*, like a bee at the lotus feet of Is'vara (S'iva). Will all the works of merit in the sea-engirdled earth come up to the liberality of this worthy *Is'vara*, or all the meritorious equal him in greatness of mind ?

As firm as the Mandara mountain, of unequalled capacities, a mango tree to the parrot of allied kings, of great generosity, the head of the Brahmans of

* *Banavase pannirchchAsiramumam vaḍḍa rávuḷamunam chhatra chchháyeya chappannad achchu pannáyamam paḍedu.*

Narigonda, fond of pleasure, a friend of good people. Such says all the world is *Is'vara*, the minister (*sandhi vigrahi*) of *Góvinda Rája.*

(*Some unintelligible, parts being defaced.*)

Resting like a bee at the lotus feet of *Govinda Raja* and possessing his favour, *Is'vara Náyaka*, the minister for peace or war, adorned with all good qualities, protector of all the learned, a pleasant moon diffusing rays of mercy, with a banner of shining white,—in the 29th year of Chalukya Vikrama, the year Svabhánu, the month Pushya, the 10th day of the moon's decrease, Friday, the day of the sun's entering the northern signs,—with his heart bent on meritorious works, thinking on the saying that there is no friend like merit—for providing sandal, incense, lights, and food for the god *Narasimha*, and for repairing his temple on the bank of the *Peragatta* tank, in the northern quarter of *Balligáve*, the royal city of the *Banavase* Twelve Thousand, which shone like nose-jewel and head-ornaments to the land of *Kuntala*, —with the consent of the citizens of the royal city Balligáve and of the five maṭhas, and the knowledge of the auspicious Daṇḍanáyaka Govíndarasa,—Nákanna, the son of Rudramayya, the son of the poet Báṇḍava, the owner of Pakkaḷeyúru, situated in the kampana Jiḍḍulige Seventy, in the Banavase Twelve Thousand, having made over, free from all imposts, with every formality, with washing the feet and pouring of water, 50 *kamma* of paddy land according to the kachchavi pole, from his rent free estate in the land of that Pakkale—(Is'vara náyaka) receiving, presented it.

And the boundaries of the land were defined as follows :—On the side of Indra (the east), the stones on which the sásanas are written. On the side of the sun's son (Yama, the south), the tank Brindeya. On the side of the lord of waters (Varuna, the west), the cultivation of the city Balli. On the side loved of Kubéra (the north), the Yeleya river. From these marks the land itself may be clearly made out.

Moreover the chief ministers of the Vanavási Twelve Thousand to give every year 1 *gadya(na)*, Brahman renters 1 *paṇa*, the royal servants 10 *visa.*

Whoso makes a gift becomes the lord of all wealth. Whoso despises and alienates it, incurs the guilt of murdering in the holy places of Ganges, Gaya, Varanás'i, and Kurukshetra,—cows, Brahmans, rishis and his own brothers : he will go through all the hells and descend to the lowest. Whoso resumes a gift made by himself or by another will be born a worm in ordure for sixty thousand years.

---

69. S'ila S'asana at Balagami, date A. D. 1075.

Size ft. 5' × ft. 1 10'.—Haļe Kannada Characters.

The Donor.	Moon.	Narasimha destroying Hiranyakas'ipu.	Sun.	Cow suckling calf.

Praise to Narasimha, who taking the form of the man-lion slew the rákshasa Hiraņyakas'ipu.

The auspicious *Chálukya* emperor, peerless in might, *Tailapa*; a combination of all splendour, *Satyás'raya; Vikramáditya*, the home of bravery; *Jaya Singha*, excellent in wisdom, a treasury of surpassing ambition, kind to all; *Trailokya Malla*, encircling (as a garland) the fortune of the world—these being famous brought the Chálukya kingdom to renown. *Bhuvanaika Malla*, his son, with qualities worthy of praise from all the inhabitants of the world, a beloved ornament to the wife his father's kingdom, his crest the dust from the lotus feet of S'iva, of the highest fame, the whiteness of the nectar of his splendid features shone into all lands.

May it be well.—While the victorious kingdom of *Bhuvanaika Malla Deva*, protector of all lands, favourite of earth and fortune, great king of kings, supreme ruler, first of monarchs, glory of the *Satyás'raya kula*, ornament of the *Chálukyas**, was continually increasing in prosperity, to endure as long as sun, moon, and stars.—

Resting at his lotus feet, shone the Vishnu-like *Ganga*, who had subdued his enemies, whose lotus feet were worshipped by other kings, who placed his commands upon the heads of hostile princes, the first hero in the world. A sea of great wealth, lord of the Brahmans, a great conqueror by the might of his hands, an ornament to Brahmans and Kshatriyas, king of kings, was *Udeyáditya*.

May it be well.—While praised by all people, born with all the privileges of Brahmans and Kshatriyas, favourite of earth and fortune, great king of kings, supreme ruler, lord of *Koļálapura*, chief of *Nandagiri*, having the ensign of a lusty elephant, having received a boon from Sómés'vara, the Ganga Cupid, a Ganga of truth, an increaser of victory, a chintámani to the desires of all people, a chief jewel in the crown of kings, *S'rimad Ganga Permmánaḍi Bhuvanayka Vira, Udeyáditya Deva* was governing the Banavase Twelve Thousand, the Sántalige Thousand, the Mandali Thousand, and the eighteen agrahá-ras, punishing the evil and protecting the good,— having subdued the mon-

---

* See note p. 14.

archs of the neighbouring countries, *Chera*, *Choḷa*, *Pándya*, *Pallava*, and exacted tribute from them; having acquired all the land as far as the four oceans and accomplished the desire to be a great conqueror; being in the enjoyment of peace and wisdom, in the royal city of *Balligáve**,—Being desirous of performing a work of merit, and having informed his lord king *Bhuvanaika Malla*, of the same,—to provide for repairs to the temple of *Narasimha*, on the bank of the *Perguta* tank, in the royal city of *Balligáve* and for the daily service of the god, in the S'aka year 997, the year Rákshasa, the month Pushya, the first day of the moon's increase, Monday, at the moment of the sun's entering the northern signs,—gave up, washing the feet of *Púrnna Nanda Bhaṭṭáraku* of that place, and pouring water,—one village Kundavige, in the Mugunda Twelve of the Banavase náḍ kampaṇa.

Whoso preserves this gift will derive the merit of presenting a thousand tawny cows in Ganga, Gaya, Kurukshétra, Váranás'i and Prayága, or of having a kolaga made, decorated with the five precious stones, for Brahmans versed in the védas. Poison is no poison, the property of the gods that is the real poison. For poison kills one man, but a gift to the gods (if alienated) kills a man with his son and descendants.

---

* *Svasti samasta bhuvanastuta, Brahma Kshatra viránvaya, s'ri prithvi vallabha, mahá rájádhirája, parames'varam, Koḷáḷapura vares'varam, Nandagiri nátham, mada gajendra lánchchhanam, Somes'vara labdha vara prasádam, Ganga Kusumáyyudam, nanniya Gangam, jayadutta rangam, sakala jana chintámani, mandalika makuṭa chúḍámaṇi, S'rímad Ganga Permmánaḍi Bhuvanayka Víran Udeyáditya Deva Banavase pannirchchhásiram Sántalige sásiramumam Manḍali sásiramum padinenṭ agrahάramumam dushṭa nigraha vis'ishṭa pratipálanadin álutium pratyanta vásigalappa Chera Choḷa Pánḍya Pallava prabhritigal aldu dáḷándu kappamam konḍu chatu vváddhi paryyantam nelanam nimichchi vijugishu vrittiyanappu keydu sukha sankathá vinodadim rájadháni Baḷḷigáveyol irddu.*

70. S'ila S'asana at Balagami, date A. D. 1071.

Size ft. 6 × ft. 2 6.—Haḷe Kannaḍa Characters.

Boar. The Yogi Gunagalla * Sun. The Trimurti in a temple. Moon. Cow suckling calf.

Supreme is the Boar form of the splendid Vishnu, which dispersed the waters of the ocean and supports the peaceful world upon its right tusk.

May it be well.—While the victorious kingdom of *Bhuvanaika Malla Deva*, protector of all lands, favourite of earth and fortune, great king of kings, supreme ruler, first of monarchs, glory of the *Satyás'raya kula*, ornament of the *Chálukyas* †, was continually increasing in prosperity, to endure as long as sun, moon, and stars—

Living at his lotus feet in *Bankapura*, entitled to the five great drums, chief of great tributaries, subduer of fierce enemies, lord of all the treasures in that place, like Náráyana in his ability to carry out his master's behests, the refuge of the learned, clothed with the garment of prudence, possessed of all learning, with a mind purified by the praise of Hara, great in giving increase to the Chálukya kingdom, a lion of independence, like a bee at the lotus feet of *Bhuvanaika Malla*, adorned with all virtues, was the great minister, senior councillor for peace and war, the Mane Verggaḍe Daṇḍanáyaka *Udeyáditya*.

At whose request, *Bhuvanaika Malla*, in the S'aka year 993, the year Virôdhikrit, the month Pushya, the 1st day of the moon's increase, Monday, at the moment of the sun's entering the northern signs,—for the ablutions and daily worship of the god *Harihaṛáditya* of the royal city of *Baḷḷigámve*, and for repairing his temple, gave up, free of all burdens,—washing the feet of *Gunagaḷḷa Yogi*, a combined light of virtue, wisdom and peace, possessor of all the blessings arising from the sound *om*,—and pouring water—one village, Bidiringeri, situated in the Jiḍḍuḷige Seventy, in the Banavase Twelve Thousand.

Whoso maintains this gift, that man shall have eternal joy. He who usurps it shall have eternal pain.

As a (sectarian) mark on the fair brow of heavenly felicity, renowned for the powers of the Advaita, shone the pure minded *Gunagalla*. As movable things spring from immovable and return again to immobility so was his mind fixed; perfect in Advaita lore, without any equal was *Gunagalla*. Enjoying unbounded happiness from the all-knowing, all-possessing, all-pervading Advaita; all things and the cause of all things was *Gunagalla*.

---

* An inscription over him as follows :—*Srímadu Gunagaḷḷa Dévara dibya múrtti.*

† See note p. 14.

The moment you acquire the consciousness "I am knowledge" is it not to experience unbounded happiness? "Save myself naught is" of this knowledge was he the treasury, the summit of Advaita, *Gunagalla.*

Joyful, undual, in the form of virtue and knowledge, without pride, a lover of the divine essence in all things and thus attached to all names was the Yógi *Gunagalla.* Enmity having broken out between desire which enters into the body and the six passions which seeking for increase abide there, they have left you; all mixed actions and self conceit you have burnt up by the roots—being thus distinguished can heavenly happiness fail you great muni *Gunagalla?*

Wedded to eternal happiness, without wish for family, having forsaken the pleasures of the senses, without desire, pure, wise and a lover of wisdom was the supremely happy *Gunagalla.* Having escaped from the seven troubles, and freed himself from ignorance and the influence of the passions, a great rishi was *Gunagalla.* Perfect in renouncing the world, looking with disgust on family, he desired a life of devoted piety, perfect peace and fortitude, and what he desired he has become, this *Gunagalla.*

In the east of Tumbigere in the celebrated Kogali náḍ . . .
in the west the abodes of Yoges'vara and Svayambhu, and in the famous city of Balipura he set up Yoges'vara, Hariharáditya, and the god called Vássayana, and built their temples,—this *Gunagalla.** In the south country he built a tank, made many divisions of land to Brahmans in the celebrated Muttúru, and built the Sidda Tirtha,—all these in the knowledge of all people did *Gunagalla.*

He taught the tatva doctrine, and saying "Can you not give up your old ways? This is the way (of truth)" thus with great boldness taught *Gunagalla.* The great muni *Gunagalla* by grace has entered on that path, can any thing then be impossible to one who with unshaken faith at all times adheres to his lotus feet? Can the desires be unfulfilled of those who receiving this doctrine, free from desire, given to kindness, are the disciples of the prince of gurus? By deep meditation on tatva the impurity of the mind may be purged away, the light of the soul will always shine as clearly as a little lamp, the favour of the feet of the guru god, obtained with due reverence, is the only thing that will endure, therefore obtain it all disciples by your piety, then happiness and good fortune will come to all.

This was written by Pratikanṭha Káma Rája.

---

* *Akkara* ‖ *Esava Kogali náḍ oḷagaṇa Tumbigereya múḍaṇa simeyadoḷage mosalya maduvisa paḍuvaṇa sime Yoges'varam Svayambhu niḷeya jasada Balipura varadoḷ Yoges'varam Hariharádityam Vássayánan emba pesara devaram devâleyangaḷam máḍisidar Gunagaḷḷa Devar* ‖

71. S'ila S'asana at Balagami, date A. D. 1035.

Size ft. 6 6′ × ft. 3 1′.—Haḷe Kannaḍa Characters.

Sun. Moon.
Linga with Votary in a temple.
Boar. Cow suckling calf.

Praise to S'iva who manifests himself clearly as objects to the sense, benefactor of the earth, creator, preserver and destroyer of the world, soul of all things, who with anger destroyed Manmatha, lord of the three worlds.

Desiring to perform the world-astounding Rájasúya sacrifice, in order to obtain the great wealth (necessary for it) . . . . the son of the king-terrifier went forth with anger, and having levied contributions there, and completed it, the Pánḍavas came to Balligámve and the five set up the temple of the Five Lingas.*

May it be well.—The king *Jaya Simha Deva*, protector of all lands, favourite of earth and fortune, great king of kings, supreme ruler, first of monarchs, glory of the *Satyás'raya kula*, ornament of the *Chálukyas*†, the perfume of the jasmine, fearful to the armies of his enemies, a lion to the elephants his rival kings, male of males, a golden ornament to the male sex, like the fire which shall destroy the world to Chóḷa, full of desire to fight with the Chóḷa rája,‡ a jewel in the garland of distinguished kings, to hostile kings a saw for their heads, a falcon (to strike them), a scorching sun (to burn them up), in brightness as the sun, in worship like Vishnu, to the ocean of kings a Baḍabánala, to the four-arrowed a thousand-armed, to the world of kings a Rudra, clothed with fame and learning, like Ráma in skill with the bow, possessed of the title *Jagadeka Malla* and all other titles—ruling in peace and wisdom in his residence at *Poṭṭalakere*—in the S'aka year 957, the year Yuva, the month Pushya, on the day of full moon, Sunday, the day of the sun's entering the northern signs, at the vyati páta :—

To *Malla Kules'vara Panḍita*—who had reached the farthest shore of the ocean of logic and all the other sciences, like the original Rudra, a young lion in tearing open with his claws the forehead of the elephants his opponents, the spontaneous wild-fire to the forest of opposing disputants, a thunderbolt to the caves of false arguers, a Badabánala to the Bauddha sea, a lightning bolt to the

---

* *Jagadas'charyada Rájasúya makham ṫyaḍal mahártha pává . ge meyda . . nripabhíshana megákshepadim pógi vastugaḷa kappaman alli konḍu magurḍḍadu Ppánḍavar Bhaḷḷigávege vand ayvarum aydu lingama nivása sthápanam máḍipar.*

† See note p. 14. ‡ *Chôḷógra kaḷánaḷam, Chóḷa bhanḍanápéksham.*

mountain of the professors of the mimámsa, a saw in cutting down the great tree of sceptics, a Garuda in opposing the great serpents the professors of the sánkhya philosophy, an osprey in the tree of his stunned opponents, a three-eyed to the triple city of sin, a grinding stone to Mádhava Bhaṭṭa, destroyer of the self conceit of Jnánánanda, a fire such as shall destroy the world to Abhayachandra, a lion to the elephant his opponents, a sealer up of the mouths of the most eloquent speakers, the limit of the point of the compass of the science of ethics, loving to defend the professors of logic, like Brahma in supporting and establishing a proposition, like the throne of Sarasvati in the assembly of the learned, like Vishnu in judgment, like S'iva in producing proof, like the flood of Ganges in his eloquence, an acknowledged master of commentators, a bee to the lotus of the excellent the device on the banner of great sanyásis, a coat of mail to the pure, a noose for the necks of a dozen of pretended pandits, a terrible meteor in the sky of his rival Digambara, distinguished by the title of *Vádi Rudra Guṇa* :—

To provide for the repairs of the temple of the Five Lingas set up by the Pándavas in the Kálámukha Bramhachári quarter of the royal city of *Balligámve* in the *Banavase* Twelve Thousand and for perfumes, incense, and daily service of the god, for food and clothing for the disciples and rishis, and for the relief of every kind of want ;—gave, free from all burdens, with every ceremony and pouring of water, in the fields belonging to *Mayúru*, 11 mattas according to the kacchavi pole, and also according to that pole 5 mattas in the garden land of the town, and under *Pergatta* 2 mattas,—altogether 18 mattas and under *Pergatta* a flower garden.

Whoso maintains this gift will secure the merit of presenting a thousand tawny cows to Brahmans at the holy bathing places of Váranási, Kurukshetra, and Prayága—and of presenting a koḷaga decked with the five precious stones to Brahmans learned in the védas, or of presenting a double headed (*i. e.* parturient) cow to a thousand Brahmans. Whoso usurps this gift will incur the guilt of killing a thousand tawny cows and a thousand Brahmans at the holy bathing places of Váranási, Kurukshetra, and Prayága. Whoso by violence seizes the land presented either by himself or by another will certainly be born a worm in ordure for sixty thousand years. The earth has had Ságara and many other kings whose empire was extensive in proportion to their gifts of land. The bridge of merit deserves your support O kings of the earth. Thus from age to age cries Rámachandra to the kings who come after him. Poison is no poison. The property of the gods that is the real poison. For poison

kills one man, but a gift to the gods (if usurped) kills a man with his son and descendants.

The feet of S'iva are worthy of worship by all the world—the works of merit enjoined in the three vedas are a refuge to the different castes. Whoso acts contrary to either of these on his head will I put my foot.

May those who do not wish to maintain this public gift be totally ruined.

Here follows another s'ásana (date? A. D. 1058) the greater part of which has been defaced.

May it be well.—Born of a race worthy of praise from all kings, *Satyá* . . . supreme ruler, lord of Kuvalálapura, chief of Nandagiri, having the ensign of a lusty elephant, ...
a Ganga of truth, the Ganga Bhíshma, the Ganga S'iva,* . . . . .
a head jewel in the diadem of great kings, the *Chálukya* (*name defaced*), in the year Vilambi, the month Pushya, the 10th day of the moon's decrease, Tuesday, at the moment of the sun's entering the northern signs, to the god of the Five Lingas set up by the Pándavas, called *Umá Mahes'vara*. . . .

(*Some defaced*)

a flower garden, and for a great car procession in the hot season, for perfumes, lights and daily service . . . one matta.

(*Rest defaced.*)

---

72. S'ila S'asana at Balagami, date A. D. 1019.

Size ft. 4 6' × ft. 2'.—Haḷe Kannaḍa Characters.

Moon. Sun.

Linga with Priest.

An attendant. Cow suckling calf.

May—the husband of *Lakshmi*, bearer of the chakra, whose vehicle is *Garuḍa*, having eyes like the lotus—the husband of *Párvati*, bearing the s'úla, whose vehicle is *Bàsava*, having an extra eye—the husband of *Sarasvati*, bearer of the pás'a, who comes riding on the swan, having eight eyes—these three, worshipped by the three worlds, grant our desires.

---

* *Nanniya Gangam* | *Ganga Gángeyam* | *Ganga sarbbanum.* See No. 69.

May it be well.—While the victorious kingdom of the illustrious *Taïlapa Deva*, protector of all lands, favourite of earth and fortune, great king of kings, supreme ruler, first of monarchs, glory of the *Satyás'raya kula*, ornament of the *Chálukyas**, the perfume of the jasmine, fearful to the armies of his enemies, a lion to the elephants his rival kings, male of males, a golden ornament to the male sex, like the fire which shall destroy the world to Chóla, full of desire to fight with the Chóla Rája, a jewel in the garland of distinguished kings, to hostile kings a saw for their heads, a falcon (to strike them), a scorching sun (to burn them up), in brightness as the sun, in worship like Vishnu, to the ocean of kings a Baḍabánala, to the four-arrowed a thousand-armed, to the world of kings a Rudra, clothed with fame and learning, like Ráma in skill with the bow, a golden ornament to the male sex, born in the auspicious *Chálukya* race,—was continually increasing in prosperity, to endure as long as sun, moon and stars.—†

Of the kings of the Chálukya dynasty by which the world had been governed, 59 sat upon the throne with great glory in the city of *Ayodhya*. Of that race was born *Satyás'raya Deva*, favourite of the goddess of victory, who ruled all the earth so that among the lines descended from Brahma the *Satyás'raya kula* was reckoned the greatest, obtaining the name of Sárvva Bhauma.‡

Descended from that *Satyás'raya kula* was the powerful lord of the earth *Núrmmaḍi Taïla*, like Indra in the extent of his possessions, a terror to his enemies, of brilliant fame, who ruled all the earth. When the earth had fallen into the hands of the Raṭṭas, he routed the Raṭṭa kings, sacked them, was as a grinding stone to the Raṭṭas, and obtained possession of the Chálukya kingdom.‡

That king *Jaya Singha*, sunlight to the groups of lotuses the Bhója kings, the king of beasts to the elephant Rájendra Chóla, what wonder that he is called the great king of kings. ‡ Dispersing the darkness his enemies, and causing his greatness to shine forth into all the world, as the morning sun mounts up above the mountain of the east so he mounted up on his throne of splendour, and subduing the increasing powers of the Kali Yuga he left it no place, the king

---

* See note p. 14. † Cf. No. 71.

‡ *Dhareyam Chálukyánnvayad arasugaḷ ekona shashṭi simhásanam áḷdar Ayodhyápura varadoḷu paramotsavadindam irddu tad vams'a bhavam* || *jaya vanites'am Satyás'raya Devam Brahma kuḷamanoḷu pina Sattyás'raya kuḷav ene sakala dharitriyan áḷdam sárbba bhauma vesar esevi negam* || *á Satyás'raya kuḷadoḷ ilásudatis'am pratápi Núrmmaḍi Taïlam vásava vibhavam ripu santrási yes'obhási sakala dhátriyan álda* || *Raṭṭara kaige virdd eḷeyum paṭṭamumam Raṭṭa rájyad arasugaḷam mumbiṭṭu taṛidoṭṭi Raṭṭa gharaṭṭam Chálukya rájya paṭṭaman ántam* || *á Jaya Singha nripálam Bhoja nripámbhoja rájanina nibha tejam Rájendra Chóḷa gaja mriga rájam Rájádhirája nenipudu piride* ||

Jaya Singha. Málava seeks in vain an opportunity of lifting himself up, at a single one of his roars Chera fled afar, Chóla he drove into the sea, and when he attempted to come out cast him in again* ; thus the splendour of his fame passed over the seven oceans and filled the regions beyond, his conquests of the eight points of the compass put to shame the regents of the points ; who in the world could stand before this king *Jaya Singha ?*

The dweller at his lotus feet, *Kundamarasa*, the son of *Iriva Bidanga Deva*, entitled to the five great drums, Mahá Mandales'vara, the ruler of the chief city of Banavási, having obtained a boon from the favour of Chámunda, a lion to the elephants his enemies, like S'iva receiving the worship of good men, white with streaming benevolence as an elephant (with the moisture on his forehead,) first in the assembly, terrible as lusty elephants, a cage of adamant to any who took refuge with him, a driving hook to the elephants his enemies, like the sun to the darkness his enemies, a man as good as his word,† in war like Ráma, in honour like mount Méru, the sole champion of the world, clothed with wisdom and valour, the circle of his camp caused all the points of the compass to move, a grinding stone to his enemies, a diadem to the brow of all the petty kings, chief of all the umbrellas‡,— ruling with equal justice § the *Banavase* Twelve Thousand, the *Sántali* Thousand, and the *Hayve* Five Hundred, as far as the western ocean, was in the enjoyment of peace and wisdom in the city of *Balipura* ;—in the s'aka year 941, the year Siddhárti, the month Pushya, the 2nd day of the moon's increase, Sunday, at the auspicious moment of the sun's entering the northern signs.—

Having repaired the temple of the god *Múlasthána Nandikes'vara*, gave, washing the feet of *Múliga S'ivas'akti Pandita*, accomplished in all the kinds of devotion, *yama, níyama, ásana, pránáyáma, pratyáhára, dhyána, dhárana, mauna, anushthána, japa, samádhi*, ‖ —to provide for the daily service of the god and future repairs of the temple—

Near the land formerly belonging to the temple, in the corner of the plain in the lane south west of the city, a paddy field of 12 mattas according to the katsavi pole,—and the uncultivated ground south of the southern trench of the paddy field, one matta ; its boundary mark, a ditch on the west,—and to the north of the northern trench of the paddy field, one matta of uncultivated ground ; its boundaries, on the north, the northern waste weir of the Kari tank, on the east the well below the Balli field,—and in the plain near the land

---

* *Málavam elumam puduke gattisid attareyatti Cheranum Cholanumam samudradolag arddidudarddidandam.*

† *Nudidante ganda.* ‡ *Sattigana chattam.* § *Ubhaya sámayadi* ‖ See Nos. 8 and 38.

belonging to another god, two Balli paddy fields of two mattas,—and to the north of the temple a flower garden of 30 kammas, and two tanks which stretch from the south to the east of the temple, and under the tanks an areca garden of one matta,—and at the northern waste weir of the tanks to the south of the Haḍidala tank a flower garden of 50 kammas.

Moreover for the worship and honour, and daily oblation of the companion god *Chaturmukha* (Brahma) and for the repairs of his temple, to the east of the spring under the Are tank formerly belonging to the temple, one matta 50 kammas,—and for a flower garden 40 kammas round the temple,—and south from the temple two streets, the boundary-marks of which are on the west and north long ponds, and on the south and east the high road,—and west from the temple two tanks and the land belonging to them, bounded north and west by the north-west-street, east by the Balli pond,—and in that place north from Bádumbe a flower garden of 40 kammas.

(The s'ásana stops abruptly here, and is probably not quite complete.)

73. S'ila S'asana at Balagami, date A. D. 1075.

Size ft. 3 6' × ft. 1 7'.—Haḷe Kannaḍa Characters.

Sun. Linga with Votary. Moon.

Nandi. Cow suckling calf.

May it be well.—While the auspicious *Bhuvanaika Malla Deva*, a protector of all lands, favourite of earth and fortune, great king of kings, supreme ruler, first of monarchs, glory of the *Satyás'raya kula*, ornament of the *Chálukyas** was ruling in peace and wisdom in the city of *Bankapura*.

May it be well.—The dweller at his lotus feet, the sole champion of the world, a terror to the forces (of his enemies), male of males, a saw for the heads of his enemies, a falcon to hostile kings, the wild-fire to the grove of his enemies, a lion to the elephant his enemies, like Ráma in subduing opposing kings . . . . . .

† . . . . . the year Rákshasa, the month Pushya, . . at the moment of the sun's entering the northern signs. . . for the restoration of the god Siddés'vara . . . . the son of Bhatta . . . . made with joy . . . . to enter a better world . . . . . near the glorious

* See note p. 14.

† This part of the inscription is so much defaced as to be almost entirely illegible.

Balli . . . . . a Brahman agrahára . . . . washing the feet of the teacher *Sosala*, and pouring water as approved by all people . . . in the Jiḍḍuḍige Seventy . . . . . the gift of that Brahmanála Dakshinagarasa . . . . washing the feet of the teacher Sósala, &c., . . . a rent free agrahára. . . .

Whoso maintains this gift will derive the merit of presenting all the holy agraháras. In his house will Lakshmi (fortune) and Sarasvati (learning) dwell. Whoso revokes this gift incurs the guilt of killing a Brahman. His race will be destroyed. Merit is a bridge for all and under the care of kings, therefore protect and support it, thus does Rámachandra from age to age beseech the kings that should be after him. Whoso revokes a gift presented by himself or by another will assuredly be born a worm in ordure for sixty thousand years.

(*Some defaced.*)

---

74. S'ila S'asana at Balagami, date A. D. 1158.

Size ft. 7 8' × ft. 4 3'.—Haḷe Kannaḍa Characters.

Elephant goad. Sun. Boar. VISHNU. Sword. Moon. Cow suckling calf.

Om. Praise to *Náráyana.* Supreme is the boar form of the resplendent *Vishnu*, which dispersed the waters of the ocean and bears up the peaceful world on the tip of his strong right tusk. May the three great rulers of the three worlds, *Brahma*, *S'iva* and *Vishnu*, grant us success.

May *Kes'ava* (Vishnu), the husband of Lakshmi, who by his might acquired the empire of Bali, who combines in himself all the glory of the ten incarnations, surrounded by the conch, the vajra and the lotus in his hands, being favorable to his worshipper *Kes'ava* the general of the army, grant him to live till the destruction of the world. On the summit of the waves of the milk sea he reposes on his extensive couch the serpent Adisesha. While thus the remover of sins was reposing in the sleep of yoga, his mind being directed to the creation of the world, as if his power had assumed a separate bodily form, from the lotus of his navel sprang in submission *Brahma.*

On surveying the circle of all the worlds created in order by *Brahma*, the most beautiful is the middle one (the earth)—in that world the most pleasing region is the delightful *Jambu Dvipa*—and in that dvipa the most excellent is the *Bharata* land—and in that land the *Kuntala* country the most worthy.

The sovereigns of this *Kuntala* country, the *Chá|ukya* race, were they not born from the full vessel in the shining left hand of *Brahma*, who sprung from the lotus navel of the resplendent Vishnu ? *

Of that race the original (*prabhavam*), king *Tallapa*, dispersing his enemies, secured the sovereignty, and exerting a power double that which his enemies obtained from the infernal regions, subdued the Rattas who had overrun the whole world, rescued it out of their hands, removed a great calamity and brought fame to the *Chálukya* race. After him, his son, the ever prosperous king *Satyás'raya* ruled the land. And following after him, his younger brother's son ruled the land, the proud *Vikramárka*. After him reigned his younger brother, with fame as bright as the pleasant moon, emperor of all the lands surrounded by the seven oceans, the worthy *Appayya*. Then that monarch's younger brother *Jaya Simha*, a destroyer of the lineage of hostile kings, a thunderbolt weapon to the mountain of the anxieties of the learned, the remover of the afflictions of the earth. *Ahava Malla*, the son of Jaya Simha, then ruled the lady earth, whose tresses are the groves of honge trees, whose throat and neck are garlanded with the stems of young areca palms, whose bosoms are the swelling mountains. The next king was that ruler's son *Somes'vara*, then *his* younger brother, king *Permmanaḍi*. The son of this king (followed), *Bhuloka Malla*, praised in all the world. His son, *Jagadeka Malla* next obtained the land, who left *Málava* without possessions, forced *Pallava* to hold the sprout, *Láṭa* to place his hands together on his forehead, increased the troubles of *Kalinga*, terrifying all with his fearful might. Then his younger brother, *Núrmmaḍi Taila*, an abode of dignity, a lion in the destruction of the elephants the groups of his enemies, possessed of very great renown.

At that time was *Bijjala* king, who bore up the whole world with the strength of his might, whose sharp sword was as a serpent swallowing up the air of the breaths of his boasting enemies, making all wonder whence it came—from whom all the learned obtained great joy, of whom it might be said that the world was surrounded by the ears of his elephants.

The saying that heroes should possess the earth was then made good, for

---

* *Kan* || *Parama Hari nábhi kamalodaradoḷ janiyisida vinuta Chaturásyana bhásuratara savyetaradoḷ pari ghaṭin udayisududalte Cháḷukya kulam* ||

as if the whole world were destined for the Cháḷukya race, from the southern ocean to the boundary of the north was the place of their encampment* . . . . What a wonder was this, that he caused elephants to fight like men and to feel affection for him, this *Bijjala Deva* famous for his strength. (*Some illegible*).

May it be well.—While the victorious kingdom of the powerful emperor *Tribhuvana Malla Bijjala Devarasa*, entitled to the five great drums, great king of kings, lord of the city of *Kálanjara*, having the flag of a golden bull, with the damaruga, túrya and nirghóshana (kinds of drum), a sun to the lotus of the *Kaḷachurya* race, invincible hero, in honour as mount Meru, a light among great warriors, an elephant goad to the mighty, master of elephants, a cage of adamant to those who claimed his protection, in bravery like Rávana, to strange women like a brother, Malla of the S'anivára Siddagiri Durga, in war like Ráma, a lion to the elephant his enemies, having the title *Nissanka Malla* and many other titles †—was continually increasing in prosperity, to endure as long as sun, moon, and stars.—

Resting like a bee at the lotus feet of this king, was *Kes'i Rája* Danḍádísa, raised to greatness from the thunderbolt weapon of Brahman virtue not falling upon him, a lord over many kings, a treasury of ever increasing power. The descent of this jewel of commanders was as follows :—

In the race of Brahma, having a perfect knowledge of the Parama Brahma, a joy to all the rishis, was born the celebrated Brahmárshi, an ocean of virtue, *Bharadvaja*. Among the many great Brahmans descended from him, there appeared *Bárunda Rája*, a treasury of all Brahman virtues, a procurer of immeasurable merit, of a fame which reached the tusks of the elephants supporting the corners of the earth, of high qualities praised by the learned, of undying glory. His wife was the jewel of women, known through all the world as *Muddi Akka*, a new Sarasvati in all learning, a permanent resting place of all good qualities.

To those two were born the following children—*Márappaiya*, whose life was like that of Manu and the munis, *Váma Deva*, of a beauty and glory like that of Manmatha, *Bibi Rája*, a general praised of all people, of great prudence, the worthy *Kes'ava*, an abode of generosity, *Vishnu Deva*, a cause of prosperity to all the learned who sought his protection.

---

* *Kan* || *Husiyalu víra bhójyá vasundhará yemba vákyam ene dhareyam sádhisidam tenkabdhiye baḍaga síme Chálukya kaṭakav én embadu.* The saying referred to I am told is a popular prophecy still current, as follows :—*Nandan Anandayor madhye víra bhójá vasundhará.* Between the years Nanda and Ananda the world will become a hero's.

† See note p. 66.

On examination the junior of the (first) four yet their equal, and the senior of the last two, was *Kes'ava Rája*, reported a mine of every good quality, of unspotted fame. His wife *Pampá Devi*, in beauty, greatness, devotion to her husband, and skill in every kind of work, put to shame (respectively) the goddesses Rati, Párvati, Arundhati, Bhárati, and shamed the wives of all other chieftains.

Their son, for whose daily distribution of charity the entire number of wise men was not sufficient, for whose devotion and pilgrimages all the goddesses and holy bathing places did not suffice, for whose circumambulations and penances all the temples of Vishnu and the other great gods were too few, for whose erection of chatras and watersheds the world was too small, for whose fame the space between the points of the compass was too confined, *Háranamarasa*, obtained the worship of all the good and was a moon to the ocean of his race. His wife, who if well considered was equal in greatness to Earth, in wifely devotion to Síta, in fortune to Lakshmi, was *Durgá Dévi*.

To those two, was born *Kes'ava Deva*, a treasury of power, whose virtuous life the Krita yuga made its excuse and came to an end, whose pointed speech the arrow of Ráma made excuse and turned aside, of the daylight of whose splendid fame moonlight made an excuse and vanished. "If I rest here henceforth engaged in supporting the earth, how shall I procure the fame of being a Karna (celebrated for liberality), or how obtain the name of a S'uḍraka for heroism, can I come short in this ?" thus disputes the hand with the mind of *Kes'ava*, Dandanátha. "Combining and creating is Brahma's care doubtless, but the preservation of all things is it not mine ?" thus said *Kes'ava* to himself—what a marvel was he in the world ? To be of good birth is considered fortunate, or a man is fortunate who has gained distinction, but the term "fortunate man" has become a jest, and of little account is the fortunate man who shines forth as great in gifts, for the merest pauper who but wished for a sight of this personification of the highest benevolence rose up fortunate. How fortunate then was the land in which dwelt this Danḍanátha *Kes'ava* with wisdom of such power.

At the mere threat of this mighty Kes'a Rája, were brought into subjection *Sanka male*, on saying I want that land he gained *Sántálige*, *Rachche Malla's* territory, *Gávaṭúru*, *Mogala Náḍu*, *Sirivúru*, and to the east of the *Vanavási* hill-fort took *Raṭe*, *Haive* and the famous *Gutli* height.*

---

* *Munidaḍe Kési Rája pritanes'varam ájnege sádyaváytu Sanka male, sanda Sánṭalige korvvadar uro enalága Rachche Mallana nele Gávaṭúr Mmogala náḍ Sirivúr Vanavási durgga púrvva sawésan irdda konḍa Raṭe Haive negalteya Gutti heltaḷam* ॥.

Manmatha seeing this immortal commander *Kes'ava's* superlatively beautiful form, divested himself of shape and in disgust remains disembodied; the lion beholding the power with which he subdued all, fled in anger to the depths of the forest; at the contemplation of his continually increasing greatness and splendour, the sun daily rises and falls in agitation. "*Karna* gave lands that were waste (say they), *S'ibi* gave a ship but in anger, *Dadíchi* gave bones," but that people might not thus asperse him, *Kes'ava* used to give only gold pagodas (*hongaḷane*). In war, by blows of the sword wielded by the powerful arm of the commander *Kes'ava*, all the hostile kings being exhausted, their wives full of affection gave up themselves to save their husbands' lives, and by this assembly of women was first brought into use the rule of sanctuary at snakes' holes.

As *Krishna* possessed two wives, *Lakshmi* the daughter of the sea, and *Satyabháma*,—and as *S'iva* had two wives, *Párvati* and *Ganga*,—so the all praised *Lakshmi Devi* and, shining with fortune, *Siri Devi* became wives to *Kes'ava* and obtained the praise of all the world.

His prime minister was famous, without a peer in the world, a prince of liberality, as the resplendent kalpa-vriksha in granting the desires of the learned, a pleasant moon to the lotus of his race, on whose lotus countenance the amorous bees of female eyes rested with delight, in every member a collection of perfect virtue, acquainted with all justice, a lion to the elephants his enemies, of the highest and keenest prowess. Speech without falsehood, liberality without hoping for return, conduct which never violated peace, kindness which never failed, such were the natural qualities of *Narasinga Náyaka.*

And among his great men were—*Tikkarasa*, chief of the counsellors, a Brihaspati in discerning what was right to be done, rich in an ever increasing fame, promoter of the fortunes of his dependents. *Pratihasta*, who never withdrew his hand from liberality (a play on the name). *Kammarasa*, whose unspotted fame was like the light of the moon and filled all the points of the compass with its brightness, celebrated in all the world. *Rechcharasa*, celebrated in all the world as pure in character, pure in descent, an abode of deeds of purity, master of the purest justice, filling all the points of the compass in succession with the pure splendour of his fame. *Chaṭṭi Rája* who shone in all the world as the good accountant among the royal chief accountants, performing all the duties of Brahmans, resting like a bee at the two lotus feet of Vishnu, of great ability in dealing with enemies and with the learned. *Udárasa*, a head jewel among the accountants, a chintámani to the assembly of the learned, a sun shining in the firmament of his race, of great renown in all the world, and virtuous in life. *Potarasa*, who had studied and understood many plays and poems, whose lotus hand was praised by the bees of the minds of the learned, a draught of intoxicating delight to the best spirits of his race, a head accountant. *Mahadeva Náyaka*, an accountant, a bee at the lotus feet of Kedáres'vara, ever repeating the praises of S'iva, whose life was like that of Manu. *Náchi*, praised continually by strangers, having secured the light of Lakshmi's eyes. *Soma*, whose affection was towards good and able men among his subjects. *Govinda*, who held Vishnu continually in his unmoved breast. *Mártáṇḍa*, the brightness of whose fame illumined the globe of the firmament of his race.

While associated with all these high officers and chief accountants of the royal presence, the Daṇḍanáyaka *Kes'ava Deva*,—a chintámani in granting the desires of all those who claimed his protection, a head jewel to his race—was in the royal city of *Balipura*, punishing the evil and rewarding the good in the *Banavase* Twelve Thousand :—one day, when seated in the centre of a great assembly, surrounded by all the ministers, royal attendants and people of the city,—one who knew the most auspicious moments, and was acquainted with all works of merit—

He was descended from the great *Maríchi*, who sprung from the mind of the lotus-born (*Brahma*), and whose son was *Kas'yapa*, in whose line was born the general of the army *Revana*. His son was the lord *Somanátha*, whose son was the great lord *Chaṭṭi Rája*, a protector of judgment. His wife was *Mádiakka*, and his son *Rechana*, ever desirous of obtaining merit.

Recharasa, commenced a discourse upon piety, which (discourse) was an enemy to sin, a breaker open of the mind, a stage for the highest Lakshmi to dance upon, a great wave from the boundless ocean of heavenly joy. His speech was as follows—

"This country has existed through many ages, and is known in all the world for the chatras, pleasure gardens, temples, groves of spreading trees, and water sheds provided by the great commanders who formerly ruled in it. This city of *Balipura* is the secure abode of merit. The god *Kes'ava* being established here would be a work of the greatest merit. If well considered, merit beyond what all holocausts, sacrifices, incantations and appointed acts of devotion can procure will be obtained by the setting up here of the image of the god *Kes'ava*. Moreover, therein may be obtained the prosperity arising from a gift of land, and of the crops and vegetation grown thereon, and of its continually increasing produce."

"Therefore may you (be pleased to) establish here a town, named *Kes'ava-pura* in honour of your majesty, and in it a temple to the god *Víra Kes'ava*—then will you obtain in the present world pure fame, in the next state of existence the fullness of merit, and in the end supreme felicity."

When he thus spoke, expressing the very thoughts of the jewel of commanders, that crowning ornament of rulers, bearing these words in remembrance obtained in the southern quarter of *Balipura* a piece of land fertile to produce, all manner of fruit, a very extensive region as level as a mirror, from *Sarves'vara Paṇḍita*, the áchári of the Five Lingas erected by the *Páṇḍavas*, and from the Hergaḍḍe *Soyanna*, and from the senabhova *Kannaṇṇa*, and all their connections, in presence of the seṭṭi, the nagaras, the five maṭhas and the three puras—pouring water—

And in that pleasant land, arranging and transforming to the utmost timber and stone, as if striving to add to all the variety of forms in which Brahma had created wood and stone, the great commander *Kes'ava*, shining with exceeding devotion, built for the god *Kes'ava* an abode filled with beauty and a joy to the sight. And on a large piece of land in front of that temple, this treasury of the benefits derived from charity, in the fullness of his heart's pleasure, built a town and named it *Vírakes'avapura*. Then the jewel of commanders, gave that town, filled with commodious houses, having cots in each chamber containing the softest beds, and for the sake of heaven donations of money attached, to the Brahmans, that it might bear fruit.

This done, that *Virakes'avapura* was everywhere praised as the indigenous place of growth for kalpa-vrikshas, as like svarga a place for the continual cultivation of all the vedas, a mine of purity and virtue, a place in which to acquire the most exalted merit—and was as a newly made anklet for the goddess earth, adorned with the nine jewels.

Then for the superintendence of the vrittis in that town—on investigation *Ekkalarasa* had acquired a great name in the world as a treasury of heroism, a treasury of valour, an overflowing treasury of pure renown for judgment, a treasury of liberality. This mine of all good qualities, a moon in raising the fortunes of the Ganga race,* *Ekkalarasa*,—his chief minister *Kámaya*, and his minister for peace and war *Mahádeva*,—gaining the consent of all the chief authorities of the Jiḍḍudige Náḍ, having received from their hands, with pouring of water and all ceremony, the village of *Belvaṇi* together with all the (taxes) *maṇṇaya*, *áya*, *dáya*, and *kirukula* ;†

---

* See note p. 160.

† See note p. 77.

In the presence of the Paṭṭaṇa Sávi of the royal city Balipura, *Kirtti Seṭṭi* and *Mēbi Seṭṭi* and all the other *Nagaras* of *Dharma S'iva Déva*, áchári of the five *maṭhas*, *Múliga Madhukes'vara Paṇḍita Deva*, áchári of the Hiriya maṭha S'ri Jagadeka Malles'vara; *Sarves'vara Paṇḍita Deva*, áchári of the Five Lingas; *Jnána S'akti Pandita*, áchári of Tripurántaka of Herggaḍe *Soyimarasa*, of that place; *Váma S'akti Paṇḍita*, áchári of the Koḍi maṭha of Herggaḍe *Vennamarasa* of that place; and of the seven Brahmapuris—with the assent of the mahá pradhána *Kasapaya Náyaka*, a promoter of all works of merit—the mahá pradhána *Kesimayya*, Herggaḍe Danḍanáyaka of the Banavási Nád,* accompanied by his accountants—in the S'aka year 1080, the year Bahudhánya, the month Pushya, the day of full moon, Monday, the day of the sun's entering the northern signs, at the vyati-páta, during an eclipse of the moon—for the worship of the god *Vira Kes'ava* of the auspicious *Kes'avapura*, for the repetition of the service, for the daily oblation and offering of food, for maintaining the perpetual lamp, for a splendid car procession and assembly or fair in the month Chaitra, and for any other fresh ceremonies,—gave in the manner approved by all—

To those of the Brahmapuri of Kés'avapura, accomplished in all the holy actions—*yama*, *niyama*, *svádhyáya*, *dhyána*, *dhárana*, *mauna*, *anusṭhána*, *japa*, *samádhi*, † diligent in maintaining the perpetual sacred fire, and in serving Brahmans, gurus and gods; versed in the six tarkas, the mímámsa and other sciences; faithful in performing the six religious acts—*yajana*, *yájana*, *adhyayana*, *adhyápana*, *dána* and *pratigraha*—having performed the agnishtóma and the seven other kinds of sacrifice; familiar with many puránas, and the itihása connected with them, commentaries, poems, plays and many modes of skill; praised by learned poets in many languages, an authoritative debater, the enchantment of whose knowledge attracted to him the hearts of all the learned, whose speech was as if engraved on stone, whose fame shone like the rays of the sun, whose body was purified by the avabhrita (a purifying ablution at the termination of a sacrifice) and the settled abode of all happiness,—namely to the god Jagadeka Malles'vara two shares (*vritti*)—to the god of the Five Lingas two shares—to the god Kedára two shares—to the Brahmans 38 shares—for the pújári one share—for the garland-seller one share—altogether 46 shares, in the village of Belvaṇi.

---

* *Samasta dharmmoddhárakam mahá pradhánam Kasapayya Náyakan anukúlateyoḷam mahá pradhána Banavase náḍa herggaḍe danḍanáyakam Kesimayyam.*

† See note p. 16.

And *Tailaha Devarasa*, possessed of all titles, mahá mandales'vara, a moon in raising the fortunes of the Ganga race, * a promoter of all meritorious acts—his sister's husband *Yeraharasa*, and *Hadavala Gangana*—rising up, in order to renew the gift of their father (*boppam*) *Yakkalarasa*, released that village from (the imposts) *manneya, áya, dáya, kánike, kirukula*,† and pouring water at the feet of the god Kes'ava, gave them up as a gift with enjoyment for three generations. And the great minister, *Kesimaya* Dandanáyaka, washing the feet of his priest (*tammárádhyarappa*) the royal guru *Váma S'akti Deva*, accomplished in all the holy actions—*yama, niyama, svádháya, dhyána, dhárana, mauna, anusthána, japa, samádhi* ‡—a lover of the learned, patron of the assemblies of skilful poets, spending his time in gifts of food, gifts of gold, gifts of virgins, gifts of cows, gifts of lands, gifts of encouragement, gifts of medicine, and other gifts ; holding the unequalled vedas as a jewel, distinguished for his investigation of the sciences and idol rituals, born in the line of the rishi *Gautama*, a servant at the lotus feet of the god *Dakshina Kedáres'vara* of Balipura—and pouring water, gave to him the control (*áraykeyumam*) of that place as a Brahmapuri.

Besides which, Heggade *Sávimarasa* gave for the *áya* from the *umbali* (or rent free) land of Belvani a paddy field of one matta, according to the *maragundi* pole, and to the god *Kes'ava* a paddy field of one matta. After deducting for the *gaudike* the Guru Deva and the Heggade will divide what remains among the mahájans (or Brahmans).

In this, each share of land (*vritti*) belongs to the occupant of the house to which it is attached, but the shares of houses unoccupied belong to the god. Among these vrittis, the bhatta-vritti one, the khandika-vritti one, the agnishtóyi-vritti one, and the pújári and máligara-vrittis—altogether five vrittis will be granted and enjoyed. The boundaries of that town :—on the east the row of resting stones (for loads) near the basadi (Jain temple) of Hemmádi ; on the south, the northern limit of the cultivated land belonging to Bhagavati ; on the west, the land belonging to the Five Lingas ; on the north, the land of the Hemmádi basadi.—

(Furthermore) as a *tala vritti* for that god, obtaining it from Little Baligámve, the village of the god Kedára, with worship of the feet of that god, he presented for the daily service, for a splendid car procession in Chaitra, for the daily offering of food to the god, and for feeding daily five Brahmans from other parts, one matta of paddy land according to the kacchavi pole under

---

* *Ganga vams'a várddhi varddhana sudákaranum.*

† See note p. 77.

‡ See note p. 16.

the Narapati Ságara,—and for maintaining the perpetual lamp, one oil-mill in the city besides, to that god.

(*Here follows another grant, made* 21 *years later.*)

May it be well.—In the 3rd year of the Karachurya emperor, *Nissanka Malla Sankama Deva*, the year Vikári, the month Chaitra, the day of full moon, Monday, the time of the equinox, at the vyati páta, during an eclipse of the moon—the mahá pradhána senádhipati, the Banavase Náḍ Herggaḍe Danḍanáyaka *Kes'i Rája*, who if considered was a treasury of fortune and wealth, as Yama's weapon of punishment in taking the lives of hostile kings, a casket for the jewels of good qualities, a sun to the lotus garden of poets and men of learning. The growing fame of the commander Kés'ava shines beyond the elephants at the points of the compass, and laughs at Indra's royal elephant.

This *Kes'i Rája* Danḍanáyaka—for the worship of the god Kes'ava which he had set up, repetition of the service, for the daily oblation, for maintaining the perpetual lamp, for the procession in Chaitra and the games and fair, for any fresh ceremonies, for a throne for the god, and for feeding twenty Brahmans from other parts, and for repairs of the temple—directed that the land left to the god *Somanátha* in *Banḍanike* in the Nágara Khanḍa Seventy, should be attached to both and used in common.

And in the presence of *Sampakarasa*, mahá manḍales'vara, lord of the *Gupta* race—of *Jayadévarasa*, worshipper of the feet of Garges'vara, skilled in the management of armies, and his minister *Vásudeva Náyaka*, . . . of the mahá manḍalés'vara, sun to the lotus of the *Kadamba* race, having the favour of Jayanti Madhukes'vara, having the title Nigalanka Malla and many others, *Toppadevarasa*, and his minister *Tikkaya*,—and surrounded by his retinue, his great tributary *Sanka Gauḍa*, and the chiefs of the Nágara Khanḍa Seventy, at the feet of the god *Kes'ava*, receiving from their hands the *manneya*, *áya*, *dáya*, *kirukula*, *kánike*,*—pouring water, presented them to the god *Kes'ava* and the god *Somanátha*—

(*Some illegible.*)

Whoso maintains this gift will secure the merit of presenting a thousand tawny cows in the holy bathing places of Váranási, Kurukshétra, and . . . . and of presenting a kolaga adorned with gems to Brahmans learned in the four vedas. Whoso protects this gift as long as sun, moon, stars and sky endure, obtains the merit of presenting a thousand tawny cows to Brahmans at Váranási,

* See note p. 158.

Gaya, and Kurukshétra. Whoso alienates a gift made by himself or by another will be born a worm in ordure for sixty thousand years.

(Rest illegible.)

75. S'ila S'asana at Balagami, date A. D. 1202.

Size ft. 3 6' × ft. 2.—Haḷe Kannaḍa Characters.

Sword. Cow suckling calf. Sun. Linga with Priest. Moon. Nandi.

Adored be S'ambhu, beauteous with the chamara-like crescent moon kissing his lofty crest, the original foundation-pillar of the city of the three worlds.

May it be well.—In the 11th year of the *Yádava* emperor, possessed of all titles, *Víra Ballála Deva*—the year Dundubhi, the month Chaitra, the 13th day of the moon's increase, Monday,—*Bendi Seṭṭi* of *Hári Honnugunda* near the royal city of *Balligámve*, gave on the south of the river-ford a paddy field of 10 kammas, for the daily oblation to the god *Pralames'vara (?)*, and for repairs of the temple, washing the feet of *Bherunḍes'vara*, priest of the five maṭhas, and of *Máliga Madhukes'vara*, priest of the old maṭha, and pouring water.

Whoso maintains this gift will derive the merit of presenting a thousand tawny cows, and of presenting a thousand Brahmans in Váranási with kolagas adorned with jewels. Whoso usurps this gift will incur the guilt of slaying a thousand Brahmans and a thousand tawny cows in Váranási. This gift let all kings and Brahmans carry into effect.

76. Virakal at Balagami, date unknown.

Size ft. 2 4' × ft. 1.—Haḷe Kannaḍa Characters.

Linga with Priest. The hero in the presence.

(The inscription on this stone is entirely illegible.)

The hero borne to heaven by celestial nymphs waving chamaras.

The hero with shield and broken sword. Horseman riding over bodies. Nandi.

77. S'ila S'asana at Balagami, date A. D. 1077.

Size ft. 6 × ft. 1 6'.—Haḷe Kannaḍa Characters.

Linga with Priest. Nandi.

Adored be S'ambhu, beauteous with the chamara-like crescent moon kissing his lofty head; the original foundation-pillar of the city of the three worlds.

The great Chálukya emperor *Tailapa*, peerless in might; *Sátyás'raya*, an abode of dazzling splendour; *Vikramáditya*, a combination of the most exalted bravery; *Jaya Singha*, a treasury of ambition to excel; *Trailokya Malla*, a collection of all the fortune in the world,—these being famous brought renown to the *Chálukya* kingdom.

(*Some illegible.*)

May it be well.—While the victorious kingdom of *Tribhuvana Malla Deva*, protector of all lands, favourite of earth and fortune, great king of kings, supreme ruler, first of monarchs, glory of the *Satyás'raya kula*, ornament of the *Chálukyas**—was continually increasing in prosperity, to endure as long as sun, moon, and stars—and he was ruling in peace and wisdom† in his residence of *Tagiri*.

The dweller at his lotus feet; May it be well.—Entitled to the five great drums, chief of great tributaries, subduer of fierce kings, . . . a moon to the group of lotuses his brothers, patron of the assemblies of good men, a jewel in the cluster of good qualities, in liberality like king Nala, chief ruler in all the earth, like Adisesha upholding the world, like Brahma in skill, a lion in bravery, a jewel-mirror to the good, a protector of those who depend upon him, a punisher of the evil, a lusty elephant to the groups of creeping lotuses his enemies, of a mild countenance, fame his banner, great in ambition to excel, a bee at the lotus feet of the illustrious Tribhuvana Malla Deva, invested with titles and degrees of all kinds, the mahá senádhipati, mahá pradhána Daṇḍanáyaka *Barmma Devarasa*;

In the 2nd year of Chálukya Vikrama, the year Pingaḷa, the month Mágha, the day of full moon, Monday, at the auspicious moment of the moon's eclipse—for the ablution and daily offering to the god *Mallikárjjuna* which Pújári Linganna of the royal city of *Balligámve* had set up—and for digging a tank and for a chatra—gave, with pouring of water and every ceremony, one village *Háravúru*, situated in the Jiḍḍuḷige Seventy.

---

* See note p. 14. † See note p. 2.

This gift is a gift from all the heads of the garland-sellers, they in particular will maintain and carry into effect the gift.

Whoso maintains this gift will derive the merit of presenting a thousand tawny cows in Prayága, Váranási, Agritírtha, or Kurukshétra, and of presenting kolagas made of gold and silver to a thousand Brahmans versed in the four vedas, washing their feet. Whoso usurps this gift incurs the guilt of slaying a thousand tawny cows, and a thousand Brahmans versed in the four vedas, in the holy bathing places of Ganga, Gaya, Váranási, and Kurukshetra. Whoso usurps a gift made by himself or by another shall assuredly be born a worm in ordure for sixty thousand years. The bridge of merit deserves your support, O kings of the earth. Thus from age to age cries Rámachandra to the kings who come after him.

Maylayya, washing the feet of Pavitra Rája Pandita, and pouring water, set up this s'ásana.

---

78. S'ila S'asana at Balagami, date A. D. 1071.

Size ft. 4 9' × ft. 2.—Haḷe Kannaḍa Characters.

Linga with Priest.

Adored be S'ambhu, beauteous with the chámara-like crescent moon kissing his lofty head; the original foundation-pillar of the city of the three worlds.

May it be well.—While the victorious kingdom of *Bhuvanaika Malla Deva*, protector of all lands, favourite of earth and fortune, great king of kings, supreme ruler, first of monarchs, glory of the *Satyás'raya kula*, ornament of the *Chálukyas* *—was continually increasing in prosperity, to endure as long as sun, moon, and stars—

Living at his lotus feet in his residence of *Bankapura*, entitled to the five great drums, chief of great tributaries, subduer of the fiercest opponents, lord of all the treasures in that place†, like the son of Yugandha in carrying out his master's orders, a refuge to the wise, clothed with judgment and wisdom, possessed of all learning, great in prowess, able in war, a bee at the lotus feet of Bhuvanaika Malla Deva, a combination of all good qualities, was the great minister, senior councillor for peace and war, Mane Verggaḍe Danḍanáyaka *Udayáditya*.

Completely defeating the Málava king who had raised his enmity, and all those who had secretly conspired against the throne and against the guru, and

---

* See note p. 14.

† *A' sthána vastu náyakam.*

seizing their property and women laden with jewels he handed them over to his emperor—thus by his judgment and his mighty prowess he was renowned as the subjecter of the three worlds—this *Udayáditya* Dandádhinátha. His mind unstained by fear, his speech quite free from pride, his body full of radiance, a treasury of all wealth, his conduct without any admixture of evil—thus reputed, what a fame was his, this chief jewel of commanders, *Udayáditya*.

Who placed themselves under his protection had nothing to fear from men, who accepted his support had nothing to fear from poverty, who turned to attack him in war surrendered their lives—if considered, how great was he in might and fame, the commander *Udayáditya*. He subdued Male secure of victory, like Vishnu himself in the attributes of might, an ornament to the face of those who answer wisely, *Udega Dandádhis'am*.

At the request of *Udayáditya* the mighty hero, thus entitled to all honors and praise—the king *Bhuvanaika Malla Deva* and all his ministers, in the S'aka year 993, the year Viródhakrit, the month Pushya, the 1st day of the moon's increase, Monday, at the auspicious moment of the sun's entering the northern signs,—for the bathing and daily offering to the god *Mallikámodes'vara* of the royal city of *Balligámve*, for repairs of the temple, for any fresh ceremonies, for the food of the ascetics who resort to it—gave, washing the feet of the owner of the place * *Somes'vara Pandita*, the disciple of Chandra Bhúshana Pandita, accomplished in all the holy acts, *yama, niyama, svadhyáya, dhyána, dhárana, mauna, anushthána, japa, samádhi*†—and pouring water—one village, *Hange*, in the Nágari Khanda Seventy; and of the paddy land of the royal city of *Balligámve*, 4 mattas—free of every burden.

Whoso maintains this gift derives the merit of presenting 12,000 double-faced cows in the holy bathing places of Váranási, Kurukshetra, Prayága. Whoso usurps this gift incurs the guilt of slaying 12,000 cows and Brahmans learned in the four védas in the holy bathing places of Váranási, Kurukshétra, Prayága, and of the five great sins. Whoso usurps a gift made by himself or by another shall assuredly be born a worm in ordure for sixty thousand years. The earth has had Sagara and many other kings; according to their (gifts of) land so was their reward. The bridge of merit deserves your support O kings of the earth. Thus from age to age cries Rámachandra to the kings who come after him. Poison is no poison. The property of the gods that is the real poison. For poison kills one man, but a gift to the gods (if usurped) kills a man with his son and descendants.

* *Alliya sthána pati.*

† See note p. 16.

79. Virakal at Balagami, date A. D. 1079.

Size ft. 5 3′ × ft. 3 4′.—Haḷe Kannaḍa Characters.

The hero in the presence. Linga with Priest. Nandi.

May it be well.—While the victorious kingdom of *Tribhuvana Malla Deva*, protector of all lands, favourite of earth and fortune, great king of kings, supreme ruler, first of monarchs, glory of the *Satyás'raya kula*, ornament of the *Chalukyas**—was continually increasing in prosperity, to endure as long as sun moon and stars—

When the dweller at his lotus feet—May it be well—in the 4th year of Chálukya Vikrama, the year Siddhárti, the month S'rávana, the 5th—by order of the Piriya.

The hero being borne to heaven by celestial nymphs, some waving chamaras.

Dandanáyaka *Anantapálayya*, the Daṇḍanáyaka *Govindarasa* was ruling the *Banavase* Twelve Thousand—

By the Daṇḍanáyaka Gòvindarasa's order, the cows (*turu*) of Balligáve being seized, the watchman *Kaniya Reva Náyaka*

The hero armed with sword and shield killing another similarly armed, and driving off a herd of cattle. The herdsman in terror turning to escape.

killing several Malaharu, and returning the cows, attained to the world of gods. Who wins in war gains spoil, who falls enjoys the celestial nymphs. What fear then of death in war ?

---

80. S'ila S'asana at Balagami, date about A. D. 1020.

Size ft. 7 3′ × ft. 2 8′.—Haḷe Kannaḍa Characters.

Boar. Linga with Priest. The whole in a temple. Cow suckling calf.

(*The most important part of this s'ásana is quite illegible.*)

Adored be *S'ambhu*, beauteous with the chámara-like crescent moon kissing his lofty head ; the original foundation-pillar of the city of the three worlds. *Om*. Praise—Praise to S'iva and Ganapati.

While the auspicious *Jagadeka Malla Deva*, protector of all lands, favourite of earth and fortune, great king of kings, supreme ruler, first of monarchs,

---

* See note p. 14.

glory of the *Satyás'raya kula*, ornament of the *Chalukyas**, the perfume of the Jasmin, a lion to the elephants his rival kings, male of males, a golden ornament of the male sex, a world destroying fire to the fiercest kings, a kalpavriksha to the learned, ... was ruling in peace and wisdom† in his residence of . . *Ilila-kere* . . .

(*Much illegible*).

. . the time of the sun's entering the northern signs— . . .

. . accomplished in all the holy exercises, *yama*, *niyama*, *svádhyáya*, *dhárana*, *mauna*, *anusthána*, *japa*, *samádhi* ‡ . . . . .
for incense and daily service of the god, and for food and clothing to the rishis resorting there . . . .
under the Bende tank 12 mattas according to the kacchavi pole— . .
2 mattas . . . .

Whoso maintains this gift will secure the merit of presenting a thousand tawny cows to Brahmans at the holy bathing places of Váranási, Kurukshétra and Prayága—and of presenting a kolaga decked with the five precious stones to Brahmans learned in the védas.

Whoso usurps this gift will incur the guilt of killing a thousand tawny cows and a thousand Brahmans at the holy bathing places of Váranási, Kurukshétra, and Prayága. Whoso by violence seizes the land presented either by himself or by another will certainly be born a worm in ordure for sixty thousand years. The earth has had Sagara and many other kings; according to their (gifts of) land so was their reward. The bridge of merit deserves your support O kings of the earth. Thus from age to age cries Rámachandra to the kings who come after him. Poison is no poison. The property of the gods that is the real poison. For poison kills one man, but a gift to the gods (if usurped) kills a man with his son and descendants.

Let none revoke this public gift. Who does so will be cursed in the world to come, incur the guilt of killing Brahmans and cows in Váranási and go to the hell Ajaraja.

(*Some illegible.*)

---

* See note p. 14. † See note p. 2. ‡ See note p. 16.

81. Virakal at Balagami, date A. D. 1286.

Size ft. 6 6′ × ft. 2 9′.—Haḷe Kannaḍa Characters.

(*The greater part of the inscription illegible.*)

Moon. Sun.

Crocodile? Crocodile?

. . . . son of Velambika . .

. . in the year Pingaḷa, the month Srávana, the 5th day of the moon's increase . . .

The hero and his wife in the presence. An attendant.

Linga with a Priest on each side in a temple.

Nandi fanned by an attendant.

In the 16th year from the beginning of the reign of the mighty emperor *Rámachandra*, king of kings, a Vishnu among other monarchs, of great prowess—the year Vyaya . . .

The hero and his wife ascending to heaven in a car, attended by celestial nymphs with chamaras, and celestial musicians playing on drums. A male attendant holding on by the flag-staff at the top of the car, a female attendant seated below the heroine.

. . *Náṇes'vara* and his life's lamp (*práṇa s'aki*) *Bommáyi*, who through devotion to her husband went out with him to the battle, . . . in the fight they obtained heaven . . .

The hero, with insignia of rank, and armed with sword and shield, fighting against men similarly armed. His wife in a graceful attitude eagerly watching the fight, guarded by a spearman. On the left a horseman galloping on to the field. On the right a single combat between two men armed with javelins, one bearing on his shield the device of a lion, and the other that of a boar.

Six female figures around a fire (?) gazing at the hero with uplifted hands as in astonishment.

82. Virakal at Balagami, date A. D. 1284.

Size ft. 5 9' × ft. 2 1.'—Haḷe Kannaḍa Characters.

May it be well.—From the beginning of the victorious reign of the *Yadava* emperor *Vira Rámachandra,*

The hero in the presence. Linga with a Priest on each side. Nandi.

the 14th year, the year Tárana, the month Chaitra, the 3rd day of the moon's increase, Sunday.—May it be well—Bhayana Narasaya of the Vira Bananju dharma, leading the army of Balligáve

Celestial musicians.

against Siddhiyara Kuppaya, and surrounding him, *Viramaya Deva*, destroying soldier upon soldier, cutting them down, hacking them in two, raging about and striking off many heads, went to heaven.

The hero ascending to heaven in a car, celestial nymphs with chamaras holding on by rings.

The hero, with insignia of rank, wrestling hand to hand with a man holding a spear. Attendants on each side, one on horseback.

---

83. Virakal at Balagami, date about A. D. 1160.

Size ft. 4 6' × ft. 2.—Haḷe Kannaḍa Characters.

Sun. Moon.

The hero in the presence. Linga with Priest. Nandi.

May it be well.—While the powerful emperor *Bijjaṇa Devarasa* was ruling in peace and wisdom*—

When by order of Padmarasa Danḍanáyaka of the Banavase Náḍ,—the cart (*banḍi*) of Váma S'akti Deva, worshipper of the feet of (the god) Dakshina Kedára Devà, having been seized, *Báchaya Náyaka*, the watchman of Konavalli, fighting, went to heaven; on which his son-in-law

The hero ascending to heaven with a triumphal sword-dance, attended by celestial nymphs with chamaras.

Báchayaka, setting up a stone, raised a lamentation for the hero.

The hero armed with javelin and shield contending with a great number similarly armed, one turning to load a jinjal. A man of rank behind on horseback, with armed attendants.

---

* See note p. 2,

84. S'ila S'asana at Balagami, date A. D. 1096.

Size ft. 6 4' × ft. 2 8'.—Haḷe Kannaḍa Characters.

Nandi. | Sun. | Linga with Priest in a temple. | Moon. | Cow suckling calf.

Adored be *S'ambhu*, beauteous with the chámara-like crescent moon kissing his lofty head*; the original foundation-pillar of the city of the three worlds.

While the victorious kingdom of *Tribhuvana Malla*, protector of all lands, favourite of earth and fortune, great king of kings, supreme ruler, first of monarchs, glory of the *Satyás'raya kula*, ornament of the *Chalukyas* *— was continually increasing in prosperity, to endure as long as sun, moon, and stars; and he was ruling in peace and wisdom†.—

Among the Chalukyas the senior (*piriyam*) was king *Tailapa*; after him the promoter of valour, king *Trailokya Malla*; then followed *Vikramáditya Deva*, a beloved monarch, superior to them in skill, in bravery, in great expeditions, in liberality, in his body of god-like brightness, and in fame.

Taking *Tribhuvana Malla* as his master was the chamúpa *Kálidása*, a terror to the fiercest enemies, ruler of all the world, filled with fame, bearing S'iva on his head, full of wrath towards his enemies. Confronting in battle the Láḷa king, the Magadha, Nepála, Pánchála and Páṇḍya kings, he took from them their fame, and when they brought an immense number of elephants, women and horses, and sought the help of that Chálukya emperor, this terror of his enemies, *Kálidása*, obtained the merit.

This lord's uncle (father's younger brother) was the commander *Sarva Deva*, acquainted with joys surpassing those of Indra, and always devoted to pleasure. Thus was that illustrious *Sarva Deva* a pleasure to the hearts of good men and his people; a mine of mercy, he acquired a fame as white as the swan, and his country was celebrated like him.

As the moon rises to enlighten the world plunged in the ocean of evil, so in the *Vatsa gotra*, sprung from the race of the lotus-born (Brahma), casting a radiance over the *Kamma kula*, was born an extraordinary hero, praised by all.

To this general *Chávunḍa* and his wife *Kelayakabbe*, who was like another Lakshmi, was born, giving them great joy, *Nága Varmma* Dandádhipa, praised by all. *Nága Varmma's* wife *Nágiyakka* was a Párvati, S'iva's queen, in affection for her husband, Brahma's Bhárati herself in eloquence, Lakshmi in good fortune—so said all the world.

---

* See note, p. 14.

† See note p. 2.

As to S'iva and his consort Párvati were born Ganga and Kumára, so from the love of *Nága Varmna*, the treasury of wisdom (*vidyá niddhi*) and the fortunate *Nágiyakka* were born the lord *Sarva Deva* and the commander *Chávunḍa*. May Lakshmi, honored by them, give them all fortune as long as sun and moon endure. Like Ráma and Lakshmana may *Sarva Deva* and *Ráya* live in the world with great affection, and like a row of lamps cast the light of blessing on both sides (their ancestors of both lines). May the god who is lord of all, whose pair of feet are worshipped by all the celestials, whose crest is the crescent moon, the husband of Párvati, whose locks are the skies, the remover of all sin, S'iva,—to *Sarva Deva* and the enlightened *Chávunḍa Ráya*, versed in all the learning of the Brahmans—grant increase of power and authority. May S'iva, the remover of sins, the law giver, the supreme spirit, the creator of all, the protector of all, shelter with affection *Sarva Deva* and *Ráya*.

The Mandara mountain is supported by Vishnu, the Amara river (Ganges) by the Mandara mountain, the ocean by the Amara river, the earth by the ocean. But is the Mandara mountain a fit comparison for him? In greatness it may be. Is the ocean? In capacity. Is the earth? In endurance. But in bravery and heroism this *Chávunḍa Ráya's* qualities surpass them all.

The younger (brother) of this illustrious Ráya was *Chidda*, in generosity a kalpa-vriksha, lord of several lands, in greatness like the ocean, in firmness like the great (mountain) Méru.

The earth flooded with polluting streams of blood was unable to move, Brahma hid himself, the ocean left its bounds and fled, through the astounding feats performed in war by the unequalled and surpassing *Sarva Deva*, who had overcome death from the flattery of strange women, not a man of two words (double speech), a protector of all who claimed his protection whether friends or foes.

His word was like mount Méru, in tearing in pieces the bodies (of his opposers) he was like the enemy of lusty elephants (the lion), in granting the desires of his people a young kalpa-vriksha, his wealth was composed of whatever the poor desire (he gave away everything in charity), to sin he was an increasing judgment-fire, in beauty peerless—how can I describe the greatness of this mighty *Sarva Deva*.

To this mine of humility and ornament of the learned, *Sarva Deva*, was *Sántala Devi* wife, noted among women as the unequalled Lakshmi for devotion to her husband.

To this jewel of affectionate wives *Sántikabbe* and the mine of generosity *Sarva Deva*, was born a son, the powerful and illustrious *Sovi Deva*. When by the favor of Somés'vara of the city of Pulikara, *Somes'vara* was born, great and settled fortune came to the whole family of *Sarva Deva*. A moon to the ocean of the learned, an ocean of poetic conceptions, in eloquence a garden of flowers, to courtesans a Manmatha (Cupid), a terror in the field of battle, was that *Soma*.

How excellent then was *Sarva Deva*, the god of whose desire was S'iva, his protector and master the Chálukya emperor, his father *Nága Varmma* revered by all the good, his mother the pure *Nágiyakka*, his priest Váma Deva Brati the equal of the Vámana incarnation, his brothers *Ráya* and *Chidda*, his son the great *Sovi Deva*, all friends of good people.

The mighty *Sarva Deva*, a bee at the lotus feet of S'iva, was a helper of the race of good gurus, able to remove the sins of all his line.

A descendant of the excellent Kálámukha Chakravartti muni of great wisdom, *Kás'míra Deva*; the chief disciple of *Trilóchana Munindra* was *Vares'vara Deva*, with a body purified by penance, devoted to piety, a jewel of pandits, worshipper of the feet of S'iva the god of gods. On the good advice of this *Vares'vara Muni*, a destroyer like Yama of all evil deeds, the lord *Sarva Deva*, with a pure mind, built a temple for the great and celebrated *Tripurántaka* in *Valligráme*, which was as a crown or a golden bowl for the god. The favorite of the goddess of fortune, *Sarva Deva*, erected a residence for *Sarvés'vara*, and crowned it with a golden dome, such that it seemed as if Indra's car had stopped in the royal city of *Bali*, as the most charming spot in all the earth. In this the choicest spot in the world, the celebrated *Valligráme*, as who should say this is Méru, this is Kailása, there dwells *Sarva Deva* who like Brahma set up a pillar from earth to sky—thus made he a temple with great joy, and decorated it with all manner of ornament for the god Sarves'vara.

May it be well—The Dandanáyaka *Sarva Devarasa* entitled to the five great drums, lord of many tributaries, a great and brave commander, granting the desires of the learned, a moon to the race of the Brahmans, a mount Róhana to the jewels of good qualities, an ornament to the good, careful of his master's orders, pleasing the mind of his lord, destroyer of the pride of his enemies, walking according to the rules of morality, of unshaken courage, with these and all other titles—in the 21st year of Chálukya Vikrama, the year Dhátu, the month Pushya, the 5th day of the moon's increase, Sunday, the day of the sun's entering the northern signs, at the vyatipáta—for the pleasure and the daily offering of the god *Sarves'vara* which he had set up in the royal city of

Balligráme, and for food and clothing to the rishis who resort thither—assembled with all his ministers, and having obtained the permission of the emperor —gave, washing the feet of *Vares'vara Deva Panḍita*, accomplished in all the holy acts, *yama*, *niyama*, *svádhyáya*, *dhyána*, *dhárana*, *mauna*, *anushṭhána japa*, *samádhi**—and pouring water, so as to be approved of all—as a gift to Parames'vara—in the vritti of the place in the Balli plain, a paddy field of one matta, and in the Nágari khanḍa Seventy, the village Háruvadeppa.

Whoso maintains this gift will secure the merit of presenting a thousand tawny cows to Brahmans at the holy bathing places of Váranási, Kurukshetra, and Prayága—and of presenting a kolaga decked with the five precious stones to Brahmans learned in the vedas, or of presenting a double headed (*i. e.* parturient) cow to a thousand Brahmans. Whoso usurps this gift will incur the guilt of killing a thousand tawny cows and a thousand Brahmans at the holy bathing places of Váranási, Kurukshetra, and Prayága. Whoso by violence seizes the land presented either by himself or by another will certainly be born a worm in ordure for sixty thousand years. The bridge of merit deserves your support O kings of the earth. Thus from age to age cries Rámachandra to the kings who come after him.

(*Some illegible*).

---

85. Virakal at Balagami, date A. D. 1102.

Size ft. 5 10′ × ft. 1 10′.—Haḷe Kannaḍa Characters.

Sun. Moon.

The hero worshipping. Linga with Priest.

Praise.—Adored be *S'ambhu*, beauteous with the chámara-like crescent moon kissing his lofty head; the original foundation-pillar of the city of the three worlds.

May it be well—*Permmaḍi Deva*, entitled to the five great drums, mahá manḍales'vara, chief of the great city of *Kolálapura*, having received a boon from the favour of the goddess Padmávati,

The hero, with a torch in each hand, ascending to heaven in a triumphal dance, attended by celestial nymphs with chámaras.

May it be well—In the 27th year of Chálukya Vikrama, the year Chitrabhánu, the month Phálguna, the 1st day of the moon's decrease, Monday—the army of *Beḍara Vibharasa* coming to plunder by invitation of

* See note p. 16.

the Raṭṭas, the king's soldiers without taking food chastised a thousand braves and took their lives—*Kelaya Náyaka* turning back fatigued,

The hero, armed with sword and shield, killing a man on horseback. Figures prostrate on both sides,

Bijjaya Náyaka, the son-in-law of that Náyaka, following him and pleasing him, begged for the post of danger, and fighting with five Beḍar kings who had besieged Háruvanahalli and Kedára, beating and piercing them, obtained heaven.

Who wins in war gains spoil, who falls enjoys the celestial nymphs, and his fame is for ever established. What fear then of death in war ?

---

86. Virakal at Balagami, date A. D. 1170.

Size ft. 4 10′ × ft. 1 9′.—Haḷe Kannaḍa Characters.

Moon — Sun

The hero in the presence. — Linga with Priest. — Nandi.

Om.—Praise to S'iva—May it be well—In the 5th year of the powerful *Kalachurya* emperor *Ráya Murári Sovi*, the year Khara, the month S'rávana, the last day of the moon's decrease, new moon day, Monday—while *Dási Seṭṭi* and *Voyáḷi Holeya Náyaka* the son of Muddauve, herdsmen of the royal guru *Váma S'akti Deva*, were coming with a herd of cows in the Sandadi road of *Saliyúru*, some powerful leaders of robbers fell upon them.

The hero borne to heaven by celestial nymphs waving chamaras.

To describe the courage of him who fought with them and obtained heaven :—

The men who armed with bows fell upon him at a distance from the chief city, he cut in pieces and pierced with sharp arrows. Singling them out when greatly enraged they would not submit, having come from the slaughter of experienced warriors, he pulled them out and taking his sword struck down those robbers, and killing them in fight, dragged their bodies about, the hero *Holeya*. The apsara nymphs enamoured of him and saying 'He is ours' came down from the sky, bathed his feet, took him up with great joy and bore him away, singing 'What a marvellous rare hero have we obtained'—while all the people on earth exclaimed 'áhá !' Fortune.

A spirited fight of men armed with bows and arrows.

---

87. Marked by the Photographer as missing.

---

88. S'ila S'asana at Balagami, date A. D. 1114.

Size ft. 8 2′ × ft. 4 1′.—Haḷe Kannaḍa Characters.

S'iva, Vishnu, Brahma,

Nandi. each in a temple. Cow suckling calf.

Om. Praise to S'iva. Adored be *S'ambhu*, beauteous with the chámara-like crescent moon kissing his lofty head; the original foundation-pillar of the city of the three worlds. Supreme is the boar form of the resplendent Vishnu, which dispersed the waters of the ocean and supports the peaceful world upon its right tusk.

Govinda Rája, the head jewel of the Vaishnavas prays as follows—May he the splendid, the eternal, the husband of Lakshmi, shining with all worlds in his loins, praised of all the gods, reposing on the serpent, of endless incarnations,—protect us.

From the golden lotus in the lord of Lakshmi's shining navel, of which O wonder! his lotus face was like a reflection, sprung Brahma. From the mind of Brahma came forth before the creation nine (the nava Brahma) able to confer fortune, the brightness of whose bodies filled the points of the compass, abodes of pure qualities. From these sons of the mind of Brahma descended the shining jewels of the *Chaḷukya* race, the peerless monarchs who ruled the world.

After them (*avarim balikke*)—As the great boar in the beginning scattered the ocean and by his might raised up the world which was sunk in the waters, so delivering earth from the dominion of the enemies who had subdued it, he took the government of the world, the Sárvva bhaumi *Taila*. His lotus head he made an offering at the feet of Lakshmi, and by his might putting to shame the ocean as if to say, Is that the limit of the world? he extended the Chalukya kingdom to the very points of the compass and ruled over it. A nail to the heart of his enemies, a light to the greatness of his race, his fame was a celestial Ganges which like a mount Himálaya he supported, thus shone *Taila*, bravery his nature.

An emanation (or brightness) of the goddess of victory, his dearest son, of heroic conduct, *Satyás'raya*, an abode of all the royal virtues, (next) ruled the sea-encircled world. His son *Vikrama*, of unequalled bravery, who as Indra himself made all other emperors bow to him, a combination of the bravery of all the regents of the points of the compass, then ruled the world. His younger brother next ruled the earth, who caused all to say, Why mention the tortoise (as supporting the world)? Did the ten incarnations deliver the earth from trouble? But he did, *Núrmmaḍi*, superior to them all, greatest of all the great in the battle field. His son *Jaya Simha*, then ruled the earth, by whose creeper-like sword all enemies were subdued, who lorded over many countries reduced by his force of elephants. His son *Ahava Malla* next ruled the lady earth, whose swelling bosoms are the mountains, whose necklace round her throat are the stems of the lofty areca palms, whose soft waist are the young sprouts of plants. The elder brother of the world-renowned Ahava Malla, a chief of men, praised by all the world, *Bhuvanaika Malla* (next) ruled.

Then that king's younger brother *Vikramárka* ruled, unshaken by fear, the sea-encircled peaceful earth, filled with the spoils of victory, a proud umbrella among the first of warriors.

While he was ruling this middle world—whoever through fear of his dreadful warfare did not oppose him, whoever threw themselves on his protection, whoever sought his favour, or whoever did not fall at his lotus feet and do him obeisance, the *Sauvíra*, *Abhíra*, *Andhra*, *Golla* kings, he knew how to look upon with kindness or with a terrible frown, the king *Vikramárka*. The *Chola* king he forced to go without clothing, the *Pallava* king to have his hands full of sprouts, the *Andhra* king to go into caves, the *Singhala* king's heart of wicked designs to evaporate, the *Málava* king to give up his garland, the *Ghúrjara* king to shrug his shoulders, (all plays upon the words)—thus did he treat them with his continually increasing power, *Vikramádilya Deva*. If he but stood up to make war, the hostile kings, though powerful to subdue others, knowing that destruction would befall themselves and their armies, asked themselves what use of lusty elephants, what of our great army, what of all our arrows, what of all these attendant people? His great uplifted sword, which none were able to stay, terrified all the kings with its *jalajala* noise, and forced the goddess of victory to attend on it ever. Just as tender boys seeing their reflection in water turn and run away in fear, so the hostile kings and their elephants ran away at the mere sight of the great Chálukya prince. As the *Láḍa* king ran away, the *Chola* king seized his ear and shook it, while the *Kaḷinga* king asked where his own lost kingdom was. What fear then did he produce, this causer of weeping to kings.

While with such a name he was ruling in peace and wisdom* in his residence at *Kalyáṇa-pura*—

The dweller at his lotus feet—a kalpa-vriksha born in human form, offspring of all the merit of gifts to Brahmans in former existences, a fruit from which other merit producing trees might be propagated, a beautiful swan in the Mánasa

* See note p. 2.

lake of the hearts of learned poets, an ornament to all who were freed from sin, of great liberality, thus praised with great affection by all people was *Anantapála*.

Full of the piety of faith in S'iva, praised by all people, an abode of fame, able to subdue and put to death a crore of Rávanas if they would stand up against him, the home of victory, his might was so great what use of swords, there was no limit to his qualities of greatness. Seeing his warfare Adiséshа delighted trembles, and assists him in collecting wealth for his lord (the emperor). As the sea so he (Anantapála) causes the commanders who hinder his sacrifices (labors) to drink poison and presents Lakshmi (fortune) to him who rules him, thus the sea too befriends him.*

Living at his lotus feet like a royal swan, looking on him as his patron god, among Brahmans the foremost, the best man in the world, compelling (by his brightness) the other inferior commanders to hide in the forest all the day-time, spontaneously a friend to the good, an abode of virtuous life, praised by all the people in the world, the youthfulness of Lakshmi which was at his command he made over to the learned, that *Govinda Rája* Dandá dhipa.

With a patience, majesty, famous learning, power of command and wisdom such as did not exist in all the line of the lotus-born, enlightening the world, like a sword in the hands of the Chalukya kings, was *Govinda* Dandádhipa. Although he wished to live (peacefully) according to his own inclinations, the other commanders all said with great fear, 'We know his mind that it is always engaged in thinking how with his great power to cut in pieces the armies and all the property of the fiercest among the tributary kings, and (destroy) their very seed; therefore we must not approach his person which dazzles like the sun.' Though in his mind cherishing mercy and not how to destroy his enemies, if he sent but a messenger to any part, their minds foreboding the destruction of their kingdoms, the other kings with hearts full of terror came at once in haste to see him. How great among the powerful was this *Govinda* Dandádhipa. As if burning the points of the compass, thus with blood-shot eyes did his groups of elephants, resembling those at the points of the compass, exert themselves in the destruction of his enemies, while his angry eyes with their ruddy flames, which were as a scarlet wafer on the forehead of the queen of the points of the compass, burnt up the enemies' country and reduced them to a state of primeval desolation—thus powerful was the peerless *Govinda Rája*.

* The allusion here is to the occurrences connected with the churning of the ocean.

Quickly washing away the stain of the ignorance of the other generals who commanded in the palace of the king *Vikramárka*, he shone with the brightest purity, this *Govinda Rája* Dandádhis'a. Hostile kings from all quarters coming to prostrate themselves before him and receive his commands, he stripped the walls of the points of the compass of all their decorations this *Govinda Rája*. Where remained there an enemy's country that it might be said it is in death, or in calamity, or where there was a confluence of people? How great then in war was the king *Govinda*.

His father was *Dási Rája*, a great hero praised by all the world; his mother *S'omala Devi*, a joy to her relations, true of speech, devoted to her husband; his god was Vishnu, the chief of the gods; thus purifying the *Pará-s'ara* gotra, how great in the world was this king *Govinda*.

May it be well.—While the mahá pradhána, Mane Verggaḍe Danḍanáyaka *Govindamayya*, entitled to the five great drums, chief of tributary kings, chief of the great generals, granting the desires of the worthy, like a bee at the lotus feet of the lord of Lakshmi, like Kumáraswámi in the front of war, pleased to horripilation with hearing the law, whose fame was as bright moonlight to the water-lilies the eyes of the queen the points of the compass, a terror in the field of battle, a right arm of victory to *Tribhuvana Malla*, a sun to the high mountain of the Brahman race, possessed of these and all other titles—was ruling the *Banavase* Twelve Thousand, the *Sántaḷige* Thousand, two six hundreds, the *vaḍḍa rávuḷa* and *pannáya*,* in the royal city of *Balipura*—Vishnu sported in the great waters in the mighty expanse of the milk sea, while unable for the tepid breeze to come forth from the lotus (the navel of Vishnu) shone Brahma in its centre like its ovary. With affection did Vishnu gaze at the gentle smile of the resplendent Lakshmi, surrounded with shining large shells and branches of creeping coral, above which rose the spray like a rampart of the thorny kétare flowers.

This chief general, whose pure auspicious form was praised by all, of extensive fame, caused to be made two twelve-faced disks (images of the sun), full of radiance and dazzling to behold. And he made a pure tank of water such that it was as if his sea had come there with Vishnu, or through love for the daughter whom Vishnu bore (Lakshmi), being called by her.

(Also) may it be well—To 25 mahájans (chief Brahmans), accomplished in the holy acts—*yama, niyama, svádhyáya, dhyána, dhárana, mauna, anusthána, japa, samádhi*, †—purest of all the inhabitants in the world, distinguished

---

* *Banavase pannirchchhâyiramum Sántaḷige sáyiramum eraḍḍáṛunúṛam vaḍḍa rávuḷamum pannáyamuman áḷuttam irddu.* See note p. 79.

† See note p. 16.

by their excessive attachment to the worship of Vishnu, with hearts close to the throne of the feet of Vishnu, occupants of the sky in virtue of its being filled with the celestial Ganges of their fame, devoted to the performance of the Brahman penances, celebrated in the world for personal purity, causing Indra himself to tremble from their Indra-like greatness (through penance), as Brahma himself to the vedas, illuminators of the Brahman race, whose curse never failed, enlightening like a lamp the treasury of universal merit, of purest bodies—in the 39th year of Chálukya Vikrama, the year Jaya, the month Chaitra, full moon day, Sunday, the day of an eclipse, at the vyatipáta, the time of the equinox,—as a gift to Paramesvara, and writing a copper s'ásana—gave, with washing of feet, pouring of water and every ceremony, free of all burden, with enjoyment for three generations—the Savati khaṇḍa plain of the *thala-vritti* of the royal city of *Balipura.*

The boundaries of that tract—west, the weir of the Bengere tank and the Heggaṭṭa halla; north, the Arasakatte and Indragere; east, the boundary of Govindapura; south, Baligaḍa and the west of the Sarasvati garden.

(*Some illegible.*)

And near the Heggaṭṭa halla, for the daily oblation to the god, for the worship, the repetition of the service, a procession in Chaitra and for repairs of the temple, granted 8 mattas, 4 flower gardens, 4 oil mills, 4 shops, 4 betel and mango gardens, the carriers of loads (*héṛu vokkaḷinge*) being freed from *hejjunka, vaḍḍa rávuḷa, varddhá dána,* and *talaṛa sunka.**

Whoso preserves this gift is as if he had made it himself: whoso destroys this gift incurs the guilt of slaying cows and Brahmans. Poison is no poison. The property of the gods that is the real poison. For poison kills one man, but a gift to the gods (if usurped) kills a man with his son and descendants.

(*Rest illegible.*)

---

* See note p. 79. *Varddhá dána* would appear to mean gift on promotion or increase; *talara sunka,* local customs duties levied by the watchmen.

89. S'ila S'asana at Balagami, date A. D. 1195.

Size ft. 4 6′ × ft. 2.—Haḷe Kannaḍa Characters.

Sun. Moon.

Cow suckling calf. Linga with Priest. Nandi.

Om. Adored be *S'ambhu* beauteous with the chámara-like crescent moon kissing his lofty head; the original foundation-pillar of the city of the three worlds. May the ocean of goodness, the jewel of deliverance from domestic troubles, the giver of treasures to Kubera, the adorned with all good qualities, the remover of sin, the husband of Gauri—grant the desires of his worshippers.

May it be well.—May that illustrious one, the remover of all fear, worshipped by the assemblies of gods and rákshasas, ... a jewel to the race of all kings, possessed of all titles . . . . . . an ocean of good qualities, the mighty king of the earth—be victorious as long as sun, moon, and stars endure.

The greatest of all is the line of the *Yádava* dynasty . . .
(*A considerable portion of the s'ásana in this place is almost entirely illegible*—the name occurs of *Víra Ballâḷa* bhúpam).

May it be well—A lord of all the lands belonging to the Kshatriyas living in *Sidda-kshetra*, an abode of the pleasure of Sarasvati, a new moon to the lotuses his enemies, causing pleasure to the lotus hearts of those who serve Siddes'vara adorned with the half moon, whose image is in the chief city that shines surrounded with pleasure gardens and the shelter of young creepers, skilled in making all kinds of gifts, holding a conch in his hand—many kings were the servants of his feet.

From the great sage *Vasishtha* did his race originate. . . . . and *Kratana* a son was born, speaking pleasantly to all people,—a light to the race of the Brahmans, was that great commander. To that *Kratana* by favor was born *Kumára*.

He in the S'aka year 1117*, the year Ananda, the month Márgas'ira, the day of new moon, first of the moon's increase, Monday, at the vyatipáta,—for the pleasure and every kind of service of the god *Siddes'vara*, gave to the greatly renowned *Deva S'iva Paṇḍita* at that time there, washing his feet and pouring a libation—gave along with the *nidhi*, *nikshepa*, *jala*, *taru*,

* *Saka nṛipa samvachharamm árabhya s'atádhika sahasropari sapta das'ame.*

*páshána**—lands belonging to the city and lands belonging to Siddápura—gave with affection, the great rája washing his feet so as to shew the yava (or lucky marks in the toes)—gave, pouring water in the manner approved by all.

The gift which he thus privately made, with the pouring of water from a kalas'a, became celebrated among all people and gained him the glory of a giver of lands. In war like S'ibi, good deeds were his distinction, conqueror of all his foes, to women a Manmatha, was that *Kumára*. Adorned with all good qualities, an abode of growing good fortune, of pure extended fame, clothed with a pure body. With his terrible words the clouds were forced to come near and the pleasant streams flowed down from the mountains filled with lusty elephants. Skilled in all the science of weapons, possessed of a splendid army, he was surrounded in war by neighbouring kings and friends. Having made images of Soma and Uma he caused the place called *Agnes'vara*, adorned with groves and hills, with fruits ripening in their season, and with all holy actions, to be celebrated among all people.

The boundaries of *Prasiddhipura*, as determined by the Kshatriyas of that town, were—east, the cultivated land of the Brahma stream—west, a hedge of bamboos, namely the hedge of bamboos included between the jáli tree at the end and the mark of the creepers—south, the enclosure of the Berundés'vara temple to the mark of the jáli tree of *Ballipura* and the boundary of the temple of the god Avimuktés'vara—north, *Heggaṭṭa*—these four boundary pillars extend as far as Kiru Baligáve.

The boundaries of the field—east, the southern waste weir of *Hávalgajje*—south, *Nidugolla*—west,, the Baduva tank-bund of *Obbaddi*—north, the southern arm of the paddy land of the god Indraprastha Varáha, adjoining the stream.

. . . a paddy land of one maṭṭa, and under the tank bund of the god Rames'vara 4 flower gardens and paddy land of one maṭṭa.

Whoso preserves this gift will obtain merit. Whoso destroys it incurs the guilt of slaying a thousand Brahmans and a thousand cows. Whoso revokes by violence the land presented either by himself or by another will certainly be born a worm in ordure for sixty thousand years.

Om.—Praise to S'iva.

---

* See note p. 3

90 Virakal at Balagami, date A. D. 1158.

Size ft. 3 11′ × ft. 1 10′.—Haḷe Kannaḍa Characters.

The hero in the presence. | Linga with Priest. | Sun and Moon. | Nandi.

Om. Praise to Siva—May it be well—The powerful *Kalachurya* emperor *Bijjala Deva*, possessed of all titles . . . in the year Bahudhánya, the month Kártika—

The hero being borne to heaven by celestial nymphs waving chamaras.

the last day of the moon's decrease, new moon day, Tuesday—*S'ivayanapura Kalla Náyaka* fighting with many in the *Koḍi* hollow, and beating them, joined the gods.

Who wins in war gains spoil, who falls enjoys the celestial nymphs. What fear then of death in war to him who loves the moment of close fight?

The hero, armed with bow and arrow, overcoming two others similarly armed, one of whom is falling at his feet. A row of cattle on the left.

91. Virakal at Balagami, date about A. D. 1160.

Size ft. 3 6′ × ft. 1 8′.—Haḷe Kannaḍa Characters.

The hero in the presence. | Moon. | Linga with Priest. | Sun. | Nandi.

May it be well.—In the victorious kingdom of *Bijjana Deva*, the emperor powerful by his own might, Malla of the S'anivara Siddhagiri durga, in war like Ráma, unequalled hero,—

The hero being borne to heaven by celestial nymphs waving chamaras.

while Banavase náḍ was under the government of Kariya Kesimayya, at that time . . . his servant *Nágánna*, doing him service,* went to the world of gods.

The hero, armed with shield and sword, fighting two others armed with shields and javelins.

* *Sévaka Nágannas áḷutana máḍi sura loka práptanádam.* The ambiguous term *áḷutana*, meaning both *government* and the duty of an *áḷu* or servant, is skilfully used to enhance the importance of the person whose death is here commemorated.

92. Virakal (?) at Balagami, date A. D. 1046.

Size ft. 3 6′ × ft. 1 11′.—Haḷe Kannaḍa Characters.

Two Naga or semi-serpent forms, male and female, the latter holding the former's sword.

The faces are very expressive and each is surrounded by nine serpent hoods, an unusual number. Each body terminates in three serpent coils.

May it be well.—While the Mahá Manḍales'vara, *Ch*. . . *ḍa Ráyarasa* was ruling in peace the *Banavase* Twelve Thousand,—in the year 968, the year Vyaya, the month Márgas'ira, the 13th day of the moon's increase, Friday—*Soma Dása,* the son-in-law of the Seṭṭi of the royal city of Balligámve, Nága Deva, . . *Nágiyabe* uniting . . . .

---

93. Virakal at Balagami, date (?) about A. D. 1115.*

Size ft. 3 9′ × ft. 2′.—Haḷe Kannaḍa Characters.

Moon.

Linga with Priest. Nandi.

(*The inscription in this part all knocked off*).

The hero being borne to heaven by celestial nymphs waving chamaras.

Who wins in war gains spoil, who falls enjoys the celestial nymphs. What fear then of death in fight to him who must at some moment give up all? When pressing into that square fort (*chovukada kóṭe*) . . .

The hero on horseback, putting to the sword some others with densely matted locks. One of them with blood flowing from a terrible wound across his body from shoulder to shoulder.

---

* The lowest bas relief closely resembles that of No. 96.

94. Virakal at Balagami, date A. D. 1183.

Size ft. 4 3′ × ft. 1 11′.—Haḷe Kannaḍa Characters.

Moon. Sun.

The hero in the presence. Linga with Priest. Nandi.

May it be well.—The 8th year of the era of the powerful *Kalachurya* emperor, *Ahava Malla Deva*, great lord of the earth, an abode of all bravery, equal to Náráyana—the year S′obhakrit, the month Bhádrapada, the 13th day of the moon's decrease, Monday—the commander—

The hero being borne to heaven by celestial nymphs, all wearing tiaras, some bearing chamaras.

having scared away elephants, crocodiles, and large bodies of monkeys that they should not fall on him, attacking a bear (*bhallúka*), and spearing it, cut it in pieces.

What can I say of bravery like Ráma's! . . .

The hero with the aid of dogs destroying some large animal (? a bear). Two men (or ? women) turning away paralysed with fear.

95. Virakal at Balagami, date A. D. 1180.

Size ft. 3 9′ × ft. 2.—Haḷe Kannaḍa Characters.

The two heroes in the presence. Linga with Priest. Nandi.

May it be well.—In the reign of the *Kalachurya* emperor, *Ahava Malla Deva*—the year S′árvari, the month Kártika, the 1st day of the moon's decrease, Sunday—when *Somana* of Mágunḍi—

The two heroes seated in a car, attended by celestial nymphs bearing chamaras.

besieged . . . the Náyaka of Hála holale and slew him, *Ketama* the son of Hiḷḍeya Náyaka, being behind, killed many and went to the world of gods. The chief of the country inviting the ryots of the city . .

(*Rest illegible.*)

The two heroes under canopies, fighting with horsemen of rank. In the hand which bears his shield, the foremost hero holds by the hair a head of beautiful features, a striking contrast to his own, which are hideous, even in the celestial car.

96. Virakal at Balagami, Date A. D. 1115.

Size ft. 3 5′. × ft. 2 2′. Haḷe Kannaḍa Characters.

The hero in the presence. Linga with Priest. Nandi.

May it be well—While the favorite of the goddess of victory, the powerful . . . emperor . . . . . in the 39th year of Chálukya Vikrama, the year Manmatha, the month Bhádrapada, the 14th day of the moon's increase, Monday— .

The hero being borne to heaven by celestial nymphs bearing chamaras.

when *Govindarasa* making war upon the southern . . . and burning Kallúru, stationed his army in the . . . fort, the bold *Bopeya*, son-in-law of . . . paya Náyaka, killing many, went to the world of gods.

The hero on horseback, with an attendant bearing his umbrella, putting to the sword a number of others whose bodies exhibit terrible wounds.

---

97. Virakal at Balagami, Date A. D. 1199.

Size ft. 3 5′. × ft. 1 9′.—Haḷe Kannaḍa Characters.

Sun. Moon.

The hero in the presence. Linga with Priest. Nandi.

The following day the king's army was destroyed*

The hero being borne to heaven by celestial nymphs bearing chamaras.

May it be well—In the 8th year of the powerful *Yádava* emperor, *Víra Baḷḷáḷa Deva*, the year Raudri, the month . . the last day of the moon's decrease, Monday . . . *Sirina* the son of *Bommeya*, . . . killing many went to the world of gods.

The hero on foot, armed with sword and shield, encountering a horseman armed with a spear and riding over prostrate forms.

---

* This sentence has the appearance of being a more recent addition.

98 S'ila S'asana at Balagami, date about A. D. 680.

Size ft. 3 6′ × ft. 1 10′—Púrvada Haḷe Kannaḍa Characters.

An Elephant.

May it be well—While *Vinayáditya*, the refuge of kings, favorite of earth and fortune, great king of kings, supreme ruler, great monarch, was ruling the earth—*

Pogilli Sendraka, a subduer of great kings, ruling in *Jiluguru*, presented for the decoration of (the god) Periyadísa (?), with pouring of water and every ceremony, having informed his rája, the property of those who die without heirs †—the various authorities giving their consent (namely), the priest of Valligáme Kedára, the priest of the Auraliya temple, the priest of the Vedevaḷḷi temple, Ravichandra the chief of Alaruvalli, Sokka gámunda, Yedeya gámunda, the great gámunda and gávaḍḍis of Moleya, the gámagi of Andagi.

Whoso covets this gift incurs the guilt of the five great sins and of killing a thousand cows, ...

Whoso shall piously maintain it will rise with all his line . . .

Whoso preserves this gift shall enjoy the supreme delight . . .

99. S'ila S'asana at Taldagundi, date A. D. 997.

Size ft. 4 6′ × ft. 2 1′.—Haḷe Kannaḍa Characters.

Sun.

Linga with Priest. Nandi.

May it be well— While the victorious kingdom of the illustrious *Ahava Malla*, protector of all lands, favorite of earth and fortune, great king of kings, supreme ruler, first of monarchs, glory of the *Satyás'raya kula*, ornament of the *Chalukyas*‡—was continually increasing in prosperity.

The dweller at his lotus feet—May it be well—*Bhímarasa*, entitled to the five great drums, a close attendant on *Tailapa*, possessed of many elephants and forces, a cage of adamant to those who claimed his protection, was ruling the [*Banavase*] Twelve thousand, the *Sántalige* Thousand, the [eighteen] agrahāras . .

* *Svasti s'rí Vinayáditya rájás'raya, s'rí prithivi vallabha, maháráj́ádhirája, paramesvara, bhaṭára, prithivi rájyam keye.* Cf. T. S. 3 *and* 5.—This part is clear, but owing to the minuteness of the photograph some of the rest is more or less uncertain.

† *Aputraka poradu.*

‡ See note p. 14.

The dweller at his lotus feet, receiving tribute from all the kings, shining in the office of a great minister, the Malla Rája, the auspicious *Perggaḍe Ká* . . . *ya*, in the s'aka year 919, the year Hevilambi, the month Vais'ákha, the 8th day of the moon's decrease, Sunday,—it being stated that his giving of the control of the forty manneyas (? freehold villages) near the river was false . . from not having given the right to all the water, obtained from the hands of Devayya forty gadyánas and gave up the care of the manneya. That this may not fail, the witnesses are the eighteen agraháras, the seven officials of Jidda, the priests of both sects in the forty manneya of the river, the senabhova Polla . mayya.*

Whoso maintains this gift . . . a thousand tawny cows in Váranási, Gaya, Prayága . . .

---

100. Virakal at Taldagundi, date A. D. 1196.

Size ft. 4 6' × ft. 2 8'.—Haḷe Kannaḍa Characters.

The hero in the presence. Sun. Linga with Priest in a temple. Moon. Nandi.

May it be well—In the reign of the *Kalachurya* emperor *Ráya Murári Sovi*—the year Viródhikrit,† the month As'víja, the 8th day of the moon's decrease, Sunday—the Banavase náḍ Hergaḍe Danḍanáyaka, *Chálikya Kesimaya*, pursuing a band of robbers, in a village of the Sántalige náḍ—

The hero ascending to heaven in a triumphal dance, attended by celestial nymphs, some bearing chamaras.

Kálaya Náyaka, the son of Mukkandara Sovi Seṭṭi, ornament of the *Halisanda* race, cutting in pieces their horse, and killing many, recovered the cows and went to the world of gods.

His sons *Sómaya* and *Bammaya*, with great faith and humility, set up this stone—(*rest illegible*).

The hero on foot, armed with sword and shield, encountering a horseman armed with a sword. Another horseman behind him, and a figure falling at his feet.

---

* *Nadiyoḷage nálvattaṛa manneya káyimmanna biṭṭam pusi . . bhadakke sarvva nir odha geydoḍ átam tanage kuḍalilladi Devayyana kayoḷ nálvattu gadyáṇa ponnu kond átanam áldala manneyamam biṭṭu koṭṭ adanin tappodakke sákshi padinenṭ agrahárammum Jiddan álga ḷvarum nadiyalege nálvattu manneyar ubhayanmata devaroḍam senabhova Polla . . mayya* ||

† Probably a mistake for Virodhi, as Virodhikrit would not fall within Ráya Murári Sovi's reign.

101. Virakal at Taldagundi, date? A. D. 1189.

Size ft. 7 6′ × ft. 2 6.′—Haḷe Kannaḍa Characters.

Dvarapalaka * | A Jain Tirthankara. † | Dvarapalaka.

May it be well—While the favorite of earth and fortune, great king of kings, supreme ruler, first of monarchs . . *Billaha Rája* was ruling the Banavase Náḍ in peace and wisdom ‡—in the year of the S′aka king, the year Sa .

Figures very indistinct. Probably the hero being borne to heaven by celestial nymphs.

(The inscription in this part quite illegible.)

The hero in front of a large herd of cattle, and with a drawn sword, encountering a number of archers.

102. S′ila S′asana at Taldagundi, date A. D. 1157.

Size ft. 7 3′ × ft. 3 3′.—Haḷe Kannaḍa Characters.

Cow suckling calf. | Sun. | Sword. | Linga with Priest. | Moon. | The donor.

Om. Praise to him who with affection wears the crest of the moon, the giver of wealth, praise to *S′ambhu* who holds in a perpetual embrace the joyful *Uma*. May the chiefs of all the gods, by their power lords of the three worlds, *Brahma, Is′ána* and *Janárdana*, grant our desires. May S′iva's wife, the womb of the earth, and S′iva in whose loins the creation rests—*Párvati* the mother of the world, and *S′iva* its lord and father—protect us.

S′iva is first, S′iva middle, and S′iva without a second, the end—being the universal protector he is sovereign of mind and life, and the divine soul in all things. The auspicious god of Kailása, first of the deities, lord of the sound *Om*, embracing earth, moon, sun, Yama, wind, sky, fire, water, and Brahma, without birth, husband of *Párvati*, having the world as his car, the fountain of mercy, known by the twanging sound of his bow, king of the gods, the master of Daksha—into this *S′iva* my mind enters.

* This is a female figure, and stands a step lower than the other.

† There appears to have been some inscription at the base of this figure, which is too much defaced to be made out.

‡ See note p. 2.

This mother (Párvati), the genitrix of the twice-born (Brahmans), hearing the glorious order of *Mahádeva*, first of all the illustrious rishis, lord of the syllable *om*, for the unending work of the creation of the three worlds, shone at his left side obedient to the words, and conceived the desire for the essences from which was produced the greatness of the world.

From the lotus in the navel of the lotus-eyed (Vishnu) came forth the generator of the birth of the world, the husband of Sarasvati, with his womb (*sic*) of light. From that lotus, by the intent of *Vishnu*, worthy to be worshipped by the three worlds, that the three worlds should praise him, were produced the three worlds, filled with gods, animals and men. But as if these were grown old and not pleasing, Brahma created a land of surpassing merit.

On the globe of the world, which princes sport with, taking in their arms laden with sounding ornaments, like a Linga placed on its throne (or pedestal) shone *Jambu dvípa* to the eyes, surrounded with numerous and extensive oceans —and in that region the most glorious was the *Kuntala* country. In that land of exalted merit (*karmma bhúmi*), in the dvápara age, the seed of works of merit produced fruit a hundred crore fold, which shall grow for ever.

After the Kshatriyas who sprung from the arms of Parames'vara, the *Chálukya* race became renowned.

Of that Chálukya race, the son *Tailapa* was a king renowned; his son was the king *Sattiga*; whose son was the king *Vikramánka*; equal to him was *Jaya Simha* his younger brother; whose son was *Ahava Malla*; whose son was *Núrmmadi*; whose son was *Soma*; whose son was *Jagadeka Malla*; whose son was the king *Taila*.

In this manner the kings of the Chálukya line having ruled in order, at that time:

May it be well—Entitled to the five great drums, Mahá Mandales'vara, lord of the chief city *Kálanjara*, having the ensign of a golden bull, having the great sounds of the damaruga, túrya and nirghoshana, a sun to the lotus the *Kalachurya* race, able in war, in honor as mount Méru, as a god to the fighting-men, an elephant goad to the bravest (of his foes), a cage of adamant to those who claimed his protection, in bravery like Rávana, to strange women like a brother, the Malla of the S'anivára Siddagiri durga, in war like Ráma, a lion to the elephant his enemies, Nis's'anka Malla, possessing these and many other titles*—was the powerful emperor *Bijjana Devarasa*, whose greatness and bravery were as follows—

* See note p. 66.

Considering that the world was in his hand, looking upon all like the pleasant moon, of marvellous splendour in the field of battle, possessing the wealth of all the points of the compass, with teeth like the jasmine, of mild disposition, causing joy to all by his speech, reckoning virtuous qualities as his life although all such qualities were in him, with his body stretched out as far as the elephants at the points of the compass he plucked out their tusks and gained a great fame, the king *Bijjaṇa*.

The dweller at his lotus feet was the mahá pradhána, the Banavase náḍ Danḍanáyaka *Kes'imayya*, whose lineage was as follows.—
Bearing the burden of all his line like Girijes'a, of unequalled bravery, *Hoḷala Rája*, increasing in splendour from the glory of king Bijja, was his father, his mother *Dugganabbe*, shining with the brightness of the moon—thus was he a glory of the *Bharadvája* tribe, a light to the *Aravinda* náḍ, no ordinary man. In beauty of person the son of Indra, in good fortune Manmatha, in morals Manu, in understanding Brahma, in helping and protecting others the emperor S'ibi, in worth, majesty and profundity Raghu Ráma, thus is he considered and described with great joy by people on both sides of the earth.

The most distinguished of his ministers were—*Narasimha Deva*, of great wisdom ; *Mahádárya*, an ocean of good qualities ; *Tikkarasa*, foremost in gifts, of great dignity, without an equal.

His revenue accountants, some regarding him with affection and some with the obeisance due to a treasury of wisdom, *Chaṭṭi Rája* governed and protected—(namely) *Mailári Danḍanátha* of rapidly acquired fame ; *Polarasa*, a treasury of liberality ; *Chánakya*, gainer of all lawful profit ; *Soma*, a collection of all fortune. And among those *herggaḍe karanas*, of sincere mind and blameless life, were—having embraced the path of Manu, of great liberality, *Ebbe Rája* ; of inestimable qualities *Revana* ; *Soma*, unshaken, majestic and pure ; *Mártánḍa*, of shining fame ; *Nagoydi Rája*, of a renown worthy of all praise ; the skilful *Mallappa*, a just and good king—all of them experienced in the path of virtue.

While the mahá pradhána *Kes'ava* Danḍanáyaka, surrounded with all these his ministers, royal attendants, chief men, servants, people of the city, and chief accountants, was ruling the *Banavase* Twelve Thousand, punishing the evil and rewarding the good, residing in the royal city of *Ballipura*,—one day when in the midst of the assembly, with a few attendants round him, one at his feet watching with great fear to receive his wishes, one who himself received obeisance from others—

From the lotus born (Brahma) was descended a lord of many, *Kas'yappa*; from him was born *Abja* who obtaining the great *Paritapati* (as wife) became renowned. He had (a son) the prudent *Soma*; from whom a mighty emanation was *Chaṭṭi Rája*, a protector of all who sought refuge with him. His wife was *Mádiakka*. To these two was born *Rechanna*, destined to acquire all merit.

He commenced a discourse (as follows) on merit, which, filled with eloquent words and skilful arguments, pleased the lotus heart of all people as the rays of the sun bring delight to the lines of lotuses.

"Thus adapted to the increase of merit are the greatness of gifts of land, and gifts of villages, the distinction of gifts of food, the glory of gifts of learning. (The advantage of) each one of these may be described as follows:

"Of all gifts a gift of land is the best, this frees from all sin, this obtains svarga Thus say the learned who are acquainted with the secrets of merit—'Those who perform penances, those who perform sacrifices according to the s'ástras, the followers of truth, those who know many sciences, those who reverence and love gurus and gods, will not go beyond (to a higher heaven than) donors of land.' No gift is equal to gifts of land, no treasure is equal to land, no other gift is so allied to truth, as than untruth no sin is greater.

"From the gift of villages with all the crops and waters belonging to them, free of all burden, if presented from love to S'iva, listen and I will relate the merit one obtains. Shining like a crore of suns, surrounded by crores of celestial nymphs, in a car such as is promised to those who make crores of gifts, filled with all he may desire, accompanied by twenty one generations of his line, shall he come to my world (says S'iva) and there for time without end live in the enjoyment of all delights.

"There is nothing better in the world than food, neither has there been nor will there ever be; food is the cause of the world being what it is, all in the world depends on food, therefore whoso makes a gift of food is as if he made a gift of life. It is more meritorious than even a gift of life, therefore he who makes a gift of food obtains the merit of all gifts.

"The Brahmans and others of the four castes, the four religious orders, Brahma and all the gods, are engaged in gifts of learning. Whoso performs incantations and penance, what man soever with ability instructs disciples, by these no greater can be bestowed, they have made all gifts. Whoso supplies students with food, applies unguents to their bodies, furnishes them with clothes, gives them alms, to him all his desires will be fulfilled, of this there is no doubt. Whatsoever merit arises from pilgrimages to holy bathing places, whatsoever arises from performing sacrifices according to the s'ástras, a crorefold greater merit shall he obtain who makes gifts of learning."

Listening to the glory of the various kinds of gifts by which those who are tormented with many sins may free themselves, his mind being filled with piety and prepared, inquiring for a place where such a gift might worthily be made, and coming with *Recharasa* to a village named *Stháṇugúḍha*, a gift of the golden-wombed (Brahma) whose wisdom is full of desire for the creation of all worlds, a place of shelter for 32,000 Brahmans, shining with the images of Pranavés'vara and other gods made by Brahma, purified by the residences of Brahma, Aditya and others created by the four-faced (Brahma) and other gods, surrounded by many shining pleasure groves situated near it—this he decided on as a suitable place for the performance of a work of merit—and as if to increase the love of meritorious works he already had, saying 'I will cause it to be done', rising up from the place of the assembly, he came, along with his accountants, and first performing all manner of worship to the god *Pranaves'-vara* of the *Stháṇugúḍha* village—

And then in the presence of the Vedánti Svayampáki Deva, of the 32,000 mahájanas (Brahmans) of the agrahára reverenced by all the náḍ, the *Stháṇugúḍha* village,—accomplished in the holy acts, yama, niyama, svádhyáya, dhyána, dhárana, mauna, anushṭhána, japa, samádhi,* diligent in performing the agnihótra and other sacrifices, and in serving gurus, Brahmans and gods, versed in tarka, mimámsa and many other sciences, devoted to all kinds of merit, diligent in performing the agnishṭóma and seven great sacrifices, of a fame that dazzled like the sun, with bodies purified by the bathings after many sacrifices—and of the Deva the Herggade karanam of the place, of the *Nágara Khaṇḍa* worthies, *Baḍanike Sovarasa*, *Nakana*, *Goidana*, Begúra *Keta Gávuṇḍa*, Megundi *Sanka Gavuṇḍa*, Malavalli *Keta Gávunda*, *Konavalli Prithivi Seṭṭi*, *Kiruvaḍi Masani Seṭṭi*, these and other the *Nágara Khaṇḍa* chiefs and head men, and the Herggades and accountants of that *Kampana*—

For the pleasure and worship of the god and the daily service, the enthronement, the offerings and oblations, for a procession in Chaitra and attendant sports, and for any fresh ceremonies,—together with four Veda khandika, two Bhaṭṭa vritti, and for learned teachers of Kannaḍa letters† six khandikas for the food, clothing and chatra for the teachers and students—with the consent of *Kasapaya Náyaka* his governor.‡

---

* See note p. 16. † *Kannaḍakshara sikshe ghaḷiyár*—(*ghaḷiyár*, accomplished persons.)

‡ Cf. note p 159.

Kes'ava Dandanáyaka and his accountants, in the S'aka year 1079, the year Is'vara, the month Pushya, full moon day, Monday, the day of the sun's entering the northern signs, at the vyati-páta—pouring water, gave, with enjoyment for three generations—the village of *Hiriya Tagulaṭṭi* in the Kampana Nágara Khanda Seventy of the Banavase Twelve Thousand, and to the south-west of *Thánagundúru*, the Kónavane plain—purifying the four boundaries according to the ancient custom.

The settlement there made was as follows—to the god *Múlasthána* of *Tagulaṭṭi*, one matta; for the freehold land of the Gauḍa two mattas; in the *Konavane* plain, the Rig-veda khanḍika one, the Yajur-veda khanḍika one, the Kalpa khanḍika one, the Sáma-veda khanḍika one, for the teachers of language and grammar one khanḍika, the Prabhákara-vedánta khanḍika one, for the separate heads of the different schools of logic three mattas, for the Vedánti Svayampáki Svámi one matta, for the *davasigaru* one matta, for the garland makers of the flower-garden 20 kammas—altogether 5 mattas 20 kammas.

And of the paddy produced on the remaining land, the equivalent of one fourth part, after deducting one year's crop for the daily worship and offerings to the god—and of the residue of the paddy and of the money obtained from *Tagulhaṭṭi*, devoting one (fourth) part to the god—the remaining paddy and money are for daily feeding 30 Brahmans who eat in the god's chatra, the disciples of the 8 khanḍikas, reckoning 6 to each, 48 khanḍika disciples, the pújári and mányaru (servants) of the god 2—altogether 80— . .
For three female cooks (*báṇasúttiyaru*) 6 gadyána for their keep, and 6 paṇa for cloths (*sírege*), for 50 disciples 2 paṇa each for cloths, altogether (?) 10 ra . . . for an oil bath once a week, and for feeding 30 extra Brahmans on Mondays 4 gadyánas, for daily oblations 5 gadyánas, for the teacher of Kannaḍa 5 gadyána, for teachers of the s'ástra to boys, for teachers of the puránas, for those who maintain the sacred fire, for the presenters of akshati and sandal, and of betel and nut (*támbúla*) to the Brahmans who have been fed in the khandika chatras.

And from half the money obtained in *Tagulhaṭṭi* for the god,—from the gardens which *S'icharasa*, *Haṭṭagára*, *Boḍarasa*, *Mahadeva*, the agents (*kajjangalu*) presented—and from the seven vritti to the east of Siddahalli given by the faithful, there shall be performed daily *gaddige púje*, worship with incense, oblations and the perpetual lamp; and one thousand burnt offerings of gingeli seed (*tila homa*).

And from month to month, on the two 8th and two 14th days of the moon, on new moon and full moon days, at the vyati-páta and equinoxes (*sankramana*),

—at these auspicious times, first performing all the usual daily services, then the teachers of the s'ástras will recite the *S'ántyadhyáya*, the 6th of the *S'iva-dharma*; and according to the rules therein making a maṇḍala in front of the god, with the proper incantations place on it offerings of food (*bali*)—and pronounce a blessing on the reigning sovereign (*des'avanáḷva kshatriyánmam*), on cows and Brahmans, and the principal director of the ceremonies.

And whenever they happen in the year, on the maháparvas, the two equinoxes and the two solstices, on the eclipses of sun or moon, at the full moon days in Asháḍha, Kárttika, Mágha and Vais'ákha, on which occasions the service performed brings as much merit as worship for six months—at those auspicious times, beginning with a thousand *gaddige púje* (worship of the god's throne), then performing the *punyáha váchane* (repeating praises of the day and purifying the assembly by sprinkling), and the s'ástra khanḍikas separating the guru-manḍala, vidyá-manḍala and S'iva-manḍala—these three manḍalas worshipping, shall recite the *s'ánti adhyáya*.

And the four veda khanḍikas, filling four purified pots with water; and taking perfume drugs, gall of cattle, the five kinds of sprouts (*viz.*, those of the mango, wild fig, banyan, sacred fig, and waved leaf fig), five kinds of bark, the five products of the cow (milk, curds, ghee, urine and dung), cardamoms, sandal-wood, &c; will put those into them, and place them towards the four points of the compass, and repeat the verses in praise of *S'iva* from the four vedas. The *gaddige púje* being thus ended—

Then making before the god eight libations, and anointing him with the *pancha gavya* (the five products of the cow above mentioned) and the *panchámrita* (*viz.*, milk, curds, honey, ghee, and cocoanut-milk); will mix the flour of wheat and rice in warm water coloured with turmeric, and then bathe the god with kus'a-water, sandal-water, flower-water, pure-water, gold-water and jewel-water.

After that the vedic priests, taking up those four pots, will approach, repeating the verses of the Rig-veda commencing with the word *samudra*, and with their arms performing the auspicious bath, will place upon the god the five sweet perfumes (*viz.*, two kinds of civet, scented vermilion powder, superfine camphor, and musk). Then according to the s'ástras, decorating him, and tying on the sacred thread, making the offerings of *madhu-parka* (a dish of plantains, honey and curds). and *áchamaniya* (a little water), and worshipping him with flowers, fruits and food, with burning of incense and lights, and waving of lamps,—they will place in four metal plates lamps made of the five kinds of colored rice, each with three wicks, and wave them three times before him, with hymns of praise, with the sound of all the drums, the conchs and horns.

And at the three seasons (morning, noon and evening) after making an oblation of rice, milk and sugar, of cakes and other eatables; and presenting betel-leaf and areca-nut; they will offer around that oblation balls made of sugar as a *bali*. Then shall they come and worship all the gods of the village.

And at the *uttaráyana* (the equinox in which the sun enters the northern signs), anointing the god with 100 palas of ghee, and making a large garland of flowers containing 1008 blossoms of the blue water-lily, they will worship him therewith.

And at the full moon in Mágha they will make an oblation of ghee, and in Chaitra, after performing high service, will seat the god on a high car, and take him to visit the reigning prince, exhibiting the umbrella, the chámaras, the great banner, the standards, the vessels and the mirrors; sounding all the most auspicious musical instruments, conchs and horns, as well as those in daily use; displaying all the pictures, &c., which daily surround the god. And after making a grand illumination they will return and cause all to be placed in their positions again.

Thus shall the king who rules our nád and his chief accountants and the 32,000 remit the dues in their several places and maintain the gift. Thus will they gain all the regions procured by the merit of reading the Sáma-veda, of making gifts, and of reading the Yajur-veda. Thence enjoying the pleasures of the Rudra-loka, and for endless ages dwelling there in happiness, they will then obtain an eternal, indestructible, undisturbed place in the dwelling of the god Soma-nalina (S'iva), and there abide in everlasting joy.

Of making a gift or continuing it, the continuing it is the best, for he who makes a gift obtains svarga, but he who continues it obtains final beatitude.

(*Some illegible.*).

103. S'ila S'asana at Taldagundi, date A. D. ? 1191.

Size ft. 6 3' × ft. 3 9'.—Haḷe Kannaḍa Characters.

Sword.	Sun.		Moon.	
Cow suckling calf.	Dvara-palaka.	Linga under a canopy.	Dvara-palaka.	Votary.

Adored be Hara . . . . Praise to S'iva, the husband of Párvati, having the crest of the crescent moon, destroyer of the sins of all people, served by rishis, by whom all the world has been adorned, wearing serpents as his ornaments.

May it be well—While the powerful emperor, *Víra Ballála Devarasa*, protector of all the world, favorite of earth and fortune, a sun in the firmament of the *Yádava* race, a chintámani to the desires of all, Rája of the *Male Rájas* (hill rájas)* . . —was ruling his kingdom in peace and wisdom†—at that time;

In the world great with all good things, and surrounded by the girdle of the sea filled with the high waves of the Ganges, shines *Jambu-dvipa*, conspicuous with the rich country of *Kuntala*. In it, ornamented with pleasure groves grateful to the minds and eyes of men, with clustering branches and fruit, and with lakes surrounded with lines of lotuses covered with buds and leaves, were the pre-eminent lands of Kedára, whose king, the chief of many countries, of which *Banavase* was the first, *Mukanna Kaḍamba*, born to confer benefits on the world, rejoicing in gifts, to the Brahman race in the south . . . selecting from Ahichchhatra agrahára 12,000 Brahmans purified by agnihotras, belonging to 32 families, bringing them thence and placing them before him, sought out for them a holy spot, celebrated in the four ages, pure, distinguished by Pranames'vara and others, by Five Lingas established by Brahma and other gods, and made there an agrahára named *Sthánarudrapura*.‡

---

* Cf. note p. 7. † See note p. 2.

‡ *Svasti pras'asta samasta vastu vistára Gangottunga taranga sangatam aparárṇava baḷuḷa jaḷa vaḷaya valayita vasumatí s'ubha prades'a vis'esha rúpa Jambúdvípa kánta Kuntaḷa maṇḍala maṇḍana sakala jana mano nayanábhirámárámáneka s'áka phala púga kuḍmala daḷa vimaḷa kamaḷa kuvalaya vilási sarovara vara taṭáka taṭa kalita kaḷama kedára Kedároddáma des'angaḷarasam Banavase modal enisid aneka maṇḍes'varam Mukkanna Kaḍambam jagad anugraha vigraham dána vinodi dakshiṇa pathadoḷu vipra kulama . . keyi . . . deyidanta deyade naḍad Ahichchhatrágraháraman árádhisi sádhisi paḍada panirsásirágnihotra pavitra dvátrims'at vipra kuṭumbamam munditṭu tandu chatur yuga prasiddha vis'uddha chatur ábhidhána Chaturmukha pratishṭhita Praṇames'vara pramukha sura pratishṭhita Pancha Lingálingita tírtha kshetradoḷu nóḍi máḍida mahágrahāram Sthánarudrapurada páṛavol ad entene* ‖

To describe it—Filled with the sounds of groups of parrots, with fields of paddy, groups of lotuses, and bowers of spreading creepers, abounding in beautiful gardens, melodious with full grown cuckoos—this place thus glorious, as if, resolved that no other should equal it, had fixed that bound as a charm, lay near the mountains. But as if fearing that surrounded by mountains it would be dark, Indra, the splitter of mountains, had removed the mountains to a little distance from that *Tánagundúru*.

In its groves were the sandal with its comely leaves, the young red sandal, the cocoanut palm, the clove tree, the citron, the champaka, the neem tree (*margosa*), the mimusops elengi, the as'oka, the areca palm, the boswellia thurifera, the fragrant jasmine, and the mango.

In it were professors skilled in medicine, in sorcery (or magic), in logic, in the art of distorting people by incantation, in poetry, in the use of weapons, in sacrificing, . . . and in the art of cookery to prepare the meals. .

While its groves put to shame the groves of Nandana, such was the glory of that great agrahára that all the surrounding country prayed to be taught in the four vedas, their six vedángas, the three rival divisions of mímámsa, the tarka and other connected sciences, the eighteen great puránas, the making of numerous verses of praise, the art of architecture, the arts of music and dancing, and in the knowledge of all the four divisions of learning which were possessed by the Brahmans of the *Sthánagundúru* agrahára.

Oblations of food, milk and curds, rich milk, pudding of rice, these all abound in this village, thus did each pair of gods ever sing to each other throughout the night.

To describe the Chakradhara of the learned of that village—Having by the circle of his wisdom relieved the village of great trouble and thereby bestowed a benefit upon it, he had received the honorable name of *Chakraya*.

Whose race was as follows:—Filling the whole world with his fame as the glory of the 32,000, giving protection to many multitudes of Brahmans, of great virtue, the essence of piety, diligent in worshipping gods and Brahmans, was the Brahman lord *Mákimaya*. In virtuous life equal to the sons of Manu, possessing a knowledge of all sciences, true in speech, distinguished in the assembly, of great and secure wealth, born in the race of Brahma, worthy of obeisance from all, for the utterance of whose praise all the learned were unequal, renowned in the Vis'vámitra gotra, thus illustrious was *Máki Rája*. To the assembly of the learned, and to those who were under his protection, to those who were his friends, and to all who were worthy, like a cluster of fruit he granted all their desires as soon as ever they approached him.

Thus having like as Govinda appeared in the world as a kalpa-vriksha and gained a great name, the learned *Máki* obtained a son, a possessor of all virtue. And his son obtaining praise from all people, a moon to raise the fortunes of his family, the Brahman *Mákimaya* rose in the world.

His offspring was as follows—As king Pándu had five sons, so to him also were born five sons—*Vámana*, *Trilochana* of unequalled greatness, *Is'vara*, *Dinagopa*, and *Nrisimha*. That these were benefactors to the world and an ornament to their race, to render them this praise did all the earth love. Among these five the most illustrious, understanding the divine method, was the Brahman named *Trilochana*—like the tender sprout which the hand has caught, or a kalpa-vriksha, so among his illustrious brothers was he the first.

Of a disposition the praise of all, possessed of virtue, character, worth, a relative of all the good, with a form like the forms of those who were the embodiments of all the vedas and s'ástras (the ancient rishis), knowing the glory and the attributes of the two lotus feet of S'iva, who could equal thee, *Trilochana*, adorned with the gem of all good qualities.

Of a piety which consecrated the image of *Pranames'vara* shining like a new Brahma, this *Trilochana*, with an excess of ardour like one possessed had overcome all jealousy between Lakshmi aud Sarasvati, and gained the favor of both.—May our minds be thus free from impurity, our dispositions devoted to acts of merit, our desire a birth place of all good qualities—so did all the Brahmans pray.

His mother's family was also fortunate, descended from *Kes'ara*, grantor of benefits to all, whose son was *Bácha*, whose son was *Vámana*, a light upon the people. Among his daughters and grand-daughters the most renowned was *Mábikavve*. She was the chief wife of *Mákimaya*, and as to her were born five sons, she is Kunti herself was it said. How great then by fortune was *Trilochana*. To the goddess Rati in beauty, to Sarasvati in wisdom, to Párvati in majesty, to Arundhati in chastity, was she equal, and even greater merit had she obtained in the world, this mother *Márbyavve*.

Thus born of pure descent by his ancestors in both lines, and being the abode of prudence, morality, humility, vaidika (religious devotion), laukika (worldly wisdom), virtue, docility, kindness, liberality and many other qualities

—that *Trilochana Deva* thus thought within himself, 'I must obtain a pure merit which shall endure as long as moon and stars'—whereupon Prayága Paramés'vara appearing to him in a dream in unequalled glory, and saying, 'As in former times Nrisimha was in the pillar at the desire of Prahláda, so will I be in this stone' vanished. To the god *Mádhava* thus established, in the S'aka year 1113, the year Siddhárti,* the month Chaitra, the 11th day of the moon's increase, Sunday, at the vyatipáta, the time of the equinox—*Vámaya*, *Trilochana Deva*, *Is'vara Deva*, *Govinda Deva*, and *Narasingha Devo*, these five, worshipping the feet of the chief Brahmans in the 32,000 country and gaining their consent—gave in permanence, free of every burden, for the decoration of the god Mádhava and the temple processions (*angabhoga* and *rangabhoga*), from their vritti in the southern plain, namely in the paddy land near the tank, the Maragundi paddy-field of 60 kammas—and from their garden on the northern side 60 kammas.

Whoso preserves this gift will obtain eternal merit; whoso thinking evil usurps it, incurs the sin of killing cows and Brahmans in Váranás'i and Kurukshetra.

Moreover for preserving the perpetual lamp before the god *Mádhava* the *Settis* who were his worshippers sold to the hands of *Trilochana Deva* 5 kammas of garden land.

Their glory was as follows—Excelling in all kinds of learning, ignorant of falsehood, passing their time so as not to fail in obtaining a better world. . . .

(*Some illegible.*)

104. S'ila S'asana at Taldagundi, date A. D. 1107.

Size ft. 4 × ft. 2.—Haḷe Kannaḍa Characters.

The donor. Moon. LINGA. Sun. Cow suckling calf.

Adored be *S'ambhu*, beauteous with the chámara-like crescent moon kissing his lofty head; the original foundation-pillar of the city of the three worlds.

May it be well.—While the kingdom of *Tribhuvana Malla*, protector of all lands, favorite of earth and fortune, great king of kings, supreme ruler, first of monarchs, glory of the *Satyás'raya kula*, ornament of the *Chalukyas*†—was increasing in prosperity to endure as long as sun and moon—

* There is a discrepancy of 8 years between the name and the number of the year, besides which the latter has the appearance of 1173 which would not fall within the reign of Víra Ballála.

† See note p. 14.

While the servant of his feet, subduer of hostile armies, master of all the treasures in that place, sun to the lotus the race of Brahmans, the mighty Daṇḍanáyaka *Anantapála* was ruling in peace the Two hundred and the *Banavase* Twelve thousand.

Possessor of the favor of that mahá pradhána the Bánasa Mane Verggaḍe *Anantapála*, an abode of fortune, and living at his lotus feet :—

To the abode of all sound wisdom . . . *Rája* and his wife *Nilabbe* was born *Dási Rája*, a sun to the firmament of the *Parás'ara* gotra, a favorite of all through his fame, a jewel of good qualities. He was the father, and the treasury of all excellence *Somámbika* his mother. While that jewel of good qualities, protector of the learned, of a resplendent fame illuminating the water-lily the earth, the Ranaranga Bhairava, like Vatsa to poison, a kalpavriksha to poets, the powerful Daṇḍanáyaka *Govinda Rája*, was protecting the Banavase Twelve thousand, the *vaḍḍa rávula*, the *perjjunka*, and the two *bilkoḍe**, in the enjoyment of peace and wisdom†.

A dweller at his lotus feet, whose native place was the *Vedala* village given by Ráma in the *Antarvedi*, containing eight thousand inhabitants, whose father was *Mádhava Bhaṭṭa*, his mother *Jánaki*, his gótra the *Vatsa*, his sister *Irabba*, his younger brother *Soddela*, cousin to the Dandanáyaka *Goydarasa*,—the landholder *Trivali Bhaṭṭa*, having come to greatness in the most excellent *Tánagundúru*; in consequence of a discourse on merit, made request of the 32,000, saying 'Grant me some land that I may construct a tank here'.‡ They agreeing thereto, and giving him land near the northern road of the village, he in the 32nd year of Chálukya Vikrama, the year Sarvajit, the month Chaitra, the 3rd day of the moon's increase, Thursday—having excavated a tank and obtained therein abundance of water, built there a temple, and for erecting a watershed and presenting (passengers) with gruel (*ambali*), and for men for letting out the water from the tank and for men to examine the tank,—gave to the hands of *Maduki* 50 kammas below the tank according to the kacchavi pole, and also to the hands of Madu Deva for a garden 13 kammas—altogether 63 kammas—performing all the rites of worship to the 32,000.

This gift may the 32,000 maintain and the Herggaḍes protect.

---

* See notes p. 79 and 80. † See note p 2.

‡ *Mahá vaḍḍa grámam Táṇagundúralu perggatanam geyuttam irdu dharmma prasangadi kereyan agaḷisalu bhúmiyam kuḍivendu múttirchchhásirakke binnapam géya prasanna chittarági.*

Whoso maintains this gift will derive the merit of presenting tawny cows to Brahmans. He who alienates it incurs the guilt of killing Brahmans and cows. Whoso usurps the land presented by himself or by another shall assuredly be born a worm in ordure for sixty thousand years.

Jánaki being the mother who bore him, the celebrated Mádhava Bhaṭṭa his father, the hero, the home of wisdom, the lord Goyda Rája his cousin, he was as if Brahma had created him to obtain for the Vatsa gotra the reverence of all the other gotras. How illustrious then was he by nature.

Whoso thinks to rob *Pranames'vara* will fall into the great sin.

---

105. S'ila S'asana at Taldagundi, date A. D. 1028.

Size ft. 3 4' × ft. 0 11'.—Haḷe Kannaḍa Characters.

A figure holding an umbrella in one hand, and a club in the other

Cow suckling calf.

May it be well.—While the kingdom of *Jaya Simha Deva*, protector of all lands, favourite of earth and fortune, great king of kings, supreme ruler, first of monarchs, glory of the *Satyás'raya kula*, ornament of the *Chálukyas*,* *Jagadeka Malla*, was increasing in greatness and splendour—

In the S'aka year 950, the year Vibhava, the month Pushya, the 5th day of the moon's increase, Sunday, the day of the sun's entering the northern signs,—with the approval of all the 32,000 of the immemorial (*anádi*) agrahára of *Sthánakundúru*, a grant was made of 12 márus by the measure of the gaḍimba pole of the god Pranames'vara, to continue as long as sun, moon, and stars.

Whoso maintains this gift will derive the merit of presenting a thousand tawny cows to a thousand Brahmans in Váranási and Kurukshetra.

* See note p. 14.

106. S'ila S'asana at Taldagundi, date A. D. 1091.

Size ft. 3 × ft. 1 8'.—Hale Kannada Characters.

The Donor. Linga. Nandi.

May it be well.—While the victorious kingdom of the illustrious *Tribhuvana Malla Deva*, protector of all lands, favourite of earth and fortune, great king of kings, supreme ruler, first of monarchs, glory of the *Satyás'raya kula*, ornament of the *Chalukyas*,* was continually increasing in prosperity, to endure as long as sun, moon and stars—

May it be well.—The chiefs of the great agrahára which is the residence of Pranames'vara, the lord of the three worlds, set up by Brahma, praised by all worlds, the father of all, the golden wombed,—having come from Ahichchhatra 32,000 in number surrounded by 12,000 agnihotras,‡ distinguished for the holy acts yama and níyama,† and for bodies purified by plunging into the waters of the sacred bathing place made holy by the presence of the Five Lingas consecrated by Brahma, Indra, Rudra, Yama and Agni ; vessels filled with merit, intent upon the continual performance of works of merit, possessors of 144 villages in the south, deciders of disputed points in dharmma, freed from all sin by the purifying final ablution after many sacrifices, obstructors of the regents at the points of the compass, a refuge to the brave, with lotus feet worthy to be honored with gifts in assemblies of the learned, of Brahmans and kings ; a joy to the hearts of all their dependents, lions to the elephants the trembling kings, suns to the lotus of the vedánga, upánga, mímámsa and other sciences ; suns to the spreading lotuses the subjects of jurisprudence, the puránas, poetry, and dramas ; moons unfolding the water-lily buds the hearts of the people ; preservers of the glory of their race ; giving no place to anger, avarice, pride or enmity ; far from sin ; a refuge to learned men of distinction ; embodied gems of virtue ; an asylum for the foremost professors of science ; shining with a fame equal in purity to Kailása or the moon ; a circle of the jewels of wisdom ; like Himálaya in justice, courtesy, bravery, dignity, virtue, purity, rectitude, fortitude, and valour ; like Lakshmi to the lotus of the Brahman race, an immortal diadem for the fair lady the Kuntala country, performers of the six holy acts, protectors of all in distress, destroyers of all their enemies, a succour to all the destitute, a cage of adamant to all who claimed their protection ; powerful to curse or to bless ; accomplished in all the holy acts svádhyáya, dhyána, dhárana, mauna,

* See note p. 14. † See note p. 16.

‡ *Ahichchhatra samágata dvádas'a sahasra agnihotra parivritta dvátrims'at sahasra . . khya sameta.*

anushṭhána, japa, samádhi,* the 32,000 of the auspicious great and famous village of *Tánagundúru* . . . †—in the 16th year of the Chálukya Vikrama era, the year Prajotpati, at the time of the sun's entering the northern signs, Sunday—at the request of *Timmala Vásudeva*—for the daily service of the god *Yames'vara*—presented below the rising ground near the stream which descends from Kanagilu ghaṭṭa, in Kaḷachanahalli—obtaining it from the hand of *Billiya Kes'avaya*—three mattas according to the keyiguni account (?), in figures 3 matta.

Whoso maintains this gift will derive the merit of presenting a thousand tawny cows to Brahmans in Váranás'i. Whoso usurps this gift incurs the guilt of killing a thousand cows. Whoso by violence takes away the land presented by himself or by another shall assuredly be born a worm in ordure for sixty thousand years.

May it be well.—The 5 kammas for the god *Yames'vara* given to the hands of *Chandres'vara Deva*, to the south under the Indra tank of Moḷeyúru, let none encroach upon.

Whoso usurps this gift incurs the guilt of killing a thousand cows.

---

107. Virakal at Taldagundi, date about A. D. 1100.

Size ft. 5 3' × ft. 2 10'.—Haḷe Kannaḍa Characters.

The hero in the presence.	Moon	Linga.	Sun	Cow suckling calf.

(The whole of the inscription down one side of the stone being defaced,

The hero being borne to heaven by celestial nymphs bearing chamaras.

nothing continuous of any importance has been made out.)

The hero, in front of a herd of cattle, receiving a flight of arrows on his shield, and withstanding, sword in hand, a large number of assailants.

---

* See note p. 16.

† *S'riman mahi vaḍḍa gráma Tánagundúra múvattirchchhásaram.*

108. S'ila S'asana at Taldagundi, date A. D. 1045.

Size ft. 4 2' × ft. 2 1'.—Hale Kannada Characters.

I adore the god *Vináyaka*, who speedily removes all the difficulties of his worshippers.

May it be well—While the victorious kingdom of the illustrious *Trailokya Malla Deva*, protector of all lands, favorite of earth and fortune, great king of kings, supreme ruler, first of monarchs, glory of the *Satyás'raya kula*, ornament of the *Chalukyas*,* was continually increasing in prosperity, to endure as long as sun, moon and stars—

While the dweller at his lotus feet—May it be well—entitled to the five great drums, chief of all the tributaries, like Vishnu a lord over many great kings, an abode of fortune, a Badabánala to the ocean of his enemies, a lion to the elephant his foes, granter of their desires to all who came to him, a deity incarnate in supplying all the wants of rishis, a mine of liberality and kindness, a cage of adamant to those who claimed his protection, . . . a safe asylum to the learned . . . obtaining the reverence of all, a thunderbolt weapon to the race of hostile kings, to young women a Manmatha, possessed of all learning, to strange women as their son, brave as Indra, a benefactor to all his dependents, fierce to proud enemies—the auspicious Mahá Mandales'vara *Singana Devarasa* was ruling in peace and wisdom† the *Risukonda* Seventy mandala, the *Banavase* Twelve thousand, and the *Sántalige* Thousand, punishing the evil and protecting the good as far as the Western Ocean.

At that time, in the year Párthiva, the month Pushya, the 9th day of the moon's increase, Sunday, it being the day of the sun's entering the northern signs,—to provide for worship and daily service in the temple of Bhagavati Balliyabbe Devi, set up near *Balligáve*—gave a thala-vritti of 18 mattas according to the katsavi pole, and for the distribution of food, a flower garden of 6 mattas to the west of the street of that goddess.

Moreover for the ablutions, the daily offering, for feeding the attendant priests, and for repairs of the temple, gave up, on the east of the Nágarabhávi street, kammas 18—washing the feet of the priest of that place, Lakshmanes'vara Si'va Pandita, accomplished in the holy acts yama, niyama, svádhyáya, dhyána, dhárana, mauna, and anushthana,‡ with pouring of water and every ceremony, free of all burdens.

---

* See note p. 14. † See note p. 2. ‡ See note p. 16.

The eastern boundary of that thala-vritti is the small stream flowing east and south from the west of the Ara tank. The southern boundary the stream from the south side of the Ara tank flowing west. The western boundary the east bank of the thalavritti of the god Rámes'vara irrigated from the south. The northern boundary the drain which runs to the fields. The western boundary of the flower-garden is the small stream north-east of the Kabbina pond. Thence the eastern boundary is to the south of the tank of the god Báláditya Tejomártánda.

The northern boundary of the street of the Devipura is the northern well of the goddess. Thence the eastern boundary is the eastern limit of the land belonging to the god Tejomártánda. The southern boundary is the nirgundi tree to the south of the pond at the south east angle of the Devipura.

The eastern boundary of Nágarabhávi street is that well itself. The southern boundary is the path running north from the south-east angle of the street. The western boundary is the path running in that direction. The northern boundary is the large rugged rock at the north side of the street.

Whoso maintains this gift will obtain the merit of presenting a thousand tawny cows to a thousand Brahmans versed in the vedas, and of presenting double headed (*i. e.*, parturient) cows, decked with the five precious stones, at the holy bathing places of Ganges, Banarási, Kurukshetra, Prayága and Agri-tírtha. Whoso usurps it incúrs the guilt of the five great sins, and of killing in those places with his own hand a thousand Brahmans and a thousand cows.

Poison is no poison. The property of the gods that is the real poison. For poison kills one man, but a gift to the gods (if usurped) kills a man with his son and descendants. Whoso by violence takes away a gift made by himself or by another shall assuredly be born a worm in ordure for sixty thousand years. The earth has been enjoyed by Sagara and many other kings, whose reward was in proportion to their (gifts of) land. The bridge of merit deserves your support O kings of the earth. Thus from age to age cries Rámachandra to the kings who come after him.

Whoso being able to perform it withholds his hand from a work of merit, incurs the guilt of slaughtering a thousand cows. Whoso entirely alienates a gift when made, incurs the guilt of killing a crore of cows.

---

109. Virakal at Sorab, date A. D. 1193.

Size ft. 4 × ft. 1 9′.—Haḷe Kannaḍa Characters.

Sun. Moon.
The hero in the presence. Linga with Priest. Nandi.

While the victor over all kings, shining with wealth, filling with delight the apsara nymphs, first in the army of heroes, subduer of the base-born, brave in war, a collection of fortune, the auspicious *Dekkalarasa* (?) was ruling the kingdom of the earth—receiving orders from *Víra Balláḷa Deva* for war—

The hero being borne to heaven by celestial nymphs waving chamaras.

in the month Bhádrapada, the 8th day of the moon's increase, Sunday, of the S'aka year 1116, the year Pramádi,*—when *Devana Náyaka*, the guard of the village of Hoya Sakuti in the Jiddulige Seventy, slaying Hadavala Máṭaya, seized his cows, and Húhali Bira Gauḍa, and Kála Gauḍa's servant, the son of Varála Jasadoja, recovered the cows,

The hero, in front of a herd of cattle, putting to the sword a horseman. Two others contending in the background, one armed with bow and arrow, the other with sword and shield.

he killing many, pierced the horse, slew its master, and went to the world of gods. For his distinguished bravery was granted 15 kammas . . .

110. Virakal at Sorab, date (?) about A. D. 1100.

Size ft. 5 3′ × ft. 1 9′.—Haḷe Kannaḍa Characters.

The hero in the presence. Linga with Priest. Nandi.
The whole in a temple.

Adored be *S'ambhu*, beauteous with the chámara-like crescent moon kissing his lofty head; the original foundation-pillar of the city of the three worlds.

May it be well—While the victorious kingdom of . . protector of all lands, favorite of earth and fortune, great king of kings, supreme ruler, first of monarchs, glory of the *Satyás'raya kula*, ornament of the *Chalukyas*† . . by order of the Mandales'vara . . .

The hero ascending to heaven in a car, attended by celestial nymphs bearing chamaras.

---

* This is apparently an error for *Pramádicha*, which corresponds with A. S. 1116, while *Pramádi* falls 34 years earlier.

† See note p. 14.

Vikramádityarasa . . . killing many, went to the world of gods. For his bravery, . . . gave 50 kammas of paddy land.

The hero, with insignia of rank and a shield-bearer behind, discharging an arrow at a horseman of rank who is supported by other distinguished persons. A horseman, also of rank, galloping on to the field on the left.

Whoso maintains this gift derives the merit of presenting a thousand cows to a thousand Brahmans in Váranási, Gaya and Kurukshetra. Whoso usurps it is guilty of the five great sins.

Who wins in war gains spoil, who falls enjoys the celestial nymphs. What fear then of death in war to him who must at some moment give up all. He who is killed in war becomes like very Indra himself, will rise to Svarga with the pomp of a mighty king, and in the groves of Nandana enjoy all delights with the apsara nymphs. May it be well.

---

111. Virakal at Sorab, date A. D. 1283.

Size ft. 5 3′ × ft. 2 3′.—Hale Kannada Characters.

The hero in the presence. Moon. Linga with Priest in a Temple. Sun. Nandi fanned by an attendant.

Adored be *S'ambhu*, beauteous with the chámara-like crescent moon kissing his lofty head; the original foundation-pillar of the city of the three worlds.

Celestial musicians.

May it be well—From the beginning of the reign of the mighty emperor *Rámachandra Deva*, a Náráyana to the *Yádava* race, powerful by his own strength,

The hero ascending to heaven in a car, attended by celestial nymphs bearing chamaras.

the 12th year, the year Svabhánu, the month Phálguna, the 6th day of the moon's increase, Monday—while the nád officers *Soyi Deva*, and *Govinda Deva* were watching *Kuppaiya* engaged in a hand-to-hand fight, and seeing how skilfully he had been trained were greatly astonished at his prowess—*Sámanta*, the son of *Hiriya Sakuna Bella Gauda*, fighting bravely in the distance with *Jagaddála Kála Gauda* and distinguishing himself, stabbed him and went to heaven.

A warrior (? Kuppaiya) on foot, in front of a number of horsemen, (one of whom is a person of rank) having a trumpeter on one side and an umbrella-bearer on the other, killing a man on horseback armed with a lance.

Who wins in war gains spoil, who falls enjoys the celestial nymphs, what fear then of death in war to him who must at some moment give up all. The slain obtains svarga, the victor obtains the earth. Great prosperity, Fortune.

The hero, at the head of a band of spearmen, killing another leading a similar band.

---

112. Rock Inscription at Tekal, Date A. D. 1512 (?)

Size not given. Kannada Characters.

Two Foot prints. Sun Moon. Vishnu's Discus and Conch. Lotus bud. Boar. Bow and Arrow.

May it be well.—In the year 1434 of the victorious increasing era, the year Pramádícha,* the month Phálguna, the 1st day of the moon's increase,—When by order of *Deva Ráya Maháráya*, to Gopa Rája, mahá mandales'vara, ornament of the earth and of fortune, a pestle for pounding (?) Ere sámanta, the conqueror of Banasura, the setter up of Ganga Hale Sambá Ráya, ruler of (?) Pabasa, son of Sáluva Tippa Rája Vodayar —*Akhana Vodayar* and *Mádana Vodayar* gave *Tekal* to that *Sáluva Gopa Rája*—

Malappa Danáyaka and Singa Danáyaka, the ministers (*pradhána*) of *Ballála Ráya*, being angry that the arrangements formerly made by them were altered, by order of *Varada Rája*, *Gopa Rája* went to them desiring to make peace again. On which, that minister *Singa Rája*, having . . both the inner and outer forts, made them over before the face of *Varada Rája*.

On building the bastion (*kottala*) called *Rája Gambhira*, that *Gopa Rája* and his son *Tippaiya*, causing a tiger to be seized and brought forth, hunted it. Great good fortune be to the bastion where it died.

Inscription to the right of the above.

A Dog holding a Tiger by the throat.

This hound called *Sampige*, seizing and tearing open the skin of the neck of the tiger, wandered about in various places. To toti Tirumala who restored it, by order of *Varada Rája*, 3 ? of paddy land, 3 ? of field, and a flower garden were presented. This paddy land and field may be held under the written order of *Varada Rája*. May it be well.

---

* From the great discrepancy between 1434 and Pramádícha it may be conjectured that the latter should be Pramódúta which would very nearly correspond. Some parts of the translation are doubtful.

113. S'ila S'asana at Begur,* date (?) about A. D. 850.

Size ft. 7 9' × ft. 7 8'.—Púrvada Haḷe Kannaḍa Characters.

May it be well.—While the auspicious *Eṛeyapparasa*, brilliant as lightning descending among the stars in the clear firmament of the world-renowned *Ganga* race, protector of the mighty kings of *Vaḷala* and *Mekhala*, the chosen lord and possessor of the fortune of the auspicious *Taila's* dominion, adorned with the ornaments of a cluster of innumerable good qualities, of superhuman power, having despoiled all his enemies of their territories, was ruling the *Gangavádi* Ninety-six Thousand under the shadow of his single umbrella—

Desiring to fight with *Bíra Mahendra*, *Ayyapa Devanga* with his tributaries came against the whole *Nágatta* army and fought with all his footmen. When the slaughter of the battle became very great, taking to the elephant for refuge, he was pierced and died. *Ereyappa* hearing it, rejoiced, and fixing a tribute for *Iru Gange Nágatta*, set up a great s'asana to be in *Bempúru*, and gave him *Ankal náḍ* (or Kal náḍ). What that was I will describe;—Bempúru, Távagúru, Páchina, Pullimangala, Rátanilu, Nallúru, . . . Peramúru, Kádala. Thus much, with the fields and boundaries, did *Erayapa* give to . . . *Nágara*. Great prosperity! Fortune.

(? Witnesses) Nallúru Káma Gauḍa, Rájyanna, Igdalara, . . . Malliga . . .

The bas-relief, unless meant for the fight itself, seems to represent the massacre of prisoners taken in the battle, by throwing them before an elephant, probably the one captured from the enemy; as indicated by the arrows still sticking in his fore-

---

* This elaborately sculptured stone (*see frontispiece*) is now in the Mysore Government Museum at Bangalore. The following is the text of the inscription.

Svasti || *Samasta bhuvana vinuta Ganga kula gagana nimmala tárápatad iḷa minchaḷa vipuḷa Vaḷala Mekhalirala pála s'ri Tailádhipatya Lakshmís'vanum vrata pati táldal agaṇita guṇa gaṇa vibhúshaṇa vibhúshita vibhúti S'rimad Eṛeyapparasar pagevar ellaman nikshatram máḍi Gangaváḍi tombattáru sásiramuman éka chhatra chchháyeyoḷ áḷuttam irdu Bíra mahen-*

head. Those who escape destruction from the elephant are led up to be despatched by the king himself, or are speared by some of his attendants, two of whom are seated on the elephant.

The victorious king is seen on horseback, sword in hand, with mangled bodies of the slain at his side, which the crows are pecking at. He is accompanied by two horsemen, and his umbrellas (the insignia of rank,) one a triple one, are borne along with him. A herald preceding him proclaims the victory through a long trumpet, while *Váyu*, the god of the wind and regent of the north-west point of the compass, rides forth on his swift antelope to spread the news abroad.

Other celestial beings take a part in the scene. On the right, the terrible figure of the three-eyed *Bhairava* appears, borne by two attendants. He wears a garland of skulls, is half riding on one dead body and has a headless trunk of another at his feet. In his left hand he holds a human head, and with his right is gorging himself with the flesh of the victims, a portion being handed to him by a boy seated on the croup of the elephant. Above this horrid figure is one of *Káli* or a female *rákshasa* holding aloft a victim whom she is about to dash before the elephant.

On the upper part of the picture appear the *Apsaras* or nymphs of Indra's paradise, who according to the *Vira S'aiva* doctrines are the portion of brave warriors and bear them in their arms or in triumphal cars direct from the field of battle to paradise. The queen of the *Apsaras* appears seated on a throne (1), her feet resting on a footstool grotesquely carved like a man on all fours. She is attended by a female on each side holding a *chámara*, an indication of rank. On the forefinger of her left hand, she holds a bird (what bird is doubtful, it does not look like a parrot,) which another female behind is trying to entice into a cage. On the right of this part of the sculpture is the only one of the celestial nymphs who exhibits an interest in the proceedings. A warrior at her side is loading a jinjal, but for what purpose is not clear, unless to shoot at the bird before mentioned.

On the left, immediately over the king, stands a female figure under a *dhvaja stambha* or flag-staff, holding something (perhaps a bag of money denoting wealth) in her left hand. The other hand appears bound to the flag-staff, and the sculptor may have intended to represent thereby the goddess of victory or fortune as forced to attend upon and inseparably attached to the standard of the king, a common metaphor in inscriptions.

---

dranoḷ kádalendu Ayyapa Devanga sámanta sahitam Nágattarana danḍu velláde tumbe páḍiyol kádi kálaga mid balidoḍe áneyol ántiṛidu sattád ada keld Ereyapam mechchi Iru Gange Nágattara vaṭṭam gaṭṭi Bempúrvan iralu más'ásana bard Ankalnáḍ (or *Kal náḍ*) *ittan an ánu védipe Bempúru Távagúru Púchina Pullimangala Rátanilu Nallúru* . . *Peramúru Kádala initumam pola mére sahitam ittan Ereyapa* . . *Nágarange mangala mahá s'ri.*

Nallúru Káma Gauḍaru || *Rájyanna* || *Igdalara* [. . *Malligal Anjavágilu* ||

114. S'ila S'asana at Devanhalli, date A. D. 1697.

Size ft. 3 2' × ft. 3. 2'.—Hale Kannada Characters.

Sun. Vishnu's Discus. | Moon. Vishnu's Conch.

May the right tusk of the Boar form of Vishnu like a sceptre protect us, on which forming a small canopy rested the earth, surmounted by the golden peak of Meru.

May it be well.—In the year 1619 of the victorious increasing S'áliváhana era, the year Isvara, the month Mágha, the 15th day of the moon's increase, Saturday, at an auspicious moment—*Gopála Gauḍa*, son of *Kempamma* the lawful wife of *Immaḍi Sanna Baire Gauḍa*, and grandson of *Muddu Baire Gauḍa*, lord of the *A'vati* náḍ—presented for the worship of the god *Madana Gopálasvámi* [1] together with *Rukmini* and *Satyabháma* [2] of the city of *Devanapura*, which is nourished by the lotus feet of *Venkaṭes'vara* [3] and *Alamelumánga* [4]—for the daily service and processions, for the fortnightly processions, for the monthly processions and the annual processions, for the daily oblations, and illuminations, and for the distribution of food to all the officiating priests and other servants—the villages of *Melúru* and *Madalúru* in the *Vaḍagenhaḷḷi* hóbli, the villages of *Chetonhalli* and *Sogonahalli* in the *Nallúru* hóbli, a new tank near *Savakanahalli*, a new garden and *Channa Víramma's* garden.

Oil for the sacred lamps will be provided for separately, from the palace revenue.

Moreover we have given all the dues of the following villages,—for the palanquin bearers of the god and the fanners with chámaras, the two villages belonging to *Baichapura* and *Bairapura*—for the resident priests the two villages attached to *Averahalli*.

If any of these attendants absents himself his place shall be filled up, and the worship of the god be duly performed.

From whatever surplus of money or grain may remain after the performance of all the appointed services and the distribution of food to attendants, ornaments shall be made for the god. If the money should fall short for the carrying on of all the appointed services and the distribution of food to attendants, what is required shall be given from the palace, and the worship as appointed be performed.

---

[1] Krishna. [2] His wives. [3] Vishnu. [4] Lakshmi.

To all who are present at the time of the daily illumination of the god, a distribution of food (*anna prasáda*) shall be made.

At the time of the car procession 40 khandis shall be given from the palace for the feast to the Brahmans.

Whatever other ceremonies have been appointed in the former records of the temple shall also be duly performed. Whatever other ceremonies have been appointed in the former records of the palace they too shall be duly performed.

All cooking shall be done in the cook-room in which the daily offering is prepared. Whoever of the four castes of Brahmans, Kshatriyas, Vais'yas and S'údras violates this order, shall be excommunicated according to the rules of his caste.

May all who come to rule the land, whether kings of my own line or of any other, maintain this gift. To them do I prostrate myself. Land given by one's self is a daughter, that given by one's father is a sister, that given by another is a mother. Whoso protects either of these increases his own prosperity.

---

115. S'ila S'asana at Bhoga Nandi, date (?) about A. D. 750.

Size ft. 4 5′ × ft. 2 3′—Púrvada Haḷe Kannaḍa Characters.

May it be well—While, entitled to the five great drums, the descendant of the *Pallavas*, favorite of earth and fortune, ornament of the *Pallava* dynasty, S'rimat *Nolambádhirája* was ruling the kingdom of the earth*—

The auspicious *Dharmma S'akti Paṇḍita* . . *Rámaya Gámuṇḍa* five hundred ácháris . . *Haḷiyanna* the enclosure of Nandi . .

---

* Except at the beginning the inscription is very indistinct. The following is the text of the opening portion :—

Svasti samatigata-pancha-mahá-s'abda Pallavánvaya s'ri-prithivi-vallabha Pallava-kula-tilaka S'rimat Nolambádhirája prithivi rájyam geyuttam ire.

116. S'ila S'asana at Mulbagalu, date A. D. 1431.

Size ft. 5 × ft. 1.—Kannaḍa Characters.

May it prosper—May it be well.—In the year 1353 of the victorious increasing era, the year Sádhárana, the month Phálguna, the 10th day of the moon's increase—a temple for this god *Prasanna Virupáksha*, the wall of enclosure, the towers (*gopara*), the gilding of the pinnacles, the sacred tank in front, the funds for the decorations and processions, the agraháras, the mantapas, the maṭha for mendicant priests, these and all the other gifts,—through the merit of *Gaja Bedekára Devaráya Maháráya*, the son of Vijaya Ráya Maháráya—such was the service paid to this god *Prasanna Virupáksha* by the Heggaḍe Devas of the *Vishnu Varddhana* gotra, *Akhanna Dannáyaka* and *Mádanna*, the sons of *Vommayamma*.

117. S'ila S'asana at Halebid, date about A. D. 1117.

Size ft. 8 × ft. 4.—Haḷe Kannaḍa Characters.

Sun. Attendant with chamara. A Jain Tirthankara enthroned under a canopy. Attendant with chamara. Moon.

Cow suckling calf. Elephant.

May the doctrine of *Trailokya Nátha*, the supreme profound *syád váda* prevail; the Jain doctrine which is a token of unfailing success. May the sign of the moon-rise of knowledge be supreme in the world. May wealth arise from the lotus lake of Jain yógis. May the sun whose attributes are learning, wisdom and goodness, the friend of his worshippers, shine forth. May *Vijaya Párs'va Tírthes'vara*, lord of the three worlds, who cannot be reached by the efforts of pride, whose three white umbrellas illuminate the city of the world, possessor of all riches, the luminous expounder of wisdom, prevail. Eternally adored be *Om!* Reverence to *Vijaya Párs'va Jines'vara*, whose feet are illuminated by the rows of jewels in the crowns of illustrious kings prostrate before him, the teacher of merit to the three worlds, the enemy of lust, superior to birth, growth and destruction.

Prosperity to the kings of the *Hoysaḷa* race, a destroying sword to hostile kings, a thunderbolt-weapon to the fiercest.

The manner of its incarnation was as follows—From the celebrated *Brahma* sprung *Atri*, and from him *Soma*. The son of Sóma was *Purúrava*, a king of the earth praised by all the world. From him came the great king *Ayu*, then the beautiful *Nahusha*, then *Yayáti* and *Yadu*. In this line was born the celebrated *Saḷa*, surrounded by prostrate kings, a sea of all good qualities.*

The increase of the kingdom of that king *Saḷa* was brought about on this wise.—

When with joy a Jain ascetic praised by Indra, possessed of the worship of Jains, an adept in all the science of incantations, was performing sacrifice to bring into his power the goddess *Padmávati* of *S'as'akapura*, a tiger bounding forth, on the yogi saying 'Pierce it with the rod of the bow; drive it away Sala (*poy Saḷa*),' he removed that danger, whence the name of *Poysaḷa* became celebrated as the title of the *Yadu* kings—and from *Saḷa* the *s'árdúla* (tiger) became their sign (or crest).†

When this tiger crest had become theirs could the fortune of courage escape their hands? Henceforth did the *Yádava* kings under the title of *Poysaḷa* greatly increase inpower.

In that line, like the moon among the stars, or as the loftiest peak in a chain of mountains, so arose *Vinayáditya*, a conqueror over all his enemies, with a body brilliant as the sun. His son was *Ereyanga Bhúpa*, of a form like that of Manmatha, who had broken the pride of arm of hostile kings, a giver of benefits to the assembly of the learned, an abode of increasing greatness. Before the dread sword of *Ereyanga* even touched those his enemies whose bodies had not been prostrated in submission at his feet, their heads rolled off (a play on his name), and a warm stream was formed of the blood gushing from their bodies.

While all the world was filled with his praise, to *Achala Devi* and the king *Ereyanga* were born, like the Trimúrti, the king *Balláḷa*, the king *Vishnu*, and *Udayáditya*.

Among these the great king *Vishnu* becoming separately glorious, winning from his own family great affection as having brought them to fame with himself, his career was like that of Nala, Nahusha and Bharata.

---

* *Tad anvayávatáram | negaḷda Brahmanın Atri Soman esevá s'ri Somajam bhútaḷam pogaḷuttirppa Purúravorvvipati sand A'yur mmahi vallabham sogeyippá Nahusam Yayáti Yadu vemb urvvis'a santánadoḷ negaḷdam s'ri Saḷan ánatánya nikaram samyaktva ratnákaram. ||*

† *A' Saḷa nripatiya rájya s'ri samvarddhanaman eyde máḍuva bageyim vásavam vandita Jina púje sahitam sakaḷa mantra vidyá kus'aḷam || mudadim Jaiṇa bratis'am S'as'akapurada Padmávati Deviyam mantradin ádam sádhısal vikriyeyoḷe puli mel váye yogis'varam kumbhada kovind ánt adam poy Saḷa enal a bhayam poypudum Poysaḷánkam Yadu bhúpargge: á andind esedudu seḷeyim loḷa s'árddúḷa chihnam ||*

When this king *Vishnu Varddhana* had securely seated himself on the throne, he speedily possessed himself of the glory of all the kings as far as the ocean. Without stirring he acquired the whole of *Male* and all the *Tulu* country. On merely preparing to march, *Kumára-nád̤* and *Talakád̤* came into his hands. On placing one foot forward *Kanchi* came under his command. Before he had once flourished his sword the *Konga* kings gave up their elephants. What valour was his!

Who can depict the bravery of this king *Vishnu*, destroyer of the pride of arm of the *Chol̤a* king, the *Pánd̤ya* king, and the *Keral̤a* king; a lion to the male elephant the *A'ndhra* king; a gale to the clouds the *Lát̤a* and *Varát̤a* kings; a consuming fire to the grove the warlike *Kadamba* kings; a mine of unequalled bravery.*

While the mahá mand̤ales'vara, lord of the great city of *Dvárávati*, a sun to the firmament of the *Yádava* race, a head jewel among all princes, having obtained a boon from the goddess *Vásantiká* of *S'as'akapuri*, with a gently smiling countenance, enjoying the beautiful pure moonlight of his fame which laughed at the splendour of the autumnal moon or the brightness of Is'vara's smile, shining with the enlightenment of unsurpassed wisdom, the light of the jewels in whose feet was overpowered by the brilliance of the new jewels in the diadems of kings prostrate before him, having made war as far as the four oceans, having caused the points of the compass to move with the dazzling rays of his dreadful sword, like a jewelled crown to the goddess of courage, having performed the great sacrifices of the *hiranya garbha*, the *tulá purusha*†, and *as'va medha*, a marvellous kalpa-vriksha, a lover of the mistress royal policy, always causing the waves to swell (like the tide) in the oceans of *Yádava* and *Vishnu*, . . . a cage of adamant to all who claimed his protection, having a front brilliant with rows of pearls as large as myrobalans, a kalpa-vriksha to all the learned, having destroyed all his proud enemies with his victory-producing elephants, his immense armies and flights of arrows; of continually increasing wealth; his destruction of all his enemies was like the breaking up of the great floods, the coursers of the sun being borne away in the

* *Pod̤arade sádhyam áytu Male yellamum á Tul̤u des'avellamum nad̤eye Kumára nád̤u Tal̤akád̤ugalemb ivu kayge sarddwalt ad̤iy id̤e munchi Kanchi besak aydudu Vishn̤u nr̤ipam kr̤ipánamam jad̤iyade munne Konga nr̤ipar ittar ibhangal̤an ém pratápiyo* ǁ *Chol̤a nr̤ipála Pánd̤ya nr̤ipa Keral̤a bhúpa bhujával̤e padin . . . A'ndhra gand̤a gaja kesari Lát̤a Varát̤a dhárini pád̤a ghaná nilam kadana s'úram Kadamba vanágni Vishnu bhúpálanav áryya s'auryya nidhiy átana s'auryyaman ár intettipar* ǁ

† *Hiranyagarbha*—having a golden cow made large enough to admit of his crawling through it, and after that ceremony breaking it up and distributing the precious metal to the Brahmans. *Tulá purusha*—weighing himself against gold and disposing of it in the same way.

deluge and all the points of the compass filled with the sounds of their neighing; a collection of expanded merit, an unfading collection of good qualities bright as the moon or Ganges, lord of *Gandagiri*, an elephant-fever (*pákalam*) to the herd of elephants the *Pándya* kings, disturbing all the world with the noise of his armies, a destroyer of all the envious malignants who seek to raise themselves on the ruin of others, a Vishnu to the rákshasas the boasting kings, a Kumárasvámi to Tárakásura the evil kings, a follower of Brahma the good, of a body bedewed with the pure waters of mercy . . . .
a fire to the grove the *Kadambas*, to the *Vengiri* forces the final deluge, a gale to the cloud *Jaya Kesi*,—while with these and all other titles, the illustrious *Tribhuvana Malla Bhuja Bala Víra Ganga Hoysala Deva*, ruling *Talakádu*, *Kongu*, *Nangali*, *Gangavádi*, *Nolambavádi*, *Máravádi*, *Huligere*, *Halasige*, *Banavase*, *Hánungalu*, *Nádugonda*, the illustrious and unequalled *Vishnu Bhúbhuja* was holding in his arms both the lady Earth—adorned with beautiful *Kuntala*[1], with the admired *Madhya*[2], and charming *Kánchi*[3]—and Sarasvati :—

The dweller at his lotus feet—shining among the Jain kings as the ancient Indra, in firmness like Mandara, of pure descent in the Kaundinya gótra, the beloved son of *Ebi Rája*, a moon to the sea the womb of *Pompámbika* (*i. e.*, she was his mother), a great refuge for all the world, equal to Karna, in war like Indra, with splendid beautiful shoulders, with a fame shining like jasmine buds or still better like the moon or the Ganges, a place of recreation for the science of incantations, a chakóra bird to the moonlight of female faces, of a body which was as a stage for the goddess of courage to dance on, one for whose possession virtue and liberality contended, a jewel among ministers, a protector of the Jain doctrines, a head-jewel among the gems the good men, promoter of the increase of Vishnu Varddhana's kingdom, a sun to all the circle of the world, rejoicing greatly in making gifts, having obtained a boon from the goddess *Padmávati*, a ruler of the earth wed to the goddess of victory, a golden plate (or champion's medal) on the brow the brave warriors, the Hiriya Dandanáyaka of unequalled glory, was *Ganga Rája*.

. . . . . . the *Gangavádi* Ninety six Thousand . . . To that *Ganga* chamúpati and to *Nága Devi* was born . . . *Boppa* chamúpa . . .

(*All the rest of this fine and important inscription is illegible owing to shade upon the photograph.*)

1 The Kuntala country, otherwise flowing locks.

2 The Middle region, otherwise waist.

3 The Kánchi country, otherwise zone or girdle.

118. S'ila S'asana at Halebid, date A. D. 1196.

Size ft. 3 6'. × ft. 2.—Haḷe Kannaḍa Characters.

Sword. Sun. Moon.

Attendant with chamara. A Jain Tirthankara. Attendant with chamara.

Cow sucking calf. Elephant.

May the doctrine of *Trailokya Nátha,* the supreme profound *syád váda* prevail; the Jain doctrine which is a token of unfailing success. May he be supreme who is the full moon to the ocean of the Jain doctrine . . .

May it be well—While the emperor powerful by his own might, a Náráyana to the *Yáduva* race, *Víra Ballá!a Devarasa,* was ruling the kingdom in peace and wisdom—In the year Nala, the month Kártika, the 1st day of the moon's increase, Sunday—of the villages belonging to the basadi which Siddiyave, the wife of the mahá vaḍḍa byavahári Kavaḍamayya, had built for the god Sántinátha, *Appayya, Gopayya* and *Báchayya,* the sons of Mallarasaya the doctor *(vaiddigeya)*—for the worship of the god *Mallináthes'vara* of the seminary *(paṭṭas'ále)* which they had enclosed within the precincts of the basadi of that god S'antinátha, for repairs of his temple, for enlarging or improving it, for the gifts to be made therein, and for the performance of the fortnightly and daily ceremonies—giving to Rámachandra Deva, the disciple of the mahá manḍaláchárya Madaviya Balachandra Siddhánta Deva, 60 gadyánas of gold, purchased *Káluhalli* of Káraḍukere and *Bammatigaṭṭa* of Máchiyahalli.

The boundaries of that Bammatigaṭṭa are as follows:—east, the stone of the Hiḍi well; south, . . . west, the Yelcha hollow: north, the tank bund.

Also they gave 20 honnu and built with stones the north side of that tank from the south weir of the tank to the stone at the east well.

(The provision) for the daily worship of the god shall be as follows:—For cooking the *bali* (offering of food), 5 *balla* of rice, 1 *mána* of cakes, 2 *solige* of ghee; for the lamps 5 *mána* of oil; . . . for betel-leaf 2 fanams, for incense 3 fanams, for sandal-wood powder 3 fanams, the fee of the officiating priest 1 fanam.

(Moreover) to provide daily for the garland-makers 6 *ballas* of rice (they presented) 1 gadyána. For the food of one or two (persons) to remain at the *maṭha s'ále* to keep watch, 3 gadyánas. For the three *Nandis'vara* (sacred bulls or images of bulls) 1 gadyána. For the dancing-girls who come to present the offering of flowers, . . . Also for the swing, the fortnightly illumination, the ceremonies at the times of eclipses and of equinoxes, for the procession with lights, and for all other ceremonies that are required, for the *dána s'ále* (hall of gifts or distribution of food), for feeding the poor in the old temple (*basti*) within the town, and for the cook-house . . . . . . all free of every burden.

The priest of the god *S'antinátha*, the farmers (*gauḍas*) of *Káraḍu-halli*, ... will attend to the maintenance of this gift.

Whoso usurps a gift made by himself or by another shall assuredly be born a worm in ordure for sixty thousand years.

---

119. S'ila S'asana at Halebid, date A. D. 1637.

Size ft. 5 × ft. 2.—Kannaḍa Characters.

Sun. Moon.

May the doctrine of *Trailokya Nátha*, the supreme profound *syád váda* prevail; the Jain doctrine which is a token of unfailing success.

Adored be *S'ambhu*, beauteous with the chámara-like crescent moon kissing his lofty head; the original foundation-pillar of the city of the three worlds. May the dance of S'iva on the spot watered by the daughter of Brahma (the celestial Ganges) be your protection, exhausted by which the hoods of his many serpents being expanded and their mouths gaping they see in the sun's rays a mirage of water provided for their refreshment abounding with flocks of the *chakravika* bird, ...

. . . . . .

May it be well—In the year 1560 of the victorious increasing S'áliváhana era, the year Is'vara being then current, in the month Phálguna, the 5th day of the moon's increase, Thursday—while *Venkaṭádri Náyaka Ayya*, the eighth emperor in the Kali-yuga, (son) of *Krishnappa Náyaka Ayya*, resting like a royal swan at the two lotus feet of the god Channa Víra Venkaṭes'a of *Vela-puri*, born like a full moon from the ocean of nectar the Vaishnava mata, a protector of his subjects, a protector of divine images, a protector of his own dignity, a protector of his race, possessed of tributaries and all the seven royal qualities, punisher of kings who fail in their given word, the punisher of the evil, the protector of the worthy, shining with friendship and all the other modes of policy, associated with ministers characterized by all the five divisions of good council, a *ganda bherunda* to hostile kings, a head-jewel of brave Kshatriyas, a cage of adamant to those who claimed his protection, a Govinda in an ocean of victory, . . . in war a Bhíma, lord of the great city *Maninágapura*, a destroyer of the seven royal powers of hostile kings, . . . conspicuous with these and all other titles, was ruling with justice the kingdom of *Belúr*—

Bayappa Náyaka, removing the sign of the linga which Huchchappa Deva had affixed to the pillars of the temple of the god *Vijaya Párs'vanátha* of *Haleyabidu*, set up the image of Nandikes'vara, carved out of beautiful shining stone . . . .

(*Rest illegible owing to the photograph being greatly reduced and parts in shade.*)

---

120. S'ila S'asana at Halebid, date A. D. 1274.

Size ft. 3 × ft. 1 4'.—Hale Kannada Characters.

A Jain Yati

seated in a temple, with certain religious vessels on either side.

May it be well—The favorite disciple of *Mághanandi Bhattáraka Deva*, of the S'ri Múla sangha, the Des'iya gana, the Pustaka gachchha, the Kondakundánvaya, the Digales'vara baliya and the S'ri samudáya; the auspicious Nemichandra Bhattáraka Deva and Abhayachandra Siddhánta chakravarti being his díkshá guru and s'rauta guru;—*Yála Chandra Pandita Deva*, celebrated in the world for his teachings on penance (*tapa s'rutangalim*), having announced in the S'aka year 1197, the year Bháva, the month Bhádrapada, the 12th day of the moon's increase, Wednesday, at the time of noon that he would enter the tomb, addressing the four castes, and saying "Know ye not that ye will all acquire great merit? Obtain God. Om."—completing all the rites of a sanyási, and seated on the palyanka, praising the forms of the pancha parameshti, . . .

---

* *Madyáhna káladolu yemage samádhi yendum chátur varnnagalg aride nivellarum dhármmikar appudendu niyámisi Om itam Om endu sanyasana pūrttikam sakala nivrittiyam mádid palyankásanadol irddu pancháparameshtigala svarúpamam dhyánisutta sa* . . .

121. S'ila S'asana at Belur, date A. D. 1578.

Size ft. 4 3' × ft. 1 10'.—Kannada Characters.

The Vaishnava symbols

Chakra. Trinama. S'ankha.

Sun. Moon.

May it prosper. Adored be *S'ambhu*, beauteous with the chámara-like crescent moon kissing his lofty head; the original foundation-pillar of the city of the three worlds.

May *Kes'ava* ever protect you, the giver of happiness, with ruddy soles like the brilliant eye of the red waterlily, the giver of their desires to the chiefs of men and to the gods, worshipped by the great rishis, resplendent as a crore of suns.

May it be well—The year 1500 of the victorious increasing S'áliváhana era having passed, and the year Bahudhánya being current, in the month S'rávana, the 8th day of the moon's decrease, Saturday—while the great king of kings, the supreme lord and king, hero of valour, *S'ri Ranga Ráya Mahá-ráya* was ruling his secure kingdom of the world*—

The following was the grant made by *Krishnappa Náyaka*, a chief among kings, worshipper of the feet of the god Chenniga Ráya of *Velápura* the southern Váranási . . . in order that (his father) *Venkaṭádri Náyaka* might obtain merit (*dharma*), and that the mother who bore him might obtain happiness (*punya*), and that his brothers might obtain favour (*anugraha*).

Krishnappa Náyaka, a bee at the lotus feet of *S'ri Ranga Ráya*, . .

(*Rest illegible owing to reduction of the photograph*).

* *S'riman mahárájádhirája rája parames'vara s'ri vira pratápa S'ri Ranga Ráya Mahá-ráyaru prithvi sthira rájyam geyutirppalli.*

122. S'ila S'asana at Belur, date A. D. 1625.

Size ft. 4 8′ × ft. 1 8′.—Kannaḍa Characters.

Sun. Moon.

The Vaishnava Symbols
Trinnama.

Chakra. S'ankha.

May it prosper. Adored be *S'ambhu*, beauteous with the chámara-like crescent moon kissing his lofty head; the original foundation-pillar of the city of the three worlds.

May it be well—In the year 15(4)7 of the victorious increasing S'áliváhana era, the year Króḍhana, the month Mágha, the 8th day of the moon's decrease, Monday—the service of a verandah to the temple of *Chenna Ráyasvámi* of *Velapura*.

We, *Krishnappa Náyaka*, *Venkaṭádri Náyaka*, *Uliga Múrtiappa Náyaka*, and *Marina Náyaka*, in order that our grandfather *Yarama Náyaka*, our father *Peddi Náyaka*, and our mother *Betamma* may obtain merit, have built a verandah of 26 *ankanas*, and devoted it at the lotus feet of *Chenna Ráyasvámi*.

123. S'ila S'asana at Belur, date about A. D. 1600.

Size ft. 4 8′ × ft. 1 8′.—Kannaḍa Characters.

Discus. Trinnama. Conch.

(The inscription is illegible.)

124. S'ila S'asana at Belur, date about 1650.

Size ft. 3 × ft. 1 8′.—Kannaḍa Characters.

Sun. Trinnama. Moon.

Money devoted to God. Prosperity.

A command of the authorities of *Belur* to the washermen caste of the fifty-six countries, residing in the *Belur* country.

The following tax shall be collected from all your caste.—For a girl or woman a *varaha*, for a widow four *varaha* . . .

(Rest not clear the language being very corrupt.)

S'ri salepaṭ aṇa mangalam Belúra stánadavaru Belúra síme aruvatt' áru des'ada asagara játigen ákida s'ásana nimma játiyarelara u kanne vennage varahá ganḍa saitavaḷige nálu varahá . . . .

125. S'ila S'asana at Belur, date about A. D. 1380.*

Sise ft. 4 × ft. 1 6.—Haḷe Kannaḍa Characters.

(The inscription very much reduced in photographing.
The beginning is not given.)

. . . Having subdued the *Kérala, Taulava* and *Andhra* kings can you fail in accumulating mighty spoils.

That you and your enemy meet on the same battle-field is the only similarity between you, for as even the young of a swan separates the milk from the water with which it is mixed, so do all people discern in you (two) the distinction between good and evil.

When *Gunḍappa Danḍinátha* goes forth to battle who can withstand him and live?—the possessor of forces and of all the eight royal requisites, a place of destruction for thousands . . . .

. . . .

Whatever ministers refused to help him in war, reckoning that a man who refuses to assist another is as bad as a drunkard, he punished them according to his superior wisdom and thus ruled the earth.

Having encountered in battle and overcome the kings of *Anga, Ganga, Kalinga, Kaṭhara, Kamboja, Simhala* . . . *Magadha, Málava, Kerala, Jiḍḍiya, China, Joniga* . . *Chola, Pándya, Vidarbha, Sauráshṭra, Kuru, Maru, Pancha, Pánchála,* . . . *Telunga,* and as far as *Párasika,* he set up pillars of victory in *Kolahana, Kásmira,* . . *Maháboṭa, Kákamúka, Ekapáda, Gholámukha* . . . . . and in all these regions caused his name to be greatly renowned this *Gunḍa Danḍádhinátha.*

By order of the auspicious great king of kings, the supreme ruler of kings, *S'ri Víra Harihara Mahárája,*—seeing that the grants to the god *Chenna Kes'avanátha,*—favourite deity of the great king of kings *Vishnu Varddhana,* possessor of the auspicious *Velur* which is as a new Vaikuntha of the lower world, gratifier of every human desire among the crowds of worshippers who adore him, who incarnate in a body presents himself to the sight of his followers in the midst of his splendid pile—which (grants) the ancient king *Vishnu Varddhana Biṭṭi Deva* had made for the decorations, processions, and other holy ceremonies, had through lapse of time become diminished—

He restored them, and made a decree to perpetuate as long as sun, moon and stars endure, the orders for the recital of the Veda [1] which that *Biṭṭi Deva*

---

* Compare with No. 123.

had given, for the daily worship according to the *Pancha Rátra* ritual and the *Mantra Siddhánta*, the worship of the throne,[2] the enthronement for the bath,[3] the enthronement for decorations,[4] the enthronement for processions,[5] the enthronement for offerings of food,[6] the enthronement for retiring to rest,[7] for the display of the sacred emblems,[8] the ceremonial contact,[9] for the sixty four festivals of rejoicing, for the worship with flowers, the daily oblation, the daily procession, the fortnightly festival, the monthly festival, the yearly festival, the festival of purifications,[10] the festival of remaining at home,[11] the festival of the engine (or disc),[12] the festival of invoking Ráma and Krishna,[13] the festival of worship with lotuses, the swing festival, the festival of illumination, the festival in Márgas'ira, the festival in Pushya, the festival in Chaitra, the decoration with the nine gems, the decoration with new cloths and jewels, the burning of sandal perfume, the congratulation, the presentation of fruit and delicacies, the presentation of a bull, the offering of honey, the offering of seeds the display of the four divisions of the army,[14] the exhibition of the mirror and of garlands, the exhibition of dancing, the procession to the treasury, the bathing at equinoxes, at solstices, and at the time of the sun's entering a new sign,the waving of lights, the penance for defects (or omissions) in the daily service, and the penance for accidental interruptions,[15] the peace offering, the festival of bringing the god home from a distance, for these and all other festivals and ceremonies.

Moreover, at the gate which *Gam Sálár* (?) the Turk of *Kalubarige* coming, broke open and burnt*, he built a gopura and 107 chambers.

In height that tower was equal to one foot of *Purobhava* (Brahma), or to one of *S'árngina* (Vishnu). It resembled the mountains Meru, Himavan, Rumanvan, Malaya, or the highest peak of Mandara. The pinnacles on the spire shot up as far as svarga, and were marked with prints of the lotus-feet, decked with golden anklets, of hosts of *siddhas* and other celestial beings.

---

1 *Veda páráyana.* 2 *Mantrásana.* 3 *Snánásana.* 4 *Alankárásana.* 5 *Yátrásana.* 6 *Bhojyásana.* 7 *S'ayyásana.* 8 *Aupachárika.* 9 *Samspars'aka.* 10 *Pavitrotsava.* 11 *Sthána s'ayanotsava.* 12 *Yantrotsava.* 13 *Ráma Krishna japotsava.* 14 *Chaturangabala.* 15 *Nitya naimittika práyaschitta.*

* *Kalubarigeya Turuka Gams'aláranu (?) bandu muridu sudisidantha bágilu.*

126. S'ila S'asana at Belur, date A. D. 1548.

Size ft. 4' × ft. 1 5'.—Hale Kannada Characters.

Discus. Trinnama. Conch.

May it prosper—Adored be *S'ambhu*, beauteous with the chámara-like crescent moon kissing his lofty head ; the original foundation-pillar of the city of the three worlds.

May it be well—The year 1470 of the victorious increasing S'áliváhana era having passed, the year Kilaka being then current, in the month Ashádha, the 11th day of the moon's decrease, Monday,—while the auspicious great king of kings, supreme ruler of kings, hero of valour, *S'ri Víra Sadás'iva Deva Mahárúya* was in his residence of *Hampe Hastinávati*, ruling the kingdom of the world—

The grant of land which *Chikka Singappa Náyaka*, the son of *Hiriya Singappa Náyaka*, receiving it from the hands of *Krishnappa Náyaka*, the son of *Hadapada Bayyappa Náyaka*, presented to the favourite god of all the line of the kings of kings, the god *Channa Kes'ava* of *Velápura*, the Váranás'i of the south, the new Vaikuṇṭha of the lower world, was as follows.—

For the S'iva-rátri car festival of the god *Channa Kes'ava*, he gave in the *Hásana-s'íme* one village *Chikka Gaddahalli* and one village *Govindanahalli*. . . . And within the limits of these two villages all the paddy land, and the dry cultivation land, together with all the rents* therefrom, the profits of land given out on half share cultivation†, and the *ashṭa-bhoga-tējas-svámya* rights of *nidhi*, *nikshepa*, *jala*, *taru*, *páshána*, *akshína*, *ágámi*, *siddha*, and *sádhya*.‡ With the pouring of water and presentation of a coin § were they given.

May prosperity attend the gift thus made.

Of making a gift or perpetuating one, the perpetuating one is the best. He who makes a gift obtains svarga, but he who perpetuates one obtains final beatitude.

* *Suvarnádáya.* † *Várádáya* ‡ See note p. 3. § *Hiranyódaka dáná dhára.*

127. S'ila S'asana at Belur, date A. D. 1554.

Size ft. 6 4' × ft. 1 5.'—Kannaḍa Characters.

Hanuman.

* May prosperity attend it—In the year 1477 of the victorious increasing S'áliváhana era, the year Rákshasa being then current, in the month Mágha, the 5th day of the moon's increase.—While the great king of kings, supreme ruler of kings, hero of valour, *Víra Sadas'iva Mahárâya*, seated on his jewel throne, was in *Vidyánagara*, ruling the kingdom of the world—

Seeing that disputes would arise between the cultivators (*halagaru*) and the artificers (*pánchâluru*) in the presence of (the god) *Channagi Ráya* of *Belúru*, *Ráma Rájaya*, in the presence of *Tirumala Rájaya*, inquiring into the former rights of the artificers, *Ráma Rájaya* and *Tirumala Rájaya* decreed to the artificers the southern street of *Belúru*, and to the cultivators only the back row for dwellings, from the Vira Bhadra temple in the east to the southern fort on the west; and added some houses and waste lands on the south, saying, There perform your ceremonies, and build houses. The land lying between these grants . . . .

The kings who shall arise in *Vidyánagara*, in devotion to that *Channaga Ráya* may not refuse to grant the contributions to the artificers for the car and other festivals, without incurring the wrath whereby he destroys his enemies.

All of us most honorable citizens, *Ráma Rájaya*, *Bánadarasa* agent for the affairs of *Tirumala Rája*, and *Hásana Basetti* agent for the affairs of *Rámappaya*, have made the donation to the god *Channa Kes'ava* according to the decree of *Ráma Rájaya* and *Tirumala Rájaya*.

Of making a gift or perpetuating one, the perpetuating one is the best. He who makes a gift obtains svarga, but he who perpetuates one obtains final beatitude.

Whoso violates this decree given to the artificers forfeits the favor of *Chenniga Ráya*.

---

* The inscription is not free from obscurities.

128. S'ila S'asana at Belur, date about A. D. 1380.

Size ft. 6 8'. × ft. 1 9'. Hale Kannada Characters.

Adored be *Narasimha*. The command of the god *Kes'ava*, enriched as with a garland by a line of adoring gods and rákshasa chiefs, lord of *Velapura*, the city of delights. May that god Kes'ava protect us, who dwells in the ulterior part (*parárdha*) of Jambu-dvipa, shining with the combination of all good qualities, creator of all worlds, praised and worshipped by Brahma, Is'ána (S'iva) and the nava Brahma, of a form of glory, lord of the three vedas, with eyes resembling the crimson water-lily, bearer of the discus, the holy, the god who enables his devoted worshipper to win heaven.

Whomsoever the Vedántins in their hearts adore under the name of Brahma or of S'iva, or the Bauddhas under the name of Buddha, whomso the Naiyyáyikas skilled in the sacred scriptures (adore) under the name of A'tma (soul), whomso the Jainaka understand by Tanu (body), whomso the Mímámsaka call Karma (action), that god Kes'ava ever grant your desires.

That god Kés'ava preserve us from all calamity, who laughs till the final deluge (*pralaya*) at the consuming flames from S'iva's central eye, who is in the form of the kalpa-vriksha, in mercy like a great cloud, glancing like lightning over the garment that covers the breasts swelling like mountains of Lakshmi, lord of all the chiefs of the gods.

That god Kes'ava grant us happiness, who in the time of the illustrious *Hoisaṇa* kings, adorned with the collection of all good qualities, conspicuous for bodily strength,—as if the divine Vishnu sought how to obtain similar fortune, took upon himself the plan of the protection of all the world in Velanagara, the city of his servant.

The god Kes'ava of Velapura, giver of sight to the blind, who raises up the poor to royal dignity, who causes the lame to be the swiftest of the swift, makes the dumb as eloquent as Brihaspati, the barren to be crowded with offspring, the granter of all desires, alike to the residents of that country and to foreigners from abroad—protect us. The great god Kes'ava protect us, the god whom the wise Nárada hymned as follows; 'O destroyer of sin, god of gods, the supreme, remover of all sorrow, the merciful'; who dwells, the first original body of the god, in the city of Velapura, which is a shore to check the rising waters of pride.

In the three worlds which came into being from an essence (*tatva*) incomprehensible and indescribable, which are wonderful with the varieties of uncreated illusions (*máya*), did Brahma create many distinguished kings, among whom, during the Kali yuga, in order to purify the sins of the age, *Sangama* came into being.

From the union of *Sangama*, descendant of a beautiful race, with *S'arada* sprung five children, resembling five kalpa-vrikshas. The . . . of them was *Haryappa* whose . . . was *Bukka* Nripati, bearing the burden of all the world. From him sprung *Harihara*, lord of the Lakshmi of worldly fortune.

In presenting gifts of gold to Brahmans, like Karna the son of Súrya; in making gifts of lands and gifts of cows, the real Paras'u Ráma; in satisfying the desires of all, without any parallel,—thus meritorious, *Harihara* prospered.

While *S'ri Víra Vijaya Harihara Mahárâya*, great king of kings, supreme monarch, chief jewel among the ornaments of the race of kings, the Hindu raja who was paramount sovereign of the eastern, western, southern, and northern oceans, protector of the brave, a destroying serpent to kings who break their word, conqueror of the most powerful heroes; in his new capital and the chief of cities *Vijayanagara*, which shines on the banks of the *Pampa* river, amid the society of persons ever devoted to works of merit, was ruling in peace and wisdom* the kingdom of the world—

The servant living with affection at his lotus feet, an all-subjecting incantation in bringing into his power the Lakshmi of victory over hostile kings, was *Vijaya Gunḍa* Danḍanátha.

To describe his glory.—As in former times to king Das'aratha was an excellent minister Sumantra, even so to Harihara was *Gunḍa Danḍa*, the master over his enemies. Great was the fame that *Gunḍa Danḍa* had gained in the world, into the tongues of the flames of the might of whose sceptre-like arms the Yavana, Turushka, Andhra and other kings had fallen like moths, a chief of ministers, whose policy was an all pervading energy strengthened by the brightness of wisdom. Having in battle subdued all hostile kings and set their wives free, ruling the earth with justice, his ministers and gurus executing his orders, *Gunḍa Danḍádhipa* by himself grew prosperous, shining in his independence as a great light among other kings.

†While merely in his mind forming the intention of war, the king of *Anga* lost all his limbs, the king of *Kalinga* went out of his senses, the king of *Gurjara* was seized with a fever of anguish, the king of *Panchála* rushed into death, the king of *Sindhu* with his mighty forces threw himself into the sea, the *Andhra* king went blind and was as if bound though not caught in a snare, while the *Chola* king was turned into a hog.

---

* See note p. 2.

† In this and the following verse the fate of each king is described in a play of words upon his name.

Anga was beaten on the field of battle, *Kalinga* bolted from the field, *Andhra* hid himself in a cave of the mountains, *Gurjara* bellowed with cries, *Konkana* was put in a corner, *Chola* took refuge in the hills; when the victorious *Gunda* was made a commander of the forces.

Renowned as the first of great ministers, a globe on which might daily grow surpassing valour, profoundest prudence, lavish liberality, highest courage, untiring energy, wealth and fame; a benefactor and skilful administrator to the Brahmans, protector of the good, punisher of the evil; may it be well with him. Who exceeds him in merit, in prowess, and in the strength of his forces?

(*The s'ásana ends here and is evidently incomplete*).

---

129. S'ila S'asana at Hassan, date A. D. 1561.

Size ft. 6 × ft. 2.—Kannada Characters.

Worshipper. Moon. Linga. Nandi.

May it be well. I bow to the commands of the supreme *Virupáksha*, commands which without a beginning are fixed and eternal as the Siddas. Even as the furious Rudra when with the weapon of his energy he conquered and put to death the hosts of evil spirits and subdued the gods, thus victorious does *Víra Bhadra* shine. Adored be *S'ambhu*, beauteous with the chámara-like crescent moon kissing his lofty head, the original foundation-pillar of the city of the three worlds.

May it be well. The year 1482 of the victorious increasing S'áliváhana era having passed, the year Rudhiródgári being then current, in the month S'rávana, the 10th day of the moon's decrease, Monday, at an auspicious time, the ruler of the kingdom, *Sadas'iva Mahárdya*, son of the mahá mandales'vara, . . . great king of kings, supreme ruler, *Víra Pratápa Achyuta Ráya Mahárdya*, being in the city of *Hastinávati Vidyánagara*, ruling the kingdom in peace and wisdom,*—presented to the god *Virupáksha* of *Hásana*, the village of *Sattihalli*, situated within the district governed by *Ráma Rájuiya* the agent for his affairs, and within the *Hásana* country, which by right of the Náyakship was ruled by *Krishnappa Náyaka*, the son of *Singappa Náyaka*.

Moreover, many people having represented to *Krishnappa Náyaka*, the son of *Bayappa Náyaka*, with all humility, that he should secure the merit of

---

* See note p. 2.

festive processions, he presented to the god *Virupáksha* of *Hásana*, the paddy land, the fields, the great watercourse, the dam with the land under it, and arable ground belonging to the village of *Saṭṭahalli* in the *Hásana* country which (land) *Tammappa Náyaka's* brother *Bukkanna Náyaka* had leased to him, having freed them from the imposition of *kánike, kappa, jóḍi, beḍige, taḷavárike, alivu, annyáya, samaya, sankhya, bíldána, sunka,* and *saudige**.

In order that the power and merit and glory in success of great kings might accrue to *Krishnappa Náyaka* the son of *Bayappa Náyaka*, *Bukkanna Náyaka*, the son of *S'andávara Krishnappa Náyaka* and younger brother of *Tammappa Náyaka*, presented the village of *Saṭṭahalli* for the car festival of the god *Virupáksha*, erecting a s'ásana of the gift.

And the villages of *Biranahalli*, *Aaruvalli*, *Rájaghaṭṭa*, *Manḍigenahalli*, *Guḍḍenahalli*, and *Yeṛeganagilu*, belonging to the temple of *Virupáksha*—*Hallanahalli* belonging to the god *Holada Rames'vara* for the anointing and the daily offerings—*Honnénhalli* belonging to the god *Vighnes'vara*,—and the paddy land and fields under the *Hásana* tanks . . . presented, with freedom from the imposts of *jóḍi, beḍige, kánike, biráḍa, hiṭṭu, hunmi* and *bíjavari*†, to the god *Virupáksha*—they erected a s'ásana and bestowed upon the gods *Virupáksha*, *Holada Rámes'vara* and *Vighnes'vara*.

Whosoever among the kings of the Hásana country, its chiefs, *senabhovas* (accountants), *gauḍas* (farmers), subjects or officers, now consenting to consecrate these villages to the service of the god *Virupáksha*, shall at any time unjustly resume them—will incur the guilt of slaughtering cows and Brahmans in the holy city of Kás'i in the presence of the Vis'vanátha Linga on the Manikarnika bank; of incest with his mother, of killing women, and of murdering gurus. In the mahá Narakas shall he remain, enduring through many Brahma kalpas and manvantaras the tortures inflicted by the servants of Yama.

Whoso protects this gift, shall derive the merit of a crore of as'vamédhas, together with the supreme merit of those who present a thousand cows with all

---

* *Kánike*, offerings or gifts; *kappa*, tribute; *jóḍi*, a favourable quit-rent; *beḍige*, begging; *taḷavárike*, village watchman's dues; *alivu*, waste or ruin; *annyáya*, injustice; *samaya*, season or proper time; *sankhya*, enumeration; *bíldána*, transit duties, or else fallow land; *sunka*, customs; *saudige*, fire-wood.

† The foregoing note explains some of these terms: the others are—*biráḍa*, apportioning, that is, of any extra fine or assessment upon a village amongst the individuals; *hiṭṭu*, flour or pudding, that is for feeding government peons when passing through a village on duty; *hunmi*, full moon; *bíjavari*, the amount of seed required for a portion of land.

their adornments. For a hundred of celestial years shall they receive honor from the king of the world of gods, thence rising to the service of Mahes'vara in Kailása, they shall become one with the supreme spirit.

Of making or continuing a gift, the continuing it is the best, for he who makes a gift obtains svarga, but he who continues it obtains final beatitude. To lay a tax on land which has been freed is to incur the guilt of slaughtering a thousand cows. To remove the burden laid on the land is to secure residence for ages in heavenly bliss.

By *Krishna Nanjappa*, the son of the teacher *Hásana Nanjappaiya*, well versed in the Yajur veda, was this s'ásana composed, on the 4th of Ashádа. *Kálachandra* corrected it, and *Timmalachári*, a dependent of *Lakhanacharya* of the Kás'yapa gótra, engraved it.

From Major Dixon's Photographs.

II.

TA'MRA S'A'SANAS,

OR

INSCRIPTIONS ON COPPER PLATES.

130(i). Tamra S'asana at Anantapur*, Professed date B.C. 3066.

3 Plates, 4 sides.—Nandi Nágari Characters.

(*First line partially broken off. Contained the following verse.*)

May it be well.—Supreme is the boar form of the resplendent Vishnu, which dispersed the waters of the ocean and bore up the peaceful earth on the tip of his strong right tusk.

While the protector of all lands, favorite of earth and fortune, great king of kings, supreme ruler, first of monarchs, lord of *Hastinápura*, the bestower of widow-hood on the wives of the riding Bhagadatta kings, a sun to the lotus of the *Pánḍava kula*, terrible in war, an unsparing bow to *Kalinga*, a sun among males, unsurpassed hero, invincible champion on the field of battle, disgracer of *As'vapati Ráya*, slayer of *Gajapati Ráya*, smiter on the head of *Narapati Ráya*, a Révanta among skilled horsemen, tamer of the deers his neighbour kings, the daily terror of the four quarters of *Konkaṇa*, to the wives of others as a son, possessed of a flag bearing the device of a golden boar, adorned with the glory of all lines of kings, born in the *Soma vams'a*, son of the emperor *Parikshit*, the emperor *Janamejaya*, was in *Hastinápura*, ruling in peace and wisdom—

On the occasion of his coming to the south on an expedition of victory, halting the army at the confluence of the rivers *Tungabhadra* and *Haridra*, in the presence of the god Harihara, in the month Chaitra, the dark fortnight (*part of the plate broken off*) the time of the sun's going north (*part of the plate broken off*) at the vyati páta, at the auspicious time of an eclipse of the sun, when it was a half obscured, at the conclusion of the *sarpa yága* (serpent sacrifice)—to the Brahmans from *Gautama-gráma*, situated within the *Khampana Sántalige*

---

* This is known as the Gauj agrahára s'a'sana. The following is the text of the first part.

Svasti samasta-bhuvanásraya s'ri-prithvi-vallabha mahárájádhirája parames'vara parama-bhaṭṭáraka Hastinápura-varádhisvara árohaka-Bhagadatta-ripu-ráya-kántá-datta-vairivaidhavya Pánḍava-kula-kamala-márttanḍa kadana-prachanḍa Kalinga-kodanḍa ganḍa-márttanḍa ekánga-vira raṇa-ranga-dhira As'vapati-Ráya-disápaṭṭa Gajapati-Ráya-samháraka Narapati-Ráya-mastaka-tala-prahári hayárudha-prauḍha-rekhá-Revanta sámanta-mṛiga-chamára Konkaṇa-chátur-disa-bhayankara-nityakara paránganá-putra suvarṇṇa-varáha-lánchhana-dhvaja samasta-rájávalí-virájita-samálankrita s'ri-Soma-vamsodbhava s'ri-Parikshiti-chakravartti tasya putra Janamejaya-chakravartti Hastinápure sukha-sankathá-vinodena rájyam karoti dakshina-disávare digvijaya-yátreyam bijayam karomi Tungabhadrá-Haridrá-sangame s'ri-Harihara-Deva-sannidhau kaṭakam utkalita Chaitrą-máse krishna . . . karaná-uttaráyaṇa-san . . . vyati-páta-nimitte suryya-parbaṇi-arddha-grása-grahita-samaé sarppa-yágam karomi Banavási-panichcháhasra-madhye Khampaṇa-Sántalige-sáhasra-madhye Gautama-grámátu Bráhmaṇá ṣe.

Thousand in the middle of the *Banavase* Twelve Thousand—namely to *Govinda Paṭṭavarddhana* of the Kannaḍa shákhe and Gautama gotra, t *Vámana Paṭṭavarddhana* of the Kannaḍa shákhe and Vasishṭa gotra, to *Keshava Yajnadíkshita* of the Kannaḍa shákhe and Bháradvája gotra, to *Náraṇadíkshita* of the Kannaḍa shákhe and S'rivatsa goṭra, and the thirty two thousand Brahmans of many gotras sprung from the fourfaced (Brahma), coadjutors in the sacrifice—when the final offerings for the consummation of the sacrifice were being made, the Emperor being rejoiced, presented five manner of gifts, umbrellas, palanquins, a throne with guards, with *Náḍaballi*, *Bádaballi*, *Chikka Hárika*, *Doṇaḍúru*, *Talangere*, *Sulligoḍu*, *Ságara*, *Gauja*, *Sálúru*, *Bácheyanahalli*, *Champagoḍu* and *Hariyampagoḍu*, these twelve villages situated in *Gautama gráma*, together with the (imposts) *anka*, *danḍu*, *khanḍana*, *náḍu*, *biṭṭi*, *galiya*, *sunka*, and the *ashṭa-bhoga-tejas-svámya* rights—(presented these) with every ceremony and with pouring of water.*

The boundaries of those *gráma* :—On the north-east the stream at the junction of the boundaries of Gautamagráma, Banisúr and Sáliyúru ; then turning south, the joint boundaries of Gautamagráma and Sáliyúru as far as Ambaligála ; thus west, the stream which forms the boundaries of Gautamagráma and Sáliyúru ; thus south, the joint boundaries of Gautamagráma and Sáliyùru to the pond on the Uyagaḍḍe (mound) ; thus south, the joint boundaries of Gautamagráma and Sáliyúru as far as a stream. Thence the southern villages :—On the south-east, the joint boundaries of Gautamagráma, Sáliyúru and Kánvapura, to the beginning of the *vyághra* trees between the two hills ; then looking west, the joint boundaries of Gautamagráma and Kánvapura as far as the Kaduvaṭa stream ; thus west, a watercourse which meets the joint boundaries of Gautamagráma and Kánvapura ; thus west, the junction of the boundaries of Gautamagráma, Kánvapura and Maliya-úru at the Kataki mound ; thus west, the joint boundaries of Gautamagráma and Maliya-úru to the group of red stones ; thus west, the saline stream at the junction of the boundaries of Gautamagráma, Maliya-úru and Andhásara. Thence the western villages :—the salt river at the junction of the boundaries of Gautamagráma, Andhásara and Hosagunda, where it is unfordable ; then looking north, the joint boundaries of Gautamagráma and Hosagunda as far as a stream ; thus north, the joint boundaries of Gautamagráma, Hosagunda and Bidarugunji . . .

* *Chatur-mukha-náná-gotrebhyo dvatrisatu-sahasra-Bráhmaṇá sarppa-yága-púrṇṇáhuti-tad-anga-samaś mantránga-praṇámam karoti chakravatti mechchi panchánga pasáya chhatra sukhásana balada gaddige anka danḍa khanḍaṇa náḍu biṭṭi galiya sunka ashṭa-bhoga-teja-sámya* (see note, p. 3.) *Gautama-gráma tanu madhyá pravishṭa* (here follow the names of the villages) *ebam dvádasa grámátu sarba samasya dhárápúrbakam datta.*

thus north, the joint boundaries of Gautamagráma and Bidaragunji to the Kshíra kola (milky stream); thus north, the stream at the junction of the boundaries of Gautamagráma, Biduragunji and Trigadhapola. Thence the northern villages :—on the north-west, the second junction of the boundaries of Gautamagráma and Trigadhapola at the Uriya stream; then looking east, the joint boundaries of Gautamagráma and Trigadhapola to the Ketaki mound and white *malli* trees; thus east, the joint boundaries of Gautamagráma and Trigaḍhapola to the red stone; thus east, the joint boundaries of Gautamagráma, Trigadhapola and Biliyúru to Kamsagaḍḍe; thus east, the joint boundaries of Gautamagráma, Biliyuru and Madaba to the Sura kola north of the hill; thus east, the joint boundaries of Gautamagráma, Madaba and Banniúru to the bambu trees; thus east, the joint boundaries of Gautamagráma and Banniúru as far as the Sanchari stream east of the mound. Thus it ends at the eastern boundary on the north east.

Merit is a common bridge for kings. This from age to age deserves your support, O kings of the earth. Thus does Rámachandra beseech the kings who come after him.

Of making a gift or perpetuating one, the perpetuating one is the best. He who makes a gift obtains svarga, but he who perpetuates one obtains final beatitude.

(*One line broken off.*)

---

131 (ii). Tamra S'asana at Harihara, date A. D. 1354.

3 Plates, 4 sides.—Nandi Nágari Characters.

Adored be *S'ambu*, beauteous with the chámara-like crescent moon kissing his lofty head; the original foundation-pillar of the city of the three worlds.

May the elephant-faced *Vináyaka*, that benevolent one to whom the seven great oceans are as elephant-ponds for him to sport in—protect the world. May the right tusk of the Boar form of Vishnu, like a sceptre protect us, on which forming a small canopy rested the earth surmounted by the golden peak of Meru. . . . May the Varaha protect us.

There was born a king perfect in his line as a pearl, the brightness of whose fame spread to all the points of the compass, a jewel in the eyes of the most beautiful women, *Sangama* by name, worthy of being surrounded by an assembly of all the great, (a play on the name.)

From him sprung the illustrious *Bukka Rája*, a conqueror over mighty kings, king of kings, with a face illuminated by the knowledge of the sciences, of astrology, astronomy, and the vedas; glorious as Vyása, conspicuous with all splendour.

May it be well.—In the year 1276* of the victorious increasing S'áliváhana era, the year Vijaya, the month Mágha, the 15th day of the moon's increase, Monday, at the auspicious time of an eclipse of the moon;—we, *Bukka Ráya Mahárâya*, great king of kings, supreme ruler, the embodiment of justice†, have given to *Rámaṇṇa Joyisa* (astrologer), son of the eminent astrologer Mádhava Joyisa, of the Kas'yapa gotra, Badavana sútra, and Yajus s'ákhe, the town astrologer of the city of the god Harihara‡, the village of *Miṭṭaligana Kaṭṭe*, which by an order to *Miṭṭali Golla* we caused to be built on the four . . . land situated in *Harihara-Devara-pura*, attached to *Koyúru chávaḍi* in the *Uchchangi venṭhe*§—and with it the *nidhi*, *nikshepa*, *jala*, *páshána*, *akshina*, *ágámi*, *siddha*, *sádhya*, *hechchárike*,*&c.*, as well as the whole of the *ashta-bhoga-tejas-svámya* rights ¶, in sole possession (*eka bhoga*), with presentation of a coin and water.

The description of the boundaries of the said village of *Miṭṭali Golla Kaṭṭe*:—East of the village, a black stone erected in the middle of the Pándava rocks at the side of the village of Nágenúru: South of the village, two white stones near the white rocks of the village of Mudihadada Yantra: West of the village, three black stones erected on the mound of small stones at the village of Salukatte: North the row of stones, namely white stones and others, erected at the bottom of the mound of white rock belonging to Kundaváḍi.

May the s'ásana of the meritorious gift from the east onwards thus presented without reserve in the presence of Virupáksha, be enjoyed by father, son and posterity as long as sun and moon endure.

Of making a gift or perpetuating one, the perpetuating one is the best. He who makes a gift obtains svarga, but he who perpetuates one obtains final beatitude. Whoso usurps a gift made by himself or by another shall assuredly be born a worm in ordure for sixty thousand years. Land presented to Brahmans is to kings as an only sister, neither may she be enjoyed nor ravished away, (otherwise, nor subjected to taxation).

S'ri Virúpáksha (in Kannada characters).

---

* These figures are Kannada.

† *Sriman-máhárájádhirája rája-paramesvara dharma-múrti.*

‡ *Harihara-Deva-pura sthalada daivajniru.*

§ *Koyúra chávaḍige saluva Uchchangi venṭhedolagaṇa Harihara Devara purada úram bádadol iha chau vyámeda bhúmi madhyadoḷu návu Miṭṭali Gollage nirúpisi kaṭṭisi koṭṭa Miṭṭaligana kaṭṭeyandu námadheyakaváda grámavannu, &c.*

¶ See note p. 3.

132 (iii). Tamra S'asana at Harihara, date A. D. 694.

3 Plates, 4 sides.—Púrvada Haḷe Kannaḍa Characters.

May it be well.—Supreme is the Boar form of the resplendent Vishnu, which dispersed the waters of the ocean and bore up the peaceful earth on the tip of his strong right tusk.

Of the illustrious *Mánavyasa* gotra praised in all the world, sons of *Háriti*, nourished by seven mothers resembling the seven worlds, through the protection of Kárttikeya having obtained a succession of good fortune (or the succession to Kalyáṇa), having in a moment brought all kings into their subjection at one glimpse of the boar ensign obtained from the favour of the adorable Náráyaṇa, were the kings of the *Chalukya* race.—

To which (race) being an ornament, with a body purified by the final ablutions on the consummation of the as'vamedha sacrifice, was *S'ri Pulakesi* Vallabha Mahárája.—Whose son, with a pure fame gained from the conquest of the groups of the *Vanavási* and other hostile kings, was *Kirtti Varmma* Prithivi Vallabha Máharája.

His son, who having encountered in battle and defeated *S'ri Harsha Varddhana* the king of all the north, had acquired the additional title of *Parames'vara*, was *Sattyás'raya* S'ri Prithivi Vallabha Mahárájádhirája Parames'vara.

His dear son, by whose counsel and help alone had been obtained the abundance of royal spoils from hostile kings, was *Vikramáditya* Bhaṭṭáraka Parames'vara, by the flag of whose fame gained by victory over hostile kings who made war upon him associated with valiant warriors roaring with many different sounds (or in many different languages) all the points of the compass were illuminated; who after conquering the *Pallava* king whose insults threaten-

---

* *S'rimatám sakala-bhuvana-samstúyamána-Mánavya-sa-gotráṇám Háriti-putráṇám sapta-loka-mátṛibhis-sapta-mátṛibhir-abhirabhivarddhitánám Kárttikeya-parirakshaṇa-prápta-kalyáṇa paramparáṇám bhagavan-Náráyaṇa - prasáda-samásádita-varáha - lánchhane-kshaṇa-kshaṇad-vas'ikritás'esha-mahibhṛitám Chalukyánám kulam alankarishnor as'vamedhávabhritha-snána-pavitrikrita-gátrasya s'ri-Pulikes'i vallabha-mahárájasya súnúh parákramákránta-Vanavásy-ádi-para-nṛipati - manḍala-pranibaddha - vis'uddha-kirttih s'ri-Kirtti-Varmma-prithivi-vallabha-mahárájas tasyátmajas samara-samsakta-sakalottará-pathes'vara-s'ri-Harsha-Varddhana-parájayopalabdha-Parames'vara-paranámadheya Sattyás'raya - s'ri-pṛithivi-vallabha-mahárájá-dhirája-parames'varas tat-priya-sutasya Vikramáditya-parames'vara-bhaṭṭárakasya mati-sahaya-mátra - samadhigata - vijagis'a-samuchitochita-rájya-vibhavasya vividha-rasitasita - samaram-upagata-ripu-narapati-vijaya-samupalabdha- kirtti-patákávabhásita-digantasya himakara-kara-vimala-kula-paribhava-vilaya-hetu-Pallava- pati - parájayánantara - parigṛihita - Kánchipurasya prabháva-kulis'a-dalita-Choḷa-Pánḍya-Keraḷa-dharanidharánvaya-mánamána-s'ṛingasya ananya-*

ed destruction to the dynasty resembling in purity the rays of the moon, had become possessor of *Kánchipura*; by the thunderbolt of whose prowess the peak of pride of the *Choḷa*, *Páṇḍya*, and *Keraḷa* kings was split; the lotuses of whose feet were bathed with waters distilled from the jewels in the crown of the king of *Kánchi* who never had bowed to any man; lord of all the lands between the three oceans.

His son, who like as the heavenly general (Kumárasvámi) of Bálendu S'ekhara (S'iva) smote down the excessively grown might of the Daityas, so destroyed the power (or forces) of *Trairájya Pallava*; the beloved of all nations for bringing them the security which follows on victory; in his great affection for his people like Yudhishṭhira; in the possession of the Lakshmi of fortune like Vásudeva; in his driving many kings with an elephant-goad like Parasu Ráma; in being an asylum to many kings like Bharata; who had reduced to subjection *Pallava*, *Kalabhra*, *Keraḷa*, *Haihaya*, *Vila*, *Malava*, *Chola*, *Páṇḍya*, (?) *A'ḷuva Ganga*, and others—*Vinayáditya Satyás'raya* S'ri Prithivi Vallabha Mahárájadhirája Parames'vara Bhaṭṭáraka, thus commands all people.

Be it known to you all, that the S'aka year 616 having past, and the 14th year of our victorious reign being now current, our victorious army being in *Karanjapatra-gráma* near to *Harishapura*, on the full moon day of Kártíka, the bright fortnight, in accordance with the application of *Srimad A'luva Rája*—the village named *Kiru Kágamási*, in the *Eḷevolal bhága* of *Vanavási mandala*, has been granted in sole possession, free of all imposts, to *Is'ána S'armmaṇa*, son of *Mára S'armmaṇa* and grandson of *S'ri Sarmmaṇa Somayáji*, completely versed in all the veda and vedánga.

The chatra at the *Katákrita kshetra* to the west side of *Peg-Gágamási* is the limit of this beautiful kshetra; on the north east *Pulivutu* at the boundary of the village of *Sirigoḍu*; thence going onwards, *Karvva Surigoḍu*; then *Perbatu*; then . . . .

---

samavana-Kánchipati-maṇi-makuṭa-kuṭa-kiraṇa-salilábhishikta-charaṇa-kamalasya trisamudra-madhya-vartti-bhuvana-mandaládhis'varasya súnuh pitu . . . Bálendu-S'ekharasy-eva-senánir Ddaitya-balam-ati-samuddhatam-Trairájya-Pallava-balam-avashṭabhyah samasta-vishaya-pras'amanad-vihitan-manonuranjanah atyanta-vatsalatvád Yudhishṭhira iva s'ri-rámatvád Vásudeva iva nripánkus'atvát Paras'u Ráma iva rájás'rayatvád Bharata iva Pallava-Kaḷabhra-Keraḷa-Haihaya-Viḷa-Maḷava-Choḷa-Páṇḍyádyáyen-A'ḷuva - Gangádyai - mmauli - samabhṛityat-ánvitáh Vinayáditya Satyás'raya s'ri-pṛithvi-vallabha-maharájádhirája parames'vara-bhaṭṭárakas sarván evam ájnápayati viditam astu vosmábhi shoḍas'ottara-shachchhateshu s'aka-varsheshv atiteshu pravarddhamána-vijaya-rájya-samvatsare chaturddas'e vartamáne Harusha-pura-pratyasanne Karanja-patra-grámam adhivasati vijaya-skandhávare Kárttika-paurṇṇamásyá s'rimad A'luva Rája vijnápanayá.

then *Karapu Kere*; then to the south, *Halepura*

. . . .

Therefore let all future kings, whether of this or of foreign countries, considering that the glory of their life and wealth will rapidly decay, place no regard upon them; but knowing that the earth will endure as long as sun and moon, protect this land as their only daughter.

Thus hath it been said by the adorable Vyása who arranged (or separated) the vedas:—The earth has been enjoyed by Sagara and many kings. In proportions to their (gifts of) land so was their reward. Whoso makes a gift has an easy task, the maintenance of it is arduous. But than making a gift the maintenance of one is more meritorious, for the making a gift procures svarga, but the maintaining of one secures final beatitude. Whoso by violence takes away land presented by himself or by another shall be assuredly be born a worm in ordure for sixty thousand years.

This s'asana was written by the minister for peace and war, *S'ri Ráma* Puṇya Vallabha.

133* (iv). Tamra S'asana at Soraba, Professed date B. C. 3066.

3 Plates, 4 Sides.—Nandi Nágari Characters.

May it be well—Supreme is the boar form of the resplendent Vishnu, which dispersed the waters of the ocean and bore up the peaceful earth on the tip of his strong right tusk.

While the protector of all lands, favourite of earth and fortune, great king of kings, supreme ruler, first of monarchs, lord of *Hastinapura*, the bestower of widowhood on the wives of the riding Bhagadatta kings, a sun to the lotus of the *Páṇḍava kula*, terrible in war, an unsparing bow to *Kalinga*, a sun among males, unsurpassed hero, invincible champion on the field of battle, disgracer of *As'vapati Ráya*, slayer of *Gajapati Ráya*, smiter on the head of *Narapati Ráya*, a Revanta among skilled horsemen, tanner of the deers his neighbour kings, the daily terror of the four quarters of *Konkaṇa*,† like a bee to the nectar issuing from the mouth of Is'vara, skilled in the

---

* Compare with No. 130.

† To this point as No. 130. Then *chachcharya-puṭa-chácha-puṭa I'svara-mukha-kamala-vinirgata sudásálanga-brahma viṇádi-bharata-sástra-prasiddha aneka-sástra-pravina-koranṭaka byalinágárjunádi-mantra-jaya-siddha-prasiddha samudayana-mitra-pádáravinda ari-ráya-kula-vilaya-kálánala-nityakara*—continues as in No. 130.

science of music and dancing, learned in many sciences, celebrated among those who had gained their ends from the use of the Koranṭaka, Byali, Nágárjuna and other incantations, whose lotus feet are the source of an ever increasing greatness, like the fires of judgment in daily destroying the races of hostile kings, to strange women as their son, having the ensign of a golden boar, adorned with the glory of all lines of kings, born in the *Soma vams'a*, son of the emperor *Parikshit*, the emperor *Janamejaya*, was in *Hastinapura*, ruling the kingdom in peace and wisdom—

On the occasion of his coming to the south on an expedition of victory, halting the army at the confluence of the rivers *Tungabhadra* and *Haridra*, in the presence of the god *Harihara*—the month Chaitra, the dark fortnight, Monday, in Bharani mahá nakshatra, sankránti, at the moment of vyatí páta on the conclusion of the *sarpa yága*—to the Brahmans from *Pushpagaḍḍe gráma*, situated within the *khampana Eḍe-náḍ* Seventy, in the middle of the *Banavàse* Twelve thousand*—namely to *Mádhava Paṭṭavarddhana* of the Kannaḍa shákhe and Atreya gotra, *Vis'ves'vara Ghalila* of the Kannaḍa shákhe and Vasishṭa gotra, *Yogis'vara Paṭṭavarddhana* of the Kannaḍa shákhe and S'rívatsa gotra, *Vishnu Dikshita* of the Kannaḍa shákhe and Vis'vámitra gotra, and to two thousand Brahmans of many gotras, when the final rite of consummation of the *sarpa yága* (serpent sacrifice) was being performed, after the benediction, the Emperor being rejoiced, presented five manner of gifts, umbrellas, palanquins, a throne with guards, with *Bammanahalli*, *Nittakki*, *Nechhe*, *Korakoḍi*, *Annageḍḍe*, *Kodalikere*, *Ura*, *Gendana*, *Kulavalli*, and *Kaideyahalli*, these ten villages, situated in *Pushpageḍḍe gráma*, together with the (imposts) *anka*, *danḍa*, *khanḍana*, and the *ashṭa-bhoga-tejas-svámya* rights—(presented these) with every ceremony and with pouring of water.†

The boundaries of these *gráma*:—On the north east, the confluence of streams at the junction of the boundaries of Pushpageḍḍe, Kántápura and Haya; thus looking south, the stream at the joint boundaries of Pushpageḍḍe and Haya; thus south, the rapids at the junction of the boundaries of Pushpageḍḍe, Haya and Uddare. Then the southern villages:—south east, the gorge formed by the waterfall at the junction of the boundaries of Pushpageḍḍe, Uddare, and

* *Chaitra-mása krishṇa-pakshe Soma-dine Bharaṇi-mahá-nakshátre sankránti-vyati-páta-nimitte sarppa-yága-karomi Banavàse-panichháhasra-madhye khampaṇa-Eḍenáḍu-Eppatara tatu madhya Puspageḍḍeya-gráma Bráhmana &c.*

† *Chaúghamaksha náná-gotrada sahasra-dvaya-Bráhmana sarppa-yága-púrnáhuti-samaś ásirbáda-púrbakam chakravrartti mechchi panchánga pasáya chhatra sukhásana balada gaddige anka danḍa khanḍaṇa ashta-bhoga-teja-sámya* (see note p. 3.) *sarba-namasyavági Puspageḍḍiya-grámá tanu madhya pravishṭa* (here follow the names of the villages) *evam dasa grámátu dhárápúrbakam datta.*

Kúḍali ; thus looking west, the Máttriya kola at the joint boundaries of Pushpageḍḍe, and Kúḍali ; thus west the Bálaya kola at the junction of the boundaries of Pushpageḍḍe, Kúḍali and Tavanidhi ; thus west, the Labada Kaṭṭe at the joint boundaries of Pushpageḍḍe and Tavanidhi. Then the western villages :—south west, the Moliya Moraḍi at the junction of the boundaries of Pushpageḍḍe, Tavanidhi and Tekkára ; thus looking north , Srápро Ratavalli (?) at the joint boundaries of Pushpageḍḍe and Tekkára ; thus north, Mágere at the junction of the boundaries of Pushpageḍḍe, Tekkára, and Kulaga ; thus north, Uyanguḍḍe at the joint boundaries of Pushpageḍḍe and Kulaga. Then the northern villages :—north west, the stream at the junction of the boundaries of Pushpageḍḍe, Kulaga and Basa-úru ; thus looking east the stream at the joint boundaries of Pushpageḍḍe and Basa-úru ; thus east, the Pálu-gola at the junction of boundaries of Pushpageḍḍe, Basa-úru and Tanaguppe ; thus east, the bend of the stream at the joint boundaries of Pushpageḍḍe and Tanaguppe ; thus east, the stream at the joint boundaries of Pushpageḍḍe and Tanaguppe ; thus east, the stream at the junction of the boundaries of Pushpageḍḍe, Tanaguppe and Kuntapura. Thus ends the boundary eastwards at the north east.

Merit is a common bridge for kings : this from age to age deserves your support, O kings of the earth : thus does Rámachandra beseech the kings who who come after him. Whoso by violence takes away land presented by himself or by another shall assuredly be born a worm in ordure for sixty thousand years. Poison is no poison, the property of the gods that is the real poison : for poison kills one man but the property of the gods (if usurped) destroys sons and descendants.

134* (v). Tamra S'asana at Soraba, date A. D. 692.

3 Plates, 4 sides.—Púrvada Haḷe Kannaḍa Characters.

May it be well—Supreme is the boar form of the resplendent Vishnu, which dispersed the waters of the ocean and bore up the peaceful earth on the tip of his strong right tusk.

Of the illustrious *Mánavyasa* gotra praised in all the world, sons of *Háriti*, nourished by seven mothers resembling the seven worlds, through the protection of Kárttikeya having obtained a succession of good fortune (or the succession to Kalyáṇa), having in a moment brought all kings into their subjection at one glimpse of the boar ensign obtained from the favor of the adorable Náráyana, were the kings of the *Chalukya* race.—

* Compare with No. 132.

To which (race) being an ornament, with a body purified by the final ablutions on the consummation of the as'vamedha sacrifice, was *S'ri Pulakes'i* Vallabha Mahárája.—Whose son, with a pure fame gained from the conquest of the groups of the *Vanavási* and other hostile kings, was *Kírtti Varmma* Prithivi Vallabha Mahárája.

His son, who having encountered in battle and defeated *S'ri Harsha Vardhana* the king of all the north, had acquired the additional title of *Parames'vara**, was *Vikramáditya* Parames'vara Bhaṭṭáraka, by whose counsel and help alone had been obtained the abundance of royal spoils, by the flag of whose fame gained by victory over hostile kings who made war upon him associated with valiant warriors roaring with many different sounds (or in many different languages) all the points of the compass were illuminated; who after conquering the *Pallava* king whose insults threatened destruction to the dynasty resembling in purity the rays of the moon, had become possessor of *Kánchipura*; by the thunderbolt of whose prowess the peak of pride of the *Chola*, *Páṇḍya*, and *Kerala* kings was split; the lotuses of whose feet were bathed with waters distilled from the jewels in the crown of the king of *Kánchi* who never had bowed to any man; lord of all the lands between the three oceans.

His son, who like as the heavenly general (Kumáraswámi) of Bálendu S'ekhara (S'iva) smote down the excessively grown might of the Daityas, so destroyed the power (or forces) of *Trairájya Pallava*; the beloved of all nations for bringing them the security which follows on victory; in his great affection for his great people like Yuddhishṭhira; in the possession of the Lakshmi of fortune like Vásudeva; in his driving many kings with an elephant-goad like Paras'u Rama; in being an asylum to many kings like Bharata; *Vinayáditya Satyás'raya* S'ri Prithivi Vallabha Mahárájádhirája Parames'vara thus commands all people:—

Be it known to you all, that the S'aka year 614 being past, and the (?) 12th year of our victorious reign being current, our victorious army being in the village of (?) *Chitrasédu* in the *Toramara* country, the adorable sun being about to turn on his southward course, in the Ròhini nakshatra, Saturday†—on the representation of *Chitraváha* Mahárája, son of the ocean of good qualities *Upendra*, the village named *Salevoge* in the country of (?) *Eḍe* . . .

* On comparing this with the corresponding passage in No. 132 it seems evident that the engraver has omitted the name and titles of *Satyás'ráya*, which should have come here.

† *Chaturddas'ottara-shaṭchhateshu s'aka-varsheshu atiteshu pravarddhamána-vijaya-rájya-samvatsare dvádase* (?) *varttamáne Toramara-vishaye Chitrasedu* (?) *grámam-adhivasati-vijaya-skandháváre dakshiṇáyanábhimukhe bhagavati-bháskare Rohiṇi-nakshatre S'anes'vara-váre guṇa-ságarád Upendrátmaja S'ri Chitraváha* (?) *mahárája vijnápayá.*

to the north east of *Vaijoyantipura*, has been presented to *Divákara S'armmaṇa*, son of *S'ankara S'armmaṇa* and grandson of *Nága S'armmaṇa* of the Devaráta Kaushikasa gotra, a follower of the Rig veda—(presented) with pouring of water and presentation of a coin, with freedom from all imposts on account of taxes or from entry of evil persons of other sects.

Therefore let all future kings, whether of this or of foreign countries, considering that the glory of their life and wealth will rapidly decay, place no regard upon them; but knowing that the earth will endure as long as sun and moon, protect this land as their only daughter.

Thus hath it been said by the adorable Vyása who arranged (or separated) the vedas:—The earth has been enjoyed by Sagara and many kings; in proportion to their (gifts of) land so was their reward.

Whoso makes a gift has an easy task, the maintenance of one is arduous. But than making a gift the maintenance of one is more meritorious, for the making a gift procures svarga, but the maintaining of one secures final beatitude. Whoso by violence takes away land presented by himself or by another shall assuredly be born a worm in ordure for sixty thousand years. This s'asana was written by the minister for peace and war *S'ri Ráma* Punya Vallatha.

(Here follow two lines of a rudely engraved inscription very indistinct, in which apparently some official of the Banavasi country claims merit for perpetuating the gift.)

---

135 (vi). Tamra S'asana at Shimoga, date A. D. 1522.

7 Plates, 12 sides.—Nandi Nágari Characters.

Adored be *S'ri Gandhipati*. Adored be *S'ambhu*, beauteous with the chámara-like crescent moon kissing his lofty head; the original foundation-pillar of the city of the three worlds. May the right tusk of the Boar form of Vishnu, like a sceptre protect us, on which forming a small canopy rested the earth surmounted by the golden peak of Meru. May the bright form which disperses the dark clouds of all obstacles (*Ganes'a*) be favorable to us, which though in body like an elephant was not born of an elephant, but is the offspring of Agaja (Párvati) and honored by Vishnu.

Born like shining butter from the churning by the gods of the great milk sea is there a glorious one (*Chandra*) who drove away the darkness. From him sprung *Budha*, who by unparalleled penance obtained a lasting name. His son was *Purúravas*, a combination of all merit. He had a son *Ayus*, who by the might of his shoulders destroyed all his enemies. From him came *Nahusha*, whose son was *Yayati*, dreadful in war, renowned in all the world. His son was *Turuvasu*, the equal of the Vasus, born to her husband by *Devayáni*.

* In that race shone *Timma Bhúpati*, whose wife was *Devaki*. Of great fame among the *Tuluva* kings, of the Yadu line, of the family of *Krishna Rava*, was the victorious ruler *S'ekhara*, whose wife was *Bukkamá*. From this glorious one sprung the king *Narasa*, to other kings a head jewel without any flaw of weakness, as Manmatha the joy of Devaki was born from Krishna.

Which king, quickly damming (*badhva*) the swollen stream of the Káveri, crossed over it, and through the power of his might in war, taking his enemy prisoner alive, subdued his country, and here building for himself a residence in the city before named *Sriranga*, planted in the three worlds the pillar of his fame as a donor unequalled for his gifts. Who had conquered the kings of *Chera*, *Chola*, *Pándya*, the dishonored (*mánabhrashṭa*) ruler of *Madhura*, the powerful *Turushka*, the *Gajapati* king, and other kings besides these ; who had bound his orders like garlands upon the heads of all the kings as far as the Ganges, and from the eastern to the western mountains ; who had from time to time bestowed with great joy, in strict accordance with the scriptures, numerous charities in Ráme'svara and many other holy places ; who, surrounded with assemblies of the learned, had made the sixteen great gifts in the world ; who continued to multiply deeds of fame which were hymned by all the inhabitants of the three worlds.

By *Tippákshi* and *Nágalá Devi* this king *Nrisimha* had two sons,—as by Kaus'alya and S'ri Sumitra had Das'aratha,—(namely) *Vira Nrisimhendra* and *Krishna Rája* Mahipati, who excelled in bravery and modesty like Ráma and Lakshmana.

Vira S'ri Narasimha, seated on the jewel-throne in *Vijayanagara*, by his fame and policy putting to shame Nriga, Nala, Nahusha and all existing kings ; having drawn to himself the hearts of all people and praised by all the Brah-

* *Tad vams'e Devaki jánir didipe Timma Bhúpatih | yas'asvi Tuluvendreshu Yadoh Krishṇa Raváavaye | tato bhúd Bukkamá jáni Sékhara kshitipálakah || atrá samaguṇa bhrams'am mauli ratṇam mahibhujám | sarasá[illegible] ulabhút tasmán Narasá vanipálakah | Devaki nandanah Kámo Devaki nandanád iva | Káverim ás'u badhvá bahulo jala pathám yo vilanghyava s'atram | jiva gráham grahitva samita bhuja baláttancha rájyam tadiyam | kritvá S'riranga púrvam tad api nijavase paṭṭaṇam yo babháse | kirtti stambham nikháya tribhuvana bhavane stúyamánápadáná | Cheram Cholan cha Páṇḍyam tad api cha Madhurá vallabham mánabhrashṭam | viryodagram Turushkam Gajapati nṛipatim chápi jitvá tadanyán | á Gangá tiram anká pratima charama bhúbhrit aṭántar nitántasyánta kshoṇipatinám srajam iva s'irasá s'ásanam yo vyatánit |*

mans; ruled all kingdoms from the Bridge to mount Méru, and from the eastern to the western mountains.

Every variety of gift had he made in Kanaka Sadasi, in the temple of S'ri Virupáksha (at Hampe), in the city of Kálahasti, in the hill of Venkaṭa (Tripati), in Kanchi, in S'ri S'aila, in S'ona S'aila, in the excellent Harihara, in Ahobala, in Sangama, in S'ri Ranga, in the holy Kumbhakona, in the sin destroying tírtha of Mahá Nandi, in Gokarna, in Ráma Setu (Rámes'vara), and all the holy places in the world, so that they were flooded with streams of the water poured out in making his gifts. The dust raised by the hoofs of the prancing horses which accompanied him covered up the ocean . . .

. . . .

who having made the *túla purusha*, the *go sahasra*, the *hemas'va*, the *hema garbham*, the *kanaka kari ra'ham*, the *pancha langali* * and bestowed them all in gifts; who without leaving a single obstacle had protected all manner of kingdoms and of charitable donations.

At the time when this glorious king went to the abode of Indra (*i. e.* died), then *Víra S'ri Krishna Ráya* Mahipati obtained the wealth of the kingdom, and this mighty lord of heroes put on the jewelled epaulettes (*keyúra*).†

Whereupon, thinking that by the spread on all sides of this king's fame the whole universe would be absorbed, S'iva (to preserve his distinction) made an eye in his forehead, Vishnu took four hands, Brahma took four faces, Káli took an immense sword in one hand and a lotus in the other, Sarasvati held the lute. Who as if in anger lest his enemies should find a refuge on the seas, covered up the seven oceans with the dust from the broken clods thrown up by the prancing of the horses in the hosts of his army; but the water poured out in the presentation of whose numerous gifts of gold, as immeasurable as the Brahmáṇḍa or mount Méru, formed other groups of oceans in their stead. Who in order that his gifts to the poor might not be interrupted, as if to ascend to the world of gods in his bodily form seated in the chariot of the sun, had planted his cloud-reaching pillars of victory in every point of the compass, marking his conquest over all hostile kings. Who had made every kind of gift in Kanchi, in S'ri S'aila, in S'onáchala, in Kanaka Sabha, in Venkaṭádri, and in other meritorious places, having gone round them many times for the sake of good fortune; who had in many temples and sacred bathing places presented

---

* These are in order:—His own weight in gold, a thousand golden cars, a golden horse, a golden womb, a golden elephant and car, five ploughs of gold.

† *Tasmin guṇena vikhyáte kshiter Indre divam gate | tatopyavápi Víra S'ri Krishṇa Ráya mahípatih | bibharti maṇi keyúre vaiśiraka mahíbhuje |*

every variety of offering such as the *kanaka dána*, the *tula purusha*, &c. according to the ancient rites.

Who was an implacable subduer of hostile kings, powerful in protecting the globe placed on the head of A'disesha, the punisher of kings who break their word, the rejoicer of the hearts of the destitute, fierce in war, the king of kings, the supreme ruler, champion over the three kings, a terror to hostile kings, to Hindu rájás a god-like protector, the slayer of the tigers the evil, the champion of heroes, having these and many other titles, *Krishna Ráya* Kshitipati, served by the kings of Anga, Vanga, Kalinga, and many other countries, who humbly address him thus 'O great king, look on us! may you conquer! may you live long!'*—being seated on his jewel throne in *Vijayanagara*; surpassing Nriga and many other kings in his glory, his liberality, his wisdom and policy; who having acquired the wealth of all the lands from the eastern to the western mountains, and from Himavat to the Bridge had multiplied it by bestowal on the indigent and thus built up his fame:—

In the year 1444 of the S'áliváhana era, the year Svabhánu, the month Pushya, at the time of the Makara sankramana, and the Hasta nakshatra, Tuesday, presented on the banks of the holy Krishna, to a Brahman named *Tryambaka*, of the As'valáyana sútra, an ornament of the Vasishṭa vams'a, a follower of the Rik s'ákha, versed in all the vedas, vedánta and ágama; whose nature it was to make all happy, of a form beloved by all, a full moon to the Pushya nakshatra, his heart filled with the praises of Vishnu, having overcome all his enemies (or passions), a chief over all, distinguished by the protection (or embraces) of Párvati;

Presented those ornaments of the great *Ranga Rájya*, of the *Gájanúr* country and of the *Ganga Mandala nád*, celebrated in the world, of great extent, situated to the south of Súlebailu on the *Tungabhadra*, west of Sogane gráma and Ramánáthálaya, west also of Kusukuru, north of Honnahalli;—(namely) the villages famous by the names of *Grámatika*, *Kadabúru* together with its boundaries, and *Mattúru* close to Danáyaka Hosahalli, having also obtained the name of Krishnaráyapura, always filled with crops of grain; together with its four boundaries, free of all imposts; with the rights moreover of *nidhi, nikshepa, páshána, siddha, sádhya*, and *jala*; with the *akshina* and *ágámi* also †; to be held in sole possession, with all the trees, the tanks, the

* *Roshakrita-pratipárthiva-dandah s'esha-bhuja-kshiti-rakshana-'saunda | bháshege tappuva ráyara ganda | stoshakridardhishu yo rana-chandah | rájádhirája ityukto yo rájá-parames'varah | múru-ráyara-gandás'cha para-ráya-bhayankarah | Hindu-ráya-suratráno dushta-s'ardúla-khandanah | vira pratápa ityádi-birudair uchitair yutaih | álokaya Mahárája jaya jívati vádibhih | Anga-Vanga-Kalingádyaih rájabhih sevyate cha yah |*

† See note p. 3

draw wells, ponds, springs, and marsh lands; to be enjoyed by his sons and descendants in regular succession as long as sun and moon endure—with power moreover to bestow it on another, to mortgage or to sell it.*

This he bestowed, surrounded, by his purohitas and numerous wise men famous for their knowledge of the sciences, and of great authority in speech; *Krishna Deva Maháráya*, worthy of reverence from the great, bestowed with great joy, accompanied with the presentation of a gold coin and the pouring of water.

And the same *Tryambaka*, the sacrificer, the head over the chiefs, in the same year and month, and at the same time, bestowed the villages of *Grámatika* and *Kadabúru* on the learned *Hariharárádhya*, the most wealthy of the Kotís'a family, who had reached the farthest shore of the six sciences, excellent in all his qualities, a moon to the sea of Madhavárádhya (*i. e.* his son), of the Apastambha sútra, the Yajus s'ákha and the Harita gótra.

Furthermore to *Aubhala*, the son of Dandobhala, of the As'valáyana sútra the Kas'yapa gotra, and Rik s'ákha, versed in the vedas, a man of high character, he presented *Hosahalli*, *Arekatte*, and *Sangalapura*.

Moreover to the 30 vriṭṭis pertaining to *Mattúr* adding 30 more, he presented them to Brahmans learned in the vedas, whose names are here written :—(*Here follow the names, tribes and families of* 150 *shareholders*).

Its boundaries in the local vernacular :—(*des'a bháshayá*).

[*Some illegible*]

north east, the resting stones at the group of *tagu* trees; east, by the eastern hill; east, the boundary stone of Kadabúru; south east, the image stones at the Sogani village; also south east, Káchina katte, the new mound near Keritahalli and Alagere; south, the . . . banyan tree of Káchina katte; south west, the stream at the boundary of Kusukúru; north west, the Arkéshvara temple at the banyan tree of Yeraka; north, the tamarind tree near the village hedge of S'ikharapura; north east, the grazing lands belonging to the fields of the small tank near S'ikharapura; east, the young pipal tree at Harigi;

. . .

This s'ásana was composed with elegant expressions by the poet *Sabhápati*, at the request of the great king *Krishna Deva Ráya*. And *Víranácháryа*, son of Nallanna, with great joy engraved it.

Of making a gift or-perpetuating one, the perpetuating one is the best. He who makes a gift obtains svarga, but he who perpetuates one obtains final

---

* *Dánasyá dhamanasyápi vikrayasápichockitam.*

beatitude. Whoso by violence takes away land presented by himself or by another shall assuredly be born a worm in ordure for sixty thousand years. Merit is a common bridge for kings. This from age to age deserves your support, O kings of the earth. Thus does Rámachandra beseech the kings who came after him.

S′ri Virupáksha [in Kanarese letters.]

---

136 (vii). Tamra S′asana at Shimoga, date A. D. 1622.

3 Plates, 4 sides.—Nandi Nágari Characters.

Prosperity. Adored be *S′ambhu*, beauteous with the chámara-like crescent moon kissing his lofty head; the original foundation-pillar of the city of the three worlds. May *Ganes′a*, honoured by Indra and all the gods, the all-pervading, continue the protector of the worlds.

While seated on the jewel throne, the king of kings, the glorious, the supreme ruler, a lion in striking down with the powerful strength of his shoulders the groups of hostile kings, *Ráma Deva Mahárája*, a proficient in all learning, was ruling this whole world :—*

Many were the kings who dwelt under his protection, obedient to his commands and eager to promote his greatness. Among whom was a king named *Kenga*, a conqueror over all the kings who were his enemies, with the tears of whose widowed queens the earth was wet. He had a son *Hanumán*, of the highest qualities.

That king having been a donor of all manner of gifts, on a certain occasion, on a lucky day, the thought entered his mind that he would make a gift of land that should bring him good fortune. Accordingly, on the day of his son's marriage, he made a donation with pouring of water, of a village, an ornament to the earth, to the learned *Puṭṭa* of *Vijayi Bilige.*

Devoted was he to the worship of the lotus feet of S′iva, purified in mind by researches in the vedánta, having performed pilgrimages to many holy bathing places, of great liberality so excessive that Karna fled away, of such profundity that even the ocean did not seem to equal him, of the Vis′vamitra gotra the Bodháyana sutra, a follower of the Yajur veda, a chief among the learned, the son of Gangádhara.

---

* *Ratna-simhásanásino-dhiras chanḍa-parákramah rájádhirájas tejasvi yo rája-parames′varah vairi-manḍala-dordanḍa-chanḍa-khanḍana-kesari Ráma Devo mahárájas sarva-s′ástra-vis′áradhah tasmin s′ásati bhúpále dharanim sakalám imám* ||

And in the S'aka year which may be reckoned as *veda*, *ambudhi*, *s'ara* and *dróni* (*i. e.* 1544) the year Durmati, the month Vais'ákha, the third day of the moon's increase, a lucky Saturday,—the Brahman *Puṭṭappa*, a head-jewel to the learned . . . that large village which he had obtained from the great king, situated in the *Sáraga venṭhya*, within the limits of *Gájanúr*, in the *Ganga Manḍala Náḍ*, on the banks of the *Tungabhadra*, whose name was *Pargaha*, worthy of respect from all the learned, whose god was Malles'a Deva, which had another name *Turánkara*, together with its suburb named . . free of all imposts together with its four boundaries, containing many houses and gardens; with the rights of *nidhi*, *nikshepa*, *páshána*, *siddha*, *sádhya*, and *jala*; with the *akshina* and *ágámi* also*; with the beautiful trees, the tanks, the draw wells and ponds; to be enjoyed by sons and descendants in regular succession, as long as their posterity, or sun and moon should endure; with power to bestow on another, to mortgage, sell or exchange†; this the Brahman Puṭṭa, worthy of reverence from the learned, gave, with presentation of a gold coin and pouring of water, to ten Brahmans, having divided it into portions and making ten vriṭṭis. (*Here follow the names, tribes and families of the ten Brahmans.*)

Its boundaries in the language of the country:—east from the bank of Koraluhalli belonging to Lakkena Koppa; west, from the sluice of the Kusankuru tank; south, from the high mound of Kali Koppa; north, the boundary of Honnahalli. Such is the description of the four boundaries.

To this let the sun, moon and other gods be written as witnesses. For a man's character is known to the sun and to the moon, to the fire and to the wind, to the earth and to the sky, to his own mind (or conscience) and to Yama, to day and to night, to morning and to evening, and to justice (*dharma*).

Land presented to Brahmans is to kings as an only sister, neither may she be enjoyed nor ravished away, (otherwise, nor subjected to taxation). Of making a gift or perpetuating one, the perpetuating one is the best: he who makes a gift obtains svarga, but he who perpetuates one obtains final beatitude. Whoso makes a gift has an easy task, the maintenance of another's gift is arduous: but the maintenance of a gift made by another is twice as meritorious as the making a gift oneself: and by the resumption of another's gift all the virtue of one's own donations is destroyed. Merit is a common bridge for kings: this from age to age deserves your support, O kings of the earth. Thus does Rámachandra beseech the kings who come after him.

S'ri Ráma (in Kanarese letters).

---

* See note p. 3.

† See note p. 246.

137 (viii). Tamra S'asana at Shimoga, date A. D. 1672.

1 Plate, 2 sides.— Kannada Characters.

May it be well.—In the year 1594 of the glorious increasing S'áliváhana era, the year Virodhikrit, the month S'ravana, the 15th day of the moon's increase, the day of full moon,—S'rimat *Keladi Somas'ekhara Náyaka* caused the following copper s'ásana to be engraved and given to *Mudda Linga*, the *Tungabhadra* ferryman (*harugola*) and other boatmen (*ambigaru*) at *Simoge*.

You having made a request for some rent-free land (*umbali*); on condition of your keeping a *harugolu* and carrying across the passengers who come daily by the government house (*haveli*) in the Simoge fort, taking from them a fee; and on condition of your providing extra *harugolu* and rendering service to the palace whenever required by the government; we have bestowed upon you 24 pagodas of rent-free land, according to measurement with a line (*rekha pramáṇa*), in the village of *Korlahaḷḷi*, situated in *Gájanúr*.

Whatever rights belong to this land, within the boundary stones set up at the four boundaries thereof, may be enjoyed by you, in accordance with the ancient customs of the country, and the land be held in possession by you and your descendants.

But according to the *nirúpa* formerly written and given by the Karta *S'ivappa Náyakayya*, ... to *Ranga Boya Timma, Sanna Mariya*, and *Mudda* . . . . and to the three persons *Dugga Káḍa, Mogge Timma*, and *Doḍḍa Channa*, who . . . . . to these six we have granted *harugolu* * and *teppa*.†

Such is the copper s'ásana written and given, and thus much may you enjoy, rendering service to the palace.

S'ri Sadás'iva.

---

* *Harugolu*—a round basket boat covered with hides. † *Teppa*—a raft of bamboos.

138 (ix). Tamra S'asana at Shimoga, date A. D. 1714.

3 Plates, 4 sides.—Kannada Characters.

Adored be *S'ambhu*, beauteous with the chámara-like crescent moon kissing his lofty head; the original foundation-pillar of the city of the three worlds.

May it be well.—In the year 1636 of the glorious increasing S'áliváhana era, the year Vijaya being then current, in the month Chaitra, the 15th day of the moon's increase, the day of full moon, the *Badaba Murári koṭi koláhala* (?), the establisher from beginning to end of the *nishiddha* (? forbidden !) veda, devoted to the service of S iva and his gurus, descendant of Srimat *Keladi Sadás'iva Náyaka*, great grandson of *Siddapa Náyaka*, grandson of *S'ivappa Náyaka*, son of *Somas'ekhara Náyaka's* meritorious wife *Channammáji*—S'rimat *Basavappa Náyaka*, made a gift of land to *Timmanna*, of the Kaundinya gotra, the Apastambha sútra and the Yajus shákha; great grandson of Konanna, grandson of Yellanna, son of Bávanna, and younger brother of Yellanna; and caused a dharma s'ásana to be written as follows:—

The land assigned for the expenses of the god Hanumanta which we had set up, and for which we had built a temple in the agrahára established in the name of Mariyappa, in the *Gájanúr* country, in the village of *Gájanúr*, on the banks of the Tungabhadra.

For every 1¾ khandi and 3 mana in the country of Gájanúr and the village of Gájanúr 10 pagodas and 5¼ fanams; for . . .
1 pagoda and 2 fanams; from Dasohalli 3 bága; altogether 12 pagodas, (*and so on, through very minute and tedious details.*)

The balance, amounting altogether to 153 pagodas 7 fanams and 1 viss, have we given to the god; and within the boundary stones stamped with the Vámana mudre, the *ashṭa-bhoga-téjas-svamya* rights of *nidhi*, &c.*; the crops and trees; and whatever may thereon be cultivated, may you and your descendants enjoy, and as long as sun and moon endure carry on the rites of the agrahára temple. Such is the dharma s'ásana of the gift of land.

To this let the sun, moon and other gods be written as witnesses. For a man's character is known to the sun and to the moon, to the fire and to the wind, to the earth and to the sky, to his own mind (or conscience) and to Yama, to day and to night, to morning and evening, and to justice (dharma.)

Of making a gift or perpetuating one, the perpetuating one is the best. He who makes a gift obtains svarga, but he who perpetuates one obtains final

---

* See note p. 3.

beatitude. Land given by oneself should be regarded as a daughter, that given by one's father as a sister, that given by another as a mother; these it is unlawful to take for oneself.

Wheresoever a great yogi abides and devotes himself to the service of S'iva Linga, that spot is equal to all the holy bathing places, there is a man's guru.

S'ri Sadás'iva.

---

139 (x). Tamra S'asana at Tirthahalli, Professed date B. C. 3012.

3 Plates, 4 sides.—Devanágari Characters.

Adored be *S'ri Ganádhipati.* May the four arms of Vishnu protect you, which are as dark as the raincloud; which are hardened with the use of the bow S'árnga and the blows of its bow-string; which are like the pillars of the mantapa of the three worlds.

May it be well.—In the year 89 of the glorious increasing Yuddhishthira era, the year Plavanga, in the month Sahasya (Margashira), on the day of new moon, Wednesday,*— *S'ri Janamejaya Bhúpa*, the great king of kings, the supreme ruler, the valiant among heroes, born in the *Kuru kula*, in the Vaiyagrapípáda gotra,—from his throne in *Kishkindha-nagara*, protecting the various orders and religious ceremonies of all castes, made this gift of land for the worship of *Síta Ráma* adored by Kaivalyanátha, disciple of Garudaváhana Tirtha of the Munibrinda matha, situated in the Vrikodara kshetra, in Sitapura, in the west country.

The four boundaries of the Munibrinda kshetra, in which my great grandfather Yuddhishthira rested, are the following:—on the east, the western bank of the Tungabhadra flowing north; on the south, north of the confluence of streams at Agastya ás'rama; on the west, the eastern bank of the Páshána river; on the north, the south bank of the Bhinna river.

---

* *S'ri jayábhyudaye Yuddhishthire s'ake Plavangákhye ekona-navati-vatsare Sahasya-máse amavásyáyám Saumyaváre s'rimat mahárájádhirája rája-parames'varo vira-pratapa-s'ali Kuru-kulodbhavo Vaiyagrapípáda-gotrajah S'ri Janamejaya bhúpah Kishkindhá-nagaryám simhásanasthah sakala-varnás'ramá-dharma-pratipálakah pas'chima des'asya Sitápura Vrikodara kshetre tatrapi Munibrinda-mathasya Garuda-váhana Tirtha s'rimad s'ishya Kaivalyanáthair árádhita Sita-Rámasya pújártham krita bhúdána-sádhanam asma-prapitámaka-Yudhishthirádishtita-Munibrinda-kshetrasya chatus-sima-parimiti-kramah.*

The Munibrinda kshetra, situated within these four boundaries, do I give of my own free will, in order that my father and mother may attain to the Vishnu-loka, to be enjoyed by you and your disciples in regular succession, as long as sun and moon endure, along with the *tejas-svámya* rights of *nidhi, nikshepa, jala, páshána, akshína, ágámi, siddhi* and *sádhya*.* And this Munibrinda kshetra have I placed in the hands of the Yati, with presentation of a gold coin and pouring of water from the Tungabhadra, in the presence of the god Harihara, at the time of the eclipse (?). †

The witnesses to the confirmation of this s'ásana are sun and moon, wind and fire, sky, earth and water, conscience and mind, day and night, and the two (morning and evening) twilights; these have knowledge of every man's religious gifts.

S'ri Váraha (in Kannada letters.)

Of making a gift or perpetuating one, the perpetuating is the best. He who makes a gift obtains svarga, but he who perpetuates one obtains final beatitude. To protect a gift made by another is twice as meritorious as to make a gift oneself. Land given by oneself is as a daughter, that given by one's father is as a sister, that given by another is as a mother; therefore a gift of land must never be resumed. Dogs will eat what is vomited by any other creature, but not what is vomited by their own species: how much baser is he who resumes a gift himself has made. Whoso by violence takes away a Brahman's vritti, whether presented by himself or by another, shall assuredly be born a worm in ordure for sixty thousand years.

---

140 (xi). Tamra S'asana at Devanhalli, date A. D. 1584.

5 Plates, 8 sides.— Nandi Nágari Characters.

Adored be *S'ri Ganádhipati.* Adored be *S'ambhu,* beauteous with the chámara-like crescent moon kissing his lofty head; the original foundation-pillar of the city of the three worlds. May the right tusk of the Boar form of *Vishnu* like a sceptre protect us, on which forming a small canopy rested the earth, surmounted by the golden peak of Meru. May that glory (*Ganes'a*) be favourable to you, which dissipates the darkness of difficulties, which though in the form of an elephant was not born of an elephant, but is the offspring of Párvati, worshiped by the lion and by Vishnu.

---

* See note p. 3

† *Uparága samaya.*

May that glorious one (Chandra) prevail, who was born from the ocean of milk, an abode of all pleasant things, the pure and excellent. His son was Budha, and his grandson Purúravas; whose son was Ayu, whose son was Nahusha, whose son was Yayáti, whose son was Puru. From his line sprung Bharata, from whom descended S'antanu, in whose line was born the great Arjuna. His son was Abhimanyu, from whom sprung Parikshit.

From him the eighth in descent was *Nanda*, from whom the ninth was *Chalikya*. From him the seventh *S'ripati*. . . . Then came *Bhaira*, an equal of kings; from whom sprung *Bijjalendra*. The tenth in succession from him was *Víra Hammáli Ráya*, from whom the third was *Máyapurisha*.* .

. . . .

. . . . *Sámi Deva nripati* . .

. . . *S'ri Ponnamata nripa* . .

was an ornament among kings, a kalpa-vriksha to the learned, the beauty of his body was such as to draw down the Apsaras from heaven. He took to wife *Balláliká*, in whom all virtues were bound up.

To him was born a son *Ráma Rája* . . . whose crowned queen was *Lakkámbika*.

He had a son named *S'ri Ranga Rája*, who in penance surpassed his father. He obtained as wife the beautiful and virtuous *Tirumalámbika*, in the same manner as Chandra obtained Rohini.

By Tirumala Devi were born to that king three wonderful sons.

The brave *Ráma Rája*, who destroying all the hostile kings throughout the world, was ruling the whole globe after the manner of the primeval kings Bharata, Manu, Bhagirathi and others.

At sight of his liberality the kalpavriksha itself sank down . . .

Tirumala Ráya, who was of great valour, the subduer of many hostile kings, then ruled the world.

He was a chief among the famous, who offering up the fried rice of the fame of his enemies as an oblation in the flames of his own fame, shone forth as the regent of all the points of the compass; who filling the seven worlds with his fame raised it above the peak of Meru and caused it still to grow; who obtained the throne amid the blessings of Brahmans, and ruled all lands.

From whom even the kalpa-vrikshas receiving gifts, and unable to keep pace with the fame of his liberality, retired to do penance on the banks of the heavenly Ganges; who for the sake of merit had made every variety of gift in Kanchi, in S'ri Ranga, in Seshâchala, in Kanaka Sabha, in Ahobala and other

* All this is very doubtful, as well as some other passages, the inscription being too indistinct.

holy places, as well as in many temples and sacred bathing places, the gifts namely of *kanaka dána*, *tula purusha* and others, according to the s'ástras.

His son was *Vis'ákhi*, of great fame and glory, receiving the benefit of the meritorious works performed during a long period by *Vengalámba*, possessing power through the patronage of S'ri Ranga Ráya.

He had two wives, *Tirumala Devi* and *Kalamba*, who shone forth like Lakshmi and Bhúmi the consorts of Vishnu, or as Rohini and Chitra Devi the consorts of Chandra.

The stream of his fame, which took its rise in the liberality of his hands, resembling the beautiful rain-cloud, on the day of his coronation by holy Brahmans according to the sacred rites, flowed into the ten points of the compass; and by it was quenched the fire of the thirst of poverty experienced by the indigent.

S'ri Ranga Raja . . . . . .
a protector alike of his own and the enemy's army, for he granted the latter assurance of peace as soon as they besought it, his fame was in all lands, and by all people he was praised as a great politician. Glorious through the favor of the Lakshmi of heroism, lord of *Aravitipura*, master of all the world resting in the arms of A'diseshа. A chief among kings, as celebrated in the field of battle as Rámabhadra, possessed of many lofty titles, enjoying the benefit of the rites and ceremonies of many classes, foremost among the kings born in the Atreya gotra, of immeasurable fame. Possessed of immense forces of well trained cavalry, reverenced for his learning, receiving obeisance from the Raṭṭa and Magadha kings, like Dharma Ráya a master of politics, lord of *Kalyánapura*, a *Chálikya* emperor, adorned with a crown that was brilliant with rubies. To the (?) *Yeladur* king like an elephant driver, to courtezans an only lover, possessed of many fortunate titles, of a pleasing fame . . . a Manmatha overcome with pleasure-yielding beauty, punisher of kings who break their word, extending his protection over the nine continents. A great king over kings, king of fortune, supreme paramount king, subduer of the three kings, of a fame which towered above Meru, whose eyes were averted from others' wives, a terror to hostile kings, a slayer of the tigers those who asperse others, a *ganda bherunda* to the elephants the hostile kings, a moon to the devout, ... praised with folded hands by the *Kámbhoja*, *Bhoja*, *Kalinga*, *Karahata* and other kings, who salute him saying 'May you conquer, may you live long!'

This *S'ri Ranga Ráya*, a chief among kings, ruling the kingdom seated on his jewel throne; by his fame and policy putting to shame Nriga, Nala.

Nahusha and many other celebrated kings; praised by all the Brahmans from the Bridge (*setu*) to mount Meru; having won the hearts of all from the eastern to the western mountains :—

In the S'aka year reckoned as *anga, ambara, bána, indu* (1506), the year Tárana, the month Kártika, the bright fortnight, on the auspicious day of full moon, during a lunar eclipse;—presented on the banks of the river Pinákini, in the presence of the god S'ri Ráma, an abode of all good fortune, to Brahmans of many various names, s'ákhas, gotras and sútras, famous for their knowledge of the vedas; the village of *Pushpitodupura*, having another name *Baichápura*, situated in *Yelahanka nád* belonging to the *Sivana-samudra* country.

It lies east from the worthy village of Marasamudra, south east of Bisalahalli, south of Varadanapalli, south west of Dukkanapalli, west of Alika, north west of Bettenahalli, north of Surabhishapura, and north east of Kadatanamala gráma.

This fertile region, having watchmen and customs tolls, together with its four boundaries, is presented free of all imposts, together with the rights of *nidhi, nikshepa, páshána, sidha, sádhya*, and *jala;* with the *akshina* and *ágami** also; and along with numerous trees, ponds, draw wells, tanks, springs and gardens; to be enjoyed by many, descending from generation to generation in regular succession, as long as sun and moon endure; with power moreover to give away, sell or exchange.

This, on the application of the famous *Bhairavendra*—great grandson of *Sonna Baira*, who was like Indra a vanquisher of all his enemies, celebrated for his justice, a chief in the fourth race (Súdra), a follower of the fourth s'ákha (!); grandson of the king named *Bhairava*, to whom all his enemies were subject; son of *Baichappa*, an ocean of good qualities; the creator of joy to the eyes of *Náchámba*—did the king worthy of reverence from the learned, *S'ri Ranga Ráya*, surrounded by his *purohita* and other holy persons his friends, and by many learned men travellers through all the veda and vedánta; give, with presentation of a gold coin and pouring of water.

And moreover he divided the village into forty vrittis, which Bhairavendra and the king Baichiya received and distributed in order, to those Brahmans of many s'ákhas, names, gotras and sútras, learned in all the vedas, whose names are here written :—(*Here follow the names, &c., of the* 40 *Brahmans*).

The verses in this s'ásana of the famous *S'ri Ranga Rája*, skilled in policy, a master of peaceful qualities, were by his order composed by the son of Sabhá-

---

* See note p. 3.

pati, a Brahma to poets and their poems. Ganappayáchári, son of Viranna, engraved it on copper, by order of the king.

Of making a gift or perpetuating one, the perpetuating one is the best: he who makes a gift obtains svarga but he who perpetuates one obtains final beatitude. To maintain a gift made by another is twice as meritorious as to make a gift oneself: to resume a gift made by another is to lose the merit of all one's own gifts. Whoso by violence takes away land presented by himself by or another shall assuredly be born a worm in ordure for sixty thousand years. Land given to Brahmans is to kings as an only sister, neither may she be enjoyed nor ravished away (otherwise, nor subjected to taxation.) Merit is a common bridge for kings: this from age to age deserves your support, O kings of the earth. Thus does Rámachandra beseech the kings who come after him.

S'ri Virúpáksha (in Kannaḍa letters.)

---

142 (xii). Tamra S'asana at Devanhalli, date A. D. 1697.

3 *Plates*, 4 *sides.—Kannaḍa Characters.*

(*The same as S'ila S'ásana No.* 114, which see.)

143 (xiii). Tamra S'asana at Kolar, date A. D. 1761.

2 Sides.—Kannaḍa Characters.

May Mallikárjuna Svámi of Guru Parvata be favorable to us.

Sun. Linga. Nandi. Moon.

In the year 1683 of the glorious increasing Sáliváhana era, the year Vishu, the month Chaitra, the 1st day of the moon's increase, Monday :—

May it be well.—*Chikkaṇṇa S'eṭṭi* of *Dyávaráyapaṭṇa* in *Benggalúru*, *Kalasappa S'eṭṭi* of *Aralé-pyáṭe* in *Amrita Ságara*, *Vira S'eṭṭi* of *Mamúli-pyáṭe*, *Ráyanna S'eṭṭi* of *Danḍina-pyáṭe* (cantonment bazaar), with other *Des'adavaru* (Lingayets), both residents and strangers from the highways of the 56 countries; caused the following *dána sásana* (deed of gift) to be written and given to *Giri S'eṭṭi*, son of Malli S'eṭṭi of *Kaṭṭáru parvata* in the *Koḷála* country; for the benefit of the people of the 56 countries :—*

For the grains which are carried to and from *Lála-pyáṭe* and other places, through the Koláḷa country by way of *Búdiguṇṭe*, for each load going either way by the high road and stopping at the *aramane kaṭṭe* (palace custom house), we agree to give 1 *byále*, one byále in words. And this with sincere mind and soul and body, three times repeated with sincere voice, permanently and everlastingly,† to your sons, grandsons and descendants, as long as sun and moon endure, we agree to continue paying. After this manner may you enjoy and remain in comfort; in token of consent and agreement to which, we have written and given you this *dána sásana*.

To this let the sun, moon and other gods be written as witnesses. For a man's character is known to the sun and to the moon, to the fire and the wind, to the earth and the sky, to his own mind (or conscience) and to Yama, to day and night, to morning and evening, and to justice (dharma.)

To protect a gift made by another is twice as meritorious as to make a gift oneself. To seize upon another's gift is to lose all the merit of one's own. Land given by oneself is as a daughter, that given by one's father as a sister, that given by another as a mother; these it is unlawful to take for oneself.

**—munttáda staḷa parastaḷada chetur dhikku aivattáru des'ada bhárámárgada des'adavaru Koḷálada sime Katárru parvatada Malli S'eṭru komárru S'ri Giri S'eṭruvaru aivattáru des'adavarigú bekágiyiruva káraṇá barris'i koḍista dána s'yásanada kramaventendarre | adági |*

†—naḍisi konḍu baraluḷavarru | trikaraṇa s'uddavági s'ri váchaka s'uddavági s'as'vita sároddáravági.

Such is the copper *dána s'ásana*, written by the son of the Doḍḍa Pyáṭe Shánbhog Gopálaiya.

The signatures of the parties to this gift here follow in token of consent (*vapita*). *44 signatures in Kannaḍa.*
2 signatures in Mahratti.

---

144 (xiv). Tamra S'asana at Kolar, date A. D. 1698.

2 Sides.—Telugu Characters.

Sun. Linga. Ganes'a. Nandi. Moon.

May it be well.—In the year 1620 of the victorious increasing Sáliváhana era, the year Bahudhánya, the month Jeshṭha, the 7th day of the moon's increase :—

Prithvi Saṭṭi, and the royal minister *Bháskara*, possessors of garland-like strings of titles made illustrious by the name of each, worshippers of the lotus feet of Ganes'vara and Gauris'vara (Siva), ever striving to subdue the modern sins of *Jambu-dvipa*, abodes of fortune and wealth ; together with other chief *ayyávali* and all the *sálumála*, and those of the 56 countries, both residents and strangers, from the four points of the compass ; namely, from *Gúlúru, Hebbúru, Tumukúru, Kallúru, Kaḍapam, Chitanipalle, Hulikallu, Mágaḍi, Gudcramáranipalli, Solúru, Tyámagonḍla, Bengalúru, Pedda Balápuram, Chinna Balápuram, Galapálya, Jidipalle, Guḍibanḍa, Chillagaṭa, Kadiripanáyinipálya, Birangikottakota, Madalapalle, Kolála, Mulavái, Kottakoṭa, Másti, Bágalúru, Kangondi, Punganúru, Madalapalle, Gunḍugallu, Shivanagalu, Múginàyinikoṭa, Penagonḍa, Varanikotlapalle, Kandigere, Chikanáyinipalle, Huleru, Harati, Hircvúru, Ayamangala, Mattoḍuvu, Bándvaram, Matávaram, Basavanahalli, Hale Jávani, Hosa Jávani, Gabaluru, Upuhalli, Nágamangala, Santtas'ivara, Kundaripi, Nallúru, Malarájyam, Kanchi* and other places ; gave the following general *s'ásana* to the Des'a, *Mudra Virappa* of *Koláta*.

Whereas it was formerly agreed between you and us, that for all loads carried by bullocks or other animals of burthen, coming to Koláta either from the east or the west, we should pay you for grains, areca nut, chillies, spices, cotton cloths, blankets, ghee, oil, sugar and other such articles, at the rate of

4 pagodas for 100 loads according to the Government account; and for salt, or split grains, 2 pagodas for 100 loads according to the same account; and for loads brought by the Korachars, either east or west, 3 fanams 1 byále for 100 loads according to the same account; and for loads of other miscellaneous articles, 1 viss for each load: and you having enjoyed the same:—

And whereas now the Des'adaru from the four quarters assembled at the Yaḍepalli custom house, have agreed to sell their goods wholesale (or in the lot) while the counting is going on; we therefore authorize you either there or at your own place in Kolála to take a certain quantity (indefinite!), which may you enjoy,* and be in comfort, you, your sons, grandsons and descendants, in regular succession, as long as sun, moon and stars endure, bringing fame to this country. Such is the general s'ásana given to you.

To maintain a gift made by another is twice as meritorious as to make a gift oneself. To resume a gift made by another is to lose all the merit of one's own.

Here follow 24 signatures in Telugu.

---

145 (xv). Tamra S'asana at Mulbagalu,† date A. D. 1431.

2 Sides.—Telugu Characters.

S'ri Prasanna Virúpáksha.

Prosperity. May it be well. In the year 1353 of the victorious increasing S'áliváhana era, the year Sadárana, the month Phálguna, the 10th day of the moon's increase; gifts having been made to this god *Prasanna Virúpáksha* of a temple, a wall of enclosure, towers, gilded pinnacles, a Manmatha tank, funds for the decoration, procession and display, agrahára villages, manṭapa, a maṭha for mendicant priests, and for all other sacred purposes; by merit of *Gaja Beṭekára Deva Ráya Maháráya*, son of *Vijaya Ráya Maháráya*: the *Heggaḍe Devas* of the Vishnu Vardhana gotra, the sons of Vommayamma, *Akhana Danáyaka* and *Mádana Danáyaka*, in order to obtain the merit of making gifts and all other kinds of merit, gave to the god *S'ri Prasanna Virúpáksha*, to

---

* *Yi prakáram appaná ichchivunṭimi ganaka á prakáram anubhavista vunṭiri sarinte yipuḍu chatur dikula Des'amváru Yaḍepalle kaṭalo kúḍi níku koneghaṭam amme peṭalo gállúrpupuḍamaṭa níku sari poina stalamandu ainá sari niroḷála staḷamandu ainá sare yi prakáram magamayattu koni &c.*

† Compare with S'ila S'ásana No. 116.

provide for the distribution of food, for illuminations, for daily processions, for fortnightly processions, for monthly processions, for a car festival, and for all other decorations, processions and displays necessary to be performed, the following villages, with pouring of water :—

In the *Muluvai* country, *Virúpákshapura* 1, *Gudehalli* 1, *Suradevihalli* 1, *Mahadevanahalli* 1, *Kudevanahalli* 1, together with the *Kunchibande* well 1. These have we given, along with the *divya bhoga svámya* rights, within the four boundaries of these villages, namely, the *nidhi*, *nikshepa*, *jala*, *taru*, *páshána*, *akshína*, *ágámi*, *siddha*, *sádhya** ; with also all the dues payable in money and all the dues payable in kind.

Such was the meritorious gift offered to the god *S'ri Prasanna Virúpáksha*, by *Akhana Danáyaka* and *Mádana Danáyaka*, the sons of *Vommayamma*.

To maintain a gift made by another is twice as meritorious as to make a gift one's-self. Whoso by violence takes away land presented by himself or by another shall assuredly be born a worm in ordure for sixty thousand years.

---

146 (xvi). Tamra S'asana at Belur, date A. D. 1117.

7 Plates, 12 sides.—Haḷe Kannaḍa Characters.

Ever adored be Kes'ava and S'iva, the givers of rewards, the witnesses of the deeds of men, worshipped by the three worlds.

From Brahma, who sprung from the lotus the navel of Vishnu, was born Atri; from Atri was born Chandra ; his son was Budha ; his son was Purúravas; from Purúravas sprung Ayus, from him Nahusha, from Nahusha Yayati, from Yayati Yadu. In the Yadu line were born many kings.

In this celebrated line there arose a famous king *S'ala*, who in a certain forest being addressed on account of a terrible tiger by a great muni thus, *Poy Sala* (strike, Sala !), from that speech of the muni's obtained his royal name.

Among the *Poysalas*, lords of Dvárávati, possessors of the tiger banner, born in *S'as'apura*, was *Vinayáditya* Bhúpati. Depriving all his enemies and their forces of their living, he caused them to scream out with the blows of the

---

* See note p. 3.

† *Khyáteshu teshu nripatih kathitah kadáchit kas'chit vane munivareṇa S'alah karáṇam s'árddúlakam prahṛi Poy Sala ity ato bhút tasyábhidá muni vachopi chamúra lakshmanı|| tato Dvárávati náthá Poysalá dvípi lánchhanáh játáh S'as'apure teshu Vinayáditya bhúpatih |*

blade of his sword. In giving joy to all the world he was like the moon, in causing all to fear him by his punishments like Yama, in help to the virtuous and in benefit to the world like Krishna, illuminating the circle of the world with the brightness of his fame.

. . . who causing the Lakshmi of victory to settle on the lotus of his white canopy, and the Lakshmi of valour to dance on his powerful arms skilled in smiting down his enemies, made the fame of the king who had punished all his enemies to shine into all the points of the compass.

The *Konkaṇigar* (people of Konkaṇa) he caused to lament and flee, saying "Is this man's sword vowed to the destruction of us all?" thus did he fearlessly ravage them, *Vinayáditya.**

More beautiful than the rays of the moon, the splendour of the milk ocean, or the brightness of Meru, *Keliyabba* was the object of his love.

As the junction of Ganges with the ocean produces merit to all, so the union of these two brought joy to all, for to them was born a son *Ereganga*, celebrated as the crowning-point of those who were embodiments of all good qualities.

When he entered upon the conquest of the northern regions, he first took into his hands the kingdom formerly conquered by *Bhoja Ráya*, chief among the *Máḷava* kings mighty of arm, as if taking the *ápos'ana* (or sip of water) preliminary to a feast. † By the fire of his anger all the country was first scorched and then consumed, which brought to mind the way in which the agniyástra of Ráma caused the ocean to burn. †

Achala Devi, calmer than the sea, and celebrated throughout the world for her virtues, became his queen.

To this queen, pure in descent in both lines, possessed of all the lucky marks, and to this king of virtuous life were born three fortunate sons, *Balláḷa*, *Vishnu* and *Udayáditya*.

Among those who observe the rules appointed by the s'ástras, among those who understand the pure science of the mind, among the learned and the meritorious, they gained the praise of being the foremost, and worthy of the kingdom.

Supreme is *Vishnu Deva*, the favourite of the Lakshmi of great victories, joyfully inclined to the cultivation of dancing and other sciences, delighting in

---

* *Konkaṇigar ivana khaḍgada kankaṇav idu nammanelavo muligisug enutam bhonkolu kedaruvinam nis's'ankam pariyiṭṭan alte Vinayádityam.* ‖

† *Dhárádháro bhujabalavatám Máḷavádhis'varáṇám Bhojenojo vijita ripuṇḍvarddhitá yá prasiddhá sábhúd ápos'ana mahita bhú bhojane yasya púrvam Kauberás'á vijaya samaye varṇṇyáte kim ea virah.*‖

deep conversation in the assembly of those noted for their wisdom, possessor of self-acquired fame which was an ornament to the world. An abode of deep and secret counsels, of so great power, that the tortoise which supports the world unable to bear its burden bent down in impotence leaving the earth to be borne up by the sword wielded by his powerful shoulders. The smoke of his sacrifices ascended in such clouds to heaven that Indra, fearing a rival, made him monarch of the lower world. Devoted to the worship of Vishnu, kind to all, in making gifts and bestowing rewards his hands were an astonishing picture, but in punishing his enemies severe, in all other deeds deserving of reverence from the whole world.

Having by the might of his arms first acquired the wealth of the *Hoysala* kingdom, taking up the circle of the points of the compass, he gained possession of *Talakáḍu* and of *Ganga Rájya*, being the first to rule them, this *Vishnu Bhúpála*, the raiser of the fortunes of the Yadu race.

The Lakshmi of victories gaining great increase by the power of his arms, he burnt the capital city of the *Gangas*, this powerful king *Vishnu* called *Bhujabala Ganga.* *

May it be well.—Entitled to the five great drums, mahá mandalesvara, lord of the city of *Dvárávati*, the gilder of the pinnacle of the *Yadu* race, the foundation-pillar of the lofty mansion of Lakshmi, the unconquered hero, the source of inconceivable victories, having obtained a boon from the goddess *Vásantika*, devoted to the shining lotus feet of Vishnu, his breast covered with the tokens of unsurpassed fortune and glory, engaged in daily increasing works of merit, whose footstool creaked with the weight of the lotus feet on which rested the faces of numerous vassal kings making obeisance before his throne, whose kingdom was cooled by the rays of his white canopy, fanned by groups of *chámaras* which looked like a cluster of favours from Lakshmi, pleased to horripilation at the recital of the valor and refined tastes of the *Sauvira* kings, † his cheeks bright with the rays from his large earrings set with all manner of gems won in victory over his enemies, by his wealth drawing down the divine Indra to gaze upon such glory, his breast adorned with rows of pearls whose radiance spread to his armlets (or epaulettes), given up to the acquisition of

---

* *Modaloḷ Voysaḷa rájya Lakshmi yodavam toḷ balpinim taḷdi tannudayam ranjipe tanna balvodeva . . . miṛe dis'á chakraman ottikonḍu Talakáḍam Ganga rájyakke tám modaládam Yadu vams'a varddhana karam S'ri Vishnu Bhúpálaka ‖ Pingade tóḷuḷu kórvam alangire Jaya Lakshmi lakshmi varddhise suṭṭam Gangara kuṛupina puramam tunga balam Vishṇuvemba Bhujabala Ganga ‖*

† *Sauvira sarasa vira kathá karṇṇan ottirṇṇa harsha pulaka santánanum* |

fame. Filled with benevolence, by the victory obtained in many wars his powerful arms were like the bands of the casket enclosing his world-renowned valour, and his waving sword was as a fetter binding the Lakshmi of victory to himself. His palace resounded with the humming of the bees flocking to the flowers of varied hue bound in the hair of the lovely ones who waited on him. His mind was as peaceful as that of the lady royal policy, like a stage was it for the display of the Lakshmi of valour, or a pleasure garden for her to rest in. Considerate of the welfare of the kings who sought refuge with him, skilled in the art of dancing and in the various modes of music, fond of engaging in argument according to the rules of logic, well trained in the rules of grammar, skilful in examination of the wisdom of the vedas, he was a casket for the gem of his mind, which was honoured by all the puranas. The world being trodden to dust with the troops of his *Kambhoja* horses, having filled space with the groups of his victorious standards, an unequalled thunderbolt weapon in splitting the great rock the *Pándya* king, an adept at the game of war in overthrowing the *Tulu* kings, a Bhairava in destroying the armies of *Jagat Deva*, like Yama in stringing his bow, Váyu in uprooting the brahma tree the king *Narasimha*, the favourite of the yoginis for satisfying the thirst of their lips with the blood from the heads of the *Kala* kings, a garuda in destroying with his sword the serpent the *Vengiri* king, master over *Mala Rája*, a young elephant in breaking through the plantain grove the two armed *Kunta*.

Possessor of the city of *Talavana* acquired by his own might, subduer of the *Konkonga* country, having easily overcome *Nolambavádi*, having gained possession of *Kolálapura*, having uprooted *Kovatúru*, having terrified *Tereyúru*, having passed beyond *Vallúru*, and caused *Kanchipura* to tremble; erector of numerous lofty temples, richly decorated, for *Vijaya Nárayana* out of the wealth acquired by his powerful arms, having filled the whole Brahmánda with his fame, punisher of the *Malapas*, making war accompanied only by veteran troops . . . . conspicuous in valour, S'rimat *Tribhuvana Malla Bhujabala Víra Ganga Vishnu Varddhana Poysala Deva*, protecting in the shelter of his mighty arms all the region lying between the *padiya* (lower) ghat of *Nangali* on the east; *Kongu*, *Cheram*, *Anamale* on the south; the *Bárakanúr* ghat road of *Konkana* on the west; and *Sávimale* in the north :— *

---

* *Kámbhoja váji ráji sancharana tarala dharaní valayanum | vijaya kadaliká kadamba chhumbita viyal valayanum | Pándya ganda s'aila nirbbhedanákáladambholiyum | Tulu nripála hridaya vilalana prakata rana keliyum | Jagad Deva bala vilaya bhairavanum | adiyam ávalepa rúpa lopa nipuna chápanum | Narasimha brahma bhúja bhanja prabhanjananum | Kalapá*

While—along with his queen;—May it be well. Beautified with all the marks indicative of fortune, a collection of all grace, a Lakshmi sprung from the milk ocean of *Balipura*, pure with an unspotted life, like the rays of the moon in raising the tide of love in *Vishnu Varddhana's* breast, like a bough of the kalpa vriksha to the learned men and others attendant on her, of a beautiful lotus face from which issued the nectar of excellent, pure, pleasing and seasonable words, having great joy in worshipping the lotus feet of *Párvati*, her mind stored with knowledge as the womb of the earth is with gems, whose sidelong glances resembled the playful waves of the salt ocean, a crowning ornament of finished dancers, an amulet (or talisman) in preserving domestic order, to her fellow queens as a raging elephant, distinguished by these and many other titles: S'rimat *Piri Arasi* (chief queen), *Paṭṭa Mahádevi* (crowned queen) *S'ántala Devi*:— *Vishnu Varddhana Poysala Deva*, from his palace in the great city of *Veldpura*, was ruling the kingdom in peace and wisdom:—

In a lofty pile,* adorned with all the signs of fortune, resembling the science of grammar for it too was based upon sútras (otherwise lines); resembling the vedas for the number of feet in each line was fixed; resembling the wearer of the moon (S'iva) in being adorned by Párvati (otherwise rare and large stones); resembling the Tri Vikrama avatára in prevailing by great strides (otherwise rising up directed by skill); resembling the four-faced (Brahma) who sprang from the lotus (this was an abode of Lakshmi who loves the lotus); resembling Devendra (who has a thousand eyes) in dazzling the sight; resembling the great chains of mountains built up from the beginning on a firm foundation; resembling a lake shining with water-lilies; resembling Kailása in being marked with the footprints of S'iva's bull (otherwise spots favorable to works of merit); in being free from the quality of támas (otherwise darkness); in being filled with pillars; in being free from the quality of rajas (otherwise dust); in being of great reputation; in being free from the

---

laka pálacha. ka s'oṇitápántushṭa yogini manoranjananum | Bengiri bhujanga bhanga kara khaḍga khaga rájanum | Mala Rája rájanum | irundoḷ kunta kadali vana vidalana karála s'unḍálanum | átmikrita Taḷavanapuranum | angikritá Kon Konga vishayanum | avalambita Noṇambavádiyum | úrikṛita Koḷálapuranum | unmúlita Kovatúranum | uttaraḷita Tereyúranum | ullanghita Vallúranum | utkampita Kánchipuranum | bhujabaláwashṭambha sambhúta vitta vrachita vichitra vijaya Náráyaṇottunga bhavanum | yas'ah prasara paripúrṇna padmajánḍanum | Maḷaparoḷu ganḍanum | subhaṭa samarakeḷiloḷanum | . : . munniṛivanum s'auryyam Meṛavanum enisida s'rimat Tribhuvana Malla Bhujabaḷa Vira Ganga Vishṇu Varddhana Poysaḷa Devaru múḍalu Nangaliya paḍiya ghaṭṭa | tenkalu Kongu Cheram Anamale | paḍuvalu Konkaṇada Bárakanúra ghaṭṭa vádi | baḍagalu Sávi male yindoḷagáda bhúmiyam bhujabaḷávashṭambhadim parıpálisuttam.||

* All the similes in this passage involve a play upon the words.

quality of satva (otherwise ?) in being filled with lions and elephants (among the decorations); in being easy of access resembling the sea in its deep and peaceful interior ; resembling mount Meru the resting place of Dhruva Ráya (having large chambers); resembling the circle of the moon in being filled with nectar (otherwise mortar); resembling the sun . . . ; resembling the sky adorned with stars (otherwise gems); adorned with numerous gilded pinnacles, towering up in innumerable storeys :—

Having with pious faith set up the god *Vijaya Náráyana*, from the white lotus of whose navel sprang Brahma the creator of the worlds, the brother to Balabhadra whose power was exhibited in the flood of the river Yamuna turned back by the plough-share held in his mighty hands, whose breast covered with the round shining drops which fell upon it when the amrita was churned out resembled the sky adorned with stars, who in his boar form separated the waters of the ocean with a kick of his toe-nail and danced on the muddy floor of Pátála, who was the ally of the *Pándavas* in releasing the world from its burden of giants, who as Tri Vikrama compassed the earth in a stride going up the running creeper which sprung up from the presentation water poured out by Bali, who as Devendra by various means destroyed the race of cruel rákshasas, who in the form of a tortoise took up the Mandara mountain which the world was unable to bear up when the gods and goddesses were churning, in whose capacious interior are enclosed all living things, glorious though his form is unknown, near and yet distant, absent yet ever present, deep and yet lofty, minute and yet immense, easy of approach, ever profoundly peaceful, limited and yet infinite, in the form of Param Brahma :—

Vishnu Varddhana Poysala Deva, in the S'aka year 1039, the year Hevilambi, the month Chaitra, the 5th day of the moon's increase, Monday; in order to provide for the daily service, the divine decoration, and the ceremonies of the three watches of the gods S'ri *Vijaya Náráyana*, S'ri *Channa Kesava* and S'ri *Lakshmi Náráyana*; for the support of S'ri Vaishnavas, of Brahmans, of learned men to write the prayers and songs, of garland makers, of dancing girls for illumination, and of all kinds of temple servants; presented with all due rites, the *kirukula*, together with the temple dues of god and goddess,* and the customs and tolls within the four boundaries of the vrittis (or shares) he had made and presented with pouring of water at the

* *Devi devana káṇike sahita | s'ri pádadalli dhárá púrvakam máḍida vritti Vélápurada biḍu chatus síme sunka pannáya sahita |*

sacred feet from the waste land of *Velapura* ; 12 dwelling houses (?) in Devalige nád ; *Basavanahalli* in that nád ; in Kodigi nád 12 *bárasi* (?) ; *Nidugunda* with its villages ; in Abbidore Tagere nád 2 *hasudegalu* (?) with villages ; in Balavi nád . . . . . . *Agalúru* . . . ; in Yamana nád 12 *morasu* (?) ; in *Beku nád*, *Kesakad* with its villages ; in Vyasa nád, *Bodagere* and *Banteyanahalli* ; in those two náds united, *Devanúru* with its four boundaries ; in *Hiriya Muguli* 5 vrittis ; these, with all the taxes, he presented with all obeisance at the holy lotus feet of him who performed the Tri Vikrama avatár. And also certain monies and the offerings of the pious, he assigned for repairs of any cracks or injuries to the temple.

Moreover, besides these, S'ri *Vishnu Varddhana Poysala Deva*, reckoned as the eleventh incarnation, in order to perpetuate his government and extend his dominion, presented the following lands, with observance of all due rites, in the presence of the god S'ri *Vijaya Náráyana*, to 120 Bhattas who should perform the great sacrifices, the oblations and offerings, *Hiriya Muguli* with *Bikanahalli*; to 21 Bhattas *Beneyúru* and *Areyahalli* with *Kelayabehalli*; to 32 S'ri Vaishnavas *Nittúru* in Tagere nád.

Adored be Náráyana.

(*The following appears to be a different grant, made subsequently*).

His son, the chief king of the Yadu race, of great fame, his valour his wealth, a lion in destroying the elephants the kings who forsake works of merit and walk in their own ways, was *Narasimha*.

From him, by his crowned queen (*patta mahádevi*) *Achala Devi*, was born the great king *Ballála*. He was a great hero, dispersing the darkness which had covered up works of merit he caused them to shine forth, delighting in the nectar which issued from the lotus feet of the god Kes'ava. Like as S'iva set up Kailása which Das'amukha was in the act of bearing away on his shoulders, so establishing many works of merit which had been swept away in the rapid stream of the Kali yuga. Chief of the wrestlers in the field of battle is *Víra Ballála Bhúpa*. May the king Ballála prevail, the protector of the whole world, to the white lotus of whose fame the world was as the ovary (!) . . . shining as the enchanter of enchanters, his doors securely fastened, his lodges filled with guards and archers, his ramparts high, surrounded with a moat—the lake named Vásudeva tírtha. Being the favourite of Vijaya Náráyana, he gained the empire of the south ; the champion who took *Uchchingi*, which in length and breadth can be compared within the limits of the lower world to a second sky alone, and was celebrated in the three worlds ; and afterwards, when *Pándya* cast himself on his protection, restored him his kingdom ; thus both in destroying and in protecting was he greatly celebrated this *Vira Balláḷa Deva.**

To maintain a gift made by another is twice as meritorious as to make a gift one-self: he who makes a gift procures svarga, but he who maintains one secures final beatitude. Merit is a common bridge for kings: this from age to age deserves your support, O kings of the earth. Thus does Rámachandra beseech the kings who come after him.

The writing of *Baravaráchárya Súrya.*

Adored be Náráyana. Great prosperity. Fortune.

Víra Balláḷa Deva, the chief among the *Maldpas,* . . . (gave) *Kadala* with its villages . . . . .

(*Another grant, made in* (?) *A. D.* 1235,)

In the year Ananda, the month Chaitra, the 5th day of the moon's increase, Sunday, *Nárasinga Deva,* the son of S'rí Víra Pratápa chakravarti S'ri Víra Somes'vara Deva, presented to the god *Channa Kes'ava* of Belúru, the village of *Chikka Go* . . . situated in Nekku náḍu, with pouring of water. Great prosperity.

The chief among the Malapas, S'ri Víra Somes'vara (*? signature*).

---

146 (xvii). Tamra S'asana at Belur, date A. D. 1382.

5 Plates, 8 sides.—Devanágari Characters.

The s'ásana of the dues to be given to the god Kés'ava of *Velúr* . . the great minister *Mudaya Danḍanáyaka.*

May it prosper. Adored be *S'ambhu,* beauteous with the chámara-like crescent moon kissing his lofty head; the original foundation-pillar of the city of the three worlds. When Vináyaka seized on the disk of the rising sun, taking it for a red gourd, his proboscis, resembling the stem of an opening lotus, was as brilliant as the rays of the sun.

May the lord Kes'ava be favorable to your prosperity, the lord of *Belanagara,* adorned with splendid garments, the chief jewel in the crown of the *Hoysala* kingdom. *S'ri Hari. Om.*

---

* *S'ri vijayádi s'abda viḷasan Náráyaṇang oldu kalvasadim tenkaṇa chakra máḷisidam i Balláḷa bhúpálakam | ataḷim pátáḷavenṭum desegaḷ agaladind uddadim vyomadind irvageyágalu perchchi múṛum bhuvanadoḷ esev Uchchingiyam konḍa ganḍam maguldum Pánḍyam s'araṇ bokkaḍa karuṇisi tad rájyamam koṭṭu múṛum jagadoḷu vikhyáti vettu haraṇa bharaṇadim Vira Balláḷa Devam |*

Chandra was a sovereign whose orders were worn by all kings as their crowns. From the ocean of that Soma vams'a sprang *Bukka* Mahipati. Under the rule of Nala, Nahusha and other kings the earth was *rájavati* (tending towards a good king), but when Bukka reigned it became *rájanvati* (possessed of a good king.)

To this *Bukka Ráya,* whose fame was like a pure lotus of unequalled fragrance and filled with nectar which opened to all the points of the compass, and on which the sky rested like a bee, was born a son, *Harihara,* the raiser of the fortunes of his house, resembling in ability Kumára, the son of S'iva. An ocean of morality, his dictates none were able to transgress, and the regions under his rule none were able to trespass upon.

He conquered *Chola*, *Kerala* and *Páṇḍya*, obtaining a fame in the South, which was a mirror to his lotus face. His victorious expeditions, though made when the sun is brightest, caused the days to appear ever cloudy to the *Yavanis* (the wives of Muhammadans) through their blinding tears. O wonder! Even the kalpa and other bountiful trees did not obtain so great a praise from people, for he excelled the kalpa vriksha, the Earth and mount Meru, each in its chief characteristic.

As Ráma had Sumantra, so he had a minister *Muda Dandes'a*, who had been his father's adviser, and had with ease subjected all his enemies. He put to shame Yugandha in obtaining for his master the decoration of numerous chains of precious stones; and invading the territories of many powerful kings, stopped them in their haste to get away, and seized them alive (as a snake charmer does a snake). The agrahâras he had presented were as ornaments on the face of the ladies the points of the compass, and like garlands of perfect pearls the Brahmans in them. The little lakes of the fears of those against whom he marched were absorbed in the dust thrown up by his armies, and they lost themselves in the great ocean of his fame.

To him, thus upholding the laws broken through by other kings, and protecting his subjects as his children, all the cultivators and merchants, with great joy, agreed to pay taxes as in the days of Bharata.

That all may understand, the particulars of these are here written in the Karṇáṭa language.

In the S'aka year 1304, the year Dundubhi, the month Kártika, the 10th day of the moon's decrease, Sunday; May it be well . . . .

. . . . praised throughout the world, chief of men, . . . as Devendra to all the points of the compass, five hundred *vira s'ásana* distinguished by all good qualities, beautiful with a virtuous life, incarnations of heroism, possessed of justice, humility and wisdom, protectors of the Banajigas of the four quarters . . . . .

promoters of fruitful works of merit, greatly reverenced, of strong patience, favorites of the mistress fame, exalted by the fortune of being distinguished descendants in the line of Baladeva and Vasudeva in the race of the moon, lords of *Ahichhatra*, men of virtue, men of prudence and discrimination, first of heroes, revered by all, superintendents of all the works of merit and demerit in the southern Varanás'i, abodes of all virtues, a capital for great kings, the birth place of many people, the fragrance of the jasmin, with these and other titles, worshippers at the lotus feet of the gods Ganes'vara and Gaures'vara: from *Vijayanagari*, *Hastinávati*, *Dorasamudra*, *Gutti*, *Penagundi*, *Adabani*, *Udayagiri*, *Chandragiri*, *Muluváyi*, *Kanchi*, *Padavidda*, *Chadurangapaṭna*, *Mangalúru*, *Bárakúru*, *Honnávara*, *Chamsháura*, *Araga*, *Chandragutti*, *Arsikere*, *Huligere*, *Nidugallu*, *Chimatanakallu*, *Tarigekallu*, *Janani*, *Sarikaṭṭe*, *Tilakalámbi*, *Singapaṭṭana*, and other places, the pettas under their control; all the cultivators (*halaru*), the companies of merchants, the *mummuri daṇḍa*, and all the receivers of village dues (the village servants) .

. . . .

having assembled in the presence of the two lotus feet of the god *Virupáksha*, and set up the diamond chámaras, having seated themselves and come to a common agreement:—To *Mudaga Daṇḍanáyaka*, the *mahá pradhána*, the promoter of merit in the Kali yuga, the upholder of justice, the doer of virtue, being appointed for the management of the affairs of the 56 countries, we have with great joy presented the *Prithivi Sheṭṭi-ship* (mayoralty of the kingdom) and the *Dundu svámya* (the dues payable by each class).

The annual dues are as follows: Immovable property: for light assessment villages 1 *byále* per *gadyána*, for villages cultivated on half share, 1 *byále* per *gadyána* according to the rent payable in money; for rice and grain 2 *bala* per *khanḍuga* for government and private shares united. Particulars of the dues payable on grain carried by pack bullocks: for the *nava ratna* (? nine kinds of grain) 2 *fanams* per *gadyána* reckoned on the price. Perfumes: fresh camphor 1 *hága* per *kuruju*; *panne* (?) 1 *byále* per *kuruju*; musk 1 *byále* per *tola*; the red flower *crocus sativa*, 1 *hága* each; dark sandal chips 1 *aḍḍa* per *tola*; sandalwood 1 *hága* per *tola*, ...
wedding cloths 1 *visá*; white cloths 80 pieces to a *malavi*, 1 *aḍḍa*; silk cloths 1 *aḍḍa* per . . raw silk, 1 *hága* per *tola*; spun cotton 1 *aḍḍa* per *malavi*; cotton 1 *hága* per *malavi*; wool, 1 *hága* per *malavi*; sack cloth 1 *visa* per piece (*paṭṭe*); rugs and carpets 1 *hága* per *malavi*; pal-

myra leaves (for writing upon) 1 *hága* per *malavi*; *góni* 1 *hága* per *malavi* of pieces. Grains : for these six kinds, *nellu*, *jola*, *rági*, *navane*, *baragu* and *sáve*, 1 *byale* per load. Split grains : *godhi*, *kaute*, *ellagase*, *kusabe*, *hesaru*, *uddu*, *togari*, *huruvalli* and other pulses, 1 *hága* per load. A load of rice 1 *byále*; a bullock load of untaxed grain from other countries 1 *hága*; a load of buffalo ghee 1 *aḍḍa*; a load of salt 1 *byále*; a load of jaggory 1 *hága*; a load of sugar 1 *aḍḍa*; a load of areca nut 1 *hága*; a load of betel leaves for chewing 1 *hága*; a load of chillies 1 *aḍḍa*; turmeric, garlic, cummin seed, fenu greek, mustard . . 1 *hága* . . . . 1 *hága* per cartload; green ginger . . . . . per load; dye seeds 1 *hága* a load; all other kinds of seed 1 *hága* a load; . . . .

Betel vines 1 leaf daily per row; areca nut trees 1 nut daily for each line; timber 1 *byále* a cart load; straw and firewood 1 *byále* a cart load; . . . . . Country bred horses 1 *byále* a *gadyána*; elephants 1 *hága* per *gadyána*; camels 1 *byále* a *gadyána*; female servants 1 *byále* per *gadyána*; carts 1 *byále* per *gadyána*; bullocks 1 *byále* a head; buffaloes 1 *hága* a head; goats, sheep and other such cattle 1 *visa* according to the excise rate; servants 1 *hága* a year for each person; chargers of the troopers 5 *pana* a year for each horse; great officials, from 10 up to 100 *honnu*; field slaves (*jitgara*) 1 *pana* a year for each; . . . . .

These various dues whoso desires happiness will pay. Whoso opposes and refuses . . . . . baser than the lowest menials.

Virtue is of more merit than a thousand horse sacrifices.

(Signatures in Kannaḍa characters.)

Sálu Múleyavaru.

S'rí Ganes'vara Navares'vara Devaru.

---

147 (xviii). Tamra S'asana at Belur, date A. D. 1262.

5 *Plates*, 8 *sides.—Devanagari Characters.*

May the boar form of Vishnu protect, who smiling beheld Lakshmi mount upon the world, taking it for a budding lotus, when, supported on his long tusk resembling the stem of a lotus in the lake, it sparkled with the play of its ocean waves.

From the lotus navel of Vishnu, whose locks were illuminated by the rays of the jewels in the thousand heads of the serpent on which he reclines, issued Brahma, the creator of all things movable and immovable, on whose countenance Sarasvaṭi dwells, a female swan in a group of lotuses. Then was born the possessor of the bow and arrows composed of flowers (Manmaṭha), adored by all the groups of deities. From Brahma's mind came forth a son Atri, resembling S'iva save in his three eyes, of great wisdom. From him sprung Chandra, a friend to the ocean in raising its tides, a crest jewel to S'iva the enemy of the three cities (of the rakshasas) and the guru of the world. Since Budha was born to Chandra, Manmaṭha wanders over the world discharging his arrows at random.

In this fortunate race was born Yadu, chief of the mighty, illuminating all the points of the compass with the increase of his fame. Then was born the king *Sala*, who purified all the points of the compass, washing them clean with the great ocean of his fame . . .

He, once on a time, being in *S'as'apura*, going to pay adoration to *Vasantika* the goddess of his family, drew near to a rishi abstracted in penance, when a tiger appeared. Enraged at seeing them, its eyes glaring forth like flames, its waving tail lashing all the points of the compass, its claws as sharp and long as razors, it roared upon the muni. On this, the muni saying in the Karṇáṭa language '*Hoy Sala*', gave him an iron rod, with which he quickly slew the tiger. Afterwards, the tiger having obtained svarga (!), its eyes being closed in rage, it became the sign on the banner of all the kings of that race. All his descendants also from that saying were called *Hoysalas*, just as from *Yadu* they were formerly called *Yádavas*.

In that race was born *Vinayáditya*, who with his hands caused the lotus of the world to open. From him was born the king *Ereyanga*, flooding the earth with the water dropping from the temples of his towering lusty elephants, a great victor in the field of battle. From him was born *Vishnu*, who seemed as if his own original (or a divine incarnation), protector of all the world, surpassing by his valour the fame of Indra's conquest of the points of the compass. From him was born *Narasimha*, who reduced all his enemies to servitude with the unsparing edge of his sword, and fulfilled the desires of all who sought his bounty.

His son was *Ballála*, whose enemies are even to this day thrown into a fever on hearing his name whispered in their ears, whom his subjects have not yet forgotten as the granter of all their desires, with whose fame the heavenly Ganges still contends for the superiority, renowned for his destruction of the *Mallas* of the hill forts (*giri durga*).

From him was born *Nrisimha*, possessor of no less fortune than his father, an abode of all good qualities, honored beyond even his own desires, a lion skilled in striking down the elephants his enemies. When he became king, the earth brought forth on all sides without sowing, not forced by labor but through love of his goodness. His sword, which was stained with the brains of mighty and powerful kings beheaded by him, he cleansed in the river of the blood of elephants, camels . . . . and by bringing forth the *Chola* king who had been overwhelmed under the clouds of dust raised by the march of hosts of enemies, and setting him up again in power, gained great renown, as the setter up of the Chola king, the overthrower of the Páṇḍya king. The whole region in front of his fields of battle was strown with elephants, horses, and footmen . . . . . .

His son was *Soma*, who churned the ocean of his enemies with the Mandara mountain of his right arm, whose valour laughed at that of gods and Daityas. Through fear of him all kings left their thrones—terrified by the tramping of the troops of his lines of horse, by the twanging of his powerfully drawn bows, by the war cries of his hosts, by the dreadful sound of his great drums which burst open the doors of the hearts of his enemies—and concealed themselves in forests, living in huts made of branches, or in the hollows of trees. His chief queen was *Bijjali*, an abode of all pleasure, adorned with all rare qualities, a jewel among women, an ornament to the world, to move in the neighbourhood of the brightness of whose toe-nails made the wives of other kings honorable (!); she shone like the moon in the rays of her moonlight fame.

To her was born the king *Nrisimha*, whose gifts put to shame the kalpavriksha, whose possessions put to shame Devendra, whose fame put to shame the heavenly Ganges, whose increasing wisdom put to shame Brihaspati the guru of the gods, whose power put to shame S'iva with the bull for his vehicle, an eye in his forehead and terror in his decrees, an abode of all good qualities. Which king *Narasimha* was as a banner of victory to the three worlds ; when his heart was set upon war with mighty enemies, the courtezans of svarga at once decked themselves for the crowd of kings who would fall before him. Which king in the field of battle bursts through and through the lines of elephants, cutting in pieces horses and horsemen, breaking into fragments the groups of chariots on which are mounted valiant warriors, whose heads he smites off. Who with great joy fulfills the desires of all, whose sharp sword-edge is a creeper spreading into all the world, this *Narasimha* is supreme ruler of all the earth, a lion to the herds of elephants his enemies.

Of a pure and marvellous career, entitled to all honors in the highest degree, like the rays of the sun in dispersing the darkness his enemies, *Narasimha* Mahipála, whose dominion was like the earth surrounded by the ocean, whose pair of lotus feet were brightened as in an illumination by the rays from the thick set jewels on the crowns of his tributary kings, dwelling in his own *Hoysala* country, in the royal city of *Dorasamudra*, an abode of all fortune, in the kingdom bestowed upon him with affection by his father and filled with all royal wealth :—

In the S'aka year 1184, the year Durmati, the month Chaitra, the 12th day of the moon's increase, Monday, gave, at the time of making various gifts, the village named *Bellúru*, belonging to the *Kalkuni* country, together with its well known boundaries, and the associated villages, and with the *ashta-bhoga-tejas-swámya* rights of *nidhi*, *nikshepa**, *taṭáka*, *árama*† and all other rights.

There was a valiant commander *Vishnu*, an ocean to the gems of fortune and fame, related to the friend of the ocean (Chandra, *i. e.*, he was of the lunar race). He had a wife La . . . an abode of all good qualities, as devoted to him as moonlight to the moon, skilled in drawing to her the hearts of all. From him was born the commander *Perumála*, a Yama to the groups of proud enemies, by his liberality outvying the emperor Bali, in justice Dharma Ráya himself, whitening the world with the brightness of his pure unequalled fame. His form, pure as the rays of the moon, gave joy to all, his fame purified the three worlds like the stream of the heavenly Ganges, his speech was as the breeze from the *Maleya* mountains rejoicing the hearts of the weary, a chintámani to all who sought his bounty.

To this *Perumála*, an abode for the love of Ráma and Krishna, in the constant enjoyment of Lakshmi, born in the Atri-vams'a, a great favorite with his sovereign, *Narasimha* Mahipati presented the village of *Bel'úru* for the purpose of making it an agráhara.

And that *Perumála* Daṇḍanátha, naming that village *Hoysaḷa Narasimhapura*, and forming it into 86 vrittis, gave it with pouring of water to Brahmans of many gotras, versed in the Rig, Yajus, Sama and Atharva vedas with the vedangas, and pandits in all branches of learning.

The particulars of this, to the same effect, are given in the Karṇáṭa language, that all may understand.

May it be well.—The protector of all lands, praised by all the learned, the abode of all good qualities, the favorite of earth and fortune, impossible to be possessed by fear or avarice, the king of kings, the supreme ruler, lord of

---

* See note p. 3. † *Taṭáka*, ponds: *aráma*, groves.

the city of *Dvárávati*, the sun in the sky of the *Yádava* race, a crowning ornament to the wisest, king over the *Male* rajas, remover of the distresses of those who take refuge with him, of a brilliant fame resembling the dazzling thunderbolt, a *ganda bherunda* to the chief of the *Maleyas*, the invincible hero, a sun to the darkness his enemies, the sole champion of the world, the hero of the field of battle, obtainer of fortune on S'anivára (?), wise as Brihaspati, *Malla* (wrestler) of the hill forts, splitter open of the hearts of his enemies, in war a Ráma, in conflict a Bhima, a lion to the elephants his enemies, opener of the waterlily of the Yádava race by the moonlight of his bounty, destroyer of the *Magara* kingdom, setter up of the *Chola* kingdom, overthrower of the *Pándya* kingdom, *Nissanka Pratápa Chakravarti Hoysala Bhuja Bala S'ri Vira Narasimha Devarasa*;

In the S'aka year 1184, the year Durmati, the month Chaitra, the 12th day of the moon's increase, Monday; presented the vritti *Bellúru* of Bellúru in *Kalukuni* nád, and the villages on that channel, *Hálehálu*, *Mávinakere*, *Godiyahalli*, *Honakodanahalli*, *Ariyahalli*, *Kavunakote*, *Nelligere*, *Devahalli*, *Koppa*, *Genasamudra*, *Náyakittiyahalli*, *Kaliveya Sitakareyakere*, *Bommakkana Mádiyahalli*, *Chakkana Kodiyahalli*, *Yeriyahalli*, *Kasavanakatte*, *Dásanahalli*, *Kareyahalli*, *Nerilakere*, *Duggadoddanahalli*, *Yelaparatigere*, *Kariyajiyanahalli*, *Belakalli*, and *Migoyahalli*, these being the principal, together with the well known boundaries, and (*here follow a number of detailed measurements and dues thereon payable from the above*) (presented) to his dear friend (*manomitra*) *Perumála Dandanáyaka*, with pouring of water, for the purpose of making an agrahára, together with the *ashta-bhoga-tejas-swamya* rights of *nidhi*, *nikshepa*, *tatáka*, *aráma* and all other rights.*

May the gift made by the king *Narasimha* endure as long as the earth and mountains, as the sun and moon.

To tax a rent-free village is to incur the guilt of slaughtering a crore of cows: removing the taxes laid on a village will procure the highest heaven. Of making a gift or perpetuating one, the perpetuating one is the best: he who makes a gift obtains svarga, but he who perpetuates one obtains final beatitude. Whoso usurps a gift made by himself or by another shall assuredly be born a worm in ordure for sixty thousand years. Merit is a common bridge for kings: this from age to age deserves your support, O kings of the earth. Thus does Rámachandra beseech the kings who come after him.

Great prosperity attend it. Fortune.

S'ri Vira Narasimha Devasya.

* See note p. 273.

148 (xix). Tamra S'asana at Eelur, date A. D. 1278.

3 Plates, 4 sides.—Devanágari Characters.

May the boar form of Vishnu protect, who smiling beheld Lakshmi mount upon the world, taking it for a budding lotus, when, supported on his long tusk resembling the stem of a lotus in the lake, it sparkled with the play of its ocean waves.

From the lotus navel of Vishnu, whose locks were illuminated by the rays of the jewels in the thousand heads of the serpent on which he reclines, issued Brahma, the creator of all things movable and immovable, on whose countenance Sarasvati dwells like a female swan in a group of lotuses. Then was born the possessor of the bow and arrows composed of flowers (Manmatha), adored by all the groups of deities. From Brahma's mind came forth a son Atri, resembling S'iva save in his three eyes, of great wisdom. Afterwards from the eyes of Atri issued Chandra. In whose line was born Yadu, chief among the mighty.

Afterwards was born *Sala*, an ornament to all the line. He being in *S'as'ipura*, was doing obeisance to the rishi in the temple of the goddess *Vasantika* in the forest, when a tiger came forth filled with rage; which that king, who was as brave as a lion, speedily slew, the rishi having said to him in the Karnáta language "*Hoy Sala*", and given him an iron rod.

The tiger then obtained svarga, its eyes still open with rage. And it became the sign on the banner of all that line.

In that race was born *Vinayáditya*, a great king, who with his arms caused the lotus of the world to open.

Then was born *Ereyanga*, flooding the earth with the water dropping from the temples of his towering lusty elephants, a great victor in the field of battle. From him was born *Vishnu*, a protector of all the world, an abode of all justice, who speedily subdued all inferior enemies and seized their kingdoms. From him was born *Narasimha*, from whom was born *Víra Ballála*, reverenced throughout the world. From him was born *Narasimha*, who set up the *Chola* king, and thereby gained great renown.

From him was born *Soma*, whose power laughed at the gods and rákshasas, who had churned the ocean of his most powerful enemies with the Mandara mountain of his right arm. His chief queen was *Bijjali*, an abode of all pleasure, adorned with all rare qualities, a jewel among women, an ornament to the world, to move in the neighbourhood of the brightness of whose toe-nails made the wives of other kings honorable (!) ; she shone like the moon in the rays of her moonlight fame.

She bore the king *Nrisimha*, whose gifts put to shame the kalpa-vriksha, whose possessions put to shame Devendra, whose fame put to shame the heavenly Ganges, whose increasing wisdom put to shame Brihaspati the guru of the gods, whose power put to shame S'iva with the bull for his vehicle, an eye in his forehead and terror in his decrees, an abode of all good qualities. Supreme is *Narasimha*, the ruler of the world, a lion to the herds of elephants his enemies.

Narasimha Mahipála, possessed of all the highest titles, dwelling in his own *Hoysala* country, in the royal city of *Dorasamudra*, an abode of all fortune, in the kingdom bestowed upon with affection by his father and filled with all royal wealth*:—In the S'aka year 1200, the year Bahudhánya, the month Mágha, the 14th day of the moon's decrease, Monday ; in the course of making various other gifts ; the village named *Hebbála* in the *Konga náḍ*, together with its associated villages, assessed at a rental of 648 pagodas ; in order to provide for the taxes which the *Karṇáṭa* people resident in *Kás'i* had to pay; for the alms and chatra expenses ; for the distribution of food and other religious works ; *Narasimha Deva*, who was the security for maintaining the worship of the god, presented to the god *Vis'ves'vara* and to those dwellers in *Kás i*, with pouring of water.

To the same effect in the *Karṇáṭa* language, that all may understand.

May it be well—The protector of all lands, the favorite of earth and fortune, the king of kings, the supreme ruler, the lord of *Dvárávati*, the sun in the sky of the *Yádava* race, a precious jewel protecting all, king over the *Male* rajas, *ganḍa bherunḍa* of the *Malepa* chiefs, the unshaken hero, the sole champion of the world, the unassisted hero, *Malla* of the S'anivára Siddigiri-durga, in war a Ráma, a lion to the elephants his enemies, utter destroyer of the *Magara* kingdom, setter up of the *Chola* kingdom, overthrower of the *Pándya* kingdom ; *Nissanka Pratápa Chakravarti Hoysala Bhuja Bala S'ri Vira Narasimha Devarasa*.

In the S'aka year 1200, the year Bahudhánya, the month Mágha, the 14th day of the moon's decrease, Monday, having settled the *Hebbála* vrittis, bestowed *Hebbála* in Konga náḍ, with the villages on that channel, according to the rules for giving s'ásanas, with enjoyment for three generations, yielding 232 pagodas, (&c., *particulars of the rentals*,) altogether 648 pagodas ; to

---

* *Soyam samasta-pras'asti-sahito Narasimho mahipála svakiya-Hoysala-manḍale nikhila-lakshmi-nivásas'rayám svajanaka-prema-pratishṭhápita-prájya-rájyasampadam-Dhorasamudrákhyám nija-rájadhánim adhivasan!!*

provide for the taxes which the residents from all parts in *Váranás'i* must pay to the *Turahkas* (Muhammadans); for the daily offering to the god Vis'ves'vara, for the chatra, the distribution of food and all other religious works.

That *Narasimha Devarasa* having divided it into vrittis, remitted the taxes and *gopindalana* (?), and freed it from all imposts, presented the village named *Hebbala*, within the *Konga nád*, assessed at an annual rental of 648 pagodas; for the residents from all parts in *Váranás'i*, and for the daily offering to the god Vis'ves'vara and for all other religious works; to endure as long as sun, moon, stars and sky.

(*Some illegible.*)

S'ri Vira Narasimha Devasya.

149 (xx). Tamra S'asana at Hassan, date A. D. 1335 (?)

3 *Plates*, 4 *sides*.—*Nandi Nágari Characters.*

(*The plates are cracked and very indistinct.*)

May *Ganapati* grant protection, the son of Hara, having the face of an elephant, a sun in dispersing the darkness of difficulties. May the adorable original Boar form of Vishnu grant prosperity, by whom being embraced the Earth greatly rejoiced.

From the ocean of milk was born Chandra, the younger brother of Lakshmi. In his line was born Yadu, by whom, worthy to rule, the world was blessed as the ground is blessed by the rainy season.

Afterwards in that race was born the king *Sangama*, freed from the heap of sins. His sons were *Harihara*, *Kampa Ráya*, *Bukka Mahipati*, *Márappa* and *Muddapa*.

(*Some illegible.*)

. . . valiant as Arjuna among the Pándavas, he mounted one of the regent elephants at the points of the compass and set out on an expedition of victory: dreadful as Yama, many kings fell before him as he thus marched forth; the *Konkana* king suffered great disgrace; the *Ghurjaras* were seized with trembling; the *Kámbhojas*, *Andhras* and *Kalingas* were defeated.

. . . king of kings, supreme ruler, victorious in battle with many kings, possessed of all titles, chief over mighty kings, a terror to hostile rulers, a godlike protector of the Hindu rajas, adorned with all royal wealth.

His capital city was *Vijaya[nagara]* . . . . .

His chief queen was *Gaurámbika*, adorned with all good qualities, her heart fixed on the lotus her husband, . . . resembling S'achi the consort of Indra, or Savitri or Chhaya . . . . . . in song and music excelling the apsaras . .

By her he had a son, a punisher of the evil and protector of tho good, in the form of Harihara . . . .

In the S'aka year computed as *chandra*, ... the year Yuva, the month Margashira, the 7th day of the moon's increase, an auspicious day, the mahá parvani; on the banks of the *Tungabhadra*, in presence of the good Virúpáksha, the giver of happiness; the beautiful village of *Kankuvalli*, fertile with crops, having acquired the name of *Hariharapura*, situated in Kunchabaddu, a place of merit, within the limits of Narasimhapura, west of the celebrated Hebbuhalli . . . . . . east of the Shaila peak, ... near Madvachala, on the north side and near to Dodda Betta; together with its associated villages *Hosahalli*, *Shigurahalli*, *Bairakalli*, and *Kachanahalli*; has been presented to . . . . son of a Brahman of the Yajus s'akha . . . . . .

The king *Harihara*, excelling Brihaspati in wisdom, made this gift on a 7th day, a sankramana, to endure as long as sun, moon and stars, with presentation of a gold coin and pouring of water; together with the *nidhi* and *nikshepa*, as long as sun and moon endure.

The four limits of that excellent agrahára are for the general benefit here written in the *Karṇáṭa* language.

(*Much illegible.*)

Of making a gift or perpetuating one, the perpetuating one is the best: he who makes a gift obtains svarga, but he who perpetuates one obtains final beatitude. Land presented to Brahmans is to kings as an only sister, neither may she be enjoyed nor ravished away, (otherwise, nor subjected to taxation). Merit is a common bridge for kings: this from age to age deserves your support, O kings of the earth. Thus does Rámachandra beseech the kings who come after him.

S'ri Virúpáksha (in Kannaḍa letters).

150 (xxi). Tamra S'asana at Hassan, date A. D. 1406.

3 Plates, 4 sides.—Nandi Nágari Characters.

Adored be *S'ambhu*, beauteous with the chámara-like crescent moon kissing his lofty head; the original foundation-pillar of the city of the three worlds. Supreme is the bee that buzzes around the temples of Vináyaka, which resembles a heavenly drum sounding for the removal of difficulties. Adored be the Boar, which as in sport tossed up the earth, bristling with its plants and trees as if pleased to horripilation with the game.

There was a king named *Sangama*, a cluster of good qualities, a moon in raising the tide of the ocean of happiness.

His son was *Bukka Ráya*, in whom the world became possessed of a good king, who by his excellence obtained the title of *Rájendra*.

To the great king Bukka Raya was born a son *Harihara*, as to S'iva was born a son Mahasena from Gauri. He having acquired the city named *Vijaya*, became the sovereign of all the lands surrounded by the ocean.

(*Some illegible*)

His son was *Deva Ráya*, devoted to the protection of his subjects, under whose orders were all hostile kings reduced. While this king *Deva Raya* was ruling the world, the creeper of his fame spread through all the earth, and rising to svarga, derided Devendra and the groups of deities.

Deva Ráya shines forth as ruler of the undivided world, having smitten down all his enemies with his might, and having adorned the Brahmans. Of a mighty command emulating that of Indra and the other regents of the world, his wealth and power surpassed theirs.

This great victor in battle and slayer of his enemies, at the time of his coronation, having distinguished a village with his own name, presented it to some chief Brahmans, celebrated throughout the world for their learning, having forms like deities, versed in the vedas and s'ástras, devoted to the performance of the six great rites, having over come their passions, and continually praising God in their minds.

May it be well.—The year 132(?8) of the victorious increasing era being current, in the year Vyaya, the month Kartika, the 10th day of the moon's decrease, Monday, the Bhadrapada (nakshatra), the Priti yoga and Bava karana; at the conjunction of all these auspicious signs, *S'riman Mahárájádhirája Parames'vara S'ri Víra Pratápa Deva Ráya Mahárája*, at the time of his coronation,* made a gift of an agrahára, containing . . vriṭṭis, distinguished by his own name as *Pratápa-Deva-Ráyapura*, in the *Bháskara kshetra*, on the banks of the *Tungabhadra*, in the Hemakúṭa (mountain), in the presence of the god S'ri Virúpáksha, to Brahmans versed in the vedas and s'ástras, with presentation of a gold coin and pouring of water, to endure as long as sun and moon.

The names of the Brahmans who received vriṭṭis are here written. (*The names, tribes, &c., of 38 Brahmans follow*). Of this newly acquired agrahára of Pratápa-Deva-Ráyapura are these Brahmans the light, the great yogis who have been separately described above.

The description of the four boundaries of the agrahára given by us is here written in the language of the country that all may understand.

Description of the four boundaries of of Handiganahalli, the coronation agrahára of *S'ri Vira Prauḍha Devaráyapura*:—The large rock standing at the level of the water in the middle of the bend of the Handigana tank; thence west, the stone planted in the middle of the pond at foot of the western hill; thence east, the line of stones set up south of Haivinahalli, and the stone inscribed with a linga and a crocodile; thence east, the large watercourse running north-east from the southern bank of the stream in the great forest; thence east, the buffalo swamp west of the stream at the north-east gate; thence north (*and so on the details being very tedious*).

Such is the *dharma s'ásana* of the coronation agrahára *Pratápa Devaráyapura*, within the four limits of Handigana-kere; presented with the *ashṭa-bhoga-tejas-swámya* rights of *niddhi, nikshepa, jala, páshána, akshina, ágámi, siddhi* and *sádhya*†; with freedom from customs duties, money taxes, and all other imposts; at the auspicious time of coronation, in the *Pampa kshetra*, in presence of the god S'ri Virúpáksha, with presentation of a gold coin and pouring of water.

Merit is a common bridge for kings: this from age to age deserves your suport, O kings of the earth. Thus does Rámachandra beseech the kings who come after him. Land presented to Brahmans is to kings as an only sister, neither may she be enjoyed nor ravished away, (otherwise, nor subjected to taxation). Whoso usurps a gift made by himself or by another shall assuredly be born a worm in ordure for sixty thousand years.

S'ri Virúpáksha (in Kannaḍa letters).

---

* *Paṭṭábhisheke samaye.*

† See note p. 3.

III.

VARIOUS INSCRIPTIONS,

From Original Sources.

151. Tamra S'asana at Mercara,* date A. D. 466.

3 Plates, 8 in. × 3·2 in., 4 súles. Seal, an Elephant.—Púrvada Haḷe Kannaḍa Characters.

May it be well.—Success through the adorable *Padmanábha*, resembling (in colour) the cloudless sky.

A sun illumining the clear firmament of the Jáhnavi (or *Ganga*) *kula*, distinguished for the strength and valour attested by the great pillar of stone divided with a single stroke of his sword,† adorned with the ornament of a wound received in cutting down the hosts of his enemies, of the Kanváyana gotra, was Srimán *Kongaṇi Mahádhirája*.

His son, inheriting all the qualities of his father, possessing a character for learning and modesty, having obtained the honours of the kingdom only through his excellent government of his subjects, a touchstone for (testing) gold the learned and poets, skilled both in expounding and practising the science of politics, the author of a treatise on the law of adoption,‡ was Srimán *Mádhava Mahádhirája*. His son, possessed of all the qualities inherited from his father and grandfather, having entered into war with many elephants (so that) his fame had tasted the waters of the four oceans, was Srimad *Hari Varmma Mahádhirája*. His son, devoted to the worship of Brahmans, gurus and gods, having humbled himself at the feet of Náráyana, was Srimad *Vishnu Gopa Mahádhirája*. His son, with a head purified by the pollen from the lotuses the feet of Tryambaka, having purchased his kingdom by personal strength and valour, daily eager to extricate merit from the thick mire of the Kali yuga in which it had sunk, was Srimán *Mádhava Mahadhirája*. His son, the beloved sister's son of *Krishna Varmma Mahádhirája*,—who was the sun to the firmament of the auspicious *Kadamba kula*,§—having a mind illuminated with the increase of learning and modesty, of indomitable bravery in war, reckoned the first of the learned, was Srimán *Kongaṇi Mahádhirája*.

To Vandaṇandi Bhaṭára, the disciple of Guṇanandi Bhaṭára, who was the disciple of Janánandi Bhaṭára, who was the disciple of Síḷabhadra Bhaṭára, who was the disciple of Abhananda Bhaṭára, who was the disciple of Guṇachandra Bhaṭára, of the Koṇḍakundánvaya, the line of gurus to the Datta

---

* For fac-simile see *Indian Antiquary*, I, 362.

† *Sva-khaḍgayka-prahára-khaṇḍita-mahá-silá-stambha-labdha-bala-parákramodáraṇo.*

‡ *Dattaka-sútra-vrittir-praṇetán.*

§ *Srimad-Kadamba-kula-gagana-gabhasti-málina-Krishna-Varmma-mahádhirájasya priya-bhágineyo.*

(? adopted son) named Avinita;* in the year 388, the month Mágha, Monday, the nakshatra being Sváti, the fifth day of the bright fortnight; (the village) named *Badaṇeguppe*, situated in the middle of the Eḍenáḍ Seventy, in the Púnáḍ Ten Thousand, being obtained by *Avinita Mahádhirája Bhadatta*, minister of the sovereign of all the continents. for the S'rí Vijaya Jinálaya of *Talavana-nagara*,—assigning twelve kaṇḍugas in each of the six associated villages, *ambali* and the *tala vritti* of Talavana-pura, twelve kaṇḍugas in Pogarigere, and twelve kaṇḍugas with the enjoyment of royal rights in Pirikere,—he presented the charming (village).†

The boundaries of the village of *Badaṇeguppe*:—east, a red stone, Gajasele, the *Satti* post at the junction of the three paths of Karivalli, Koṭṭagara and Badaṇeguppe: south-east, a bank covered with bandhuka bushes. Then the southern boundaries, a thicket of milk-hedge, a balkani tree: again west, a line of many medical plants, then the pond at the junction of the three paths of Badaṇeguppe, Koṭṭagara and Multagi, then Chanḍigála: as far as a clearing-nut tree at the south west. Then the western boundaries, a [peduldel] tree, a [sántareti] banyan tree, thence the bed of the stream: again to the north, a line of many medical plants, and a bank covered with the rose-apple: again north-west, the temple tamarind tree. Thence the group of neggilu at the junction of the three paths of Badaṇeguppe [multagi], Koleyanúru and Dásanúru, [niduvelanga]: thence the hill which protects the north of the village of Gajasele and the descent to the large stone; again east, a line of many medical plants, then a [kadapaltegála] banyan tree: again north east, the bank at the junction of the three paths of Badaṇeguppe, Dásanúru and Polmada, the [kodigaṭṭi] tamarind tree, and so the mound of [kentaramba] which joins the eastern boundary.

Witnesses thereto:—Perbba Kavaṇa, the man who is a friend in all things to the line of the Ganga Rájás.‡ Maru Gareya Sendrika, Ganjenád Nirggunḍa Maṇiyugureya, servants § of Nandúla Simbáladapa.

---

* *Avinita-námadheya-Dattasya desiga-gaṇam.*

† *Ashṭa-asiti-uttarasya trayo-satasya samvatsarasya Mágha-másam S'omavaram Svati-nakshatra suddha panchami akaḷa-varsha-prithuvi-vallabha-mantri Taḷavana-nagara-S'ri-Vijaya-Jinálakke Pú-náḍu* 10 (an old cave numeral) *sahas'ra Eḍe-naḍu-saptari-*(? *ti*) *madhye Badaṇeguppe náma** *Avinita-mahádhirája-bhadattena paḍiyeṛáṛ oḍam úr úroḷ pannir kkaṇḍugam geydu ambalimaṇṇum Taḷavana-puradoḷ taḷa-vittiyaman Pogarigeṛeyoḷ pannir kkaṇḍugam Pirikeṛe-yoḷam rájamánam anumodana pannir kkaṇḍugam manoharam dattam.*

Jinálakke, which would mean 'for the Jain war' (*ála*), is probably a mistake for *Jinálayakke* 'for the Jain temple.'

‡ *Ganga-rája-kula-sakalásthayika-purusha.*

§ *Bhrityáyám.*

Country witnesses * :—Tagadúru Kulugova, Gaṇiganúru Tagada, Algoḍate Nandaka, Ummatúru Beḷḷúra Aḷageya, Badaṇeguppe Beḷḷúra Deggiviya.

(Signature (?) of three letters).

Whoso by violence takes away land presented by himself or by another shall be born a worm in ordure for sixty thousand years. The earth has been enjoyed by Sagara and other kings: according to their (gifts of) land so was their reward. Poison is no poison, the property of the gods that is the real poison: for poison kills a single man, but a gift to the gods (if usurped) destroys sons and descendants. Merit is a common bridge for kings: this from age to age deserves your support, O kings of the earth. Thus does Rámabhadra beseech the kings who come after him. Written by *Visvakarmma.*

152. Tamra S'asana at Hosur†, date A. D. 762.

5 Plates, 8 in. × 3 in. Seal, an Elephant—Haḷe Kannaḍa Characters.

May it be well.—Success through the adorable *Padmanábha*, resembling (in colour) the cloudless sky.

A sun illumining the clear firmament of the Jáhnavi (or *Ganġa*) *kula*, distinguished for the strength and valour attested by the great pillar of stone divided with a single stroke of his sword,‡ adorned with the ornament of the wound received in cutting down the hosts of his cruel enemies, of the Kanváyana gotra, was Srimat *Kongaṇi Varmma Dharmma Mahádhirája.* His son, inheriting all the qualities of his father, possessing a character for learning and modesty, having obtained the honours of the kingdom only for the sake of the good government of his subjects, a touchstone for (testing) gold the learned and poets, skilled among those who expound and practise the science of politics, the author of a treatise on the law of adoption,¶ was Srímán *Mádhava Mahádhirájá.* His son possessed of all the qualities inherited from his father and grandfather, having entered into war with many elephants (so that) his fame had tasted the waters of the four oceans, was Srímad *Hari Varmma Mahádhirájá.*

His son, devoted to the worship of Brahmans, gurus and gods, praising the feet of Náráyana, was Srímán *Vishnu Gopa Mahádhirája.* His son, with a head purified by the pollen from the lotuses the feet of Tryambaka, having by personal strength and valour purchased his kingdom, daily eager to extricate

* *Desa sákshi.* † For fac-simile, cf. *Ind. Ant,* II, 156. ‡ See note p. 281. ¶ See note p. 281.

the ox of merit from the thick mire of the Kali yuga in which it had sunk, was Sríman *Mádhava Mahádhirája*. His son, the beloved sister's son of *Krishna Varmma Mahádhirája*,—who was the sun to the firmament of the auspicious *Kadamba kula*,*—having a mind illuminated with the increase of learning and modesty, of indomitable bravery in war, reckoned the first of the learned, was Srímán *Kongaṇi Mahadhirája*. His son, named *Avinita*, possessed of the three powers of increase, who had brought anxiety to the face of Yama on account of the smallness of the residue left after the countless animals offered to him as a tribute (namely) the brave men consumed in the sacrifice of the face of the many wars waged for *Andari*, *A'lattúr*, *Paurulare*, *Pennagara* and other places, author of a commentary on fifteen sargas of the Kirátárjuniya,† was called *Duvvinita*.

His son, the lotuses of whose feet were dyed with the balls of honey shaken from the lines of bending bees, the clustering savages, rubbing against one another, was named *Mushkara*. His son, of a pure wisdom acquired from his being the abode of fourteen branches of learning, distinguished for his skill among those who teach and practise the science of politics in all its branches, a rising sun in dispersing the clouds of darkness his enemies, bore the celebrated name of *S'ri Vikrama*. His son, whose broad chest bore on itself the emblems of victory in the shining scars of wounds received in many battles inflicted by the tusks darting like lightning of huge elephants, possessed of the quintessence of all the sciences, having gained the three objects of wordly pursuit, the glory of whose virtuous life each day augmented, was *Bhú Vikrama* by name.

Moreover, he who had defeated in *Bhime'sa gráma* the *Pallavendra Narapati* trodden to powder by the feet of a hundred elephants maddened with the stream of blood issuing from the door of the breast of the Bhaṭṭára (or warriors) forced open by his numerous weapons‡, was named *Vilanda Rája*, called *S'ri Vallabha*, in the enjoyment of fortune obtained by victory in a hundred fights. His younger brother, whose lotus-feet were irradiated with the brilliance of the jewels in the crowns of numerous prostrate kings, who was to fortune as a husband chosen by herself, was surnamed *Nava Káma*, beloved of the good, his fame in destroying hostile kings the theme of song. Of which *Kongaṇi Mahárája*, whose other name was *S'ivamára*, the grandson, the groups of the toes of whose feet were illuminated with a rainbow light from the rays of the jewels set in the bands of the crowns of prostrate kings, who had fixed his faith on Náráyana, raging with fury in the front of war horrid with the assault

* See note p. 281. † *Kirátárjuniya-panchadas'a-sargga-ṭikákáro.*

‡ *Apichá nána-heti-prahára-prathigaṭita-bha ṭáran-kaváṭṭáṭṭita-srigbhárásváda-pramatta-dvipa-s'ata-charaṇa-kshoda-sam-narddha-Bhimes'a-gráme-Pallavendrah-narpatim-ajayad yo.*

of heroes, horses, men, and elephants, was *Bhíma Kopa.* No less a captivator of the glances of young women the most skilled in the joyful art of love than a subduer of the world, laden with spoils of victory gained in many most arduous wars, a lion to the herd of elephants the hostile kings, was *Rája Kesari.*

Moreover, a sun greatly illumining the clear firmament of the *Ganga kula*, a terror to hostile kings, a protector of the fortunate ways of good men, who having obtained the name of a good king shone like a sun over all kingdoms, ... lord over kings who were wed to fortune, a shining head-jewel to the brow of kings, with his bow resembling Káma or Ráma the son of Das'aratha, in bravery a Paras'u Ráma, in great heroism Balári, in great splendour Ravi, in government Dhanes'a, of a mighty and splendid energy, the most glorious all-in-all, to all things living Brahma himself, the king whom all the poets in the world daily praise as the creator Brahma, the middle of whose palace continually echoed the sounds of the holy ceremonies which accompanied his daily rich gifts, among the favourites of fortune named the first,* was *Prithuvi Kongaṇi Mahárája.*

By whom, considering that all things in this world are as transient as a bubble, the S'aka year 684 having passed, residing in *Mányapura*, from his victorious camp, in the month Vaís'ákha, during an eclipse of the moon in the constellation Vis'ákha, on Friday, † to Mádhava S'armma, a resident of Táthúr, son of Mára S'armma, of the Kás'yapa gotra, follower of the Vájasaneya veda, was given in the *Gúdalúr* . . . . in the *Gúdalúr* . . . . in the 14 villages of *S'ripura*, 12 khanḍikas in each village, with the seed for sowing, of land fit for the cultivation of rice and other grain; a store-house for seed grain only, with (power of) three mortgages; . . . . 2 khanḍika of garden land, with seed for sowing; together with 30 khanḍika of forest land fit for the cultivation of drugs (or pepper) &c., with seed for sowing. The whole of this, freed from all imposts, was given with pouring of water.

Witnesses to this gift: the existing chiefs of the Ninety-six Thousand country.‡

---

* *S'ri-purusha-prathama-námadheyena.*

† *Tenedam akhilam-budbudachal jjniva-lokam-avalokya chatur-as'ity-uttareshu shat-chhateshu S'aka-varsheshu samatiteshu Mányapuramm-adhivasati-vijaya-skandhávare Vais'ákha-máse soma-ggrahaṇe Vishákhá-nakshatre S'ukravára.*

‡ *Gúdalúr-mmaṛiyáchi Gúdalúr-ppa-u-i S'ripuram iti chaturshu grámeshu grámam-prati dvádas'a khanḍika vapana-sammita s'alv-ádi-vapana-yogyam bhúmi tri-kudaba-sammitá vapana mátram griha sthánam trims'a kudaba sammitam múrpa . . dvi khanḍika vapana-sammitam toṭa-kshetram trims'at khanḍiká vapana-sammitam priyangvádi-vapana-yogyam-áraṇyan cha dattam etat sarvvam sarvva pariḥá-opetam udaka púrvvam dattah asya dánasya sákshiṇah Shannavati sahasra vishaya prakṛitayaḥ.*

Moreover thus is the sloka delivered by Manu:—Whoso usurps a gift made by himself or by another shall be born a worm in ordure for sixty thousand years. To make a gift oneself is easy, to maintain another's difficult; but of giving or of maintaining a gift, the maintaining a gift is the best. The earth has been enjoyed by Sagara and many kings; according to their (gifts of) land so was their reward. Poison is no poison, a gift to the gods that is a dreadful poison: for poison kills one man, but a gift to the gods (if usurped) kills sons and descendants. Whoso protects it will derive the merit thereof.

Written by Vis'vakarmma.

---

153. Tamra S'asana at Nagamangala,* date A. D. 777.

6 Plates, 10 sides. Seal, an Elephant.—Haḷe Kannaḍa Characters.

The whole genealogical portion, down to *Prithuvi Kongaṇi Mahárája*, is word for word the same as No. 152. Thence the continuation is as follows:—

By whom, the S'aka year 698 having passed, and the 50th year of his glorious and powerful reign being then current, residing in *Mányapura*, from his victorious camp:—†

Praised as the chief protection of the S'ri Múla (the Jains), of the Nandi Sanghánvaya, the Eregittúr gaṇa, and the Múlikal gachcha, rejoicing all the world with his combination of the rays of auspicious good qualities, resembling another *chandra* (or moon), was there a guru named *Chandra Nandi*. His disciple, whose ability was worthy of protecting the assembly of the learned, a second *Kumára* worthy to rejoice the heart of *Parames'vara* (otherwise the greatest sages) was the munipati named *Kumára Nandi*. His disciple, who understood the essence of all sciences, who had acquired the fame of possessing wealth but for the assembly of the learned, was the great muni *Kírtti Nandyáchárya*. His dear disciple, the beloved of the lotus-lake of the disciples, a sun in illumining the sky of the virtuous actions of good men daily praised for their great learning, was *Vimala Chandráchárya*.

Through the instructions in law of this great ṛishi, having become the confounder of S'rimad *Báṇa*, (or the *Báṇa kula*),‡ in sweeping away all cause

---

* For fac-simile see *Ind. Ant.* II, 156.

† *Ashṭa-navaty-uttareshu (sha)ṭchhateshu S'aka-varsheshv atíteshv átmánah-pravarddhamána vijayais'varyya-samvatsare pancha-s'attame pravarddhamáne Mányapuram-adhivasati-vijaya-skandhávára.*

‡ *S'rímad Báṇa kaḷakalah* or *kula kalah.*

of fear like the flood of a great river, who with the sceptre in his hands had broken down the groups of trees his enemies,* was *Dunḍu*, first of the name, the *Nirgunda Yuva Rája*. His beloved son, who through his knowledge of politics had destroyed without exception the groups of his enemies, a friend to all the world, of a life pleasant to be heard of, making good use of thought, word, and deed, was *Parama Gúla*, first of the name, the *S'ṛi Prithuvi Nirgunda Rája*.

His wife, born of the beloved daughter of *Pallavádhirája* by *Maru Varmma*, an ornament of the *Ságara kula*, was *Kundavvi* by name. In her husband's house did she grow up, daily promoting works of merit; and she erected a Jain temple, an ornament to the north of *S'rípura*, a glory to all the world.

For the repairs of any cracks or defects in which, for erecting any new portions, for the worship of the god, and for the gifts and charities—on the representation of that *Prithivi Nirggunda Rája*—the *Maharajádhirája Paramesvara*, united with (his queen) *S'ríja* superior to *Lakshmí*, made a grant of the village of *Ponnaḷḷi*, belonging to *Nirgunda*, with freedom from all imposts. Its boundaries:—on the east, the white stone rock of *Noḷibela*; on the south-east, *Paṇyangere*; on the south, the bank of the water course of the *Belgalli*-tank and the *Dilla*-tank; on the south-west, the rocky ground of white stone at *Jaidaráke*; on the west, the tank of the *Henkevi* weavers; on the north-west, the piles of stones at *Puṇuse* and *Goṭṭagáḷa*; on the north, the great bend of the water course of the *Sáma*-tank; on the north-east, the *Kalambetti* hill.

And he further gave other land on the north-east, (viz) in the plain of the *Dunḍu Samudra* a small garden of 12 *kanduga*; in the share of *Nallu Rája*, the chief of *Mannampale*, 2 *kanḍuga*; on the west of the *táṇḍa* of the *Dunḍu* chief, one *táṇḍa*; in *Kammargatti*, in the plain of *S'rívura*, 2 *kanḍugas*; under the *Kaḷani* large tank 6 *kanduga*; in the pasture-land of the *Ẹrepúli* tank 20 *kanduga*—this is dry-cultivation land; and in the north-west corner of *S'rívura*, in the middle of *Devangeri*, a site for 30 separate houses.

Witnesses to this gift: The 18 existing chiefs.

Witnesses to this gift: The existing chiefs of the Ninety-six Thousand country.†

Whoso through avarice seeks to resume this gift, incurs the guilt of the five great sins: whoso maintains it acquires all merit. Moreover by *Maru*

* *Váhá-danḍa-manḍalágra-khanḍitári-manḍaḷa-druma-shanḍo.*

† *Asya dána sákshinaḥ ashṭadas'a prakṛitayah. Asya dánasya sákshiṇaḥ Shannavati sahasra vishaya prakṛitayah.*

hath it been said : whoso by violence takes away land presented by himself or by another shall be born a worm in ordure for sixty thousand years. He who makes a gift has an easy task ; the maintenance of another's gift is arduous : but to maintain a gift is more meritorious than to make one. The earth has been enjoyed by *Ságara* and other kings : according to their (gifts of) land so was their reward. Poison is no poison, the property of the gods that is the real poison : for poison kills a single man, but a gift to the gods (if usurped) destroys sons and descendants.

By *Visvakarmmácharya*, an abode of all learning, skilled in painting pictures,* was this *s'ásana* written.

Though it be but four *kaṇḍuka* of rice seed . . . . or two *kaṇḍuka* of waste land, it should be protected in the same manner as a gift to a Brahman.

---

154. Tamra S'asana at Mallohalli,† date A. D. 454.

3 Plates, 7¼ in. × 1¼ in., 6 sides. Seal, an Elephant.—Púrvada Haḷe Kannaḍa Characters.

May it be well.—Success through the adorable *Padmanábha*, resembling (in colour) the cloudy sky.

A sun illumining the clear firmament of the Jáhnavi (or *Ganga*) *kula*, possessed of the wealth of the glory of the kingdom conquered by the might of his own arm, of distinguished fame through striking down the *anila* (or *níla*) *stambha*, a wild fire in consuming (?) *Baṇa* the stubble of the forest,‡ was S'rímat *Kongaṇi Varmma Dharmma Mahádhirája*.

His son, inheriting the qualities of his father, author of a treatise on the law of adoption,§ adorned with the wound acquired by entering into many wars, of a wealth and glory protected by Bhagavat, was Srímat *Mádhava Adhirája*.

His son, whose fame acquired by (his) many elephants had tasted the waters of the four oceans, skilled in riding on the best elephants and the best horses, the destroyer of hosts of enemies, was S'rimat *Hari Varmma Mahárája*.

His son, endowed with the group of qualities inherited from his father and grandfather, in kingly policy the equal of Bṛihaspati, his mental energy unimpaired to the end of life, of a valour equal to that of S'akra (Indra), was Srímad *Vishnu Gopa Rája*.

---

* *Chitrakalábhijnena.*

† For fac simile see *Ind. Ant.* V. 136.

‡ *Banaiti-gahana-kaksha-praddha-davágni.*

§ See note p. 282.

His son, like Kubera in the merit of smiting his enemies in great wars, a young (or rising) sun, his favour and his anger like nectar and like poison, his sins destroyed by religious rites and numerous gifts of cows, gold, lands, and other things ; of widespread fame for his renewal of Brahman endowments long since destroyed ;* as performing the sacrifice of many wars, the sole sacrificer (in the world) ; like Indra of valour invincible, like Kubera wonderful in the possession of heaps of treasure inexhaustible, like Yama in his arrows which destroyed the battlements of the neighbouring chiefs, of mighty victorious valour, was *Mádhava Rája.*

By his son *Kongani Rája* was given to Káda Svámís'va, a Taittiríya Brahman, chief of the Hiranya-kes'i sútra . . . . . .

. . . . to Tippúra Káda Svámi was given, in the manner of a Brahman endowment, 10 *kanḍuga* of paddy land below Melúr tank, freed from all dues of the eighteen kinds,† and formed into a Brahman vritti with pouring of water ; for the increase of merit and health was it given.

In pursuance of which, in the year Jaya, the 29th of the wealth of the great victories increased by himself, (namely by) S'ríman *Kongaṇi Mahárája*, of the Kánváyana gotra,—of a might invincible by any in the world, chief in affection for the Brahmans, devoted to the worship of the lotus feet of Hara (Siva),—the moon being in the S'ataya nakshatra, to Káda Svámís'va of the Mádela gotra . . . .

. . Let this land be continued without hindrance to Káda Svámi, the beloved of the Madala (gotra) : such is our command, which whosoever transgresses is a sinner worthy of corporal punishment.‡

Moreover thus is the sl'oka delivered :—Whoso seizes upon land presented by himself or by another, will incur the guilt of slaughtering a hundred thousand cows. To give much oneself is easy, to maintain another's gift is difficult ; but of giving or maintaining (another's gift) the maintenance (of another's) is more meritorious. The earth has been enjoyed by Sagara and many kings ; according to their (gifts of) land so was their reward.

Whoso is a follower of the Mahárája . . . . .

. . . 12 *kanḍugu* ; this all should respect and preserve . . . .

those famed for their adherence to virtue.

---

* *Chiropahrita-brahmádeya-pradána-prakhyáta-yas'ah.*

† *Ashṭádas'a-játibhih-sarvva parihâraih.*

‡ *Etad ::samachchhásanam akramet sa pápah s'arîran daṇḍam arahati.*

155. Tamra S'asana at Mallohalli,* date A. D. 513.

5 Plates, 9 in. × 3½ in. 8 sides.—Púrvada Haḷe Kannaḍa Characters.

Success through the adorable *Padmanábha*, resembling (in colour) the cloudless sky.

A sun illumining the clear firmament of the Jáhnavi (or *Ganga*) *kula*, distinguished for the strength, fortune and valour acquired by the great pillar of stone divided with a single stroke of his sword, adorned with the ornament of a wound received in battle while cutting down the hosts of his terrible enemies, of the Kánváyana gotra, was Srímat *Kongaṇi Varmma Dharmma Mahádhirája*.

His son, inheriting all the qualities of his father, with a character for learning and modesty, having obtained the honours of the kingdom only for the sake of the good government of his subjects, of great understanding improved by acquaintance with the best principles of the substance of various sciences, a touchstone for (testing) gold the learned, skilled among those who thoroughly expound and practise the science of politics, maintaining a due distinction between friends and servants, the author of a treatise on the law of adoption, was S'rímán *Mádhava Mahádhirája*.

His son, possessed of all the qualities inherited from his father and grandfather, having entered into war with many elephants (so that) his fame had tasted the waters of the four oceans, of wide-spread renown sprung from his riding on lusty elephants and horses, of great wealth acquired by the use of the bow, was Srímad *Hari Varmma Mahádhirája*.

His son, devoted to the worship of gurus, cows, and Brahmans, praising the feet of Náráyana, was Srimad *Vishṇu Gopa Mahádhirája*.

His son, with a head purified by the pollen from the lotuses the feet of Tryambaka, with two arms grown stout and hard with athletic exercise, having purchased his kingdom by his personal strength and valour, bearer of a sharp . . beloved by rákshasas whose lips were black with hunger, a reviver of the custom of donations for long-ceased festivals of the gods and Brahman endowments,† daily eager to extricate the ox of merit from the thick mire of the Kali yuga in which it had sunk, was S'ríman *Mádhava Mahádhirája*.

His son,—the beloved sister's son of *S'ri Kṛishṇa Varmma*, the sun in the firmament of the auspicious *Kadamba kula*, and anointed with the final ablu-

* For fac.simile see *Ind. Ant.* V. 138.

† *Chira-pranash'a-deva-bhoga-brahmádeya-visargga-ayaṇa-káriṇa.*

tions of continual *asvamedhas*—who received his royal (or coronation) anointing on the couch of the lap of his divine mother,* possessed of the three powers of increase, enjoying the essence of the three objects of worldly desire without one interfering with the other, fearless though surrounded with all the bands of tributary chiefs whom he had subjected, having parties of councillors attached to him by continual affection and gifts, having a mind purified with the increase of learning and modesty, follower of the lives of the kings of the Krita yuga, his wide-spread fame acquired by victory in many wars covering the three worlds like the unbroken expanse of a milk ocean, bold to give without stint, his inviolable commands placed upon the heads of foreign kings subdued by his invincible might, surpassing Kubera in the growth of his wealth increased in many ways, a mine of many glorious qualities, reckoned the first of the learned, the joy of the hearts of his beloved ones, in not transgressing the bounds of respect resembling the ocean adorned with gems, like Yama in punishing according to desert, like the sun in the greatness of his glory, like Vaivasvata Manu devoted to protecting the South in the maintenance of castes and religious orders, the friend of all, of high birth, was S'rímat *Kongaṇi Mahádhirája.*

By his son named *Avinita*, whose broad chest was embraced by the beloved daughter of *Skanda Varmma*, the *Punnáḍ Rája* who herself had chosen him though from her birth assigned by her father, according to the advice of his own guru, to the son of another; having by the growth of the three powers of increase brought into subjection all the bands of tributary chiefs; having brought anxiety to the face of Yama on account of the smallness of the residue left from the animals offered up by him as a tribute (namely) the brave men consumed in the sacrifice of the face of the many wars waged for *Andari*, *A'lantúr*, *Pauruḷare*, *Pernnagara*, and other places;—by (this) S'rímat *Kongaṇi Vṛiddha Rája*, having the name of *Durvvinita*, the ruler of the whole of *Pánnáḍ* (? *Pákháḍ*) and *Punnáḍ*, like Vaivasvata Manu able for the protection of the castes and religious orders which prevailed in the South, the friend of all, of high birth:—the year Vijaya being current, the 35th of the victories and wealth increased by himself; was given,—to S'rímad *Deva Sarmma* of the Kásyapa gotra and follower of the Vájasaneyi, (also) called *Mahádeva*, promoter of the race of that sun of the world named S'rímat *Valmiki*,—Bempurís'vara-stána named Keḷale, with pouring of water.

(Moreover) on the north-east, wet land, 4 *khaṇḍis*; of the wet land of the Krishna pond, above—3 *khaṇḍis*, below—6 *khaṇḍis*; of the land east of the

* *Janani-devatánka-paryyanka-evádhigata-rájyábhishekasya.*

Penna river 15 *khandis*, (bounded) on the south by a big tree, south-west by an as'vatta (tree), north-east by a jambu tree, further north-east by the Nakule pond; of the land on the west 12 *khandis*; on the north-west of the wet land of the big pond 7 *khandis*; thus much did he piously give to Mahádeva.

Moreover by Manu hath the s'loka been delivered: Whoso seizes upon land presented by himself or by another shall be cast into terrible darkness for sixty thousand years. The earth has been enjoyed by Sagara and many other kings: according to their (gifts of) land so was their reward. To make a gift oneself is easy, to maintain a gift made by another is difficult; but of giving or maintaining (another's gift) the maintenance (of another's gift) is more meritorious. A gift made with pouring of water, one enjoyed for three generations, one maintained for six generations, such may not be resumed; neither the gifts of former kings.

---

156. Tamra S'asana at Harihara,* date (?) A. D. 350.

3 Plates, 6½ in. × 2¾ in., 4 sides.—Seal, an Elephant.—Púrvada Haḷe Kannaḍa and Devanágari Characters intermixed.

May it be well—Success through the adorable *Padmanábha*, resembling (in colour) the cloudless sky.

A sun illumining the clear firmament of the Jáhnavi (or *Ganga*) *kula*, of mighty valour acquired by the pillar of stone divided with a single stroke of his sword, ... resplendent as a jewel on the forehead, was S'rimán *Konguli Varmma Dharmma Máhádhirája*.

His son, was *Vishnu Gopa Mahárájádhirája*.

His son, the lord of *Koláḷapura*, a sun to the *Ganga kula*, having the sign (or crest) of a lusty elephant, having received a boon from the goddess Padmávati,—in the middle of the excellent *Talavana-pura* which he was then ruling,† in the (?) S'aga year . . . the year Sádhárana the month Phálguna, full moon day, being Sunday,—within *Devanúr* in *Káre, náḍ*,—*Ráma Deva*, the good son of Madhi Gavuḍa of the Yarakula (caste), having slain He . . and with great devotion conducted *Rája Malla's* wife and guards thither, (he) being pleased thereat, bestowed the following land: ‡

---

* For fac-simile see *Ind. Ant.*, VII. 172.

† *Tadangáḷḷáda parama Talavanapura madye.*

‡ *Káre náḍa Dhevanuramuḷagge Yarakuladha Madhi gavuḍana s'u putta Ráma Dhevanu He . . ran iṛidhu Raja Mallana henḍati bhanṭar avanu bal valátind oppisidh allige mechchu goṭṭa bhúmi.*

The eastern boundary runs along a field of black soil, a tamarind tree and a pond, to the banyan tree at the common boundary of the guard house and Devanúru; the southern boundary runs by the tamarind tree of the shining pond and the old water course to the wood-apple tree at the common boundary of Kalkonte and Devanúru; the western boundary runs by a tamarind tree to the tamarind tree at the common boundary of Badanevála and Devanúru; the northern boundary runs by a tamarind tree and field of black soil to the common boundary of Alaṇivanchi and Devanúru, and thus ends on the north east.

Witnesses :—He of the Eḍenaḍ Seventy, witness.*

---

157. Tamra S'asana at Bangalore,† date A. D. 481.

5 *Plates, 7¾ in. × 2¼ in., 8 sides.—Seal gone.—Púrvada Haḷe Kannaḍa Characters.*

May it be well.—Success through the adorable *Padmanábha*, resembling (in colour) the cloudless sky.

A sun illumining the clear firmament of the Jáhnavi (or *Ganga*) *kula*, master of countries born from the rapidity of his own victories, adorned with the ornament of a wound obtained in war with hosts of terrible enemies, of the Kánváyana gotra, was S'rimat *Kongaṇi Varmma Dharmma Mahádhirája.*

His son, inheriting all the qualities of his father, possessing a character for learning and modesty, having obtained the honours of the kingdom only for the good government of his subjects, a touchstone for (testing) gold the learned and poets, skilled among those who thoroughly expound and practise the science of politics in all its branches, preserving due distinction between friends and servants, author of a treatise on the law of adoption‡ was S'rimat *Mádhava Mahádhirája.*

His son, possessed of all the qualities inherited from his father and grandfather, having entered into war with many elephants so that his fame had tasted the waters of the four oceans, of a glory acquired from the equal skill with which he rode on elephants and horses, of enormous wealth acquired by the practice of the four modes of policy, was S'rimad *Hari Varmma Mahádhirája*

His son, devoted to the worship of gurus, cows and Brahmans, praising the feet of Náráyana, was S'rimad *Vishnu Gopa Mahádhirája.*

---

* *S'ákshiṇám Eḍenáḍe Eppattga s'ákshi.*

† In the Museum. The last plate is missing.

‡ See note p. 282.

His head purified by the pollen from the lotuses the feet of Tryambaka, his two arms grown stout and hard with athletic exercises, having purchased the kingdom with his personal strength and valour, the reviver of many thousands of long-ceased donations for the festivals of the gods and endowment of Brahmans, performer of the offering of first fruits (*ágrayaṇa*),* both his arms shining with the gems of hard knobs produced by the drawing of his bow for the destruction (or against the deer) the fear of the enemy, his race illuminated by his great and wide-spread glory, was S'rimat *Mádhava Mahádhirája*.

The beloved sister's son of S'ri *Kirshna Varmma* Mahádhirája—who, being anointed with the final ablutions of a completed as'vamedha, was the sun to the firmament of the auspicious *Kadamba kula*—having obtained his royal (or coronation) anointing on the couch of the lap of his divine mother,† enjoying the essence of the three objects of worldly desire without one interfering with the other, of a mind purified by the acquisition of learning and modesty, his fame acquired by the conquest of many mighty kings surrounding the three worlds like the unbroken expanse of the milk ocean, a lake to the lotus of compassion for the bees the eyes of fair women disturbed by the shower of Káma's arrows, reckoned the highest theme of poets, the ablest among the most able, was S'rimat *Kongaṇi Mahádhirája*.

By his son, successor to the qualities of his father, his broad chest embraced by the arms of one who desired him though assigned by her father to the son of another,† surrounded by bands of feudatories from all sides subjected by the growth of the three powers of increase, having parties of counsellors attached to him by constant affection and gifts, having with the sharp sword in his hand cut down the hosts of his enemies and with his arms plucked them up by the root, of a form glorious with virtue and set with the gems of the daily improving qualities of the best of men, though not matured in age yet possessed of ripe virtue, a mine of clusters of distinguished qualities, in punishing according to desert the superior of Vaivasvata, able in protecting the castes and religious orders which prevailed in the South,‡ a friend to all, of good descent, of the highest religious merit, praising the feet of the adorable Vishnu,—what more? the Yudhishṭhira of the Kali yuga, S'rimat *Kongaṇi Mahárája*, in the third year of the great wealth increased by himself,§ the month S'rávaṇa . . . . to the Somayáji *Vása S'armma*, a resident of *Mahásenapura* . . .

(Rest illegible; last plate wanting).

* *Chira-pranashṭa-deva-bhoga-brahmádeyáneka-sahasra-visarggágrayaṇa . . . káriṇa.*
† See No. 155.
‡ *Varṇṇás'ramábhilakshana-dakshiṇá-dis'ábhigoptum-pariyáplavatá.*
§ *A'tmana-pravarddhyamána-vipulais'varye tritiye savatsare.*

158. Tamra S'asana at Bangalore,* date (?) A. D. 444.

3 Plates, 11 in. × 6¼ in., 4 sides. Seal, a Boar.—Nandi Nágari Characters.

Adored be *S'ambhu*, adorned with rays of the moon's digits, ... a mighty tree of bounty.

May it be well. While the protector of all lands, favourite of earth and fortune, great king of kings, supreme ruler, first of monarchs, lord of *Kalyáṇa-pura*, bestower of widowhood on the wives of the elephant-riding *Bhagadatta* kings, a sun to the lotus of the *Chálukya kula*, terrible in war, a bow to *Kalinga*, a sun among males, unsurpassed hero, invincible champion on the field of battle, disgracer of *As'vapati Ráya*, slayer of *Gajapati Ráya*, smiter on the head of *Narapati Ráya*, tanner of the deers his neighbour kings, the daily terror of the four quarters of *Konkaṇa*, to the wives of others as a son, having a flag with the device of a golden boar, adorned with the glory of all lines of kings, born in the *Soma vams'a*,—*S'ri Víra Noṇamba* chakravartti, was in *Kalyáṇa-pura* ruling the kingdom in peace and wisdom :—

On coming to the south on an expedition of victory, halting the army at *Henjaru-gráma*,† in the S'aka year 366, the year Táraṇa, the month Phálguṇa, the dark fortnight, Wednesday, at the time of new moon,—the chief (*múliká*) *Gangaváḍikára*, the *vaḍḍa byavahári* of the Chalukyas, *Maro Saṭṭi*, of Haluháḍi-gráma, situated in the khampana Kundu-náḍ Seventy, in the Gangaváḍi Ninety-six Thousand—having in the Henjaru battle pierced the horse and brought down *Kilva Ráya*—presented five manner of gifts, an umbrella, a palanquin, an escort, a throne, and, together with the (imposts) *anka*, *daṇḍa*, *khanḍane*, and the *ashṭa-bhoga-teja-sámya* rights, with every ceremony, the following land ;‡—4,000 *salage* of rice land, according to . . . . the Múlasthána Deva land 500 *salage* of rice land, Bhalári land 500 of rice land, the goldsmith's land 200, the carpenter's land 200, the barber's land 100, the door keeper's land 100, the . . . land 100.

The boundaries from the north east are as follows :—the Kembbare stream at the joint boundaries of Beluhura and Haluháḍi ; thence south, the banyan

---

* In the Museum. For fac-simile see *Ind. Ant.* Compare with Nos. 130 and 133.

† *Henjaru-grámátú kaṭakam utulitam.*

‡ *Gangaváḍi - chhánnavati -sahasra-madhya khampana- Kundu-náḍu-Eppatara-tatu-madhye Haluháḍi-grámá múliká-Gangaváḍikára Chalukiyara vaḍḍa-byavahári Maro Saṭṭi Henjaru bbavaradalu turakav iridu Kilva Raya manna úna panchánga pasáya chhatra sukhásana bbala gaddi anka daṇḍa khanḍaṇe ashṭa-bhoja-teja-sámya sarba-namasya datta bhúmi.*

tree at the joint boundary of Beluhura and Haluhâḍi; thence south, the white pond at the common boundary of Beluhura, Kadilavágila and Haluháḍi; thence south, the deep pond at the joint boundary of Kadilavágilu and Haluháḍi; thence south, the Chenchari stream at the joint boundary; thence south as far as the Parala mound at the joint boundary of Kaḍilavágila and Haluháḍi. Thence the southern boundaries:—on the south east, the stones of the Svayambhu vritti at the common boundary of Kaḍivágila, Karaváḍi and Haluhádi; thence west, as far as the Chanchari stream at the joint boundary of Karaváḍi and Haluháḍi; thence west, the new stones at the joint boundary. Thence the western boundaries:—on the south-west, the Parala tank at the common boundaries of Kereváḍi, Mangalúr and Haluháḍi; thence north, as far as the Chanchari (stream) at the joint boundary of Mangalúr and Haluháḍi; thence north, the Kaḍaba river at the common boundary of Mangalúr, Hanameváḍi and Haluháḍi; thence north, the group of mixed rocks at the joint boundary of Hanemaváḍi and Haluháḍi. Thence the northern boundaries:—on the north-west, the banyan tree and stream at the common boundary of Hanemaváḍi, Bellúr and Haluháḍi; thence east, as far as the mound at the joint boundary of Bellúr and Haluháḍi; thence east, the white pond at the joint boundary; thence east as far as the . . . at the joint boundary of Bellúr and Haluháḍi; thence east, the Kembare mound at the common boundary of Bellúr, Baluhára and Haluháḍi; thence east, the kalpa tree at the joint boundary of Beluhára and Haluháḍi; thence east it ends at the north east.

Witnesses:—Talakád Hanuvanu, Mangalúr Negavanu, Bbellúr Kachchuvara, Kaḍilavágila Vasyara.

The writing of the skilful Odváchári.

Whoso usurps a . . . . or an inch of land shall go to Naraka and there remain till the final deluge.

Approved (*oppe*)—*Ari-Ráya-mastaka-tala-prahári* (smiter on the heads of hostile kings).

---

159. Tamra S'asana at Hosur,* date about A. D. 640.

3 Plates, 9 in. × 3½ in., 4 sides. Seal, a Boat.—Púrvada Haḷe Kannaḍa Characters.

May it be well. Of the Mánavya gotra, sons of Hárití, brought up by the group of mothers, worshippers of the feet of Svámi Mahásena, were the *Chalukyas*.

To whose completed kingdom the successor, an ornament of his race, his body purified by the final ablutions of the horse sacrifice, was the celebrated *Paulakes'i*, whose second name was *Raṇa Vikrama*.

After him was *Satyás'raya*, the conqueror of *Harsha Varddhana*.

By his own dear son, in his own language (*sva bháshayá*) called *Ambera*, it is thus commanded :†—On the full moon of Mahá Mágha, at the sangama tírtha, during the eclipse of the moon, with presentation of golden coin and pouring of water,—to thirteen of the A'treya gotra, five of the Kaus'ika gotra, three of the Kás'yapa gotra, three of the Kauṇḍinya gotra, three of the Kaus'ika gotra, two of the Sávaṇṇika gotra, one of the Bháradvája gotra, one of the S'aunaka gotra—to these great Brahmans, learned in all the vedas, constant performers of the six rites, altogether thirty-one Brahmans, is given in the *Koṇikal* district, the village called in its (or his) own language *Periyáḷa*.

The sloka delivered by Manu is an example :—The earth has been enjoyed by Sagara and many kings: according to their (gifts of) land so was their reward. Whoso takes away land given by himself or by another shall be born a worm in ordure for sixty thousand years.

---

* For fac-simile see *Ind. Ant.* VII.

† *Sva-priya-sutá sva-bháshayá Amberety ávijnápita san.*

160. Tamra S'asana at Vokkaleri,* date A. D. 758.

5 Plates, 9½ in. × 5½ in., 8 sides. Seal, a Boar.—Púrvada Haḷe Kannaḍa Characters.

May it be well. Supreme is the Boar form of the resplendent Vishnu, which dispersed the waters of the ocean, and bore up the peaceful earth on the tip of his strong right tusk.

Of the Mánavya gotra praised in all the world, sons of Háriti, nourished by the seven mothers the mothers of the seven worlds, through the protection of Karttikeya having acquired a succession of good fortune (or the succession to *Kalyáṇa*), having in a moment brought all kings into their subjection at one glimpse of the boar ensign obtained from the favour of the adorable Náráyaṇa, were (the kings of) the auspicious *Chaulukya* race.

To which (race) an ornament, his body purified by the final ablutions of the horse-sacrifice, was S'ri *Paulakes'i* Vallabha Mahárája.

Whose son, with unsullied fame gained by the conquest of the groups of the *Vanavási* and other hostile kings, was S'ri *Kírtti Varmma*, favourite of the earth, great king.

His son, who encountering in battle S'ri *Harsha Varddhana* the lord of all the north, by defeating him acquired the title of Parames'vara, was *Satyás'raya*, favourite of earth and fortune, great king of kings, supreme lord.

His dear son, perfect in wisdom and reverence, his sword his only aid; making his own the wealth which his father, alone, mounted simply on his splendid horse Chitrakanṭha and desiring to conquer all regions, had won, together with that inherited from three generations; rejoicing in splitting with the thunderbolt of his valour the mountains the *Páṇḍya*, *Choḷa*, *Keraḷa*, *Kalabhra* and other kings from the sky to their base; whose lotus feet were kissed by the crown of the king of *Kánchi* who had never bowed to any other man; was *Vikramáditya Satyás'raya*, favourite of earth and fortune, great king of kings, supreme lord and sovereign.

His dear son, who as Tárakaráti (Kumárasvámi) the son of Bálendu S'ekhara (S'iva) to the forces of the Daityas, so captured the proud army of *Trairájya* the king of *Kánchi*; levier of tribute from the rulers of *Kavera*, *Párasíka*, *Simhala* and other islands; possessed of the *Páḷi dhvaja* and all other marks of supreme wealth, which by churning all the kings of the north

---

* For fac-simile see *Ind. Ant.* VII.

he had won and increased ;* was *Vinayáditya Satyás'raya*, favourite of earth and fortune, great king of kings, supreme lord and sovereign.

His dear son, having in youth acquired the use of all the weapons and accomplishments of a great king ; uprooter of the clumps of thorns (springing up) among the kings of the south of whom his grandfather was the conqueror ; exceeding in valour in the business of war his father who desired to conquer the north, he surrounded his enemies and with his arrows destroyed their elephant forces ;† war his chief policy ; with his glad sword causing the hosts of his enemies to turn their backs ; in the same manner as his father attacking and putting to flight the hostile kings and capturing from them the Gangá, Yamuná and Páḷi flags, the emblems of the great ḍhakka drum, rubies and lusty elephants ; with difficulty stopped by destiny ; by his valour exciting the country ; ‡ in removing kings who cherished evil designs, like Vatsa Rája ; desiring not the assistance of another ; in setting out and with his own arm conquering and subjecting the whole world, a lord like Indra; by the three modes of policy, by breaking the pride of his enemies, by generosity, and by his invincibility, having become the refuge of the world ; having acquired a kingdom resplendent with the Páḷi dhvaja and all other tokens of supreme wealth ; was *Vijayáditya Satyás'raya*, favourite of earth and fortune, great king of kings, supreme lord and sovereign.

His dear son, who upon being anointed as the self-chosen of the Lakshmi of the dominion of the whole world obtained great energy ; who, determined to root out the *Pallavas*, the obscurers of the splendour of the former kings of his line, and by nature hostile, going with great speed into the *Udáka* province, slew in battle the *Pallava* named *Nandi Pota Varmma* who came against him, captured his defiant lotus-mouthed trumpet, his drum called Roar of the Sea, his chariot, his standard, immense and celebrated elephants, clusters of rubies which by their own radiance dispelled all darkness,§ and entering with-

* *Karadíkṛita-Kavera-Párasíka-Simhaḷádi - dvipádhipasya sakalottara-patha-nátha-mathanopárjjitorjjita-páḷi-dvhajádi samasta-páramaisvaryya-chinhasya.*

† *Dakshines'á-vijayini-pitámahe-samunmúlita-akhila-kaṇṭaka-samhatir uttará-patha-vijigishor-guror-agrata-eváhava-vyápáram-ávaran-naráti-gaja - ghaṭa - páṭana-vis'íryyamáṇa-kṛipáṇa-dháras.*

‡ *Gangá-Yamuná-páḷi-dhvajapaṭa-ḍhakká-mahás'abda-chinhá-máṇikya - matangajádín-pitṛisát-kurvvan paraih-paláyamáner-ásádya katham-apividhi-vasád apanito pratápád eva vishaya-prakopam.*

§ *A'tma-vams'aja-púrvva-nṛipati-chchháyápahárinah prakṛity-amitrasya (k) Pallavasya samúlottúlanáya-kṛitamatir ati-tvarayát Udáka-vishayam-prápyábhimukhágatan Nandi-Poti-Varmmábhidánam-Pallavam-raṇa-mukhe-samprahṛitya prapalásya-kankamukha-váditrá-samudraghoshábhidána-vádya-vis'eshán khaṭvánga-dhvaja-prabhúta - prakhyáta-hasti-varán sva-kiraṇa-nikara-vikása-nirákṛita-timiram-mánikya-rásin-cha hastekritya.*

out destruction *Kánchi*, the zone (*kánchi*) as it were of the lady the region of Agastya's abode (i. e. the south), acquired the great merit of covering with gold Rája Simhes'vara and other *deva kula* sculptured in stone, which *Narasimha Pota Varmma*—the protector of poor and indigent Brahmans rejoiced by the bestowal of continual gifts—had made (or created); the sovereign who by his invincible valour having withered up *Páṇḍya*, *Chola*, *Kerala*, *Kaḷabhra* and other kings, was residing in *Jayamambha*, the embodiment of a fame as brilliant as the pure light of the autumn moon, situated on the shore of the southern ocean called the Rolling Ocean, whose shores were strewn over and glittering with marine heaps composed of clusters of pearls scattered from their shells by blows from the snouts of crocodiles resembling mighty elephants;* was *Vikramáditya Satyás'raya*, favourite of earth and fortune, great king of kings, supreme lord and sovereign.

His dear son, in youth well instructed in the use of arms, perfect in subduing the six kinds of passions; who, through the joy which his father felt on account of his good qualities, having obtained the rank of Yuva Rája, prayed for an order, saying 'Send me to subdue the king of *Kánchi*, the enemy of our race', and immediately on obtaining it, marched forth and going against him, broke the power of *Pallava*,—who unable to make war on a large scale took refuge in a hill-fort,—and capturing his lusty elephants, his rubies, and treasury of gold, delivered them to his father; thus in due time having obtained the title of Sárvva-bhauma,† the lotus of his feet covered with the pollen the gold dust from the crowns of lines of kings prostrate before him through reverence or fear; *Kirtti Varmma*, favourite of earth and fortune, great king of kings, supreme lord and sovereign, thus commands all people:—

Be it known to you from us, that the 679th s'aka year having passed, and the 11th year of the increase of our victorious reign being current;‡ from our

* *Kalas'abhava-nilaya-harid angan-ánchita-kánchiya-mána Kánchim avinásya pravis'ya santata-pravritta-dáná-nandita-dvijja-dinánátha-jano Narasimha-Pota-Varmma-nimmápita-s'ilámaya-Rájasimhes'varádi-deva-kula-suvarṇa-rási-pratyarpaṇoparjitojita-puṇyah nivárita-pratápa-prasara-pratápita-Páṇḍya-Choḷa-Keraḷa-Kaḷabhra-prabhriti-rájanyaka-kshubhita-kara-malara-karahata-dalita-s'ukti-mukta-muktáphala-prakara-márichi-jála-vilasita-velákula-Ghúrṇamánárṇábhidháne dakshiṇárṇave s'arad-amala-s'as'adhara-visada-yas'o-rás'imayam Jayamambham atishṭhipad.*

† *Sva-guṇa-kalád(h)-ánandita-hridayena-pitrá-samáropita-yauva-rájyah sva-kula-vairiṇam-Kánchipate-nnigraháya mám-preshaya ity ádes'am-prárthya labdhvá tadanantaram eva krita-prayánas-san abhimukham-ágatya prakás'a-yuddham-kartum-asamartha-pravishṭha-durggam Pallavam bhagna-s'aktim kritvá matta malangaja máṇikya suvarṇa kotir ádáya pitre samarpitaván evam kramena prápta sárvvabhauma padah-*

‡ *Nava-saptaty-uttara-shaṭ-chhateshu S'aka-varsheshu atiteshu pravarddhamána-vijaya-rájya-samvatsare ekádasi varttamáne.*

victorious camp stationed at the village of Gaviṭṭage, on the northern bank of the Bhímarathí river, on the full-moon day of Bhádrapada, on the application of *S'ri Dosi Rája*, is given to Mádhava S'armma, the son of Krishna S'armma, and grandson of S'ri Vishnu S'armma, of the Kámakáyana gotra, versed in the Rig and Yajur vedas, together with Nengiyúr and Nandi, the village named *Suḷḷiyúr*, situated in the *Pánungal* district, on the southern bank of the Aṛadoṇe river, in the midst of the villages of Támaramúge, Pánungal, Kiṛuvaḷḷi and Bálavúru.

This let future kings, whether of our own or of any other race, reflecting that life and wealth are fleeting, preserve as long as sun, moon, earth and ocean endure, as if a gift made by themselves and thus perpetuate their glory. And by the adorable Vyása, arranger of the vedas, hath it been said: The earth has been enjoyed by Sagara and many kings: according to their (gifts of) land so was their reward. To make a gift oneself is easy; to maintain another's that is the difficulty: but of making a gift or maintaining one, the maintaining a gift is the best. Whoso resumes a gift made by himself or by another shall assuredly to born a worm in ordure for sixty thousand years.

By the great minister for peace and war, S'rimad *Aniváṛita Dhananjaya Puṇya Vallabha* was this s'ásana written.

---

161. Rock Inscription at Sravana Belgola, date (?) about 100 B. C.

Púrvada Haḷe Kannaḍa Characters.

May it be well. Success through the adorable *Varddhamána*, a *tirthankara* by his own merit, an embodiment of the nectar of the peace of acquired *siddhi* (the fruit of penance); refuge of both the upper and lower worlds, himself all things movable and immovable, by his own energy pervading the worlds of both mind and matter; having obtained inconceivable greatness and supreme honor throughout the world, having acquired the great *arhantya* in the group of worthies who have become *tirthankaras*: moreover whose undisputed (and indisputable) doctrine, overcoming those of the other disputing sects, is supreme in *S'ri Vis'ála*, and a security to the world.*

---

* *Tadanu S'ri Vis'áleyaj-jayatyadya jaggadhitam tasya s'ásanam avyájam praváḍi mata s'ásanam* ||

After the great sun *Mahávíra* had gone down,—an abode of glorious qualities which illuminated all worlds, a great orb of a thousand brilliant rays, which, dispersing the darkness, caused to unfold the lotus of the faithful multiplying in the lake of the supreme Jain faith :—(there arose) the adorable great rishi *Gautama gaṇadhara*, his personal disciple *Lohárya*, *Jambu*, *Vishnu Deva*, *Aparájita*, *Govarddhana*, *Bhadra Báhu*, *Vis'ákha*, *Proshṭhila*, *Kshatrikárya*, *Jayanáma*, *Siddhárta*, *Dhṛitishena*, *Buddhila* and other gurus.

Bhadra Báhu Svámi, of the illustrious line and direct descent of these great men, who by virtue of his severe penance had acquired the essence of knowledge ; having, by his power of discovering the past, present and future, foretold in *Ujjayini* a period of twelve years of dire calamity (or famine), all classes of the people leaving the northern regions took their way to the south under the rishi's direction.*

And in the countries they traversed might be counted many hundreds of villages filled with ruins, among which appeared remains of human bodies, money, gold, grain, cows, buffaloes and goats. But when they had reached a mountain with lofty peaks, whose name was *Kaṭavapra*—an ornament to the earth ; the ground around which was variegated with the brilliant hues of the clusters of gay flowers fallen from the beautiful trees ; the rocks on which were as dark as the great rain-clouds filled with water ; abounding with wild boars, panthers, tigers, bears, hyenas, serpents and deer ; filled with caves, caverns, large ravines and forests ;—that moon among the *ácháris*, perceiving that but little time remained for him to live, and fearing on account of his present mode of life, announced to the people his desire to do the penance before death, and dismissed them so that none were left. Then, with one single disciple, performing the *sanyasana* on stones covered with grass, by degrees he quitted his body and attained to the state of the seven hundred rishis.†

May it prosper, this Jina s'ásana.

---

* *Mahávira savitari parinirvṛite bhagavat paramarshi Gautama gaṇadhara sákshách-chishya Lohárya Jambu Vishnu-Dev Aparájita Govarddhana Bhadra-Báhu Visákha Proshṭhila Kshatrikárya Jayanáma Siddhártha Dhṛitishena Buddhiládi guru paramparena kramábhyágata mahápurusha santati samavadyotitánvaya Bhadra Báhu svíminám Ujjayinyám ashṭánga-mahá-nimitta-tatvajnena traikálya-dars'ina-nimittena dvádas'a-samvatsara-kála-vaishamyam upalabhya kathite sarva-sanghah uttara-pathád dakshina-patham prasthitah árshenaiva.*

† *Atah áchárya . . . . jívita-s'esham alpatara-kálam avabudhyádhvanah suchakitah tapas-samádhim árádhayitumáprichchhya niravas'eshená sangham visṛijya s'ishyeṇaikeva pṛithulakastírṇa talásu s'ilásu sva-deham sanyasyárádhitaván kramena sapta-s'atam ṛishiṇám arádhilam iti.*

162. Rock Inscription at Sravana Belgola,*

date (?) about A. D. 200.

Púrvada Haḷe Kannaḍa Characters.

Rapidly scattering like the rainbow, like clustering flashes of lightning, or like a dewy cloud ; to whom are the treasures of beauty, pleasure, wealth and power secure ? Should I who love the chief good, remain attached to this world ? Thus saying, he assumed the state of a sannyási, and by his virtue the eminent muni *Sena Pravara* reached the world of gods.†

---

163. S'ila S'asana at Gulganpode, date (?) about A. D. 300.

Size 4¾ ft.×4¾ ft.—Púrvada Haḷe Kannaḍa Characters.

May it be well. While *S'ri Mahávali Baṇarasa*,—born in the *Mahávali kula*, (?) doorkeepers to Parames'vara the lord over gods and demons, praised by all three worlds,—was ruling the kingdom of the world :—

A brave heart dying has merit in a son, his lord has merit in the enterprise which shewed his valour. Thus, like a brave man, *Viyaḷa Vijyadhara*, at the command of the great lord who ruled him, pursuing that *Marigára*, pierced him : then there being no footing for the horse, dismounting from the horse, he went down walking, and joining fight, fell. To him is given for a livelihood Kula Nallúr free of all imposts. ‡

Whoso usurps a gift made by himself or by another shall be born a worm in ordure for sixty thousand years.

---

* For fac-simile see *Ind. Ant.* II, 266.

† *Sura chápam bôle vidyul lategaḷa teṛa vôl manju vôl tôṛi begam piridhu s'ri rúpa lîlá dhana vibhava mahá rásigaḷ nillav árgge paramarttha mechche nán i dharaṇiyul iraván endu sanyasana gayduru satvannaḍi Sena Pravara munivara deva lokakke sandár.*

‡ *Svasti sakala-jagat-trayábhivandita-surásurádhisa-Parames'vara - pratihárikrita- Mahávali-kulotbhava S'ri Mahávali Baṇarasam prithuvi rájya geye | manas urar aḷi kaype maganam prabhu kaype tuḷi geva santan | ganḍa paḍi vapa Viyaḷa Vijyadhara tannan áḷva prabhu-mera besased á Marigáran aṭṭi iṛidu kuduregе páhg illa áge kudure-ind iḷidu naḍad iḷid oṭṭi keydu bíldan-avage bál-gaḷvu koṭṭodu Kula Nallúr savva parihára.*

164. S'ila S'asana at Gulganpode, date (?) about A. D. 500.

Size 6 ft. × 4½ ft.—Púrvada Haḷe Kannaḍa Characters.

May it be well. While *S'ri Mahávali Báṇarasa*—a great king Vikramáditya, who as a mount Meru of victory received from other kings the celebrated name of Báṇa Vijyádhara—was ruling the kingdom of the world :—

Pekkiri Voradoga Rája, of great beauty, of the highest valour, a mount Meru of bravery, by command of the great lord who ruled him, fighting in *Manchindi-úru* and causing the whole of the beseiging force to retreat ; his army being weary, he, unshaken as a mountain, marched on, and coming up with the chiefs, pierced and drove them off and fell. His army, putting off their arms in the town near which they had come, raised a lamentation and made a gift to yield an annual income for him.

Whoso through avarice, covetousness or envy usurps it and lets that waste be uncultivated, shall incur the guilt of the five great sins.

To him in whose name this gift stands, to him shall be given five ploughs, with release from fighting.

---

165. S'ila S'asana at Anantapur, date A. D. 1079.

Haḷe Kannaḍa Characters.

May it prosper.—While the victorious kingdom of the protector of all lands favourite of earth and fortune, great king of kings supreme lord, first of monarchs, glory of the *Satyas'raya kula*, ornament of the *Chálukyas*,† S'rimat *Tribhuvana Malla Deva*, was increasing in prosperity to endure as long as sun, moon, stars and sky ; and he was in his residence at *Kalyáṇa*, ruling the kingdom in the enjoyment of peace and wisdom :—‡

---

* *Svasti tasya s'ri-Vikramáditya-jaya-mero-mmahibhrit Báṇa Vijyádhara khyáta-námadheyasya rájabhi S'ri Mahávali Báṇarasar prithuvi rájya geye aṇi-chelvan aṇuma parákraman vira mahá meru Pekkiṛi Voradoga Rájan tannan áḷva prabhu meru besase Manchindi úrul kádu vaṭṭiya samasta balamu mógeṛtare tamma paḍe geṭṭu beṭṭan adare tamid irane naḍadu náyakaruḷ taḍa iṛidu óḍisi bildan tamma paḍe baḷikke band úroḷ gaḷagonḍ attu avange vas'otpattiyáge dáya goṭṭodum á deguḷum biḷádeyu yo parahate lobhán mohát pramádád vá sa panchabhi mmahadbhi pátakke yukto bhavati. I dhammad id ávaṇa perund avvange koṭṭodu ai guḷa kaḷani parihára.*

† See note p. 14.

‡ See note p. 2.

And his younger brother, praised in all the world, prince of the world-renowned *Pallava* race, supreme lord and valliant sovereign of the *Yuva rájya*, an ornament to *Vikrama*, lover of the Lakshmi of victory, head jewel of the *Chálukyas*, in war the three-eyed, of pure Kshattriya descent, powerful as a rutting elephant, master of patience, to the forces of hostile kings . . . . . S'rimat *Trayalokya Malla Vira Noḷamba Pallava Permmanaḍi Jaya Singha Deva*, was ruling the *Baṇavàse* Twelve Thousand in the enjoyment of wisdom :—*

The dweller at his lotus feet, entitled to the five great drums, master over great feudatories, great and fierce Danḍanáyaka, benefactor to the learned, purifier of his race, the sole friend of the world, . . . a jewel of truth, in prudence Brihaspati, vowed to prosperity, to others' wives as a son, ... the abode of all good qualities, the joy of both kings,† worshipper of the feet of S'rimat Trayalokya Malla Víra Noḷamba Pallava Permmánaḍi Jaya Singha Deva, subduer of hostile forces, possessed of these and all other titles, the mahá pradhána, the senior Danḍanáyaka for peace and war,‡ *Tambarasa*, ruling the *Sántalige* Thousand and the agraháras, punishing the evil and protecting the good :—

The royal agent for that nád having favoured his commands to *Máchi Rája* :—§

A blossom to all the world was *Sindaváḍi*—and among its agraháras the most charming was *Kambagála Beḷgali*, a jewel to which ornament of the earth, born in the Atreya gotra, of great fame, was the lord *Máchi*. That mahá purusha, born to Somanáthayya and Abbakabbe, possessor of all good qualities, purifier of his gotra, friend of the wise, *Máchi Rája*, acting according to the orders of the royal agent, set up on the north east side of the tírtha in the north east of the royal city *Andásura*—the god Máches'vara, the god A'ditya, and the god Vishnu, in the 3rd year of Chálukya Vikrama, the year Siddarthi, at the time of uttaráyana sankránti ; and washing the feet of *Ananta S'iva Panḍita*, perfect in *yama*, *niyama*, *svádhyáya*, &c., ¶ (rest not copied).

---

* *Tad ánujam svasti samasta-bhuvana-stúyamánam loka-vikhyáta-Pallavanvaya-s'ri-mahí-vallabham yuva-rájya-rája-parames'vara-vira-mahes'varam Vikramábharaṇam Jaya-Lakshmí-ramaṇam Chálukya-chúḍámaṇi kadana-trinetra-kshatriya-pavitram matta-gajanga-rája sahaja-manujam ripu-ráya-kaṭaka-súra . . . kálam s'rimat Trayalokya Malla Vira Noḷamba Pallava Permmanaḍi Jaya Singha Devar Banavàse pannirchchhásiramumam sankathá vinoda-dim rájyam geyuttam ire.*

† *Ubhaya-ráya-santosam.*

‡ *Hiri-sandhi-vigraha-danḍanáyakam.*

§ *A' náḍa rájádyakshapa besanam Máchi Rájange deya geydu kuḍe !*

¶ See note p. 16.

166. S'ila S'asana at Nirgunda, date about A. D. 1250.

Haḷe Kannaḍa Characters.

Fortune. Adored be *S'ambhu*, beauteous with the chamara-like crescent moon kissing his lofty head; the original foundation-pillar of the city of the three worlds.

May it be well. While, entitled to the five great drums, the Mahá Maṇḍales'vara, lord of *Dvárávati-pura*, a sun to the firmament of the *Yádava* race, a head jewel among all princes, champion among the *Maḷparu*, adorned with the name of *Poysaṇa* and many other splendid titles, S'rimat *Tribhuvana Malla Víra Ganga Hoysaṇa Deva*, was growing in prosperity to endure as long as sun, moon, stars and sky: and he was ruling the *Gangaváḍi* Ninety-six Thousand, punishing the evil and protecting the good, in the enjoyment of peace and wisdom :—*

In the S'aka year 987, the year Nala, the month Pushya, the 5th day of the moon's increase, Thursday, the time of the sun's entering the northern signs :—While the offspring of the *Ganga* race celebrated in all the world, Konguḷi Varmma Dharmma Mahárájadhirája, a tree of bounty to his dependents, lord of *Koḷála-pura*, valiant prince, having the crest of a lusty elephant, distributor of gold, having obtained a boon from Padmávati Devi, the Ganga Cupid, a Ganga of truth, promoter of victory, sun to the lotus of the *Ganga kula*, the Ganga Bhishma, ... worshipper of the feet of S'iva, subduer of hostile forces, a bow to the proudest, . . . scatterer of his enemies, the sole hero, . . . a cage of adamant to his dependents, a lion to the elephants his enemies, in war a close fighter, a saw to his enemies, to others' wives a brother, . . . adorned with all titles, S'riman Mahá Manḍales'vara *Gangarasa* was ruling the *Arabala* Seventy, and the *Meláḷa manṇeya*, punishing the evil and protecting the good :†—

* See note p. 2.

† *Samasta-vasumati-tala-khyátam Gangánvaya-prasútam Konguḷi-Varmmo-Dharmma-Maharájádhirója vandi-jana-kalpa-bhuja Koḷálapura-varádhis'varam víra-mahes'varam madagajendra-lánchanam vinayoga-kánchanam Padumávati-Devi-labdhar-vara-prasádam . . .. dámodam nanniya-Gangam jayad-uttarangam Gango-kula-kamala-márttanḍam Ganga-Gángeyam kas'a-gamakiváḍi-vágindreyam S'iva-pádárádhakam para-bala-sádhakam ganḍa-prachanḍa-kodanḍa . . . para-bala-dúrttan ekyánga-viran . . s'aranágata-vajra-pinjaram vahirini-kunjaram âhava-jaṭṭa- laṭṭam vayiri-gharaṭṭam para-nári-sahodaram . . samasta-námávaḷi-samálankrita-sametam S'rimanu Mahá Manḍales'varam Gangarasaru Arabalav-eppattumam Meláḷa-manṇeya-sahitam dushṭa-nigraha-s'ishṭa-pratipálanadind áluttam ire.*

The capturer of *Nangali, Kongu, Singha-male, Ráyapura,* and *Talakáḍu;* living in *Bengiri;* displaying the greatness of his might in *Koḷḷagiri, Balare, Valúru, Chakragoṭṭa, Uchangi, Viráṭa, Poḷalu, Bankapura, Banavāse* and *Koyatúr,* he reached the highest standard of valour—*Vishnu Varddhana.**

His eldest son was *Narasingha* Bhúpálaka. His standards reaching as far as the peaks of *Devagiri,* his valour displayed as far as (?) Vahnáchala . . . . may he prevail in the earth, S'ri *Narasimha* Bhúpati. In autumn the disturber of other kings, in happiness like Bálachandra, dwelling in pleasure like Indra, ornament of the Yadu kula, delighting in war with his enemies, of secure and growing glory, exalted by his own victories, lord of the world, was *Narasimha* Bhúmipála, the established favourite of Lakshmi, the Hokkasala (? Hoysala) lord.

His son, the power of whose arms was as follows:—The favourite of victory, his two feet planted on the heads of all kings, . . . mighty to subdue enemies unmoved by others . . . . was *Balláḷa Bhúpálaka* . . . . *Balláḷa* nripála.

While, thus celebrated, the Mahá Mandales'vara, ... of *Talakáḍu, Gangavádi, Noṇambaváḍi, Banavase,* and *Hánungalu,* Bhujabala Víra Ganga, unassisted hero, Malla of the Sanivára Siddigiri-durga, in bravery like Ráma, of unshaken valour, *Hoysaṇa Víra Balláḷa Deva,* punishing the evil and protecting the good in the *Gangaváḍi* Ninety-six Thousand, was in his residence at *Dorasamudra,* ruling the kingdom in the enjoyment of peace and wisdom† :—

May it be well. While the protector of all lands, favourite of earth and fortune, great king of kings, supreme lord, the sun in the firmament of the Yádava race, the head ornament of all princes, Malla of the Male Rájas, champion among the Mallapas, *gaṇḍa bheruṇḍa,* immovable warrior, unassisted hero, sole hero of the earth, Malla of the Sanivára Siddigiri-durga, in bravery like Ráma, a lion to the elephants the hostile kings, the uprooter of the *Magada* kingdom, the disgracer of the *Páṇḍya* kingdom, the setter up of the *Choḷa* kingdom,‡ the emperor of unshaken valour, *Hoysaṇa Bhujabala Víra Somes'vara Deva* was ruling the kingdom in the enjoyment of peace and wisdom† :—

---

* *Nangali Kongu Singhamale Ráya-pura Talakáḍu kondavá Bengiri-vási Koḷḷagiri Balare Valúru Chakragoṭṭav Uchangi Viráṭanam Poḷalu Bankapuram Banavāse Koyatúr tunga parákraman negaḷdu vikrama nikala Vishnu Varddhanam* ‖

† See note p. 2.

‡ See note p. 7.

The servant of his feet, was *Vijaya Náyaka* of *Nirugunḍa,* whose greatness was as follows :—

. . . of great fierceness to the enemy's army . . . was *Baṭṭaya Náyaka*, the chief support of his lord in the field of battle. The servant of his feet :—In wealth like Kubera, having no equal in the world, was (?) *Devánka Seṭṭi*, devoted to him with affection. To that Des'i Seṭṭi and the jewel of women Chandalángana, like a young rising sun, was born a son . . . To describe the greatness of his qualities :— . . . . in liberality a kalpa vriksha, in brightness the sun, in greatness mount Meru, ... was the lord *Nala Seṭṭi*. Like as the river Ganges in wrath descended on the head of S'iva and spread over the world, so did the creeper of the fame of *Ballála Seṭṭi* fill the world. He, restoring without any stint the ruined places and bestowing them on Brahmans, obtained the name of Badigere Mala in the world. As Lakshmi to Vishnu, so to him was Devama the wife. To whom, in consequence of their vows, was born their eldest son *Nalli Seṭṭi*. A light to his race, in the form of justice, of immeasurable greatness, he was as a pure shining mirror, *Nalle Seṭṭi* . . . . for the decoration and processions of the god Siddhanátha Deva, for the bathing and daily offering, for the procession in Chaitra, and for repairs of his temple, presented, below the Hiriya kere (*rest not copied*). . .

---

167. Tamra S'asana at Karigatta, date A. D. 1680.

3 Plates, 4 sides.—Devanágari Characters.

May the Boar protect us, on whose right tusk the earth rested with joy, surmounted by the peak of Hemádri like a canopy.

From the lotus navel of Vishnu, filled with all auspicious qualities, the husband of Lakshmi, was born the progenitor of the world (Brahma). From him Atri, from Atri Chandra, from Chandra Budha, from Budha Puru, from Puru Ayu, from Ayu Nahusha, from Nahusha Yayáti, from Yayáti *Yadu* Bhúpati, whose descendants grew to power in the region around *Dváraka-nagara*.

Certain of those born in this race, coming to the *Karṇáṭa* country to visit Ramáramaṇa, the god of their race, who is the glory of the height of

Yadugiri; seeing the beauty of the country, they settled with great desire in *Mahishúra-pura* for the protection of the people.*

From them, of famous character, imposing his commands on the heads of tributary kings, sprang *Deva Rája Mahipati*. As to Das'aratha, so to him were born four sons. The first of them was *Dodda Deva Rája*, like Ráma himself in receiving daily service from his brothers, like Indra himself in daily protecting the *vibudha* (deities, otherwise the learned), the refuge of highest merit, of great valour in destroying the forces of the proudest enemies, perfect in the science of overcoming hostile kings, thus was he rightly called Deva Rája (i. e. Indra). His virtuous wife *Amritámba*, as Síta bore Kus'a and Lava, so bore *Chikka Devendra* and *Kanthírava Mahipati*.

Placing his feet on the heads of all kings, filling all regions with his wealth, and thus protecting all his subjects, displaying the path of virtue, ever creating happiness in the world, *Chikka Devendra* was without doubt like Chandra (the moon) himself. In the east, defeating in war the *Pándya Chokka Bhúpa*, he captured the great *Tripura* which was in his possession, and also *Anantapuri*. In the west, overthrowing the *Kelali* kings, who were under the power of the *Yavanas*, he took *Sakales'apura* and *Arakalgúdu*. In the north, defeating *Ranadúlá Khán*, he seized *Ketasamudra*, *Kandikere*,, *Handalagere*, *Gúlúru*, *Tumukúru*, and *Honnavalli*. Overcoming *Mushtika*, who was supported by the *Morasas* and *Kirátas*, he captured *Jadakanadurga*, and gave it the name of *Chikka Devaráyadurga*. From *S'rimushna* he removed the original varáha, which had been thrown down by the Yavanas, and took it to *S'rírangapatna* through devotion to Vishnu. Defeating *Timmappa Gauda* and *Rámappa Gauda*, he captured *Maddagiri*, *Midages'i*, *Bijjavara* and *Channaráyadurga*.

He, while seated on the jewel throne in the *Paschima Ranga nagara*, governing the kingdom with reverence for gods and Brahmans, the S'aka year reckoned as *indu*, *bindu*, *anga* and *chandra* (1601) having passed, and the year Siddharti being current, in the month Saha (Kartika), on the 2nd day of the moon's decrease, the anniversary of his father's death, in the presence of *Venkates'a*, god of gods, dwelling in *Níláchala* on the northern branch of the *Káveri*;—for the purpose of providing for the performance to him of all manner of ceremonies and worship, presented to four chief Vaishnavas four freeholds, namely, (*here follow their names, &c.*)

To these has this támra s'ásana been given. And the details of the grant are here written in the language of the country. (*Rest not copied*).

---

* *Tasyám kritáva'árah katichana Karnáta-des'am ájagmuh Yadugiri-s'ikharábharanam kula-daivatam ikshitum Ramáramanam asya des'asya saubhágyam avalokya samutsukáh asmin prajáh pálayanto Mahishúra-pure vasan.*

168. Tamra S'asana at Tonnur, date A. D. 1723.

18 Plates, 34 sides.— Devanágari Characters.

Reverence to *S'ri Rámánuja.* May the Boar be ever the protection of the three worlds, which raised up the earth from the ocean, supporting on the tip of his tusk the tortoise on which rests A'disesha, and on him the elephants at the points of the compass, on them mount Meru, and on it the earth resembling a flower, overspread by the sky. May the primeval Boar be your protection, which raised up from the ocean the earth whose forests stood up as if she were horripilated with joy at being lifted by her lover. May the tusk of the boar form of Vishnu protect you, on which rests the earth covered with ranges of snowy mountains resembling canopies.

On the leaf of the banyan was he (Vishnu) reposing, the creator, preserver and destroyer of the universe, the birthplace of all fortune, the subduer of all evil, that one supreme, whose assistants are Brahma and Lakshmi. From the lotus of his navel sprang the golden wombed (Brahma); from whom, of celebrated character, sprang Atri, to whom were obedient Vishnu, Brahma and Siva. From his eyes was born Chandra, who dwells on the head of the three-eyed (S'iva) garlanded with the constellations, the original of the Kshatriya race. From him sprang Budha, from him Pururava, from him Ayus, from Ayus Nahusha, from Nahusha Yayáti, from Yayati *Yadu Bhúpati*, whose descendants occupied the city of *Dváraka.*

Of that race some came to the *Karnáṭa* country to visit Ramáramaṇa their *kula deva*, the glory of the height of Yadugiri. Seeing the beauty of the country and desiring to dwell there, they settled in *Mahishúra-pura.**

From them sprang *Beṭṭa Cháma Ráṭ*, a mill for grinding the wheat his enemies, who gained the new title of Ambara Gaṇḍa. To him were born three sons—first, *Timma Rája* Mahipati; second, his brother *Krishna Bhúpati*; the last, his brother *Cháma nripa*, possessed of all good qualities, the victor in battle over *Timati Venkaṭa* the general of *Ráma Rája*.

He (the last) had four sons, who though unequalled by any others in the world were equal among themselves, promoters of victory as if the embodiment of the four modes of royal policy. The first of them, *Rájadharádhirája*, thrashed the proud lord of *Kárugahalli* on the field of battle with his riding whip, and conquering *Tirumala Rája* took *S'rirangapaṭṇa*, and seating him self on its throne acquired the dominion of a Sárvabhauma. His younger brother was *Beṭṭada Cháma Rája*, who with the fire of his valour consumed

---

* See note p. 310.

all the hostile kings, who slew immense numbers on the field of battle with wounds resembling the sacred thread. His younger brother was *Deva Rájendra*, to whom, as Jishnu to Vishnu, the younger brother was *Cháma Rája*.

To *Deva Rájendra* were born four sons, as to Das'aratha. The first of them was *Dodda Deva Rája*, a very Rama himself, whom all his brothers daily served through devotion, pure, of good character, full of merit, grateful, performer of his vows, giver of gifts, benevolent, of great bravery, celebrated for merit and fame. The second was *Chikka Deva Rájendra*, who, in mind, speech, and life resembling Lakshmana, was devoted to his brother. The third was *Deva Rája*, second to none in his good qualities, a kalpa vriksha to his dependents. His younger brother *Mariya Deva*, of great virtue, performer of good actions, was of great devotion to his elder brother,—who, being generous, an ocean of mercy, heroic, a sea of friendship, brave, while he ruled the world its happiness was like that under the government of Ráma.

To the elder brother *Dodda Deva Rája* the celebrated *Amritámba* was wife, who, as Sita bore Kus'a and Lava to Rama, so to this king bore *Chikka Devendra* and *Kanthirava Mahipati*. Of them the elder, *Chikka Devendra*, of good qualities, brave, skilled in all knowledge, generous, was as celebrated as Upendra. By him was the Chandra vams'a greatly exalted, more than by Yayáti, Vikrama, or any of the kings of old. To him was wedded the Lakshmi of victory, a sea of all good qualities, the self chosen lord of fame.

In the world were none greater than *Chikka Deva*; if there were, none were more worthy; if there were, none could stand before him in battle; if there were such, none were more ready to forgive a fault. At mere sight of this punisher of the evil and protector of the good, his enemies became motionless with fear; on account of whom Vishnu through love for the earth became the sword in his hand, with which cutting down the forces of his enemies he drew out their entrails, and smiting down proud kings, protecting others, conquering the lord of *Madhura*, imitated the sports of Krishna. Entering the field of battle and knocking off the crowns of the hostile kings, his sword danced about, while the Lakshmi of the victory of his arms sang. As if he were wedding the Lakshmi of victory, the jewels fallen from the crowns of kings were gems for her, the varied shreds of their gay dresses were as decorations for her . . . . his sword dropping blood was as a female bestowing the Kashmir árati, a support to the vine of victory, the destroyer of proud hostile kings, a joy to his dependents. In a dream was this sword given to him by Vishnu, by which he slew thousands of kings. Terrible as Máya, or S'ambara, or Indrajit, or Máricha, he went forth and conquered many districts about (?) *Dilli* and *Bhágangara* and obtained the name of unequalled hero.

S'ambhu lost his valour, *Kutupu Sháh* lost all hope, *Ikkeri Basava* trembled, *Ekoji* absconded alone, *Dádoji* . . . when *Chikka Deva* nripati came forth to war. The . . . in one direction, the *Turukas* on one side, the *Marasas* in the middle, the group of *Arayas* in another place, the *Tigalas* all round, the *Kaṭakas* in one part, the *Malegas* in one quarter,—thus did he make offerings of these to all the points of the compass, and acquire a lofty fame ; and speedily destroying all the groups of kings, and taking tribute from *Kutupu Sháh*, obtained great glory in the world. As the animals in the forest flee at sight of the lion, as the dove flees at sight of the hawk, as the hare flees at sight of the tiger, as the snake flees at sight of the kite, thus did all the kings flee at sight of *Chikka Deva* as if a new created Narasimha.

Male of males, champion over the sons of boasters, champion over those who oppose with arms, punisher of kings who break their word, champion over the bravest in war, possessed of these and many other titles, was *Chikka Deva Rája*.

Bala chakravarti gave to Vishnu but one world, which had belonged to many ; Narayana gave to the Brahmans but a few sayings of those from his lips ; the sun gives but a few rays to the earth for which he takes a return : but *Chikka Deva Rája* gives without stint and takes nothing back. The moon gives away one less than 16 digits one by one till nothing is left him, but *Chikka Deva Rája* gives away the 16 shades (or standards of gold) and yet is as rich as before. For the worthy among his dependents he provided permanent abodes in *S'riranga*, the *Yadu* hills, *Anjanagiri*, *Kanchi*, *Víkshavana*, *Setu*, *S'ankhamukha*, *Darbhasa'yana*, *Kumbhakona*, *Kás'i*, *Dvárávati pura*, *Jagannátha*, and *Prayága*. The story of Prithu in face of him became vain, Nala lost his name, Raghu's fame was diminished, what mention then of Kártavírya ? When *Chikka Deva Rája* ruled the world where was the glory of Dilípa ?

Among the worthiest of women, beloved as Lakshmi by Vishnu, so to him was his wife *S'ri Devamámba*. In devotion to her husband S'ri Devamámba was the first of all women, her good qualities eclipsed those of Sudakshina, like the embodiment of the energy of Vishnu, or none else than the incarnation of his mercy, born to protect the world. To describe her virtues even the many tongues of A'disesha would fail, how then can one tongue suffice ? While along with her, this famous king *Chikka Deva* nripati was ruling the world for a long time, having conquered all the neighbouring kings, protecting Brahmans, gods, friends, the learned and his dependents—he was to the world like the lord of Lakshmi.

To that king Chikka Deva by his wife Devamámba was born, as if an emanation from Vishnu, a son *Rája Kanṭhiravendra*. He was in virtue Ramachandra himself, in uprooting the groups of hostile kings like an elephant, in keeping to rules like a perfect poet, in good qualities Vishnu himself. From Kausalya was born Rama with the face of the moon, from Devaki was born Krishna with a face like a jewelled mirror, but as if Narasimha reflecting that he was born from a pillar with a face of terror had again been born from this Devamámba, so was *Rája Kanṭhirava*. Lakshmi dwelt in his side glance, Sarasvati in his face, faith in the lotus feet of Vishnu in his mind, the earth in his arms, the Lakshmi of liberality in his hands, the radiance of the gems in the crowns of kings in his feet, the learned in his house, his fame in the three worlds.

Having divided the whole of his kingdom into four parts, the first he gave to Brahmans, the second to the gods, the third as gifts of merit, the fourth retaining for himself, he ruled the world. In his reign good food was distributed in every village, so also in every village were there temples in which daily there were processions, in every road were groves and watersheds. Having great joy in all learning, like Yama in devoting to the flames all hostile kings, filled with all good qualities. A moon to the ocean of the royal race, brave, having the title Dharani Varáha, the unmoved in the field of battle, in the assemblies of women a Manmatha, the son of Chikka Deva Rája.

The wife of Kanthirava Raja was *Chelvájamámba*, celebrated in the world as in devotion to her husband like Sita to Rama. In qualities, name, patience, character, merit, beauty, faith in Vishnu, she eclipsed all the world.

To her by Kanthirava Rája, as from Devaki was born Krishna to protect the world, so was born *Kṛishna Rája*. At the time of his birth, Chikka Devendra obtained a higher name as a conqueror, in his hands were the signs of the chakra, s'ankha and kamala—shewing him to be Krishna himself; his fame increased from day to day as the moon fills up her digits; while an infant all kings prostrated themselves at his feet as the great mountains place he rays of the sun on their heads as soon as he rises; as Krishna when an infant taking two or three steps carried the world in his hand, so as soon as he began to walk about the house all kings hastened to bring their tribute and fall at his feet.

Sovereign of the throne of the western Rangarája-nagara, his mind placed at the lotus feet of Náráyana, his feet reverenced by the crowns of hostile kings, making the protection of gods and Brahmans his chief duty, displaying all the qualities of Chikka Deva Bhúpaja, namely nobility, respect, wisdom, gentle speech, power, kindness, valour, skill, generosity,—through faith in whom, and keeping his sign in his hand, by the favour of Krishna, this grandson was born to Chikka Deva; thence was Krishna rightly his name, and had he Rukmini and Balabhadra he would have been Krishna himself.

By daily processions having obtained the favour of the god of Pashchima Ranga, and by protecting the families of all his friends, and by terrifying all hostile kings, this *Krishna Rája* became as it were the Vibhíshaṇa of the world.

Daily rising at dawn, praising the lotus feet of Vishnu, repeating without omission his thousand names, daily performing the agni hotra, daily bestowing a cow and money on Brahmans, he then listened to the itihása and kathas. Thus filled from the streams of water poured out with his daily offerings, the Kaveri ran with gold and carried his fame to every land.

For the lord of the Yádava mountain, the protector of his race (*kula náyaka*) he caused to be made a crown, set with the nine gems—and for Sampatkumára, his processional image, he caused to be made a jewelled coat.

A'disesha is the lord of Pátáḷa, but his subjects the Bhogis have nothing to eat but wind; Indra is the lord of svarga, but the gods there have to watch for an offering by some one before they can obtain nourishment: but while *Krishna Rája* rules the world, all his subjects receive good food, handsome raiment, perfumed scents, gold and jewels, and chámaras. To obtain even in suraloka the kalpa vriksha, the chintamani and the cow of plenty is very difficult; but here to all who require them are given jewels, cows and trees. Is there then in all the world so great a lord as *Krishna Rája?*

His gifts putting to shame the kalpa vriksha, his wealth putting to shame Indra, his fame putting to shame the divine Ganges, his wisdom putting to shame Brihaspati, his valour putting to shame the flame of S'iva's central eye, thus of true greatness is *Krishna Rája*.

* *Srinivása yati*, of the S'ri Vaishnava mata was his guru.

His paṭṭa mahishi was *Deváǰamma*, besides whom he had eight wives, in whose several names he caused to be made eight *sarasu* (tanks) in the eight tírtha of the Yadu mountain. And he not only established agraháras in his own name, but one in the name of his mother *Chelváǰamámba*, and repairing the temple of Vishnu established an agrahára in the name of his grandmother *Deviramma*.

* From this point an abstract only is given, as the verses continue in the same strain.

* After inquiring after all the best and most fertile spots in his own kingdom of *Karnáṭaka*, he discovered that the most suitable residence for Vaishnavas was the region half a yojana south of Yadugiri, north of the Kávéri, north-west of Níládri, east of the hill at the (?) Lakshmantirtha (*Rámánujánghri s'ri tírtha taṭákádri*)—the residence of Lakshmi Náráyana, beautiful, of genial climate, having the name *Hoysala Des'a.*

In it is the city of *Yádava puri*, protected by *Vishnu Varddhana*, purified by the pollen the dust from the lotuses the feet of *S'ri Rámánuja*, its god Lakshmi Náráyana the benefactor of the faithful, to the east of whose temple is the temple of S'ri Yádava Náráyana Vasanta Gopála Deva.

Considering that between these two temples he should establish agraháras, he made two agraháras, each consisting of four streets, each filled with rows of houses. And in order that the ceremonies and processions of both gods might be duly performed, he invited Brahmans from many countries to come and take up their residence there ; namely, such as were patient, of good character, versed in the veda and vedánta, professors of the Rik, Yajur and Sáma vedas, professors of the s'ástras, acquainted with the s'rauta and smárta ceremonies, performers of the agni hotra, free from anger and other evil passions, of good descent, family men, acquainted with the essence of both vedánta, acquainted with the Dráviḍa prabandha, S'ri Vaishnavas, Mádhva Brahmans and Advaita Brahmans.

For the residence of whom, and support of their families, he formed vrittis attached to each house, to endure as long as sun and moon, and marked out the boundaries.

Which, in order to have written down in a támra s'ásana, signed by his own hand and sealed with the varáha mudra, he sent for *Rámáyana Tirumalárya*, a Vaishnava of the Kaundinya gotra and a poet, and directed him to compose a s'ásana grantha. In accordance with which order, the following s'ásana, approved of by both donor and donees, was written by him.

The Sáliváhana S'aka year reckoned as *veda, arnava, ritu, kshiti* (1644) having passed, the year Shubhakrit being current, in the month Margashira, full moon, Tuesday, Brahma yoga, A'rdra nakshatra, Bálava karaṇa—on this auspicious day, the chief of the Vaishnava kings, the moon being eclipsed in the constellation under which Rámánuja was born, in order to increase the Brahmans in Yádava nagari which had been the residence of that yati, already the resort of many Brahmans versed in the veda and vedánta :—

---

* Here the translation is resumed.

Among the Yádava kings who came from Dvárávatí nagara the embodiment of the fruit of merit, the kalpa vriksha to his dependents, a thunderbolt weapon in cutting off the wings of the mountains his enemies, punisher of those who claim to have a title,* a ganda bherunda to the elephants the hostile kings, an elephant to the plantain garden his opponents, a sun in dispersing the clouds of his enemies' forces, placing his commands on the heads of tributary kings, a gale to the clouds the *Mahárásh{t}ra* kings, a wild fire to the withered forest the *Turushkas*, skilled in punishing the mighty *Pándya*, a lion to the herds of elephants *Chola* and *Kerala*, a pleasure giving rain-cloud to the chakora birds his dependents, S'rímad Rájádhirája S'rí Bhúpála Parames'vara Praudha Pratápa Víra Narapati, of the A'treya gotra, an ocean of good qualities, of the As'valáyana sútra, chief of the Kshatriyas, of the Rik shákha, grandson of Chikka Deva Rája, son of Kanthírava kshitíndra, the unequalled *Krishna Rája*, a kalpa vriksha in continual gifts: assigned to Brahmans (described as before), making vrittis, with houses and groves, certain villages:—

In the *Hoysala Des'a*, the *Kuruvanka* nád is the most charming: in which, of the agraháras he made, the first was *Yádavapuri*, known to all people as *Tondanúru*, in which is the great Chelvadevámbudhi (lake); [the second] *Atikuppe*, both large and populous villages—with their hamlets *Honnenhalli*, *Marahalli*, *Sámagondanahalli*, *Heruhalli*, *Harikalale*, *Ichanahalli*, *Náduboyanahalli*, *Hemanvalli*, *Hanumanakatte*, *Chikkavanhalli*, *Chikka Hosahalli*, *Teginahalli*, *Kanchinakere*, *Murukanahalli* and its koppalu, *Hakkimanchanahalli*, *Ganganahalli*, altogether 17 subordinate villages, or with their two chief villages 19 villages, fertile, populous, having bridges and tanks, yielding double crops, all bearing sugar cane, of good soil, filled with groves and hamlets. These, forming into 112 vrittis for Brahmans, he distributed them to each one so that each had an equal share of best, middling and inferior soil. Also, having 112 houses securely built by masons, he filled them with furniture and grain, &c., for one year; provided one milch cow in milk with its calf for each house; and for the decoration of the children of the vritti-holders, gave to each, silk cloths, shawls, sets of earrings, finger rings, &c., to the number of 20 of each, and bestowed them on the residents of the agrahára of *Yádavapuri*. In the fort of *S'rírangapatna*, whose walls are purified by the washing of the waves of the holy Kávéri, the residence of Paschima Ranga, the Gautama kshetra, in the presence of Ramáramana (Vishnu) reposing with S'rí Devi and Bhú Devi on his couch the serpent A'disesha, making a vow that he

* *Birudentembara gandah.*

presented this pious gift to Brahmans in order to gain the favour of the lotus feet of Lakshmi Náráyana, calling the Brahmans separately, he presented them with the vrittis, with pouring of water and presentation of a coin, repeating they are no longer mine (*ná mama ná mama*).

The names and particulars of those Brahmans for three generations are here written (here follow the names, &c., with a repetition of the grant. Then usual dharma s'lokas).

By the poet *Tirumalárya*, daily reader of the Ramáyana and Bhárata, a composer of poetry in Karṇáṭa, Samskrita and A'ndhra, skilled in singing (*gándharva*), was this s'ásana composed so as to gratify all people.

S'rí Krishna Rájah.

---

169. Tamra S'asana at Melkote, date A. D. 1724.

5 *Plates*, 8 *sides.—Devanágari Characters.*

(The whole of the first part down to the date corresponds with No. 168. Thence the continuation is as follows) :—

May it be well. In the 2nd aparárdha of Brahma who was born from the lotus navel of Vishnu, in the first part of his day, in the varáha kalpa, the 7th manvantara, the 28th yuga, the beginning of the Kali yuga, the S'áliváhana s'aka, the year reckoned as *bhúta*, *arṇava*, *anga*, and *kshiti* (1645) having passed, and the year Krodhi being current, in the month Pushya, the 12th day of the moon's decrease, Wednesday, under the constellation Anurádha, the vriddhi yoga, the bálava karaṇa, the uttaráyaṇa, the sun being in Makara,—on this auspicious day, in the morning, the chief of the S'ri Vaishnava kings, the obtainer of merit among the Yádava kings who came from Dvárávati-nagara, a kalpa vriksha to his dependents, a thunderbolt weapon to the wings of the mountains the hostile kings, champion over those who claim to have a title,* a gaṇḍa bheruṇḍa to the elephants the hostile kings, an elephant to the plantain, garden his enemies, a sun in dispersing the dark clouds his enemies' forces, placing his commands on the heads of tributary kings, a gale to the clouds the *Mahárásḥṭra* kings, a wild fire to the withered forest the *Turushkas*, skilled in overthrowing the powerful *Páṇḍya*, a lion to the elephants the *Chola* and *Kerala* kings, a whirlwind to the clouds the *Kelale* kings, S'rímad Rájádhirája S'rí Bhúpála Parames'vara Prauḍha Pratápa Víra Narapati, born in the

---

* See note p. 317.

A'treya gotra, an ocean of good qualities, of the As'valáyana sútra, chief among the Kshattriyas, of the Rik s'ákha, grandson of Chikka Deva Rája, son of Kanṭhírava Kshitíndra, the unequalled *Krishna Rája*, a divine kalpa vriksha in daily bestowing gifts :—

For the purpose of having all the ceremonies of the three seasons performed for the lord of Hastagiri, in order to provide the necessary funds, articles and persons therefor ; and in order to provide for the ceremonies of the daily offering to Varada Rájasvámi, and a manṭapa, a grove and a pond for the procession in Vais'ákha in the name of his mother Cheluvájamma and his father's mother Deviramma ;—inquiring after twelve villages which were populous and provided with a tank, within his own territories, near to Kánchi, and having found such according to his wishes on the banks of the river in the *Kárimangala*-nád belonging to *Vírabhadra Durga*, namely, in the *Pannirkola* hobli, the villages of *Páparpaṭṭi*, with its tank, *Yaṭṭiganahaḷḷi*, *A'cháradahaḷḷi*, *Kamalanáyakanahaḷḷi*, *Gollappanáyakanahaḷḷi*, *Múdehaḷḷi*, *Balúru*, *Paratihaḷḷi*, *Belachánahaḷḷi*, *Sajjalahaḷḷi*, *Vepalahaḷḷi*, *Nallappanáyakanahaḷḷi* ; in order that these 12 fertile villages might be devoted to him who eternally resides in Kánchi to remove the troubles of the faithful, *Appratima Krishna Rájendra Chandra* ; in the fort of *S'rírangapaṭṇa*, whose walls are purified by the waves of the holy *Kávéri*, the residence of Pas'chima Ranga, the Gautama kshetra ; in the presence of Ramanáramana who reposes with S'rí Devi and Bhú Devi in happiness on the serpent S'esha ; sending for *Rámánuja Yatís'vara*, the son-in-law of Saumya, and saying " You, your disciples, and their descendants, daily perform without break all the ceremonies which we have stated for Varada, taking for the purpose the profit arising from these villages," presented these villages, with pouring of water and presentation of a coin, repeating they are no longer mine (*ná mama, ná mama*).

The boundaries and description of the villages presented by Krishna Rája for the ceremonies at Kánchi, are here written in the Karnátaka language.

(After repetition of much of the above, continues thus) :—also within the four boundary stones of these villages marked with the s'ankha and chakra, the rice land and dry fields, the gardens and store houses, the dams and embankments, the dry cultivation and the wet cultivation, the poor rent-free land and the waste, half the quit rent due to the Virabhadra Durga revenue authorities from the dancing girls of the north temple, the tax on blacksmith's houses, the tax for . . of the hill, the tax of the *palliga* caste, the tax for child birth, the tax on naming a child, the fees due to Gopálasvámi ; and of the customs, the money remaining after deducting the duty on laden bullocks ;

with the *jitagára* (slaves), the salary of the kambli makers, the internal transit duties, the duty on all crops, the duty on the profits of cloth sales, the duty on iron, the duty on tobacco, and all other rights.

And in that *Páparpaṭṭihalli*, the rents from the market, the customs dues, and the fees from the Thursday fair; with all similar rights in the 12 villages. Also the old freehold in *Anantagiri* in *Atti-náḍ*, namely the village of *Vepapunḍi*, with the duties levied therein on the crops,* &c. &c., (concludes in the usual manner).

---

170. S'ila S'asana at Banavasi, date A. D. 1068.

Haḷe Kannaḍa Characters.

May it be well. While the favourite of earth and fortune, great king of kings, supreme lord, first of monarchs, ornament of the *Chálukyas*,† S'rimat *Trailokya Malla Deva* was ruling the kingdom of the world :—

May it be well. While, the power and glory of his race being established as far as the peaks and caves of Himavat the emperor of all mountain ranges, a blazing sun in the sky of the celebrated *Kadamba kula*, his two lotus feet surrounded with the crowns of foreign kings, the lord of *Banavási-pura*, having the monkey flag and the lion signet, the five great drums and the five great decorations, the ruler of eighty four cities, having an eye in his forehead, descendant of a race consecrated by the performance of eighteen as'vamedhas in strict accordance to the rules, a mine of virtue, having obtained a boon from . . . Devi, in the enjoyment of happiness, having obtained the promise of

---

* *Yi grámagaḷa yallegaḷalli s'ankha chakránkitavági pratishṭápitavágiruva chatus síme yalle gallugaḷige voḷagágiruva gadde beddalu tóṭa tuḍike aṇe achchukaṭṭu káḍárambha nirárambha káṇi beḷige Virabhadra durgada aṭṭhavaṇige teruva baḍa devasthánada ara dási vúlaga mánya kammárara toṭṭi terige beṭṭada poḍina terige palligara játi terige bála terige náma gáṇige Gopálasvámi vartane sunkakke saluva paṭṭaḍi yéru sunka tegadu bákila haḍa jitagáraru kambaḷagára sambaḷa voḷapálu sunkakke saluva á sakala pairu pommige saluva javaḷi lábhádáya pommu kabbinada pommu hogesoppina pommu muntáda á sakala svámya yi Pápárpaṭṭu grámada pêṭe suvarṇádáya sunka pommu yi péṭeyalli kaṭṭuva Brihaspativára sante huṭṭuvaḷi sahá yi 12 grámada á sakala svámya Aṭṭi-náḍa Anantagiri sthaḷadallu púrva dattavági sarvamányavági naḍadu baruva Vepapundi gráma 1 yidaralliyú aṭṭhavaṇige saluva pairu sunka pommu devasthánagaḷige svalpa pairu dattammaṇihya paikakke saluva rujádi gúḷa kaiváḍa muntáddakke saluva pairugaḷu sahá.*

† See note p. 14.

moksha having the name victor in war,* and other titles, S'ríman Mahá Mandales'vara *Kirtti Varmma Deva* was ruling the Banavási Twelve Thousand :—

In the S'aka year 990, the year Kílaka, the month Chaitra, the 1st day of the moon's increase (rest not copied).

---

171. Tamra S'asana at Bangalore,† date A. D. 1253.

5 *Plates,* 14¼ *in.* × 9½ *in.,* 8 *sides.—Nágarí Characters.*
Seal, 4 *in. diameter, a Wounded Tiger,* ¾ *in. relief, with* (?) *a Saláki; moon above, sun below.*

Om. Obeisance to *S'iva.* May the original Boar be your protection, on whose tusk rests the earth, lifted up as if a fruit plucked from the tree. O tongue, thee do I reverence, aid me in worthily proclaiming the glory of the royal line.

From the lake the navel of Vishnu, powerful to create the universe and devoted to the protection of the three worlds, sprang a lotus on which Lakshmi rests with great joy. Thence was born Brahma, sporting on the waves of the sea of the vedas, by means of Sarasvati having come to the married state and become a house holder. From whose mind, discerning the modes of all rites whether plain or obscure, the cause of the creation of the world, was born Atri of supreme excellence. From whom was born Chandra, giving joy to all the world with his rays filled with nectar. From him many lines of kings take their rise.

Of whom the kings of the *Yadu* race are celebrated in the puráṇas, the possessors of many countries acquired by their valour, skilled in all royal accomplishments and methods of government, through the merit of their great sacrifices and penance entitled to a throne in svarga.

Of the kings of this race who in regular descent were ruling the world, a mighty king named *Sala* arose.

---

* *Samasta-kula-mahídharam-chakra-chakravarti-mahima-Himavad-girindra-rundra-s'ikhara-sthala-sthápita-nijánvaya-s'akti-prabhava prakaṭíkṛita-Kadamba-kulámbara-prachaṇḍa-márttáṇḍam para-nṛipati-makuṭa-ghaṭita-charaṇáravinda-yugalam Banavási-pura-varadhís'varam sáká-charendra-dhvajam simha-lánchhanam permádi-pancha-ghoshaṇam permáḍi-pancha-bhúshaṇam chatur-ás'iti-nagarádhishṭitam laláṭa-lochanam jagad-vidhita-ashṭádas'ás'vamedha-díkshita-kula-prasútam satya-ratnákaram . . jya-devi-labdha-vara-prasádam sarasa-vinodam moksha-labdha-varam samara-jaya-námádi-pras'asti-sahitam.*

† In the Museum.

He once on a time went into the forest near *S'as'apura* in order to visit Vásanti, the goddess worshipped by all the kings of his family. Seeing there the great muni, doing reverence to him, he sat down a moment. Then, while unarmed he was engaged in the worship of the goddess and reverence of the muni, a cry of wild beasts arose, and a fearful tiger bounded forth, its claws powerful enough to tear up mountains, its long tongue swinging about with desire to swallow some one, the fiery sparks from its eyes burning up its eyelashes.

That muni, exclaiming in the language of his country *Hoy Sale!* (strike, Sala!) gave him a saláki, with which he slew it. From that the name of *Hoysala* came to all the kings of his line; and the tiger going to svarga, was adopted as the sign on the flag of all that line, who being ever ready for war, able in stringing and discharging their bows, at very thought of them all their enemies trembled.

(The genealogy is continued as in other inscriptions down to *Soma,* and continues:)

In the Bháradhvaja kula, descendant of the Soma vams'a, was born *Viṭṭarasa,* possessed of all good qualities, a great warrior. To him the celebrated *Buḍanáchi* was wife. From whom was born a daughter *Somala,* in beauty superior to Rati, in removing the troubles of her dependents equal to Lakshmi. She became the crowned queen of *Soma Mahipati;* being filled with devotion, by her gifts putting to shame the kalpa vriksha, her fame ascended up to heaven along with that of *Soma Mahipati.*

That king thus fortunate, whose glorious career was known in all countries, *S'ri Somes'vara Bhúmipála,* residing in the prosperous royal city *Vikramapura,* which he had established for his own pleasure in the *Chola Manḍala* conquered by the power of his own arm; in the year Paridhavi, the month Phálguna, new moon day, during an eclipse of the sun; in consequence of a discourse on the gifts proper to be made on that day, giving to the village of *Madanampalli* together with *Mattikaṭṭa,* situated in the *Kallukani-náḍ* another name *Somalápura* in honour of his paṭṭa mahishi Somala Devi, and forming there 70 vṛittis at a rental of 140 nishkas (pagodas), presented them for the performance of the ceremonies of the god he had set up in that town, to Brahmans of various gotras, with pouring of water.

This matter, in order to be clearly understood, is here written in detail in the Karnáṭa language.

(After repetition of all the titles and epithets) *Hoysala Bhujabala Víra Somes'vara Devarasa,* in the S'aka year 1175, the year Paridhávi, the month

Phálguna, new moon day, during an eclipse of the sun (made the grant as given in the original at foot, * many of the terms being unknown).

May this gift of *Somes'vara* kshmápati endure for many *yugas* and *kalpas*, as long as the sun rides in his chariot, as long as the sea rolls with waves, as long as male and female rivers and lakes and ponds flow, as long as the earth stands firm, as long as the sky with its constellations lasts, as long as Setu and Meru continue.

Whoso usurps a gift made by himself or by another shall be born a worm in ordure for sixty thousand years. Merit is a common bridge for kings, this deserves your support from age to age: thus does Rámachandra beseech the kings who come after him.

S'rí Víra Somes'varasya.

---

172. S'ila S'asana at Somnathpur, date A. D. 1270.

Haḷe Kannaḍa Characters.

May the supreme male be your protection, who in the form of the Boar raised up the earth from its humbled condition, buffeted by the waves of the sea, and tossed it up as in sport on the tip of his strong right tusk. May the Boar form of Hari be your protection, which smiled at Lakshmi wandering among the lotuses springing from the lakes on the bosom of the earth supported on his right tusk.

From the lotus navel of Vishnu sprang Brahma, the creator of the worlds. From him sprang Atri, fearful in penance. From his eyes sprang the moon-

---

* *Kallukaṇi náḍa Madani tanna káluvalli sahita modalu g* 18 *p* $1\frac{1}{4}$ $\frac{1}{16}$ *á náḍa Mottikaṭṭa tanna káluvalli sahita modalu g* 8 *p* $5\frac{1}{4}$ $\frac{1}{16}$ *antu úru eraḍakkam modalu g* 25 *p* 8 *vaṭṭa* (exchange) *p* $6\frac{1}{4}$ $\frac{1}{16}$ *sáda g* 1 *p* $2\frac{3}{4}$ *paṇa* 2 *ra sese mánya ba laha g* 2 *p* $8\frac{1}{4}$ $\frac{1}{16}$ *kumára g* 1 *p* $3\frac{3}{4}$ *nivandha g* 1 *p* $2\frac{3}{4}$ *s'ri karaṇa p* $9\frac{3}{4}$ $\frac{1}{16}$ *sunka* (customs) *g* 5 *p* 1 *pannáya p* $8\frac{1}{4}$ *aḍike* (areca nut) *lakka* 1 *kkam g* 5 *paṇa vondara sese g* 4 *p* 5 *kanḍikevaṇa p* 4 *vóvata g* 22 *p* $8\frac{1}{2}$ *yéra sese g* 6 *p* $2\frac{3}{4}$ *áneya sese g* 13 *p* 8 *toḷapu g* 4 *nalládhu sallettu g* 8 *p* 2 *beḍa dere Madaniyake g* 6 *p* $5\frac{1}{4}$ *Mattikaṭṭada bhóge g* 3 *p* $2\frac{3}{4}$ *kháṇa nivandha p* $4\frac{1}{2}$ *kaluku p* $1\frac{1}{2}$ *kadireya sese g* 21 *p* $\frac{3}{4}$ *kumára málike p* $6\frac{1}{4}$ $\frac{1}{16}$ *vijaya víra vana p* 3 $\frac{1}{16}$ *koḍati vaṇa p* 2 *khánasa* . . . . *kkam g* 8 *p* $\frac{1}{4}$ $\frac{1}{16}$ *bhatta bhaṭṭa ko* $8\frac{1}{2}$ *kham g* 1 *p* $\frac{3}{4}$ *ellu sa* 2 *ko* . . . *g* 1 *p* $\frac{3}{4}$ *jóla sa* 1 *ko* 18 *má* 2 *káruṇya biṭṭiya bhandi g* 4 . . . *gaṇadu pottara g* 1 *p* $2\frac{3}{4}$ *ettitu pottara p* $3\frac{3}{4}$ *antu gadyáṇa* . . . *Madani gúḍida Mattikaṭṭavannu tamma paṭṭadarasi Sóvalá Déviyarige s'reyorthavági á úrannu Sóvalápuravendu hesar iṭṭu Bráhmaṇarige vṛi* 62 *Rigveda khanḍika vṛi* 1 *Yajur veda khanḍika vṛi* 1 *Sáma veda khanḍika vṛi* 1 *á úralli távu pratishṭheya máḍida dévarige vṛi* 2 *kerege vṛi* 2 *antu eppattu vṛittiyági máḍi í kula maryádeya g* 140 *nu prati varsha aramanege tettu bantági* &c. [*N. B. g* stands for *gadyána* (pagoda), *p* for *paṇa* (fanam), *ko* for *kolaga.*]

like glory Chandra. From him many lines of kings took their rise: among whom of glorious qualities and celebrated career was Yadu.

From him innumerable kings descended: among whom was born *S'ala*, of great glory, by the might of his arms possessed of all the earth. He once on a time, being in his own *S'as'apuri*, went forth to do reverence to Va'santi, his *kula devati*, and to the *siddha* who dwelt by her side, when a powerful tiger rushed out desiring to devour him. But on the siddha saying in the Karṇáṭaka language '*Hoy S'ala*' he slew it, and from that time all the kings of his race obtained that name.

In that race arose *Eṛeyanga*, who by his gifts put to shame Karṇa. His son was *Vishṇu*, acquainted with all the rites prescribed in the vedas. His son was *Narasimha* Bhúpati; to whom was born *Ballála* Mahívallabha, praised as the bestower of every gift on his dependents. To him *Nṛisimha* Bhúpati was son, the setter up of *Choḷa*, by his great power and wisdom in government protecting *Púṇḍya*.

From him was born *Soma*, like another *soma* (or moon), the lord of all things moveable and immoveable on the earth, the subjector of all his enemies, whom all the sciences had made their resort. To that *Soma*, as Ganga to the ocean, so *Bijjala* was wife. To these two was born *Narasimha*, resembling a kalpa vriksha, slaying all his enemies with his terrible sword, his fame having filled all the points of the compass and gone to the utmost limits of the ocean, at sight of whose gifts the kalpa vriksha trembled, Karna lost his name, and the kámadhenu was covered with shame.

Once on a time, when dwelling in the city of *Dorasamudra*, the lion of kings *Narasimha* was seated in the council, there began a discourse on gifts of merit; when the head among the many learned men present, the friend of the tributary kings, the chief adviser of Narasimha Bhúpati, the minister *Soma*, rose up from his seat. To *Malli Deva*, an officer in the army, the subduer of the flames of the enemy's power, (? he desired to give) his daughter in the first bloom of her youth; and also (another) to *Chikka Ketaya*, able in war, whose might none could withstand: these Narasimha Bhúpati cherished like sons. On that minister *Soma*, the son of his elder sister, coming and doing obeisance, that moon of the Yadu race (the king), discerning all that was in his mind, gave him his desire. And moreover, to provide for the worship of the gods he had set up in the agrahára he had established, presented to him 3000 . . . which that *Soma Daṇḍes'a* taking, made therewith all the necessary arrangements; the particulars of which are here published in the Karṇáṭa language.

May it be well. While the protector of all lands, favourite of earth and fortune, great king of kings, supreme lord, lord of *Dvárávati-pura*, sun to the lotus of the *Yádava kula*, head ornament of the wise, king over the *Male Rájas*, champion among the *Malepas*, ganḍa bherunḍa, unshaken warrior, sole hero, terrible in the field of battle, Malla of the S'anivára Siddigiri durga, in bravery a Rama, a lion to the elephants his enemies, a rare embodied Manmatha, the setter up of *Chola ráya*, the protector of the *Páṇḍya* kingdom, the exterminator of the *Magara* kingdom, the setter up of columns of victory from *Setu* to *Vindhya*, unequalled for valour, S'ri Vishnu Varddhana Pratápa Chakravarti Hoys'ala Bhujabala *Srí Víra Nárasimha Devarasa* was in his residence at *Dorasamudra*, ruling the kingdom of the world in the enjoyment of peace and wisdom :—

His dear son *Soma Dhannáyaka* (made provision) for the offerings and decorations, the daily processions, the processions on holy days, for repairs of the temple and the food of the rishis who resort thither, of Kes'ava Deva and the other gods he had set up in the Vaishnava quarter of the great agrahára he had established in his own name. And the dues of the places which that *Narasimha Deva Arasa* in the S'aka year 1192, the year S'ukla, the month A'sháḍa, the 12th day of the moon's increase, Wednesday, had given with pouring of water ; — and the dues of the places which the great minister, *gáyi gopála, ganḍa penḍára manḍalika*, a champion over the (?) Júba great manḍalíka, a Devendra of Danḍanáthas, in the use of the sword Svayambhu a Trinetra of the sword, a Rekhá Revanta in riding the most unmanageable horses, subduer of the enemies' forces, (?) born to be an adopted son ;* delighting in gifts of food, distinguished for gifts of gold, the senior Danḍanátha, a sun upon the eastern mountain, a blossom on the boon-giving creeper of the gods, *Someya Dannáyaka* had given within those limits with pouring of water :—the sons-in-law of that Dannáyaka, *Malli Deva Dannáyaka* and *Chikka Ketaya Dannáyaka*, distributed for the offerings of those gods, for extra expenses, and for the living of the temple Brahmans, in the following manner :—

May it be well. In the year Dhátu, the month As'viyuja, the 3rd day of the moon's increase, Sunday, for the gods in the great agrahára reverenced by all, a treasury of learning, *Somanáthapura*, (namely), the gods Prasanna Kes'ava, Ganḍa Penḍára Gopála, Varada Janárdhana, and within the precincts (*prákára*) the six Brahma &c., twelve Kes'ava &c., twelve Hamsa Náráyaṇa &c., ten Matsyā &c., twelve Sankarshaṇa &c., twelve Krishna avatára ; and on the bank of the Kávéri, the gods Lakshmi Narasimha, Yoga Náráyaṇa ; and

* *Svikárasárodaya.*

the god Sárangapáṇi of Malavaḷḷi: the rent of the places belonging to the endowments of all these gods are confirmed to that Somanáthapura, (namely) a land rent of 210 gadyáṇas. And of the 21 vrittis which the Dannáyaka gave, together with the dues of the *banḍúra* of that town, deducting the half vritti of the garden, with the rice field and dry land to the east of the . . . sluice, which is under and belongs to the Bannasamudra Bágilúr channel— the remaining 20½ vrittis are for all the teachers of science (*sarva s'ástra upádhyáyarige*). Or, including the half vritti which all those men of science (*s'ástradavaru*) obtained in exchange from Mandigeya Kávanna, altogether 21 vrittis—of which, 7 being for the S'aiva quarter, the remaining 14 vrittis (*rest not copied*).

---

173. S'ila S'asana at Heggere, date (?) A. D. 1094.

Haḷe Kannaḍa Characters.

Elephant. Dvara-palaka. A'dinatha. Dvara-palaka. Cow.

May the doctrine of *Trailokya Nátha*, the supreme profound *syád váda* prevail; the Jain doctrine which is a token of unfailing success. May it be well. The doctrine of S'ri *Vardhamána* . . . . the *Konḍakundánvaya*.

Of which a servant,—may it be well— the protector of all lands, favourite of earth and fortune, great king of kings, supreme lord, first of monarchs, glory of the *Satyás'raya kula*, ornament of the *Chálukyas*, S'rimad Bhúvallabha Ráya *Permmaḍi Deva*, while in his residence at *Kalyána*, punishing the evil and protecting the good in the seven and a half lakh country, was ruling in the enjoyment of peace and wisdom :—

The dweller at his lotus feet :—the fire of whose anger raging *dhagil, dhagil, dhagil*, in the city of his enemies; blazing *garil, garil, garil* on the heads of his enemies; burning *chimil, chimil, chimil* in their bowels; who could war against the Rája of the *Male Rájas*? His son, causing the badabánala fire of the ocean to tremble, eclipsing the fire of S'iva's frontal eye, deriding even S'iva who burnt Káma and swallowed the poison, a consuming fire of valour, was *Vishnu Bhúpálaka*.

May it be well. While the *Hoysala* kingdom of—entitled to the five great drums, Mahá Mandales'vara, lord of the city of *Dvárávati*, sun to the lotus of the *Yádava kula*, ornament of great kings, champion among the Malepas—

the hero who took *Taļakáḍu,* Bhujabala *Vishnu Varddhana,* was increasing in prosperity to endure as long as sun, moon, stars and sky :—

His son, whose greatness was as follows :—like a god enjoying the pleasure of the gods, the complete lord of Lakshmi, of glory exceeding that of the elephant kings (*dvipa rája*), a lion to the elephants the hostile kings,—was S'rí *Narasimha* Bhúpa, the . . . of victory.

The servant of his feet :—a bee with its mind fixed on the perfume of the golden lotus the feet of Jina—which are ruddy with the light of the jewels set in the crowns of the residents of svarga, an ocean of . . , whose eyebrows are black with the smoke of the offerings made in his worship—a sun to the lotus the worthy and his friends, as the foam on the waves of the Ganges rises up at the sight of the moon so his fame ascending into all the regions of space, terrible in war, of unequalled bravery, (&c., &c.) lord of the city of *Hulyara,* a moveable kalpa vriksha born from the ocean of the womb of *S'ántala Devi,* the son of *Sámanta Bhaṭṭa,* (after a great number of praises of his valour, continues) the remover of the kunkuma from the foreheads of the *Maleya* women, the remover of the kastúri of the *Cholika* women, a belt to the *Láṭa* women, a garland between the shining breasts of the *A'ndhra* women, a jewelled armlet to the *Gúrjara* women, a bee kissing the lotuses the faces of the haughty *Gauḍa* women of true virtue worthy of all praise, a jewelled mirror to the moonlike faces of the *Karṇáṭaka* women ; a terror to his fellow kings, smiter on the head of those who claim to be champions (*gandanka tala prahári*), slayer of those who oppose him, knocker down of those who call themselves great, shaker of the world, champion over the wrathful, a bherunḍa to the sharabha the hostile kings, the pounder of the tributaries, a chintámani to the learned, the subduer of the pride of the rutting elephant *Ayyana* (?), lord over all the world, long live *S'ri Bhaṭṭa Deva Sámanta*.

(Much more in the same strain, calling him Kali Biṭṭi Deva).

To describe his descent :—The chief queen (*agra mahishi*) of Sthira Gambhíra *Noļamba* was S'rí Devi. From his destroying at one blow the confederation of his enemies so that they should not unite together, he obtained the title of *Víra-tala-prahári.* Having displayed in the army of the Chálukya king *A'hava Malla* the valour of the great, he received thence the title of great.*

* *Intenis'i negalda Biṭṭi Devánvayadentendoḍe* || *Sthira Gambhíra Noļamban agra mahishi S'rí Deviyam tad vipotkararam tágaḍe bandu bandiviḍiyalu tad vairi sanghátamam baradi deydila prahâradoļé kondand ittan á bhúpaná laradi víra-taļa-prahári-vesaram dhátri taļam bannisalú* || *Cháluky-A'hava Malla nripálana kaṭakadoļ doḍḍankamunam lileyoļ páḍedan adaṭam pális'i doḍḍanka baḍivanemb í birudam* ||

To his son *Ahu Malla* and *Honnavve* was born *Sámanta Bhíma*; to describe whom :—When *Vishnu Bhúpati* with a large force of horses and elephants stood ready for battle and was sounding the instruments, being in his army, he slew S'ítagara Gaṇḍa by his valour, and thence received from the king the title of S'ítagara Gaṇḍa in the world, this Kali Bhíma.†

To him was born a younger brother *Sámanta Malla*, of good character, possessed of all the qualities described as belonging to the Jina márga, beloved by *Govi Deva*, of great bravery. As if Yama having swallowed all his victims, unable to digest them, had vomited them forth again, such was the condition of the enemies slain in battle by *Huliyara Bhaṭṭa*. Slaughtering the elephants of the hostile kings, and satisfying the furies with the blood flowing from the headless corpses of those slain by him on the field of battle, thus greatly excited was the wrath of *Sámanta Bhaṭṭa*. His younger brother was *Govi Deva*, the creeper of whose fame spread into all the world (&c., &c.)

To describe the wife (*sati*) of *Sámanta Bhaṭṭa* :—The colour of her body like that of the emerald and the diamond mixed (!), the locks of her hair like the blue sapphire (!), she was as if all the jewels had been born in the form of *S'ántale*. Whatever virtues are united in the Mahes'varágama, the Jina-s'rí-dharmma, the Sad-Vaishnavágama, and the Bauddhágama, in the possession of all these she had no equal.

Narasimha Deva Mahipa governs with the aid of Sámanta Govinda, Hiriyambhaṭṭa, his own mother the celebrated Sátavve, Mandaradaiya, Bhú-máchi Deva, and Hiriayya Muttayya Bhíma, but who is greater than *Vishnu Sámanta*, says all the world.

To this *Biṭṭi Deva*, whose glory was equal to that of Kailása, this Bhujabala *Narasimha Mahipa*, gave *Hennegere*, for the support of the elephants (*gaja brayakk endu*).

Which, S'riman Mahá Sámanta *Govi Deva*, of the S'rí Múla sangha, Des'iya gaṇa, Pustuka gachcha, and Koṇḍakundánvaya; of the Bhádráyana hill; in order that his wife *Mahádevi Náyakiti* might obtain eternal happiness; washing the feet of S'ri Máṇika Nandi Siddánta Deva, the disciple of Guṇachandra Siddánta Deva, gave for the eight manner of ceremonies of the *basadi* of Jína Párs'va Deva of *Heggere*, and for the food of the rishis.

And *Sámanta Biṭṭi Deva*, the good son of *S'ántala Devi*, that he might obtain eternal happiness; in the (?) 18th year of Chálukya Vikrama, the month

† *Ari madhurári s'indura ghaṭá vighaṭogra mrigendra Vishṇu bhúpatiya runakke rága vadavutt iral átana biḍinalli tán s'ítagara gaṇḍanam paridu kondadhaṭim paḍedam mahipanim s'ítagara gaṇḍan emba biridam Kali Bhíma nilátalágradoḷu* ||

Jeshṭa, the 5th day of the moon's increase Monday, at the Sankramana ; gave to the basadi *Savaṇagere*. Whose boundaries (&c.).

And *Heggaḍe Jakkanna*, in order that his mother-in-law *Mahádevi Náyakiti* might obtain eternal happiness (another gift).

174. S'ila S'asana at Sindigere, date A. D. 1138.

May the doctrine of *Trailokya nátha*, the supreme profound *syád váda*, a token of unfailing success, the Jain doctrine prevail.

May it be well. While the victorious kingdom of the protector of all lands, favourite of earth and fortune, great king of kings supreme lord, first of monarchs, glory of the *Satyás'raya kula*, ornament of the *Chálukyas*,* S'rímat *Tribhuvana Malla Deva*, was increasing in prosperity, to endure as long as sun, moon and stars :—

The dweller at his lotus feet :—May it be well. Entitled to the five great drums, Mahá Manḍales'vara, lord of *Dvárávati-pura*, sun in the sky of the *Yádava kula*, head ornament of kings, champion among the *Malapas*, adorned with these and many other titles, S'rimat Tribhuvana Malla *Vinayáditya Poisala* was governing all the territory included between *Konkaṇa*, *Bhaḍada-vayal-náḍ*, *Talakáḍu* and *Sávi-male*, punishing the evil and protecting the good. In the breasts and the brains of the *Malapar* did the fear of him spread, when he lifted his hands to smite the heads of the *Malapar*.

The beloved of the mind and eyes of that Manḍalesvara, to strangers and to the citizens like herself the embodiment of eternal merit, thus praised in the world, that *Keleyavvarisi* was the protection of the people, the kingdom and the king.

While these two, in the enjoyment of peace and wisdom, were in their residence at (?) *Sosulya*, ruling the kingdom, *Keḷayala Devi*, cherishing *Mariyáne Danḍanáyaka* as her younger brother, *Vinayáditya Pois'ala Deva* being also present, gave in marriage to *Mariyáne Danḍanáyaka*, *Adekavve Danḍanáyakitti*, conferring on him also the lordship of *S'indigere* in *A'sandi náḍ*, in the S'aka year 961, the year Sarvajit, the month Phálguṇa, the 3rd day of the moon's increase, Monday.

---

* See note p. 14.

Thus having made the gift of a virgin and the gift of land, with pouring of water, while maintaining them with merit; to the world-renowned Pois'ala king and the lotus-like Keleyabbaris'i, was born and grew celebrated in the world Víra Ganga *Ereyanga* nripa. Of unequalled merit, a third Márutti, a fourth Ugra-vahni, a fifth Samudra, a sixth Púgane, a seventh Ubrades'a, an eighth Kuládri, a ninth Hasti of unparalleled liberality, a tenth Nidhi-prabandha, who can utter the praises of *Ereyanga Deva* ?

(To him and) to *Achala Devi*, praised as the A'di Bhoga, were born the heroes *Balláḷa* kshoni-vallabha, *Vishnu* dharitri-vallabha, and the chief of warriors *Udayáditya*.

While *Ballaḷa* nripála . . . . by the speed with which he defeated the combination of proud enemies having obtained the title of (?) Bágibalu Deva, was in the enjoyment of peace and wisdom in the royal city *Belapura*, governing the kingdom: to *Mariyáne Danḍanáyaka* and *Chámavve Danḍanáyakiti*, who resembled a second Lakshmi, were born *Padmala Devi, Chávali Devi* and *Boppa Devi*. These three becoming highly accomplished in sciences, in singing and dancing; and of a fame which made them worthy of three kings; *Balláḷa Deva* married the three virgins on the same day in the same marriage hall; and in the S'aka year 1025, the year Svabhánu, the month Kartika, the 10th day of the moon's increase, Thursday, as a marriage gift, having again conferred on *Mariyáne Danḍanáyaka* of the second generation, S'indigere, together with the lordship thereof, with pouring of water, was maintaining the same :—

As Vishnu, with eyes like the blue waterlily, a face like the lotus, and a gently smiling countenance, displaying the power of his arms in the bright moonlight of his fame which filled the three worlds, delighting in the overthrow of those who have forsaken the paths of justice, S'rí *Vishnu Bhúpa* was shining like a sun in the world. When anger makes him frown all kings are destroyed; in the sport of his victorious expeditions what countries he overran! what lands resounded with his praise! what kings he overcame! even as far as the shores of the ocean; thus gaining possession of all the world—*Vishnu kshitís'a*.

May it be well. Entitled to the five great drums, Mahá Manḍales'vara, lord of *Dvárávati-pura*, born in the *Yádava kula*, a head jewel among the jewels the *Chálikya* manḍalíka,* through worship of the feet of Achyuta (Vishnu) having obtained the glory of Jishnu, by nature of a valour which went be-

* *Yádava-kulodaya Chálikya-maṇi-manḍalíka-chúḍámaṇi.*

yond the regents of the points of the compass; causing the wives of hostile kings to miscarry at the sound of his victorious conch; having obtained a boon from Vásantiká Devi; the daily bestower of gifts; by the performance of unequalled *hiranya garbha* and *tulá purusha* * and a thousand sacrifices having satisfied the manes of his ancestors, the gods, gurus and Brahmans; on account of his valour being without any opponent and thus having acquired the title of Adhirája Vishnu; sprung from the sea of the Yádava kula, the line of Vijaya Náráyana; like Brahma in re-creating the world out of chaos; like Kumáraswámi among the learned; . . . . . to others' wives a son; daily receiving the blessings of all people for his justice and thus increasing in prosperity; unequalled in war; having by the power of his arms subdued *As'vapati*, *Gajapati* and other kings and obtained numerous horses, elephants, and jewels, and thus being in the enjoyment of the Lakshmi of an heroic kingdom; the abode of Sarasvati; a Bhairava of the final deluge to the *Choḷa kula*; a lion to the elephant *Keraḷa*; a Baḍabánala to the ocean the *Páṇḍya kula*; a wild-fire to the sprouts of the creeper the fame of *Pallava*; a s'arabha to the lion *Narasimha Varmma*; his unshaken valour a well into which fell the deer the (?) *Kalapála* and other kings; a terrible bow of victory in cutting off the *Kalapála*; an ornament of victory born for the destruction of the lines of proud boasting kings; glorious in the possession of *Kánchipura* in which he had sounded his terrible *ḍinḍima* (drum); shaking down the houses in the cities of many kings by the thundering sound of his *bheri* (drum); squeezing as if in his hand *Dakshina Madhura-pura*; having by his general burnt *Jananátha-pura*; with a look of his eyes removing the poverty of the world; the manifest Vishnu; lord over all the world as far as the ocean; free from fear as from avarice; while, possessed of these and other titles, S'rímat Kambigoṇḍa† Vikrama Ganga *Vishnu Varddhana Deva*, punishing the evil and protecting the good in the *Gangaváḍi* Ninety-six Thousand, the *Nolambaváḍi* Thirty-two Thousand and the *Banavási* Twelve Thousand, was ruling the kingdom in the enjoyment of peace and wisdom :—

The dwellers at his lotus feet:—seeds on the noble tree the office of chief ministers of the whole kingdom; bees at the lotus feet of Arhat Parames'vara; adorned with the gems, quietness, self-control, meekness, humility, heroism, skill and other good qualities; like half moons in possession of the flag embellished with the title of Mahá-prachaṇḍa-Daṇḍanáyaka obtained from

---

* See note p. 215.

† Perhaps this should be *Kanchi goṇḍa*, the capturer of Kanchi.

the race of Kambigonḍa Vikrama Vishnu Vardhana Deva ; decorated with the earrings the Lakshmi of the *syád váda* ; of great happiness arising from the daily anointings of the Jina púja ; delighting in gifts of the four vedas ; resembling the eyes of the Lakshmi of pure wisdom ; mutual friends ; were the mahá pradhána *Mariyáne Danḍanáyaka*, and, reckoned the first lord of Bharata, *Bharates'vara Danḍanáyaka*. These, without any difference in opinion, as if the embodiments of goodness, like Bhíma and Arjuna, or Lava and Kus'a, though two were as if of one form.

[Their praises continue at great length, comparing Mariyáne to a young elephant (*mari áne*), &c., &c. The following is an abstract of important particulars].

The wife of *Mariyáne* was *Jakkanavve*. Their son was *Mariyáne Danḍanáyaka*, whose wife was *Yakkaṇi*.

Bharata surpassed *Chálakya* as a minister, his god was Trailokya-nátha Parama Jina, his guru *Mághanandi* Bratipati.

The following was the genealogy of *Bharata Danḍanáyaka* and of his elder brother *Mariyáne Danḍanáyaka* :—Descended from the Bháradvája gotra, was *Kákarasa* Danḍanátha, sole lord of the *Ganga* kingdom and the *Pois'ala* kingdom. His wife was *Ambi*. His sons were *Nánkaraṇa* chamúpa and *Mariyáne*, (?) born to give the Ganga kingdom to the Pois'ala king. His daughter Danḍanáyakitti *Dekavve* had two sons, the *dharmabharma Dhákarasa* and *Mábhana* Danḍanáyaka. Dhákarasa's wife was *Hammále*. Their sons were *Mariyáne* vibhu and(?) *Dhakaráji* chamúpati. *Mábhi Rája's* daughter became the wife of *Bharates'a* Danḍanáyaka, the younger brother of *Mariyáne*. To her, *Chávallave Danḍanáyakitti*, were born the Danḍanátha *Ereyanga* and the Chamúpati *Ballu*. Ballu's wife was *Padmala Devi*, and he also had *Chavala Devi* and *Boppale*.

Thus *Mariyáne Danḍanáyaka* and *Bharataṇa* were grandsons of the sons of Balluva, the son of Yareyanga, the son of Nemana, the son of Dhákarasa, the son of Mábhana Danḍanáyaka, the son of the senior *Mariyáne Danḍanáyaka* ; and of the daughters of Boppala Devi and others up to Padmala Devi.

* While, with the descendants of this long and honoured line connected with the kings of his race, S'rí Kambigonḍa Vikrama Ganga *Vishnu Vardhana Pois'ala Deva*, having *Mariyáne Danḍanayáka* and *Bharataṇa Danḍanáyaka* as judges (*satyádhikárigalu*), treasurers, and chief advisers,

* The foregoing genealogy is far from clear. From this point the translation is resumed.

was dwelling in happiness in the royal residence at *Dorasamudra*, and governing the kingdom :—in the S'aka year 1060, the year Paingala, the month Pushya, the 10th day of the moon's increase, Sunday, uttaráyana sankránti—among the great gifts of the *tulá purusha*, in the presence of *Bharatammaiya Dandanáyaka*, approving of the name of *Bittiyanna*, (he) depositing 500 honnu at the feet of the Deva, and receiving the lordship of Dadiganakere Baggavali ; erected a basadi in S'indigere, the inheritance from their ancestors, which *Mariyáne Dandanayaka* and *Bharatana Dandanayáka* had received with pouring of water, (for which basadi), among the great gifts, *Vishnu Varddhana Deva*, pouring water with his own hands presented to Madhuchandra Deva, the junior mantravádi of Ganda Vimukta Siddhánta Deva, áchári of the S'rí múla sangha, the Des'iga gana, the Pustuka gachcha, and Kondakundánvaya,—the following land :—under the old tank four kanduga of rice land, under Távare gatta a garden sufficient for 20,000 betel vines, in the village of Mávinakere two oil mills, with the dung heaps and customs dues, to endure as long as sun, moon, stars and sky, (Imprecatory verses).

(Here follows another gift made at the same time, in which, being under the Chálúkya king Tribhuvana Malla Deva)—S'rimat Tribhuvana Malla, the capturer (*gonda*) of *Talakádu, Kongu, Nangali, Gangavádi, Nolambavádi, Banavási, Hanungalu*, and *Halasige, Bhujabala Víra Ganga Pois'ala Deva*, being in the royal residence at *Dorasamudra*, ruling the kingdom of the world in the enjoyment of peace and wisdom :—the mahá pradhána, senior treasurer, *Mariyáne Dandanáyaka*,—son-in-law of Sovarasa Da. the son of Bávarasa Da. and son of Dhákarasa Da. the son of the senior Mariyáne Da.—united with the mahá pradhána Dandanáyaka *Bharata*, obtains for the basadi of Sindigere, the place of their inheritance, with pouring of water from the hands of *S'rí Vishnu Varddhana Hoys'ala Deva*, the village of *S'ravanángihalli*. (Concludes with its boundaries, and imprecations).

175. S'ila S'asana at Yelandur, date A. D. 1654.

May the lord of Gauri, whose chest is marked with the *kunkuma* from the bosom of Gauri, the ocean of mercy, joyfully give happiness to *Mudda Bhúmipa*.

82

To the south of Himáchala is ***Nílagiri.*** There, while Kapila ríshi was performing penance, with the water of the Deva Ganga in his vessel, Nandís'vara appearing, said, "O great muni, pour forth the water in your vessel towards the north, and it shall become a river of merit, bestowing on all people present and eternal happiness." At this command, saying, "I will do it," he poured forth the water of his vessel to the north, and gave it the name of *Suvarṇávati.*

On the banks of that stream is a city, whose glory is as follows :—Brahma desiring to create a place free from all the evil passions, it became so filled with brightness, that he gave this rare city the name of *Eleyindúru* (city of the young moon) in the world.

And the eight petals of the lotus that city, were—on the east, *Svetas'ílá-dri,* the abode of Gangádhara ; on the south east, the *Mallinátha* mountain near *Tárápura ;* on the south, the *Suragi* hill, bright with the residence of . . . ; on the south west, the *S'ankares'vara* mountain, the abode of . . . ; on the west, the mountain adorned by *Mal-likárjuna* near *Bannúr ;* on the north west, the *Sambhulinga* mountain ; on the north, *Prathama S'rís'aila,* glorious on account of Malles'vara ; on the north east, the *Nirmmala* mountain, the abode of Nílakaṇṭha. These eight moun-tains being its eight petals, that city was in the middle of them like the eye of the lotus.

Thither Parames'vara coming, and saying "I will protect it," in each of the four yugas was worshiped under a different name and different colour, as follows :—in the Krita yuga as Tripurántaka, white as crystal, he was wor-shipped by Jamadagni ; in the Treta yuga as Nílakaṇṭha, of a tawny colour, he was worshipped by Raghunátha ; in the Dvápara yuga as Lokes'vara he was worshipped by the sons of Páṇḍu ; in the Kali yuga as Gaures'vara, of the colour of sapphire, he was worshipped by the kings of *Padi-náḍ.*

For *Singha Deva Bhúpa,* not only built his temple and worshipped there, but while with the glory of the lord of Lakshmi, in the form of Manmatha, like the son of Devendra and the king Ráma, an ornament to the race of kings, filled with all learning—ruling over the Ten Náds (*Padi náḍugaḷu*), in the S'aka year 1490, the year Vibhava, knowing the glory of Gaurís'a the mine of goodness, that king presented for (the support of) his worship the celebrated town of *Ganaganúru,* without any estimation of its value, so great a donor was he in the world.

His younger brother, praised by all the world for his spotless fame, was *Cháma nripála,* a new Manmatha : whose famous sons were *Nanja Rája* and *Tirumala Rája.*

And that Nanja Rája's elder brother *Tirumala Rája* presented *Vaḍeyarapura*, and near to it *S'enaguṇḍala*; and with great joy that excellent king also gave to Gaurís'vara *Chinchanapura*.

That king's son, a mine of virtue, ever filled with merit, governing with great skill the portion of the world called *Padináḍu*, like a bee at the feet of S'iva, the refuge of beggars, how did he shine in the world among kings, *Muddendra Bhúpálaka*.

And in the S'aka year 1576, the year Jaya, that *Mudda Bhúpati*, with joy obtaining gardens, rice fields and tanks, presented them to the joy of Gauri, the lord of Kantugiri; how was be celebrated for liberality in the world. And this ornament of kings built for Gaurisa a gopura, several temples, and a manṭapa; and set up the Pancha Linga to Gaurinátha with great splendour. And for this his faith he obtained family, kingdom and fame from S'iva.

Ras'ika Panḍita, the son of Bommanna Panḍita, wrote this for *Muddu Bhúpa* so as to please him. May S'iva grant to *Muddu Rája* sons, grandsons and great grandsons; elephants, chariots and horses; gold and jewels and splendid treasures; with virtuous and liberal wives; free him from all troubles and diseases; impart to him wisdom, health and strength, learning and . . for ever.

Than making a gift oneself, to maintain another's is twice as meritorious: whoso resumes a gift made by another loses all the benefit of his own. Whoso usurps a gift made by himself or by another shall be born a worm in ordure for sixty thousand years. Of making a gift or preserving another's, the maintaining another's is the best: making a gift procures svarga, but preserving another's gives eternal happiness.

Description of the lands and rights presented by *Mudda Rájaiya* for the enjoyment of the god Gauripati:—In the rice fields of *Yelandúru*,—to the (?) mirror holders (*darpaṇadavarige*) 1 , to the presenters of the wave offering of rice and turmeric (*pasúriyavarige*) 1 , to the presenters of the wave offering of lights (*gumbhártiyavarige*) 1 , to the illuminators (*mangaḷa dipadavarige*) one, to the lamp wavers (*mangaḷáratiyavarige*) two khandiga, to the dancers one khandiga. In the rice fields of *Yariyúru*—to the headman of . . . (*veḷada s'eruvegáranige*) one khandiga, to the chámara holders one khandiga, to the (?) bricklayers one khandiga, to the garland maker one khandiga, also a garden; for the special offerings on Mondays, Fridays and Dhanurmása, two khandiga, for the . . . offering to Amma one khandiga. In *Hosahalli* agrahára—to the cymbal beaters 100 bhúmma, to the beaters of the maddale drum, 100 bhúmma. In *Gandahalli*—to the singers 100 bhúmma, to the dancers 100 bhúmma.

In *Yalandúru*, *Yariyúru*, *Maddúru*, *Gumbaḷi*, *Ammaḷe*, *Homma*, *Honnúru*, *Kesavattúru*, *Agara*—in these villages, a svámya of one kolaga per khandi, and one kolaga per 100 bhúmma, of rice land ; one bundle of cotton per 100 bhúmma of black soil ; two baḷḷa per 100 bhúmma of *rasabhanḍa* ; ten balls of jaggory per 1,000. Whoso resumes the villages, gardens, rice lands or dues granted by the *Padináḍu* kings, will incur the guilt of slaughtering cows in Kás'i, of incest with his mother, of drinking spirits, and other such sins.

Obeisance to S'ri Gauris'a. May it endure.

INDEX.

The figures within brackets refer to the Introduction.